PATRICK T. CONLEY

Liberty and Justice

Liberty and Justice:

A History of Law and Lawyers in Rhode Island, 1636–1998

Patrick T. Conley

Rhode Island Publications Society 1998

Dedication

No one is more mindful than the author that this book, despite its bulk, is not a comprehensive survey of Rhode Island legal history, and should not be judged as one. The tyranny of Time and the paucity of secondary sources have dictated the select-essay format. Such a topical treatment necessarily slights or excludes many talented and prominent lawyers and jurists whose careers do not coincide with the subject matter of the essays herein. This deficiency applies especially to recent and current practitioners. To these brothers and sisters before the Bar, I extend my regrets and apologies and dedicate this book to them.

First printing, 1998

For information write:

Rhode Island Publications Society
1445 Wampanoag Trail
East Providence, Rhode Island 02915

Printed in the United States of America
ISBN 0-917012-99-2

Typography & design by Clifford Garber
Cover design by the author and Z Design Group

CONTENTS

FOREWORD

IN THIS WORK entitled *Liberty and Justice*, Dr. Patrick T. Conley, the noted Rhode Island historian, has set forth a compilation of essays and excerpts from treatises and books which chronicle the history of Rhode Island law and lawyers from the founding of the colony in 1636 down to the present time. The book consists of three parts and thirty-one chapters. No aspect of Rhode Island legal history has been overlooked.

This volume contains a panoramic overview of the legal history of our state that should be invaluable both to scholars and to students of the law. Dr. Conley has brought together in this compilation numerous sources of historical and legal information. In each instance he has provided an introduction that places the essay or excerpt in the overall historical context. In some instances his introduction may correct factual material on the basis of Dr. Conley's own intensive research on the subject matter.

This compilation was commissioned as the defining work in celebration of the 100th anniversary of the Rhode Island Bar Association. It is an excellent symbol not only of the centennial of the organized bar but of 362 years of Rhode Island legal history. No portion of the centennial observance and celebration will be of such enduring value as this book. On behalf of the Rhode Island judiciary and the members of the bar of this state, I express our deep appreciation to Dr. Patrick T. Conley for his magnificent effort and splendid literary achievement.

Joseph R. Weisberger
Chief Justice

ACKNOWLEDGMENTS

ANY BOOK is the product of several hands and many influences. Though I alone appear on the title page, that billing would be impossible without the assistance of others whose help I gratefully acknowledge. My longtime colleague Al Klyberg, director of the Rhode Island Historical Society, freely granted me permission to reprint several articles from *Rhode Island History* and made the marvelous graphics collection of the Society and the graphics curators available to me. Dr. Hilliard Beller, my editor for two decades, performed in his usual precise and meticulous manner. Linda M. Gallen, my legal secretary, efficiently typed much of the text; it was her first book but not her last, unless carpal tunnel syndrome has done her in. Ellen Rossano, a former student, persuaded me to write this book (against my better judgment) and performed such diverse tasks as organizing the material, overseeing the production, preparing sponsor profiles, and guiding the book on each stage of its journey; Cliff Garber designed the book, chose and set the type, prepared the scanned art, and put the pages together on his Macintosh; if the book possesses any aesthetic appeal, the credit is theirs. Again fulfilling its overlooked mission, the Rhode Island Publications Society became cosponsor of the book when the project's future appeared uncertain, and it then assumed the task of distributing the finished product. Gratitude also is due to the generous legal sponsors who purchased pages at the end of this volume and thereby helped to underwrite the cost of publication.

Finally, I would express my thanks to Thomas Wilson Dorr, Charles E. Gorman, Amasa Eaton, Robert Emmet Quinn, William H. Edwards, and Justice William E. Powers, whose exploits in the field of Rhode Island legal and constitutional development commanded my admiration and inspired my efforts.

Patrick T. Conley

INTRODUCTION

In format this history is basically an anthology. Given the status of Rhode Island legal history, no other type of general survey would be possible on short notice. The state's legal literature is deep in constitutional, judicial, and administrative studies but shallow in most other areas of law. The building blocks required for a comprehensive, detailed history of Rhode Island law, in the manner of Lawrence M. Friedman's *A History of American Law*, have not yet been fashioned by lawyers or historians. The recent opening of the Supreme Court Judicial Records Center in Pawtucket and the consequent ordering of the state's voluminous legal records may provide the incentive as well as the opportunity for researchers to delve into the varied and unexplored recesses of the state's legal past.

It is a poor workman, however, that faults his tools, so I have employed another means of surveying Rhode Island's legal development, at least broadly, if not deeply or comprehensively. That device is the select essay approach, quite common in various fields of law. It was used, for example, in the multivolume series of selected essays published earlier in the century by the Association of American Law Schools in such areas as Anglo-American legal history and constitutional law.

Rhode Island's unique (seventeenth- and eighteenth-century) and turbulent (nineteenth- and twentieth-century) constitutional history has prompted a large body of writing, so constitutional and political history predominate in the sections reprinted herein. To achieve balance, however, I have endeavored to locate and reproduce articles for nearly every legal appetite—crime, law enforcement, business, the role of women, family law, civic and civil rights, admiralty, torts, administrative law, and the legal profession itself.

The selections also include biographical profiles of eighteenth-, nineteenth-, and early-twentieth-century lawyers to demonstrate the changes time has wrought in the training and practice of members of the bar. To these are added the intimate anecdotal accounts of practicing professionals (like Abraham Payne, Ed Smith, and myself) with first hand knowledge of the events and personalities they describe. As with all anthologies, the quality of the research and writing is uneven. To enliven the text I have added a good supply of illustrations and captions, because many of the essays did not have visuals in their original version.

Like Gaul, this book is divided into three parts, and like Caesar's division, mine is also arbitrary. Nonetheless, Caesar's description was useful for understanding the general terrain of his subject, and my categories should suffice for that purpose as well.

Part One, "From Colony to State, 1636–1790: The Foundations of the Law," encompasses the colonial origins of Rhode Island law from the drafting of the founding documents to the assumption of statehood in 1790 under the federal Constitution. During this era major legal themes included the development of a body of internal law for the governance of a New World frontier commonwealth; the relationship between the colony and the mother country and the delineation of their respective powers; the establishment of intercolonial relations; the Americanization of the common law and its gradual replacement by local statute; the adjustment to the laws of trade and commerce under the mercantilist system; the formulation of the federal theory of empire and its corollary, dual sovereignty; the establishment of independence; the creation of a new federal union under a national constitution; and the determination of Rhode Island's role within that union of states.

Part Two, "From Statehood through the Nineteenth Century, 1790–1898: The Law as an Instrument of Change," describes the transformation of our legal system from one that had been fashioned to regulate a small, homogeneous, dispersed, agricultural and commercial society where interpersonal relationships predominated in economic and social life to a system designed to regulate the increasingly impersonal, heterogeneous, complex, urban-industrial society that took shape in Rhode Island during the nineteenth century. The most obvious legal change produced by what historian Peter J. Coleman describes as "the transformation of Rhode Island" was the replacement of the royal charter as the state's basic law with a popularly written (in the narrow sense) state constitution to serve the needs of a rapidly expanding nineteenth-century commonwealth. But this era was marked by many subtle, less convulsive changes that dramatically transformed such areas of the law as torts, contracts, equity jurisprudence, business organizations, and the role of government in economic life.

Gradually the major direction taken by the nineteenth-century legal system was away from the preindustrial and antidevelopmental common-law values of the eighteenth century. As political and economic power shifted to commercial and industrial groups, these entrepreneurs began to forge an alliance with the legal profession to advance their own interests through a transformation of the legal system. This transformation both aided and ratified a major shift in power in an increasingly market-oriented economy.

As Professor Morton J. Horowitz has demonstrated in his Bancroft Prize-winning book *The Transformation of American Law, 1780–1860*, nineteenth-century American jurisprudence was marked by the rise of legal formalism—a movement away from the subjective, utilitarian, flexible, and instrumentalist conception of the law to an objective, rigid, standardized system increasingly divorced from the subjective influences of politics, morality, and equity.

Rhode Island traveled this road towards formalism. Some of its attorneys, such as James K. Angell, Henry Wheaton, and Samuel Ames, became part of the "treatise tradition," an important change in legal consciousness. According to Horowitz, the earlier efforts at legal commentary, "modeled after Blackstone and designed for the nonpracticing gentlemen lawyer, emphasized jurisprudence, constitutional law, and political science. By contrast [James] Kent, and even to a greater extent, his successors in the treatise tradition, like Joseph Angell and Joseph Story, generally sought to write high quality technical handbooks for practicing lawyers." These legal treatises were thought to demonstrate the "scientific" nature of law and show that law should proceed not from will but from reason. Through its "black letter" presentation of supposed "general principles," the treatise sought to resolve all controversy over policy while promoting the ideal of a logical, symmetrical, and inexorable system of law.

Formalism also believed that the course of American legal change should, if possible, be developed by courts and not by legislatures. It is no accident that James K. Angell's colleague Samuel Ames established judicial independence—at least as the final interpreter of law—by his landmark decision in *Taylor* v. *Place* (1856), described by C. Peter Magrath in one of my selected essays.

In the Gilded Age, of course, Rhode Island's burgeoning industrial economy wrought dramatic changes in business law, especially in the areas pertaining to contracts, insurance, financial institutions, and corporations. The railroad and the system of urban mass transit impacted the law of negligence and eminent domain, while the mechanization of factories and the brutal conditions of factory life not only affected the law of negligence but also gave rise to a system of labor law.

By the end of the nineteenth century a combination of legal formalism, the increasing complexity of the economic system, the revolution in transportation and communication, and the increasing size and diversity of Rhode Island's population led not only to a substantial increase in the number of practicing attorneys but also to development of an organizational impulse among them to strengthen their professional status, to regulate their conduct and interaction, and to give them increased influence through unity.

I have entitled Part Three "The Modern Era, 1898–1998: The Law as a Profession," because the century described within those chronological parameters coincides with the organization and operation of the Rhode Island Bar Association. In 1905, shortly after the beginning of this era, the Bar Association assumed a leadership role in the creation of Rhode Island's modern judicial system, an event described by Chief Justice Joseph R. Weisberger in one of the included essays. Through its role in formulating standards of conduct for lawyers, setting educational requirements for the practice of law, interacting with government in the shaping of legislation, and disseminating information about the law and its constant evolution, the bar has been a major force in Rhode Island life during the course of this century. Today, with a membership in excess of 4,800, the Bar Association is the largest professional organization in the state.

But, of course, the past century of Rhode Island legal history is much more than the story of professional bonding and judicial structure. This era has been characterized by a legal explosion that has made the laws so voluminous and complex that the general practitioner of 1898 has become as rare as the California condor (and much less conspicuous). The dimensions of that explosion can be grasped by comparing the three digests, or compilations, of the general laws in operation at the end of the eighteenth, the nineteenth, and the twentieth centuries. The historic *Digest of 1798*, the first codification of state (as opposed to colony) law, consisted of one volume containing 652 pages. *The Digest of 1896*, assembled on the eve of our modern era, had 1,447 pages but was still one volume, despite the aforementioned developments in nineteenth-century law. In 1998 the present compilation—the *General Laws of 1956*, as consistently enlarged and amended—spans thirty volumes, with over 21,000 pages of text.

The transformation from laissez-faire to the regulated economy and the greatly enlarged role of government in the social order are the primary factors accounting for this vast expansion in the volume and complexity of legislation and law. Legal theorists describe this epochal development as "the revolt against formalism" and "the rise of legal realism" and its offshoots, a sort of "sociological jurisprudence." The growth of regulation has spawned governmental bureaucracy, which in turn has given a hothouse growth to administrative law and procedure, or, as critics contend, the substitution of system for substance.

The mushrooming of modern law has pressured practitioners to specialize—to know more and more about less and less, as one wag described it. Gone are the days of the true generalist, described in Abraham Payne's late-nineteenth-century *Reminiscences of the Rhode Island Bar*. Today's high-tech law firm of aggregated specialists is as far removed from the sole practitioner of 1870 as the village blacksmith of that year was different from Mr. Goodwrench and his crew.

The present era has also been characterized by constitutional turmoil culminating in constitutional calm (with the exception, perhaps, of the current flap over the separation of powers). The modernization of our state's basic law and the impact of that process on the structure of government are the only twentieth-century legal topics that have been addressed by legal historians. Incredibly, all other aspects of our twentieth-century legal system are yet to be analyzed by historians (if any there be) of Rhode Island legal development.

In editing the following pieces, I have taken the liberty to correct not only typographical and grammatical errors but also obvious misstatements of fact. This remediation has been done unobtrusively, without the use of pedantic paraphernalia calling the reader's attention to the change. Where my interpretation of the topic is more expansive than that of the original (or differs slightly), I have presented such information in my introductory essay. Those introductions are intended to place each of the essays in historical context, and, in the case of constitutional history, to give some degree of cohesion and continuity to the volume—qualities that anthologies inherently lack.

My editorial introductions often contain a bibliographical or historiographical commentary to lead the reader or prospective researcher towards more in-depth knowledge of the subject being presented. The reader should also be aware that many of these selections in their original form contained scholarly documentation that has been omitted from this reprint. These essays are marked with an asterisk in the listing of sources at the end of this volume. The serious researcher is urged to consult the original, unexpurgated version.

It has been an honor to compile this commemorative history and to participate significantly in the centennial observance of the Rhode Island Bar Association. If this work gives pleasure to my fellow attorneys and whets the appetite of legal historians, it will have served its intended purpose.

Patrick T. Conley, J.D., PH.D.
June 19, 1998

Part One

From Colony to State, 1636–1790: The Foundations of the Law

1

This general introduction to the governmental and legal system of early Rhode Island reveals certain salient, unique, and curious aspects of the state's development. Owing largely to the influence of Samuel Gorton, Rhode Island based its original legal system on English rather than Biblical law, in contrast to the practice of the surrounding Puritan colonies. Also, the original towns combined to form the colony and secure a patent and a charter. In most other English colonies a charter preceded settlement.

Unlike most American states, Rhode Island did not establish a county system of government. Instead, counties were used only for the organization of militia and the administration of the judicial system. Despite the absence of county government, however, democratic localism prompted the residents of each county to host regular sessions of the General Assembly in their respective county courthouses. This system of rotating the legislature reached full swing by the end of the eighteenth century and continued until the mid-nineteenth century, when a constitutional amendment limited Assembly sessions to Providence and Newport. Thus Rhode Island, the smallest state, had five concurrent capitals—Newport, Providence, East Greenwich, Kingston, and Bristol—for more than a half century. All five of its historic statehouses have survived.

The dominance of the General Assembly is made apparent in Conley's essay. This historic condition was modified but not repudiated by the state constitution of 1843. Rhode Island's most significant feature, however, is the religious liberty that prevailed from its founding and its "lively experiment" with the revolutionary doctrine of establishing separate spheres of operation for the church and the state. This essay was adapted from Conley's introductory essay in *The Statehouses of Rhode Island* (1988) and is fully documented in Conley's *Democracy in Decline* (1977), a detailed analysis of Rhode Island's early constitutional development.

The Colonial Foundations of Rhode Island's Legal System

Patrick T. Conley

Creating the "Lively Experiment"

If we disregard the tribal organizations of Narragansetts, Wampanoags, Niantics, Nipmucks, and Pequots (as do most American historians, to their discredit), government in Rhode Island began when religious exile Roger Williams and about a dozen disciples founded Providence in the spring of 1636. During the town's early months, civic affairs were conducted by a fortnightly meeting of "masters of families," or "householders," who considered matters relating to the "common peace, watch, and planting." As the number of settlers increased, a formal government became necessary, so Williams and the initial settlers drafted articles of self-incorporation in 1637. Then these "masters of families" entered into a mutual compact creating a "town fellowship." The major features of these first governmental agreements, the fundamental papers of Providence town government, included the vesting of administrative control in a majority of the householders and the all-important proviso that such control was to be exercised "only in civil things." This latter clause reflected Williams' desire to establish a colony based on the then revolutionary principle of religious liberty and the separation of church and state.

This 1884 engraving by T. F. Hoppin depicts the landing of Roger Williams on the west bank of the Seekonk in the spring of 1636. Sheltered by the Wampanoags and welcomed by the Narragansetts, Williams established Providence as an experiment in religious liberty.

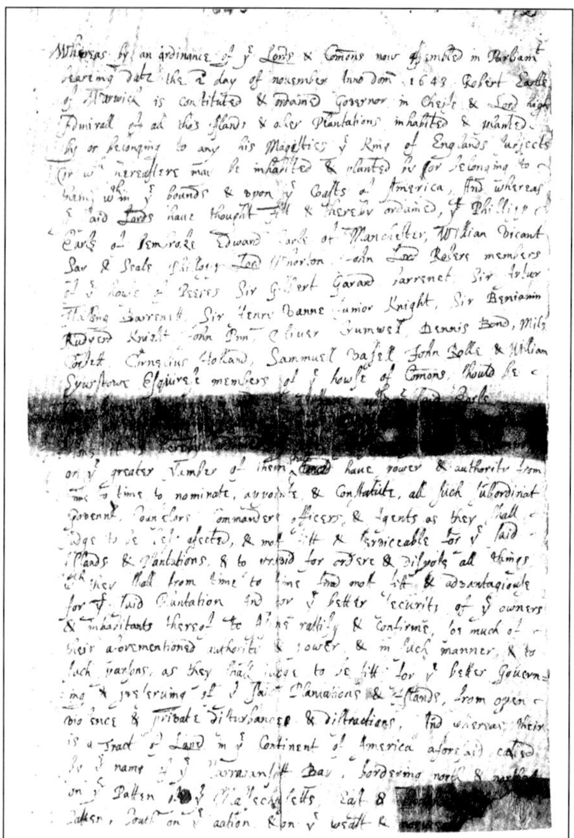

The parliamentary patent of 1644 served as Rhode Island's first instrument of government. Its use of the words "approved and confirmed" rather than "granted" in connection with right to the land was a vindication of Williams's controversial belief that the deeds given to him by the Indians were valid.

Other dissenters soon followed Williams to the Narragansett Bay region, and two additional towns took root: Portsmouth (1638), founded by William Coddington in concert with Antinomian preacher Anne Hutchinson, and Newport (1639), established by Coddington after a squabble with the fiery woman the Puritans called the "American Jezebel."

Legal title to the lands on which the early towns were planted rested only upon deeds from the Narragansett chiefs, or sachems, because Williams had been so bold as to declare that the king of England's authority to grant these New World lands to English colonists rested upon "a solemn public lie." This view, though just, was unacceptable to the neighboring colonies of Plymouth, Massachusetts Bay, Connecticut, and New Haven. The more orthodox Puritans of those colonies, angered by the defiance of Rhode Island's religious outcasts, began to cast covetous eyes upon the beautiful Narrangansett Bay region, which, they said, had been transformed by Williams, Hutchinson, Samuel Gorton, and their kind into "a moral sewer."

To unite the towns against this threat, to thwart Coddington's political designs, and to secure parliamentary protection for his holy experiment, Williams journeyed in 1643 to England, then on the verge of civil war, to secure a patent that would unite the settlements of Portsmouth, Newport, and Providence into a single colony and would officially confirm the settlers' claims to the lands they held by Indian purchase. Williams obtained the desired patent from Robert Rich, earl of Warwick, and his parliamentary Committee on Foreign Plantations. Significantly, the patent lacked the royal seal, for King Charles I had already begun to lose power and control over the parliamentary opposition. Still, Williams' patent of 14 March 1644 became the first legal recognition of the Rhode Island towns by the mother country.

In 1642 volatile Samuel Gorton—another freethinking and quarrelsome religious leader—had succeeded in developing to the south of Providence a mainland settlement which he eventually called Warwick. Here, as in Providence, liberty of conscience prevailed. Although his new town was not mentioned in the patent, Gorton sought and eventually secured its inclusion under the patent's protective provisions, despite the vigorous attempts of Massachusetts to annex the Warwick settlement.

The two island towns of Portsmouth and Newport also embraced the legislative patent, and representatives of the four communities met initially on Aquidneck Island in November 1644. Under this patent Rhode Island began its unique system of rotating its legislative sessions. At one such meeting, held at Portsmouth in May 1647, the colony's lawmakers drafted a famous legal code. According to Charles McLean Andrews, the leading historian of colonial America, "the acts and orders of 1647 constitute one of the earliest programmes for a government and one of the earliest codes of law made by any body of men in America and the first to embody in all its parts the precedents set by the laws and statutes of England."

The 1647 assembly elected officers, established a system of representation, and devised a legislative process containing provisions for both local initiative (repealed in 1650) and popular referendum. Then it enacted the remarkable code, an elaborate body of criminal and civil law prefaced by a bill of rights. Finally, for the administration of justice, the productive assembly established a General Court of Trials with jurisdiction over all important legal questions. The president, who was the chief officer of the colony, and the assistants, who represented their respective towns, were to possess the jurisdiction heretofore exercised in matters of minor and local importance.

The code and the court system of 1647 would serve as the cornerstones of the judicial establishment of both the colony and state of Rhode Island. Thus did the four original towns and their inhabitants combine to create a fairly systematized federal commonwealth and deal a temporary blow to the forces of decentralization.

Stormy seas still lay ahead for the Rhode Island ship of state, for no sooner had a semblance of internal unity and stability been created than two external dangers arose, one of which menaced the colony's landed possessions and the other its very existence. The first danger resulted from the claims of the Connecticut-based Atherton land company to much of present-day Washington County; the second and greater threat arose from the restoration in 1660 of the Stuart dynasty to the throne of England. The Restoration rendered doubtful the legal validity of the parliamentary patent of 1644 and placed Rhode Island in a precarious position because of her close ties with the antimonarchical Commonwealth and Protectorate of Oliver Cromwell.

SIMPLICITIES DEFENCE

against

SEVEN-HEADED POLICY.

OR

A true complaint of a peaceable people, being part of the Engliſh in New England, made unto the ſtate of Old England, againſt cruell perſecutors

United in Church-Government

in thoſe parts.

Wherein is made manifeſt the manifold out-rages cruelties, oppreſſions, and taxations, by cruell and cloſe impriſonments, fire and ſword, deprivation of goods, Lands, and livelyhood, and ſuch like barbarous inhumanities, exerciſed upon the people of Providence plantations in the Nanhyganſet Bay by thoſe of the Maſſachuſets, with the reſt of the united Colonies, ſtretching themſelves beyond the bounds of all their own Juriſdictions, perpetrated and acted in ſuch an unreaſonable and barbarous manner, as many thereby have loſt their lives.

As it hath been faithfully declared to the Honourable Committee of Lords and Commons for Forrain Plantations, whereupon they gave preſent Order for Redreſs.

The ſight and conſideration whereof hath moved a great Country of the Indians and Natives in thoſe parts, Princes and people to ſubmit unto the Crown of England, and earneſtly to ſue to the State thereof for ſafeguard and ſhelter from like cruelties.

Imprimatur, Aug. 3d. 1646. Diligently peruſed, approved, and Licenſed to the Preſſe, according to Order by publike Authority.

LONDON,

Printed by *John Macock*, and are to be ſold by *George Whittington* at the blue *Anchor* neer the Royal *Exchange* in *Cornhil.* 1647.

In this 1647 pamphlet entitled *Simplicities Defense...*, Samuel Gorton (1592–1677), founder of Warwick, denounced the Massachusetts officials who had tried to wrest his settlement from him. Gorton's knowledge of the English common law enabled him to exert significant influence on early Rhode Island legal development.

Fearful for its legal life, the colony commissioned the diligent John Clarke of Newport to obtain royal confirmation of its right to exist. After an exasperating delay stemming from Rhode Island and Connecticut's conflicting claims to the Narragansett Country, Clarke, with the assistance of Connecticut agent John Winthrop, Jr., secured from Charles II the royal charter of 1663. This coveted document was immediately transported to Rhode Island, where it was received by the grateful colonists in November 1663.

The sixty-five-hundred-word instrument had the legal form of a corporate or trading company charter. It devoted relatively brief space to the organization of government, but it did provide for the offices of governor, deputy governor, and ten assistants. The original holders of these positions were named in the charter itself, but their successors, called magistrates, were "to be from time to time, constituted, elected and chosen at-large out of the freemen" of the colony (or "company"). The charter also provided that certain of the freemen should be "elected or deputed" by a majority vote of fellow freemen in their respective towns to "consult," to "advise," and to

Dr. John Clarke (1609–1676), a Newport physician and Baptist preacher, served as Rhode Island's colonial agent in London and, with the help of Connecticut's John Winthrop, Jr., secured the royal charter of 1663.

"determine" the affairs of the colony together with the governor, deputy governor, and assistants. It entitled Newport to six of these "elected or deputed" representatives; Providence, Portsmouth, and Warwick received four each; and two were to be granted to any town which might be established in the future. Though an equitable apportionment in 1663, this provision would become a source of grave discontent in the early nineteenth century.

The governor, deputy governor, assistants, and representatives (or deputies) collectively were called the General Assembly. Each member of this body had one vote. The Assembly, with the governor presiding, was to meet at least twice annually, in May and October. The only charter-imposed qualification for members was that they be freemen of the colony.

Rhode Island's legislature was endowed by the charter with extraordinary power. It could make or repeal any law, if such action was not "repugnant" to the laws of England, set or alter the time and place of its meetings, and grant commissions. Since there was no separation of powers, it could

The royal charter of 1663 made Rhode Island a self-governing colony.

exercise extensive control over the judicial affairs of the colony, prescribe punishments for legal offenses, grant pardons, regulate elections, create and incorporate additional towns, and "choose, nominate and appoint such ... persons as they shall think fit" to hold the status of freemen. In comparison, the governor was weak and the mere executive agent of the Assembly.

The royal charter mandated annual elections for all at-large officers of the colony (the posts of recorder, sergeant, treasurer, and attorney had been created earlier by statute); provided for the raising and governing of a militia; and established acceptable boundaries (which included the Pawcatuck River as the western line of demarcation). Further, the document asserted, with language not unknown in other colonial charters, that inhabitants of the colony "shall have and enjoy all liberties and immunities of free and natural subjects... as if they ... were born within the realm of England." This clause and its alleged violation would cause the mother country serious difficulties a century hence.

Finally, the charter's most liberal and generous provision bestowed upon the inhabitants of the tiny colony "full liberty in religious concernments." The document commanded that no person shall be "molested, punished, disquieted, or called in question for any differences in opinion in matters of religion" that "do not actually disturb the civil peace of our said colony."

This guarantee of absolute religious liberty was a vindication of Williams' beliefs and royal recognition of the fundamental principles upon which the Providence Plantation was founded—absolute freedom of conscience and complete separation of church and state. As Williams observed, this liberality stemmed from the king's willingness to "experiment" in order to ascertain "whether civil government could consist with such liberty of conscience." This was the "lively experiment" upon which the government of Rhode Island was based—an experiment that prompted some to observe that Massachusetts had law without liberty but Rhode Island now had liberty without law.

King Charles II (1630–1685) returned from exile in France to assume the throne of England in 1660. In the immediate aftermath of this restoration, he granted Rhode Island a very liberal charter, making the colony self-governing, and guaranteeing it "full liberty in religious concerments."

Survival and Growth

In the period from 1663 to 1681, the practice of governmental rotation ceased temporarily. During these early years of the charter regime, all sessions of the legislature were held in Newport, often in private homes. Rotation resumed in 1681 and followed a very irregular pattern. Newport remained by far the most frequent site, but occasional sessions were held in Providence, Warwick (until 1741), and Portsmouth (until 1739). Kingstown (not divided into North and South until 1723) hosted its first meeting in 1698, but it did not become a regular site until a 1733 law directed the Assembly to convene in South Kingstown every other October.

From 1696 onward, the colony began to achieve a measure of stability. In that year the General Assembly developed more systematic and workable procedures and formally became bicameral, dividing into the House of Magistrates, or Senate, and the House of Deputies (Representatives). In imitation of the English Parliament, the deputies assumed the task of preparing the tax bill and choosing their own speaker and clerk. Two years later, in 1698, Samuel Cranston was elected governor. During his twenty-nine-year tenure, by far the longest of any Rhode Island governor (he died in office on 26 April 1727), Cranston established internal unity and brought his colony into a better working relationship with the imperial government in London.

During the Cranston regime, the colony's western boundary dispute with Connecticut was resolved in Rhode Island's favor. A second important territorial development, with a direct impact on Rhode Island's network of colony houses, was the creation of the county system in 1703. By that date the Assembly had incorporated five towns in addition to the original four: Westerly (1669), New Shoreham (1672), Kingstown (1674), East Greenwich (1677), and Jamestown (1678). The five mainland communities were assigned to the County of Providence Plantations, while the four island settlements were included in Rhode Island County (later called Newport County). From the outset, however, these counties were merely militia districts and units of judicial administration, not separate layers of government as they are in nearly all other states.

In 1729, six years after Kingstown was divided into North and South, King's (later Washington) County was created, with South Kingstown its seat. The readjustment of the colony's eastern boundary with Massachusetts in 1746 brought Tiverton and Little Compton into Newport County and Cumberland into Providence County. It also prompted the creation of Bristol County from the former Massachusetts communities of Bristol—which became the county seat—and Warren, which then included present-day Barrington. This new judicial unit of less than twenty-five square miles became, and remains, America's second smallest county. The General Assembly did not include Bristol in its rotation scheme until December 1797.

Rhode Island's fifth county, Kent, was set off from the southern tier of Providence County in 1750. A 1759 statute mandated annual meetings of the legislature in East Greenwich, the new county's shire town. That community had first hosted a session of the Assembly in February 1735.

Governing from the Five Colony Houses

The five counties created between 1703 and 1750 influenced the operations of Rhode Island's government for more than a century. Each of these governmental units prompted the construction of a county house in which the General Assembly could meet and the courts deliberate. Because the legislature rotated its sessions from county seat to county seat, each of these buildings became, in effect, a colony house and each county seat became a capital. On the first Monday in May, each newly elected legislature convened and organized at the Newport Colony House, the largest, oldest, and most imposing of these citadels of government.

More frequently and for a much longer duration than they served as seats for the colony's legislative and executive branches, Rhode Island's county facilities housed its judiciary as well. By the charter's general charge to the legislature "to appoint, order and direct, erect and settle, such places and courts of jurisdiction, for the hearing and determining of all actions, cases, matters and things ... as they shall think fit," the basic law of 1663 did not fundamentally alter the judicial structure of 1647. The General Court of Trial was retained, and in 1664 the Assembly ordered that its sessions be held semiannually with the governor or deputy governor and at least six assistants presiding. From time to time several inferior courts were also created.

Because legislative and judicial functions were for a time combined in the same body of men (namely, the governor, deputy governor, and assistants), the General Assembly often exercised functions now considered the exclusive domain of the judicial branch. Almost any part of the judicial process was open to its inspection and possible correction.

The rearrangement of the court system in 1729, through the use of three counties (Newport, Providence, and King's) as units of judicial administration, was a change of primary importance. The lowest tribunal in this county-based structure was the local court of the justice of the peace. This agency, in continuous session, had original jurisdiction in minor matters and bound over more serious offenders to the higher courts of general sessions of the peace. These courts, established in each county, were conducted semiannually by all the local justices of the peace or any five of them, and they were empowered to try all criminal cases, capital crimes excepted. Their decisions could be appealed to the highest court. They in turn exercised appellate jurisdiction over all petty offenses originally triable by a justice of the peace.

The courts of common pleas were civil courts, on the same level as the courts of general sessions, conducted by "judicious" persons chosen by the Assembly from their respective counties. These appointees, upon their selection, were elevated to justiceship of the peace. The jurisdiction of these courts, which was both original and appellate, extended to the trial of nearly all civil actions arising in the county. They conducted business semiannually together with that of the courts of general sessions.

The General Court of Trial, renamed the Superior Court in 1746, sat at the apex of the county system. Held at Newport, it consisted of the governor, deputy governor, and assistants. The Superior Court of Judicature, Court of Assize and General Gaol Delivery (the forerunner of the present Supreme Court) possessed original jurisdiction in certain major cases, but its primary function consisted in reviewing appeals from decisions of the courts of general sessions and the courts of common pleas. Petitions from decisions of the Superior Court, however, were often entertained and acted upon by the General Assembly, and occasionally appeals from the court's verdict were accepted by the king in council.

In February 1746, the governor and assistants were removed from the bench of the Superior Court and replaced by one chief justice and four associates, but this change did not significantly diminish legislative influence. Judges could still be members of the Assembly, so those deputies or assistants appointed to the bench usually retained their legislative posts. Furthermore, the Assembly annually appointed all judges. During the session preceding the 1746 Superior Court Act, the legislature established a formal procedure for receiving, "hearing and determining" petitions praying relief from court decisions, thus strengthening and reaffirming its appellate powers, which were similar to those possessed by the English House of Lords. These practices endured for the remainder of the colonial period. In fact, the petition process and the system of annual appointment persisted until the establishment of the state constitution in 1843.

The development of executive power under the charter of 1663 was comparable to the growth of judicial autonomy: both were repressed by the powerful legislature. Apart from making the governor the presiding officer of the General Assembly and granting him the right to convene special sessions of that body, the charter bestowed upon him few exclusive powers of significance. He had no appointive power, for that important prerogative resided in the legislature, and even the governor's charter-conferred position as commander in chief of militia was carefully circumscribed by the Assembly.

By 1750, Rhode Island's five counties—Providence, Newport, King's (Washington), Bristol, and Kent—had been established, but only as units of judicial administration. This map by historian John H. Cady shows the boundaries of the counties and the early towns.

2

Edwin S. Gaustad, professor emeritus at the University of California, is a leading authority on the history of religion in America. Among his works are *A Religious History of America* and the *Historical Atlas of Religion in America*. The following essay on the legacy of Roger Williams is taken from Gaustad's *Liberty of Conscience: Roger Williams in America* (1991). It attempts to trace the historical reputation of Williams and his influence on Anglo-American thought and practice in the realm of church-state relations.

The Rhode Island founder's basic theme, embodied in his book *The Bloudy Tenent of Persecution*, is that religious persecution, often implemented by the state, is a principal cause of bloodshed and war. Among the most significant conclusions reached by Williams in this and other writings are these: (1) any attempt by the state to enforce religious orthodoxy "stinks in God's nostrils," because it perverts God's plan for the regeneration of souls and is productive of persecution and religious wars; (2) God has not favored any particular form of government, and it is therefore to be inferred that forms of government will vary according to the nature and disposition of the people governed; (3) political and, especially, religious diversity is inevitable; and (4) the human conscience must be completely emancipated through the establishment of religious liberty and the separation of church and state.

Contrary to Rhode Island folklore and the writings of Vernon Parrington, Samuel Brockunier, and other early-twentieth-century historians alluded to by Gaustad, Roger Williams was not an exponent of democratic theory. Despite Williams's belief in spiritual freedom, in his capacity as a civil ruler the founder of Providence insisted upon strict adherence to civil law to prevent chaos. In this sphere Williams was not a political radical, but rather a traditionalist whose approach to governance was authoritarian. This view of Williams is most persuasively propounded by Edmund S. Morgan in *Roger Williams: The Church and the State* (1967).

In the following essay, the final chapter in Gaustad's perceptive intellectual biography of Williams, the author summarizes three hundred years

Roger Williams was banished into this winter wilderness in January 1636 by Puritan leaders because of his unorthodox views advocating the complete separation of church and state. This mid-nineteenth-century romantic painting by Peter F. Rothermel depicts Williams departing from Salem armed only with Bible and staff.

of commentary on the intrepid "Seeker" and evaluates Williams and his historiography. Gaustad avoids the pitfall of presentism while deftly depicting Williams as a man of the 1600s who nevertheless remains vitally relevant to late-twentieth-century America because of his passionate concern for religious liberty.

Roger Williams and His Legacy

Edwin S. Gaustad

When the Massachusetts General Court took its historic action against Roger Williams in 1635, John Cotton remarked that Williams had not been banished so much as he had been "enlarged" to the whole country beyond. None would be more surprised than Cotton himself to learn that this indeed turned out to be the case. By assuming responsibilities for the colony of Rhode Island, Roger Williams was forced to wrestle continuously with the implications of liberty of conscience, with the heartaches as well as the opportunities such liberty brought. And by making his two charter-seeking trips to London, Williams forced many others in England to reflect on the possibility that liberty itself might be "enlarged."

The Rhode Island charter of 1663 acknowledged that the citizens of that small colony had it "much on their hearts (if they may be permitted), to hold forth a lively experiment." That experiment was to test the proposition that religious liberty could exist side by side with civil security and even prosperity. King Charles II and his royal advisers seemed ready in 1663 to place their bets on that possibility, blazing the way for freedom in religion in these words:

> That our royal will and pleasure is, that no person within the said colony, at any time hereafter, shall be any wise molested, punished, disquieted, or called in question, for difference in opinion in matters of religion, [that] do not actually disturb the civil peace of our said colony; but that all and every person and persons may, from time to time, and at all times hereafter, freely and fully have and enjoy his and their own judgments and consciences in matters of religious concernments.

The Reverend John Cotton (1584–1652) was a leading Puritan clergyman and Roger Williams's principal theological antagonist.

The charter further specified that such freedom was not to be understood as a "liberty to licentiousness and profaneness," nor was the civil peace to be disturbed. Roger Williams praised this charter, finding the limitation wholly congenial to his own commitment to "civility" within the social order. More surprisingly, others well outside of Rhode Island found the charter praiseworthy as well.

In 1664 the "Lords Proprietors" of New Jersey, Lord John Berkeley and Sir George Carteret, offered a formal Concession and Agreement that promised settlers of this land, recently seized from the Dutch, the same liberty of conscience in the very same words. No person would be in any way "molested, punished, disquieted or called in question" for any difference in religious opinion or—the New Jersey document added—practice. But again, such liberty was no license for licentiousness or for disturbing the civil peace of the society.

The very next year Charles II granted a charter for the whole of Carolina that demonstrated that the words of the Rhode Island Charter had so soon acquired a special status of their own. Once more the proprietors were authorized to grant a liberty that assured that none would be in any way "molested, punished, disquieted, or called in question for any differences in opinion or practice in matters of religious concernments." "Practice" had by now become a standard partner to "opinion."

The usual proviso was added concerning licentiousness and civil peace; otherwise all persons might enjoy "freely and quietly" their "judgments and consciences in matters of religion." When later that year, the Lord Proprietors spelled out their agreement with potential settlers, in treating religion these titled gentlemen thought they could do no better than repeat the very same words.

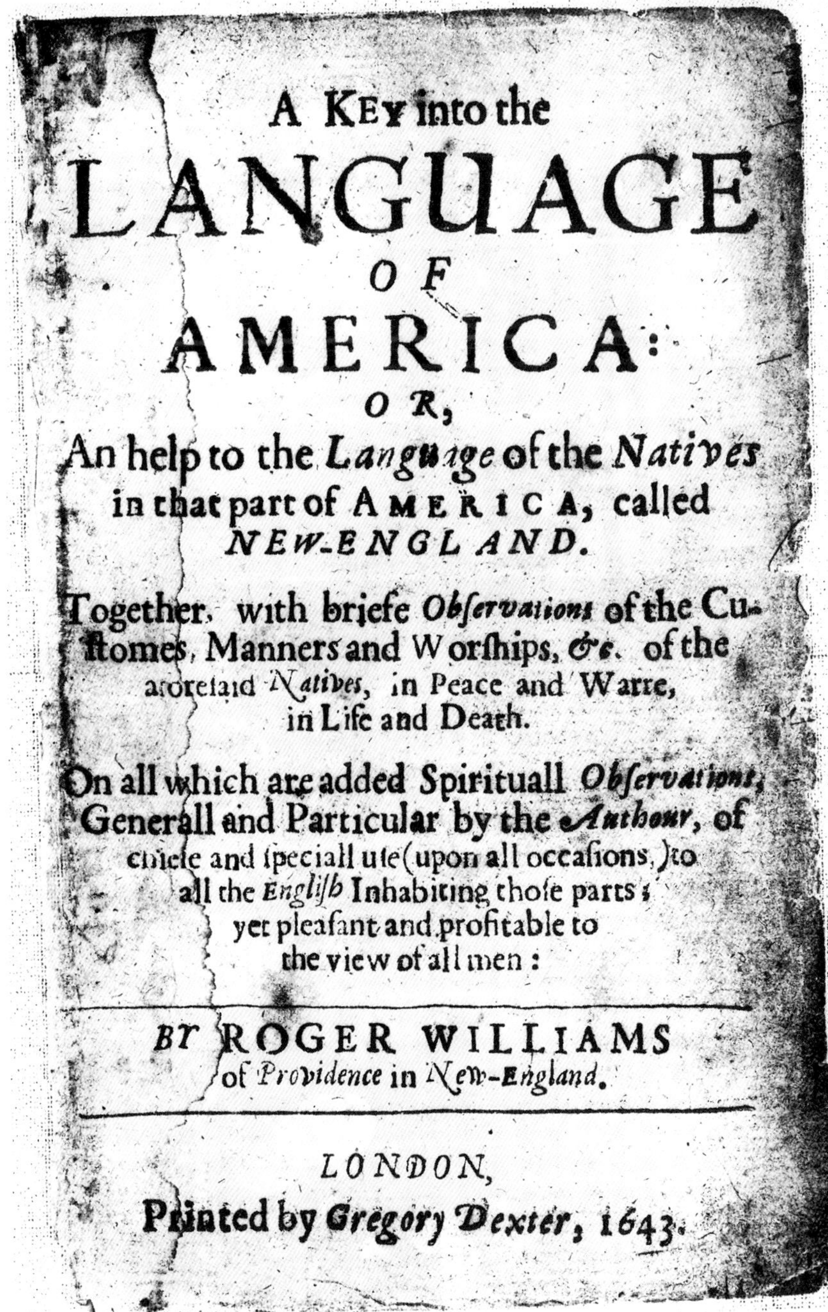

A KEY into the
LANGUAGE
OF
AMERICA:
OR,
An help to the *Language* of the *Natives* in that part of AMERICA, called *NEW-ENGLAND.*

Together, with briefe *Obſervations* of the Cuſtomes, Manners and Worſhips, *&c.* of the aforeſaid *Natives*, in Peace and Warre, in Life and Death.

On all which are added Spirituall *Obſervations*, Generall and Particular by the *Authour*, of chiefe and ſpeciall uſe (upon all occaſions,) to all the *Engliſh* Inhabiting thoſe parts; yet pleaſant and profitable to the view of all men:

BY ROGER WILLIAMS
of *Providence* in *New-England.*

LONDON,
Printed by *Gregory Dexter*, 1643.

In addition to his spiritual ministry to the Native Americans, Williams was concerned with their language and customs. On his return to England in 1643 to secure the parliamentary patent, Williams published his *Key into the Language of America*, the first English-language dictionary and ethnography of an American Indian people.

The colony of New Jersey being divided into two halves in the seventeenth century, West New Jersey felt obliged to issue its own guarantee of liberty of conscience in 1677. Showing a little more originality in wording, this document went beyond "disquieted" and "molested" to declare that no person, on account of religion, would be "in the least punished or hurt, either in person, estate, or privilege." But then, originality exhausted, the statement followed the Rhode Island charter closely in affirming that all persons may "from time to time and at all times, freely and fully have and enjoy his and their judgments and *the exercise of their* consciences in matters of religious *worship*." The italicized words indicate West New Jersey's modifications, it being clear that "practice" or "exercise" needed to be explicitly included as an integral part of religious liberty. Religion was more than mere opinion; to allow persons to think freely but not act freely in religion made no sense to the libertarians of the seventeenth century nor to the libertarians who would follow.

Pennsylvania needed to follow no one else's handbook or model when it came to religious liberty. For that colony's founder, William Penn, had in 1670 published his own manifesto, *The Great Case of Liberty of Conscience*. There Penn made it clear that this liberty had to be more than a liberty of mind: it must include, he wrote, at a minimum the "exercise of ourselves in a visible way of worship." So when a dozen years later Penn's colony came into being, it is not surprising that guarantees to religious liberty were spelled out, and spelled out in quite modern-sounding terms, to both *him* and *her*. No person living "peaceably and quietly under the civil government, shall in any case be molested or prejudiced for his or her conscientious persuasion or practice," this enactment being laid down in 1682. Penn also added that "he or she" would not be compelled at any time "to frequent or maintain any worship, place, or ministry whatever contrary to his or her mind."

John Milton and Roger Williams would both rejoice that the coerced tithe for the support of a hireling ministry was, at least in Rhode Island and Pennsylvania, a thing of the past. Anglicanism continued to enjoy tax moneys in Carolina and New Jersey—despite the assurances of religious liberty—until after the American Revolution. And in New England, of course, the legal tithe on behalf of Congregationalism continued well into the nineteenth century. Even in Pennsylvania religious liberty was assured only to those "who shall confess and acknowledge one almighty God to be the creator, upholder, and ruler of the world." The words of Rhode Island's charter were sometimes more faithfully copied than was the reality for which Roger Williams stood; nonetheless, the Western world was steadily moving further and further away from the "bloody tenent" [of religious persecution, as Williams called it].

John Locke gave that world (especially the English-speaking portion of it) a healthy nudge along its path toward freedom when in 1689, six years after Williams' death, he published his *Letter on Toleration*. Of course, that word *toleration* would have pleased Williams no more in 1689 than it did when Parliament had used it a generation or so before. Liberty was more than toleration, freedom more than a concession. Despite that unassailable fact, however, much of what Locke stated in his powerful Latin epistle would have greatly warmed the heart of the man who had said most of it a half century before. "I regard it as necessary above all to distinguish between the business of civil government and that of religion," Locke wrote, "and to mark the true bounds between the church and the commonwealth." This encapsulated much of what Williams had repeatedly declared, at far greater length, both in London and in Boston.

The civil magistrate, Locke continued, must concern himself only with civil goods, never with the salvation of souls. "It does not appear that God ever gave any such authority to one man over another as to compel other men to embrace his religion." The power of the magistrate lay in compulsion, while the power of religion lay in persuasion. Locke, who wrote persuasively himself about human understanding, added that "such is the nature of human understanding that it cannot be compelled by any outward force. Confiscate a man's goods, imprison or torture his body: such punishments will be in vain." (Williams could only have regretted that John Endecott, also in his grave, was not in a position to hear those words.) The whole of civil government, Locke concluded, "is confined to the care of the things of this world, and has nothing whatever to do with the world to come."

As for the church, Locke contended in words that would make every Separatist happy that it was strictly a "free and voluntary society." No one was born into it, no one could be compelled to it, no outside force could legislate for it. It is a union based on mutual consent, and one must have full freedom to join it as well as full freedom to depart from it. But someone will say, Locke wrote, that it is not a true church unless it has bishops and presbyters. Sounding much like Roger Williams, Locke stated that in quarrels of this sort we should look to the New Testament for an answer—and there we find the following: "Where two or three are gathered together in my name, there am I in the midst of them" (Matt. 18:20). The presence of Christ, not the dignity of church officers or the exact propriety of church ordinances, makes it a church. And where and how is Christ truly present? The answer to that question every voluntary association of worshipers has to determine for itself.

The church has the right of excommunication, Locke agreed, but excommunication means only that: placing one outside of a community of believers. Such a person, set out from one community, has a full right to join another; he should receive no "rough treatment," nor be injured in either body or estate. Christians should not mistreat each other on the grounds of religious errors, nor churches abuse each other—for who truly knows the error? Only the "Supreme Judge of all men, to whom also alone belongs the chastisement of the erroneous." Churches have no jurisdiction in earthly matters, Locke pointed out, "nor are fire and sword proper instruments for refuting errors or instructing and converting men's minds." Those tempted to think otherwise would do well to look to history, said Locke—as Williams had before him. Just consider "what limitless occasions for discords and wars, how powerful a provocation to rapines, slaughters, and endless hatreds" has the spirit of religious persecution brought down upon all humankind.

One need not look to antiquity or to medieval history to find these lessons sharply drawn. England offered all the examples necessary for Locke, as it had for Williams, of the bloodiness as well as the utter irrationality of state-coerced religion. We need only observe "how neatly and promptly under Henry, Edward, Mary, and Elizabeth the clergy changed their decrees, their articles of faith, their form of worship, everything, at a nod from the prince." Obviously, the rulers could not all have been right, and they may very well all have been wrong. But even assuming that any civil magistrate at any given time did chance to be correct, this altered the case against compulsion not one whit. "I may grow rich by an art that I dislike; I may be cured of a disease by remedies that I distrust; but I cannot be saved by a religion that I distrust or by a worship that I dislike." Religion and force can never be properly joined; they were and are in essence totally incompatible; in the end, a person "must be left to himself and his own conscience." Or, as they said in Pennsylvania, to his or her own conscience.

Locke, whose influential political treatises on government were published in this same year, exercised enormous influence in England and, later, in America. In justifying the Glorious Revolution of 1688, he

The Reverend Cotton Mather (1663–1728), grandson of the Reverend John Cotton, was a devout conservator of the Puritan religious tradition and the author of a detailed ecclesiastical history of New England in which Roger Williams fared badly.

helped his countrymen explain their deposing of King James II (who had succeeded his brother Charles II in 1685) and their choosing of William and Mary as their joint sovereigns. He also encouraged the passage of the Toleration Act of 1689, which ended the persecution of Protestant dissent, though it stopped well short of establishing a full freedom for all religious opinion and practice that did not disrupt the civil peace. The seventeenth century did not achieve a total liberty in religion, but by its final years the terrifying ideas that Roger Williams had described in 1644 had lost much of their terror.

The Eighteenth Century

So far as the lasting reputation of Roger Williams went, the eighteenth century did not get off to a promising start. In 1702 Cotton Mather of Massachusetts published in London his *Magnalia Christi Americana; or, The Ecclesiastical History of New England.* In that impressive historical work, Williams does not come off well. On the other hand, Mather's scorn of Williams was expressed with such verve and panache that no one, even now, can resist quoting him, the end result being that even modern students may learn of Rhode Island's maverick chiefly from that one source. Before Rhode Island, of course, Williams was a wild maverick in Massachusetts, and that seized most of Mather's attention. As historian and scholar, Mather would prefer "to leave a veil than a scar upon the memory of any person," but some people were too memorable to ignore. Mather's history would be but "an unfinished piece" were Roger Williams to be left out.

And so Mather began, very artfully, with an anecdote. In Holland, Mather had heard, a windmill in 1654 had been forced by extraordinarily high winds to turn faster and faster until the stone became so hot that it set the mill on fire, and then—those same high winds operating—the whole town was set ablaze. And so to the moral. "But I can tell my readers that, about twenty years before this, there was a whole country in America like to be set on fire by the rapid motion of a windmill in the head of one particular man." The "whole country" was Massachusetts, and the "particular man" was, to be sure, Roger Williams, and Cotton Mather was, to be equally sure, not one of his great admirers.

Williams had "less light than fire in him," Mather observed, that fire bringing him to the hot point of opposing the civil magistrate's enforcement of the First Table. That, said Mather, would have "opened up to a thousand profanities" and turned the Bay Colony into a "sink of abominations." Not content with that, however, "this hot-headed man publicly and furiously preached" against the Massachusetts charter "on an insignificant pretense of wrong thereby done unto the Indians." And, of course, he objected to a religious oath being administered to irreligious men. "These crimes," Mather noted with some relief, "at last procured a sentence of banishment upon him." Whereupon, Williams proceeded with others to the "gathering of a thing like a church" and the founding of a hodge-podge colony that contained "Antinomians, Familists, Anabaptists, Antisabbatarians, Arminians, Socinians, Quakers, Ranters—everything in the world but Roman Catholics and real Christians."

Cotton Mather did give Williams credit for his work with the Indians and his relationships with Massachusetts officialdom following his banishment. In fact, in several respects Williams "acquitted himself so laudably," Mather conceded, "that many judicious persons judged him to have had the 'root of the matter' in him, during the long winter of his retirement." Mather was particularly impressed, of course, by Williams' contesting against the Quakers, an effort in which "he maintained the main principles of the Protestant religion with much vigor." It was just too bad that this had not been his life's work, too bad that he had found it necessary, not to tilt at windmills, but to turn himself into an overheated one.

If Mather spoke for a great deal of Massachusetts in 1702, a Rhode Island clergyman and historian spoke for much of his colony a generation later in offering a rather different assessment of Williams. John Callender, graduate of Harvard (class of 1710), was ordained as a Baptist minister in 1718, one of the Congregational clergymen assisting in that ordination being none other than Cotton Mather. Accepting the invitation of the Baptist church in Newport (John Clarke's church) to become its pastor in 1731, Callender remained in that office until his death in 1748. In 1739 he wrote *An Historical Discourse, on the Civil and Religious Affairs of the Colony of Rhode-Island and Providence Plantations*, an invaluable account and the colony's only published history for a century after.

Callender praised not only Williams but the principles for which he fought. "I take it to have been no dishonor to the Colony," he wrote, "that Christians of every denomination were suffered to lead quiet and peaceable lives, without any fines or punishments for their speculative opinions, or for using those external forms of worship they believed God had appointed." Bigots, he added, may call this confusion and disorder, but Roger Williams knew what was truly the most "monstrous disorder"—namely, "trampling on the consciences" of humankind. Williams, said Callender, was "one of the most disinterested men that ever lived, a most pious and heavenly minded soul"—perhaps exactly what one would expect a Rhode Islander and Baptist to say.

But what about a Quaker in eighteenth-century Rhode Island? What kind of evaluation might Roger Williams expect from that source? Stephen Hopkins, many times governor of the colony between 1755 and 1768 and later signer of the Declaration of Independence, compiled materials for a history of Rhode Island that never was completed. In portions that he did publish in the 1760s, Quaker Hopkins acclaimed Roger Williams as deserving all honor for "having been the first legislator in the world... that fully and effectively provided for and established a free, full, and absolute liberty of conscience." Williams made that "beneficent principle" the "chief cornerstone of his infant colony," so much so that when Massachusetts asked Rhode Island in 1657 to cooperate in stamping out Quakerism. Williams' colony swiftly replied that it had "no law among us" that made any such religious persecution possible.

Hopkins was often enough governor himself, as Williams had been, that he clearly understood what havoc liberty of conscience could make for administrators. It even created problems for the economy and social order.

Every "human felicity," Hopkins noted, "has some attendant misfortune." And of liberty of conscience this was conspicuously true, for it " hath ever been found to produce some disorders, factions, and parties." If one looked for a remedy for these "mischiefs," it could be found only in the "personal virtue and steady perseverance of the wise and good" among Rhode Island's citizens. Only this would ever be sufficient to "withstand the headlong passions of the giddy multitude." Roger Williams' task, said Hopkins, was on the one hand to "guard and maintain that sacred liberty and freedom they had established, and on the other, to prevent and suppress the licentiousness too naturally flowing from it." It was Hopkins' task as well, and perhaps the peculiar task and burden of democracy everywhere.

As Hopkins was publishing segments of his incomplete history in the pages of the *Providence Gazette*, another movement gave a greater reputaion to the colony and ultimately to its founder. The College of Rhode Island, later Brown University, chartered in 1764, was to a considerable degree the creation of the Baptists, those in Rhode Island and far beyond. But it was never intended to be a narrowly sectarian institution, inhospitable to those of other denominations or of none. Indeed, in language as forceful as can readily be imagined, the charter specified that "into this liberal and catholic institution shall never be admitted any religious tests; but, on the contrary, all the members hereof shall forever enjoy full, free, absolute, and uninterrupted liberty of conscience." Not until nearly another century had passed did either Oxford or Cambridge admit dissenters into their midst. In the ringing affirmation of the Brown charter, the spirit of Roger Williams may be discerned, even as it may be discerned twelve years later when the colonies agreed in July 1776 to declare their independence from England. Rhode Island had already issued its own declaration [renouncing George III] two months before.

The Reverend Isaac Backus (1724–1806) was an influential Baptist writer and preacher. During the second half of the eighteenth century, Backus became one of the leading American proponents of church-state separation in the tradition of Roger Williams.

In the period of the American Revolution, the historical reputation of Roger Williams received its greatest boost from a New England Congregationalist become Baptist: Isaac Backus. A native of Connecticut, Backus during the Great Awakening became a pro-revivalist New Light who separated from the official establishment of his home colony. Gradually he came to reject the notion of infant baptism, becoming by 1756 a Baptist pastor in Middleborough, Massachusetts, and remaining so to the end of his long life in 1806. In 1777 he published the first volume of his major work, *A History of New England with Particular Reference to the Denomination of Christians called Baptists*. Quite consciously, Backus sought to rescue Roger Williams from what he regarded as undue neglect, especially in the wider circles outside of Rhode Island. And writing at a time when the American Revolution was underway, Backus also thought that Williams' theme of liberty deserved every possible emphasis.

Gathering a great many documents himself, including twelve of Roger Williams' own letters, Backus was in a position to tell a far fuller story than anyone had before. Indeed, he wrote what almost amounted to a biography of Williams, though the data were immersed in a general historical development and in Backus' own theological commentary. Quoting extensively from manuscript sources, Backus helped to preserve some lost material and called attention to even more. He emphasized Williams' role in creating the country's first Baptist church in Providence, and he emphasized his total dedication to religious liberty. "The first founder and supporter of any truly civil government upon earth" was the encomium that Backus placed upon the head of Williams, adding that he knew of no other person coming to New England in the same period "who acted so consistently and steadily upon right principles about government and liberty as Mr. Williams did."

More than praising Roger Williams, Isaac Backus imitated him in pleading for religious liberty as well as for profound personal piety in the late eighteenth century. When all America in 1774 was alarmed about a tax on tea, Backus thought that Massachusetts would do well to be equally alarmed about a tax on conscience—that is, the tithe collected by force to support the Congregational ministry, whether one attended that ministry or not. It was true, Backus acknowledged, that one could appeal to the state to receive a special exemption by proving that one supported some other church. But even that gave the state an authority over conscience that it did not deserve to have. The legislators of Massachusetts held that no violation of conscience was involved, for the tax was of a purely civil nature. Not so, replied Backus. If the state's clergy were truly "Christ's ministers, he has made laws enough to support them; if they are not" Christ's ministers, then what magistrate has the courage to point that out, while still collecting the taxes? We dissenters, we Baptists, Backus told the Massachusetts legislators face to face, ask only what is legitimately ours: "we claim charter rights, liberty of conscience." In 1779, Backus even suggested a bill of rights that Massachusetts might append to its constitution, a bill making it clear that "every person has an unalienable right to act in all religious affairs according to the full persuasion of his own mind, where others are not injured thereby."

So New England had a strong libertarian Baptist voice during the Revolution and after, as did the heavily populated state of Virginia. Following the religious excitement of mid-eighteenth century known as the Great Awakening, the number of Baptists grew rapidly; heretofore, they had been a small and not particularly aggressive body of believers. With a renewal of pietism and a removal of the Anglican establishment (notably in Virginia), Baptists flourished, and in their flourishing they waved the banners of religious liberty with vigor and effect. In the course of the American Revolution, Virginians moved early against continuing tax support for the Church of England. But in moving toward a full freedom in religion, the pace was slowed by those (for example, Patrick Henry) who thought that some connection between church and state needed to be retained. Thomas Jefferson and James Madison thought otherwise but needed popular support to carry the legislature along with them. Baptists led in that support, petitioning their representatives to defeat the Patrick Henry plan and support Jefferson's Bill for Establishing Religious Freedom.

Madison's justly famous *Memorial and Remonstrance*, presented to Virginia's House of Burgesses in 1785, helped turn the tide in favor of Jefferson and in favor of religious liberty. Madison (like Williams) argued

Thomas Jefferson (1743–1826) was the author of Virginia's famed Statute for Establishing Religious Freedom.

that in matters of religious conscience citizens are accountable to God alone, not to man, and that the civil magistrate was no competent judge of religious truth, nor could he rightfully "employ Religion as an engine of Civil policy." Establishments of religion do far more harm than good to both the civil and ecclesiastical realms, Madison argued. They tend to erect either a spiritual or a political tyranny; "in no instances have they been seen the guardians of the liberties of the people." Should not all America (like Rhode Island) be an asylum "to the persecuted and oppressed of every Nation and Religion," or must we now after winning our own liberty erect "a Beacon on our Coast," warning all sufferers for conscience "to seek some other haven"? For Madison, that question had only one correct answer, and that answer came the next year in the form of Jefferson's long-delayed bill, at last passed in 1786.

Jeffersonian rhetoric required neither earlier documents nor earlier champions of religious liberty. Nevertheless, his statute did echo language of both Rhode Island's and Pennsylvania's charters as it provided that "no man shall be compelled to frequent or support any religious worship, place or ministry whatsoever, nor shall be enforced, restrained, molested, or burthened in his body or goods, nor shall otherwise suffer on account of his religious opinions or beliefs." Jefferson did not even worry about liberty as an excuse for licentiousness or profaneness or about threats to the civil peace. For him, as for Madison and Williams, the greatest threat to civil peace was not liberty of conscience but the farce of "fallible and uninspired men" setting themselves up as inspired and infallible judges of the consciences of others: war, rapine, ravishment, treachery, and torture—every student of recent history knew the bloody results.

So in 1786 Virginia had a Statute for Establishing Religious Freedom. In 1787 the new nation had a constitution to send out for ratification; here Rhode Island was not first, but last, this concern for too strong a central government also reflecting the spirit of Roger Williams and Rhode Island's "giddy multitude." That the Constitution would be ratified at all was far from clear in the early months of 1788, as many persons worried especially about the absence of any federal bill of rights. The Constitution expended too much time saying what government could do, not enough making clear what limits were being placed upon that government, especially with respect to human rights. Virginians, who had their own Declaration of Rights, were among those concerned that an even stronger government did not explicitly restrain itself. Madison, lobbying earnestly for ratification, soon discovered that Virginians in large numbers would vote against the Constitution unless it had a bill of rights.

He learned this in conversation with, among others, John Leland, a Baptist itinerant preacher of great force and great conviction with respect to the separation of church and state. Agreeing with Madison that church establishments had done far more harm than good, Leland declared that all persecution, inquisition, and martyrdom derived from one single "rotten nest-egg, which is always hatching vipers: I mean the principle of intruding the laws of men into the Kingdom of Christ." If one had to choose between persecution and state support, the former should instantly be chosen. "Persecution, like a lion, tears the saints to death," Leland observed, "but leaves Christianity pure; state establishment of religion, like a bear, hugs the saints but corrupts Christianity." Would the United States, like virtually all of Europe, have a national church and form a corrupting alliance with institutional religion? What guarantee did the Constitution provide that it would not?

This uneasiness led Madison to agree with Leland and other constituents that if the Constitution were ratified, Madison would personally pledge that the first order of business in the newly elected Congress would be the drawing up of a bill of rights. Virginia did ratify, though narrowly, and James Madison as a member of the House of Representatives did execute his pledge. In 1789 the first ten amendments to the Constitution were submitted to the people for their approval, the very first phrase of the very first amendment specifying that "Congress shall make no law respecting an establishment of religion, or prohibiting the free exercise thereof." By 1791 that amendment, along with all the others, had become fundamental law for the nation. Though it was a major milestone, neither Jefferson nor Madison nor others "distressed of conscience" would relax. "I have sworn upon the altar of god," Jefferson wrote in 1800, "eternal hostility against every form of tyranny over the mind of man." Jefferson believed that such tyranny had historically been exercised most often by religion. Roger Williams would only have wished to add that religious tyranny had been even bloodier with respect to the bodies of all humankind.

The Nineteenth Century

The most famous wall in American history belongs to Jefferson, not to Williams. With similar but not identical concerns, both men wanted a clear division between the civil and ecclesiastical estates. Williams spoke of it as "the hedge or wall of separation between the garden of the church and the wilderness of the world." Jefferson spoke of it as "a wall of separation between church and state." No evidence demonstrates that the latter statement was dependent on the former, but the interests of both "parties"—pietist and deist—could on occasion happily coincide.

That coincidence led, in fact, to Jefferson's penning of the phrase. Baptists in Connecticut wrote to Jefferson to congratulate him on his election in 1800 to the presidency of the United States. As dissenters in New England, these pietists appreciated Jefferson's dedication to religious liberty in general and to their liberty against the Congregational establishment in particular. Jefferson, like Williams, distrusted religion wedded to power and despised those clergy who seemed more interested in wealth and position than in truth and humble service. Congregationalists, for their part, distrusted Jefferson, whom they saw as their enemy so far as the establishment of religion was concerned. In this, they were correct, for Jefferson eyed all official religion with keen suspicion, convinced that its practitioners looked for any way possible to circumvent or nullify the First Amendment.

Baptists, being powerless, aroused less suspicion, though Jefferson was surprised that in their letter they asked him to set aside a day of fasting so

James Madison (1751–1836) was the author of *The Memorial and Remonstrance against Religious Assessments* (1786) and the principal architect of the religion clauses of the First Amendment.

that the nation might heal its wounds from a bitterly divisive campaign between him and John Adams. Jefferson would declare no such day of fasting or feasting or anything else pertaining to religion, for to do so would be to add more fuel to the dangerous mixture of religion and politics. On the other hand, he did not want to ignore a letter from faithful supporters in Connecticut—where he had so few. Thus, he composed a careful reply, telling these pietists that he shared their view that religion was solely a matter between the believer and the Deity, with government standing quite aside. One owed to the state no account whatsoever concerning one's faith or worship, as the Constitution now made clear. "I contemplate with solemn reverence," Jefferson wrote, "that act of the whole American people"—that is, the First Amendment as ratified by the people. Then Jefferson gave his special spin to the amendment by describing its force as "thus building a wall of separation between church and state."

Jefferson, who had fought for so long in Virginia for religious freedom, would now fight for its preservation and fortification at the national level. Even with that precious amendment, religious liberty depended on an approving public, for public opinion, he argued, could itself become a kind of inquisition. During his eight years in the presidency as well as in many letters written in retirement at Monticello, Jefferson tried to remold people's minds to accept, perhaps even glory in, the possibility set forth in Rhode Island's 1663 charter: "to hold forth a lively experiment, that a most flourishing civil state may stand and best be maintained... with a full liberty in religious concernments." Jefferson devoutly wished to keep that Rhode Island experiment—now the American experiment—lively.

Jefferson was succeeded in the presidency by his colleague in the battle for religious freedom, James Madison. A scholarly and brilliant statesman and the most powerful mental force at the Constitutional Convention, Madison, when still in his early twenties, cried out against that "diabolical, hell-conceived principle of persecution" which he saw being practiced in his own Virginia neighborhood. In jailing some itinerant Baptist preachers, Anglicans unwittingly created a powerful enemy of all bloody swords wielded in the name of religion. His *Memorial and Remonstrance*, written when he was all of thirty-five years of age, made his position more explicit and firm. Then in his "generalship" of the First Amendment, Madison thought even more deeply about the questions of liberty of conscience, his own proposed draft including that favorite word of Roger Williams, *conscience*. Madison offered this initial version: "The Civil Rights of none shall be abridged on account of religious belief or worship, nor shall any national religion be established, nor shall the full and equal rights of conscience be in any manner, nor on any pretext infringed." Three months of discussion, debate, and modification would transpire before the much shorter form of the First Amendment's religion clauses emerged.

Thus eight years of a Madisonian presidency added to eight years of a Jeffersonian presidency worked to set the liberty of religion on as firm a foundation as possible. Not everyone was convinced. Indeed, counter-pressures continued throughout the nineteenth century, including some persistent official establishments of religion. For the First Amendment specified only what Congress could or could not do, not what paths the individual states might follow. Connecticut, for example, continued its establishment until 1818, when it was overturned in a very close vote. This prompted Jefferson to rejoice (in a letter to John Adams—they now were friends again) that "this den of priesthood is at length broken up, and that a protestant popedom is no longer to disgrace American history and character." No longer in Connecticut, that is, for establishment continued for yet another fifteen years in Massachusetts. By the time it fell, neither Adams nor Jefferson could rejoice, for both had passed from the scene.

The deists did not speak for all the American people; in fact, they spoke for very few. The pietists, who came much closer to representing the broad public, made religious liberty real not so much by talking about it as by living it. In the westward expansion of the first half of the nineteenth century, along the ever-shifting frontier, religion moved with a freedom that belied all fear about how a nation could survive without a national church—or without at least some government protection of and support for the many churches. As it turned out, churches divorced from the state proved to be even more lively as they carried on the lively experiment; in the words of the Rhode Island charter, church members proceeded to "freely and fully have and enjoy his and their own judgments and consciences." To be sure, those judgments and consciences could be and often were wrong, conspicuously so in the case of the nineteenth-century alliances with nativism and defenses of slavery. In the long run, however, even so strong a defender of "official religion" as Lyman Beecher agreed that the voluntary system turned out to be far better for the whole country: it cut churches loose from the state and "threw them wholly on their own resources and on God." And that was where reliance needed to be, not upon heavy-handed civil magistrates who still had difficulty distinguishing between incivility on the one hand and impiety on the other.

In general, those denominations did best that loved the state least. Baptists, Methodists, Disciples of Christ (a group of frontier origin in the 1830s) and others who had never known establishment and never cared for it took to this new freedom with alacrity and joy. It was as though they had suddenly broken free of all oppression, restraint, and political disfavor. The two major colonial establishments, Congregationalism and Anglicanism, on the other hand, reacted quite differently. Now suddenly unburdened, these two denominations felt suddenly heavy with the weight of fiscal responsibility. This was particularly true of the Anglicans, now Episcopalians, for whom disestablishment came abruptly, even harshly. In Virginia after the Revolution, Episcopalians bemoaned their dreary and outcast state: ministers unpaid, churches not maintained, "and there is no fund equal to the smallest want." For them, rcligious liberty was, at best, a mixed blessing.

The future, however, belonged to those who reveled in the freedom, splashed in it like adolescents at the swimming ponds. They would build their own churches without the help of anyone, they would ordain their own clergy without the authority of synod or benefit of university, they would arrive at their own creed innocent of most history and most theology. By the time Andrew Jackson became president in 1829, it had become the age of the people in politics no less than in religion. In a sense, the nation had decided between Roger Williams and John Cotton, and Cotton had lost.

Not everyone was happy with the way things had turned out. John Quincy Adams, for one, was certainly unhappy with how the election had turned out in 1828, for he was obliged to turn the presidency over to a rude westerner and Indian fighter. But this Adams was no happier about the way the contest between Cotton and Williams seemed to be turning out. When years later he had to prepare an address for the Massachusetts Historical Society, he discussed Roger Williams and the colony for which he was responsible and indicated that he did not care much for either. Williams, wrote Adams in 1843, came to Massachusetts "sharpened for controversy, a polemical porcupine from Oxford, an extreme puritan, quilled with all the quarrelsome metaphysical divinity of the age." *He* was the aggressor, Adams averred, not the Bay Colony, certainly not John Cotton, and "I cannot acquit him." Moreover, "his excommunications were all intolerant, his refusal to take the oath of allegiance was factious, his preaching against it seditious." Why at this time had the nose of John Quincy Adams been tweaked somewhat out of joint about Roger Williams?

The answer lay in a volume that had appeared a few years earlier. Written by a Massachusetts historian, it nonetheless seemed to take the part of the Narragansett colony against the Bay Colony. "It has in recent times," Adams wrote, "become a sort of literary fashion to extol the character of Roger Williams by disparaging" the character of Massachusetts. Though dead more than a century and a half, the "polemical porcupine" still had power in his quills. What had irritated Adams was the first volume of George Bancroft's monumental *History of the United States*, which emerged in 1834, the whole ten volumes being completed some forty years later. A graduate of Harvard and a native son of Massachusetts, Bancroft alienated Adams by being both pro-Williams and pro-Jackson. In Bancroft's view, the age of the people had indeed arrived, automatically making heroes out of all those who had resisted entrenched privilege and aristocratic power.

Williams, more a political than a theological figure for Bancroft, emerged as "the first person in modern Christendom to establish civil government on the doctrine of liberty of conscience, the equality of opinions before the law." (Williams might have appreciated the compliment, but he would have despised the use of the term *Christendom*.) Williams, Bancroft added, "would permit persecution of no opinion, of no religion, leaving heresy unharmed by law, and orthodoxy unprotected by the terrors of penal statutes." Writing in the romantic mode, Bancroft went on at length about the virtues of Roger Williams, even of Rhode Island and "the excellency of the principles on which it rested its earliest institutions." Bancroft's credentials as a Massachusetts man were certainly in danger of being challenged, especially as he launched into the following peroration: "Let, then, the name of Roger Williams be preserved in universal history as one who advanced moral and political science, and made himself a benefactor of his race." It remained to be seen whether Williams, who had endured countless persecutions, would survive such ebullient praise.

More praise was on its way, for example, in the form of biographies that began to appear, the first in 1834 (by James D. Knowles), the second (by Romeo Elton) in 1853. In 1860 the president of Brown University, Francis Wayland, joined in the chorus by praising Williams' "stern love of individual liberty." At this point Williams had not yet had any monuments erected to him; there was not even a marker over his grave, its exact location being uncertain. But, said Wayland, "there are some men whose monuments are everywhere, who are known as wide as civilization." The Pilgrims in America, Wayland added, sought liberty for themselves; Roger Williams in America sought "liberty for humanity."

If the first half of the nineteenth century brought both the age of the people and the freedom of religion to full flower, the second half of that century brought in a world to which Roger Williams would have been a stranger: large cities, great factories, millions of immigrants, and a loss of cultural authority for religion. As Americans advocated and exercised their liberty, they gave little thought to the parable of the wheat and the tares in determining the proper limits for either church or state. Biblical arguments moved out of the public sphere into the private domains of denominations and seminaries. So also arguments about the stature and significance of Roger Williams tended to become the concern of the churches only.

On the whole, Congregationalists felt obliged to defend the role of John Cotton and Massachusetts, while Baptists felt a similar obligation to defend Roger Williams and Rhode Island. In 1876 Congregationalist Henry Martyn Dexter published an argumentative tract entitled *As to Roger Williams and His "Banishment" from the Massachusetts Plantation. With a few further words concerning the Baptists, the Quakers, and Religious Liberty.* To summarize the contents in fewer words than the title, Williams persecuted Massachusetts, not the other way around. A Baptist pastor in Providence, Henry Melville King, responded with an equally argumentative tract that defended the reputations of Roger Williams, John Clarke, and Obadiah Holmes while attacking the reputation of Massachusetts and the five-volume production of its current apologist historian, John Gorham Palfrey. At the end of the century, the denominational spat continued, with Congregationalist Leonard Bacon (*History of American Christianity*, 1897) squared off against Baptist Albert H. Newman (*A History of the Baptist Churches in the United States*, 1894).

Meanwhile, Roger Williams was being rescued by scholars in the academic world, and by one scholar in particular, Moses Coit Tyler. Despite his Congregational and Yale background, Tyler gave Williams very high marks. In 1878 he published his influential *History of American Literature during the Colonial Time*, a work that soon became the standard critical evaluation of the literary production for the years from 1607 to 1765. Tyler found Williams most refreshing, conceding that this might be because one became "rather fatigued by the monotony of so vast a throng of sages and saints, all quite immaculate, all equally prim and stiff." Williams, by contrast, moved with an easy swing, escaped "the paste-board proprieties," vented his impetuosity, and indulged his indiscretions. He was, in short, a man of "singular vitality." And by 1878, Tyler thought that Williams had in fact carried the day. "The world, having at last nearly caught up with him, seems ready to vote—though with a peculiarly respectable minority in opposition—that Roger Williams was after all a great man, one of the true heroes, seers, world-movers, of these latter ages." The "peculiarly respectable minority" did not disappear in the nineteenth nor in the twentieth century, but to the extent that Tyler's evaluation prevailed, the nineteenth century ended on a high note for the "polemical porcupine."

The Twentieth Century

Not to be outdone, the twentieth century likewise opened on a high note. In 1902 Irving B. Richman published a two-volume history entitled *Rhode Island: Its Making and Its Meaning.* Its meaning, it turned out, derived directly if not solely from the life and work of Roger Williams. Williams was, Richman wrote, "by moral constitution a humanitarian, and by mental an idealist." Along with that, however, he was a "commonwealth builder, and his building was according to his qualities." Williams built Providence and made possible the colonization of Aquidneck Island, Richman noted, and "his doctrine of Soul Liberty" pervaded all. One year later another Brown University president, W. H. P. Faunce, echoed Richman's sentiments but added some of his own, as well as those of James Russell Lowell, a poet and essayist of the previous generation. Lowell had commented that seventeenth-century New England could boast of only two great spirits: John Winthrop, Sr., and Roger Williams. Faunce agreed, adding that as Columbus gave substance to the theories that the world was round, so Williams gave substance to the theories that religious liberty was the friend rather than the enemy of the civil state. In his battle with John Endecott, Williams faced the sunrise and the future, Faunce concluded, while Endecott faced "the sunset and the dark."

In thc first third of the twentieth century, many thought that the future did indeed lay with Roger Williams. Reform-minded historians of the Progressive era lauded liberty and promoted the cause of human dignity. In their reading of the national past, the Puritans emerged as enemies to these causes; indeed, Puritan-bashing became the fashion. As the historical fortunes of Puritanism declined, those of Roger Williams rose. Anyone that the Puritans criticized or banished must have done or thought something right. So Williams came to be identified with democratic reform and social progress.

In 1927 Vernon L. Parrington published the first of three volumes under the general title of *Main Currents in American Thought.* A student of both literature and history, Parrington—like Isaac Backus—sought to rescue the reputation of Williams, but not as a pietist or theologian so much as a democrat and political liberal. Roger Williams was, Parrington declared, "primarily a political philosopher rather than a theologian," and this he meant as high praise. Of an acute mind, Williams stood out as "the teacher of Vane and Cromwell and Milton, a forerunner of Locke and the natural-rights school, one of the notable democratic thinkers that the English race has produced." Determined to outmatch George Bancroft, Parrington expanded on the virtues of this seventeenth-century Separatist transformed into a twentieth-century democrat. "England gave her best," Parrington wrote, when she sent us Roger Williams. "A great thinker and a bold innovator, the repository of the generous liberalisms of a vigorous age, he brought with him the fine wheat of long years of English tillage to sow in the American wilderness." Parrington, who enjoyed his metaphors, pressed them for all they were worth, and sometimes beyond. But then he abandoned his agricultural allusions to state more directly, if extravagantly, that Williams was "certainly the most generous, most open-minded, most lovable of the Puritan emigrants—the truest Christian amongst many who sincerely desired to be Christian." After that eulogy, little remained to be said of John Cotton except that "his dreams and aspirations lie forgotten in the grave of lost causes and forsaken faiths."

While other Progressives were not so effusive, the votes—as Moses Coit Tyler would say—came in heavily on the side of Williams. In his massive *Colonial Period of American History* (1934), Charles M. Andrews even entered the denominational fray long enough to dismiss Henry Martyn Dexter as a biased witness when it came to Roger Williams, one whose historical judgments inspired no confidence in this area. Later in the 1930s, the concern for liberty took on a particular focus—namely, the suspicion of and antagonism toward the rising power of fascism and communism. Partisans for democratic liberty gathered in all who might conceivably be enlisted on their side, and a major biography of Roger Williams appeared in 1940 under the title *The Irrepressible Democrat* (by Samuel H. Brockunier).

Following World War II intellectual history enjoyed a renaissance, with historians taking seriously the content of all ideas, even theological ones. Inspired by the labors of Harvard's Perry Miller, scholars gave up Puritan-bashing as a favorite indoor sport. But the fact that the Puritans received far more serious and sustained scholarly attention did not mean that Roger Williams' stock went down. The battle was no longer partisan. Now the key was whether theology ought once again to be read, weighed, and understood. With respect to Roger Williams, Miller took the lead here as well, publishing in 1953 a small but highly influential book entitled *Roger Williams: His Contribution to the American Tradition.* With some scorn, Miller dismissed the notion of Williams as "the precursor of Jefferson, of liberalism and of rationalism." Miller, who understood Williams as theologian first and political theorist second, changed the direction of scholarly studies. He influenced many, notably Ola E. Winslow, whose excellent biography of Williams appeared in 1957, and Edmund S. Morgan, whose first-rate extended essay was published a decade later.

In the broader culture, meanwhile, Roger Williams continued to attract attention. The U.S. Supreme Court even granted him a footnote as it decided in 1962 that a state-mandated prayer for New York's public schools was a violation of the First Amendment. (In the 1940s the Court made that Amendment applicable to the states, which is only one reason that religion cases now tumble over each other onto the judicial dockets.) Justice Hugo Black, speaking for the Court, noted that men and women had crossed the ocean to escape from "officially established state religions and religious persecution in Europe." They emigrated to America in order to be able to pray when and how they pleased, in terms of their own faith, not in terms of the faith of the civil magistrates. And that seemed the appropriate spot to nod in the direction of Roger Williams who (said Black in a footnote) was "perhaps the best example of the sort of man who came to this country for precisely this reason."

More than two decades later, the Court considered an Alabama law that authorized a moment of silence in the public schools for the purpose of "meditation or voluntary prayer." The Court decided in 1985 that this too was unconstitutional, although the opinion was not unanimous. Justice William Rehnquist vigorously dissented, rejecting not only this particular decision but also the tendency "for nearly forty years" to read the Constitution and its Bill of Rights as though Roger Williams, Thomas Jefferson, and James Madison were the primary authors of or authorities on it. The "wall of separation" was, Rehnquist argued, a misleading metaphor, and, having appeared in a private letter, it was totally without constitutional force. The First Amendment did not require the government to be strictly neutral with respect to religion, the justice stated; it only prohibited a national church or sectarian favoritism. Since the Alabama case dealt with prayer, Rehnquist thought it apropos to note that even George Washington proclaimed national days of thanksgiving and prayer. "History must judge," Rehnquist concluded, "whether it was the father of his country in 1789, or a majority of the Court today, which has strayed from the meaning of the Establishment Clause."

In 1985 Rehnquist was a dissenter and an associate justice. By 1990 he was less often a dissenter and served now as chief justice. In a case heard that year relating to religious free exercise, the justices pulled back from their jealous regard for the religious minority, the "distressed for conscience." In other words, they pulled back from Roger Williams, to say nothing of Jefferson and Madison. The case, which concerned the ritual use of peyote by two members of the Native American Church, resulted in a sharply narrowed understanding of just how free "free exercise" should be. Writing for the majority, Justice Anthony Scalia stated that government cannot afford the "luxury" of striking down laws just because they interfered with someone's religious practices. Religious practices "not widely engaged in" will inevitably suffer, Scalia conceded, but that must be preferred "to a system in which each conscience is law." John Cotton would have agreed. Others disagreed, including dissenter Justice Harry Blackmun, who firmly stated, "I do not believe the Founders thought their dearly bought freedom from religious persecution a 'luxury,' but an essential element of liberty." Though he probably did not have Roger Williams in mind as a founder, he nonetheless would have warmly embraced the Rhode Islander's remark that, "having bought truth dear, we must not sell it cheap, not the least grain of it for the whole world."

In the past half-century, American society has become noisily and notoriously pluralistic. This has made Roger Williams more relevant, for he had strong opinions about what government should do about religious pluralism: leave it alone. Turks, Jews, infidels, papists: leave them alone.

By 1990 the list had grown much longer, but the principle remained the same. Religion has the power to persuade, never the power to compel. Government does have the power to compel, but that government is wisest and best which offers to liberty of conscience its widest possible range.

As to the year 2000 and beyond, one cannot anticipate what will happen to the reputation of Roger Williams, how praised or how damned, how distorted or how ignored he might be. For the sake of both the garden of the church and the wilderness of the world, however, the hope remains that he will not again become an exile.

3

The following essay by Glenn W. LaFantasie, an authority on both Roger Williams and the Narragansett Indians, describes Rhode Island's first major criminal manhunt and sheds light on the status of red men and white in local colonial courts. It may surprise some that in 1638 three whites could be executed for the murder of one Indian, and that Massasoit's view of felony murder prevailed over Roger Williams's more restrictive interpretation of the crime. However, such relative equality before the law was not uncommon in early New England.

Alden T. Vaughan's *New England Frontier: Puritans and Indians, 1620–1675* (rev. ed., 1979), a leading work on this subject, asserts that "when the Indian came to the Puritan's courts for civil or criminal cases, he could expect just treatment.... Case by case, the New England court records reveal no apparent discrimination against the Indian. A white plaintiff was not assured of a favorable decision, nor an Indian of an adverse one."

LaFantasie, the holder of a graduate degree in history from the University of Rhode Island, began his professional career as publications director of the Rhode Island Bicentennial Commission (ri76). Thereafter he was retained by the state attorney general's office to research the validity of the tribal claims of the Narragansetts, and he then became the associate editor of the *Correspondence of Roger Williams* (2 vols, 1988). His most important work on Rhode Island's native population, coauthored with Paul R. Campbell, is "Scattered to the Winds of Heaven: Narragansett Indians, 1676–1880," *Rhode Island History* 37 (1978), 67–83.

Murder of an Indian, 1638: Equal Treatment before the Law

Glenn W. LaFantasie

The expanse of forest between Plymouth and Providence was, in the 1630s, a no-man's land—and a perfect scene for murder.

Separating the established Pilgrim town at Plymouth harbor from the fledgling settlement founded by Roger Williams at the head of Narragansett Bay, a wilderness stretched for forty miles. So deserted was this country that no English colony asserted jurisdiction over the land. For whites who ever stopped to think about it, the wilderness loomed as a danger to be avoided, at least while their own settlements remained small enough to provide plenty of elbow-room. For Indians, the land offered abundance and a source of survival in the form of prime hunting grounds.

Trees and brush covered this land with a density broken only by occasional swamps, narrow rivers, and meandering brooks. Some cleared land, mostly near marshes in the interior, stood in stark contrast to the woodlands. A white man could get easily lost in this tangle of woods and fen, as John Billington learned in July 1621. He wandered five days in the forest and survived by eating berries and anything else he could find. By chance, he stumbled upon an Indian plantation at Manomet, south of Plymouth. Finally, the governor of the Pilgrim settlement learned of Billington's whereabouts and sent a boat to bring him safely home.

Despite the sheer desolation of this wilderness, a number of Indian paths and trails traversed the interior and by the late 1630s both Indians and whites used these primitive highways for travel and trade. From Plymouth a main trail twisted west through the forest to a place called Titicut by the Indians, then on to Cohannet, through Misquamsqueece and Seekonk, and across the Seekonk River to Pawtucket—the place of the falls. From Pawtucket, the small settlement of Providence stood only four miles south. This trail, winding and rough, linked Plymouth and Providence together, though as a means of communication the Indian path only may have reminded the Separatists at Plymouth and the religious dissenters in Providence of the great distance existing between them, both physically and ideologically.

In the summer of 1638 along this trail an Indian was murdered by a group of white men. And although the Indian victim held no great office among his people, though he personally wielded no power or authority in his lifetime, his death sent sudden shockwaves rippling throughout southern New England and brought Indians and whites into a confrontation that nearly erupted in a war of revenge and pride.

Massasoit Ousamequin (ca. 1580–1661), chief sachem of the Wampanoags, greeted the Pilgrims in 1621, sheltered Williams in early 1636, and fathered the famous King Philip. After the killing of Penowanyanquis, he applied the doctrine of felony murder to justify the execution of all perpetrators. Massasoit's statue (shown here), by Cyrus O. Dallin, stands atop Cole's Hill in Plymouth, Massachusetts.

In July 1638, Mixanno, the son of the sagacious Canonicus, chief sachem of the Narragansett Indians, decided to send a gift to the English magistrates at Plymouth. He intended the gift as a symbol, an expression, of Narragansett friendship with the whites. Indians in seventeenth-century New England shared a lively fascination for white man's goods—material items that were sometimes practical (such as knives and cloth), sometimes ornamental (such as trinkets and clay pipes). One sure way to receive English commodities was to first offer a token in Indian goods. Mixanno, however, chose not to bring his gift to Plymouth himself. For the job he selected an Indian named Penowanyanquis, a personal messenger or a manservant. Whatever his status, he was not a Narragansett; Penowanyanquis was a Nipmuck Indian.

This original deed for Providence Plantations to Roger Williams from Narragansett sachems Canonicus (who signed with a bow) and Miantonomi (who signed with an arrow) was executed on March 24, 1638, and confirmed earlier verbal grants of land. Close cooperation between natives and the English marked the early years of the Rhode Island Colony.

The Nipmucks were, like the Narragansetts, part of the Algonquin family of nations. They inhabited lands that today comprise central Massachusetts and northwestern Rhode Island. During the years 1616 to 1621, a catastrophic plague struck the natives of southern New England—including the Nipmucks and the Wampanoags—and decimated the Indian population. But this epidemic of unknown origin and variety left the already powerful Narragansetts unscathed. Realizing the plague presented opportunities better than war ever could, the Narragansetts simply expanded their domain and exerted control over their less fortunate neighbors who were in no position to resist the incursion. Thus the Nipmucks became tributaries of the Narragansetts, conquered people governed by the leaders of a traditional enemy.

Mixanno entrusted Penowanyanquis, the Nipmuck, with the task of delivering his gift to the English. Carrying three beaver skins and some Indian beads, Penowanyanquis left Narragansett country (the southern part of present-day Rhode Island) and followed the Indian trail toward Plymouth.

Penowanyanquis faced a number of dangers traveling alone in the forest between Narragansett country and Plymouth colony. This land was the hunting grounds of the Wampanoags—enemies of both the Narragansetts and the Nipmucks. Massasoit, the wily chief sachem of the Wampanoags, resented the audacious Narragansetts for their expanding empire and showed only contempt for the Nipmucks, whom he considered weak and unworthy. Intertribal feuds and the possibility of meeting unfriendly Indians were not the only danger, however. During the 1630s, incidents of white malevolence toward Indians increased steadily. Some unsavory English did not think twice about whipping Indians they thought impudent or robbing goods and property from Indians they considered push-overs.

As a result, Penowanyanquis probably felt a certain uneasiness when he encountered a group of four white men on the trail as he traveled toward Plymouth. When no interchange occurred, the Indian continued his journey unmolested and unharmed. Penowanyanquis finally arrived in Plymouth safely and he completed his appointed duties without mishap.

But on the trail where he had left them, the four white men—Arthur Peach, Thomas Jackson, Richard Stinnings and Daniel Cross—devised a plan, a scheme that included Penowanyanquis as their victim. These men were already fugitives, only one step ahead of the law. All four had fled Plymouth and their positions as indentured servants.

Indentured servants in Plymouth colony formed the backbone of the settlement's labor force. Although contracts were usually voluntary, working conditions were often strenuous and demanding. A laborer might be compensated with a sum of money or might work to pay off a debt, to educate a child, or even to learn a trade as an apprentice. Stinnings in 1635 hired himself out to Robert Bartlett for nine years and the contract terms specified that upon completion of his indenture he would receive from his master two suits of clothing and a modest sum of money. Stinnings was known as an "apprentice" but the exact nature of his work is not revealed in the records of Plymouth colony.

Edward Winslow (1595–1655), to whom Arthur Peach was indentured, was a governor of Plymouth Colony on three occasions. In 1621 he had negotiated the first treaty with Massasoit. Winslow was a foe of Samuel Gorton, but a very effective liaison between the English and the Indians.

Even less is known about the terms of indenture for the other three men who comprised the motley group along the trail, probably because contracts for servants were usually executed informally as verbal agreements. This may have been the nature of Peach's contract with his master Edward Winslow. The historical records do not mention the names of Jackson's or Cross's employers, although one of these servants was apparently bound to master John Barnes of Plymouth.

Runaway servants disrupted the organization of the Pilgrim work force and frequent desertions represented the worst and most chronic problem with which masters had to contend. In 1633, for example, Thomas Brian, a servant of Samuel Eddy, had run away for five days but had turned up lost in the woods. He was tried for this offense and sentenced to be "privately whipped before the Governor and Council" of the colony. Later that same year, Will Mendlow had received a similar punishment for running away and "attempting uncleanness" with a maid servant. Abandonment of servitude involved only grim rewards unless, of course, a servant escaped for good.

Having broken the terms of their agreements, the four fugitives from Plymouth realized that they would be safe from the long arm of Pilgrim justice only when they reached sanctuary beyond New England's borders. But it is not clear, except in the case of Peach, why these men left Plymouth in the first place.

Peach had good reason to flee Plymouth. A respected member of the community, he had served the English well as a member of the militia in the Pequot Indian War of 1637. Because Plymouth colony took no active role in the war (a force of fifty men raised to fight the Indians received word that the war had ended just as the men were ready to march), Peach's militia service meant that he probably had settled first in neighboring Massachusetts Bay sometime in the 1630s. After the war he made his way to Plymouth and became indentured to Edward Winslow, a former governor of the colony. Contemporary opinions differed, but it seems that Peach was initially well-liked in the Pilgrim settlement. Governor John Winthrop of Massachusetts Bay described Peach as "a young man of good parentage and fair condition." Soon after Peach's arrival in Plymouth, however, trouble began.

Though he made arrangements to work for Governor Winslow, Peach demonstrated a remarkable lack of enthusiasm for manual labor. He became lazy, even at times idle, yet he also enjoyed lavish spending and his debts soared. Bad as this was, Peach managed to get himself involved in even worse trouble—and scandal.

He took a liking to Dorothy Temple, a house servant indentured to Stephen Hopkins, one of Plymouth's admired leaders. Hopkins's wife Elizabeth disapproved of Peach and suspected that he and Dorothy were having an illicit love affair. Elizabeth Hopkins convinced her husband that Peach should be forbidden to see Dorothy. So the dutiful Hopkins warned him to stay away from both the young woman servant and the Hopkins homestead.

The warning came too late. Dorothy was pregnant and she informed Peach that she carried his child. Faced with certain punishment for the crime of fornication, he decided to desert this hapless girl, the indignant Hopkins, his master Winslow, and the entire Plymouth colony.

Somehow he pursuaded Stinnings, Jackson and Cross to accompany him in his flight. Whether these men had also violated Plymouth law or whether they had grown tired of their working conditions and surroundings is not known. Whatever their circumstances, the three servants followed Peach out of town in the dead of night and the four fugitives tried to find their way along the Indian trails to the west. Peach, ringleader for the group, had set their course for the Dutch colony of New Netherlands on the Hudson River, an area where they would be free from Pilgrim authority.

When these men encountered Penowanyanquis on the trail, they had already grown desperate and worried. For one thing, they were not quite sure of their whereabouts and they had already succeeded a number of times in getting lost. For another, the appearance of an Indian in the woods was not particularly comforting to any white man, especially runaway servants. The English magistrates often employed Indians as agents to track down fugitive servants. In 1633, both Thomas Brian and Will Mendlow had been captured and returned to Plymouth by Indians working for the colony.

The fears of Peach and the others did not diminish as they watched Penowanyanquis pass on his way toward Plymouth. If they no longer wondered about this Indian's mission, they still had to face the uncertainty of the wilderness beyond. With no money, their journey would be arduous, perhaps even impossible. They needed a plan—some way to insure their effort to move further west.

Peach provided the solution. Obviously the Indian they had met was on his way to trade the beaver skins and beads for English goods. And after completing his barter, the Indian would probably follow this trail on his journey home. Peach then conceived his plan to wait at a point along the trail for the Indian to return. The four men could easily overpower the native, steal his goods, and be quickly gone. As originally formulated, Peach's plan may or may not have included premeditated murder.

At a place the Indians called Misquamsqueece (present-day Seekonk, Massachusetts), Peach and his partners in crime made camp and waited. Peach probably had no idea that they camped only twelve miles east of Providence or that technically he and his compatriots were already beyond the recognized legal jurisdiction of Plymouth. The place they had chosen to commit their nefarious deed was, by chance, a virtual no-man's land. It was a spot described by Roger Williams as "fit for an evil purpose."

The four white men waited two days for Penowanyanquis's return. Finally the Indian approached laden with English treasures—three bolts of cloth (called "coats") and five fathom of wampum (Indian money made from shellfish that was also used as a medium of exchange by English colonists).

As Penowanyanquis neared the camp, Peach beckoned him to join them around their campfire. The Nipmuck obliged, Peach offered him a pipe, and the group shared a brief interlude of tobacco smoking. Suddenly the prevailing cordiality changed and Peach abruptly informed Penowanyanquis that he was about to be murdered and robbed.

This outburst by Peach surprised his companions and they quickly argued against killing the Indian. Peach, however, felt no pangs of conscience. He boasted that he had previously killed many Indians, implying that the murder of this one would involve no great loss to humanity. Stinnings, Jackson and Cross continued their protests, however. When they could not dissuade Peach from killing the Indian, the three followers retreated from camp and left the ringleader to do his handiwork.

Peach drew his rapier from its scabbard and lunged toward Penowanyanquis. The sword pierced the Indian's leg and punctured his stomach. Peach removed his weapon and made another thrust. This time he missed and Penowanyanquis sprang backwards out of Peach's reach. One white man with rapier in hand came to Peach's assistance and lunged at Penowanyanquis from behind. This second assailant also missed the struggling Indian and instead plunged his blade firmly into the ground.

Penowanyanquis saw his opportunity and took it. In seconds he was upon his feet and he threw himself into the swamp at the edge of the white men's camp. The four Englishmen were right at his heels and they cornered him. As one white man jabbed with his sword, Penowanyanquis quickly rolled aside. Without delay the Indian bounded to his feet and ran deeper into the swamp. Seriously wounded and almost totally exhausted, Penowanyanquis collapsed in the murky marsh. He heard his white pursuers approaching slowly. Using all his remaining strength, he pulled himself to cover and lay silently in the recesses of the swamp.

Frantically Peach and his accomplices roamed the bog in search of their victim. But in this thickest part of the woods, there was no sign of the wounded Indian. He had disappeared without a trace.

Back at their camp, the Englishmen packed their gear in haste and snatched the Indian's three coats of cloth and wampum. They resumed their journey west along the Indian trail toward the Seekonk River and the fields of Pawtucket.

Though only a few miles from Pawtucket, the white men somehow wandered off the main trail. Lost and running low on supplies, they finally emerged from the forest maze at Pawtucket Falls on the Seekonk (Blackstone) River and they camped nearby. Desperate and unsure of how long they could last without replenishing their supplies, the men hailed some passing Indians and inquired about local white settlements where they might find some help. This time Peach restrained himself and treated these Indians without threats of violence.

One Indian, unaware the Englishmen had committed a crime, soon passed through Providence and reported the plight of the four lost white men to Roger Williams, the leader and founder of the small settlement of religious dissenters and exiles. Williams had been cast out of Salem in 1635. As a member of the Puritan ministry, he had advocated the implementation of new religious duties, and on specific points, an overhaul of Puritan religious and civil practices. As a voice crying in the wilderness, he also stood apart from other Puritans by espousing a belief that title to land in New England belonged to the Indians and that the only way whites could own land was for them to buy it. Williams respected the natives and found them endlessly fascinating. He learned the Narragansett language, studied Indian customs, and became a trusted friend of most Indian leaders residing in southern New England.

Despite the harsh sentence and treatment Williams had received from his kindred whites in Massachusetts Bay, he characteristically turned the other cheek and maintained a close friendship with Governor John Winthrop of Boston. Williams also offered Christian kindness to all travelers, red and white, who passed by or near his modest house in Providence.

When word came that four Englishmen teetered on the brink of starvation at their camp four miles north of Providence, Williams immediately dispatched messengers (probably Indians) to deliver food and provisions. Williams also sent along an invitation for the men to visit him in Providence. Peach and his associates were grateful for the unexpected supplies but they were curt and evasive in answering Williams's inquiries. They declined his invitation to Providence. Peach concocted a ruse for Williams's benefit by saying that he and his friends had traveled from Pascataquack (Maine) and had been lost for five days.

Not easily discouraged, Williams sent another messenger with a second invitation. Again Peach refused by explaining that he and his colleagues were tired and badly in need of rest. The fugitives remained at their camp but Peach probably realized he would soon run out of excuses for Williams. So far, no one knew about their dastardly crime, but if the Indian's death became known, Williams would surely be among the first to hear about it. It seemed that Peach and the others could not avoid a brief visit with the Providence preacher.

The four men appeared on Williams's doorstep the following day. Peach explained that the men had not accepted Williams's invitations because William Blackstone, an Anglican clergyman who had settled in the Pawtucket area, had warned them of hostile Indians known to be prowling the woods between Pawtucket and Providence. When Blackstone informed them it was safe to travel, they made their way to Providence to pay their respects and to thank Williams for his kindness.

Williams accepted their story. Actually he was preoccupied, engaged in some letter writing when the men arrived. He paid more attention to finishing his compositions than he did to their explanations. Williams, in fact, was a prolific correspondent and his letters were carefully constructed tomes that spared not even the slightest detail. Completing this current batch of letters, he realized that the arrival of Peach and his friends might provide a convenient means for delivering the correspondence to Connecticut, where these men said they were destined. Williams gave his letters to Peach for delivery and he promised to find someone to guide them to Connecticut in return for their service as postmen. Unsuspectingly, Williams provided these men with an escorted escape from justice. But their crime was about to be revealed.

As darkness fell over the swamp on the evening of the assault, Penowanyanquis—wounded and tired—mustered all his strength and began to drag himself back to the path. The next morning three Indians discovered him. Still alive, though badly hurt, Penowanyanquis related the story of the four Englishmen who had attacked and robbed him. The three Indians immediately set out for Pawtucket and inquired there about the white men. The Indian communications line began to hum with news of the attack and Peach somehow learned, even before Williams did, that he and the others were being sought. That night, while Williams still had no cause for suspicions, Peach and his accomplices "got on hose and shoes" and left Providence.

After Williams discovered that the four men had gone, an Indian brought him word of the attack on Penowanyanquis. With his usual burst of energy, Williams relayed the message to the Narragansett sachems Canonicus and Miantonomi and he requested their assistance in apprehending the four Englishmen. At the same time he gathered a few townspeople together and sped into the forest to help the wounded Indian.

Penowanyanquis was still alive when Williams arrived and the preacher dressed the wounds as best he could. With the help of friends who accompanied him, Williams carried the dying Indian to Providence. Penowanyanquis suffered severe pain and he continuously cried out "Muckquachuckquand," the name of a god who had appeared to him in a vision during his youth.

In Providence, the Indian was attended by Thomas James and John Greene. But there was little they could do. Penowanyanquis had lost too much blood and had contracted a fever. Weak and hardly able to speak, the Indian related his story in minute detail and identified his assailants. He may have then requested his Indian friends to take him from Providence so he could die elsewhere. Here the historical records are annoyingly incomplete. Williams left no account of Penowanyanquis's death, so it appears that he was not present when the Indian died. This added a further complication to events that transpired.

Meanwhile, Peach and his accomplices arrived at the Indian village of Miantonomi, the chief sachem who lived about twenty miles south of Providence and not far from the western side of Narragansett Bay. Knowing their escape plan had been seriously jeopardized, the Englishmen asked the sachem for transportation across the bay to the white settlement of Antinomians on Aquidneck Island. Perhaps they hoped the religious differences between Aquidneck and Plymouth would be enough to make extradition impossible. They told Miantonomi nothing about why they wanted to go to Aquidneck, although Peach showed the sachem the packet of letters Williams had given him to deliver to Connecticut. Peach let Miantonomi think the letters were addressed to Aquidneck and that he was Williams's official courier.

The Narragansetts, by all appearances, were only too happy to assist a friend of Williams. Miantonomi ordered the outfitting of a canoe and instructed some Indians to escort Peach and his followers across the bay. After landing on Aquidneck, the Indians did not depart. Instead they brought Peach and the others directly into the tiny Portsmouth settlement.

After the four Englishmen had been introduced to the Portsmouth leaders, the Indians demanded that Peach and his followers be immediately arrested and charged with Penowanyanquis's murder. Obviously Roger Williams's messenger had reached the Narragansett chiefs before the four murderers arrived at the Indian village. The transportation provided by the Indians had actually been part of a plan to turn the four Englishmen over to the nearest white authorities. William Bradford, one of the Plymouth magistrates, later noted with admiration that the Indians had carried out the plan with such "subtlety" that Peach and his accomplices never suspected "their fact had been known" all along. The Aquidneck residents complied with the Narragansetts' demands. Peach and the others were held in custody as the Portsmouth leaders tried to figure out exactly what was going on.

As the situation became obvious, the Portsmouth leaders resented being stuck in the middle. Williams informed the island residents that the men should be returned either to Plymouth or Massachusetts Bay for trial. But he was not sure under which colony's jurisdiction these men came. First, the murder had been committed in an area that he knew did not belong to Providence, but he did not know if it belonged to Massachusetts Bay or Plymouth. Second, the men had last resided in Plymouth, which meant they had broken Plymouth law. It was a confusing mess with no precedent upon which to rely and Williarns, in frustration, appealed to Governor Winthrop for an opinion.

Aquidneck was left the problem of what to do with the prisoners. Moreover, the people of Portsmouth grew increasingly concerned about Indian threats of reprisals against the English in revenge for Penowanyanquis's death. Slowly tremors began to shake and threaten the English living within the vicinity of the Narragansett Indians.

The murder of Penowanyanquis aroused the Narragansetts to a fever pitch. At first the Indians grew fearful because they believed that Penowanyanquis's death was the first step in an English plot to commit wholesale slaughter of Indians around Narragansett Bay. This fear was not as preposterous as it might sound. A year earlier a combined force of English from Connecticut and Massachusetts Bay had marched against the Pequot Indians. On the banks of the Mystic River, the English soldiers—assisted by Narragansett and Mohegan allies—surrounded a stockaded Pequot fort. The fort was burned and the allied force annihilated the Pequot defenders—men, women and children. Those not killed by musket ball or arrow were burned in the inferno of the fort's interior. Pequot casualties totaled between three hundred and seven hundred. Most Narragansetts at the Pequot fort refused to fight because they disagreed with the noxious English commanders and their merciless tactics. For those who stayed to watch the devastation, the results were sickening. After the battle the Narragansetts were heard to moan "mach it, mach it," words that becried the wickedness and waste of the slaughter. The Narragansetts needed no better lesson in how far English ruthlessness could go.

Now, a year later, with the Pequot nation virtually exterminated, the Narragansetts feared it was their turn to experience the wrath of the English. Williams informed the Indians they had nothing to fear and assured them they were safe. Still, rumors raced through the Narragansett country and many Indians thought it might be wise to attack the English before any more time passed. A crisis and a potential for war loomed over southern New England.

Finally cooler heads prevailed. Miantonomi warned the English that some Narragansetts wanted revenge and that it would be best for every white man to be a little more cautious than usual. Yet he also learned who among his people had circulated threats against the English and he let it be known that any violence against the whites would be regarded as a breach of Indian law. He also spread the word that he believed the English would see justice done.

Winthrop replied to Williams's inquiry about which colony had actual jurisdiction over the prisoners. He believed the easiest way out of the tightening vise would be to turn Peach over to the Indians and allow the natives to dispose of him in whatever manner they chose, short of torture. The other three, Winthrop suggested, could then be tried at a later date. He hoped this solution would satisfy the Indians and put an end to Narragansett threats of reprisal. Winthrop's recommendation became moot, however, when Plymouth sent word to Aquidneck that the prisoners should be moved to the Pilgrim community.

Although Governor Thomas Prence of Plymouth agreed to accept the prisoners, he, like everyone else, was not particularly happy with the notion that his colony would become solely responsible for deciding the accused murderers' fate. Prence worried about rumors that the four prisoners might appeal their case directly to England, which would leave Plymouth powerless to bring swift justice. If the trial took place in England, the Narragansetts might blame the Pilgrim colony for allowing the murderers to leave New England unpunished. Winthrop, however, assured Prence that the men could not be tried in England (presumably because the New England colonies were sovereign entities with, as yet, no established procedures for appeal to the crown). So Prence informed the residents of Aquidneck that the prisoners should be transported to Plymouth as soon as possible.

When they received Prence's message, the Aquidneck Island settlers probably breathed a sigh of relief. They too had suffered from the pressure created by the crisis. The leaders of Aquidneck, seeking to rid themselves of the suspected Englishmen's unwanted presence, had made persistent pleas to Williams for the prisoners to be transferred to Providence for temporary incarceration. But Williams shared the fears of most whites and he wanted nothing more to do with Peach and his accomplices.

The crisis grew to unwieldy proportions. Throughout southern New England whites trembled at Indian threats, while Indians quaked at the thought of English attacks similar to the one leveled against the Pequots at the Mystic River fort. When Roger Williams described the crisis as a "great hubbub in all these parts," his characteristic understatement conveyed little of the actual confusion, paranoia and terror that pervaded the entire countryside.

Some uneasiness dissipated, however, when Plymouth finally requested the delivery of the prisoners. Arrangements were made quickly to transport the men, but somehow precautions and plans went awry. One of the prisoners, Daniel Cross, escaped from Aquidneck by boat. Only three men arrived in Plymouth to await trial.

Shortly, reports came to Plymouth that Cross had found sanctuary with some English settlers in Maine. How he managed to travel such a great distance safely is still a mystery. It is possible that his escape was planned and executed by persons who also provided some means of safe passage to Maine. Governor Prence sent a warning to the English harboring Cross that the fugitive had to be returned to Plymouth. Defiantly, the settlers of the northern province refused. John Winthrop was not surprised. He believed the English residents of Maine represented the worst element in New England (even far exceeding the "heretics" who inhabited Aquidneck Island, for instance). Refusal to extradite Cross typified their manner to "countenance... all such lewd persons as fled from us to them."

By early September the trial of Peach, Jackson and Stinnings began. The court selected twelve men to sit on the jury and hear testimony. The records of the proceedings are sketchy and provide only a miniscule amount of detail. As soon as the trial began, all three defendants confessed to committing the murder of Penowanyanquis, yet these admissions did not completely satisfy the court. Consequently, the Plymouth jurists summoned various individuals to testify. Overriding every other concern, the court worried about its authority to hear the case at all. And the court magistrates confronted a rather knotty question—no one had actually seen Penowanyanquis die. No one could be sure if these men should be tried for murder or a lesser charge of assault.

The testimony soon ended any doubt. Roger Williams, taking time from his busy schedule and activity as a diplomatic mediator between the colony of Connecticut and the Narragansetts, went to Plymouth to give testimony. Thomas James, who had examined the wounded Penowanyanquis in Providence, accompanied Williams and together they convinced the jury that the Indian indeed had been mortally wounded. Desiring corroborative evidence, the court tried to persuade two Indian friends of Penowanyanquis to present further evidence. At first these two unidentified Indians refused to attend the court sessions in Plymouth because they still believed the English were conspiring to slaughter Indians. Finally Plymouth authorities convinced them to appear at the trial and assured their safety. Before the court, the Indians swore that if Penowanyanquis had not truly died from his wounds, then they would be willing to give up their own lives at the hands of the English.

Now no questions remained. On September 4, 1638, the court declared

Peach, Jackson, and Stinnings guilty of murder and robbery. And following the tenets of Pilgrim law, the jury sentenced the guilty parties "to be hanged by the neck until their bodies were dead."

Some people in Plymouth were shocked and others were saddened by the severity of the sentence. Bradford observed that "some of the rude and ignorant sort" were incredulous that Englishmen would be "put to death for the Indians." Others in Plymouth may have simply regretted that men of their own kind, despite their obvious ruthlessness, had come to such an end. Only one execution had occurred in Plymouth during the eighteen years of the settlement's existence. In 1630 a jury had found John Billington—the same man who had once lost himself in the forest—guilty of "wilful murder" and he was subsequently hanged.

Now the same fate awaited Peach, Jackson and Stinnings. On the day the trial concluded, the three men were led to a hilltop (later known as "Gallows Hill") and were publicly hanged. Winthrop reported that "two of them died very penitently, especially Arthur Peach." The third, unnamed in the surviving records, must have resisted his executioners or perhaps in some way broke the solemn demeanor of the occasion.

In the crowd that gathered on Gallows Hill, Roger Williams and some Narragansett Indians witnessed the execution. When it was over, the Indians displayed great satisfaction and remarked to Williams that the execution helped to prove English sincerity and trustworthiness.

For the time being, the execution served a practical purpose by maintaining the peace. The deaths of Peach, Jackson and Stinnings averted the eruption of a frontier war. And for the first time in the annals of American history, white men had been brought to justice for committing a heinous crime against an Indian. Unfortunately the trial and execution of Peach and his accomplices set no lasting precedent.

The trial and execution did reveal that whites could recognize the necessity of enforcing equal justice under the law, even if as in this case the enforcement of justice resulted, in large part, from white fear of Indian reprisals and anxieties caused by the inherent pressure of the crisis. Still, it appears that the court, jurors, and residents of Plymouth acknowledged—if only in this fleeting instance—that justice was an end for which to strive, no matter if that justice served whites or Indians.

Ironically this point was best expressed at the time not by any Englishman, but by a local Indian. During a visit with Williams just before the trial commenced, Massasoit, sachem of the Wampanoags, proclaimed that all four Englishmen were guilty. Williams, however, replied philosophically that only one of them was truly guilty, the one who had actually committed the murderous deed. Massasoit disagreed. True, he said, only one man wounded the Indian, "but all lay in wait two days, and assisted." The guilt had to be shared by all.

Miantonomi, who assisted English authorities in the apprehension of Peach and his associates, was himself murdered in the wilds of eastern Connecticut in 1643 by the Mohegans under Uncas, their chief, in accordance with the wishes of Connecticut Puritan leaders. The sachem's killing is reconstructed in this nineteenth-century engraving from *History of the Indians of Connecticut*, by John DeForest.

Adulteries, Murthers, Robberies, Thefts,
Wild Indians punish these!
And hold the scales of justice so,
That no man farthing leese.
When Indians heare the horrid filths,
Of Irish, English Men
The Horrid Oaths and Murthers late,
Thus say these Indians then,
We weare no Cloaths, have many Gods,
And yet our sinnes are lesse:
You are Barbarians, Pagans wild,
Your land's the wildernesse.

—Roger Williams (1643)

4

Anne Marbury Hutchinson (1591-1643) was the central figure in what Massachusetts Puritans called the Antinomian Heresy. The word *Antinomian* means "against the law," and it was used by Puritans in a perjorative way to characterize Hutchinson's belief that one's conformity with religious laws and formalities (godly behavior) was not a sure sign of salvation. Instead, Hutchinson emphasized the "covenant of grace"—the indwelling of the Holy Spirit within a believer—and seemed to imply that such an individual had an immediate knowledge of the will of God. This view, which foreshadowed the tenets of Quakerism, threatened the Puritan belief in the Bible as the ultimate source of religious knowledge, and it caused her critics to assume erroneously that Antinomianism was a justification for civil disobedience that freed adherents from their obligation to follow moral and civil law.

Anne Hutchinson's gender intensified opposition to her theology. The Bay Colony leaders were unwilling to separate the issue of the validity of her teachings from the fact that she, a "mere woman," was expressing them. The male clerical establishment started with the assumption that her ideas could be no better than their source. A woman might legitimately conduct a private religious meeting, but only if the membership was exclusively female. No sooner had Anne Hutchinson assumed the leadership of a mixed gathering then she was accused of "unnatural" behavior. Though not the major issue in the Antinomian controversy, gender clearly played a role in this politically charged theological dispute.

In a farcical trial Anne was convicted of "traducing the ministers and their ministry," and she was eventually banished to that haven for dissidents—Rhode Island. In 1638 she became a cofounder of Portsmouth along with her husband, William, and one of her prominent adherents, merchant William Coddington. This brilliant and dynamic woman's final years were especially tragic. She became embroiled in political disputes with Coddington and other religious refugees, and on the death of her husband in 1642 she was left with the burden of supporting those of her fourteen children who were still minors. She took herself and the younger members of her family to present-day Westchester County, New York, and settled near

Anne Hutchinson (1591–1643), like Roger Williams, was banished from the Massachusetts Bay Colony because of her religious beliefs. Her sect was labeled *Antinomian*, a word that meant "against the law." This derisive name resulted from Hutchinson's belief that salvation came through faith and the indwelling of the Holy Spirit (a "covenant of grace") rather than through observing the formality of church rules or civil law. This statute of Hutchinson by sculptor Cyrus Dallin stands in front of the Massachusetts statehouse.

Pelham Bay. Here she and several of her children were killed by Indians in 1643. The Hutchinson River and Hutchinson River Parkway are the enduring reminders of her brief stay.

Hailed as America's first notable female leader, Hutchinson never gave her prosecutors the satisfaction of seeing her spirit broken: "Her repentance is in a paper," complained one Massachusetts magistrate, "but... not in her countenance."

Anne Hutchinson's example inspired other early Rhode Island women to assert their individuality and equality in matters of religious belief. In 1638 Mary Verin of Providence defied her abusive husband Joshua to attend services conducted by local Baptists. Her "boisterous and desperate" spouse (as Roger Williams described him) was disfranchised in May 1638 for his forcible interference with Mary's religious practices when the Providence town government decreed that "Joshua Verin, upon the breach of the covenant for restraining the liberty of conscience, shall be withheld from the liberty of voting till he shall declare the contrary."

Mary Dyer of Portsmouth (1611–1660) also figured prominently in the religious life of early Rhode Island. At first an avid follower of Hutchinson, she made the short transition from Antinomianism to Quakerism and became a devout witness to her new faith. When she attempted to preach the principles of Quakerism in Boston, she was banished, only to return again and again. After her fourth offense she was hanged on June 1, 1660. When offered her life if she would leave Massachusetts and return no more, she said, "Nay, I cannot; for in obedience to the will of the Lord God I came, and in His will I abide, faithful to the death."

Richard Brandon Morris, a major American historian and a leading authority on law and constitutional development in early America, wrote this essay in 1952 during the Cold War and at the height of another inquisition called McCarthyism. It appears in his anthology *Fair Trial: Fourteen Who Stood Accused, from Anne Hutchinson to Alger Hiss*. Later Morris achieved distinction for his books on the Confederation era, as editor in chief of the *Encyclopedia of American History*, and as coeditor of the *New American Nation Series*.

Jezebel before the Judges: Anne Hutchinson Tried for Sedition

Richard B. Morris

It could have been today instead of 1637. Allowing for differences in political climate, the sedition trial of Anne Hutchinson before her judges at Cambridge could have been staged at Foley Square, New York, any time during the last few years. But Anne Hutchinson would have had a different sort of trial. The accused would still have no guarantee that her judges would judge her dispassionately, or that the jury would be uninfluenced by the inflammatory outpourings of the press. She could still not be certain that her prosecutor would not seek political advantage from her conviction. Nonetheless, she would be shielded against prejudice and hysteria to a degree unknown among the Puritan theocrats. She would be presumed innocent up to the moment when by the unanimous verdict of a trial jury she might be convicted on evidence establishing her guilt beyond a reasonable doubt. The bulwarks constructed over the course of the past three hundred years for the protection of the innocently accused would safeguard her rights.

By our standards, Anne Hutchinson did not get a fair trial in 1637. She might today.

During times of acute political tension orthodoxy becomes a test of loyalty. People who have heterodox ideas and try to do something about them find themselves in jeopardy. People like Anne Hutchinson. It is then that the courts rouse themselves to determine the point at which ideas translated into action become an imminent danger to the state. In totalitarian states people who openly attack the leaders and foment a political opposition are liquidated out of hand or accorded the kind of trial designed to serve as a sounding-board for the state's propaganda machine. Anne Hutchinson's trial much more closely resembled a typical political trial conducted behind the iron curtain than the sort of judicial proceeding we now have a right to expect in our own country.

To understand why Anne Hutchinson became the greatest political issue in the history of early Massachusetts, we must find out how this emigrant to the New World was able to win so many followers to her camp in so brief a time. That she was a woman of rare intelligence, superabundant physical energy, and great personal magnetism even her enemies grudgingly conceded. From her father, who had been imprisoned for rebellion against church laxity, she had inherited a stubborn pride and an integrity of mind. A strong streak of mysticism, which colored both her personality and her views, explained her unbridled ethusiasms. In the mother country she had come under the spell of the learned John Cotton, who preached at the fashionable St. Botolph's Church at Boston, in Lincolnshire. Renowned as one who "loved to sweeten his mouth with a piece of Calvin before he went to sleep," Cotton was conspicuous among the Cambridge-trained Puritans for his scholarship and eloquence. Like other leading Puritans of his day he had dedicated himself to the task of cutting out what they termed the gangrene of impure doctrine from the body of the Church of England. He would have dropped many of the doctrines and practices the church had taken over from Roman Catholicism. But the English ecclesiastical authorities deemed Cotton's theological surgery to border on malpractice. Denounced to the Court of High Commission in 1632, Cotton fled to Massachusetts, that haven for discontented religious rebels.

Cotton's most devoted follower was disconsolate at his going. Before long a revelation from Isaiah came to Anne Hutchinson: "Thine eyes shall see thy teachers." She interpreted this as an order to leave her comfortable world and share the fate of her pastor in that little Utopian commonwealth which was being builded on the shores of New England. At the time of her exodus she had been married twenty years and had a sizable family. Her husband, William, was characterized by Winthrop, her enemy, as "a man of very mild temper and weak parts, and wholly guided by his wife." He seems to have followed unquestioningly the leadership of his spouse, whom he cherished as "a dear saint servant and of God."

Anne and her family settled in Boston, a tight little frontier town of a thousand souls. But if she expected peace she was soon disabused, for the populace was jittery and suspicious. And with good reason. They were well aware that the enemies from without the colony, seeking to annul the charter, seemed to be on the verge of success. Horror stories filtering in from outlying settlements told how the savage Pequots were scalping saints and sinners indiscriminately. Despite the expulsion from the colony, some years before, of that unreconstructed pagan Thomas Morton of Merrymount, discordant elements were not discouraged from settling. Take the learned Roger Williams, for example. From his pulpit at Salem he "divulged new and dangerous opinions against the authorities of the magistrates." Recognized in our day as a liberal and a democrat, Williams's comtemporaries were wont to think of him as a "wild Ishmael, his hand against every man." In 1636, in the dead of winter, Williams was expelled and forced to make his way through the wilderness to Rhode Island.

Scarcely had the colony had time to recover from the Williams affair when a far greater peril threatened its internal security. Anne Hutchinson was too active a mind to sit back and succumb to the ordinary routine of household drudgery. She began to have meetings in her front parlor, to which the women of Boston flocked. Starting out with discussions of child care and nursing problems, she soon moved into the realm of theology, where she was temperamentally most at home. Now, one would hardly expect a bluestocking in Boston to be looked upon with favor in those pioneer days. John Winthrop, a founding father, summed up the feeling of the more conventional when he observed that this "godly young woman of special parts" had gone astray "by occasion of her giving herself wholly to reading and writing." Had she "attended her household affairs and such things as belong to women, and not gone out of her way and calling to meddle in such things as are proper for men, whose minds are stronger," that antifeminist magistrate continued, "she had kept her wits and might have improved them usefully and honorably in the place God had sent her." But Winthrop never succumbed to Anne's charm.

People soon crowded into her meetings to hear her capsule version of the long Sabbath sermons, which seldom escaped the sharp barbs of her wit. Save for her hero, John Cotton, the ministers failed to rise to the impeccable standard she set. She was particularly scathing in her criticism of the Reverend Mr. Wilson, pastor of the First Church of Boston, who shared that congregation with John Cotton, its teacher. When Wilson rose to preach, Mistress Hutchinson walked out of the meetinghouse, and other members of the congregation contemptuously turned their backs on him. From sneering silence the congregation soon turned to open defiance. In every meetinghouse the pastors were shocked to find their interpretations openly challenged. The Reverend Thomas Weld complained: "Now, after our sermons were ended at our public lectures you might have seen half a dozen pistols discharged at the face of the preacher," so numerous were the objections "made by the opinionists in the open assembly against our doctrine delivered. Now the faithful ministers of Christ must have dung cast on their faces," he continued in Biblical vein, "and be no better than legal preachers, Baal's priests, Popish factors, Scribes, Pharisees, and opposers of Christ himself!"

Meantime Mistress Hutchinson's following grew. "It was strange to see how the common people were led" to condemn the Reverend Mr. Wilson, Winthrop caustically commented, for matters that "divers of them did not understand." Another hostile critic, Edward Johnson, satirized in his *Wonder-Working Providence* the spell she cast over her admirers. "Come along with me," one of them is quoted as declaring, "and I'll bring you to a woman who preaches better Gospel than any of your blackcoats that have been at the Ninnyversity. I had rather hear such a one that speaks from a mere motion of the spirit, without any study at all, than any of your learned scholars, although they may be fuller of the Scripture." But to the thrill-starved females of Boston no one was "fuller of the Scripture" than Anne Hutchinson, and so they continued to drink at her spiritual fountain, with the result, according to Winthrop, that "many families were neglected and much time lost."

But Anne Hutchinson was not only spreading disrespect for the clergy. She was fashioning theological views that bordered close on heresy. "It was not long," Cotton Mather tells us, "before 'twas found that most of the errors then crawling like vipers about the country were hatched at these meetings" held at the home of this "virago." The Boston ministers, Cotton excepted, not only were lacking in ability, Anne charged, but labored under a "covenant of works." They were formalists, sticking to the letter of the Mosaic law and neglecting its spirit, "a company of legal professors" who "lie poring on the law which Christ hath abolished." As a result of this preoccupation with the written word, she contended, they misled the people about the most important of all issues—salvation. Sound Calvinist doctrine held that the Lord's elect alone could be saved from everlasting damnation, and in no other way than through the covenant of grace, manifested by the spirit of the Lord within them. Giving this doctrine an extremely literal interpretation, Anne Hutchinson insisted that the indwelling of the Lord's spirit was evidenced by a serenity of soul. To obtain so blissful a state, mere pietism, fasting, prayers, and outward religious observance would not suffice. In fact, even a minister of the gospel might not possess such a heaven-directed heart, and, if he did not, would be damned. The effect of her views was to subordinate the role of the formal church and to dramatize the part the individual played in his own salvation.

These were fighting words. If unopposed, they would have undermined the theocracy based upon the prestige of the ministry. How seriously Anne's followers took her charges was dramatically demonstrated at this time when the men of Boston refused to go off to the Pequot War because their chaplain, the Reverend John Wilson, was under a "covenant of works." The targets of Anne's criticism came to feel that she was hatching a dangerous heresy, known in Europe as Antinomianism and associated with the disciples of Johannes Agricola, a German tailor. Some feared that her views would bring about a reign of terror such as swept Münster when the demagogic Anabaptist John of Leyden seized the reins of power. To the conservative theocrats her doctrines were not only heretical but actually subversive.

Had Mistress Hutchinson's orbit been restricted to women, the perils probably could have been minimized. In those days women could not vote nor hold office, nor did they directly share in formulating church policy. But the spell she cast brought many members of the opposite sex under her intellectual sway, and among them some of the colony's most notable personages. Only a short time before, young Sir Harry Vane, whose father had been a privy councilor, had found it expedient to migrate to Boston because of his defiance of the church authorities. Almost immediately upon arrival he was elected Governor. Vane soon became one of Anne Hutchinson's most ardent supporters. Twenty years her junior, Sir Harry was a quick captive to her charm and learning. Ugly rumors, for which there is not the slightest supporting evidence, were spread concerning this friendship. Some thirty years later, and five years after Vane had paid with his head because Charles II considered him "too dangerous a man to let live, if we can honestly put him out of the way," the Secretary of State recorded in his official papers the canard "from Major Scott's mouth" to the effect that "Sir Harry Vane in 1637 went over as Governor to New England with two women, Mrs. Dyer and Mrs. Hutchinson, and he debauched both, and both were delivered of monsters." This political calumny is wrong in every detail except for the curious references to the miscarriages suffered during the days of their persecution by Anne and the handsome Mary Dyer, her devoted follower (later martyred as a Quaker). While even the Cavalier historian Clarendon grudgingly admitted that the "unbeautiful" Vane made "men think there was somewhat in him of extraordinary," John Winthrop soon had good reason to feel toward him much as Cromwell did at a later day when he prayed "that the Lord would deliver him from Sir Harry Vane!"

Mary Dyer (1611–1660) of Portsmouth was yet another unsuccessful litigant in the courts of Massachusetts. Her Quaker beliefs and her determination to preach them led to her death by hanging in 1660. This painting of her trial is displayed in the Social Law Library, Boston.

Anne's spell over the opposite sex brought her the firm allegiance of her brother-in-law, the Reverend John Wheelwright, who had come over from England in the late spring of 1636. She schemed to have Wheelwright selected as a third pastor of the First Church of Boston, alongside Wilson and Cotton, but Winthrop rudely scotched the proposal. Instead Wheelwright was invited to Mount Wollaston, the site where Morton's house stood before the incensed Puritans burned it to the ground. This snub was not soon forgotten by the Hutchinsonians. On January 20, 1637, a fast day set aside because of "the dissensions in our churches," Wheelwright delivered a forthright sermon in Boston which was calculated to destroy any possibility of conciliation. Pulling no punches, he excoriated those who made broad their phylacteries, enlarged the borders of their garments, loved the chief seats in the synagogues, and wanted to be called of men "Rabbi, Rabbi." His allusions were too obvious to be lost on his critics.

The authorities now felt that any further delay would be fatal. In March the General Court brought Wheelwright to trial for sedition and contempt. The opposing forces, led by Vane and Winthrop, were evenly balanced, but the clergy tipped the scales against the prisoner, who was duly convicted. Still clinging to the hope that the opposition might be pacified, the court postponed sentencing Wheelwright.

With Boston hotly pro-Wheelwright and pro-Hutchinson, the conservatives realized that in any election conducted in the capital they could never unseat Vane and his following. A motion was carried at the General Court to hold the next meeting of that body at Cambridge, then called Newtowne, a small community far less infected with the Hutchinsonian virus. The main business of that court was to be the election of the governor and magistrates. While the voters were now permitted to vote for their candidates by proxy, all parliamentary questions were decided by a viva voce vote of those present. This placed at a considerable disadvantage busy Bostonians who could not attend in person. Winthrop and Vane were the opposing candidates on election day, May 27, 1637. "There was great danger of a tumult that day," reported Winthrop, "and some laid hands on others." At the height of the fracas the Reverend Mr. Wilson, stout and fiftyish, clambered up a spreading oak and, in what was literally the first stump speech in American history, vehemently harangued the crowd to vote for Withrop. Vane and his entire slate went down to defeat. Winthrop won the governorship, Dudley was elected Deputy Governor, and [John] Endecott, a lion among the anti-Hutchinsonians, was chosen an assistant for life. In a rebellion against the new leadership, the town of Boston sent Vane, Coddington, and Hough to sit in the General Court as deputies.

One of the very first acts of the newly constituted General Court was the passage of an immigration law that imposed heavy penalties on strangers harbored without permission of the magistrates. At the time the law was passed it was known that a party of Anne Hutchinson's followers were on their way from England. This inhospitable measure, a flagrant violation of the charter, was scathingly attacked by Vane, and the arguments waxed hot and heavy in the early summer months. Finally, exasperated at the futility of further resistance, Vane sailed for England in August. At a political demonstration by the Hutchinsonians, Vane made a forthright plea for religious toleration and expressed the hope that "Ishmael shall dwell in the presence of his brethren."

But the expulsion of Wheelwright and the departure of Vane failed to stifle "the breeder and nourisher of all these distempers." Moved by a burning fanaticism, the elders were as determined as was the self-righteous Elijah to see that dogs should eat the flesh of this forthright female and that "the carcase of Jezebel shall be as dung upon the face of the field." When Anne Hutchinson's partisans now urged that the government had gone far enough in crushing the opposition, they were told off in language such as Jehu used to Joram. "What peace," that man of the Old Testament cried out, "so long as the whoredoms of thy mother Jezebel and her witchcrafts are so many?"

The government party now had Anne Hutchinson arrested and brought to trial. Hers was a political trial and must be judged by the standards of that day. Whether it was the royal government trying Raleigh, or the Puritans when in power bringing the royalists to justice, the political trials of that era were partisan affairs that would outrage our sense of fair play. Furthermore, it must be remembered that in seventeenth-century England the rules of criminal procedure and evidence were still in formation. In Massachusetts, a frontier colony less than a decade old, these rules were still more elementary. Moreover, the Massachusetts Puritans, never too cordial toward the technicalities of the English common law, looked toward the Bible for instruction in criminal matters. Even John Cotton, considered a Hutchinsonian at this time, had declared: "The more any law smells of man the more unprofitable" it is. Such theocratic views could be handy weapons for leaders engaged in a fight to maintain their arbitrary power undiminished.

From the start of Anne Hutchinson's trial certain procedural safeguards were ignored which we now consider fundamental. The prisoner was brought to trial without indictment or information, without being informed of the precise charges against her, and without even knowing what the penalty was. Since no lawyer was as yet practicing in the colony, the denial of counsel to the accused was less prejudicial in fact than it seemed on its face. But the denial of jury trial seems far more shocking. Only a year before, John Cotton had drafted a code of laws in which he did not provide for trial by jury because it was unknown in the Bible; but the authorities, regardless of their conservatism, felt this was going too far, and failed to adopt his draft. Within four years after the Hutchinson trial the colony's first written code of laws impliedly recognized jury trial and allowed the accused in criminal cases the right to elect to be tried by bench or jury.

In the absence of an indictment, the crime for which Anne Hutchinson was put on trial must be inferred from the remarks of her judges. From the record it is clear that she was tried for sedition and contempt. In a theocracy like Massachusetts, traducing the ministers constituted subversive behavior. Since only a short time before this trial the Court of King's Bench in England had declared the charter vacated, the Bay Colony rulers deemed a united front necessary to defend the commonwealth's independence. This objective, in their minds, justifiably transcended all issues of free speech and toleration. Hence, while the judges refrained from imposing the death penalty in this case, they would have felt perfectly justified in so doing. They kept this in mind when, in 1641, they adopted the Body of Liberties, the Bay Colony's first written code. Therein the death penalty was provided for any person who "shall treacherously or perfidiously attempt the alteration and subversion of our frame of polity or government fundamentally."

The scene of Anne Hutchinson's trial is now known as Cambridge. The trial was held in the meetinghouse, a rough-hewn board building, its crevices sealed with mud. Winter had descended unusually early that November. Ice was piled up along the river's banks, and in the unheated meetinghouse the temperature was appropriately frigid, considering the work that had to be done. The governor and magistrates occupied a table and chairs, while the deputies sat on rude wooden benches.

By present-day standards of judicial propriety, John Winthrop, who presided over the tribunal, should have disqualified himself, as he was the prisoner's bitterest foe among the laity. Curiously, Winthrop was generally magnanimous, but in the Hutchinson affair he assumed the dual role of judge and prosecutor with unaccustomed relish. While normally poised and dignified on other occasions, at this time he treated the spectators to frequent unjudicial outbursts of rancor and exasperation. Had Winthrop needed a model for his behavior, he might well have chosen that Puritan hero Sir Edward Coke, who went to untoward lengths in badgering and reviling Sir Walter Raleigh when that talented Elizabethan was tried for treason. The fact is that Winthrop's conduct conformed to the accepted behavior of judges and prosecutors in English state trials. A man who believed that democracy was "the meanest and worst of all forms of government" and that the only liberty which should be tolerated was that "exercised in a way of subjection to authority" could be counted on to bring the full power of the oligarchy to bear upon dissenters, whether political or religious. "The eyes of all people are upon us," Winthrop had once counseled the settlers. "If we shall deal falsely with our God in this work we have undertaken, we shall be made a story and a byword through the world." This was a major test, and Winthrop had no intention of letting the Lord down.

Had Anne Hutchinson nurtured any hope of receiving charitable treatment at the hands of her judges, it must have been quickly dissipated when she saw Winthrop flanked by his old political rival, Thomas Dudley, the Deputy Governor, on one side, and by John Endecott on the other. When Dudley died, some verses were found in his pocket which revealed that his bigotry remained pure and uncorrupted.

> Let me of God and churches watch
> O'er such as do a toleration hatch,

the Deputy Governor warned, and for his epitaph chose: "I died no libertine." The grim-visaged Endecott appeared even more fanatical in his black skullcap. His tight mouth and massive jaw, only partly concealed by a gracefully pointed beard, were double assurance that these proceedings would be carried out to a suitable conclusion. The man who cut down Morton's maypole would never brook defiance of the Bible Commonwealth.

Before her judges stood the prisoner, a woman in her late forties, bereft of counsel, as was the fashion of the time. Although she was in an advanced state of pregnancy, she was forced to remain standing. Only when "her countenance discovered some bodily infirmity" was she finally permitted to sit down.

WINTHROP: Mrs. Hutchinson, you are called here as one of those that have troubled the peace of the commonwealth and the churches here; you are known to be a woman that hath had a great share in the promoting and divulging of those opinions that are causes of this trouble, and to be nearly joined not only in affinity and affection with some of those the court had taken notice of and passed censure upon, but you have spoken divers things as we have been informed very prejudicial to the honor of the churches and ministers thereof, and you have maintained a meeting and an assembly in your house that hath been condemned by the general assembly as a thing not tolerable nor comely in the sight of God nor fitting for your sex, and notwithstanding that was cried down you have continued the same. Therefore, we have thought good to send for you to understand how things are, that if you be in an erroneous way we may reduce you so you may become a profitable member here among us; otherwise, if you be obstinate in your course, then the court may take such course that you may trouble us no further. Therefore, I would intreat you to express whether you do not assent and hold in practice to those opinions and factions that have been handled in court already, that is to say, whether you do not justify Mr. Wheelwright's sermon and the petition.

MRS. HUTCHINSON: I am called here to answer before you but I hear no things laid to my charge.

WINTHROP: I have told you some already and more I can tell you.

MRS. H.: Name one, Sir.

WINTHROP: Have I not named some already?

MRS. H.: What have I said or done?

WINTHROP: Why for your doings, this you did harbor and countenance those that are parties in this faction that you have heard of.

MRS. H.: That's matter of conscience, Sir.

WINTHROP: Your conscience you must keep or it must be kept for you.

MRS. H.: Must not I then entertain the saints because I must keep my conscience?

WINTHROP: Say that one brother should commit felony or treason and come to his brother's house. If he knows him guilty and conceals him, he is guilty of the same. It is his conscience to entertain him, but if his conscience comes into act in giving countenance and entertainment to him that hath broken the law he is guilty too. So if you do countenance those that are transgressors of the law you are in the same fact.

MRS. H.: What law do they transgress?

WINTHROP: The law of God and of the state.

MRS. H.: In what particular?

WINTHROP: Why in this among the rest, whereas the Lord doth say, "Honor thy father and thy mother."

MRS. H.: Aye, Sir, in the Lord.

WINTHROP: This honor you have broke in giving countenance to them.

MRS. H.: In entertaining those did I entertain them against any act (for here is the thing) or what God hath appointed?

WINTHROP: You knew that Mr. Wheelwright did preach this sermon and those that countenance him in this do break a law.

MRS. H.: What law have I broken?

WINTHROP: Why the fifth commandment.

MRS. H.: I deny that, for he saith in the Lord.

WINTHROP: You have joined with them in the faction.

MRS. H.: In what faction have I joined with them?

WINTHROP: In presenting the petition.

MRS. H.: Suppose I had set my hand to the petition, what then?

WINTHROP: You saw that case tried before.

MRS. H.: But I had not my hand to the petition.

WINTHROP: You have counseled them.

MRS. H.: Wherein?

WINTHROP: Why in entertaining them.

MRS. H.: What breach of law is that, Sir?

WINTHROP: Why dishonoring of parents.

MRS. H.: But put the case, Sir, that I do fear the Lord and my parents, may I not entertain them that fear the Lord because my parents will not give me leave?

WINTHROP: If they be the fathers of the commonwealth, and they of another religion, if you entertain them then you dishonor your parents and are justly punishable.

MRS. H.: If I entertain them, as they have dishonored their parents, I do.

WINTHROP: No, but you by countenancing them above others put honor upon them.

MRS H.: I may put honor upon them as the children of God and as they do honor the Lord.

WINTHROP: We do not mean to discourse with those of your sex but only this; you do adhere unto them and do endeavor to set forward this faction and so you do dishonor us.

MRS. H.: I do acknowledge no such thing. Neither do I think that I ever put any dishonor upon you.

WINTHROP: Why do you keep such a meeting at your house as you do every week upon a set day?

MRS. H.: It is lawful for me so to do, as it is all your practices, and can you find a warrant for yourself and condemn me for the same thing?

WINTHROP: There was no meeting of women alone, but your meeting is of another sort for there are sometimes men among you.

MRS. H.: There was never any man with us.

WINTHROP: Well, admit there was no man at your meeting and that you was sorry for it, there is no warrant for your doings, and by what warrant do you continue such a course?

MRS. H.: I conceive there lies a clear rule in Titus, that the elder women should instruct the younger, and then I must have a time wherein I must do it.

WINTHROP: All this I grant you, I grant you a time for it, but what is this to the purpose that you, Mrs. Hutchinson, must call a company together from their callings to come to be taught of you?

MRS. H.: Will it please you to answer me this and to give me a rule for them I will willingly submit to any truth. If any come to my house to be instructed in the ways of God what rule have I to put them away?

WINTHROP: But suppose that a hundred men come unto you to be instructed will you forbear to instruct them?

MRS. H.: As far as I conceive I cross a rule in it.

WINTHROP: Very well and do you not so here?

MRS. H.: No, Sir, for my ground is they are men.

WINTHROP: Men and women, all is one for that, but suppose that a man should come and say, "Mrs. Hutchinson, I hear that you are a woman that God hath given his grace unto and you have knowledge in the word of God. I pray instruct me a little." Ought you not to instruct this man?

MRS. H.: I think I may. —Do you think it not lawful for me to teach women and why do you call me to teach the court?

WINTHROP: We do not call you to teach the court but to lay open yourself.

MRS. H.: I desire you that you would then set me down a rule by which I may put them away that come unto me and so have peace in so doing.

WINTHROP: We are your judges and not you ours, and we must compel you to it.

MRS. H.: If it please you by authority to put it down, I will freely let you, for I am subject to your authority.

Winthrop's unjudicial counterblast would have exploded more appropriately from the parapets of the Court of High Commission, at that very time engaged in stifling the Puritan clergy at home. The Governor up to this point had come off a poor second in his duel with an expert intellectual fencer. Dudley felt called upon to take up the attack.

DUDLEY: I would go a little higher with Mrs. Hutchinson. About three years ago we were all in peace. Mrs. Hutchinson from that time she came hath made a disturbance, and some that came over with her in the ship did inform me what she was as soon as she was landed. Now it appears by this woman's meeting that Mrs. Hutchinson hath so forestalled the minds of many by their resort to her meeting that now she hath a potent party in the country. Now, if she in particular hath disparaged all our ministers in the land that they have preached a covenant of works, and only Mr. Cotton a covenant of grace, why this is not to be suffered.

Mrs.. H.: I pray, Sir, prove it that I said they preached nothing but a covenant of works.

DUDLEY: Nothing but a covenant of works, why a Jesuit may preach truth sometimes!

MRS. H.: Did I ever say they preached a covenant of works then?

DUDLEY: If they do not preach a covenant of grace clearly, then they preach a covenant of works.

MRS. H.: No, Sir, one may preach a covenant of grace more clearly than another, so I said.

MR. ENDECOTT: I desire to speak, seeing Mrs. Hutchinson seems to lay something against them that are to witness against her.

WINTHROP: Only I would add this. It is well discerned to the court that Mrs. Hutchinson can tell when to speak and when to hold her tongue.

MRS. H.: It is one thing for me to come before a public magistracy and there to speak what they would have me to speak and another when a man comes to me in a way of friendship privately. There is difference in that.

Mistress Hutchinson had now worked herself up to a pitch of righteous anger. In the words of one observer, "she vented her impatience with so fierce speech and countenance, as one would hardly have guessed her to have been an antitype of Daniel, but rather of the lions, after they were loose." The clergy who were there in force to bear witness against Anne could scarcely conceal their dismay at the way the trial was going. The fanatical Reverend Hugh Peters, who had come from Salem to further the prosecution, now broke in, declaring: "That which concerns us to speak unto you, as yet we are sparing in, unless the court command us to speak, then we shall answer to Mrs. Hutchinson, notwithstanding our brethren are very unwilling to answer." The situation was embarrassing, but Winthrop's casuistry reassured him. "This speech was not spoken in a corner but in a public assembly, and though things were spoken in private yet now coming to us, we are to deal as public."

Without further coaxing, Peters proceeded to relate how the prisoner had charged the ministry with teaching a covenant of works, going so far as to maintain that there "was a broad difference between our brother Mr. Cotton and ourselves."

"What difference do you conceive to be between your teacher and us?" Peters had insistently demanded. Cotton, she informed the elders, "preaches the covenant of grace and you the covenant of works."

Then the Reverend Mr. Wilson, who, of all the ministers, bore the greatest grudge against Anne Hutchinson, proceeded to corroborate Peters. One after another, Thomas Weld and John Eliot of Roxbury, George Phillips of Watertown, and Zechariah Symmes of Charlestown—all as unrelenting in their hostility as Peters and Wilson—rose in their turn to back up Peters's accusations. Even the gentle Thomas Shepard, minister of

Cambridge, while extremely "loath to speak in this assembly concerning this gentlewoman in question," felt impelled to assert what "my conscience speaks unto me." But he added that perhaps her heretical remarks were "but a slip of her tongue." "I hope she will be sorry for it, and then we shall be glad of it."

Dusk had descended upon the meetinghouse. But the magistrates were unwilling to adjourn on the charitable note that Shepard had struck. Summing up the day's evidence against the prisoner, the Deputy Governor turned to Anne Hutchinson and declared:

DUDLEY: I called these witnesses and you deny them. You see they have proved this and you deny this, but it is clear. You said they preached a covenant of works and that they were not able ministers of the New Testament. Now there are two other things that you did affirm which were that the Scriptures in the letter of them held forth nothing but a covenant of works and likewise that those that were under a covenant of works cannot be saved.

MRS. H.: Prove that I said so.

WINTHROP: Did you say so?

MRS. H.: No, Sir, it is your conclusion.

The wrangling was at last interrupted by the lateness of the hour. "Mrs. Hutchinson," Winthrop declared, his patience fast ebbing, "the court you see hath labored to bring you to acknowledge the error of your way that so you might be reduced. The time now grows late. We shall therefore give you a little more time to consider of it and therefore desire that you attend the court again in the morning."

The first day had gone very well for the prisoner. She had outfenced the magistrates in a battle of wits and forced the ministers into the unchristian-like stand of having publicly revealed a private and confidential conversation. Had she had the benefit of counsel learned in the law, a nice legal question might have been raised in her behalf. Although the common-law decisions of the period were indecisive, a clever lawyer might have made a good case for the position that in English law confessions to ecclesiastics were privileged communications. Of course, Mistress Hutchinson's statements to the ministers had been more in the nature of a confidential communication than a confession according to church law, and in view of the temper of the bench it is obvious that her objection would most certainly have been dismissed on technical grounds, if no others were ready to hand. But on the moral issue Mistress Hutchinson had come off with flying colors.

The Boston bluestocking's resourcefulness had not yet been fully tested. Hardly had Winthrop convened the court the next morning when Mistress Hutchinson dropped a bombshell. During the night, she declared, she had looked over certain notes of the conference that had been taken by the Reverend Mr. Wilson. This was Vane's copy, which that disappointed young statesman had turned over to his friend before sailing for home. "I find things not to be as hath been alleged," she charged. As "the ministers came in their own cause," they should be forced to take an oath. While Winthrop insisted that since this was not a jury trial the court had full discretion in the matter of the oaths of witnesses, Bradstreet piously implored Mistress Hutchinson that, had the ministers been in error in reporting her remarks, "you would make them to sin if you urge them to swear." But the prisoner was unmoved by this plea, and many members of the court supported her.

"An oath, sir," she exclaimed to Stoughton, "is an end of all strife, and it is God's ordinance."

Sneeringly Endecott broke in: "You lifted up your eyes as if you took God to witness you came to entrap none—and yet you will have them swear!"

A hurried conference took place on the bench. Finally, in a face-saving concession, Winthrop ruled: "I see no necessity of an oath in this thing, seeing it is true and the substance of the matter confirmed by divers, yet that all may be satisfied, if the elders will take an oath they shall have it given them." Even now the court hesitated to humiliate the ministers by refusing to admit their unsworn word. "Mark what a flourish Mrs. Hutchinson puts upon the business that she had witnesses to disprove what was said, and here is no man to bear witness," the Deputy Governor broke in sarcastically.

She replied with dignity: "If you will not call them in that is nothing to me."

Before that issue was finally disposed of, three defense witnesses were heard—Coggeshall, Leverett, and the Reverend John Cotton. Coggeshall, a Boston deputy, had, only a moment before, annoyed the magistrates by requesting that the ministers consult with Cotton on the propriety of their taking such an oath and had earned Endecott's sharp rebuke. "I think that this carriage of yours tends to further casting dirt upon the face of the judges." Another magistrate, Roger Harlakenden, had then exclaimed: "Her carriage doth the same!"

As a witness for the defense Coggeshall was roughly handled. Winthrop pointed out that "Mr. Coggeshall was not present" at the conference.

"Yes, but I was," Coggeshall insisted, "only I desired to be silent till I should be called."

"Will you, Mr. Coggeshall, say that she did not say so?" the Governor asked.

"Yes," was the categorical reply. "I dare say that she did not say all that which lay against her."

Coggeshall's contradiction of the ministers' unsworn version of the conference so infuriated the Reverend Mr. Peters that he shouted at the witness: "How dare you look into the court and say such a word?"

Coggeshall folded up like a spent bellows. "Mr. Peters takes upon him to forbid me. I shall be silent."

The magistrates and divines now primed their muskets for the next defense witness. Leverett, a ruling elder in the Boston church, asserted that Mistress Hutchinson charged the ministers with failing to preach a covenant of grace with Cotton's clarity. But his remarks compounded the confusion.

Both sides now readied themselves for the defense's star witness, the Reverend John Cotton, who in a way was as much on trial as the prisoner. In answer to Winthrop's summons he rose from a seat beside the prisoner. As he proceeded to give his own version of the conference, he must have seemed to the spectators like a tightrope walker crossing a yawning chasm on a swaying wire—a thrill which, like the theater, their Puritan piety forbade them from enjoying. A forthright refutation of the ministers' accusation would have earned him the lasting enmity of his envious and less gifted colleagues. But should he repudiate Mistress Hutchinson's touching advocacy and devotion, he would destroy his reputation for loyalty and integrity. The course he pursued was a blend of courage and tact.

In recalling the disputed passages between Mistress Hutchinson and the pastors, Cotton admitted that he was exceedingly uncomfortable that "any comparison should be between me and my brethren." When pressed to describe the differences as the prisoner had analyzed them, he testified that she had pointed out that he "preaches the seal of the spirit upon free grace and you upon a work." These points, to Cotton's way of thinking, did not seem "so ill taken" as they are now represented. "I must say," he added, "that I did not find her saying they were under a covenant of works, nor that she said they did preach a covenant of works."

As to the issue of their competence, the Deputy Governor asked the witness: "They affirm that Mrs. Hutchinson did say they were not able ministers of the New Testament."

"I do not remember it," Cotton replied.

The learned divine's soft answers and his conciliatory but firm testimony added up to a serious modification of the black-and-white version of the conference insisted on by the elders. Everyone present felt that a turning-point had been reached at the trial. Had the defense now rested, the Governor and his supporters would have been in an extremely awkward position.

But Mistress Hutchinson's impulsiveness was to take a great load off the consciences of the magistrates. Like other women before her, she insisted on having the last word, and her rashness proved a fatal error. When Cotton took his seat, she asked the court for "leave" to "give you the ground of what I know to be true." Recklessly she plunged ahead. "The Lord knows that I could not open Scripture," she asserted. "He must by his prophetical office open it unto me." Then, more boldly, she added: "Now if you do condemn me for speaking what in my conscience I know to be truth, I must commit myself unto the Lord."

MR. NOWELL: How do you know that that was the spirit?

MRS. H.: How did Abraham know that it was God that bid him offer his son, being a breach of the sixth commandment?

DUDLEY: By an immediate voice.

MRS. H.: *So to me by an immediate revelation.*

At this point the Deputy Governor sneered: "How! An immediate revelation!" Patiently Anne Hutchinson insisted that the Lord, through the medium of the Bible, had shown her the way; Isaiah and Daniel were cited in her support. Fortified by her faith, she shouted defiantly:

"Therefore I desire you to look to it, for you see this Scripture fulfilled this day and therefore I desire you that as you tender the Lord and the church and commonwealth to consider and look what you do. You have power over my body, but the Lord Jesus hath power over my body and soul, and assure yourselves thus much, you do as much as in you lies to put the Lord Jesus Christ from you, and, if you go on in this course you begin, you will bring a curse upon you and your posterity, and the mouth of the Lord hath spoken it."

Another version of the triad has Mistress Hutchinson warning the magistrates and elders: "Take heed how you proceed against me, for I know that for this you go about to do to me, God will ruin you and your posterity, and this whole state!"

For a moment the courtroom was stunned. So the ancient Hebrews in the synagogue of Nazareth must have reacted when they heard from the mouth of young Jesus doctrines that seemed blasphemous to their ears. No man standing on the soil of Massachusetts Bay had ever gone that far. Neither the ribald and profane Morton of Merrymount nor the eloquent and forthright Roger Williams had ever dared to invoke a curse upon the elders of the New Zion. Mistress Hutchinson's few rash words had entirely undone the effect of her own witnesses' testimony. Her judges had successfully baited her, and now they sought to spring the trap.

WINTHROP: Daniel was delivered by a miracle. Do you think to be delivered so, too?

MRS. H.: I do here speak it before the court. I look that the Lord should deliver me by his providence.

MR. HARKALENDEN: I may read Scripture and the most glorious hypocrite may read them and yet go down to hell.

MRS. H.: It may be so.

Would Cotton dare stand by her now? Everyone in the courtroom wondered. Endecott lost no time in pinning him down. Turning to the Boston divine, he asked whether he approved of her revelations "as she hath laid them down."

"I do not know whether I do understand her," Cotton answered. "But this I say, if she doth expect a deliverance in a way of providence—then I cannot deny it."

The Deputy Governor wanted a more categorical answer. "Good Sir, I do ask whether this revelation be of God or no."

MR. COTTON: I should desire to know whether the sentence of the court will bring her to any calamity, and then I would know of her whether she expects to be delivered from that calamity by a miracle or a providence of God.

MRS. H.: By a providence of God I say I expect to be delivered from some calamity that shall come to me.

WINTHROP: The case is altered and will not stand with us now, but I see a marvellous providence of God to bring things to this pass that they are. We have been harkening about the trial of this thing, and now the mercy of God by a providence hath answered our desires and made her lay open herself and the ground of all these disturbances to be by revelations.

With indecent haste Winthrop sought to keep Cotton from extricating his chief disciple.

"We all consent with you," the other judges added. Resuming the attack against the prisoner, Winthrop stigmatized Anne Hutchinson's views as "desperate enthusiasm." Endecott resented Winthrop's obvious effort to shift the attack back to Jezebel.

"Do you witness for her or against her?" he demanded of Cotton, whose answer was worthy of a medieval Schoolman.

MR. COTTON: This is what I said, Sir, and my answer is plain that if she doth look for deliverance from the hand of God by his providence, and the revelation be in a word or according to a word, that I cannot deny.

MR. ENDECOTT: You give me satisfaction.

DUDLEY: No, no, he gives me none at all.

MR. COTTON: But if it be in a way of miracle or a revelation without the word, that I do not assent to, but look at it as a delusion, and I think so doth she, too, as I understand her.

DUDLEY: Sir, you weary me and do not satisfy me.

MR. COTTON: I pray, Sir, give me leave to express myself. In that sense that she speaks I dare not bear witness against it.

MR. NOWELL: I think it is a devilish delusion.

WINTHROP: Of all the revelations that ever I read of I never read the like grounds laid as is for this. The Enthusiasts and Anabaptists had never the like.

MR. COTTON: You know, Sir, that their revelations broach new matters of faith and doctrine.

WINTHROP: So do these, and what may they breed more if they be let alone? I do acknowledge that there are such revelations as do concur with the word, but there hath not been any of this nature.

DUDLEY: I never saw such revelations as these among the Anabaptists; therefore I am sorry that Mr. Cotton should stand to justify her.

Hugh Peters burst out: "I think it is very disputable which our brother Cotton hath spoken." "It overthrows all," Winthrop solemnly added.

DUDLEY: These disturbances that have come among the Germans have been all grounded upon revelations, and so they that have vented them have stirred up their hearers to take up arms against their prince and to cut the throats of one another, and these have been the fruits of them, and whether the devil may inspire the same into their hearts here I know not, for I am fully persuaded that Mrs. Hutchinson is deluded by the devil, because the spirit of God speaks truth in all her servants.

WINTHROP: I am persuaded that the revelation she brings forth is delusion.

Then, according to the record, "all the court but some two or three ministers" cried out, 'We all believe it! We all believe it!' "

The court was ready to proceed to sentencing when Deputy Brown urged that a more severe punishment be meted out to the prisoner than that which had already been imposed on her disciples, "for this is the foundation of all mischief and of all those bastardly things which have been overthrowing by that great meeting. They have all come out from this cursed fountain." Winthrop was about to put the motion for sentence when [William] Coddington rose to his feet and made a last effort in behalf of the prisoner.

"I do not see any clear witness against her," he pointed out, "and you know it is a rule of the court that no man may be a judge and an accuser too. I would entreat you to consider whether those things which you have alleged against her deserve such censure as you are about to pass, be it to banishment or imprisonment," he continued. "I beseech you do not speak so as to force things along, for I do not for my own part see any equity in the court in all your proceedings. Here is no law of God that she hath broken nor any law of the country that she hath broke, and therefore deserves no censure."

Coddington had courageously raised fundamental issues only to be rudely handled by the Deputy Governor, who observed: "We shall be all sick with fasting." But the opposition would not be stampeded by their stomachs. Colburn openly dissented "from censure of banishment," and even the Deputy Governor refused formally to condemn Anne Hutchinson on the technical ground that the witnesses against her had not testified under oath. To "end all scruples," Winthrop ordered the elders to be sworn. There was a whispered consultation among the divines. The Reverend Messrs. Weld, Eliot, and Peters held up their hands. The Governor turned to them and put the oath: "You shall swear to the truth and nothing but the truth as far as you know. So help you God."

Anne Hutchinson's strategy had now badly backfired, for her insistence that the ministers be put to the oath merely gave them the opportunity of repeating their testimony in court for a second time and impressing it on the spectators all the more vividly. The Reverend John Eliot, some day to be renowned as the Apostle to the Indians, was most explicit in his testimony, while the other two pastors hedged somewhat.

Now the court saw no reason to delay sentence longer. The last few moments as preserved in the trial record are characteristic of the whole proceedings:

MR. STOUGHTON: I say now this testimony doth convince me in the thing, and I am fully satisfied the words were pernicious, and the frame of her spirit doth hold forth the same.

WINTHROP: The court hath already declared themselves satisfied concerning the things you hear, and concerning the troublesomeness of her spirit

William Coddington (1601–1678), a religious supporter of Anne Hutchinson, was a founder of Portsmouth (1638) and Newport (1639) and, later, governor of Rhode Island (1674–1676 and 1678). It is disputed as to whether this portrait by Charles Bird King is of Coddington or his namesake and son, who was also a Rhode Island governor (1683–1685).

and the danger of her course amongst us, which is not to be suffered. Therefore if it be the mind of the court that Mrs. Hutchinson for these things that appear before us is unfit for our society, and if it be the mind of the court that she shall be banished out of our liberties and imprisoned till she be sent away, let them hold up their hands.

All but three raised their hands. Coddington and Colborn were the lone dissenters, and one deputy declared that he could not hold up his hand "one way or the other."

WINTHROP: Mrs. Hutchinson, the sentence of the court you hear is that you are banished from out of our jurisdiction as being a woman not fit for our society, and are to be imprisoned till the court shall send you away.

MRS. H.: I desire to know wherefore I am banished.

WINTHROP: Say no more, the court knows wherefore and is satisfied.

Winthrop had the last word. In all, the trial consumed but two days as contrasted with major criminal trials today, which are seldom terminated under six weeks and not infrequently run on for many months. In sentencing Anne Hutchinson to deportation the authorities were invoking a penalty employed promiscuously against serious offenders as well as paupers and vagrants. Even strangers who were so indiscreet as to come to the Bay Colony leaving their wives behind in the old country would be summarily expelled.

The condemnation of Anne Hutchinson spurred the decision to liquidate the entire opposition party. At the time of Wheelwright's conviction some sixty leading Bostonians had signed a petition denying that Wheelwright had "stirred up sedition in us." Though the tone of their remonstrance was temperate, the signers were neither forgiven nor forgotten. Leading Hutchinsonians—Coddington and Coggeshall, who had dared to speak up for the accused at the trial—were given three months to leave the colony; others were disfranchised. Charging that "there is just cause of suspicion" that the Hutchinsonians, "as others in Germany, in former times, may, upon some revelation, make sudden eruption upon those that differ from them in judgment," the court ordered some fifty-eight citizens of Boston and seventeen from adjacent towns to be disarmed unless they repudiated the "seditious libel," by which term their petition was now stigmatized. Winthrop recounts that some of the "chief military officers" whose loyalties were suspect were now forced into line, but Captain John Underfill, the bawdy military stalwart, remained obdurate and had to be banished. If any plot had sprouted, it was nipped in the bud. As Winthrop felicitously puts it, "when they saw no remedy, they obeyed."

With calculated cruelty Anne Hutchinson was separated from her family and committed to the home of Joseph Weld, brother of her archenemy, the Roxbury divine. Throughout the winter the elders labored with her, but in vain. Finally, in March 1638, they gave her an ecclesiastical trial. Momentarily yielding to the buzzing of her tormentors, she signed a retraction of her views. Then, with characteristic impulsiveness, she recanted. "My judgment is not altered, although my expression alters!" she exclaimed. It must have been a peculiarly agreeable task for the Reverend Mr. Wilson to pronounce her excommunication and order her "as a leper to withdraw yourself out of this congregation." As she passed Winthrop on leaving the trial, that worthy muttered: "The Lord sanctify this unto you." She answered defiantly: "The Lord judgeth not as man judgeth. Better to be cast out of the church than to deny Christ!"

How Cotton, of all the Hutchinsonians, escaped the fate of the rest is a story in itself. But as a realist he saw no prospect of holding out against the wolf pack. Publicly declaring that he had been made use of as a "stalking horse," he turned against his friend and disciple at the church trial. He now savagely charged her with "all promiscuous and filthy coming together of men and women," and predicted that if she continued in her course she must inevitably become unfaithful to her husband. By such smear tactics, unworthy of a great churchman, Cotton recovered "his former splendor" in the eyes of the orthodox.

Even when she was banished from the commonwealth and had made her new home in Rhode Island, Anne's enemies still pursued her. With amazing impudence the Bay Colony authorities sent four laymen down to Anne's settlement to convince her of her errors. She made short shrift of them. As soon as they announced that they had come from Boston, she shouted bitterly: "What from the Church at Boston? I know no such church, neither will I own it. Call it the whore and strumpet of Boston, no Church of Christ!" Sprayed by this picturesque Biblical buckshot, her visitors scampered for cover.

But Anne and her brood continued to be wanderers. After her husband's death she settled at Pelham Bay, then in Dutch New Netherland, where in 1643 she and most of her family were treacherously murdered by Indians. A divine judgment, the Puritan elders called it, scarcely able to conceal their jubilation at the news that this Jezebel, their greatest foe, could no longer oppose them, at least on this earth.

The Antinomian presence on Aquidneck Island and the religious liberty that prevailed in Rhode Island encouraged the persecuted Quakers to settle in Newport beginning in 1657. By 1699 the Society of Friends was large enough to require the spacious meetinghouse depicted in this 1850s lithograph by John Collins. The building still stands at the corner of Marlborough and Farewell streets.

5

Admiralty jurisdiction is a power generally exerted by a central government rather than by its constituent members. For example, Article I, Section 8, of the United States Constitution gives to Congress the power to grant letters of marque and reprisal, to make rules concerning captures on land and water, to define and punish piracies on the high seas and offenses against the law of nations, and to provide and maintain a navy. Conversely, Article I, Section 9, containing the Constitution's express limitations on the power of the states, prohibits them from granting letters of marque and reprisal. In addition, Article III, Section 2, extends the judicial power of the central government "to all cases of admiralty and maritime jurisdiction." Concerning this grant, Alexander Hamilton remarked in *Federalist* No. 80 that "the most bigoted idolizers of State authority have not thus far shown a disposition to deny the national judiciary the cognizance of maritime cases."

Historian Marguerite Appleton, a close student of colonial Rhode Island who wrote her doctoral dissertation on "The Relation of the Corporate Colony of Rhode Island to the British Government" (Brown, 1928), views Rhode Island's creation of a court of admiralty as one of the colony's many manifestations of self-reliance and independent spirit—a bold willingness to usurp the prerogatives of the mother county if perceived necessity demanded it.

In the seventeenth century, admiralty jurisdiction was concerned mainly with the disposition of "prizes"— enemy ships and cargo captured legally under the authority of governmentally issued letters of marque and reprisal. Today this aspect of admiralty jurisdiction is rarely used. The bulk of admiralty cases in U.S. district courts concern private-law disputes affecting the shipping industry — contracts to carry goods, charters of ships, marine insurance, ship collisions and spills, seamen's or passengers' personal injuries, and salvage operations.

Two of the men involved with Rhode Island's forbidden foray into maritime law had other interesting historical connections: William Dyer was the husband of Mary, the Quaker martyr; Judge Nathaniel Byfield was the most prominent of the four incorporators of Bristol when it was established as a Plymouth Colony frontier town in 1680, after King Philip's War.

Rhode Island's First Court of Admiralty

Marguerite Appleton

Rhode Island's first Court of Admiralty, which functioned intermittently from 1653 until abolished by an Order in Council in 1704, was the natural result of the period in which England was engaged in almost incessant warfare. We find the first mention of such a court in the colony during Oliver Cromwell's War with the Dutch.

Although there was no provision in the Rhode Island Patent of 1643 for a Court of Admiralty, the arrival of a letter in 1653, brought by William Dyre [Dyer] from the Council of State, gave the necessary authority to issue privateering commissions.

> ...and the better to defend the colony against the Dutch, power is hereby given to you to raise forts and also to take and seize Dutch ships and vessels at sea as shall come in to any of your harbors or within your power, taking care that such accounts be given to the state as is usual in the like cases. And to that end you are to appoint one or more persons to attend to the care of the business.

Thus, while the power to erect a Court of Admiralty was not specifically granted, a reasonable interpretation of the letter would seem to have authorized such a court as a corollary to privateering.

Accordingly, on May 17, 1653, the General Assembly at Newport voted to make William Dyer, Joseph Sanford, President of the Assembly, and Nicholas Easton, moderator, a committee of three to "take care that the state's part of all the prizes be secured and account given." On the following day it was voted that

> ...for the tryall of prizes brought in according to the law the General Officers with three juriers of each town shall be authorized to try it. The President and two Assistants shall have authority to appoint the time, but if any fail at the time appointed, either officers or juriers, the juriers shall be made up in the town of Newport when they shall be tried. In case of any of the officers fail, then those that appear shall proceed according to the law of Alleroone.

The Assembly chose eight men as a committee of war, and granted commissions to Captain John Underhill, William Dyer, and Edward Hull as privateers.

This action came at the time when Providence and Newport were separated on account of the controversy over William Coddington's commission as Governor. The energy of the Newport Assembly in giving out privateering commissions angered Providence and Warwick. The mainland settlements feared that these commissions, which bore the name of the whole Colony, might sooner or later involve Rhode Island in quarrels with her New England neighbors. Therefore, a vigorous protest was made to Newport, to the effect that the action was "like for aught we know to set all

New England on fire, for the event of war is various and uncertain." To make sure that Providence would not be injured by such rashness, the Assembly meeting there declared that in case of trouble they would petition England for aid, and announced that no one who recognised the commissions illegally issued in the name of the Providence Plantations would be allowed to accept any position in their government until he had "given satisfaction to the respective towns of Providence and Warwick." Apparently Newport took no notice of this remonstrance; in any case, the Court of Admiralty began to function almost immediately.

Although this tribunal was called a Court of Admiralty and was ordered to proceed according to the "laws of Oleron," in reality it was simply the General Court of Trials hearing prize cases. It had the same machinery—consisting of the President of the Assembly, the Assistants, the Recorder, Treasurer, Attorney, and Sergeant, and three jurors from each town. Because such an elaborate organization—and particularly the employment of a jury—was unusual in a Court of Admiralty, and also because Rhode Island did not have a thoroughly-developed court system, it is clear that it was merely the highest civil court in the Colony asserting admiralty jurisdiction when necessary.

We know that the court tried a few cases, one of which, that of the *Swallow*, frigate, can be reconstructed with a fair degree of accuracy. About the middle of April, 1653, Captain Edward Hull of the *Swallow*, learning of the state of war, captured (in the Connecticut River) a vessel sailed by a Captain Sebada. One month later, on May 18, Captain Hull received his privateering commission from the Newport Assembly. During the interval his capture was probably hidden in one of the many inlets of Narragansett Bay. After he had waited a reasonable length of time, he produced his prize for adjudication, and notwithstanding the discrepancy between the date of the commission and the date of the seizure, it was condemned as a lawful prize. Some weeks later the owners sold the vessel to Christopher Almy for £56: 10*s*. In the mean time, Sebada had brought suit against Hull in the Court of Admiralty sitting in Portsmouth, Rhode Island, on the ground that his vessel had been taken before the captor had received his commission, and the Newport decision was reversed. Our knowledge of this case is derived in part from frequent mention in the *Rhode Island Colonial Records* of a quarrel between Christopher Almy, who had lost money through the decision of the Portsmouth tribunal, and Nicholas Easton, who refused to surrender the Colony's share of the prize money. The General Court of the Providence Plantations finally ordered Easton to relinquish "the state's part of the prizes taken in the time of the difference of the colony with the Dutch."

At least one other case was presented to this local Court of Admiralty. Captain Thomas Baxter was granted a privateering commission in the summer of 1653 in the name of the Providence Plantations. He captured the *Desire*, owned by Samuel Mayo of Barnstable, Massachusetts, on the pretext that she was trading with the Dutch. What the towns of Providence and Warwick had feared, actually happened. The United Colonies of New England quickly protested the capture of the *Desire,* and demanded justice for Mayo. They dispatched a representative to Rhode Island with instructions to find out the source of this authority to issue privateering commissions, and "what security" the colonists had "to take prizes that are brought thither and tried, and who are the judges." Unfortunately, we have no further record of the occurrence.

The war with the Dutch came to an end in 1654, and for forty years there is no further mention of such a court in Rhode Island. Although twice within the next two decades England was at war with her great commercial rival, Holland, the American colonies do not appear to have taken the offensive. During the period of peace from 1672 until 1694 no occasion called for such a court.

The Charter which Rhode Island secured from Charles II contained no clause dealing with a maritime tribunal. In spite of this, the members of the Assembly firmly believed that under the new Charter they had the right to set up one—if necessary. Governor Sanford wrote to the Lords of Trade in 1660: "concerning the court of admiralty, we answer that we have made provision to act according to the laws of England as near as the constitution of our place will bear."

Although King William's War broke out in 1689, a Court of Admiralty was not established in Rhode Island for five years. In January, 1694, Captain Hore of the *Dublin*, sailing under a commission from the Governor of Jamaica, came into Rhode Island waters with the *Saint Paul*, and prayed for her condemnation. After deliberation the Governor and Council decided that the state of war permitted the creation of such a court notwithstanding the silence of the Charter in this respect. A law was then passed which authorized them to act as a Court of Admiralty, and the *Saint Paul* was promptly adjudged a lawful prize.

This tribunal differed from the earlier one in that it was not the colonial civil court hearing prize cases. It was a special court with special powers. Although its machinery, consisting of the Governor, the Deputy-Governor, and the Assistants, was borrowed from the civil courts, a jury was no longer employed. Its function was the "condemning of prizes and other seafaring activities as occasion shall require."

The procedure in prize cases was exceedingly simple, as the trial of the right of seizure of the *Golden Bell* shows. The *Servillian,* Captain Theodorus Lovering, who had a privateering commission from Governor Beeston of Jamaica, had captured the *Golden Bell* of two hundred tons and twelve guns and had taken her into Newport Harbor. The Governor, Deputy-Governor, and Assistants examined the depositions of the crew of the *Servillian*, which had been drawn up under oath, to the effect that the vessel belonged to subjects of the French King, and that she had been seized near Newfoundland. The court then declared that the *Golden Bell* was the lawful prize of Captain Lovering, and he was permitted to dispose of her to suit himself after paying the required fees and costs.

A curious case came up in April, 1696. The same Captain Lovering sighted a small boat off the coast of Cuba and gave chase. After a few hours she was boarded without resistance, and it was then found that "there was No person on borde, Nor No other Creator [creature] but one or two hens.

Her lading or what she had on borde was only some Garlick, and fifteen jars of Muntego, and some sapadele." There was no difficulty in securing the condemnation of this derelict with her strange cargo.

Shortly before the close of King William's War, England took steps to set up Courts of Admiralty under the control of the Crown in the charter colonies. When the new Board of Trade was organized, in 1696, illegal trading and piracy were openly practised along the Atlantic seaboard. The dividing line between privateering and piracy was indeed difficult to maintain. Though the attempt was made to prevent privateering from degenerating into piracy by limiting the duration of commissions to definite periods, it was almost impossible to compel privateersmen to abandon their profitable and adventuresome business after peace had been concluded. The result was that the colonists were constantly charged with piracy as well as violations of the Acts of Trade, while the Home Government was put to no little trouble to stamp out pernicious practices on the high seas. Edward Randolph, Surveyor-General of the Customs in America, sent a memorial and a report to the Board of Trade in 1696 in which he stated his conviction that the lax enforcement of the Navigation Acts was due to the impossibility of obtaining an impartial jury in the ordinary civil courts. Therefore he strongly advocated Courts of Admiralty to try cases of illicit trade, all the officials of which should be royal appointees independent of colonial influence. His suggestion was accepted, and, after some delay in making up a suitable list of officials, commissions were issued from the Admiralty in England to colonists of the charter colonies to serve in the maritime courts.

Commissions for Peleg Sanford as judge and Nathaniel Coddington as registrar of admiralty arrived in Rhode Island in 1697. The action of the home government was greeted with manifest hostility. Governor Clarke refused to swear in Sanford, assuming that the power to establish courts of justice was exclusively secured to the Colony by Charter and by precedent. Clarke persuaded Sanford to give him his commission, showed it to the Assembly, and urged that body to submit to no outside control.

The next year the Board of Trade, alarmed by the many reports of acts of piracy on the part of Rhode Island seamen, decided to make an investigation of conditions in the Colony. In reply to the notice of the pending inquiry, the Assembly at once sent an obsequious letter to the home government explaining away the alleged misdemeanors on the favorite plea of ignorance, and picturing Rhode Island as the victim of calumny. In a speech to the Assembly, Governor Clarke expressed sentiments of rather a different character. He urged his colleagues to resist the action of the Board of Trade, which he thought constituted an attack on their chartered rights.

> "...I doe conclude" [he asserted] "it lys before this Honoured Assembly to make what preparations can be for the maintaining and indicating our just rights and privileges according to our Charter, and I will assure you there shall be nothing wanting on my part to the best of my skill and ability to maintain the same, and hope it will be all your Minds and resolutions so to doe, and I am of that opinion we had

> better like men spend the one half of our Estates to maintain our privileges than... that we with our children should be brought into bondage and slavery as I may say (for I conclude it will be but very little better) for if we did but feel or was sencible of one halfe of some other Governments suffer I doe believe we should be more vigorous to prevent what is likely to come Upon us."

Unfortunately this spirited speech—undoubtedly meant for domestic consumption only—nevertheless reached the Board of Trade and served to heighten the unsavory reputation of Rhode Island with that body. And in 1701 Joseph Dudley was commissioned governor of Massachusetts Bay, and at the same time Vice-Admiral for all New England.

The War of the Spanish Succession had already broken out in Europe; in North America its inception was reflected in noticeable war-like activity against the French. As before, Rhode Island's chief interest lay in privateering. Governor Samuel Cranston was convinced that he could issue privateering commissions, and that the Governor and Council, as in King William's War, could function as a maritime court. It was not long before Dudley seriously questioned both Cranston's authority and that of the local Court of Admiralty.

William Wanton, of Newport, received a privateering commission from Governor Cranston in 1701 and took command of the brigatine, *Greyhound*. He returned after a few weeks' cruise with three French ships of considerable size and value. The right of their seizure was being tried in the Rhode Island Court of Admiralty when Dudley interfered. He attempted to stop the proceedings because Wanton had not obtained his commission from him, and asserted that the *Greyhound* had "the face of a pirate rather than His Majesty's ship." At length, however, the prizes were condemned by the deputy-judge, Thomas Newton. Dudley, greatly annoyed, wrote to the Board of Trade that "Rhode Island absolutely will not submit to take commissions for the privateer they have set out," and that when he went there to publish his commission as Vice-Admiral, "the Governor and Council of that Island used indecent expressions saying they were ensnared and injured, nor would not give (nor have they given since) due obedience to the said commission."

His reiterated complaints of Rhode Island—it was seldom that his letters did not contain some criticism of the Colony—now produced decisive action on the part of the Home Government. The Board of Trade could not overlook the fact that the Court of Admiralty was maintained in spite of the royal decree of 1696. Queen Anne, in 1703, commanded Rhode Island to obey Governor Dudley, because the Charter did not grant admiralty jurisdiction. When this failed to achieve the desired result, the Attorney-General was consulted on the point of law involved. He reported that the Colony had not greatly transgressed, for the court in question was clearly only a temporary institution. The Board of Trade was not satisfied,

Judge Nathaniel Byfield (1653–1733), one of the original proprietors of Bristol, served as an admiralty judge with a commission from the mother country after the Rhode Island admiralty court was disallowed by the Privy Council. This portrait of Byfield is by noted colonial artist John Smibert.

Richard Coote, earl of Bellomont and governor of Massachusetts (1699–1700), wrote a scathing critique of Rhode Island's governmental system in 1699. The report resulted in the Privy Council's action against Rhode Island's admiralty court and prompted the colony to prepare its first legal code in 1705.

and in 1704 succeeded in having the local court abolished by an Order in Council declaring that the Act under which it had functioned was null and void. A royal Court of Admiralty was then formally established. The *Boston News-Letter* of May 1, 1704, printed the following announcement: "Rhode Island, April 27. The Honorable Nathaniel Byfield, Esquire, his commission for judge of the admiralty was published and admitted of here on the 25th, currant."

The process of substituting a Court of Admiralty under the control of the Crown for the local tribunal, was not accomplished without friction. This was the period when the corporate and proprietary colonies were fighting the attempts of the Home Government to vacate the charters, and the Rhode Islanders interpreted the Order in Council as only one more attack on their cherished Charter. Moreover, Governor Dudley was disliked in Rhode Island, and it is not likely that his interference in the case of the *Greyhound* had been forgotten.

Although legally the local court had now ceased to exist, Governor Cranston still considered that he had not been prohibited from granting commissions to privateersmen. In November, 1704, he issued a commission to Captain Halsey of the *Charles*, who returned from the West Indies in the spring of the following year with a valuable Spanish prize. This was being litigated before the Court of Vice-Admiralty when a serious quarrel arose over Halsey's commission. The cargo had already been landed and stored when Judge Byfield discovered that the Captain's commission had been given to him many months after the Order in Council had been received in Rhode Island. Assuming, therefore, that it was invalidated, the judge refused to proceed with the trial until he could consult with the judge of the Court of Admiralty in New York. His dictum stirred up a hornets' nest of indignation in Newport. The vessel was lying in the harbor, her miscellaneous cargo was in danger of being looted, and Captain Halsey was impatient to obtain his clearance papers. Governor Cranston, stoutly supported by the Assembly, insisted that he had been well within his rights in granting privateering commissions, and that he was determined to exercise this power of vice-admiralty as long as the Charter remained in force. In the mean time the owners of the *Charles* had petitioned Dudley to order the condemnation of the vessel. When at last the trial was re-opened, "eighteen lusty fellows" pushed into the court room and presented the registrar with a document which proved to be a justification of Governor Cranston's action. The judge refused to have it read, and the court was adjourned amid the hoots and jeers of the rough intruders. The prize was finally condemned by Judge Byfield according to Dudley's instruction, and Captain Halsey, securing a new privateering commission from Governor Cranston, sailed away on his belated voyage.

After the resentment over this incident had died down, the royal Court of Admiralty was allowed to carry on its duties with comparative smoothness, although the exact powers of the Governor in maritime matters continued to be a troublesome question. For the rest of the colonial period, Rhode Island remained under the jurisdiction of the Court of Admiralty in Boston.

The early history of Rhode Island's Court of Admiralty illustrates two interesting features of the political life of that colony: her autonomy and her independence. Her governmental machinery, never imposed from without, was developed gradually from within, and to meet practical needs. One of these obvious needs in a community whose chief interest and means of livelihood lay on the sea, was for a court having power to condemn prizes in time of war. Such a court was first created by expanding the jurisdiction of the civil tribunal.

Secondly, as a consequence of her corporate character, the Colony was more independent than other American communities. Linked but loosely to the Home Government, she was unwilling (or unable) to appreciate the value of centralized control even in matters clearly of imperial concern. Hence, the Rhode Islanders (forgetting how recently they had sought imperial protection in the shape of the Patent and the Charter against their neighbors, Massachusetts and Connecticut) interpreted the establishment of a royal Court of Admiralty as an infringement of Charter rights. They resented this reasonable administrative measure and resisted its application, accepting most unwillingly the supervision and control of the Mother Country.

6

Rhode Island's largest mass execution for crime occurred in Newport on July 19, 1723, when Captain Charles Harris and twenty-five of his crew were hanged for piracy. Harris and his men were condemned to death by an imperial admiralty court with Massachusetts Lieutenant Governor William Dummer presiding. By present standards the deck was stacked; admiralty courts had no jury and the defendants had no counsel. To support their plea of not guilty, most of the accused claimed to be "forced men"—seamen impressed into piracy after their capture by pirates. Even Harris experienced this fate. To be found not culpable, however, the defendant had to show, by clear and convincing evidence, that he had not embraced pirate ways or signed articles of association. Only ten of the thirty-six Newport defendants succeeded, thereby avoiding the gallows.

There was a touch of irony in the fact that Rhode Island was the setting for such a major pirate trial, for it had a long-standing reputation for tolerating these sea robbers. For example, during the imperial reorganization of the 1690s, reports of Rhode Island's lack of participation in the first phase of the great Anglo-French confrontation for empire, rumors that the colony was countenancing piratical activities, and repeated refusals by the colony to recognize the commissions of some admiralty court officials prompted the strict and circumspect Board of Trade to authorize an investigation of Rhode Island's activities and government. The inquiry was conducted in 1699 by Richard Coote, earl of Bellomont and governor of New York, Massachusetts, and New Hampshire (1699–1701). Bellomont was instructed to obtain copies of all the colony's laws and other public records "relating to the administration of that government." To this end the English investigator visited Rhode Island and then issued a scathing summary of conditions there. The people, he said, had a disdain for learning and were "shamefully ignorant." His report also disclosed an unjustified exercise of the judicial function by the General Assembly, violations of the Acts of Trade, usurpation of admiralty jurisdiction, and the harboring of pirates. Bellomont concluded his twenty-five-point indictment, which listed many deviations from the directives of the charter, by asserting that "his Majesty is neither honored nor served by that government, as at present it is managed."

The exhortation to the admiralty court by Advocate General John Valentine gave thanks that the Newport defendants had been "delivered up to the sword of justice" and rejoiced that now "such flagitious persons find as little countenance, and as much justice at Rhode Island, as in any other part of his Majesties's dominions."

There was sometimes a thin line between the pirate and the privateer. The latter operated against an enemy ship or port in time of war under a government license known as a letter of marque and reprisal. The same conduct in peacetime or without official sanction was piracy. Often men accustomed to privateering could not restrain or retrain themselves when circumstances changed.

Piracy was rampant in the seventeenth century. The English were known as a nation of pirates, and that tradition came to her colonies at an early date. The practice was familiar to residents of American port towns, including Newport, which at first welcomed pirate ships because they brought cheap but valuable commodities and bought supplies from local merchants. By the early eighteenth century, however, the increased activity of pirates and the boldness of their depredations became intolerable to many governments, especially that of England.

In 1713, after the conclusion of Queen Anne's War with France and Spain, the Royal Navy was unleashed against the pirates. The sea robbers were also cut off from their old suppliers in the colonial ports. Americans no longer needed to consort with pirates, because their economy prospered through legitimate commercial activity. Punishment such as that visited upon Charles Harris and his crew in Newport, a one-time pirate haven, greatly discouraged this barbarous practice. By 1730 large-scale piracy, so prevalent in the seventeenth century, was at an end.

The following excerpt is taken from a book entitled *The Pirates of the New England Coast, 1630-1730* (1923), by George F. Dow (a curator) and John H. Edmonds (an archivist). Clearly their skill was compiling rather than writing. However, lawyers accustomed to the low literary quality of depositions and transcripts may find the narrative tolerable. For more readable analyses of the golden age of piracy, consult Marcus Rediker, *Between the Devil and the Deep Blue Sea: Merchant Seamen, Pirates, and the Anglo-American Maritime World, 1700-1750* (1987); Robert C. Ritchie, *Captain Kidd and the War against the Pirates* (1986); and Frank Sherry, *Raiders and Rebels: The Golden Age of Piracy* (1986).

The Piracy Trial of Charles Harris and His Crew

George Francis Dow and John Henry Edmonds

On the 10th of January, 1722, the good ship *Greyhound* of Boston in the Massachusetts Bay, Benjamin Edwards, commander, was homeward bound. She was loaded with logwood and only one day out from the coast of Honduras where the crew had been worked hard for several weeks loading the many boatloads of heavy, thorny-growthed, blood-red wood. Early in the morning the lookout had sighted a ship headed toward them and while not plantation built she attracted no particular attention until it was seen that her course was slightly changed to conform to that of the *Greyhound*, or rather, it would seem, to intersect the course on which the *Greyhound* was sailing. As the ship drew nearer, a long look through the perspective revealed a heavily manned vessel of English build and Captain Edwards thought it best to order all hands on deck. Soon the stranger ran up a black flag having a skeleton on it and fired a gun for the *Greyhound* to bring to.

West India waters had been plagued for many years by piratical gentry and the Boston captain had heard many terrifying tales of their barbarous cruelties to masters and seamen but he was a dogged type of man and so at once prepared to defend his ship. The pirate edged down a bit and shortly gave the *Greyhound* a broadside of eight guns which Captain Edwards bravely returned and for nearly an hour the give and take continued at long gunshot without much damage to either vessel. Finding that the pirate was more heavily armed than the *Greyhound* and her decks showing many men, Captain Edwards began to reckon the consequences of a too stubborn resistance, for it seemed likely that eventually he must surrender, barring, of course, a lucky chance shot from his guns that might cut down a mast on the pirate ship. At last he ordered his ensign to be struck and hove to. Two boatloads of armed men soon came aboard and searched the ship for anything of value. The loot was not great for the New England logwood ships had little opportunity for trade or barter and the disappointment of the pirate crews was soon spit out on the men. Whenever one came within reach of the cutlass of a pirate he would receive a swinging slash across shoulders or arms, or perhaps, a blow on the head with the flat of the blade that would fell him half-senseless to the deck. By way of diversion two of the unoffending sailors were triced up at the foot of the mainmast and lashed until the blood ran from their backs. Captain Edwards and his men were then ordered into the boats and sent on board the pirate ship and the *Greyhound* was set on fire.

The rogue proved to be the *Happy Delivery*, commanded by Capt. George Lowther and manned by a strange assortment of English sailors and soldiers with a sprinkling of New England men. As soon as the men from the *Greyhound* reached her deck they were given a mug of rum and invited to join the pirate crew. This was habitually done at that time by these outlaws and frequently a nimble sailor would be forced and compelled to serve with the pirates against his will. The first mate of the *Greyhound*

This 1730 painting by an unknown artist depicts Newport harbor near the time of the Harris trial. At that time the town had emerged as the fifth most prosperous and populous commercial center in the original thirteen colonies, exceeded only by Philadelphia, Boston, New York, and Charleston.

was Charles Harris, born in London, England, then about twenty-four years old and a man who understood navigation. He, with four others, Christopher Atwell, Henry Smith, Joseph Willis and David Lindsay, was forced and Captain Edwards and the rest of his crew, with other captured men, were put on board another logwood vessel and permitted to make the best of their way home. In a day or two, Harris, beguiled by the adventurous spirit of the ship's company, was persuaded to sign the Articles of the *Happy Delivery* when again asked to do so by Captain Lowther. He proved to be so capable a man, when several captures were made, that ten days later, when a Jamaican sloop was taken, Lowther decided to retain her and give the command to Harris and to this he readily acceded.

The mate of the *Happy Delivery* was Ned Low, a young Englishman who had lived in Boston for a few years and not long before this time had deserted from a logwood ship in the Bay and happening to meet Lowther had joined him in a career of robbery and murder. Just before the Jamaican sloop was taken, a Rhode Island sloop of about one hundred tons was captured and as she was newly built was taken over by Lowther and armed with eight carriage guns and ten swivels and the command given to Low.

The career of Harris during the next fourteen months closely follows that of Lowther and Low and may be traced in the narrative of their adventures. He soon lost his sloop when it was abandoned at sea in the gulf of Matique and May 28th, 1722, when Lowther and Low separated, Harris cast his lot with Low and sailed north with him along the New England coast to Nova Scotia and then across the Atlantic to the Western Islands, where a large Portuguese pink was taken and retained and the command of the schooner *Fancy* given to Harris. These two scoundrels cruised together for some time making several captures and at length reached the Triangles off the South American coast, eastward of Surinam, and here the pink was lost while being careened and both crews went on board the schooner where Low again assumed command. Before long a large Rhode Island-built sloop was captured which Low took over and having had a falling out with Harris, the command of the schooner *Fancy* was given to Francis Farrington Spriggs, who had been serving as quartermaster.

Harris now drops out of sight for about five months. He may have been wounded or sick at the time Spriggs was given his command, at any rate, no mention of his name has been found until May 27, 1723, when he appeared off the South Carolina coast in command of the sloop *Ranger*, lately commanded by Spriggs. Captain Low was sailing in company with him in the sloop *Fortune* and together they took three ships. About three weeks before, they had captured the ship *Amsterdam Merchant*, from Jamaica but owned in New England. The master was John Welland of Boston and after he had been on board the *Ranger* for some three hours he was transferred to the *Fortune*, where Low vented his spite against New Englanders by cutting the captain about the body with his cutlass and slashing off his right ear. A month later, at the trial of Captain Harris at Newport, R. I., this Captain Welland was the principal witness against him. He deposed that he had been chased by two sloops and that one of them came up with him and after hoisting a blue flag had taken him. This was the *Ranger*, with Harris in command. He had been ordered aboard the pirate sloop and had gone with four of his men. The quartermaster had examined him and asked how much money he had on board, and he had replied "About £150 in gold and silver." This money was taken away by the pirates. Meanwhile Captain Low in the *Fortune*, came up and Welland was sent aboard to be interrogated, where he was greatly abused. The next day, after taking out a negro, some beef and other stores, the *Amsterdam Merchant* was sunk. While the three vessels were lying near each other, Captain Estwick of Piscataqua, N. H., came in sight and soon fell into the clutches of Low and Harris. His ship was plundered but not destroyed and in this vessel Captain Welland and his men at last reached Portsmouth, New Hampshire.

Off the Capes of the Delaware other minor captures were made by Low and steering eastward along the Long Island shore early on the morning of the 10th of June a large ship was sighted which soon changed its course and the two pirate sloops at once followed in pursuit. What then took place may best be told in the words of the newspaper account written at the time.

"Rhode Island, June 14. On the 11th Instant arrived here His Majesty's Ship Grayhound, Capt. Peter Solgard Commander, from his Cruize at Sea and brought in a Pirate Sloop of 8 Guns, Barmudas built, 42 White Men and 6 Blacks, of which number eight were wounded in the Engagement and four killed; the Sloop was commanded by one Harris, very well fitted, and loaded with all sorts of Provisions: One of the wounded Pirates died, on board of the Man of War, with an Oath on his Departure; thirty lusty bold young Fellows, were brought on shore, and received by one of the Town Companys under Arms guarding them to the Gaol, and all are now in Irons under a strong Guard. The Man of War had but two Men wounded, who are in a brave way of Recovery.

"Here follows an Account (from on board of the Man of War) of the Engagement between Capt. Solgard and the two Pirates Sloops: Capt. Solgard being informed by a Vessel, that Low the Pirate, in a Sloop of 10 Guns & 70 Men, with his Consort of 8 Guns and 48 Men, had sailed off the East End of Long-Island: The Capt. thereupon steered his Course after them; and on the 10th Currant, half an hour past 4 in the Morning we saw two Sloops N. 2 Leagues distance, the Wind W.N.W. At 5 we tack'd and stood Southward, and clear'd the Ship, the Sloops giving us Chase, at half an hour past 7 we tack'd to the Northward, with little Wind, and stood down to them; at 8 a Clock they each fired a Gun, and hoisted a Black Flag; at half an hour past 8 on the near approach of the Man of War, they haultd it down, (fearing a Tartar) and put up a Bloody Flag, stemming with us distant 3 quarters of a Mile: We hoisted up our Main-Sail and made easy Sail to the Windward, received their Fire several times; but when a breast we gave them ours with round & grape Shot, upon which the head Sloop edg'd Away, as did the other soon after, and we with them. The Fire continued on both sides for about an hour; but when they hall'd from us with the help of their Oars, we left off Firing, and turned to Rowing with 86 Hands, and half an Hour past Two in the Afternoon we came up with them; when they clapt on a Wind to receive us; we again kept close to Windward, and ply'd them warmly with small and grape shot; and during the Action we fell between them, and having shot down one of their Main Sails we kept close to him, and at 4 a Clock he call'd for Quarters; at 5 having got the Prisoners on board, we continued to Chase the other Sloop, when at 8 a Clock in the Evening he bore from us N.W. by W. two Leagues, when we lost sight of him near Block Island. One Desperado was for blowing up this Sloop rather than surrendering, and being hindered, he went forward, and with his Pistol shot out his own Brains.

"Capt. Solgard designing to make sure of one of the Pirate Sloops, if not both, took this, seeming to be the Chief, but proved otherwise, and if we had more Daylight the other of Low's had also been taken, she being very much batter'd; and 'tis tho't he was slain, with his Cutlas in his hand, encouraging his Men in the Engagement to Fight, and that a great many more Men were kill'd and wounded in her, than the other we took.

"The Two Pirate Sloops Commanded by the said Low and Harris intended to have boarded the Man of War, but he plying them so successfully they were discouraged, and endeavoured all they could to escape, notwithstanding they had sworn Damnation to themselves, if they should give over Fighting, tho' the Ship should even prove to be a Man of War. They also intended to have hoisted their Standard upon Block-Island, but we suppose now, there will be a more sutable Standard hoisted for those that are taken, according to their Desarts.

"On the 12th Currant Capt. Solgard was fitting out again to go in the Quest of the said Low the other Pirate Sloop, (having the Master of this with him, he knowing what Course they intended by Agreement to Steer, in order to meet with a third Consort) which, we hope he'll overtake and bring in."

—*Boston News-Letter*, June 20, 1723.

The *New England Courant* of Boston, James Franklin's paper, printed a similar account of the fight and capture and also mentioned the fact that Joseph Swetser of Charlestown was one of the men taken and that both he and Charles Harris "who is the Master or Navigator," had previously been advertised in the public prints as forced men, with one or two more of the company. A week later the *Courant* published a list of the names of the men, as follows:

"An Account of the Names, Ages, and places of Birth of those Men taken by his Majesty's Ship Greyhound, in the Pirate Sloop called the Ranger, and now confined in his Majesty's Gaol in Rhode-Island.

Names	*Ages*	*Places of Birth*
William Blades	28	Rhode Island
Thomas Powel, Gunner	21	Wethersfield, Conn.
John Wilson	23	New London County
Daniel Hyde	23	Eastern Shore of Virginia
Henry Barnes	22	Barbadoes
Stephen Mundon	29	London
Thomas Huggit	24	London
William Read	35	London-derry, Ireland
Peter Kewes	32	Exeter, England
Thomas Jones	17	Flint, Wales
James Brinkley	28	Suffolk, England
Joseph Sawrd	28	Westminster
John Brown	17	Leverpool
William Shutfield	40	Leicestershire, Engl.
Edward Eaton	38	Wreaxham, Wales
John Brown	29	County of Durham, Engl.
Edward Lawson	20	Isle of Man
Owen Rice	27	South Wales
John Tomkins	23	Glocestshire, Engl.
John Fitz-Gerald	21	County of Limerick, Irela.
Abraham Lacey	21	Devonshire, Engl.
Thomas Linisker	21	Lancashire, Engl.

Thomas Reeve	30	County of Rutland, Engl.
John Hinchard, Doctor	22	Near Edinbirgh, N. Brit.
Joseph Swetser (forc'd)	24	Boston, New England
Francis Layton	39	New-York
John Walters, Quar. Master	35	County of Devon
William Jones	28	London
Charles Church	21	Westminster
Tom Umper, an Indian	21	Martha's Vineyard
In all	30	

—*New England Courant*, June 24, 1723.

The following seven were held on board the *Grayhound* by Captain Solgard, who hoped through them to take Low. They were brought back to Newport and gaoled on July 11th. One of the pirates died in gaol on July 15th.

Charles Harris, Captain	25	London
Thomas Hazell	50	———
John Bright	25	———
Joseph Libbey	21	Marblehead
Patrick Cunningham	25	———
John Fletcher	17	———
Thomas Child	15	———

When the news of this great capture of pirates reached the seaport towns along the New England shore there was much rejoicing. Nothing like it had ever happened in the history of the Colonies and to be accused of piracy at that time, with any show of evidence, was very nearly equivalent to being found guilty, so a great gathering of people was assured for the hanging soon to follow.

Three weeks later the Honorable William Dummer, Esq., Lieutenant-Governor and Commander in Chief of His Majesty's Province of the Massachusetts Bay in New England, together with divers members of His Majesty's Council and other gentlemen from that Province came riding into the town of Newport, and with Governor Samuel Cranston of Rhode Island and other judges duly commissioned by Act of Parliament proceeded to open a Court of Admiralty for the trial of the pirates. The trial was held in the town house on Wednesday morning, July 10, 1723. The Court was authorized by Act of Parliament made 11 and 12 William III; made perpetual by Act of 6 George I. The Court organized, and then adjourned until eight oclock in the morning of the next day—when Charles Harris and twenty-seven others were brought to the bar and arraigned for acts of felony, piracy and robbery.

The facts connected with the taking of the ship *Amsterdam Merchant*, with the presence in court of the master and some of his men, were in themselves sufficient to hang the accused. Captain Solgard of the man-of-war, who had fought with the accused pirates and captured them, also testified as did his lieutenant and surgeon. The presence of these men in court together with the reputed facts of the chase and capture decided the

William Dummer (1677–1761), lieutenant governor of Massachusetts, presided at the piracy trial of Charles Harris and his crew. This portrait by Robert Feke now hangs at Governor Dummer Academy, a prestigious private school in Massachusetts.

case in the minds of the people before the evidences were offered or the verdict rendered. John Valentine, the Advocate General for the King, presented the articles which accused the prisoners of piratically surprising and seizing the ship *Amsterdam Merchant*, and carrying away beef, gold and silver and a negro slave named Dick; cutting off Captain Welland's right ear and afterwards sinking the ship valued at one thousand pounds. They were also accused of piratically attacking His Majesty's ship, the *Grey Hound*, and wounding seven of his men.

The prisoners were not represented by counsel, but they all pleaded "not guilty," and fourteen of them were ordered tried at that very session, so the Advocate General addressed the Court as follows:

"May it please your honor, and the rest of the honorable judges, of this court.

"The prisoners at the bar stand articled against and are prosecuted for, several felonious piracies and robberies by them committed upon the high sea. To which they severally pleaded not guilty.

"The crime of piracy is a robbery (for piracy is a sea term for robbery) committed within the jurisdiction of the admiralty.

"And a pirate is described to be one who to enrich himself either by surprise or open force, sets upon merchants and others trading by sea, to spoil them of their goods and treasure, often times by sinking their vessels, as the case will come out before you.

"This sort of criminals are engaged in a perpetual war with every individual, with every state, christian or infidel; they have no country, but by the nature of their guilt, separate themselves, renouncing the benefit of all lawful society, to commit these heinous crimes. The Romans therefore justly styled them, *Hostes humoni generis*, enemies of mankind, and indeed they are enemies and armed, against themselves, a kind of *felons de se*— importing something more than a natural death.

"These unhappy men satiated with the number and notoriety of their crimes, had filled up the measure of their guilt, when by the Providence of Almighty God, and through the valor and conduct of Captain Solgard, they were delivered up to the sword of justice.

"The Roman Emperors in their edicts made this piece of service so eminent for the public good, as meritorious as any act of piety, or religious worship whatsoever.

"And 'twill be said for the honor and reputation of this colony (though of late scandalously reproached, to have favored or combined with pirates), and be evinced by the process and event of this affair, that such flagitious persons find as little countenance, and as much justice at Rhode Island, as in any other part of his Majestie's dominions.

"But your time is more precious than my words, I will not misspend it in attempting to set forth the aggravations of this complex crime, big with every enormity, nor in declaring the mischiefs and evil tendencies of it; for you better know these things before I mention them; and I consider to whom I speak, and that the judgment is your honors.

"I shall therefore call the King's evidences to prove the several facts, as so many distinct acts of piracy charged on Prisoners, not by light circumstances and presumptions, not by strained and unfounded conjectures, but by clear and postive evidence: and then I doubt not, since for 'tis the interest of mankind, that these crimes should be punished; your honors will do justice to the prisoners, this colony, and the rest of the world in pronouncing them guilty, and in passing sentence upon them according to law."

Capt. John Welland then testified as to the facts attending the capture of his ship. He also said that Henry Barns, one of the prisoners at the bar, was forced out of his ship at the time it was taken and was "very low and weak" and when on board Captain Estwick's vessel (in which they had at last reached Portsmouth) Barns had tried to get away and hid himself. But the pirates threatened to burn the ship unless he was given up so Barns was compelled to go on board the pirate sloop. Barnes had cried and "took on very much" and asked the mate of the *Amsterdam Merchant* to notify his three sisters living in Barbadoes that he was a forced man and also very sick and weak at the time. The mate and the ship's carpenter confirmed the captain's testimony that all the pirates were "harnessed, that is, armed with guns, etc."

Capt. Peter Solgard, Lieut. Edward Smith, and Archibald Fisher, "Chirsurgeon" of the *Grey-Hound Man of War*, testified to the well-known facts of the engagement with the pirates and William Marsh, a mariner, made oath that he had been taken by Low's company in the West Indies the previous January and that "he saw on board the schooner at that time Francis Laughton and William—— and on board the sloop, Charles Harris, Edward Lawson, Daniel Hyde, and John Fitz Gerald, all prisoners at the Bar, and that Gerald asked him whether he would seek his fortune with him."

This concluded the testimony and the prisoners were then severally asked if they had anything to say in their own defence. Without exception each man said that he had been forced on board of Low and did nothing voluntarily.

The Advocate General then summed up the case, as follows:

"Your Honors, I doubt not have observed the weakness, and vanity of the defence which has been made by the prisoners at the Bar, and that the articles (containing indisputable flagrant acts of piracy) are supported against each of them: Their impudences and unfortunate mistake, in attacking his majesty's ship, tho' to us fortunate, and of great service to the neighboring governments: Their malicious and cruel assault upon Capt. Welland, not only in the spoiling of his goods, but what is much more, the cutting off his right ear, a crime of that nature and barbarity which can never be repaired: Their plea of constraint, or force, (in the mouth of every Pirate) can be of no avail to them, for if that could justify or excuse! No pirate would ever be convicted; nor even any profligate person in his own account offend against the moral law; if it were asked, it would be hard to answer; who offer'd the violence? It's apparent they forced, or persuaded one another, or rather the compulsion proceeded of their own corrupt and avaricious inclinations: but if there was the least semblance of truth; in the plea; it might come out in proof, that the prisoners or some of them did manifest their uneasiness and sorrow, to some of the persons whom they had surprised and robb'd; but the contrary of that is plain from Mr. Marsh's evidence, that the prisoners were so far from a dislike, or regretting their number by inviting him to join with them, and seemed resolved to live and die by their calling, or for it, as their fate is like to be. And now seeing that the facts are as evident as proof by testimony can make 'em, I doubt not your honors will declare the prisoners to be guilty."

The prisoners were than taken from the bar, the court room was cleared and the judges considered the evidence and voted that all were guilty except John Wilson and Henry Barns. The Court then adjourned for dinner and at two o'clock met and opened by proclamation. The prisoners were brought in and those found guilty were sentenced by Lieut.-Governor Dummer to be hanged by the neck until dead. Thirteen more "of that miserable crew of men," as they were characterised by the Advocate General, were then brought to the bar for trial, and Captain Welland named six of whom he recognized as having been on the *Ranger* and all had been harnessed, except Thomas Jones, the boy. John Mudd, the carpenter, said that he well remembered Joseph Sound because he said "Sound took his buttons out of his sleeves."

"Benjamin Weekham of Newport mariner, deposed, that on the tenth of March last he was in the bay of Honduras on board of a sloop, Jeremiah Clark Master, Low and Lowders companies being pirates, took the aforesaid sloop, and that this deponent then having the small pox was by John Waters one of the prisoners at the Bar carried on board another vessel; and that he begg'd of some of the company two shirts to shirt himself, the said Waters said damn him, he would beg the vessel too, but at other times he was very civil; and the deponent further saith, he saw William Blades now prisoner at the Bar amongst them.

"William Marsh deposed, that he was taken in manner as aforesaid, and that John Brown the tallest was on board the schooner, and the said Brown told him he had rather be in a tight vessel than a leaky one, and that he was not forced.

"Henry Barns mariner, deposed, that he being on board the Sloop *Ranger* during her engagement with the *Grey-Hound Man of War*, saw all the prisoners at the Bar on board the said sloop *Ranger*, and that he saw John Brown the shortest in arms, that Thomas Mumford Indian, was only as a servant on board.

"The prisoners at the bar were then asked if they had anything to say in their own defence.

"William Blades said he was forced on board of Low about eleven months ago, and never signed to their articles, and that he had when taken about ten or twelve pounds, and that he never shared with them, but only took what they gave him.

"Thomas Hugget said he was one of Capt. Mercy's men on the coast of Guinea, and in the West Indies was put on board Low, but never shared with them, and they gave him twenty-one pounds.

"Peter Cues said, that on the twenty-third or twenty-fourth of January last he belonged to one Layal in a sloop of Antigua, and was then taken by Low and detained ever since, but never shared with them, and had about ten or twelve pounds when taken, which they gave him.

"Thomas Jones said, he is a lad of about seventeen years of age, and was by Low and company taken out of Capt. Edwards at Newfoundland, and kept by Low ever since.

"William Jones said, he was taken out of Capt. Ester at the Bay of Honduras the beginning of April last by Low and Lowther, and that he has been forced by Low to be with him ever since; that he never shared with them, nor signed the articles till compelled three weeks after he was taken, and the said Jones owned he had eleven pounds of the quarter master at one time, and eight pounds at another.

"Edward Eaton said, that he was taken by Low in the Bay of Honduras, about the beginning of March, and kept with him by force ever since.

"John Brown the tallest said, that on the ninth of October last he was taken out of the Liverpool merchant at the Cape De Verde by Capt. Low who beat him black and blue to make him sign the articles, and from the Cape de Verde they cruized upon the coast of Brazil about eleven weeks, and from thence to the West Indies, and he was on board of the *Ranger* at the taking of Welland.

"James Sprinkly said, he was forced out of a ship at the Cape de Verde by Low in October last, and by him compelled to sign the articles, but never shared with them.

"John Brown the shortest said, he was about seventeen years old, and in October last at the Cape de Verdes was taken out of a ship by Low, and kept there ever since, and that the quarter-master gave him about forty shillings, and the people aboard about three pounds.

"Joseph Sound said, he was taken from Providence [in the Bahamas], about three months ago, by Low and company and detained by force ever since.

"Charles Church said, he was taken out of the *Sycamore Galley* at the Cape de Verdes, Capt. Scot commander, about seven or eight months ago, by Capt. Low, never shared, but the quarter-master gave him about fourteen pounds.

"John Waters said, he was taken by Low on the twenty-ninth of June last, out of ——, and they compelled him to take charge of a watch, and that he had thirteen pistols when taken, which was given him, and that he said in the time of the engagement with his Majesties ship they had better strike, for they would have better quarter.

"Thomas Mumford Indian said, he was a servant a fishing the last year, and was taken out of a fishing sloop with five other Indians off of Nantucket by Low and Company, and that they hanged two of the Indians at Cape

Sables, and that he was kept by Low ever since, and had about six bitts when taken."

These excuses availed nothing except for Thomas Jones, the boy, and Thomas Mumford, the Indian. The rest were found guilty and duly sentenced.

The next morning John Kencate, the doctor on board the *Ranger*, was brought to trial. The Advocate General stated that although the prisoner "used no arms, was not harness'd (as they term it) but was a forc'd man; yet if he received part of their plunder, was not under a constant durance, did at any time approve, or join'd in their villanies, his guilt is at least equal to the rest; the Doctor being ador'd among 'em as the pirates God for in him they chiefly confide for their cure and life, and in this trust and dependence it is, that they enterprise these horrid depredations not to be heightened by aggravation, or lessened by any excuse."

"Capt. John Welland deposed, and that he saw the Doctor aboard the Ranger; he seem'd not to rejoice when he was taken but solitary, and he was inform'd on board he was a forc'd men; and that he never signed the articles as he heard of, and was now on board the deponants ship.

"John Ackin Mate and John Mudd Carpenter, swore they saw the prisoner at the Bar walking forwards and backwards disconsolately on board the *Ranger*.

"Archibald Fisher Physician and Chirurgion on board the said *Greyhound Man-of-War* deposed, that when the prisoner at the Bar was taken and brought aboard the King's ship he searched his medicaments, and the instruments, and found but very few medicaments, and the instruments very mean and bad."

Others testified that the doctor was forced on board, by Low, and that he never signed articles so far as they knew or heard, but used to spend much of his time in reading, and was very courteous to the prisoners taken by Low and his company, and that he never shared with them.

The doctor himself said that he was chirurgion of the *Sycamore-Galley*, Andrew Scot, master, and was taken out of that ship in September last at Bonavista, one of the Cape de Verde Islands, by Low and Company, who detained him ever since, and that he never shared with them, nor signed their articles.

The Court then cleared the doctor and proceeded with the trial of Thomas Pownall, Joseph Sweetser and Joseph Libbey. The name of the latter is not found in the first published lists of the pirates gaoled at Newport for the reason that he was one of those detained by Captain Harris in hopes of capturing Low who had deliberately deserted them, when jointly they probably could have taken the man of war. Libbey's name appears in the published lists of those condemned and executed, as having been born in Marblehead.

At the trial of these men Doctor Kencate testified that "he well knew Thomas Powell, Joseph Sweetser and John Libbey, and that Thomas Powell acted as gunner on board the *Ranger*, and that he went on board several vessels taken by Low and company, and plundered, and that Joseph Libbey was an active man on board the *Ranger*, and used to go on board vessels they took and plundered and that he see him fire several times, and the deponent further deposed that Joseph Sweetser now prisoner at the bar, was on board the pirate Low, and that he has seen him armed, but never see him use them, and that the said Sweetser used to often get alone by himself from amongst the rest of the crew, he was melancholly, and refused to go on board any vessel by them taken, and got out of their way. And the deponent further saith, that on that day, as they engaged the man-of-war, Low proposed to attack the man-of-war, first by firing his great guns then a volley of small arms, heave in their powder flasks and board her in his sloop, and the *Ranger* to board over the *Fortune*, and that no one on board the *Ranger* disagreed to it as he knows of, for most approved of it by words and the others were silent.

"Thomas Jones deposed that Thomas Powell acted as gunner on board the *Ranger*, and Joseph Libbey was a stirring, active man among them, and used to go aboard vessels to plunder, and that Joseph Sweetser was very dull aboard, and at Cape Antonio he cried to Dunwell to let him go ashore, who refused, and asked him to drink a dram, but Sweetser went down into the hold and cried a good part of the day, and that Low refused to let him go, but brought him and tied him to the mast and threatened to whip him; and he saw him armed but never saw him use his arms as he knows of: and that Sweetser was sick when they engaged the man-of-war, tho' he assisted in rowing the vessel.

"John Wilson deposed that Thomas Powell was gunner of the *Ranger*; and the Sabbath day before they were taken, the said Powell told the deponent he wished he was ashore at Long Island, and they went to the head of the mast and Powell said to him I wish you and I were both ashore here stark naked.

"Thomas Mumford, Indian (not speaking good English), Abissai Folger was sworn interpereter, deposed that Thomas Powell, Joseph Libbey and Joseph Sweetser were all on board of Low the pirate, that he saw Powell have a gun when they took the vessels, but never saw him fire, he saw him go on board of a vessel once, but brought nothing from her as he saw, he see him once [shoot] a negro but never a white man. And he saw Joseph Libbey once go aboard a vessel by them taken and brought away from her one pair of stockings. And that Joseph Swetser cooked it on board with him sometime, and sometimes they made him hand the sails; once he saw said Swetser clean a gun, but not fire it, and Swetser once told him that he wanted to get ashore from among them, and said he if the Man-of-War should take them they would hang him, and in the engagement of the Man-of-War, Swetser sat unarmed in the range of the sloop's mast, and some little time before the said engagement he asked Low to let him have his liberty and go ashore, but was refused."

There was other testimony to much the same effect. Powell said he was taken by Lowther in the Bay of Honduras in the winter of 1721–2 and by him turned over to Low. Libbey said he was a forced man and produced a newspaper advertisement in proof. Sweetser said he was taken by Lowther about a year before and forced on board of Low. He, too, produced an advertisement to prove that he had been forced. Powell and Libbey were found guilty and Sweetser was cleared.

Hazel, Bright, Fletcher, and Child and Cunningham who had been detained on board the *Greyhound* in the later pursuit of Low, were then placed on trial. By numerous witnesses it was shown that all had been active on board the *Ranger* at the time of the fight but that Fletcher was only a boy and that Child had come on board from the *Fortune*, only three or four days before the fight. Captain Welland spoke a good word for Cunningham and said that he had got him water and brought the doctor at the time he was laying bleeding below hatches for nearly three hours with a sentinel over him. John Bright was the drummer and "beat upon his drum upon the round house in the engagement."

Thomas Hazel said he had been forced by Low about twelve months before in the Bay of Honduras. Bright said that he was a servant to one Hester in the Bay and had been taken by Low about four months before and forced away to be his drummer.

Cunningham said he had been forced about a year before from a fishing schooner and that he had tried to get away at Newfoundland but without success. Fletcher, the boy, said he had been forced by Low from on board the *Sycamore Galley*, Scot, master, at Bona Vista, because he could play a violin. There is no record of what Child had to say for himself. Fletcher and Child were found not guilty; the others were sentenced to be hanged. Cunningham and John Brown "the shortest," were recommended "unto His Majesty, for Remission."

While the pirates were in prison and especially in the interval between their condemnation and execution they were visited frequently by the ministers who afterwards stated in print that "while they were in Prison, most seemed willing to be advised about the affairs of their souls." John Brown prepared in writing a "warning" to young people in which he declared "it was with the greatest Reluctancy and Horror of Mind and Conscience, I was compelled to go with them and I can say my Heart and Mind never joined in those horrid Robberies, Conflagarations and Cruelties committed." On the day before they were executed letters were written by many of them to relatives and Fitz-Gerald composed a poem which afterwards was printed. The following verses illustrate his poetical style:

To mortal Men that daily live in Wickedness and Sin;
This dying Counsel I do give, hoping you will begin
To serve the Lord in Time of Youth his Precepts for to keep;
To serve him so in Spirit and Truth, that you may mercy reap.

. . . .

In Youthful blooming Years was I, when I that Practice took;
Of perpetrating Piracy, for filthy gain did look.
To Wickedness we all were bent, our Lusts for to fulfil;
To rob at Sea was our Intent, and perpetrate all Ill.

. . . .

I pray the Lord preserve you all and keep you from this End;
O let Fitz-Gerald's great downfall unto your welfare tend.
I to the Lord my Soul bequeath, accept thereof I pray,
My Body to the Earth bequeath, dear Friend, adieu for aye.

The gallows were set up between high-and-low water mark on a point of land projecting into the harbor, then and now known as Gravelly Point. At that time there was no street or way that gave direct or convenient access and the crowds that gathered to witness the execution went around by what afterwards was known as Walnut Street by the almshouse, or filled the boats and small vessels that lined the shore. Most of the condemned had something to say when on the gallows usually advising all people, especially young persons, to beware of the sins that had brought them to such an unhappy state. The execution took place on July 19, 1723, between twelve and one o'clock, and twenty-six men were "hanged by the neck until dead" in accordance with the sentence of the Court.

"Mr. Bass went to Prayer with them; and some little time after, the Rev. Mr. Clap concluded with a short Exhortation to them. Their Black Flag, with the Pourtrature of Death having an Hour-Glass in one Hand, and a Dart in the other, at the end of which was the Form of a Heart with three Drops of Blood, falling from it, was affix'd at one Corner of the Gallows. This Flag they call'd Old Roger, and often us'd to say they would live and die under it."

"Never was there a more doleful sight in all this land, then while they were standing on the stage, waiting for the stopping of their Breath and the Flying of their Souls into the Eternal World. And oh! how awful the Noise of their dying moans!"

The bodies were not gibbetted but taken to Goat or Fort Island and buried on the shore between high and low water mark.

Thomas Tew, a famous Newport pirate of the late seventeenth century, flew this menacing flag. Tew's descendants now live peacefully in the City by the Sea. The banner is from a sketch by historian John Millar.

7

Rhode Island widows, wives, and single women often appeared before the General Court of Trials during the late seventeenth and early eighteenth centuries, and they were the principal litigants in nearly five hundred criminal and civil cases. These women actively participated in a variety of civil actions, including debt, property, inheritance, contract, and slander. Females were also prosecuted, judged, and punished for criminal conduct ranging from adultery to murder. Unfortunately, no likenesses of any of these woman litigants survive.

In the following essay, Catherine Osborne DeCesare, a doctoral student in history at Providence College, discusses the role of women as litigants in early Rhode Island and examines how the institution of marriage and adherence to English common law governed female appearances in the colonial courtroom. This essay and the later article on divorce by Professor Sheldon Cohen differ significantly from the other studies in this anthology in that they utilize the newly organized Rhode Island court records now housed at the Supreme Court Judicial Archives in Pawtucket.

This record center was established in 1989 in order to enhance the accessibility and ensure the preservation of Rhode Islands court documents of historical value. Manuscript court records are considered to be one of the most important types of primary source material available to students of American history, and our relatively untapped court documents make up the largest and most systematic body of manuscript material available for the study of seventeenth-, eighteenth-, and nineteenth-century Rhode Island. The court system of the colony and state of Rhode Island has produced and retained over three thousand cubic feet of manuscript court records dating from 1671 to 1900. This includes over three million documents that detail over five hundred thousand court cases, including civil litigation (1671–1900), criminal prosecutions (1671–1900), divorce actions (1749–1900), and naturalization petitions (1793–1980). Of course, twentieth-century judicial records are also available at the archives for use by lawyers and historians.

Older scholars heretofore have utilized mainly *published* statutes, legislative proceedings, and court records in reconstructing Rhode Island's legal development. Such a limited data base renders some of these accounts either superficial or misleading. For example, Professor Sydney James, the foremost authority on colonial Rhode Island, asserts that Nathaniel Blagrove and Nathaniel Newdigate were the first Rhode Island lawyers, both having migrated from Bristol (then in Massachusetts) to Newport sometime around 1710. However, DeCesare's archival research identifies several seventeenth-century Rhode Island attorneys appearing before the General Court of Trials. Currently, Professor Mary Sarah Bilder of the Boston College Law School is preparing for publication an extended essay entitled "The Lost Lawyers: Legal Literacy and Legal Development in Colonial America." That well-researched essay focuses on Rhode Island and irrefutably shows, contrary to all previously published histories on the subject, that there were "many attorneys and legal literates" appearing in the courts of Rhode Island during the late seventeenth century, and that Rhode Island in that period had developed "a legal system with its own techniques for applying English law and learning." Such discoveries buttress the conclusion of Lawrence M. Friedman, noted author of *A History of American Law* (rev. ed., 1986), that "colonial history is unthinkable without [manuscript] court records."

Women and the Legal Culture of Colonial Rhode Island

Catherine Osborne DeCesare

Eunice Greenman, a single woman and a spinster by trade, was the daughter of John Greenman, a Newport cordwainer. She resided on Thames Street in Newport with the prominent Wanton family. Her employer, William Wanton, was the first of four members of the Wanton family to serve as governor of Rhode Island; his son Joseph Wanton was Rhode Island's last colonial governor. Eunice professed to have been brought up "virtuously and thereby gained ye good esteem and favour of her neighbours"; hence she believed herself entitled to a reasonable marriage settlement to "secure a comfortable fortune in the world." In May 1715 Christopher Almy initiated, in the words of Eunice, a "pretended marriage courtship." According to Eunice, as revealed in the court documents, he professed much love and affection towards her and promised to marry her.

The courtship continued, and the years passed. In March 1719 Eunice became pregnant. Still the relationship endured, as did Almy's promises of marriage. Six months later Almy arranged for the banns to be posted. Shortly thereafter, following the birth of their child, Almy, "against all his most solemn declarations…deserted…ye plaintiff refusing to marry her." Christopher's father, Captain Job Almy, apparently disapproved of the union between his son and Eunice, a servant girl; in addition to Captain Almy's mercantile ventures, the Almy family were wealthy landholders. Subsequently Christopher became betrothed to his first cousin Elizabeth Almy of Tiverton. Eunice attempted to stall and stop the marriage. She recruited local judges Henry Bull and Peleg Smith to help her. The particulars of the situation were argued and disputed before the judges, who decided to issue an injunction to postpone the marriage until Eunice's grievances were addressed in the General Court of Trials. Even so, the wedding of Elizabeth and Christopher Almy proceeded as planned in April 1720.

Governor William Wanton (1670–1733) employed Eunice Greenman, who lived in the Wanton household.

Filled with "great shame and dishonor," Eunice procured the services of attorney Jonathan Read and filed a formal complaint against her former betrothed in the General Court of Trials. Almy was represented by Nathaniel Newdigate, one of Rhode Island's premier attorneys, who had been instrumental in compiling Rhode Island's laws for publication in 1719. The defendant requested that Eunice Greenman's action be abated, or thrown out of court. The defense stipulated that the plaintiff's declaration and complaint did not adequately specify the type of action against the defendant. Furthermore, in a second attempt to abate the action, the defense cited an English statute dated the 29th Year King Charles the Second. This law stipulated that "no contracts concerning marriage shall be good to charge any person unless such contract be reduced into writing and signed by both partyes." The court disregarded Newdigate's attempts to have the case dismissed on technical grounds, and the case proceeded to trial.

Depositions collected from James Brown and John Hammett attested to the validity of Almy's procurement of the banns of marriage between himself and the plaintiff. Brown was the assistant responsible for issuing the banns to Almy. In July 1720 a writ was served to Almy by the sheriff, Jahleel Brenton, for the September session of the General Court of Trials to answer the complaint of Eunice Greenman. This was done to ensure Almy's presence at the court session.

Many depositions were filed witnessing and attesting to the character of the plaintiff. Ruth Wanton, wife of William Wanton, testified that she knew Eunice well and claimed that for four years before Eunice had had a child by Almy, she had lived with the Wanton family. During this time, Ruth continued, Eunice had behaved herself very discreetly and soberly and kept herself reserved from other men besides Almy. Ruth had noticed that Almy frequently called upon Eunice. When she enquired of Eunice the reason for his visits, Eunice told her that Almy was courting her and often promised marriage. The deposition of Elizabeth Scott reiterated and confirmed Ruth Wanton's testimony. Leah Greenman, Eunice's younger sister, came forward to state that she had overheard Almy claim Eunice's child as his own. The testimony of Lewis Mitchell confirmed that the child was indeed Almy's, and that Almy had given the infant a pair of gold buttons. Susanah Bayley, presumably a neighbor of the Greenman family, testified that in October she was called to the Greenman household by Eunice's mother, who feared Eunice would take her own life. Bayley and Eunice's mother went immediately to the bed chamber, where they found Eunice seated on the bed and crying. At that juncture, as Susanah Bayley recalled, Eunice's mother asked her daughter to give her the penknife that she was apparently holding. Eunice "pulled it out and gave it to her mother."

After each side presented its arguments, the case was put into the hands of the twelve-man jury, which weighed the evidence, found in favor of Eunice, and awarded her damages in the amount of two hundred pounds in addition to court costs. In a subsequent appeal and rehearing of the case by the General Court of Trials initiated at the request of Almy, Eunice once again received a favorable judgment and was awarded compensatory damages. After his second defeat, Almy requested that the case be appealed to the General Assembly. When the case was accordingly placed in the hands of the Assembly in June 1722, the assistants confirmed the preceding court judgments in favor of Eunice Greenman.

Were the legal and courtroom experiences of Eunice Greenman similar to those of other females living in Rhode Island during the late seventeenth and early eighteenth centuries? And if so, how? Surely we can empathize with Eunice and sense her distress, disappointment, and anger. Although she was virtually powerless to stop the marriage of Elizabeth and Christopher, Eunice successfully initiated and won civil suits against Christopher Almy. Did gender have any bearing on accessibility to the court?

As Rhode Island approaches the twenty-first century, we pause to reconsider its history and reflect upon the state's presumed distinctiveness. Even today Rhode Islanders seemingly revel in their uniqueness. How many times have we heard the phrase "Only in Rhode Island"? No doubt the concept of religious freedom in the colony was radical for the seventeenth century, but can Roger Williams's concept of a "lively experiment" be correlated to all aspects of the colony's community life? In the realm of law, was Rhode Island in fact a "lively experiment?" This paper will investigate the colony's adoption and adaptation of English legal culture during the late seventeenth and early eighteenth centuries, specifically in relation to the lives of colonial Rhode Island's women. An examination of the relationship between gender and legal culture can provide us with a vantage point for considering the question of Rhode Island's assumed exceptionalism.

Over three hundred years ago, Rhode Island and Providence Plantations consisted of fragmented and religiously diverse political settlements. Pressure from hostile neighbors forced the colonial inhabitants to draw together for their common defense. In the absence of a homogeneous and well-defined religious code, Rhode Island reverted to familiar and comfortable legal principles. Because her precarious political situation made the colony extremely vulnerable to outside interference, the earliest town leaders looked to the home government for protection and justification, and they consequently emphasized their allegiance to English law. The sixth clause of the acts and orders of 1647 declared that "we do voluntarily assent and are freely willing, to receive and be governed by the laws of England, together with the way of the administration of them." In 1673 the General Assembly reaffirmed its allegiance to the home government and declared that "this Assembly and all other Assembleys shall make lawes as agreeable to the lawes of his majestys realme of England" Established English institutions served as a model for the construction of Rhode Island's judiciary and legal system. In the implementation of legal institutions and traditions, Rhode Island's dependence on English legal culture overshadowed her uniqueness.

Under the protection of England, Rhode Island participated in a transatlantic economy as a member of the Atlantic community. As a result, the colony became increasingly influenced by political, social, and economic events in England. Crop failures, fires, wars, riots, speculation, and the use of credit all affected the economic soundness of England, and thus all of these had repercussions across the Atlantic and combined to shape Rhode Island's legal history. The fiscal expansion of the colony and the utilization of attorneys further solidified the bonds between Rhode Island and England. The volume of court activity in early Rhode Island directly reflected political and economic events not only in the colony but in England as well; for example, King Philip's War, the Dominion of New England, King William's War, Queen Anne's War, and economic depressions in England all affected the volume of court activity. Wars and political instability decreased litigation, and economic instability increased it. Rhode Island's transatlantic connections worked to limit the extent of the colony's popularly assumed peculiarity.

The judicial system in colonial Rhode Island was established soon after the founding of the colony. Out of necessity the issues of law and order were addressed to preserve the fragile and chaotic political entity of Rhode Island and Providence Plantations. The Patent of 1644 enabled the General Assembly to enact laws providing they corresponded to English law. In 1647 Rhode Island adopted an official code of law. This code represented only a small portion of the laws governing the colony, as the full body of English law was understood to be in force. Of the earliest founders, Roger Williams of Providence Plantations and Samuel Gorton of Warwick strongly advocated that the colonial government be established under the principles of English law and adhere exclusively to civil matters. The Code of 1647 was drawn predominantly from Michael Dalton's English manual for justices of the peace. Frequently citing Dalton's guide and English statutes, the code repudiated the Puritan adherence to biblical law and exhibited a propensity for English law instead.

Sir Edward Coke (1552–1634), attorney general to Elizabeth I and later a prominent jurist, influenced the development of Rhode Island's legal system which was modeled on his *Institutes*. Coke was a friend to Roger Williams and an inspiration to Samuel Gorton.

The construction of Rhode Island's laws was similar to what is found in the *Institutes* and *Reports* of Sir Edward Coke, the renowned legal scholar and defender of the common law. Coke served as Queen Elizabeth's attorney general and then had a long career as an influential member of the House of Commons. His writings quickly became an authority in the court and a useful reference tool both for scholars and for practicing attorneys. Like Coke's institutes, Rhode Island's acts and laws listed and defined criminal activity, enumerated penalties, and included a brief history of the law.

The earliest founders of Rhode Island and Providence Plantations were to some extent familiar with English legal customs, traditions, methodologies, and the writings of Sir Edward Coke. On February 10, 1634/35, Samuel Gorton was a complainant in the chancery court case of *Gorton* v. *Foster and Lambe*; on his return to London more than a decade later, he was involved in a second case, one originating from a loan of one hundred pounds that he procured from the gentleman John Duckingfield in 1634. While a student at Charterhouse and at Pembroke Hall, Cambridge, Roger Williams received the patronage of Sir Edward Coke himself.

Contrary to the code of law adopted in Rhode Island, the colonies of Massachusetts Bay, Connecticut, and New Haven combined English law and Mosaic law in the development of their judicial codes. Hebraic law surfaced in the Massachusetts Code of 1648, which frequently cited Deuteronomy, Exodus, Numbers, Leviticus, and other Old Testament references. In these New England colonies the official state church strove to enforce morality and maintain order, and hence the establishment of a rigid code was an important part of the written law. In the Massachusetts Bay Colony, assistants consulted ministers regarding legal concerns affecting the colony at large. In the colonies of New Haven and Connecticut, the ability of individuals to participate in civic affairs was determined by appropriate membership and standing in the religious community.

To some degree most people lived their lives as dictated by the letter of the law. During the colonial period, legal culture was a changing reality dependent upon the ideas and ideals of men of status. But the intention of law and the application of law do not necessarily coincide. Theoretically, Rhode Island's propensity to adopt much of the legal culture of England determined the legal standing of females in the courtroom of the General Court of Trials. In actuality, however, laws were modified and sometimes traditions were altered and expanded to allow women greater access to the court.

Whereas Rhode Island adopted much of the English judicial system, colonists modified certain of its features in response to issues particular to the colonial environment. In England, the Court of Common Pleas, Chancery Court, and King's Court often overlapped jurisdictions; minor disputes were handled by the justices of the peace, town mayoral courts, and lord of the manor courts. Rhode Island adopted a tiered judicial system created from the English model, wherein major and minor issues were decided at diVerent court levels, but the Rhode Island system was less complex. Between 1671 and 1729 the General Court of Trials met in Newport twice a year, in the spring and in the fall, and rendered decisions in criminal and civil matters that aVected the colony at large. Town courts and justices of the peace took care of minor local issues and disputes, usually under the value of forty shillings.

Specific legal procedures in Rhode Island were adapted from Dalton's guide for justices of the peace. The General Court of Trials generally adhered to English rules and legal procedural regulations. Not only did colonial Rhode Island borrow court procedures and methodologies from the English courts; in many respects the duties and functions of court personnel in England served as a model when the early colonists set up their legal system. Judges, clerks, attorneys, sheriffs, and juries were integral parts of the English legal system, and all were replicated in Rhode Island. The use of formal written complaints, pleas, answers, depositions, and writs, and even calls for abatement and the use of technicalities, bear witness to Rhode Island's conformity to English models. Indeed, the Greenman case attests to the colony's adherence to the general letter of English legal culture: the litigants were each accompanied by their chosen attorney, the sheriff delivered the writ, the judges determined points of law, and the jury decided the case.

Rhode Island towns were required to send freemen to each court session for the jury. Juries were important in Rhode Island; the vast majority of cases required a jury to determine a verdict or resolve a civil dispute. In England, jury trials were a component of the Court of Common Pleas, but a judge decided the cases in the Chancery Court. Rhode Island's propensity for jury trials represented a modification of the established English legal system. Although it appears that Rhode Island's earliest colonists may have been more familiar with the proceedings of the Court of Common Pleas than with those of the Chancery Court, in all likelihood the passion for jury trials came from the founders' experiences with the magistrates of the Massachusetts Bay Colony.

The late seventeenth and early eighteenth centuries witnessed the emergence of a legal profession in Rhode Island. Spurred by the development of the Atlantic community and the growth of mercantilism, merchants used legal experts to support their personal interests, thus creating increased opportunities for attorneys within the court system. Attorneys were present in the Rhode Island legal system almost from the onset of colonization. The Code of 1647 went so far as to stipulate that each town maintain two attorneys. By 1700 it appears that the majority of civil litigants, male and female alike, used legal counsel in cases that came before the General Court of Trials. Attorneys brought with them the technical expertise needed both to bring a case to court and to receive a favorable judgment. Evidence of technical pleadings attests to their competence. Almost every plea and answer submitted before the General Court of Trials attempted to abate on a variety of technical grounds. There is scant evidence of informal pleadings at the court. The utilization of legal counsel in Rhode Island made the colony distinctive in New England, though other colonies, including Maryland, Virginia, South Carolina, and New York, also had practicing attorneys during the seventeenth century.

Rhode Island women were excluded from participating in the realm of public law; that is, they were not allowed to sit in the legislature, draft laws, serve as members of the court, sit on juries, or vote. Female participation in the realm of private law depended upon marital status and social standing within the community. Single women, including widows, were accorded virtually the same legal rights and privileges as men: they could sue and be sued, they could own and sell property, they could enter into binding contracts, and they could bequeath their property by will. All females were considered infants, maids, or single women until they married. Marriage was considered to be a female's most important and defining life choice. Eunice Greenman anticipated the prospect of marriage to Christopher Almy, and she was nearly suicidal when he broke his promise.

Once a woman married, her legal status changed significantly. All the rights and privileges she had previously enjoyed as a single woman were removed, and she was cast into a dependent and subordinate status. *The Lawes Resolutions of Women's Rights*, published anonymously in 1632, was a lengthy guide to English laws affecting women. Its central thesis stipulated that "women have no voice in Parliament, they make no laws, they consent to none, they abrogate none." Theoretically, English common law assumed that all women were under the protection of a father, a husband, or a male guardian. *Coverture* was the common-law term used to describe the legal position of a wife. Under the letter of English common law, wives could hold no real property, nor could they alter or dispose of property without their husbands' consent, even if it was land obtained by their own inheritance. Wives could not make contracts or wills, nor could they appoint executors without their husbands' consent. All personal goods and property obtained prior to marriage became the property of their husbands. At her husband's death a widow was legally guaranteed her dower, of which the normal disposition was a third of the total estate.

As in England and all its other American colonies, women in Rhode Island could not participate in the creation, administration, or adjudication of public law. On the other hand, women were active participants in the realm of private law. Between 1671 and 1729, females were principal litigants in 491 cases, plaintiffs or defendants in 369 civil cases, and criminal defendants in 122 cases at the General Court of Trials. A comparison of male and female cases heard by this court shows that 14 percent of all criminal defendants and 10 percent of all civil litigants were females. Women participated in the same kinds of cases as their male counterparts did: they were plaintiffs and defendants and colitigants in all types of actions of case, debt, property, contract, and, to a very limited extent, slander. All were involved in criminal activity, although men were more likely to be convicted of such violent crimes as theft, assault, and murder. Females were more apt to be involved in cases of receiving stolen goods, illegitimacy, fornication, and infanticide.

When widows, wives, or single women appeared before the General Court of Trials during the late seventeenth and early eighteenth centuries, their appearances were conditioned by their marital status. On the one hand, in accordance with English common law, single women, including widows, were able to initiate civil proceedings and could be sued as individuals. On the other hand, single women—excluding widows—were more frequently suspected of and prosecuted for criminal activity than were wives and widows, who were apparently sheltered from most criminal prosecutions by the institution of marriage. Unmarried females were particularly vulnerable to crimes with moral undertones; fornication, illegitimacy, and infanticide indictments usually involved single females. In 1717 Mary Roolenburg, a single woman and a spinster, was indicted on charges of infanticide, or "murdering a bastard child born of her body." She was cleared of the infanticide charges at the General Court of Trials, but in a separate case she pleaded guilty to giving birth to a bastard child and was ordered to pay a fine of forty shillings or, if unable to pay that sum, to receive fifteen lashes. Interestingly, Eunice Greenman was not prosecuted for either fornication or bearing a bastard child.

Wives were subject to serious legal limitations and were consequently unable to answer or complain on their own behalf before the General Court of Trials. In accordance with English common law, not a single Rhode Island wife appeared before the General Court of Trials on her own behalf to invoke a civil proceeding or answer a complaint. Wives were exclusively identified in relation to their husbands. The case of *Bailey* v. *Greenman* may serve as an example. In 1724 John and Elizabeth Greenman, the parents of Eunice Greenman, were named as codefendants in a defamation case initiated by a young unmarried woman named Rebecca Bailey. According to the depositions collected, Elizabeth Greenman repeatedly uttered slanderous remarks regarding the character of the plaintiff. Attempting to resurrect her reputation, Rebecca initiated the suit and sought significant damages. Although the trouble apparently stemmed from the words of Elizabeth, her husband, John, was named as codefendant, for he was considered responsible for the actions of his wife. Sometimes wives were named as colitigants in cases stemming from the time before they were married; most of these cases concerned the disbursement of property. Contrary to common-law principles of coverture, wives could appear before the court as witnesses. Indeed, the testimony of married women—especially the deposition of Ruth Wanton, the wife of William Wanton—was integral to Eunice Greenman's civil suit. These patterns of female participation in the General Court of Trials illustrate Rhode Island's adherence to common-law principles respecting the legal privileges of females.

Two interrelated bodies of law were established and utilized in English courts: the common law was administered in the Courts of Common Pleas and the King's Bench, and equity law was administered by the lord chancellor in the Chancery Court. The Chancery Court, which was established to counter some of the inequities inherent in the letter of common law, heard cases involving wives, because wives were allowed to initiate suits on their own behalf in that court and could receive more equitable justice there than they could in other courts. Usually equity courts decided cases involving the common-law right of husbands to dispose of their wives' real and personal property. Trust agreements, marriage settlements, and the creation of separate estates were devised in the Chancery Court, a disposition that enabled wives to maintain some degree of control over their own estates.

In Rhode Island there was no separate chancery court, and thus one legal avenue open to English women—particularly wives—was not replicated in the colony. Routine matters of estate settlement and probate were administered at the town level and did not usually concern the General Court of Trials. A separate equity court for the colony, created and disbanded by acts of the General Assembly, existed from 1741 to 1743. Otherwise the traditions of the common law as adopted by Rhode Island enabled husbands to exclusively administer the financial and legal affairs of their wives.

The acts and laws generated by the General Assembly did not often apply specifically to females. However, to address the problems of desertion and lengthy periods of absence by spouses, in 1712 the General Assembly modified common-law principles by enacting legislation to allow wives to handle fiscal matters in the absence of their husbands. In the seafaring communities of Rhode Island, where men were often away from home for long periods of time, this legislation helped to prevent the impoverishment of wives and children and keep them off the town poor rolls. Under the legislation wives could manage finances only after their husbands had been away for three consecutive years.

Another modification in the law by the General Assembly strengthened the legal position of widows. In 1663 the Assembly enacted a law to allow widows the right in intestate cases to administer their deceased husbands' estates. Consequently, widows appeared far more often than maids as litigants in the General Court of Trials. Lyle Koehler has determined that in 80 percent of Rhode Island's intestate cases, the widow became the sole administrator or coadministrator of the surviving estate. By comparison, in Maine and Suffolk County, Massachusetts, the widow received the right of administration only half the time. The proportion in Connecticut was similar to that of Rhode Island.

Of the females who came before the General Court of Trials, the majority were not only widows but widows acting in the capacity of plaintiff, undeniably a position of strength in the colonial court. More than twice as many females appeared before the court as plaintiffs or coplaintiffs than as defendants or codefendants, and as plaintiffs and coplaintiffs they received favorable judgments in a majority of the claims heard in the courtroom. Evidence suggests that there was no significant gender bias in favor of women at the General Court of Trials; male and female litigants received comparable results in cases adjudicated before the court.

Was Rhode Island distinctive in the creation of its legal culture, specifically as it applied to the female segment of the population? Over the course of the late seventeenth and early eighteenth centuries, as the colony gradually came within the sphere of the expanding British Empire, issues of legitimacy and religious freedom enabled it to establish a legal system without religious biases, one modeled on the judicial system of the mother country. But although Rhode Island borrowed much of its legal culture from English sources, the circumstances of colonial society at times forced modification of the established judicial system.

The legal status of women in early colonial Rhode Island apparently reflected Rhode Island's propensity to adopt and adapt the body of English common law. On the one hand, the promotion of the common law restricted the opportunities and privileges of wives before the court, for Rhode Island's laws emphasized the subordination of wives. On the other hand, wives were in fact granted certain legal rights in the courtoom, although these rights were few and vaguely described. In response to colonial conditions, some of the laws regarding women were altered, and benefits were thereby increased for certain women. However, modifications enacted by the General Assembly did little to increase the number of wives appearing as individual litigants before the court.

Was the case of Eunice Greenman reflective of female participation before the General Court of Trials? This case was cited not only because it highlights the appearance of one woman before the court but also because it has an almost timeless quality to it, with elements that are applicable to almost any age and community. As a single woman, Eunice Greenman was legally justified in bringing a suit against Christopher Almy. Although she was unable to stop the marriage of Christopher and Elizabeth, she was awarded damages for the wrong that Christopher had done to her. Ultimately she was vindicated and received the backing of her community, as represented by the judgments of the juries and the General Assembly. Eunice Greenman was supported by her family and by the women of the community. By recording depositions, these females—single women and wives—were able to provide key testimony on her behalf, and to assert themselves as a voice in the community as well.

This courthouse was the scene of the Harris trial, and much of the litigation described in this essay. The wood-frame building was moved to make room for its more stately successor, the 1739 Colony House, shown below.

Stephen Hopkins—a lawyer and a jurist, among his many achievements—is perhaps the most significant Rhode Islander of the eighteenth century. Hopkins held the posts of House speaker, governor, and chief justice of the state Supreme Court (then known as the Superior Court of Judicature) in addition to those of delegate to the Continental Congress and signer of the Declaration of Independence.

Hopkins deserves a full-length scholarly biography, but until it is written, this brief profile by Professor Marguerite Appleton is the best personal glimpse of this many-faceted man. The essay, however, has deficiencies as well as merits. Appleton's strong Rhode Island sympathies cause her to make extravagant claims on Rhode Island's behalf. Contrary to her assertions, the state was not the first to "declare independence" on May 4, 1776; on that day it renounced personal allegiance to King George III. Nor was Rhode Island the first to ratify the Articles of Confederation; Virginia holds that distinction (though Rhode Island's approval was prompt).

Conversely, Appleton could have said more about Hopkins's *The Rights of Colonies Examined* (1764). This tract was among the first to put forth a federal theory of the British Empire—the assertion that colonial assemblies possessed sovereignty in local affairs, including taxation. Hopkins's important essay in political theory has been reprinted for present-day readers, together with a perceptive essay by historian Paul Campbell, by the Rhode Island Bicentennial Foundation.

In 1768 another Providence lawyer, Silas Downer, delivered a public discourse at the local "Liberty Tree" repudiating the recently passed Declaratory Act and denying the authority of Parliament to make any laws of any kind to regulate the colonies. In 1774 Hopkins took attorney Downer to the First Continental Congress to serve as secretary to the Rhode Island delegation, which was headed by Hopkins and Samuel Ward.

Mention of Ward and Hopkins—political rivals who had reconciled by 1774—recalls the development of a system of two-party politics in Rhode

Island during the generation preceding the American Revolution. Opposing groups, one headed by Ward and the other by Hopkins, were organized with sectional overtones; generally speaking (though with notable exceptions), the merchants and farmers of southern Rhode Island (Ward) battled with their counterparts from Providence and its environs (Hopkins). The principal goal of these groups was to secure control of the powerful legislature in order to obtain the host of public offices—from chief justice to inspector of tobacco—at the disposal of that body.

The semipermanent nature, relatively stable membership, and explicit sectional rivalry of the warring camps has led historian Mack Thompson to describe the states pre-Revolutionary political structure as one of "stable factionalism." Another historian, David S. Lovejoy, has boldly maintained that Rhode Islanders revolted from British rule not only "on the broad grounds of constitutional right to keep Rhode Island safe for liberty and property" but also to preserve "the benefits of party politics"—patronage and spoils. To Hopkins, as to other Rhode Island politicians of a later time, power and preference mattered much.

This preliminary sketch by artist John Trumbull is the only contemporary likeness of Stephen Hopkins that survives. It is reproduced with the permission of the Frick Art Reference Library.

Stephen Hopkins: Chief Justice, Governor, and Signer

Marguerite Appleton

Stephen Hopkins, Rhode Island statesman and patriot, was born on his grandfather's farm on March 7, 1707. Who would have guessed that this son of quiet, hardworking parents, a lad who never had any schooling in the accepted sense of the word, would one day be the first chancellor of Brown University, would serve as chief justice of the Superior [i.e., Supreme] Court, would be elected governor of the colony of Rhode Island for ten terms, and would be one of the famous few who signed the Declaration of Independence?

Hopkins's great-grandfather, Thomas Hopkins, had been one of the early settlers in Providence and had received a home lot in one of the distributions of land. Like the others, he built his home near the Great Salt Cove, and in all probability dug clams on the shore in front of his house, hunted in the woods that topped the hill behind him, and explored the marshes and meadows on the west side of the cove. It is not at all unlikely that at some time or other he warmed his hands at Roger Williams's fireside as he talked with the great leader.

His son, Major William Hopkins, was born in 1650. He was a young man when King Philip's War broke out. Almost all of the inhabitants of Providence fled to the safety of Newport, but young Mr. Hopkins was ever after admired and respected because he was one of those who "stayed and went not away" to defend the town as best they could. Several years later he married Abigail Whipple, daughter of Captain John Whipple, and moved to Pawtuxet. There he lived for the rest of his life, and there his son William Hopkins, Jr. was born, and also his grandson, Stephen.

On his mother's side, Stephen's great-grandfather, Lawrence Wilkinson, settled in Providence in 1657, but within a few years moved to the outlying country some ten miles northwest of the settlement. Apparently he fell in love with the countryside, for it is said that at his death he owned a thousand acres. For New England, and particularly for the colony of Rhode Island, a thousand acres represented a sizable farm. His oldest son, Samuel, was a man greatly respected in the community. A staunch Friend, having embraced the Quaker faith when the Quakers were suffering bitter persecution in Massachusetts, he was an eloquent debater on history and government and was learned in the law. He married Plain Wickenden, the daughter of a Providence minister. Samuel and his bride had six children, one of whom, Ruth, became the mother of Stephen Hopkins.

Stephen was scarcely more than a baby when his parents and their two small sons (Stephen was their second child) moved west of the "Seven Mile Line" to the newly opened land of what is today the town of Scituate. It took considerable courage to live in the thickly wooded section beyond the Seven Mile Line where only a muddy footpath connected one farmhouse with another, and the nearest doctor was some twenty miles to the east. Did young Mrs. Hopkins think about these considerations as she turned her face towards the west? Probably not, for although both the Hopkins and the Wilkinson families had originally settled in Providence, sooner or later they had moved out into the country and their primary concern became the development of their newly acquired land. Then, too, her brother, Joseph, had already taken up land not far from where she was going to live. His belief in the possibilities of the new land might have done much to influence young Mr. and Mrs. Hopkins to make their permanent home near him.

Like all country lads, the Hopkins boys—and it was not long before there were six of them—learned the straight-jacket routine of farming. The boys performed planting, weeding, and milking duties, and undoubtedly William, Stephen, Rufus, John, Esek, and Samuel were impressed into service while their sisters, Hope, Abigail, and Susanna, helped their mother with endless tasks of a farmer's wife.

During the uneventful years of Stephen's childhood there was no school for him to go to. How and when he learned the three R's is not known. Since, however, his mother was by birthright a Quaker, and since tradition has it that her father and grandfather were interested in reading and study and owned enough books to be considered a library, it seems sure that the Hopkins children learned to read and write in the commonest of all schools—at home. In addition, they were probably taught the great principles of righteous living—honesty, self-reliance, and industry, and to follow the dictates of one's conscience, or, as the Quakers express it, to follow the "guidance of the inner light." But all outdoors was a school for Stephen and his brothers. Inevitably he would acquire the indispensable knowledge of the weather and the seasons. From his uncle Joseph he learned the skill of surveying, and perhaps something of the philosophy of the country dweller, which would stand him in good stead later when he represented Scituate in the Rhode Island assembly. Young Stephen, carrying the pole and chain, tramped hill and dale behind his uncle, absorbing some valuable technical knowledge in surveying. At the same time he learned the importance of land ownership and that a man always wanted to know the extent of his fields, the exact boundaries, and how his lands marched with those of his neighbors.

Two events were red letter days in Hopkins's life; one was his marriage in 1726 to Sarah Scott, a neighbor of his grandfather who lived in Louisquisset. Young Hopkins had known her for a long time. It was a happy marriage, one blessed by seven children. Also at this time he was given a farm by his father, and for several years Hopkins led the busy life of a farmer.

The second important event occurred in 1730 when Scituate, which formerly had been a part of Providence, was set up as a separate town. This administrative change in Scituate opened the door of opportunity for Hopkins, now a young man of twenty-three. He was chosen as the moderator of the town council, and also town clerk. This position, although perhaps not one of great prestige today, was important in the "new born" town. Naturally, it was vitally necessary to have the town records, land deeds, and titles accurately written up and filed. And it was not long before he was elected as one of the representatives for Scituate in the Rhode Island assembly, which opened still further the door to his public life. For then it was that he began to get acquainted with his fellow citizens from all the towns in the colony. In 1735, he was chosen president of the Scituate Town Council. He held this position for six years and also served for five years as justice of the Inferior Court of Common Pleas for Providence County. Clearly, Mr. Hopkins was considered a man of ability and great promise.

In 1742 he decided to move to Providence for good. It must have been hard for him to take this step because he had known no other home than Scituate, and the life of a farmer. There his married life had begun, and there his children had been born. Then, too, for ten years he had played an important role in the life of the town; he knew everybody and everybody knew him. On the other hand, by 1742 many of the ties that had bound him to rural Rhode Island were gone; his grandfather, both of his parents, and his uncle Joseph Wilkinson had died, and many of his brothers and sisters had moved away. It seems likely, however, the decisive factor in the matter was his election in 1739 as speaker of the Rhode Island assembly. Obviously, it would be much easier to perform the duties of this position if he lived in town, rather than twelve or fifteen miles out in the country.

After Hopkins and his wife came to the conclusion that his future lay in Providence, he sold his farm in Scituate and moved into a little house that he had built on Towne Street (South Main Street), just a block south of Market Square. It was a modest little house, but he lived there comfortably for the rest of his life. There he talked with his friends and colleagues, penned many letters and in later life wrote pamphlets and articles for *The Providence Gazette*.

When Hopkins settled in Providence, it was a small, compact community with a population of about four thousand. Practically everybody lived side by side on Towne Street with only a sprinkling of homes south of Market Square and on the west side of the Great Salt Cove. In the long period of peace after the end of Queen Anne's War in 1713, Providence had begun to build up a very profitable trade with the West Indies, which were flung out like a pack of cards south of the tip of Florida. The chief products of the West Indian islands were sugar and molasses, and ships from the New England colonies bartered their commodities—lumber, dried fish, Negro slaves, and a few manufactured articles—for the much desired sugar and molasses. Rhode Island had one special item which was in great demand—horses. These animals, called Narragansett pacers, were bred in the Narragansett Country, and, being small and tractable, were much liked by the sugar planters. Rhode Island shipmasters used to sail from island to island; Martinique, Trinidad, Barbados, or any others where they could make the best bargain. In exchange for their mixed cargo of goods and horses, they bought sugar and molasses, which was distilled into rum and sold throughout New England. This trade was the backbone of Rhode Island's prosperity, and built the fortunes of the Malbones, the Wantons, the Champlins, and Abraham Redwood in Newport and the Tillinghasts, the Nightingales, the Crawfords, and the Browns in Providence.

Not long after Hopkins settled in Providence he made his start as a merchant in the West India trade. According to the custom of the times, Hopkins frequently became a partner with other merchants by buying shares in the vessels bound for the West Indies. Eventually, he owned several ships himself, and now and again shared ownership with his brother Esek and with his son Rufus. By degrees he became closely associated with the four Brown brothers—Nicholas, Joseph, John, and Moses—in their many and varied ventures, and his friendship with them grew ever closer and more satisfying.

Meanwhile, he had entered on the long road to political success which led to forty years of public service, and for which his inheritance had fitted him. On both sides of Hopkins's family his forefathers had taken part in the administration of the colony. His grandfather, Major William Hopkins, had served in the Rhode Island assembly for many years, and his uncle Joseph Wilkinson had held many offices in Scituate. Stephen Hopkins was to prove a shining example of this family tradition.

Increasing prosperity brought with it the expansion of Providence, and the members of the Rhode Island assembly spent much time administering local needs, such as the building of adequate roads, highways, and bridges. With his country background, Hopkins was keenly "road conscious"—the difficulties of bad roads, and the comfort of good ones. He was the proper man to call on and served on many committees for planning new highways south and west of Providence, as well as the widening and repairing of streets and roads already in use.

One of the improvements he was interested in was the cutting through of a new street east of Towne Street, half way up the hill. He saw the necessity for this very soon after he moved to town and was one of the few forward-looking men who in 1743 petitioned the assembly in favor of this new street. In spite of its speedy defeat, the petition was presented again in 1746. Although the second petition met with no more success in the assembly than before, the issue of a new street was not forgotten. For ten years it was argued back and firth until it was finally voted to undertake the project. Benefit Street was started in 1756 and completed from Power Street to Whipple's Gate two years later. Probably nobody enjoyed the upheaval more than the small boys who watched the felling of the trees, and now and again, perhaps, were allowed to ride on oxcarts as the roots and rubble were carted away. At first the street was called "Back Street," but as it turned out to be a benefit to everybody, it was rechristened Benefit Street, and Benefit Street it has been ever since.

The boundaries of the colony of Rhode Island had long been a perennial problem, in regard to both Connecticut and Massachusetts. Fortune had ordained that Roger Williams's settlement included a splendid harbor, and the neighboring colonies, Plymouth, Massachusetts and Connecticut, appreciated its safety and fitness for trade. The inexact wording of the colonial charters concerning boundaries gave rise to controversies centered around the struggle for the control of Narragansett Bay.

The mutual boundary between Massachusetts and Rhode Island on the east was claimed by both colonies by virtue of their charters. When

Plymouth was merged with the Bay Colony, Massachusetts had claimed Plymouth's share of land on the eastern side of Narragansett Bay. Since the Bay Colony was never willing to let any opportunity slip by for the acquisition of land, she therefore pressed her claim vigorously. On the other hand, Rhode Islands charter of 1663 clearly stated that her eastern boundary ran from a point three miles northeast of the head of the bay straight south to the sea. Thus she naturally asserted her right to a strip of land three miles wide on the east coast of the bay. The real value of this shoestring bit of land lay not just in acreage, but in the fact that Narragansett Bay was the "front door" of the colony, the open road to the rest of the world. Rhode Island believed that it was vitally necessary to have the bay entirely within her boundaries.

During his first years as a member of the assembly, Hopkins was appointed to more than one committee to try to solve the problem of the colony's eastern boundary. More than once he and the other members of the various committees met with the Massachusetts commissioners seeking some agreement upon the boundary. Each colony appealed to the mother country for help, and at length a royal commission was appointed to try to cut the Gordian knot. The commissioners made a careful study of the matter, but Massachusetts refused to accept their decision, and once more appealed to England. Rhode Island also appealed, and this time she won her case; Massachusetts was forced to accept the line as designated in the Rhode Island charter.

While Hopkins was busily engaged with his committee work, he was at the same time holding three other positions: clerk of the Providence Town Council, justice of the peace for Providence, and justice of the Superior Court of Judicature of Rhode Island. If one wonders how a man with no formal schooling and no legal training could carry out successfully these highly specialized legal duties, it should not be forgotten that in the eighteenth century law schools as they are known today did not exist in America. If a man owned one or two legal treatises such as Sir Edward Coke's *Institutes* or the treatise *Coke on Littleton*, which were the Bibles for lawyers, one could learn enough of court rulings and procedure to handle all but the most intricate legal problems. Undoubtedly, Hopkins did own these standard books to which he could turn for help.

The decade of the fifties brought him both good and bad fortune. At times, he must have thought that the hand of the Lord rested very heavily on him, for he lost two sons and his wife within a few months of each other. His son Sylvanus was murdered by the Indians in Nova Scotia in 1753, and about six months later another son, John, was lost at sea. Hardly had he recovered from these two blows when his wife died. His grief was in part assuaged by his marriage in 1757 to Mrs. Anne Smith. She had four children, the eldest of whom was already married. The other three with their mother came to live with Hopkins, and once more his life was filled with affection and companionship.

Meanwhile, he had become interested in an unusual project. As there was no public library in Providence, Hopkins and four of his friends decided to order from England hundreds of books of general interest that would form a "library" which they would own together, and could borrow and enjoy. When the books arrived, they found there was really no place large enough to store them, so in 1754 they sent a petition to the assembly asking for the privilege of placing them in the Council Chamber of the County House. It stated that the purchasers of these books thought that they would be a real ornament to the House, and could afford agreeable amusements to the members of the assembly in their leisure hours. Moreover, they promised to pay for the bookshelves. This request was granted, and the library was successful, but alas, five years later the County House burned down and most of the precious collection of books was lost. That the books which constituted the first "public library" in Providence had been appreciated by the members of the assembly is shown when they were raising money to rebuild the County House; they included £1,000 towards the purchase of books "to be forever kept in the town of Providence; free access unto which shall always be had by the members of the Assembly."

Although the recent years had appeared to be filled with sorrow for Hopkins, Lady Luck had also offered him a cornucopia of bounty. Perhaps the most interesting experience during this period was the Albany Congress, which he attended in 1754. This conference was called together at the suggestion of English officials because, although England and her colonies had recently defeated France, they feared that war might break out again at any time. Should this happen, England would again expect assistance from the American colonies, and she felt that an accepted plan of union and cooperation would be of immense value to her. Discussions and proposals for colonial union, therefore, were important items on the agenda.

Hopkins was undoubtedly proud to represent Rhode Island and looked forward to meeting the other delegates. For him the most rewarding event was meeting and working with Benjamin Franklin, because, like everyone else, Hopkins was an admirer of the great philosopher and scientist. The tow men took to each other at once, and their friendship lasted for the rest of Hopkins's life. He was appointed on the committee to prepare a program for union, and in this way he learned the details of Franklin's plan of union which he had brought to the Congress. Hopkins was converted to the need for intercolonial cooperation, but on his return home he was unable to convince the Rhode Island assembly of this. In fact, none of the colonies accepted the idea of cooperation and colonial union at this time, and it was many years before they were willing to work together for another cause of vital importance—independence.

He had hardly gotten back from Albany when in 1755 he became a candidate for governor of Rhode Island and was elected. His election was a great triumph because almost since the establishment of the colony the wishes of Newport—the center of wealth and prestige—had usually been the controlling factor in the choice of governor. Consequently nine times out of ten, Rhode Island governors had been Newport residents. While Hopkins was well known in Newport by 1755 and had held more than one position in the Rhode Island assembly, he was not in the inner circle of that seaport town, nor was he a member of the closely knit social group of Kings County. In sharp contrast, he was a relative newcomer to the political scene from the hinterland of Rhode Island. His election, therefore, may be said to have been due to general recognition of his ability, as well as to the backing of the Brown brothers.

Although the Seven Years War did not officially break out until 1756, it was obvious that the French were preparing for war. England, also, was on the alert, and in 1755 called on her American colonies to start preparations. When, therefore, Hopkins took office as governor in the spring of 1755, to all intents and purposes he found himself with a war on his hands. During his first term of office, his energies and those of the assembly were taken up with the problems of war, while the usual day-to-day matters were brushed aside. When war did break out in 1756, scarcely a week went by when the raising of companies of soldiers, their training, their equipment—blankets, tents, ammunition, and the like—and their transportation to points along the boundary of Canada did not occupy his thoughts and attention.

Hopkins's devotion to duty was recognized by others outside the colony. His heart must have been warmed to receive, in 1759, a letter from Colonel Henry Babcock who was in command of a Rhode Island regiment in Canada. He said, "...you must excuse me, Sir, when I acquaint you that the general as well as several other officers of distinction mention you with the greatest respect as being hearty for the defense of the country, and a firm friend...to His Majesty's interest in America."

Meanwhile, when he was campaigning in 1756 for a second term as governor, he became engaged in a bitter political feud with his opponent, Samuel Ward, who was the son of a former Rhode Island governor. Political campaigns often produce invective, and the campaign of 1756 ran true to form in this respect. Probably the animosity would have been forgotten once the election was over, had not Hopkins made the mistake of suing Ward for libel and asking £2,000 for damages. The trial was postponed several times, and Hopkins finally withdrew his suit, but the controversy was not forgotten, and the colony became sharply divided into two camps, pro-Hopkins and pro-Ward. This unhappy situation continued for several years as the two contenders for Rhode Island's highest political office faced each other again and again. Pamphlets extolling the virtues of the two antagonists were widely circulated, and a good deal of money, as well as gifts of corn, sugar, cheese, and the like, passed from hand to hand in the attempt to influence the voters in favor of one candidate or the other.

Governor and Chief Justice Samuel Ward (1725–1776) was a bitter political rival of Hopkins. The two factional leaders buried the hatchet when England threatened the colony's autonomy. Both served in the Continental Congress. A leading member of that body, Ward was presiding over the committee of the whole in March 1776 when he was stricken by smallpox and died.

The Hopkins "machine," of which the Browns of Providence were ardent members, helped to get Hopkins elected seven times, while Samuel Ward became the governor only three times—in 1762, 1765, and 1767. By 1769, both Hopkins and Ward agreed to bury the hatchet, and thereafter political peace reigned in Rhode Island.

While the war was being fought, it would seem as though there was hardly a day that Hopkins could call his own. Although burdened by political disputes and his administrative duties in the assembly, Hopkins continued to further Rhode Island's effort in the French War. He also attended a second congress in Albany, in 1755, and a year later went to Boston to a convention for consultation with the English commander in chief, the Earl of Loudoun, on the conduct of the war. Hopkins also served as a member of the Rhode Island Committee of War, and for five years (1751–56) had been serving as the chief justice of the Superior [i.e., Supreme] Court.

Although he was by now fifty years old, such was his ardor for victory over the French that on learning of the surrender in 1757 of Fort William Henry on Lake George to the enemy, he volunteered for a campaign against Canada. A group of some 200 men was quickly formed, and Hopkins was chosen as their commander. They were about to start out when the news was received that the enemy had retreated and their services, so gladly offered, were no longer needed.

At last, in 1763, the Seven Years War was over, and a new era was ushered in for the American colonies. France, now defeated in war, ceded Canada to England, and for a short time it looked as though peace and prosperity had come to stay. To be sure, the feeling of optimism did not last long, for England soon discovered that Canada was a pretty expensive luxury, because she had not only to provide for the government of her new empire, but maintain an army of occupation to keep the peace along the border between the Indians and the colonies. The inevitable result was that she was faced with the problem of finances, which she sought to solve by remodeling her policy of taxation. Thus, the colonial dreams of utopia evaporated and the struggle began between the mother country and her increasingly hostile American colonies.

During the critical years, although Hopkins occupied the governor's chair but rarely, he still played an active part in the colony. He served for five years in the General Assembly as deputy from Providence, and once more took on the duties of chief justice of the Superior Court. He also embarked on several other activities which added color and variety to his life.

The *Providence Gazette* had been founded in 1762, and from time to time Hopkins wrote articles which were published in the paper. Some, perhaps, were published anonymously, while others, according to the custom of the times, appeared under fictitious names, or merely with an initial. In 1764, he was the author of an *Essay on Trade*, which was a protest against the reenactment by England of the former Molasses Act that had imposed a duty on sugar and molasses not purchased in the British West Indies. This Act had been on the books some thirty years and had always been hated. It had never produced much revenue for England, however, as the New England merchants had continued to trade with the French and Dutch sugar planters, and had become adept at smuggling in these products. Now, to have another Molasses Act which would replace the former one and which, it was understood, was to have definite provisions for vigorous enforcement, was a bitter pill to swallow. Shortly after the *Essay on Trade* had appeared in the *Gazette*, he condensed it, and then, with a new

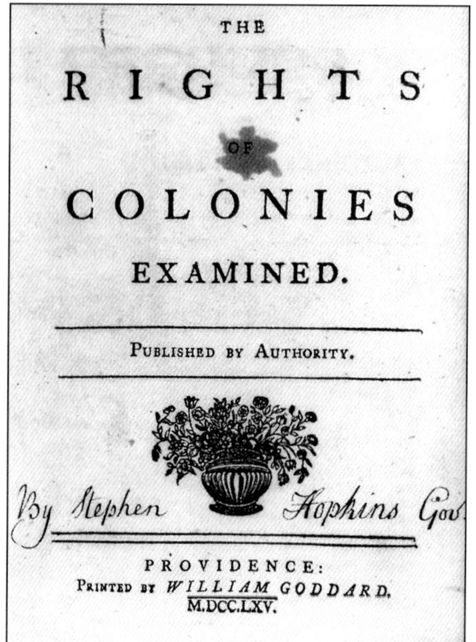
THE RIGHTS OF COLONIES EXAMINED.

PUBLISHED BY AUTHORITY.

By Stephen Hopkins Gov.

PROVIDENCE: PRINTED BY WILLIAM GODDARD. M.DCC.LXV.

Title page from the 1765 printing of *The Rights of Colonies Examined*. This treatise first appeared in 1764. Its publisher, William Goddard, was the editor of the *Providence Gazette*.

title—*A Remonstrance of the Colony of Rhode Island to the Lords Commissioners of Trade and Plantations*—the assembly voted to send two copies to Rhode Island's agent in England to be presented to the members of the Board of Trade.

Before the year was over, he took up his pen once more and wrote a pamphlet which he called *The Rights of Colonies Examined*. This was a very thoughtful exposition of the basic relationship between colonies and a mother country. His wide knowledge of history enabled him to begin with a discussion of the privileges and liberties of the Greek and Roman colonies, which privileges and liberties England had extended to her colonies, and which had been included in the charters she had granted to the New England colonies. He pointed out that "British colonists went out on a firm reliance of a solemn compact and royal promise and grant that they and their successors forever... should be partakers and sharers of all the privileges and advantages of the then, English, now British, Constitution...." With this as a background, he went on to criticize not only the tax on foreign sugar and molasses, but the proposed stamp act. He concluded by saying that "the first planters of these colonies, the American colonies, have kept due order, and supported a regular government, have maintained peace, and practiced Christianity... have demeaned themselves as loyal, as dutiful, and as faithful subjects ought...." Why, Hopkins concluded, "should the gentle current of tranquility, that has so long run with peace through all the British states and flowed with joy and happiness in all her countries, be at last obstructed, be turned out of its due course into unusual and winding channels, by which many of those states must be ruined?" This well reasoned pamphlet was published in *The Providence Gazette* and copies of it were sent to England to be printed there.

Hopkins was full of foreboding as he looked into the future, but unexpectedly he discovered a new and quite different interest. He had always been an ardent reader and had always been interested in education. He was therefore more than pleased to learn of the possibility of a college—Rhode Island College (later Brown University)—being established in Warren. With his many friends he cooperated to make this a reality, and it must have been a source of great pride to him when in 1765 he was chosen chancellor of the university, and also one of its trustees. Thereafter, Brown University and its young president, James Manning, held a very special place in his heart. And still another honor was to come his way. In 1768 Hopkins was elected a member of the American Philosophical Society.

A year later he had the once-in-a-lifetime pleasure of working with Joseph Brown in the observation of the transit of Venus. Brown had imported from England a special telescope, and the two friends and a small group of others watched the great spectacle from Benefit Street at the point not far south of College Hill [now called Transit Street]. Astronomer Benjamin West wrote an account of this and dedicated it to Hopkins, saying in the introduction that "much might be said with respect to your Honor's superior abilities in mathematics and natural philosophy; but without flattery these are the least of your achievements, when compared to your profound skill in civil police [policy], and the wise government of a people."

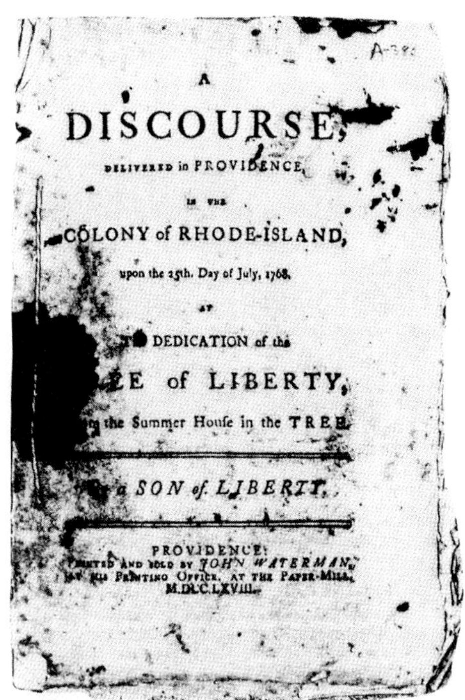

A
DISCOURSE,
DELIVERED in PROVIDENCE,
IN THE
COLONY of RHODE-ISLAND,
upon the 25th. Day of July, 1768.
AT
DEDICATION of the
E of LIBERTY,
the Summer Houſe in the TREE.
a SON of LIBERTY.
PROVIDENCE:
AND SOLD BY JOHN WATERMAN,
PRINTING OFFICE, AT THE PAPER-MILL.
M.DCC.LXVIII.

Title page of Silas Downer's 1768 Liberty Tree discourse. Downer (1729–1785), a lawyer, went through the whole list of parliamentary legislation affecting the colonies, denouncing these statutes as "infractions on the natural rights of men." He was one of the first Americans to deny publicly the power of Parliament over the colonies.

As Hopkins watched the planet glide across the sun, perhaps he had a fleeting hope that this was an omen of good fortune for the future. But such hopes were not to be realized. By this time, the differences between England and the colonies had not been ironed out in spite of a brief period of calm after the repeal, in March 1766, of the Stamp Act. The burning of the British revenue schooner H.M.S. *Gaspee* in Narragansett Bay, on the night of June 9, 1772, advertised to everybody on both sides of the Atlantic the deep dissatisfaction of the Rhode Islanders with the policies imposed by the mother country.

It could not be supposed that England would pass over this outrage quietly, and a royal commission was appointed to investigate the case and was instructed to send those convicted of the attack to England for trial. This placed Hopkins in a very serious dilemma. As chief justice of the Superior Court of Common Pleas, it was his duty to cooperate with the commissioners as they carried on their examination of witnesses. On the other hand, as a Rhode Islander, he knew who had taken part in the burning of the ship, and he was desperately afraid that his fellow colonists would be convicted. Even worse, the instructions to send the perpetrators of the vandalism to England for trial were very frightening. Like everyone else, he feared that the chances for a fair trial in England were negligible. What, then, would be the fate of these men three thousand miles away from home, who had been declared guilty of burning one of His Majesty's ships at a time when England was officially at peace with her colonies?

Hopkins took a determined stand by announcing publicly that he would not countenance the deportation of any Rhode Islander to England for trial. In the end, however, this decision was not put to the test, for, although everybody knew who had rowed down the bay on that fateful night in June, the royal commissioners were unable to get any evidence against anybody. Only one witness was found who gave straightforward testimony, but finally this was dismissed as unreliable. At length, after a year of frustrating delays, the commissioners realized that they were beaten, and the case was dismissed.

Two years after the burning of the *Gaspee*, a giant step was taken towards colonial union and independence by the calling together of the First Continental Congress in September 1774 in Philadelphia. Just which colony first suggested this important conference is not definitely known, and many colonies have claimed that distinction, but perhaps the palm should be awarded to Rhode Island. Furthermore, it is not too wide of the mark to believe that the venerable Stephen Hopkins, who had for years preached the importance of colonial union, and who had attended many colonial conferences, was the man who started the ball rolling. However that may be, it is certain that a town meeting in Providence in May 17, 1774, passed a resolution proposing a general conference to discuss the many problems facing the colonies, and for "establishing the firmest union, and adopting such measures as to them [the members of the Congress] shall appear the most effectual to answer that important purpose." A few weeks later the Rhode Island assembly passed a resolution in favor of a "Convention of representatives from all the colonies... to establish the rights and liberties of the colonies upon a just and solid foundation." At the same meeting Stephen Hopkins and Samuel Ward were chosen as delegates to the Congress.

After the Congress was called together and organized—Peyton Randolph of Virginia was chosen as president—Hopkins was appointed on two committees. The duty of the first was to draw up a paper on the rights of the American colonies, and the second committee began work on a survey of the trade and manufactures of the colonies; this would give a picture of the resources of the colonies.

While listening to the debates in the meetings of the Congress and taking part in the informal discussions which took place in the taverns of Philadelphia, he must have been heartsick to discover that the general sentiment of the members was overwhelmingly opposed to taking any radical steps against the mother country. On the contrary, the delegates were determined to keep the door of reconciliation wide open, and even after weeks of debate were in favor of only appeals to the mother country for understanding and cooperation. To carry out their decision, an "Address to the King" and a similar "Address to the People of England," expressing the attitude and thinking of the colonies, and finally a Declaration of Rights claiming the rights of the American colonists to life, liberty, and property, were prepared to be sent to England.

The only positive action taken was the organization of the Continental Association which banned importation of all British goods into the colonies, and the exportation of all colonial products to England. It was thought that this would prove to be a very strong "weapon," since it would affect the pocketbooks of the English merchants and therefore would probably create a strong sentiment in favor of the relaxation of the oppressive policies in operation against the American colonies. These measures completed the work of the First Continental Congress. After agreeing to hold another Congress, if necessary, in the spring of 1775, the delegates went home hoping against hope that the relations between England and her colonies would somehow take a turn for the better.

These hopes turned out to be forlorn indeed, and the Second Continental Congress met again in Philadelphia in the spring of 1775. The situation had by now definitely deteriorated. The nonimportation of British goods had not proved effective in softening public opinion in England; the "Address to the King" had been ignored; and the Parliament was still adamant in demanding obedience from the recalcitrant colonies to the existing laws. The port of Boston had been closed as a punitive measure after the Boston Tea Party, and for some months the town had been suffering the rigors of unemployment and food shortage, while the battles of Lexington and Concord had already taken place about a month before the Congress had been called together.

While the Congress still continued to explore all possible means of preventing a break with England, Hopkins was ready to start preparations for the worst—war. He openly said, "The gun and bayonet alone will finish the contest in which were are engaged, and any of you who cannot bring your minds to this mode of adjusting the questions better retire in time as it will not perhaps be in your power, after the first blood is shed." He admired both John Adams and Samuel Adams, and he therefore voted in favor of their candidate, George Washington, as commander in chief of the Continental Army. He also served on several committees—one for organizing the militia, a second one for procuring cannon, and a third to establish a Continental Navy. Needless to say, he was proud and pleased when he secured the appointment of his brother Esek as commander of the infant navy.

Meanwhile, Rhode Island has been traveling rapidly towards the point of no return, and preparations for war had been going on for many months—the enlistment of troops for active duty, gathering of supplies of every kind, planning for the defense of Narragansett Bay, and pondering the ever present problem of finances.

On May 4, 1776, eight weeks before the members of the Continental Congress voted in favor of the Declaration of Independence, the Rhode Island assembly, meeting [in Providence], took the momentous step of severing allegiance to the British Crown by the passage of an act declaring that

> whereas George the Third, King of Great Britain...is endeavouring to destroy the good people of this Colony, and of all of the United Colonies...it becomes our highest duty to use every means with which God and Nature have furnished us in support of invaluable rights and privileges to oppose that power which is exerted only for our destruction.
>
> Be it therefore enacted by this General Assembly and by the authority thereof it is enacted, that an Act entitled 'an Act for the more effectually securing to His Majesty the allegiance of his subjects in this his Colony, and dominion of Rhode Island and Providence Plantations,' be and the same is hereby repealed....

Thus quietly and without the fanfare of trumpets did the little colony of Rhode Island declare its independence. Never again would the records of the assembly be concluded with the phrase "God save the King"; instead, for a short time "God save the United Colonies" was used, and later, "God save the United States."

In spite of the fact that many members of Congress were haunted by the fear that the future of the colonies, without the protection of the mother country, could only mean disaster and ruin, the time had come when it was impossible to postpone the great decision any longer. A motion was presented by Richard Henry Lee of Virginia on June 7, 1776, which placed the situation clearly before the Congress. It stated "that these United Colonies are and of right ought to be free and independent states; that they are absolved from all allegiance to the British Crown, and that all political connection between them and the State of Great Britain is and ought to be totally dissolved."

Face to face at last with the decision of severing relations with the mother country, it was decided to put off action on Lee's motion for three weeks in order to enable the delegates to find out the general sentiment of the colonies on this all-important question. It was realized, however, that some preparation for the future must be made, and without further delay a committee of five was chosen to draw up a Declaration of America's position which could be voted on should Lee's motion be adopted. Another committee was also set up to devise a plan which would give the Congress the authority to work with and for the states not only on the conduct of war, but as a sort of central government after independence was secured. Hopkins was well known to be a staunch advocate of colonial union, and it was natural that he should be appointed on this committee. When its work was completed, the plan was called the Articles of Confederation.

At last, the great day arrived when, after long and thoughtful debate and some changes in wording, the Declaration of Independence was accepted and signed. Hopkins was now a feeble old man and was afflicted with what was known in those days as the "shaking palsy." His signature was shaky indeed, but his spirit was strong. He was convinced that independence offered the only solution to the problems confronting the colonies, and he believed that this would some day be won.

Soon afterwards he returned home to rest and recuperate. He was appointed a delegate for four more years, but he was forced to decline on account of his health. He could, however, help the cause at home, and for three years he worked incessantly for his beloved Rhode Island. And, indeed, "these were the times that try mens souls," for the enemy had invaded the state and occupied Newport. Proud Newport, the garden city of New England, was reduced to suffering many indignities and tribulations for three years while the British troops remained in occupation of the town.

Hopkins served on the Committee of War for two years. Its purpose was to cooperate with the other New England states for the general defense of New England. He was also a member of the Rhode Island Council of War. This proved to be an arduous assignment, because the conduct of the war rested almost entirely in its hands, and in carrying out the wishes of the assembly it met six days a week every other week. He was, to be sure, deeply absorbed in the war effort at home, but at the same time he could not forget the Continental Congress, and he kept in touch with its work through correspondence with some of his friends there.

He had been greatly interested in the Articles of Confederation which he had helped to write. Although this document had been introduced into the Congress only a few days after the Declaration of Independence had been signed, its many details had not been ironed out and endorsed until three months later. Even then,

Stephen Hopkins's house was moved from its original site on South Main Street to the corner of Hopkins and Benefit streets next to the Licht Judicial Complex. Hopkins lived in this house from 1742 until his death in 1785.

action on it was greatly delayed. It was sent to the states for ratification, and five years went by before enough states ratified it to make it official. For Hopkins, when it was at last legally in operation it was a dream come true —colonial union. It is interesting to note that Rhode Island was the first state to ratify the Articles of Confederation. A glowing testimony to Stephen Hopkins and his belief in the importance of colonial union, it could hardly have been otherwise.

In 1781 he had the great pleasure of an unexpected visit from General Washington, who had come to Rhode Island to consult with the French troops who were quartered in Newport. There, in the front parlor of his little home, Hopkins entertained the commander in chief of the Continental Army, and heard first hand the plans for the coming campaign. His friend Moses Brown, who happened to be there when Washington arrived, remarked on the unaffected friendliness of the two men as they talked together about the issues of war.

Washington's visit might be said to mark the end of the chapter of Hopkins's active life; he was by now seventy-five years old and in poor health. Moreover, it was not long after this that he suffered the loss of his wife, who died in 1782. This was hard to accept, but he was blessed by having many friends to turn to for companionship. He was very popular as he has a wealth of memories to share with his acquaintances who enjoyed hearing him tell of his varied experiences. Without question, his closest friends were the Brown brothers, who he was bound to by the ties of family, religion, literary and civic sympathies, and innumerable commercial enterprises. With Nicholas he could discuss business in general, and make plans for the future when the war was over; with Joseph there was always their untiring mutual interest in science; with John, who was very active in the General Assembly, he could keep in contact with the war effort; and with Moses he had the special bond of the Quaker faith, to which they both subscribed, as well as their love of reading and study.

He lived to hear the bell of the First Baptist Church ring all day long in 1783, announcing the glorious news that England had at last signed the Treaty of Peace, which meant that the war was over, and probably he attended the service of thanksgiving held in the Baptist Church to thank the Lord for His gift of peace with honor, and independence. By now his days were numbered, but one more honor awaited him—the award of an honorary degree of LL.D. from his beloved Brown University in 1784.

Stephen Hopkins died at home on July 13, 1785. His body was escorted to the North Burial Ground by a large group of fellow citizens from all walks of life, which demonstrated not only his manifold interests and activities, but his universal admiration as well. His monument, suitably inscribed, mentions his many public services, and his rare abilities as an individual.

9

The following essay, published in 1992 when Neil York was an associate professor of history at Brigham Young University, offers a legal analysis of the *Gaspee* affair. In it the author alludes to the major apprehension of Rhode Islanders in regard to a treasonous incident of this type: the alleged perpetrators could be tried in a remote English court in derogation of their right of trial by jury in the vicinage where the crime occurred. This removal could be accomplished because of the revival by the government of George III of an obsolete treason act passed in 1544 during the reign of Henry VIII. This "Act for the trial of treasons committed out of the King's dominions" had made possible the transportation of accused Irish traitors to England by providing that any treason committed out of the realm of England might be tried at Westminster before the King's Bench or in any English county by special commissioners appointed by the king. The parliamentary opposition, led by Edmund Burke, vainly argued that such a procedure would interfere with an accused American's right to challenge jurymen, to avail himself of counsel, and to compel the appearance of witnesses from the other side of the Atlantic. Admonished Burke: "You relax the principle of vicinage in cases of smuggling and excise; by and by, high treasons will be alleged for [justifying] taking away the privilege of a jury."

The most complete account of Rhode Island's most significant event of the Revolutionary era is Professor Richard M. Deasy's modern edition (1990) of Judge William R. Staples's *The Documentary History of the Destruction of the Gaspee*. Judge Staples (1798-1868) knew well the *Gaspee*'s significance. This learned gentleman served as an associate justice of the state Supreme Court from 1835 to 1854, and as that court's chief justice from 1854 to 1856; but it was history that was Staples's great passion. His compilation of documents pertaining to the destruction of the *Gaspee*, published in 1845, was one of four important historical works that he produced.

Since new source material has come to light during the many years since the *Documentary History* was first published, Professor Deasy undertook the

The Burning of the Gaspee, from a steel engraving by J. Rogers.

useful task of expanding and updating Staples's valuable compilation and writing an introduction to the volume that would embrace the latest scholarship and offer new insights concerning the historical significance of the *Gaspee* affair. He places the *Gaspee*'s role in the creation of committees of correspondence in the proper historical context, thus modifying Staples's claim that "the meeting of these commissioners... led to the appointment of committees of correspondence in the several colonies." Such committees first flourished at the time of the Stamp Act crisis in 1765 and exhibited "a variety of structures" from that date onward. Staples (and York in the essay that follows) would have been more accurate had it been stated that the *Gaspee* investigation raised colonial apprehensions that the ancient right of trial by jury in the locality where the alleged crime was committed would be violated by a commission that might send those accused of the *Gaspee*'s destruction to England to be tried for high treason. Such fears prompted the Virginia House of Burgesses in March 1773 to appoint a standing committee to correspond with other legislatures or their committees about activities deemed dangerous to the colonials. In a year's time all the remaining colonies except Pennsylvania had created agencies modeled on Virginia's. This network of official legislative committees of correspondence was novel, and the *Gaspee* investigation was the catalyst for their creation.

Henry VIII's law of high treason was relevant not only to the *Gaspee* incident but also to the Boston Tea Party of December 1773. Though it was the latter that served as the direct, proximate cause for the Coercive Acts of 1774—measures that led to the call of the First Continental Congress—Rhode Island's defiance in June 1772 and the ensuing cover-up staged by its citizens before the royal investigating commission in 1773 also weighed heavily on the minds of those parliamentary leaders who fashioned the Coercive (or Intolerable) Acts to punish the colonists and force them to submit. In this sense, therefore, the burning of the *Gaspee* ended the period of calm that came with the repeal of the Townshend duties (except the tax on tea) and began the third and decisive phase of colonial opposition, which inexorably led to the War for Independence. According to Professor Deasy, England's reinstatement of the old Treason Act of Henry VIII—a measure to coerce violent protesters by prosecuting them to the limit of the law of constructive treason—"had the effect of dissolving all subsidiary arguments [for dealing with dissent], of elevating tensions to the breaking point, and of insuring one last confrontation. Differences of opinion on both sides of the Atlantic over the nature of the British Empire may have been impressive before [the Crown's response to the *Gaspee*], but now they had become irreconcilable within that empire." Perhaps, suggests Deasy, the epithet "First Blow for Freedom" may fit the *Gaspee* affair after all.

There is an ironic postscript to York's article. Governor and commissioner Joseph Wanton of Newport, whom York correctly describes as critical to British customs practices and protective of Rhode Island, was later ousted from the governorship by the Rhode Island General Assembly. In May 1775 the legislature refused to administer the oath of office to Wanton—who had been reelected to the chief executive's post in the annual April balloting—because of his Loyalist learnings. With Wanton deposed, Deputy Governor Nicholas Cooke (1717–1782) of Providence ascended to the governorship, where he espoused the rebel cause.

The Uses of Law and the *Gaspee* Affair

Neil L. York

The *Gaspee* affair has become a familiar marker along the path that led to the War of American Independence. Burned to the waterline before dawn on 10 June 1772, apparently by unidentified boarders who also manhandled the crew and reputedly shot its commander, the *Gaspee* took on a symbolic importance that extended far beyond the events of the moment. The HMS *Gaspee*, after all, was a Royal Navy schooner stationed in Rhode Island waters to catch smugglers; an attack on it was an assault on the flag and therefore treason against the king.

Although the *Gaspee* affair is still overshadowed in popular memory by the Boston Tea Party, most historians of the American Revolution give it a prominent place in their narratives. True, the Tea Party led to the much-resented "Coercive Acts," which in turn led to the First Continental Congress and, more indirectly, to the bloodletting at Lexington and Concord. But the *Gaspee*'s destruction had already brought a royal commission of inquiry that prompted the forming of intercolonial committees of correspondence. Even more important, the fate of the *Gaspee*, perhaps better than the Tea Party, reflected basic, intractable problems of empire, especially confusion over the extent of local autonomy and limits to imperial authority.

The *Gaspee* affair pitted local "whig" law against an expanding conception of imperial purview: future revolutionaries against future loyalists and their British allies. It showed that law alone cannot retie broken social bonds. Law, or at least law as it was interpreted by local and imperial authorities, confused rather than clarified issues in the *Gaspee* affair. Furthermore, lacunae in the surviving record should warn us against using old narrative forms to explain what happened. Quite frankly, given the fragmentary and inconclusive evidence, we still do not know what transpired on the *Gaspee* before fire consumed it.

For those who believe in destiny, the fate of the *Gaspee* was sealed from the moment it arrived in Narragansett Bay. Rhode Island had a long-standing reputation as a smugglers' den, and the bay, with its islands, inlets, and passageways, was a natural haven for illicit trade. The colony's sixty thousand or so inhabitants were scattered along the mainland shores of the bay as well as on its islands. Providence had just over four thousand residents, while Newport boasted a population twice as large. Both towns were dominated, socially and politically, by merchants, and a fair number of them—including the wealthy Browns of Providence—were not above smuggling. Rhode Island in general was under the sway of men like the Browns and their associates; they amassed the largest fortunes and either held the highest offices or were allied by kinship and interest to those who did.

Beginning in the middle 1760s, imperial authorities endeavored to reduce smuggling in Rhode Island and elsewhere in the colonies. Smuggling had become embarrassingly widespread during the French and Indian War, even between colonial Americans and their ostensible French enemies in Canada and the West Indies. Vice-admiralty courts had been operating in British North America for three-quarters of a century; new parliamentary legislation in 1767 expanded their range of authority. The extended reach of these courts further threatened the dominion of local common-law courts, which used juries to decide cases—unlike the vice-admiralty courts, whose royally appointed judges decided cases themselves. The Royal Navy, with more ships in American waters than in former years, was expected to assist the vice-admiralty judges and customs inspectors who patrolled on shore. As an incentive to diligence, all could profit from any resulting confiscations: it quite literally paid to catch smugglers. By the time that the *Gaspee* arrived in 1772, Royal Navy vessels and cutters licensed by customs had been plying Narragansett Bay regularly for some eight years.

The factions that dominated Rhode Island politics closed ranks in opposing tighter enforcement of the navigation system. Local authorities did not help imperial officials do their jobs; even John Andrews, a Rhode Islander who had been appointed the first resident vice-admiralty judge for his colony in 1758, did not let a royal appointment get in the way of his provincial allegiance: few convictions came from his bench. Rhode Islanders had lost their fight to keep vice-admiralty courts out of the colony when it was brought within the jurisdiction of the Boston-based imperial court in 1704. They could take solace that Andrews, at least, was one of their own. Paradoxically enough, Andrews may have reinforced the tendency of Rhode Islanders to see themselves as beyond the reach of imperial law because, with his appointment, imperial law had been localized.

Governor Joseph Wanton (1705–1780) protected the *Gaspee* raiders in 1772, but his Loyalist leanings prompted the General Assembly to depose him in 1775 in favor of rebel Nicholas Cooke.

There were numerous confrontations between local residents and imperial authorities before the *Gaspee* arrived in Rhode Island. In 1771 customs collector Charles Dudley was beaten as he boarded a vessel in Newport, and he subsequently complained to the British secretary of state for American affairs, the earl of Hillsborough. Looking for an excuse to vent his own frustrations, Hillsborough notified Governor Joseph Wanton that he had received many criticisms about "the neglect of the governors and civil magistrates, in giving their assistance and protection" to members of customs. He added, pointedly, "that some of the most violent of these outrages have been committed at Newport, Rhode Island." Scarcely disguising his wish to stand Rhode Island on its figurative head, he declared that "any further exhortation" on the subject would be useless; Wanton and other leaders of the colony should worry what the "consequences" would be if the "laws of the kingdom are suffered to be trampled upon."

Wanton's response marked the chasm separating himself from Hillsborough and anticipated by a year the rift between the governor and Admiral John Montagu over the status of the

Gaspee. Acting with the permission—even at the direction—of the powerful General Assembly, Wanton disputed Dudley's charge. He countered that Dudley may have been exceeding his authority and that if he was attacked, it was by drunken sailors, not by the good citizens of Newport. Wanton had been a customs collector in Newport earlier in his career and had been set upon at least once by a crowd for trying to seize a cargo, but he had left those years behind. Well into his sixties when he became governor in 1769, he was a prominent merchant and probably a smuggler to boot. His father had sat as governor; so had an uncle and a cousin. Hardly intimidated by Hillsborough and uninterested in courting his favor, Wanton registered a complaint of his own:

> And now My Lord, permit me, in turn, to complain of the officers of His Majesty's customs in America, for the abusing and misrepresenting the colony of Rhode Island and its officers; for how unkind and ungentlemanly-like, is it for officers, sent abroad by the crown, to reside in the colonies, by every means in their power, to traduce and even falsely accuse His Majesty's faithful subjects of the colony, to their sovereign and his ministers of state.

Hillsborough and Wanton were nibbling at the edges of a jurisdictional dispute. As far as Rhode Islands leaders were concerned, anything that occurred within the borders of the colony—an area that included the waters of Narragansett Bay—was a provincial matter under the jurisdiction of local law. The Rhode Island General Assembly had said as much in the midst of the Stamp Act crisis when, imitating the Virginia House of Burgesses, it resolved

> THAT HIS Majesty's liege People of this Colony have enjoyed the Right of being governed by their own Assembly in the Article of Taxes, and internal Police; and that the same hath never been forfeited, or any other way yielded up, but hath been constantly recognized by the King and the People of Britain.

Rhode Island officials enjoyed virtual autonomy in local matters, but neither Crown nor Parliament had intended to exclude imperial authority. By charter, Rhode Island was expected to uphold English law, including the Navigation Acts. In practice, except for the years under the Dominion of New England, Rhode Islanders before the 1760s had by and large been left alone to enforce local legislation as well as acts passed by the British Parliament and applied to them.

The language of the 1663 charter was vague. Under it the General Assembly was enjoined from passing legislation inimical to the laws of England. Yet the charter stated ambiguously that Rhode Island's laws should "be not contrary and repugnant unto, but, *as near as may be*, agreeable to the laws of this our Realm of *England*." Did that mean the stipulation was not binding? Rhode Island did not routinely send its laws to London for review, so the matter was never clarified. Moreover, Rhode Islanders elected all of their own officials, from the governor on down, and through the General Assembly they were empowered to set up their own courts. Those courts had authority over "all Actions, Cases, Matters, and Things, happening within the said Colony and Plantation." A rather extensive grant of autonomy, this, a concession to the unavoidable need for local law enforcement. And as legal scholars have shown, colonial Americans in general—not just Rhode Islanders—came to see the custom of local enforcement as a constitutional right, unalterable except with their consent.

The *Gaspee* had been built as a sloop. By the time Lieutenant William Dudingston assumed command in 1768, a second mast had been added and the vessel had been rerigged as a schooner. Just under fifty feet long, the *Gaspee* carried eight small guns and a crew of twenty or so men. Before Dudingston took up his station in Rhode Island, he had patrolled the Delaware River and, after that, the waters in the vicinity of Martha's Vineyard. He managed to offend local residents both in Pennsylvania and on the Vineyard through his aggressive acts and bombastic talk. Assigned to Narragansett Bay in March 1772, he wasted no time in alienating Rhode Islanders as well by stopping, searching, and occasionally seizing vessels.

According to Deputy Governor Darius Sessions, many residents had been "disquieted" by the schooner's commander. Writing from Providence, Sessions informed Governor Wanton, in Newport, of the widespread distress caused by the *Gaspee*'s presence. Sessions told Wanton that he had consulted with the chief justice for the province, Stephen Hopkins, who advised him "that no commander of any vessel has any right to use any authority in the body of the colony, without previously applying to the Governor, and showing his warrant for so doing." After reading Sessions's letter, Wanton dispatched an informal summons, carried by a sheriff, to Dudingston. In it Wanton told Dudingston to wait on him "without delay" and bring along any authorization he might have from the customs commission empowering him to operate in Rhode Island waters. Dudingston penned a response and entrusted it to one of his men. He reminded Wanton that they had met, that the governor had not asked to see his orders or authorization then, and that in any case as a Royal Navy officer he was not obliged to show Wanton anything.

Not surprisingly, Wanton was offended by Dudingston's terse response. In a second note he told Dudingston that he was not satisfied and that he still expected to see the lieutenant's commission. Dudingston sent Wanton's summonses, along with his own explanation, on to his commander in chief, Admiral John Montagu, in Boston. He told Montagu that he had shown Wanton his "orders from the Admiralty and your first order to put myself under your command and a deputation from the Commissioners of Custom," but not any specific orders from Montagu. He had thus been conscientious and, he added, cautious, for he had heard that there were those in Newport who "talked of fitting and arming a vessel to prevent my carrying any seizure to Boston." He claimed that writs were being prepared against him, that he could not safely send a boat ashore, and that "every invention of infamous lies calculated to inflame the country is put in the newspapers."

Dudingston no doubt phrased his letter very carefully in writing to Montagu, who would brook no interference by local authorities in naval affairs. Had the lieutenant shown Wanton his orders and had Wanton forgotten? Had he not but thought he did? Or did he lie to Montagu in order to get the admiral provoked at Wanton? We do not know.

As Dudingston probably hoped, Montagu fired off a very curt note to Wanton, telling him he was ashamed of the way Dudingston had been treated. "It is your duty, as a governor," lectured the admiral, "to give him your assistance, and not endeavor to distress the King's officers for strictly complying with my orders." Furthermore, he warned, if Dudingston or any other naval officers suffered "any molestation in the execution of their duty," those guilty of such acts should be sent to him in Boston. Dudingston had told him there were plans afoot in Newport to outfit a vessel to interfere with the *Gaspee*; if such a move were made, rumbled Montagu, he would take those involved and "hang them as pirates." To this communication Wanton replied, icily, that Dudingston had not shown him "any orders from the admiralty or from you," and "as to your attempt to point out what was my duty as Governor, please to be informed, that I do not receive instructions for the administration of my government, from the King's admiral, stationed in America."

In effect, neither man accepted the authority of the other, and each was convinced that the law was on his side. Montagu had nothing but disdain for Wanton's use of a sheriff to summon Dudingston. "I would advise you not to send your sheriff on board the King's ship again, on such ridiculous errands," chided the admiral; to which Wanton retorted, "I will send the sheriff of this colony at any time, and to any place, within the body of it, as I shall think fit." Wanton undoubtedly felt personally affronted, but he also believed that his legal status as governor—not just his personal honor—had been impugned. When he duly reported his dealings with Dudingston and Montagu to the earl of Hillsborough, he emphasized the legal correctness of his stand. He had acted, he stressed, because "gentlemen of established character, and whose loyalty to their sovereign is not to be questioned," had complained that a schooner with no clear authority had been harassing merchant vessels "within the body of the colony." At their request he had pursued the matter "as was consistent with law." Wanton told Hillsborough he was still not convinced that Dudingston had any right to act "before he communicated to me, or some proper authority, his commission for doing so." The governor insisted on this point, knowing full well Montagu's differing opinion and that of the secretary himself, who had shown his concurrence with the admiral's view in his letter to Wanton in connection with the Dudley incident the preceding year.

Equally as important, Wanton hotly denied that the people of Newport were arming a schooner to attack the *Gaspee*; any claim that they were was "a malicious misrepresentation." It is most unlikely that Wanton was being coy here, although—true enough—when the *Gaspee* was later boarded, the incident took place twenty miles up the bay from Newport and involved men not from Newport but from the Providence area. Yet, even if Wanton did not know of any plans or if, in fact, there were no plans at this date to take action against the *Gaspee*, Wanton's feelings were probably common knowledge. The governor had assured Hillsborough that he would assist the "king's officers" in the "legal discharge of their trust"; apparently he distinguished acts by imperial agents that required his support from those that did not. As Wanton saw it, Dudingston was operating beyond the navy's purview; not only was he outside the protection of Rhode Island law but he had actually violated it. That, and the knowledge that Wanton was supported by his deputy governor and by the province's chief justice, may have emboldened those who eventually did board the *Gaspee*. Indeed, without that knowledge they may not have made the attempt.

The *Gaspee* was not the only warship on patrol in Rhode Island waters; the frigate *Lizard* and the sloop *Beaver* also sailed Narragansett Bay. On the morning of 9 June 1772 all three vessels were in the south bay, with the *Gaspee* anchored off Newport. The *Gaspee* set off alone to the north, headed toward Providence. Perhaps because there was no pilot on board and Dudingston was venturing into the unfamiliar Providence River, the vessel ran aground five miles below Providence on Namquit Point sometime around mid afternoon. Dudingston decided there was nothing he could do until early the next morning, when the stranded schooner might be lifted off by high tide. That evening he posted a guard before he and the rest of the crew went below. Not long after midnight the sentry (or sentries) on deck heard and then saw in the darkness a number of approaching rowboats. He (or they) hailed the boats and urged Dudingston to come up. Once topside, Dudingston too called out, then advised whoever was coming near to stay clear and not attempt to board. The boats continued to close on the *Gaspee* as words were shouted back at Dudingston. Dudingston had ordered the crew to arm themselves, and shots were fired from the *Gaspee* at the boats; at least one shot was fired from the boats in reply. During this exchange Dudingston was wounded. Men from the boats clambered aboard the schooner and chased the *Gaspee*'s crew below; then, one by one, the crew was brought back on deck, bound, and rowed ashore near Pawtuxet. Just before dawn a few of the marooned sailors, now well over a mile away from Namquit Point, saw that the *Gaspee* was afire, and they watched as it continued burning to the waterline.

Abraham Whipple (1733–1819), a highly successful privateer captain in the French and Indian War and a soon-to-be hero in the War of Independence, led the flotilla of eight longboats to Namquit Point and the stranded *Gaspee*. Whipple was the brother-in-law of Stephen and Esek Hopkins. His portrait by Edward Savage hangs at the U.S. Naval Academy in Annapolis.

Word of the *Gaspee*'s destruction spread quickly. Later on the morning of 10 June, Deputy Governor Darius Sessions, accompanied by vice-admiralty judge John Andrews, turned up at the Pawtuxet house where Dudingston and some of his crew had been left. Sessions wanted to interview Dudingston. Wounded, embarrassed, not knowing which, if any, local officials to trust, and anticipating a court martial where he would have to explain himself, Dudingston demurred. With his grudging permission Sessions talked to others from the

GEORGE R.

By the KING.

A PROCLAMATION:

FOR the diſcovering and apprehending the Perſons who plundered and burnt the *Gaſpee* Schooner; and barbarouſly wounded and ill treated Lieutenant *William Dudingſton*, Commander of the ſaid Schooner.

WHEREAS We have received Information, that upon the 10*th Day of* June *laſt, between the Hours of Twelve and One in the Morning, in the* Providence *or* Narrowganſet *River, in Our Colony of* Rhode-Iſland *and* Providence Plantations, *a great Number of Perſons, armed with Guns and other offenſive Weapons, and led by Two Perſons, who were called the* Captain *and* Head-Sheriff, *in ſeveral armed Boats, attacked and Boarded Our Veſſel called the* Gaſpee *Schooner, then lying at ſingle Anchor in the ſaid River, commanded by Our Lieutenant* William Dudingſton, *under the Orders of Our Rear-Admiral* John Montagu, *and having dangerouſly wounded and barbarouſly treated the ſaid* William Dudingſton, *took, plundered and burnt the ſaid Schooner:*

WE, to the Intent that ſuch outrageous and heinous Offenders may be diſcovered, and brought to condign Puniſhment, have thought fit, with the Advice of Our Privy Council, to iſſue this Our Royal PROCLAMATION: And We are hereby graciouſly pleaſed to promiſe, that if any Perſon or Perſons ſhall diſcover any other Perſon or Perſons concerned in the ſaid daring and heinous Offences, abovementioned, ſo that he or they may be apprehended and brought to Juſtice, ſuch Diſcoverer ſhall have and receive, as a Reward for ſuch Diſcovery, upon Conviction of each of the ſaid Offenders, the Sum of *Five Hundred Pounds*. And if any Perſon or Perſons ſhall diſcover either of the ſaid Perſons who acted as, or called themſelves, or were called by their ſaid Accomplices, the Head-Sheriff or the Captain, ſo that they, or either of them, may be apprehended and brought to Puniſhment, ſuch Diſcoverer ſhall have and receive, as a Reward for ſuch Diſcovery, upon Conviction of either of the ſaid Perſons, the further Sum of *Five Hundred Pounds*, over and above the Sum of *Five Hundred Pounds* herein before promiſed, for the diſcovery & apprehending any of the other common Offenders, abovementioned; and if any Perſon or Perſons concerned therein, except the Two Perſons who were called the Head-Sheriff, and Captain, and the Perſon or Perſons who wounded Our ſaid Lieutenant *William Dudingſton*, ſhall diſcover any one or more of the ſaid Accomplices, ſo that he or they may be apprehended and brought to Puniſhment, ſuch Diſcoverer ſhall have and receive the ſaid Reward or Rewards of *Five Hundred Pounds*, or *One Thouſand Pounds*, as the Caſe may be; and alſo Our gracious Pardon for his ſaid Offence. And the Commiſſioners for executing the Office of Treaſurer of Our Exchequer, are hereby required to make Payment accordingly of the ſaid Rewards. And We do hereby ſtrictly charge and command all Our Governors, Deputy-Governors, Magiſtrates, Officers, and all other Our Loving Subjects, that they do uſe their utmoſt Diligence in their ſeveral Places and Capacities, to find out, diſcover and apprehend the ſaid Offenders, in Order to their being brought to Juſtice. And We do hereby command that this Our Proclamation be printed and publiſhed, in the uſual Form, and affixed in the principal Places of Our Town of Newport, and other Towns in Our ſaid Colony, that none may pretend Ignorance.

GIVEN at Our Court at St. James's, *the Twenty-Sixth Day of* Auguſt, 1772, *in the Twelfth Year of Our Reign.*

GOD ſave the KING.

Printed by SOLOMON SOUTHWICK, Printer to the Honorable the Governor and Company of the Colony of *Rhode-Iſland* and *Providence-Plantations*, in *New-England*.

This proclamation of King George III offered a reward for information concerning the destruction of the *Gaspee*.

Gaspee assembled there. Sessions went so far as to take depositions from three of the crew. None of them could identify the boarders. Sessions reported what he had learned to Wanton in a letter the next day, and that was not much: the *Gaspee* had been boarded, its commander had been shot, he and his crew had been dumped on shore, the schooner had burned, and none of the boarders had been identified—no names, no physical descriptions.

The General Assembly was not in session at the moment, so Wanton, after consulting with members of his council, issued a proclamation on 12 June "strictly charging and commanding all His Majesty's officers" in the colony "to exert themselves with the utmost vigilance, to discover and apprehend the persons guilty" of this "atrocious crime, that they might be brought to condign punishment." He offered a reward of one hundred pounds for information leading to a conviction.

Wanton then notified Hillsborough of the "unwarrantable transaction," assuring the secretary that "the conduct of those who committed this outrage" was "universally condemned" and that, quoting his own proclamation, the "utmost vigilance" would be used to bring the perpetrators to justice. Yet he also wrote—at even greater length—that the people of Rhode Island had been "insulted without any just cause" and that their trade had been interrupted in an "oppressive manner" before this incident. Wanton's message clearly implied that the incident would not have happened if "those officers who have been sent into this colony" had behaved with "prudence and discretion."

From the tone of Wanton's report Hillsborough may have concluded, quite rightly, that the governor was not all that interested in uncovering what had happened to the *Gaspee*. Hillsborough, Lord North, and other members of the ministry were appalled, as was George III. Hillsborough soon after left office and the more moderate earl of Dartmouth replaced him; but Dartmouth too was distressed, and he concurred in the appointment of a royal commission of inquiry to investigate the affair. The commissioners were instructed to gather evidence and see to it that those formally accused were sent to England, possibly to be tried there for committing "High Treason" by "levying war against His Majesty." Attorney General Alexander Wedderburn, who with Solicitor General Edward Thurlow had recommended that the assault be considered treasonous, thought the *Gaspee* business "five times the magnitude of the Stamp Act" disturbances. Accordingly, the king approved a much more substantial reward than that offered by Governor Wanton: five hundred pounds for anyone giving evidence leading to a conviction; one thousand pounds and a pardon to any participant who would identify the ringleaders (and who had not been the one to shoot Dudingston).

Rhode Islanders reacted with hostility to the appointment of a royal commission and the planned trial of the accused in England. Writing to the *Newport Mercury*, "Americanus" scorned the commission as a "star chamber," a "court of inquisition" dangerously "vested with the most exorbitant and unconstitutional power." Dire warnings printed in the *Providence Gazette* and *Newport Mercury* turned up in other colonial newspapers as well. Belying the claim to objectivity printed on its masthead—"Open to ALL PARTIES but influenced by NONE"—William Rind's *Virginia Gazette* was notable for its pro-Rhode Island sympathies. Another Virginia paper reprinted a piece from the *Providence Gazette* that characterized the boarding of the *Gaspee* as merely an "unhappy scheme"; Dudingston, the author complained, had previously treated Governor Wanton "with great indignity," and his behavior while on patrol "was so *piratical* and provoking that Englishmen could not patiently bear it." The commissioners were implored not "to make any Concession in Submission whereby a Precedent shall be introduced and established which may be fatal to the Freedom of their own Constitution and the Liberties of America." Virginia in fact became so agitated over the affair that leading burgesses called for the forming of intercolonial committees of correspondence. By the end of the year ten colonies had such committees in place.

As it turned out, Rhode Islanders and Virginians need not have worried. The commissioners convened in Newport on 4 January 1773, adjourned after less than three weeks, then reconvened on 1 June and submitted a final report on 22 June, all without identifying a single soul that could be brought to trial. No one would be formally accused, much less sent to England. Whoever had been among the boarders of the *Gaspee* could breathe easier after 22 June. Thus ended the "time of terror."

The commissioners were probably foredoomed to fail. Part of the problem lay in the composition of the commission itself. The five men appointed were Robert Auchmuty, a vice-admiralty justice in Boston; Peter Oliver, chief justice of Massachusetts; Frederick Smyth, chief justice of New Jersey; Daniel Horsmanden, chief justice of New York; and Governor

Wanton of Rhode Island. No doubt the North ministry moved cautiously before making its choices, and yet the choices it made showed the impossibility of the situation. The first four commissioners could be trusted as faithful adherents of empire, but, especially in the case of the three chief justices, these men were also attached to the law. Officially they were directed to identify suspects and bring them to justice on the basis of legal evidence, not political retribution. If the ministry had other expectations it did not say so.

Wanton's inclusion may have been a political necessity, and yet the commission had been formed in the first place because Hillsborough and his colleagues did not trust the governor to carry through with an investigation. They likewise probably did not trust the General Assembly, the courts, or the local grand juries. Nonetheless the commissioners were told to work closely with Rhode Islanders because "the civil magistrates and officers" were "entrusted with the power and authority to arrest and commit to custody" those who were accused. The commissioners could find suspects, and those suspects, once formally accused, could be put in the custody of Admiral Montagu in Boston for passage to England. Still it was up to the local authorities to actually arrest the suspects, and they could do so only after indictments were handed down by a Rhode Island court or grand jury. How likely were such indictments and arrests? In 1765 the Assembly had claimed the constitutional right to police Rhode Island; four years later it voted that all trials for crimes committed in the colony should be held there. In both instances it could contend that it only asserted rights first guaranteed by the 1663 charter and claimed by the General Assembly that same year. Therefore neither Wanton nor the General Assembly could be expected to accept a change in venue. Chief Justice Hopkins, when empowered by the Assembly to use his discretion in the matter, reportedly proclaimed that "for the purpose of Transportation for Trial... he would neither apprehend by his own Order nor suffer any executive Officer in the colony to do it."

The commission's deliberations had been preceded by a court martial held in October 1772 on a warship in Portsmouth harbor, England. Testifying before a panel of nine captains, Dudingston and five of his crew gave their version of events. Although there were some differences in their accounts, they agreed that before the *Gaspee* ran aground it had been sailing to Providence to pick up crew members returning from Boston, where they had taken a prize ship; that the approaching boats had been warned off repeatedly, but the men on them boarded the *Gaspee* anyway; that under Dudingston's orders the sailors had armed themselves and fired at the boats, after which shots were returned; that Dudingston was wounded during the exchange of fire; that they had been put ashore and later saw the *Gaspee* aflame; and finally, according to Dudingston and his midshipman, William Dickinson, that one of the two leaders had been called the sheriff. During Dickinson's testimony, when the midshipman was asked if any of the boarders had been wounded, Dudingston "acquainted the Court that he was informed that one of the People in the Boats was privately buried ashore."

When asked, Dudingston defended the actions of his crew; for their part the crew concurred that Dudingston had done his "utmost." Captain Linzee of the *Beaver* appeared briefly to corroborate Dudingston's claim that he had no reason to suspect his ship would be attacked. All were found blameless and the court martial proceedings were closed. Dudingston's career was not ruined by the *Gaspee* affair; on the contrary, Dudingston was soon after promoted to captain and ended his days as a rear admiral.

Dudingston was not required to return to Rhode Island and give evidence before the royal commission, despite the commission's having requested that he do so. The lords of the Admiralty determined that a personal appearance was unnecessary. Dudingston's testimony before the court martial had been substantially the same as his written report to Admiral Montagu on 12 June, a copy of which the commission possessed. Dickinson and one of the other four crewmen were sent to testify, but that is all. The Admiralty had not even assembled the full *Gaspee* crew for the court martial or made any effort to gather detailed information for the commissioners' use. Either the Admiralty preferred that this embarrassing matter be forgotten quickly or it underestimated how tenacious Rhode Islanders would be in obstructing the commission's way.

Dickinson and seaman Bartholemew Cheever appeared before the commissioners on 1 June 1773. They told basically the same story they had related in Portsmouth, this time in more detail. Cheever again averred that he could not name any of the boarders, but that those "who acted as principals were called the head sheriff and the captain; and one of them was called constable." He claimed that he had seen two of the boarders in Pawtuxet sometime afterward. Dickinson provided a description of the "captain" and the "sheriff": the former "was a well set man, of swarthy complexion, full face, hoarse voice, and wore a white cap, and appeared rather above the common rank of mankind"; the latter "was a tall genteel man, dressed in blue clothes, his hair tied behind, and had on a ruffle shirt."

John Brown (1736–1803), Providence merchant prince, financed Stephen Hopkins's political ventures, organized the attack on the *Gaspee*, furnished the *Katy* (renamed *Providence*), one of the first ships of the U.S. Navy, and manufactured cannon at Hope Furnace for the rebel cause.

Dudingston had noted in his 12 June report to Montagu that those he had seen most closely "appeared to be merchants and masters of vessels" and "were in every respect armed, and commanded with regularity, by one who personated the sheriff." This had been a vague description at best; now, a year later, Dickinson was far more precise. Here was specific testimony the commission could use! Or could it? Dickinson, apparently separated from the rest of the crew after being put ashore from the *Gaspee*, had made his way to Boston and had actually recited his first description to Admiral Montagu on 11 June, the day after the incident. Dickinson's testimony that there had been a head sheriff and a captain involved was reflected in the royal proclamation of 26 August calling for witnesses to come forward and identify them. Montagu had also sent a copy of Dickinson's statement to Governor Wanton. Wanton had responded the next day by sending Montagu the depositions taken by Darius

Sessions and by pointing out that "you will perceive that there is a material difference between them and the account" given by Dickinson. Dickinson had been more vague in that first account, mentioning "two ring-leaders" and the presumed presence of a "head sheriff" and a "captain." He had given no physical descriptions. As a member of the commission before which Dickinson appeared the following June, Wanton could well have dismissed Dickinson's more elaborate version as confused or perhaps even tainted.

Indeed, both sides may have been guilty of trying to manipulate the evidence. This was especially so in the case of Aaron Briggs, a runaway indentured servant. Within a month of the *Gaspee*'s destruction Briggs turned up on board the *Beaver* and Captain Linzee, the commander, sent the transcript of a statement by Briggs on to Admiral Montagu in Boston. It was this deposition, even more than that of Dickinson, that excited the admiral because Briggs singled out people by name. "Although it comes from a negro man," Montagu wrote Wanton and Hillsborough, "it carries with it an appearance of truth." It agreed to Montagu's satisfaction with what he had gleaned from the reports of Dickinson and Dudingston, and Briggs's presence among the boarders had been confirmed in a separate statement by Patrick Earle, one of the *Gaspee*'s seamen. As Briggs told it, he had been forced to join the group that boarded the schooner. He identified five participants: John and Joseph Brown of Providence, Simeon Potter of Bristol, a "Doctor Weeks" of Warwick, and a "Mr. Richmond" of Providence. "It appears to me," Montagu apprised Hillsborough, "that these people were the ringleaders of the piratical proceeding." In fact, according to Briggs, John Brown was in command and had fired a musket at the *Gaspee*, after which he saw Dudingston fall.

Briggs repeated all of this for the commission in more detail soon after it began meeting in January 1773. In a noteworthy change, he stated explicitly that John Brown had shot Dudingston. Briggs's claim that he was with the boarders was again corroborated by Earle two days later. Earle could not remember anything about the others involved, except that he had heard one referred to by name as Potter.

The runaway servant had been sequestered on board the *Beaver* much of this time—some seven months—to keep local authorities from getting to him. They were nevertheless prepared, because Montagu himself had sent a copy of Briggs's deposition to Governor Wanton in July. Within days of receiving it, Wanton had obtained refutations from Briggs's master, the master's father-in-law, and two indentured servants who swore that Briggs had been asleep between them in the same bed that night. These counterclaims were laid before the commission. Eventually added to them was a letter from Darius Sessions stating that "it is impossible (I think) that there can be a word of truth" in Briggs's story, and that when he interviewed crew members the morning of the incident, none of them—including Patrick Earle—could identify anyone. It was, they had all agreed, too dark to see individuals clearly or even to tell if the boarders were Negroes or white men with blackened faces. If crew members were now saying something different, "their testimony is absolutely false."

What is more, Daniel Vaughan testified to the commission that Captain Linzee had tied Briggs to the mast of the *Beaver* and was prepared to whip him unless he named names. Vaughan came very close to claiming that Linzee had coerced Briggs into saying what he wanted to hear, in effect fabricating evidence for Admiral Montagu. Vaughan also noted that he had told this to Sessions and that Sessions had met with him at the suggestion of John and Joseph Brown and Barzillai Richmond (probably the Richmond whose first name Aaron Briggs had not known). Like Wanton before he joined the commission, Sessions only collected testimony that cast doubt on those who implicated individuals in the *Gaspee* raid.

With Briggs, the commissioners heard conflicting testimony. Had Sessions, Vaughan, the Browns, and Richmond connived and conspired? Had the others who spoke against Briggs? The commissioners could disregard the depositions of those who challenged Briggs and ask the colony's Superior Court to hand down indictments against the Browns and the others named by the runaway, but they did not do this. Perhaps they did not believe that the indictments would be issued, or perhaps they too did not believe Briggs. Wanton had dismissed Briggs as a reputable witness before the commission was even formed; he had no reason to change his mind thereafter. Daniel Horsmanden confided to Dartmouth afterward that Briggs's testimony was useless because the servant showed himself to be a "prevaricator." The commissioners consequently did not pursue the lead Briggs gave them.

What transpired with Aaron Briggs echoed what had taken place before. On 12 January, Stephen Gulley, a Smithfield farmer, had appeared and testified to the commission that he had been told by a friend, who had heard from someone else, that "Browns" had been involved in the destruction of the *Gaspee*. His testimony of thirdhand hearsay was followed in rapid succession by deponents contending that the conversation he recounted never took place and that he was an opportunist looking to cash in on the reward being offered by the Crown. The commission did not act on Gulley's assertion or on the other shreds of evidence offered to it in January or at the second session in June.

Even without the evidence given to discredit those who came forward, obtaining a conviction in an English court for a capital offense may well have been impossible. The discrepancies turned up by the commission would most likely have turned up again in court. Furthermore, there is no guarantee that the commission's task would have been simpler or that indictments, trials, and convictions would have followed if Dudingston or members of his crew had identified suspects. The effect might have been just the opposite; the task of Wanton, Sessions, Hopkins, and their obstructionist colleagues could have been made easier.

According to long tradition and a few later accounts, John Brown led the boarders. What if Brown had led the raid and Dudingston or someone else identified him? If Dudingston or any of his crew had disclosed this information to Sessions when he looked in on them the morning of 10 June, events could have taken a markedly different course. Remember that Sessions did not report to Wanton until 11 June what had happened the day before. I think we can safely assume that in the interim Sessions had talked with most of the leading men of Providence, including, perhaps, the men who boarded the *Gaspee*—John Brown probably among them. They might have agreed to take a calculated risk and deny any involvement, hoping that no eyewitnesses would turn up, that none of their number would betray them, and that provincial officials, from the governor on down, would use local law to shield them. Had they been identified from the outset, the law could have been employed quite effectively. Sessions's 11 June 1772 letter to Wanton would have been phrased differently, justifying rather than condemning that "very disagreeable affair." Instead of lamenting the incident in his correspondence to Montagu and Hillsborough, Wanton could have backed Brown and the rest, with the law—local law—behind him.

Justification could have started with the question of the right to board. John Brown was sheriff of Bristol County and had been since 1771. The *Gaspee* had run aground in neighboring Kent County, but close enough to the county line bisecting the Providence River to justify his rowing out to inspect the scene. Of the others identified by Aaron Briggs, Simeon Potter sat for Bristol in the General Assembly; Joseph Brown sat for Cumberland. Given the propensity of Rhode Islanders to use local law as their most basic defense, Potter and Brown, if brought under suspicion, might have made some argument about their "right" of inspection because they were public officials. For that matter, all those who accompanied John Brown might have claimed that they were his deputies on official colony business, understandably concerned about what Dudingston was doing. The General Assembly would presumably have backed them.

Even if Brown had acted on his own, he would have been endorsed afterward by Governor Wanton and Chief Justice Hopkins. Beyond the matter of jurisdiction, there was also the factor of kinship and community. Brown was married to Hopkins's niece; his family had strong business ties with Wanton. Corroborated by Dudingston's own testimony or that of his crew, Brown could have established that he had identified himself as sheriff, that Dudingston had refused to allow him on board, and that the crew of the *Gaspee* had fired first; he and his party had fired only in response, in self-defense. He could have either accepted responsibility for shooting Dudingston or, just as easily—citing the account in Dickinson's deposition—contended that Dudingston's own men had shot him in the confusion. Since neither Dudingston nor any of his crew had actually seen how the blaze had started on the schooner, Brown could also have testified that it had started accidentally and that he and his companions had left only after trying to extinguish it. Or he could have contended that, as he understood it, the *Gaspee* had been operating in Rhode Island without authorization and was destroyed as any other pirate vessel might have been. Either way, Dudingston could have ended up looking worse, Rhode Islanders would have been even more confident that they were in the right, and imperial authorities would have appeared impotent.

Unidentified and therefore not given the explicit sanction of local law, the *Gaspee* boarders were nevertheless protected by local authorities, even as those authorities claimed to be appalled and even as they disingenuously promised London their assistance. As John Phillip Reid has noted, the *Gaspee* affair can be viewed as another example of the kind of "competing legal cultures" that he found in Massachusetts at the time of the *Liberty* riots in 1768. If the people of Massachusetts "accepted the constitutional premises that underlay opposition to British rule, they could also accept the constitutional premise justifying manipulation for the legal process to oppose that rule." So too, Reid concluded, with the people of Rhode Island: a mob like that assembled in the *Gaspee* affair could be seen as an agent of higher law as well as of local prerogative, a *posse comitatus* acting to protect the liberties of the people. Had any members of that posse gone to trial, they may well have lied even when offering sworn testimony. With fundamental freedoms at stake, they could, with clear consciences, deceive those they believed had made an illegal, unconstitutional application of the law.

Of the five *Gaspee* commissioners, Wanton was the only one fully satisfied with the results of their inquiry. All three of the chief justices who sat on the commission believed that Rhode Island's virtual autonomy and the uncooperativeness of its officials made their task impossible. "As to the government (if it deserves that name), it is a downright democracy," Daniel Horsmanden complained to Dartmouth soon after the January 1773 adjournment. Rhode Island, he worried, was in a "state of anarchy" because all provincial officials were at the mercy of the people: "The Governor is a mere nominal one, and therefore a cipher, without power or authority; entirely controlled by the populace, elected annually, as all other magistrates and officers whatsoever."

In his own dispatch to Dartmouth, written during the same period, Frederick Smyth lamented that Rhode Islanders smuggled in "egregious excess" and that Dudingston, a good officer, had been maligned. The assault on the *Gaspee*, "though perpetrated at a place and in such a manner as without all doubt the actors must be known to some hundreds of the inhabitants of the colony, is hitherto kept so profoundly secret that all our enquiry has been ineffectual to fix with certainty upon any particular person concerned in the outrage, and to keep this matter a secret is now become a common cause." In his history of the rebellion, penned some years later while in a London exile, Peter Oliver echoed Horsmanden and Smyth and added that the outcome of their inquiry had only encouraged the "colonists to play the same Game again, upon the first Opportunity."

Smyth and Oliver probably would have agreed with Horsmanden's suggestion that Rhode Island's charter be revoked so that the colony could be brought under more effective imperial control. Horsmanden urged that Rhode Island be joined with Connecticut to form a single colony under a royally appointed governor. The better sort in both colonies, he believed, would welcome the change, because they had long groaned under a "motley administration." Nonetheless, Horsmanden was not as harsh as Smyth and Oliver in criticizing the proceedings of the commission. He was convinced that Dudingston had provoked the people, and he believed that

Wanton was a fair man, not part of any conspiracy. Unlike Smyth, who was willing to give credence to Aaron Briggs's testimony, Horsmanden thought it unreliable if plausible. Indeed, he may have detected in it the attempt of Captain Linzee to make sure that indictments were handed down against those he had decided were guilty. Possibly it was Horsmanden, working with Wanton and Auchmuty, who composed the final report to the Crown. If so, Smyth and Oliver went along with them. Although Oliver returned to Massachusetts before the report was signed and officially submitted, Smyth stayed to the last and had reputedly let it be known that "he was come to judge according to Law and Right, and not to be the Executioner of Ministerial vengeance." Even Oliver, whatever his personal feelings, eventually concurred with his onetime colleagues.

Hence the wording of the commission's findings, dated 22 June 1773. Stating that they had used "the utmost assiduity" to discover the truth, the commissioners readily conceded that their efforts were "not attended with the success ardently wished for by all." They did not know who planned or executed the attack and could only conclude that it was done on the spur of the moment, very "suddenly and secretly." As best they could determine, the *Gaspee* had been boarded by "a number of armed people, many of whom, by their dress, appeared much above the rank of common people, and were accompanied by several negroes and others." These boarders wounded Lieutenant Dudingston, treated his crew with "great barbarity," and plundered and then burned the vessel. Beyond that, they could say nothing about the events of 10 June 1772.

They went on—possibly at Wanton's insistence, though with at least the acquiescence of two others—to write some fairly sharp words about Dudingston and Linzee. They observed that Dudingston would not talk to Darius Sessions and had refused, initially, to allow his men to be interviewed; more importantly, Dudingston was much at fault for what had happened because he had failed to report to Governor Wanton and because, "in some instances," he had shown an "intemperate, if not reprehensible zeal to aid the revenue service," a zeal that pushed him to "exceed the bounds of his duty." Linzee they castigated for his "contemptuous," "unjustifiable" treatment of civil authority and (in reference to Aaron Briggs) for his overzealousness in extracting "from a weak, or wicked mind, declarations not strictly true." The commissioners also noted that they had passed their findings on to the Rhode Island Superior Court, which handed down no indictments. In making this last observation they intended no criticism of the court; on the contrary, the tone of their report indirectly supported the court's inaction.

It is hard to imagine any other outcome. If the king and his ministers had wanted above all else to obtain convictions and make an example of those who boarded the *Gaspee*, then the commission was ill-suited for that task. The North ministry could have explored other options, as Lawrence DeVaro noted in his study of this affair. It might, for instance, have empowered the commission to issue indictments itself; or it might have formed a second commission to act as a special court of oyer and terminer, thereby avoiding a jury trial in Rhode Island or England. With one commission reinforcing the other and local authorities left out, perhaps more leads would have been followed, more depositions taken, more summonses issued. With Wanton not named to the first commission and the second composed of British jurists, there may have been indictments, then trials and possibly even convictions.

Vaguely worded imperial laws could have been interpreted to the advantage of Dudingston; conflicting local laws could have been set aside as irrelevant because subordinate, or invalid because in contravention. Dudingston had confessed to Montagu in May 1772 that he feared he himself was breaking imperial law by taking prizes to Boston instead of before John Andrews, the vice-admiralty justice in Rhode Island. Dudingston took prizes to Boston because he had been warned by customs collectors not to expect convictions in any Rhode Island court. The 1767 law that he thought he might have violated stated that

> all Forfeitures and Penalties inflicted by any Act or Acts of Parliament relating to the Trade or Revenues in the *British* Colonies or Plantations in America, may be prosecuted, sued for, and recovered in, any Court of Vice-Admiralty appointed, or to be appointed, and which shall have Jurisdiction within the Colony, Plantation, or Place, where the cause of such Prosecution, or Suit shall have arisen.

A sympathetic judge could have ruled that the Boston vice-admiralty court had jurisdiction over prizes seized in Rhode Island. The vague wording — "may" and "to be appointed" — would have made it simple for him. Or if he chose not to use that clause, he could have turned to the next one, which allowed a customs official to appeal any case not decided to his satisfaction to the vice-admiralty court of his choosing, "any Law, Custom or Usage, to the contrary notwithstanding." Such a reading would not have helped Dudingston, who had not gone to Andrews's court first, but it could have helped others in the future who appealed immediately to the Boston court after losing a case before Andrews or one of the Rhode Island common-law courts. This 1767 statute could have been used in a trial on the particulars of the *Gaspee* incident to make a sweeping statement of broadened imperial power, even for formally setting aside the 1673 statute that allowed prize cases to be prosecuted in any "court of record" in the colonies. Given the confusion over jurisdiction and conflicting testimony, however, conviction for treason and a sentence of death would still have been almost unthinkable. There were just too many mitigating circumstances and complicated questions of law.

It is quite possible that by 1773, as Admiral Montagu reportedly lamented, "British Acts of Parliament will never go down in America unless forced by the point of a sword." Even so, Whitehall and Westminster were reluctant to use the full force of imperial law and did not talk of using the sword, despite the gravity of the *Gaspee* affair. To that extent London's reaction to the destruction of the *Gaspee* was more a matter of old habits than any indication of a new policy to come. That new approach was not taken until after the Boston Tea Party, and in Massachusetts, not Rhode Island. The charge of treason, the offering of huge rewards, and the appointment of a special commission notwithstanding, the North ministry did not pull out all the stops to punish Rhode Island and put someone on trial.

Although Hillsborough and Dartmouth did not think that Rhode Island authorities could be trusted to investigate the *Gaspee* incident, they gave no plenary powers to their special commission, they named Joseph Wanton to it despite Hillsborough's distrust of the governor, and they made the commission dependent on Rhode Island law officers and politicians to get anything done. Before expressing amazement at all of this, we should remember that when another ministry had sent troops to Boston to quell civil disturbances four years earlier, those troops did not have a mandate to patrol the town; they had to rely on provincial officials to define their responsibilities. In 1772, as in 1768, the boundaries of imperial law and local law were still being drawn.

If Wedderburn and Thurlow had been clear in their August 1772 opinion that the attack on the *Gaspee* had been high treason, they were ambiguous on the question of jurisdiction. The offenders, these law officers determined, could be indicted "either here or in Rhode Island taking that Assertion of the Governor to be true that the Ship was stationed within the Body of some County in that Province." In strictly legal terms there is nothing muddled about such reasoning, but law does not exist in a vacuum. Politically their opinion was too imprecise; if pressed, Rhode Islanders could have seized on it to challenge the validity of any trial held outside the colony.

Convinced that they were legally beyond the reach of the commissioners anyway, three Rhode Island lawyers had considered refusing to appear before them. "We know them not as a Court vested with any legal Power," they wrote to Stephen Hopkins. "The least Notice therefore taken of their Summons would be a partial Acknowledgment of their Jurisdiction," and to "acquiesce" in that "would entail an eternal Infamy on those, who ought to be acquainted with the Principles of the Constitution." Their ringing condemnation of the commission disturbed and worried Hopkins. His fierce words to the General Assembly notwithstanding, Hopkins preferred a flanking movement to a frontal assault. He urged the three to muffle their objections. The lawyers went through the motions of cooperating and wrote notes to the commissioners, but they did not go to Newport in January 1773. John Andrews, the vice-admiralty justice, gave a similar response. As a Rhode Islander first, a royal appointee second, he stayed home in Providence.

No imperial official ever pieced together what happened on the *Gaspee*, nor has any historian since. There are many unreconciled differences and large gaps in the record. Had the *Gaspee* simply run aground while pursuing the packet *Hannah*, as was claimed by the *Providence Gazette* at the time, and by two of the self-professed boarders many years later? Dudingston said he had heard that one of the boarders was killed; no one else said anything of the kind. Who was right? Of even greater interest, did someone call out to Dudingston and say he had a warrant for the lieutenant's arrest? Did he in fact have one and then tear it up the next day after talking with Darius Sessions? Or did the boarders, with no warrant, blacken their faces and row with muffled oars, intent on destroying the schooner regardless of the consequences? Who were the boarders, and how many local officials were involved in the subsequent cover-up? Would Rhode Islanders, led by their governor, have taken up arms to prevent anyone from being transferred to England for trial? These and many other questions are left unanswered. Until they are, we will not know what the men who boarded the *Gaspee* intended to do and, therefore, how daring they actually were or what role their understanding of law played in their decisions.

Even so, we can use the *Gaspee* affair to illustrate the vagaries of the past as well as the underlying problems of empire. And regardless of the indefinite information that was gathered after the affair, the destruction of the *Gaspee* and the appointment of a royal commission to investigate it had a most definite impact on the Revolutionary movement. What happened on the *Gaspee* was a mystery to four members of the commission that investigated the matter; it remains a mystery to us now, albeit for rather different reasons. It is, perhaps, a mystery that will never be solved.

The *Gaspee* raiders planned their caper at Sabin's Tavern at the corner of South Main and Planet streets in Providence. The historic structure, shown in this 1870s photo, was demolished in 1891.

10

Because Patrick Conley, the author of this essay, served as volunteer chairman of the state commission to celebrate the bicentennial of the Constitution, the article that follows had many settings: as a copiously illustrated booklet, as a contribution to the *Rhode Island Bar Journal*, as an article in *Rhode Island History*, and as a chapter in the author's book *The Constitution and the States: The Role of the Original Thirteen in the Framing and Adoption of the Federal Constitution* (with Dr. John P. Kaminski).

The role of the original states in the creation of the national government is often minimized by late-twentieth-century political writers and theorists, but this view is perplexing when one considers certain facts associated with the founding of the federal government. It was the states that dispatched delegates to Philadelphia, where the framers voted not as individuals but as members of their state delegations. For example, when two of New York's three representatives—Robert Yates and John Lansing, Jr.—departed early from the convention, New York was left without a quorum, and Alexander Hamilton was left without the power to register his state's approval of the final draft. With Rhode Island absent, the unanimous declaration thus had only eleven, rather than thirteen, affirmative votes. And when the thirty-nine signers affixed their names to the famous document, they did not sign randomly, but by state delegation in a north-to-south succession—New Hampshire to Georgia. The clause introducing those signatures reads, "Done in Convention by the Unanimous Consent of the States present."

Despite the famous phrase "We the People," the Constitution was not ratified by national plebiscite or local referenda, but by state-called ratifying conventions. According to the provisions of Article VII, the document became operative only when nine states had given their approval.

In the state ratifying conventions, especially that of Rhode Island, the major concerns of opponents were the threats that the new basic law posed to existing state sovereignty and its failure to include a bill of rights. When amendments were drafted to deal with these alleged defects, the changes required approval by two-thirds of the House of Representatives and passage by a similar margin in the Senate, whose membership was chosen by the state legislatures. That upper chamber, apportioned on the basis of state equality, represented not the people but the states. Then, when the proposed revisions cleared the congressional hurdles, they needed ratification by three-fourths of the states to become part of the basic law of the land.

Not only was the role of the states central in framing, ratifying, and revising the Constitution, but the document itself was permeated with the influence of state constitutions and local precedents. No fewer than eighteen different state constitutions preceded the federal constitution (some states having experimented with more than one basic law by 1787). According to the calculations of historian Donald Lutz, "The states are mentioned explicitly or by direct implication 50 times in 42 separate sections of the U.S. Constitution." Further, Lutz observes, "anyone attempting to do a close textual analysis of the document is driven time and again to the state constitutions to determine what is meant or implied by the national constitution."

The point of this recitation is to show the importance of state action in creating the Constitution and the Bill of Rights. In this era of national supremacy, the key role played by the states is a fact often forgotten by those of us who witnessed the passing of dual federalism. That system, however, is a historic reality that explains why the first century of American constitutionalism was dominated by the struggle between the states and the national government over their relative powers.

Anyone who studies the ratification process will immediately recognize the theme of diversity and realize the inadequacy of simplistic generalizations in explaining the Constitution's origins. Delaware wanted a strong central government to establish order and command respect abroad; Georgia sought security through union; New Jersey and Connecticut desired relief from interstate tariff levies; Pennsylvania, led by its business interests, sought economic stability and commercial growth. Conversely, prosperous New York was content with the existing system; North Carolina wanted to maintain states' rights; and obstinate Rhode Island fought to preserve its liberty and autonomy. Factions, issues, and motives differed from state to state, so when ratification was finally achieved, the new Union could truly be characterized as "one out of many." Such pluralism is still a salient feature of American life.

STATE *of* RHODE-ISLAND, *&c.*

In GENERAL ASSEMBLY, *February Seſſion*, A.D. 1788.

An ACT ſubmitting to the Conſideration of the Freemen of this State, the Report of the Convention of Delegates for a Conſtitution for the United States, as agreed on in Philadelphia, the 17th of September, A. D. 1787.

WHEREAS the Honorable the Continental Congreſs did heretofore recommend to the Legiſlatures of the reſpective States, to appoint Delegates to meet in Convention, at Philadelphia, in May, A. D. 1787, to make ſuch Alterations and Amendments in the preſent Confederation of the United States as would tend to promote the Happineſs, good Government and Welfare of the Federal Union: And whereas the ſaid Delegates, on the 17th Day of September, 1787, did agree upon, and report to the Congreſs of the United States, a Form of a Conſtitution for the United States of America: And whereas the ſaid United States in Congreſs aſſembled did, by a Reſolution paſſed the 28th Day of September, A. D. 1787, tranſmit ſaid Report to the Legiſlature of this State, to be ſubmitted to the Conſideration of the People thereof: And whereas this Legiſlative Body, in General Aſſembly convened, conceiving themſelves Repreſentatives of the great Body of People at large, and that they cannot make any Innovations in a Conſtitution which has been agreed upon, and the Compact ſettled between the Governors and Governed, without the expreſs Conſent of the Freemen at large, by their own Voices individually taken in Town-Meetings aſſembled: Wherefore, for the Purpoſe aforeſaid, and for ſubmitting the ſaid Conſtitution for the United States to the Conſideration of the Freemen of this State:

BE it Enacted by this General Aſſembly, and by the Authority thereof it is hereby Enacted, That the Fourth Monday in March inſt. be, and the ſame is hereby appointed, the Day for all the Freemen and Freeholders within this State, to convene in their reſpective Towns, in Town-Meetings aſſembled, and to deliberate upon, and determine each Individual (who hath a Right by Law to vote for the Choice of General Officers) by himſelf by Poll, whether the ſaid Conſtitution for the United States ſhall be adopted or negatived.

AND be it further Enacted by the Authority aforeſaid, That the Town-Clerks in the reſpective Towns ſhall forthwith iſſue their Warrants, for the convening of the Freemen and Freeholders to meet, on ſaid Fourth Monday of March inſt. at ſuch Place where the Town-Meetings are uſually holden: And the ſame ſhall be directed to the Town-Serjeants and Conſtables of the reſpective Towns, who ſhall cauſe Notifications to be ſet up in the moſt public Places of Reſort within ſuch Towns; and alſo ſhall repair to the uſual Place of Abode of the Freemen and Freeholders in ſuch Town, and give them Notice of the Meeting aforeſaid, for the Purpoſe aforeſaid. The ſaid Town-Serjeants and Conſtables to have particular Diſtricts pointed out to them, to warn the Freemen and Freeholders, ſo as not to interfere with each other's Diſtrict, that all the Freemen and Freeholders may, if poſſible, have Notice and attend accordingly. And upon the Convention of ſaid Freemen, they ſhall appoint a Moderator, who ſhall regulate ſuch Meeting; and the Voices of the Freemen and Freeholders ſhall be taken by Yeas and Nays, and the Town-Clerk of each Town ſhall regiſter the Name of each and every Freeman and Freeholder, with the Yea or Nay, as he ſhall reſpectively give his Voice aloud, in open Town-Meeting, and ſhall keep the Original in his Office, and ſhall make out a true and fair certified Copy of the Regiſter aforeſaid, with the Yeas and Nays of each and every Perſon thereon, and carefully ſeal the ſame up, and direct it to the General Aſſembly, to be holden by Adjournment, at Eaſt-Greenwich, in the County of Kent, on the laſt Monday of March inſt. and deliver the ſame to One of the Repreſentatives of ſuch Town, or other careful Perſon, who will take Charge of the ſame, to be delivered to the ſaid General Aſſembly, then and there to be opened, that the Sentiments of the People may be known reſpecting the ſame.

AND it is further Enacted by the Authority aforeſaid, That in Caſe it ſhall ſo happen that the ſaid Fourth Monday of March inſt. ſhall prove to be ſtormy or boiſterous Weather, ſo that the Freemen and Freeholders in general cannot conveniently attend, the ſaid Town-Meeting may adjourn, from Day to Day, not exceeding three Days, ſo that the Voices of the People may be taken.

AND it is further Enacted by the Authority aforeſaid, That the Secretary ſhall forthwith tranſmit to each Town-Clerk of the reſpective Towns within this State a Copy of this Act.

A true Copy:

Witneſs, HENRY WARD, *Secretary.*

[PROVIDENCE: Printed by BENNETT WHEELER.]

This call by the General Assembly authorized the only popular referendum on the federal Constitution conducted by any state.

First in War, Last in Peace: Rhode Island and the Constitution, 1786–1790

Patrick T. Conley

Founded in 1636 by Roger Williams and his associates upon the principles of religious liberty and separation of church and state, seventeenth-century Rhode Island became a haven for radical Protestant sects, especially Baptists, Antinomians, and Quakers, and persecuted religious refugees, such as Portuguese Jews and French Huguenots. The colony, dubbed a "moral sewer" by orthodox and intolerant Massachusetts Puritans, developed a dissenting tradition and prided itself on being "the home of the otherwiseminded." During its early years Rhode Island repeatedly fought off attempts by land-grabbing and resentful neighbors to reduce its already diminutive size.

To guarantee its legal right to exist, Dr. John Clarke secured for the colony an extraordinarily liberal charter from King Charles II in 1663. Not only did this document proclaim "full liberty in religious concernments," but it also set up a self-governing commonwealth wherein all local officials, from the governor and assemblymen to the viewer of fences and the corder of wood, were either chosen directly in town meeting by the freemen (i.e., those qualified to vote on the basis of residency, age, sex, religion, and land ownership) or appointed on an annual basis by the elected representatives of the people.

No other English colony possessed such a refreshing combination of religious freedom and local self-government. This condition persisted throughout the colonial era, evoking criticism from English observers. On the eve of the War of Independence, Chief Justice Daniel Horsmanden of New York, investigating the burning of the British revenue ship *Gaspee* by Providence dissidents, disdainfully described Rhode Island as a "downright democracy" whose governmental officials were "entirely controlled by the populace," and conservative Massachusetts governor Thomas Hutchinson lamented to George III that Rhode Island was "the nearest to a democracy of any of your colonies."

Rhode Islanders of the Revolutionary generation and their individualistic forebears were themselves ever mindful that they enjoyed near autonomy within the empire and broad powers of self-government within their colony. They were also keenly aware that their self-determination flowed in large measure from the generous charter of Charles II. Thus they harbored a passionate attachment to that document and stoutly defended it against all comers. They allowed it to weather the Revolutionary upheaval (when eleven colonies discarded their English charters) and retained it as the basic law of the state until 1843, a point far beyond its useful life. Most Rhode Islanders apparently shared the opinion of attorney and educator David Howell, who in 1782, while serving as one of the state's popularly elected delegates to the Confederation Congress, made the following boast: "As you go Southward, Government verges towards Aristocracy. In New England alone have we pure and unmixed Democracy and in Rhode Island... it is in its perfection."

Rhode Island was a leader in the American Revolutionary movement. Having the greatest degree of self-rule, it had the most to lose from the efforts of England after 1763 to increase her supervision and control over the American colonies. In addition, Rhode Island had a long tradition of evading the poorly enforced Navigation Acts, and smuggling was commonplace.

Beginning with strong opposition in Newport to the Sugar Act (1764), with its restrictions on the molasses trade, the colony engaged in repeated measures of open defiance, such as the scuttling and torching of the British customs sloop *Liberty* in Newport harbor in July 1769, the burning of the British revenue schooner *Gaspee* on Warwick's Namquit Point in 1772, and Providence's own "Tea Party" in Market Square on March 2, 1775.

On May 17, 1774, after parliamentary passage of the Coercive Acts (Americans called them "Intolerable"), the Providence Town Meeting became the first governmental assemblage to issue a call for a general congress of colonies to resist British policy. A month later, on June 15, the General Assembly made the colony the first to appoint delegates (Samuel Ward and Stephen Hopkins) to the anticipated Continental Congress.

A week after the skirmishes at Lexington and Concord in April 1775, the colonial legislature authorized a fifteen-hundred-man "army of observation" with Nathanael Greene as its commander. Finally, on May 4, 1776, Rhode Island became the first colony to renounce allegiance to King George III when its legislature, sitting at Providence, passed a bold renunciation act. On July 18, meeting at Newport, the Assembly ratified the Declaration of Independence.

Surprisingly, Rhode Island's initial response to a plan for a permanent central government was cordial. Such a proposal was advanced by the ad hoc Continental Congress in 1777 and embodied in the instrument known as the Articles of Confederation. The Articles were drafted, debated by the Congress, and placed before the rebellious states in November 1777. Delegate Henry Marchant of Newport bore this first national constitution to Rhode Island and urged its acceptance at a special session of the General Assembly in December. The question of adoption was deferred to the February 1778 session, and at that conclave the state gave the Articles its unanimous assent. Three amendments were suggested, but these were merely recommendations and not prerequisites for ratification.

Rhode Island was so uncharacteristically obliging because several of its towns were under British

This May 4, 1776, act renouncing allegiance to King George III (but not declaring independence) kept Rhode Island in the vanguard of the Revolutionary movement.

An Act repealing an Act, entitled, "An Act for the more effectual securing to his Majesty the Allegiance of his Subjects, in this his Colony and Dominion of Rhode Island and Providence Plantations, and altering the Form of Commiſſions, of all Writs, Proceſſes in Courts, &c.

AN ACT repealing an Act, intitled, "*An Act for the more effectually ſecuring to his Majeſty the Allegiance of his Subjects, in this his Colony and Dominion of* Rhode-Iſland *and* Providence Plantations;" and altering the Forms of Commiſſions, of all Writs and Proceſſes in the Courts, and of the Oaths preſcribed by Law.

WHEREAS in all States, exiſting by Compact, Protection and Allegiance are reciprocal, the latter being only due in Conſequence of the former: And whereas *GEORGE* the Third, King of *Great-Britain*. forgetting his Dignity, regardleſs of the Compact moſt ſolemnly entered into, ratified and confirmed, to the Inhabitants of this Colony, by His illuſtrious Anceſtors, and till of late fully recognized by Him--and entirely departing from the Duties and Character of a good King, inſtead of protecting, is endeavouring to deſtroy the good People of this Colony, and of all the United Colonies, by ſending Fleets and Armies to *America*, to confiſcate our Property, and ſpread Fire, Sword and Deſolation, throughout our Country, in order to compel us to ſubmit occupation and because it had incurred enormous military expenditures which might be partially absorbed by the new central government. Rhode Island instructed its delegates to ratify the Articles if eight other states should do so, and in the event that any alterations were advanced, these delegates were empowered to accept whatever changes were approved by nine of the states. Rhode Island further promised that it would be bound by any alterations agreed to in this manner by its delegation. No changes were made in the Articles, however, and the state's representatives unhesitatingly signed the form of ratification in Philadelphia on July 9, 1778, hailing the document as "the Grand Corner Stone" of the new nation.

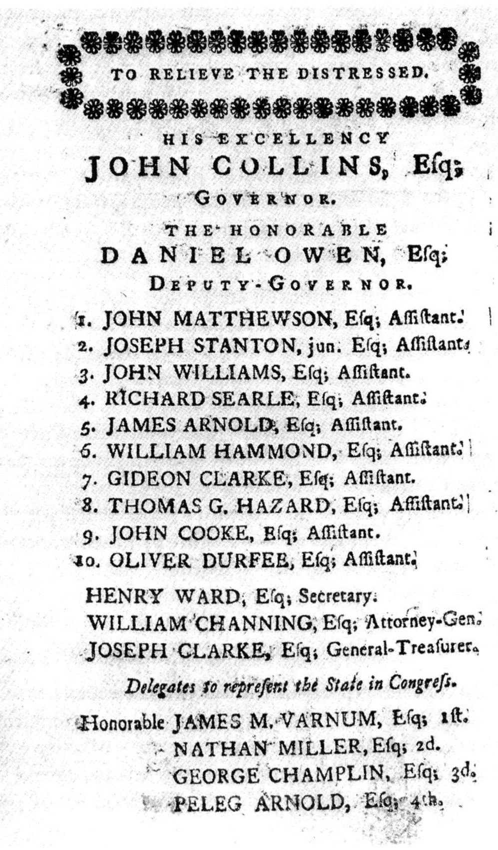

TO RELIEVE THE DISTRESSED.

HIS EXCELLENCY
JOHN COLLINS, Esq;
GOVERNOR.

THE HONORABLE
DANIEL OWEN, Esq;
DEPUTY-GOVERNOR.

1. JOHN MATTHEWSON, Esq; Assistant.
2. JOSEPH STANTON, jun. Esq; Assistant.
3. JOHN WILLIAMS, Esq; Assistant.
4. RICHARD SEARLE, Esq; Assistant.
5. JAMES ARNOLD, Esq; Assistant.
6. WILLIAM HAMMOND, Esq; Assistant.
7. GIDEON CLARKE, Esq; Assistant.
8. THOMAS G. HAZARD, Esq; Assistant.
9. JOHN COOKE, Esq; Assistant.
10. OLIVER DURFEE, Esq; Assistant.

HENRY WARD, Esq; Secretary.
WILLIAM CHANNING, Esq; Attorney-Gen.
JOSEPH CLARKE, Esq; General-Treasurer.

Delegates to represent the State in Congress.

Honorable JAMES M. VARNUM, Esq; 1st.
NATHAN MILLER, Esq; 2d.
GEORGE CHAMPLIN, Esq; 3d.
PELEG ARNOLD, Esq; 4th.

In April 1786 the newly formed Country party advanced this slate in its successful campaign to overthrow the mercantile leadership of the General Assembly and embark upon a paper-money plan "to relieve the distressed."

In the succeeding twelve years Rhode Island would seldom act with such compliance toward the federal union. In fact, Rhode Island exhibited an obstinacy in the national council which proved exasperating to many of its sister states. Its initial contrariness consisted in a flat rejection of the proposed Continental Impost (or tariff) of 1781, despite the efforts of Thomas Paine and other prominent figures to enlist the state's support. Rhode Island's most blatant demonstration of defiance was its repeated refusal to ratify the federal Constitution of 1787.

An acquaintance with the political setting in which Rhode Island's contest over the Constitution took place is essential to an understanding of the ratification controversy. The principal political fact of life was the dominance in state affairs of the so-called Country Party. This faction, led mainly by legislators from the rural and agrarian towns, had swept into power in the annual spring elections of 1786 on a paper-money platform. The victory constituted somewhat of a political revolution because it transformed the legislature from a merchant-dominated body to one in which the interests of the farmer took precedence.

The Country Party made good its campaign pledge and immediately authorized the issuance of £100,000 ($333,000) in paper money. Historians now realize that the primary purpose of the paper emission was to alleviate the tax burden which weighed heavily on the owners of real property, and that the payment of private debts in paper was merely an incidental byproduct of this successful program. However, contemporary creditors and many members of the state's mercantile community were not so well informed, and thus paper money was a chief source of controversy in local politics from 1786 through 1791. It engendered the dispute which precipitated the landmark court case of *Trevett* v. *Weeden*, and it served as the bond of union for the dominant Country Party—an organization which opposed the ratification of the Constitution of 1787.

With the exception of its response to the Annapolis Convention of September 1786, Rhode Island exhibited a wariness towards all attempts

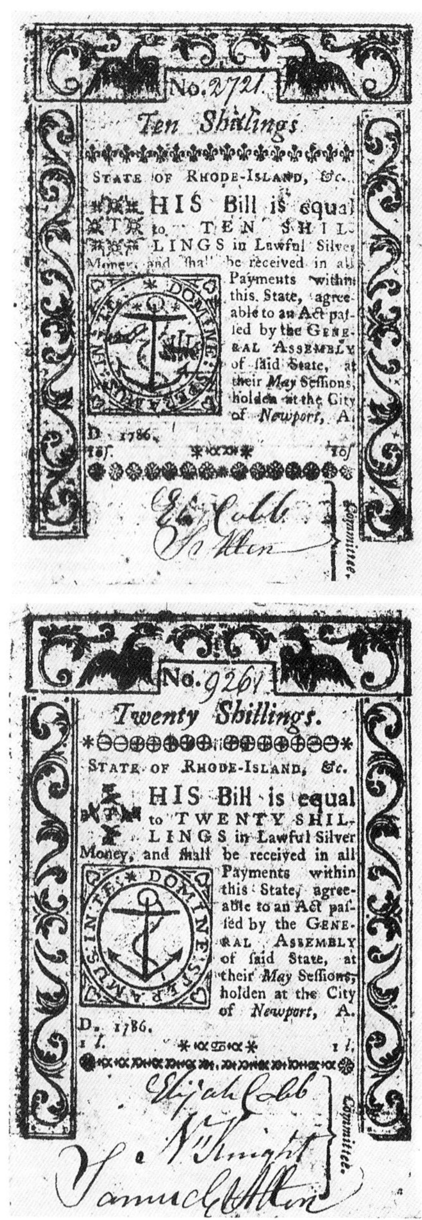

The Country party issued these paper-money bills in 1786 to fulfill its campaign pledge. The act forcing acceptance of the bills led to the famous court case of *Trevett* v. *Weeden* (1786). Paper-money advocates delayed action on the Constitution because of its ban on such state bills.

at forming a stronger central government. Just prior to that Maryland gathering, the state had expressed a desire to secure uniform and centralized regulation of commerce to protect its reexport trade from the tariffs of her neighboring states. Because that important but limited action was the only topic on the proposed agenda at Annapolis, Rhode Island dispatched two delegates. These commissioners, Jabez Bowen and Samuel Ward, Jr., had journeyed as far south as Philadelphia when they received news that the abortive four-day conclave had adjourned.

In the following year, when a call was issued for a more broadly empowered convention to discuss all matters necessary "to render the constitution of the Federal government adequate to the exigencies of the Union," the Country Party was firmly entrenched. Consequently, the state failed to vote on the February 1787 resolution of the Confederation Congress to hold the Philadelphia Convention, and when that momentous assembly convened, Rhode Island was the only state to boycott its proceedings. Three times an attempt to dispatch delegates was rejected by the suspicious General Assembly. Rhode Island's absence was protested both by the deputies (i.e., state representatives) from Providence and Newport and by General James Mitchell Varnum and Peleg Arnold, the state's delegates in Congress, but to no avail.

On September 15, 1787, just prior to the completion of the federal convention, Country Party governor John Collins offered to the president of the Confederation Congress Rhode Island's feeble excuse for nonattendance at the Philadelphia sessions. Collins declared that since the freemen at large had the power of electing delegates to represent them in Congress, the legislature could not consistently appoint delegates to a convention which might be the means of dissolving that Congress. In view of the broad power which the Rhode Island legislature was accustomed to exercise, Collins's remarks seemed evasive indeed. A spirited rejoinder signed by the Newport and Providence deputies reminded the governor that the General Assembly had dispatched delegates to the Continental Congress, ratified the Declaration of Independence, and accepted the Articles of Confederation without a popular referendum. Their arguments, though sound, were fruitless.

When the federal convention completed its labors on September 17, 1787, it transmitted the Constitution to Congress with the recommendation that the document be submitted to the states for ratification by popularly elected conventions. Congress (with Rhode Island absent) complied with this suggestion and gave the states official notice of its action.

The Rhode Island legislature took the new Constitution under advisement at its October 1787 session. It thereupon voted for the distribution of a thousand copies of the proposed document to allow the freemen "an opportunity of forming their sentiments" upon it. This approach was consistent with the Country Party's practice of governing by referendum.

With most of the freemen thus apprised of the federal charter's contents, the February 1788 session assembled. Then, to the consternation of Federalists within the state and without, the Assembly authorized a popular vote on the Constitution and scheduled it for the fourth Monday in

March. This ratification procedure was irregular and contrary to the recommendations of the Philadelphia delegates, but the legislature was not deterred by this departure from the norm. In fact, the February session specifically rejected a motion to call a ratifying convention. Over the course of the next twenty-three months, a total of eleven such efforts would be spurned.

The popular referendum on the Constitution was held according to schedule. Although the result was predictable—243 for and 2,711 against—the margin of defeat is deceptive. The Federal port towns of Providence and Newport boycotted the referendum; just one vote was cast in the former community and only eleven were registered in Newport, and these ballots, with one exception (in Newport), were cast by Antifederalists. The only towns in the Federalist column were the bay settlements of Bristol (26–23) and Little Compton (63–57). The critics of the Constitution, however, registered lopsided victories in many rural communities, among them Glocester (228–9), Coventry (180–0), Foster (177–0), and Scituate (156–0).

The total vote in this referendum was 2,954, as compared with the 4,287 who had voted in the well-contested gubernatorial election of 1787. Newport and Providence accounted for most of the abstainers, for these towns, according to fairly reliable estimates, together had between 825 and 900 freemen in 1788. Yet it is obvious that even if these communities had turned out en masse for the Constitution, it would have been rejected by an impressive plurality. Eight weeks later New Hampshire became the ninth state to ratify the federal document, but despite the rejoicing over this event in Providence, the chances that Rhode Island would follow the lead of her more amenable brethren seemed extremely remote. Antifederal sentiment ran high. On the Fourth of July 1788, some Antifederalists even formed a mob to prevent Providence Federalists from celebrating the progress of ratification.

During the early summer of 1788, the crucial states of Virginia and New York also fell in line, but Rhode Island was unrelenting. In March 1789, as the new federal government prepared to convene, the General Assembly for a fifth time rejected a motion to call a ratifying convention. In May the issue was sidestepped, and in the June and October sessions it was rejected again.

The only other holdout at this late date was North Carolina, a state which, like Rhode Island, was settled by outcasts and was noted for its individualism and separatist tendencies. On November 21, 1789, the Carolinians at last capitulated and left Rhode Island alone and, in effect, an independent republic.

As the year 1790 dawned, the pressures on the Antifederalists increased, and the prospects for at least a convention grew brighter. The opponents of the Constitution had shown signs of wavering in the early October session when they voted to print and distribute among the towns 150 copies of the twelve amendments to the Constitution which had been recommended by the new Congress of the United States. Ten of these would become the Bill of Rights.

State of Rhode-Iſland and Providence-Plantations.

In GENERAL ASSEMBLY.

January Seſſion, A. D. 1790.

An ACT *for calling a* CONVENTION, *to take into Conſideration the Conſtitution propoſed for the United States, paſſed on the 17th of* September, *A. D.* 1787, *by the* GENERAL CONVENTION *held at* Philadelphia.

B*E it Enacted by this General Aſſembly, and by the Authority thereof it is hereby Enacted,* That the New Conſtitution propoſed for the United States, paſſed on the 17th of *September*, A.D. 1787, by the GENERAL CONVENTION held at *Philadelphia*, be ſubmitted to the People of this State, repreſented in a STATE CONVENTION, for their full and free Inveſtigation and Deciſion, agreeably to the Reſolve of the ſaid Convention: That it be recommended to the Freemen of the ſeveral Towns, qualified to vote in the Election of Deputies to the General Aſſembly, to convene in their reſpective Towns, in legal Town-Meeting, on the Second *Monday* in *February* next; and then to chooſe the ſame Number of Delegates as they are entitled to elect Deputies, to repreſent them in the ſaid Convention: And that the ſaid Convention be holden at *South-Kingſtown*, on the Firſt *Monday* in *March* next.

And be it further Enacted by the Authority aforeſaid, That the ſaid Convention be and hereby is empowered, and fully authorized, finally to decide on the ſaid Conſtitution, as they ſhall judge to be moſt conducive to the Intereſts of the People of this State: And that the ſaid Convention cauſe the Reſult of their Deliberations and Proceedings, relative to the aforeſaid Conſtitution, to be tranſmitted to the PRESIDENT of the United States of *America*, as ſoon after the Riſing thereof as may be.

It is Voted and Reſolved, That his Excellency the Governor be and he is hereby requeſted, to tranſmit a Copy of this Act to the Preſident of the ſaid United States immediately.

It is Ordered, That the Secretary cauſe Copies hereof to be tranſmitted to each Town-Clerk in the State, without the leaſt Delay.

A true Copy:

Witneſs, HENRY WARD, *Sec'ry.*

PRINTED BY *J. CARTER.*

Attorney Henry Marchant sponsored this January 1790 act to call a ratifying convention. When Governor John Collins supported it, his Country party repudiated him.

In the January session the Federalist minority was further encouraged when the legislature, after two unsuccessful efforts, narrowly passed a bill, introduced by Henry Marchant, authorizing a ratification convention to meet on March 1, 1790, at South Kingstown. Four-term governor John Collins, who was always cool towards Antifederalism, courageously incurred the wrath of his own Country Party when he cast the deciding vote on Marchant's measure and broke a 4–4 Senate deadlock. He was not renominated by his political associates.

The election of delegates for this convention went unfavorably in the view of Marchant, a Newport Federalist. Two weeks before the session convened, he prophesied its outcome: "The Antie's are about ten majority. I have hopes however they will not totally reject the Constitution, but I think they may adjourn it over our General Election."

Marchant's intuition was correct. The convention met and considered both the Constitution and the twelve amendments thereto proposed by Congress. In addition, it adopted a "declaration of rights" and advanced eighteen other constitutional amendments. These were sent to the freemen for consideration.

The major points of discussion during the six-day March session were the allocation of representatives, direct taxation, the slave trade, the method of adopting future amendments, the ratification of the congressionally proposed Bill of Rights, and the power of the convention to adopt the Constitution. Although some Antifederalists had mellowed, a majority of them were resolved to resist the Constitution to the bitter end. Merchant-prince John Innes Clark, one of the four Federalist delegates from Providence, observed that "we have as determined a set of men to oppose it as ever were combined together." On Saturday, March 6, over the protests of the Federalists, the gathering adjourned until May 24 by a vote of 41–28, a margin which was a fairly accurate indication of the relative strength of the anti- and pro-Constitution factions.

During the interim between sessions the spring elections were conducted, and the Country Party (minus Governor Collins) scored its fifth consecutive victory. At the head of its ticket was Arthur Fenner of the distinguished Providence clan. So formidable and prominent was Fenner and so potent was his party that the Federalists endorsed him rather than arouse the ire of the Country majority on the eve of the ratification convention.

Despite this success and the Antifederal majority of approximately a dozen in the seventy-member convention, several critics of the Constitution were beginning to find their position no longer tenable in the face of increasing pressure from within and without the state. When the ratifying body reconvened, the Constitution's adherents, led by Marchant, Benjamin Bourne of Providence, and William Bradford from the port town of Bristol, pushed vigorously for its acceptance. Finally, after five days of political jousting, Bourne moved (in the words of convention secretary Daniel Updike) "for the grand question of adopting or rejecting the federal government." At 5:20 p.m. on Saturday, May 29, the motion squeaked through by a vote of 34–32.

In the May session of the ratifying convention, attorney Benjamin Bourne (1755–1808) made the crucial motion to conduct a vote on the adoption of the Constitution. In August 1790 this Providence delegate won election as Rhode Island's first United States congressman.

The contest was so close that a full convention might have reversed the decision. The three absent delegates—Edward Hill and Ray Sands, representing remote New Shoreham (Block Island), and Job Durfee of Portsmouth—appear to have been Antifederal, while Country Party chieftain Daniel Owen of Glocester was prevented from voting, except to break a tie, by virtue of his position as convention chairman. The margin of acceptance was narrower than that of any other state, and Rhode Island was one of only three states in which the delegates voting for ratification represented fewer people than those voting against it. But an inch was as good as a mile.

Soon after this momentous action, the formal bill ratifying and adopting the Constitution was approved by the convention. This measure also gave assent to eleven of the twelve amendments to the Constitution proposed by Congress and boldly offered twenty-one additional amendments.

At its June session the General Assembly gave its necessary approval to the Bill of Rights, established procedures for the election of federal senators and representatives, and chose Theodore Foster, a moderate Providence Federalist, and Joseph Stanton, Jr., an Antifederal leader from Charlestown, as Rhode Island's first United States senators. Foster was the brother-in-law of Governor Fenner, a fact which helped him gain the support of the Country Party. When Benjamin Bourne, a champion of the Constitution, won the August contest for the state's lone seat in the House of Representatives, Rhode Island at last became a full participant in the new federal union.

Although the principal events of this turbulent period are fairly discernible, the motives behind Rhode Island's long-term opposition and then grudging acceptance of the Constitution are multiple and complex. Certainly, the paper-money controversy contributed to the state's rejection of the new federal instrument. The Country Party came to power on a pro-paper platform in 1786, and this agrarian faction, led by Jonathan Hazard, Joseph Stanton, Jr., John Collins, Job Comstock, and Daniel Owen, firmly held the reins of political power from May 1786 until well after the reluctant ratification of the national document by Rhode Island in mid-1790. Although the party was not monolithic, it was dominant and cohesive, and the major opposition to the Constitution emanated from its ranks. In Rhode Island the Country Party served as an effective and organized vehicle of Antifederalism.

When the ratification process began, Rhode Island was too deeply enmeshed in the paper-money program to back out, and Article I, Section 10, of the federal document, forbidding states from making anything but gold and silver coin a tender in payment of debts, might have forced her to do so. The financial chaos that would have resulted from the abandonment of the paper program before it had run its course would have made the existing financial situation seem peaceful and orderly by comparison.

Speculating on the possibilities of ratification, William Ellery, Continental loan officer in Newport, several times expressed the view that the Country Party would "wait till they shall have completely extinguished the State debt" before accepting the Constitution. It was Ellery's contention that ratification would not take place before the "accursed paper money system" had run its course.

In Rhode Island there was a definite correlation between the pro-paper towns and those which opposed the Constitution, but Antifederalism and advocacy of paper money were not synonymous. Such an equation admits of too many exceptions and incongruities. Although the same towns and the same individuals who favored the paper money also opposed the Constitution, a comparison of the vote on the constitutional referendum with the votes for the Country Party candidates in 1786 and 1787 seems to indicate that the sentiment against the Constitution was noticeably greater than the normal strength of the Country Party.

In the light of these considerations, we must identify other factors in addition to the currency controversy to adequately understand the intensity of Rhode Island's Antifederalism. Additional economic motives for the state's resistance are strongly in evidence. The most important of these was the fear that exorbitant taxes on land and polls would be levied by the new national government to pay the public debt and the allegedly high salaries of federal officials. Unprecedented and burdensome state taxes on land were in large measure responsible for the paper-money emission, and the landholders' dread of similar federal taxes was to a considerable extent responsible for Rhode Island's opposition to the new federal union.

This apprehension was evidenced by the serious attention the question of direct taxes on land and polls received in the March 1790 ratifying convention. It was further exhibited in three constitutional amendments (VII, VIII, and IX) proposed and approved by that convention. In suggested amendment VII, Rhode Island joined New York in urging that "no capitation or poll tax shall ever be laid by Congress"; in amendment VIII, she joined six sister states in requesting a prohibition on the laying of direct taxes except after the failure of a federal requisition upon the states; and in proposed amendment IX (one of five that were unique to Rhode Island), the state, as an insurance measure, recommended that "Congress shall lay no direct taxes, without the assent of the legislatures of three fourths of the states in the Union."

Of the economic reasons for Rhode Island's reluctance to adopt the Constitution, it would appear that a fear of heavy taxes on land and polls probably influenced more voters than any other single factor. Perhaps former deputy governor Jabez Bowen, a leading Federalist, summed up the situation as well as any contemporary in the following letter to George Washington:

> The Towns of Newport, Providence, Bristol etc. with the whole Mercantile interest in the other Towns in the State are Federal, while

> the Farmers in general are against it. Their opposition arises principally from their being much in Debt, from the Insinuations of wicked and designing Men that they will lose their Liberty in adopting it; that the Salaries of the National Officers are so very high that it will take the whole of the Money Collected by the Impost to pay them, that the Interest and principal of the General Debt must be raised by Dry Taxation on Real Estate, etc.

As Bowen's observation indicates, there were ingredients in Rhode Island's Antifederalism in addition to those of an economic nature. Bowen spoke of the loss of "liberty," which seemed to many a necessary consequence of ratification. A consideration of this pervasive belief brings us into the sphere of what might be termed political, philosophic, or ideological motivations for Rhode Island's suspicion of the proposed federal union, and these motives were of great and, perhaps, transcendent importance.

Rhode Island had a strong tradition of individualism, separatism, democracy, and liberty, both civil and religious. It harbored a long-standing distrust of government too far removed from the people, together with an attachment to popular control of government, that one historian has termed "democratic localism." These principles were not endangered by the Articles of Confederation, to which the state readily assented. The Articles gave the people of a state—or, more precisely, their legislature—close control over delegates to Congress. Under the Confederation, members of Congress were annually appointed in a manner prescribed by the state legislature, they were subject to recall, and they were paid by their respective states. Under the Articles, as in Rhode Island, the executive was weak and the legislature supreme.

In addition to these features, the Articles, of course, exalted state sovereignty. In all important civil matters Congress was dependent upon the voluntary compliance of the state legislatures to carry out its recommendations, and the approval of all states was necessary to amend our inflexible first frame of government.

This system was rejected by the Constitution in ways too familiar to enumerate, and Rhode Island disapproved of the change. Some of her specific objections were contained in the twenty-one amendments to the new federal document offered by the Rhode Island ratifying convention of March 1790. These amendments revealed a deep suspicion of the new central establishment, a suspicion that had been increased by the failure of the proposed Constitution to contain a Bill of Rights.

Rhode Island's first suggested amendment requested a guarantee to each state of its sovereignty and of every power not expressly delegated to the United States by the Constitution; amendment II attempted to limit federal interference in a state's conduct of congressional elections; amendment XII prohibited as "dangerous to liberty" standing armies in time of peace; amendments XIII and XIV called for a two-thirds vote of those present in each house to borrow money on the credit of the United States or to declare war; amendment XVIII subjected senators to recall and replacement by their state legislature. Rhode Island was so fearful that the newly created federal system would develop beyond control that it offered a unique amendment (IV) which would have required all changes in the Constitution after 1793 to receive the consent of eleven of the thirteen original states. Those congressionally advanced amendments which eventually became the Bill of Rights, of course, won the state's support.

In an official communication to Congress in September 1789, the General Assembly quite adequately and accurately expressed the ideological basis of the state's Antifederalism:

> The people of this State from its first settlement, have been accustomed and strongly attached to a democratic form of government. They have viewed in the new Constitution an approach, though perhaps but small, toward that form of government from which we have lately dissolved our connection at so much hazard and expense of life and treasure.... We are sensible of the extremes to which democratic governments are sometimes liable, something of which we have lately experienced, but we esteem them temporary and partial evils compared with the loss of liberty and the rights of a free people.

This was not mere rhetoric. Just as Rhode Islanders were quick to protest an alleged abridgement by England of their individual and collective freedom, so also did they resist an anticipated curtailment of their "liberty" and autonomy by the Founding Fathers. Self-determination in late eighteenth-century Rhode Island was a way of life, and no portion of it would be easily surrendered, as the contest over ratification dramatically revealed.

Another formidable factor contributing to the strength of the state's Antifederalism was a strong hostility toward slavery—a hostility that pervaded the state. This attitude was intense among Rhode Island's sizable Quaker community, but it was shared by others as well, perhaps to atone for past sins. Opponents of slavery realized that the Philadelphia Convention had compromised on this issue, and they were aware that the Constitution thrice gave implied assent to the institution through the clauses on representation, fugitives, and the slave trade. In particular, the twenty-year prohibition on federal legislation banning the foreign slave traffic was a concession too great for many Rhode Islanders to accept.

Only five weeks after the adjournment of the Philadelphia conclave, the General Assembly passed an act, initiated by the influential and irrepressible Quakers, prohibiting any Rhode Island citizen from engaging in the slave trade. In vigorous language, this statute termed the nefarious traffic "inconsistent with justice, and the principles of humanity, as well as the laws of nature, and that more enlightened and civilized sense of freedom which has of late prevailed." A constitution which gave temporary protection to this trade was not an instrument to be warmly embraced.

Thus the state's antislavery contingent took refuge in Antifederalism, and during the critical year 1790 this connection nearly thwarted ratification. Fortunately, however, there were some abolitionist leaders who began to see the difficulties inherent in Rhode Island's continued rejection of the Constitution. One such man was the influential Quaker Moses Brown of the famous mercantile family. Despite some initial misgivings, he embraced the Federalist cause by 1790. Early in that fateful year Brown toured the state, talking with Friends at the various monthly meetings in an attempt to overcome their opposition. His campaign seems to have met with limited success, but the antislavery objections to the Constitution were by no means dispelled when the March session of the ratifying convention assembled.

Slavery engendered much discussion and debate at this South Kingstown meeting. In fact, the slave-trade provision of the Constitution provoked such opposition that an amendment (XVII) was specifically proposed and approved exhorting Congress to ban the traffic immediately. Rhode Island was the only state to suggest such an amendment to the federal Constitution during the ratification struggle.

Some local opponents of slavery doggedly maintained their Antifederalism until the end. When the Providence Abolition Society, founded in February 1789, received its charter from the state in June 1790, the list of incorporators revealed that ten of its signers were members of the May ratifying convention. The antislaveryites included President Daniel Owen and Antifederal floor leaders Joseph Stanton, Jr., and Job Comstock. Only three of these ten abolitionist delegates voted to accept the federal document on May 29.

Finally, Rhode Island's hostility toward the Union was conditioned in part by the Union's hostility to Rhode Island. Since the days of Roger Williams, when Rhode Island was dubbed a moral sewer by her haughty Puritan neighbors, the state had been subjected to the slings and arrows of outraged "foreigners." In the decade of the 1780s, however, this abuse from without reached unprecedented proportions. Beginning with Rhode Island's initial rejection of the Impost of 1781 and continuing through the paper-money era, the state and its citizens were subjected to an endless stream of invective. Rhode Island newspapers of the day were replete with verbal barbs reprinted from distant presses. The Confederation Congress attempted to unseat Rhode Island delegate David Howell for his strenuous opposition to the impost; later, after the paper-money issue, the state was caricatured as the "Quintessence of Villainy" and as an example of "democracy run rampant." Such harsh actions and words of condescending "foreign" critics were most distressing to Rhode Islanders.

During the Constitution-making process the Federalists took Rhode Island to task. For them the state symbolized the danger to order posed by popularly controlled state legislatures. From the outset, when the *Massachusetts Sentinel* described Rhode Island's absence from the Grand Convention as a "joyous rather than a grievous" circumstance, to the end of the ratification struggle, when some proposed the state's dismemberment and absorption by the surrounding states, Rhode Island endured repeated insult. Even the temperate James Madison found Rhode Island exasperating. "Nothing can exceed the wickedness and folly which continue to rule there," he exclaimed. "All sense of character as well as of right have been obliterated."

The most eloquent censure of all came from Connecticut, from the pens of a foursome who later joined a group of literati known as the Connecticut Wits. Their contribution to Rhode Island's litany of shame was a long poetical satire entitled the "Anarchiad, 1786–1787."

> Hail! realm of rogues, renown'd for fraud and guile,
> All hail; ye knav'ries of yon little isle.
> There prowls the rascal, cloth'd with legal pow'r,
> To snare the orphan, and the poor devour;
> The crafty knave his creditor besets,
> And advertising paper pays his debts;
> Bankrupts their creditors, with rage pursue,
> No stop, no mercy from the debtor crew.
> Arm'd with new tests, the licens'd villain bold,
> Presents his bills, and robs them of their gold;
> Their ears, though rogues and counterfeiters lose,
> No legal robber fears the gallows noose.
> . . . .
> Each weekly print new lists of cheats proclaims,
> Proud to enroll their knav'ries and their names;
> The wiser race, the snares of law to shun,
> Like Lot from Sodom, from Rhode Island run.

These derisive epithets caused anger and resentment in Rhode Island. They produced a banding together of the citizenry, especially in the country towns, against the outside agitators. The Federalists won few friends in Rhode Island with their abusive tirades.

As the foregoing discussion reveals, Rhode Island's opposition to the Constitution stemmed primarily from an adherence to the paper-money program, aversion to direct taxation, attachment to "liberty" and the principles of direct democracy, a detestation of slavery, and adverse reaction to "foreign" criticism. These obstacles for a time seemed insuperable. However, there were countervailing forces at work in this era which eventually produced a tenuous triumph for the cause of Federalism.

Several of these forces were operative from the inception of the controversy; others developed gradually as the tides of change left Rhode Island high and dry outside the Union. From the outset, the existence within the state of Continental Loan Office certificates (i.e., U.S. government bonds) in the face amount of $524,000 provided an important source of support for a new, more stable and fiscally responsible national government that could honor its debts. The major repositories for these securities, Providence and Newport, were also the major strongholds of Federalism.

Ratification would benefit not only those private creditors of the national government who held these certificates but a number of the coastal towns as well. Exposed communities such as Newport, Middletown, Portsmouth, Jamestown, Tiverton, Little Compton, Bristol, and Warren held substantial claims against the United States for war damages. Newport, Middletown, and Portsmouth, in fact, had audited claims amounting to $719,280 out of a state total of $899,100. The establishment of a government with effective taxing power would enhance their chances for compensation, but it appears from the slow conversion of these communities

(Newport and Bristol, of course, excepted) that the claims were a peripheral rather than a decisive consideration.

The mercantile community favored ratification because it had come to realize the importance of unified national control over interstate and foreign commerce. The proliferation of interstate tariffs and the failure of the Confederation diplomats to secure commercial treaties with such important nations as England and Spain as a result of the Articles' weakness in the area of commercial regulation would be remedied by the new Constitution. Effective central direction and encouragement of commerce, the merchants felt, would enhance the state's economy and their personal fortunes as well.

Finally, ratification presented the prospect of a protective tariff to the small but growing and influential class of mechanics and incipient industrialists who were concentrated mainly in Providence. In the spring of 1789 the newly created Providence Association of Mechanics and Manufacturers appointed a committee of correspondence to dispatch circular letters to similar groups in other states lamenting Rhode Island's obstructionism and expressing an "anxious desire and fervent prayer that this State may speedily take measures to be reunited under the Federal Head and thereby enjoy the benefits [presumably in the form of a protective tariff] of that Government."

John Howland, a Providence civic leader, wrote a detailed account of Rhode Island's ratification struggle in his published memoirs. He was active in the formation of the Providence Association of Mechanics and Manufacturers, a group that supported the Constitution because it provided for national regulation of commerce.

As of March 1788, these economic factors notwithstanding, the only Federalist communities were Providence, Newport, and Bristol, the state's principal seaports, plus the coastal town of Little Compton. Certain developments in 1789 and 1790, however, gradually swung the bay towns of Portsmouth, Middletown, Tiverton, Jamestown, Warren, and Barrington into the Federal camp. These were joined by Westerly, a minor port and shipbuilding town on the southwestern coast.

Surprisingly, Hopkinton, Westerly's adjacent but interior neighbor to the north, made a last-minute switch to Federalism, as did inland but shipbuilding Cumberland on the Blackstone River in the state's northeastern corner. Warwick, an agrarian town on the upper bay, had its delegation evenly split in the May 1790 convention.

Among the factors accounting for the slow attrition in the Antifederal ranks were the incessant labors of the Federalist press, which dramatized the need for union. Notable propagandists for adoption were Bennett Wheeler's *United States Chronicle* (Providence), John Carter's *Providence Gazette*, and Peter Edes's *Newport Herald*.

In addition, Rhode Island felt increasingly isolated as the inexorable ratification movement toppled the opposition in state after state. George Washington's snub of Rhode Island during his triumphal New England tour in the fall of 1789 emphasized its ostracism. The state's isolation was further accentuated, and Rhode Island wavered markedly, after North Carolina ratified in November 1789.

The proposal by Congress of a Bill of Rights, coupled with the state's submission of its own amendments, gave the Federalist cause a perceptible lift and deprived the "Antis" of a formidable objection, while the prestige and integrity of the new federal officials, especially President Washington, lessened the fears and suspicions Antifederalists harbored toward the new governmental system. Moses Brown, for example, persuasively argued that the nature of the government would depend more upon the caliber of the men who were sent to administer it than on the Constitution itself.

A severe jolt was delivered to the Antifederalists when Providence threatened to secede from the state unless Rhode Island joined the Union. This drastic but well-considered step was proposed in the Providence Town Meeting on May 24, 1790, and embodied in instructions to that town's convention delegates. If the Constitution was rejected or a decision thereon unduly delayed, the Providence delegates were empowered to meet with those from Newport and other interested towns to discuss means by which the pro-Constitution communities could apply to Congress "for the same privileges and protection which are afforded to the towns under their jurisdiction."

The principal proximate cause for Rhode Island ratification was the economic coercion exerted upon the state by the new federal government. Within weeks after the first Congress set to work, William Ellery of Newport began his campaign to persuade the national legislature to lower the economic boom on Rhode Island. Ellery, a staunch Federalist, was commissioner of the Loan Office and a signer of the Declaration of Independence. He was in frequent contact with Connecticut congressman Benjamin Huntington and Connecticut senator Oliver Ellsworth, urging them to abandon "a policy of leniency" toward Rhode Island. Repeatedly he advised them that the Antifederalists "must be made to feel before they will ever consent to call a convention," and they could be made "to feel... by subjecting the goods, wares, and manufactures of this state" to the same high duties "as foreign States not in alliance with the United States."

Although such duties would hurt the Federalists in the port towns, the result would be worth the sacrifice, claimed Ellery. As time went on, he suggested ways to hit the Antifederalists more directly. Place duties on the produce of the country folk, he advised; stop their "lime, flaxseed, and barley" from entering the neighboring states duty-free, and "the Antis will... be compelled by a sense of interest to adopt the Constitution." Further, "Congress should require an immediate payment of a sum of money from the State with an assurance that if [it is] not collected an equivalent will be distrained." The sum to which Ellery referred was Rhode Island's share of the Revolutionary debt. A call for immediate payment would necessitate the reinstitution of high taxes on land.

Prodded by Ellery's shrewd observations, Congress began to move. In July 1789 it enacted a tariff program which subjected "all goods, wares, and merchandise" which Rhode Island exported to other states to foreign duties if such merchandise were not of Rhode Island "growth or manufacture." The state immediately petitioned for a suspension of these duties, and Congress, to Ellery's dismay, relented. In mid-September an act was passed holding the discriminatory levies in abeyance until January 15, 1790.

Just as this period of grace expired, the Rhode Island General Assembly approved, not by coincidence, the act calling a ratifying convention. Immediately Governor Collins informed the president and Congress and requested a further suspension. The patient Congress again complied. On February 8, 1790, Rhode Island's privilege was extended "until the first day of April next, and no longer."

At this juncture Vice President John Adams, the Senate's presiding officer, began to show signs of exasperation. Just prior to the South Kingstown convention, he confided to Providence merchants John Brown and John Francis that he was "really much affected at the obstinate infatuation of so great a part of the People of Rhode Island." Then he admonished, "If the Convention should reject the Constitution or adjourn without adopting it, Congress will probably find it necessary to treat them as they are, as Foreigners, and extend all the laws to them as such.... If the lime, the barley and other articles, whether of foreign or domestic growth or manufacture, should be subjected to a Duty, it would soon show your People that their interests are in the power of their neighbors."

When the March ratifying convention adjourned without issue and the Country Party swept the April elections, more drastic pressures, such as those of which Adams warned, appeared necessary. On April 28, 1790, a five-man Senate committee was created "to consider what provisions will be proper for Congress to make in the present session, respecting the State of Rhode Island." Among the membership of this group were Ellsworth and Caleb Strong of Massachusetts. Ellery now reiterated his bold plans to coerce the Antifederal majority, and he urged prompt action. "It is my opinion," he stated, "that the Convention will adjourn again unless you do something which will touch the interest of the Antis before the Convention meets."

With Senator Ellsworth in the lead, the committee heeded Ellery's admonition. On May 11 it reported a two-point program imposing a prohibition on all commercial intercourse between the United States and Rhode Island, effective July 1, and demanding an immediate payment, eventually set at $25,000, on the state's Revolutionary debt. A bill encompassing those recommendations was drawn, and on May 18, after long debate, it passed by a vote of 13 to 8. Noncompliance with the requisition could, perhaps, offer sufficient pretext for a resort to military force by the United States.

According to Senator William Maclay of Pennsylvania, a vigorous opponent of the measure, some were induced to support it "to get two Senators more into the House on whose votes they can reckon on the question of residence." He was referring, of course, to the current controversy over the permanent location of the national capital. This consideration, however, was of secondary importance. As it headed for the House, Maclay observed that the bill "was meant to be used in the same way that a robber does a dagger or a highwayman a pistol, and to obtain the end desired by putting the party in fear."

Rumors regarding the measure appeared in the press in Providence just prior to the convention. This community had long been apprehensive that the federal duty act would become operative against Rhode Island. Now, in view of the Senate's even more drastic action, Providence decided to employ that long-contemplated resort—secession—if ratification were not forthcoming.

Unquestionably, some of the reluctant bay towns, such as Portsmouth, were also moved by the sustained politico-economic pressure of the federal government. There is no doubt that it was a decisive factor in Rhode Island's ratification on May 29. The strategist Ellery, who was animated by a not uncommon blend of principle and patronage, was later rewarded by the new central government for his efforts on its behalf when he received the prized appointment of collector of customs for Newport.

This analysis of Rhode Island's ratification struggle reveals that the commercial interest (including some farmers who produced crops for export, but excluding many Quakers) generally supported the Constitution, while the agrarian elements opposed it. As one historian has stated, "The Federal tide in Rhode Island rose slowly from Providence and Newport to engulf the other bay towns."

The greater fervor for paper money in the interior towns and the stronger fear of direct taxes on land fueled the farmer's Antifederalism, while the relatively large amount of Continental securities held in the mercantile towns, the war damage claims of the Narragansett Bay communities, and the commercial coercion of Congress induced the merchant and his economic allies to support the new federal establishment.

A final factor, attitudinal in nature, was perhaps more significant than any other in explaining Rhode Island's response to the handiwork of the Philadelphia Convention. The rural folk in the country towns held provincial, localistic, and democratic beliefs. Their outlook rendered them slow in grasping or accepting the full significance of the momentous events transpiring on the national stage. Most of the inhabitants of these communities were agrarian-minded. Their remote environment and their often inferior social status had shaped their ideology, and that ideology predisposed them to distrust the power of government, especially a government far removed from local and popular supervision and control.

The mercantile interests, on the other hand, were more cosmopolitan and politically sophisticated. Their mode of life brought them into contact with people of other states, making them less suspicious, broader in outlook, more inclined to realize the necessity of change and less disposed to fear it. The commercial-minded Federalists believed that the government must be strong and centralized if it were to function creatively in advancing the general welfare and dispensing justice. Moreover, they felt it must have both positive powers to enlarge opportunities and coercive powers to prevent groups or sections from indulging their own interests, passions, and errors at the expense of the commonwealth. Theirs was the idea of nationalism which found ever-increasing expression under the Constitution of 1787.

When the members of the commercial community of merchants, bankers, artisans, mechanics, and exporting farmers saw their enterprises deprived of the protection of the United States and shorn of the benefits of her commercial treaties, and when their commerce was faced with heavy duties laid upon it not only by Europe but by the United States as well, they grew more determined in their Federalism.

These Federalists—men like William Ellery, John, Nicholas, and Moses Brown, Henry Marchant, Jabez Bowen, and Benjamin Bourne—worked for both private gain and public good. They regarded their advancement and their endeavors as essential to the nation's prosperity and growth. Time and the Founding Fathers were on their side. Thanks to their exertions, Rhode Island rejoined the union which had left it behind and embarked with the nation upon a new era of political and economic development.

The Washington County Courthouse (shown in this early sketch prior to additions and renovations) was the site of the March 1790 session of the ratifying convention.

11

The following essay was written as a chapter in *The Bill of Rights and the States*, the author's general survey of the evolution of liberties in the colonial and Revolutionary history of the fourteen states that considered the federal Bill of Rights in the years from 1789 through 1791. It attempts to describe Rhode Island's contribution to the development of American liberty.

Americans, of course, did not invent individual liberty or write the first document to guarantee it. The basis of human freedom can be found much earlier in such disparate sources as the Bible; the political culture of the classical world; the natural-law and natural-rights doctrines as formulated by ancient, medieval, and early modern writers; the rhetoric and the rationale of such movements as the Renaissance, the Reformation, and the Enlightenment; social-contract philosophy; and, especially, England's common law, its Whig libertarian tradition, and its great freedom documents—Magna Carta (1215), the Petition of Right (1628), and the Bill of Rights (1689).

Despite these impressive antecedents—all of which influenced the development of personal freedom in America—the actual experiences of Americans, as colonists, rebels, and constitution-writers, were at least as important in the formulation, assertion, expansion, and institutionalization of our individual liberties as any remote or foreign source. The American colonial and Revolutionary struggle for freedom and self-determination was the major influence in the shaping of our Bill of Rights. That struggle took many forms: the colonists against the British government; dissenting individuals or sects against established churches; slaves against their masters and against the codes that bound them; the poor and middle class against the wealthy; the underrepresented backcountry against the dominant coastal areas; second-class citizens against freemen; popularly elected legislators against royal or proprietary governors; or, simply, those out of power against those who held it.

The contest for liberty advanced on many fronts. Americans inserted rights into their colonial charters; they extracted them from proprietors;

they enacted them in their legislatures; they expanded or defended them in their courts; they asserted them in the press; and they lived them in their everyday lives. During the Revolutionary era, political pamphleteers proclaimed these rights; ministers preached them; *ad hoc* protest committees demanded them; delegates in Congress petitioned the Crown for them and then asserted them in declaring their independence; and legislatures and constitutional conventions enshrined them in the basic laws of those eleven states that scrapped their royal charters to frame written constitutions.

Liberty and self-government developed more quickly in some colonies than in others. In a few it grew because their charters almost thrust autonomy upon the first settlers. In some colonies—Rhode Island, New Jersey, and, especially, Pennsylvania—benevolent founders provided their settlers with substantial rights; but in less fortunate colonies, incompetent, arrogant governors engendered fear and animosity and thereby inadvertently stimulated the development of self-government and an increasing demand for the protection of rights. The ruling elite ensconced in some colonial assemblies and councils refused to share power equitably with the new and growing backcountry, creating intracolonial divisions that occasionally erupted into armed rebellion. No matter what form the oppression took, once resistance developed to counter it, the rhetoric of rights often assumed a life and reality of its own.

Because the story of how liberty developed in the English-speaking colonies of North America is complicated by the fact that there were really thirteen different stories (fourteen when Vermont is included), *The Bill of Rights and the States* examined the evolution of American liberty in each colony and state. This approach reveals not only that the formulation of rights was more indigenous than imitative but also that the development of freedom in the various states was different and uneven. Self-government grew sporadically throughout colonial America. There was no central coordination, no general theme carried out in one colony and then transmitted to another and another. The situation was more individualized and amorphous than that. Rights prominent in one colony, for example, could be ignored in another, while certain colonies and states nurtured particular rights. New Yorkers championed freedom of expression; Rhode Islanders passionately defended religious liberty and church-state separation; Delawareans showed an unusual preoccupation with the right to keep and bear arms; Massachusetts men stoutly objected to unreasonable searches and seizures; Vermonters led the way in abolishing slavery; Rhode Islanders and North Carolinians exalted states' rights as an antidote to centralized power; and Pennsylvanians and Virginians pioneered in asserting a broad range of individual freedoms.

Colonial Americans had a seemingly irresistible urge to codify their rights and privileges. Only occasionally did their English forefathers attempt such an audacious act; only when pushed to the extreme by the perceived despotism of the monarch did the English commit their rights to paper. For the most part the rights of Englishmen remained enshrined in the common law, where they were known and available to trained lawyers who regularly drew upon them.

Perhaps Americans wanted their rights codified because of the lack of a written authoritative commentary on the common law and the paucity of trained attorneys. Even before some immigrants left England, but usually within a decade after settlement, colonists drafted fundamental documents outlining the rights of individuals. These compilations were not meant to enlarge or supplant the common law; they were meant, rather, to be expressions of the ancient rights embodied in it. By compiling these rights, the colonists were making them more accessible, and thus the people might be better able to restrain the arbitrary acts of governors, courts, and legislatures.

In 1776 Virginia codified many of these liberties in its Declaration of Rights. Other states followed Virginia's example. During the debate over the ratification of the Constitution, many state ratifying conventions, including Rhode Island's, responded to Antifederalist demands by proposing amendments to the Constitution protecting liberties from the power of the new federal government. James Madison and the first federal Congress reformulated these proposals in 1789 in drafting a federal bill of rights for state approval.

Despite the diversity so evident from state to state, common themes are apparent. The residents of every colony invoked their "rights as Englishmen" and demanded (in language often derived from their royal charters) "all the liberties and immunities of free and natural subjects as if they were born within the realm of England." Trial by jury, with its accompanying procedural protections, was the preeminent English right that Americans sought to preserve. This effort was not only for the benefit of the accused and the protection of property. The American concept of trial by jury may well have gone beyond the English right because it also pertained to the governmental role of the citizen as juror; in the period when juries decided both law and fact, the jury itself served as the guardian of the people against unjust or unconstitutional laws and administrative actions.

After 1764, Americans began asserting their right to secure property from regulations and taxes imposed without their consent. This widespread concern both for the sanctity of private property and for legislation by consent sparked the movement for self-government and independence in which Rhode Island played a leading role.

In conclusion, reference should be made to a well-researched and imaginative article by attorney Kevin Leitao—"Rhode Island's Forgotten Bill of Rights," *Roger Williams University Law Review* 1 (Spring 1996), 31–61—in which the author examines the "Declaration of Rights" drafted and approved by the 1790 state convention called for the specific and limited purpose of ratifying the Constitution of the United States.

Admitting that his essay "is largely a thought experiment," Leitao believes that by "applying the principles of popular sovereignty, the Declaration of Rights could have been enforced in Rhode Island" as state law. I strongly disagree. This declaration was clearly an expression of concern by the ratifying convention's Antifederal majority to the United States Congress regarding the threat to liberty posed by the new government of the United States. A textual and contextual analysis of the document can yield no other conclusion. No one at that time or since considered it otherwise, and the General Assembly (which never ratified the Declaration of 1790) neither included it in the public laws or based its 1798 statutory bill of rights upon it.

Finally, the principles of popular sovereignty alluded to by Leitao were repudiated by the Rhode Island and the U.S. Supreme Courts in the aftermath of the Dorr Rebellion. As Leitao asserts, the Declaration of Rights did indeed apply to the "people of the state," but it was intended to protect them not from their local officials but from the novel and distant central government whose potential appetite for power was then unknown.

The Bill of Rights and Rhode Island

Patrick T. Conley

Atop Rhode Island's present statehouse stands the Independent Man, a state symbol and its most famous piece of statuary. This heroic figure recalls the individualism, autonomy, democratic localism, self-reliance, and entrepreneurial leadership that characterized Rhode Island during its colonial, Revolutionary, and early national periods. The Man's looming presence evokes the spirit of Rhode Island's formative era when defiance in defense of liberty was a way of life.

The home of the "otherwise-minded," as critics called the tiny colony, reacted to the verbal barbs of traditional or conservative critics with a curious mixture of pride and resentment. Though a "moral sewer" to the Puritans, a "downright democracy" to the exasperated Royalists of the pre-Revolutionary years, and "Rogues' Island" to the Federalists of 1787, Rhode Island presented a much different image to its own people. For seventeenth-century ministers Roger Williams and John Clarke, Rhode Island was a "lively experiment" in religious liberty; for eighteenth-century politician, judge, and congressman David Howell, its government was "pure and unmixed Democracy... in its Perfection"; according to George Bancroft, famed nineteenth-century historian (and Newport summer colonist), "no where in the world were life, liberty and property, safer than in [colonial] Rhode Island."

Most early Rhode Islanders apparently accepted these enthusiastic self-assessments, because rights-related controversies among Rhode Islanders were rare, especially prior to statehood. The wayward colony possessed a corporate charter whereby the freemen elected the governor and the entire legislature, and hence there was never a struggle for power or rights with a royal governor or a proprietor or between upper and lower houses of the General Assembly.

Though the legislature was supreme, members of the lower house (deputies) were chosen semiannually by their respective town meetings, and members of the upper house (assistants) were elected with the general officers annually on a colonywide basis. Such frequent elections ensured that government always rested on popular consent. Rhode Island had no established church and, therefore, no struggle between dissenters and an entrenched orthodoxy. Suffrage was broadly based, office-holding was open to all voters, and representation was generally equitable; thus colonial Rhode Island experienced no class conflict between the politically dispossessed and a ruling aristocracy; and urban-rural antagonisms were not severe until the decade of the 1780s. In sum, colonial Rhode Island was relatively free of the abuses and inequalities that spawned rights-related controversies elsewhere in British America, and those who did suffer varying degrees of discrimination or deprivation—Roman Catholics, Jews, Native Americans, and blacks—were either too few or too impotent to press for reform. Rhode Island women also acquiesced in their subordinate legal and political role.

Disputes with the mother country occasionally involved the question of rights, but England's "salutary neglect" of self-governing Rhode Island minimized such confrontations, and when challenges to liberty were raised, most concerned autonomy or property rights rather than attempted abridgments of those individual liberties detailed in the Bill of Rights. A notable exception, as we shall see, was the threats England posed to the right of trial by jury when it embarked upon the administrative reorganization of its North American empire after 1763.

In retrospect, Rhode Island, from its origin in 1636 until its enactment of a statutory bill of rights in 1798, was less convulsed with rights-related agitation than one might expect, given the contentiousness of its founders —Roger Williams, Anne Hutchinson, William Coddington, John Clarke, and Samuel Gorton. In large part this relative tranquility resulted from the success of these founders in establishing a safe haven for those distressed for the sake of conscience and in creating a popularly based government that effectively reconciled religious liberty with civil order.

Of the salient rights-related issues in early Rhode Island history, religious liberty and church-state separation are preeminent and will occupy an important part of our survey. They are the principles that gave this tiny commonwealth its reason for existence. In the second half of the eighteenth century, the ownership of private property and trial by jury became the most endangered rights, and thus the ones most debated. These issues too will be examined.

Chattel slavery, a cruel and blatant disregard of rights, existed in Rhode Island for over a century prior to the passage of an act in 1784 decreeing its gradual abolition, and Rhode Island merchants dominated the American trade in African slaves. Slavery will be considered also, for our discussion of freedom must include its denial as well as its expansion.

Finally, this survey will deal with the right to vote, called by one of its historians "the first liberty," because it was usually antecedent to the exercise of other basic political and legal rights associated with the status of freemanship. Although religion, juries, property, and suffrage do not constitute the entire range of rights in early Rhode Island, they are its highest peaks and slavery its deepest chasm. Let us now examine that topography of freedom.

"Soul Liberty"

Rhode Island's experiment in soul liberty began in January 1636, when the Puritan magistrates of Massachusetts Bay banished dissenting clergyman Roger Williams into the winter wilderness. An avowed Separatist from the Church of England, the Cambridge-educated Williams was ousted for attacking the cornerstones upon which the Puritans' Bible commonwealth was built—the theology of the covenant and the use of civil magistrates to enforce that theology.

A vital area of disagreement between Williams and the builders of the Bay Colony was that Williams considered some religious doctrines propounded by the Puritans to be a prostitution of theology. His alternative to the orthodox Puritan approach was a cause for his exile. This alternative was a major element in Williams's notions of religious freedom and the separation of church and state, principles that found their expression in Rhode Island's basic law.

Roger Williams's challenge to covenant theology revolved around a method of interpreting the Bible, specifically the relation of Old Testament to New, which is called typology. His version of the typological method was based upon a belief that everything in the Old Testament is merely a prefiguration of the New Testament, that each event in the history of Israel could be understood only when it came to fruition in the life of Christ, and that the Old Testament lacked literal and historical content.

In its practical application to the life of Massachusetts Bay, this complex method of Biblical exegesis had important consequences. Among other things, Williams's method of interpreting the Scriptures was at variance with the historical mode of typological interpretation upon which covenant theology rested. Orthodox typology held that the Old Testament was simultaneously a literal *and* a spiritual work. On the literal level, Israel's scriptural theocracy provided the eternal pattern of civil justice; on the spiritual level, Israel, as the Promised Land, prefigured Christ. Orthodox typology thus intermingled the church and the civil state, and it supported the Puritan contention that the Christian magistrates of Massachusetts Bay could enforce religious conformity by basing their actions on similar powers exercised by the Biblical Israelites.

Being of a purely spiritual nature, Williams's brand of typology disputed the Massachusetts Puritan belief that any political or social arrangement could be legitimized by reference to a similar arrangement described in the Old Testament. Specifically, Williams denied the right of the Massachusetts magistrates to use the civil power to enforce religious conformity, a right claimed on the basis of Israelite precedent. It was Williams's contention that the events and the laws of Israel, having found completion in the New Testament, were without exception purely moral and ceremonial, and not to be emulated by seventeenth-century New Englanders.

Another crucial theological disagreement between Williams and the Massachusetts Puritans stemmed from their divergent views of the Ten Commandments. These divinely revealed injunctions were divided into two "tables": the first table—commandments one through four—was concerned with God and the worship of God, and was called "ceremonial"; the second—commandments five through ten—was directed towards governing human relations, and was called "moral."

Pointing out that judges and kings in the Old Testament state of Israel enforced both tables, Puritan divine John Cotton and his associates contended that this function continued to be valid. According to their interpretation, the task of enforcing the first table (worship of God) resided with civil magistrates and ministers acting in concert.

Williams believed that Jesus had abrogated this Hebraic system. He contended that Christ had set forth new laws of worship which had stripped judges, kings, and civil magistrates of their right to enforce ceremonial provisions of the first table. These matters now belonged purely to the spiritual realm. "Soul liberty," to use Williams's phrase, pertained to the first table; it was exclusively an affair of private conscience, and the magistrate had no jurisdiction whatsoever in this area.

As a result of these interpretative efforts, Williams concluded that the temporal power exercised over the religious sphere in the Old Testament was merely the archetype of spiritual power in the New, and thus, whenever the modern state attempted to enforce conformity of religious belief, it was acting in an unjustifiable manner. That false assumption of power, asserted Williams, had led and would continue to lead to persecution and religious wars. Williams's obsession with religious persecution and its baneful effects upon both spiritual and civil life occupies a prominent place in his thought and furnished the theme for one of his major works, *The Bloudy Tenent of Persecution* (1644).

The fiery minister's typological approach had liberty of conscience as its logical corollary, and it contributed substantially to Williams's dogma of separation of church and state. It is important to note that the theologically obsessed Williams sought this separation not to protect the state from the dominance of the church but to free the church and the individual conscience from the interference and coercions of the state. Williams's religious creed thus led him into the political sphere, where he was essentially a traditionalist who believed in stability and deference. As historian Edmund Morgan has observed: "So far as the political order was concerned, Williams had really only one revolutionary statement to make. He denied that the state had any responsibility for the only form of life which has absolute importance—the life of the soul."

Indicative of how strongly Williams felt about state domination of the church, in one burst of vituperation the polemical theologian asserted that such a condition would render the church, "the garden and spouse of Christ, a filthy dunghill and whore-house of rotten and stinking whores and hypocrites." Obviously Williams did not take the issue of separation lightly.

Among the conclusions that historians have drawn from Williams's earthy and passionate theological writings, the following seem to be the most significant: (1) any attempt by the state to enforce religious orthodoxy "stinks in God's nostrils" because it perverts God's plan for the regeneration of souls, and it is productive of persecution and religious wars; (2) God has not favored any particular form of government, and it is therefore to be inferred that forms of government will vary according to the nature and disposition of the people governed; (3) political and, especially, religious diversity is inevitable; and (4) the human conscience must be completely emancipated through the establishment of religious freedom and the separation of church and state.

Perry Miller, noted historian of early American religious thought, has said that Williams "exerted little or no direct influence on theorists of the Revolution and the Constitution, who drew on quite different intellectual sources, yet as a figure and a reputation he was always there to remind Americans that no other conclusion than absolute religious freedom was feasible in this society."

In his *Religious History of the American People* (1975), Professor Sydney Ahlstrom supports Miller's view. Calling Rhode Island "the first commonwealth in modern history to make religious liberty (not simply a degree of toleration) a cardinal principle of its corporate existence and to maintain the separation of church and state on these grounds," Ahlstrom then observes that "Rhode Island seems to illustrate in an almost tragic way the... dictum, often voiced by historians of science, that premature discoveries are uninfluential." For Miller and Ahlstrom, Williams is to Madison, Jefferson, and the Enlightenment-era framers of the First Amendment as Leif Eriksson is to Columbus: prior in time but lacking in influence.

Other recent historians of American religion and constitutionalism—including Mark DeWolfe Howe, Martin E. Marty, Edwin S. Gaustad, and Glenn W. LaFantasie (editor of a recent edition of Williams's unpublished letters)—hold a contrary view. According to these scholars, the Founding Fathers were well aware of the Rhode Island system of disestablishment and soul liberty, which was still intact under the same frame of government when the Bill of Rights was drafted and ratified; the guarantees in Rhode Island's famed charter of 1663 influenced similar grants of religious liberty in the proprietary charters of East Jersey, West Jersey, and Carolina issued shortly thereafter; and Williams's views on religion and the state were distilled and reiterated by Algernon Sydney and other English writers of the Whig libertarian tradition with whom our Founding Fathers were quite familiar.

Williams was also associated with an Anglo-American Baptist tradition of separationism and soul liberty, drawing his inspiration from that tradition and strengthening it with his writings and example. Throughout the colonial and founding eras, as historian William G. McLoughlin has shown, the tradition was maintained, refined, and modernized by the heroic determination of a coterie of lesser-known Baptist ministers and promulgated to the world of the Founding Fathers by the Reverend Isaac Backus (1724–1806), a prolific author and itinerant Baptist preacher who roamed the byways of southern New England spreading the gospel of separationism. Though McLoughlin recognizes Williams's slight influence on Backus, he feels that the optimistic, evangelical Backus—more than Williams, Madison, or Jefferson—influenced the predominant American church-state tradition, which McLoughlin styles "the 'sweet harmony' of a Christian nation."

Perhaps Professor Martin Marty has said it best: the American church-state outlook has issued "chiefly from two parallel, often congenial, sometimes conflicting, and occasionally contradictory positions"—the Rhode Island dissenting tradition, with its Biblical base, initiated by Williams, and the eighteenth-century Virginia Enlightenment tradition, rooted in natural law and natural rights, expounded by Jefferson and Madison.

Despite Marty's balancing act, however, Mark DeWolfe Howe has effectively carried the historical controversy into the realm of current legal and constitutional jurisprudence. Asserting that the U.S. Supreme Court, "in its role as historian, has erred in disregarding the theological roots of the American principle of separation," he contends that "the predominant concern at the time when the First Amendment was adopted was not the Jeffersonian fear that if it were not enacted the federal government would aid religion... but rather the evangelical hope that private conscience and autonomous churches, working together and in freedom, would extend the role of truth." Citing Roger Williams's letter to the Reverend John Cotton, wherein the Rhode Island exile coined the metaphor "hedge or wall of separation between the garden of the church and the wilderness of the world," Howe maintains that "when the imagination of Roger Williams built the wall of separation, it was not because he was fearful that without such a barrier the arm of the church would extend its reach. It was, rather, the dread of the worldly corruptions which might consume the churches if sturdy fences against the wilderness were not maintained." Yet, in making the wall of separation a constitutional barrier, the modern Supreme Court has failed to realize that "the faith of Roger Williams played a more important part [in the genesis of the First Amendment] than the doubts of Jefferson."

While one may endlessly debate the question of Williams's impact on the First Amendment, his influence on Rhode Island's basic law is indisputable. All of the state's founding documents bear the indelible impress of his fundamental beliefs. The Providence town compact of 1637, that settlements first frame of government, gave political power to the original "householders" but contained the all-important proviso that such control was to be exercised "only in civil things." A more detailed "plantation agreement" of 1640 reiterated this limitation; and the colonial patent that Williams obtained for the original towns in 1644 from the Long Parliament gave implicit sanction to the separation of church and state.

The culmination of this pioneering process, however, was Rhode Island's royal charter of 1663, obtained from King Charles II by tenacious Newport Baptist John Clarke, an important religious leader whose views closely paralleled those of Roger Williams. This document allowed the establishment of a self-governing colony wherein all local officials, from the governor and assemblymen to the viewers of fences and corders of wood, were either chosen directly in town meeting by the freemen or appointed on an annual basis by the elected representatives of the people.

The charter's most liberal, generous, and unusual provision, however, bestowed upon the inhabitants of the tiny colony "full liberty in religious concernments." The document commanded that "noe person within the sayd colonye, at any time hereafter, shall bee any wise molested, punished, disquieted, or called in question for any differences in opinione in matters of religion."

This guarantee of religious liberty was a vindication of Williams's beliefs and royal recognition of the fundamental principles upon which the Providence Plantation was founded—absolute freedom of conscience and complete separation of church and state. As Williams observed, this liberality stemmed from the king's willingness to "experiment" in order to ascertain "whether civil government could consist with such liberty of conscience." This was the "lively experiment" upon which the government of Rhode Island was based.

Because such a free and open governmental system prevailed in seventeenth-century Rhode Island, the colony became a haven for Baptists, Separatists, Antinomian followers of Anne Hutchinson, Gortonians, Quakers,

An Act for Declaring the Rights and Priviledges of His Majesties Subjects within this Colony.

No Free-men to be Imprisoned, or deprived of his Liberty, &c. But by his Peers, &c.

BE IT ENACTED *By the General Assembly of this Colony, And by the Authority of the same it is hereby Enacted*, That no Free-man shall be Taken or Imprisoned, or be deprived of his Free-hold, or Liberty, or Free Customs, or Out-Lawed, or Exiled or otherways Destroyed, nor shall be passed upon, Judged or Condemned, but by the Lawful Judgement of his Peers, or by the Law of this Colony; And that no Aid, Tax, Tailage, or Custom, Loan, Benevolence, Gift, Excise, Duty or Imposition whatsoever, shall be Laid, Assessed, Imposed, Levied or Required of or on any of His Majesties Subjects within this Colony, or upon their Estates, upon any manner of Pretence or Colour whatsoever, but by the Act and Assent of the General Assembly of this Colony.

No Tax or Duty to be raised, but by the General Assembly.

AND that no Man, of what Estate and Condition soever, shall be put out of his Lands and Tenements, nor Taken, nor Imprisoned, nor Disinheretd, nor Banished, nor any ways Destroyed, nor Molested, without being for it brought to Answer by due course of Law; And that all Rights and Priviledges Granted to this Colony by His Majesties Charter, be entirely kept and preserved to all His Majesties Subjects residing, in or belonging to the same; And that all Men Professing Christianity, and of Competent Estates, and of Civil Conversation, who acknowledge, and are Obedient to the Civil Magistrate, though of different Judgmnts in Religious Affairs (Roman Catholicks only excepted) shall be admited Free-men, And shall have Liberty to Chuse and be Chosen Officers in the Colony both Millitary and Civil.

No Person to be Deseised of his Lands, or otherwise molested, but by due Course of Law.

All Persons of Estates, and Obedient to the Magistrate, to have liberty to Elect, and be Elected to Offices.

February, 1783.

IT is further Resolved, That the Town-Treasurer of *South-Kingstown*, who is committed to Gaol at the Suit of the General-Treasurer, be and he hereby is ordered to be discharged from Gaol.

BE it Enacted by this General Assembly, and by the Authority thereof it is Enacted, That all the Rights and Privileges of the *Protestant* Citizens of this State, as declared in and by an Act made and passed the First Day of *March*, A. D. 1663, be and the same are hereby fully extended to *Roman Catholic* Citizens; and that they being of competent Estates, and of civil Conversation, and acknowledging and paying Obedience to the civil Magistrate, shall be admitted Freemen, and shall have Liberty to choose and be chosen civil or military Officers within this State: Any Exception in the said Act to the contrary notwithstanding.

Roman Catholics admitted to the Rights of Citizenship.

A 1719 statute denied freemanship to Roman Catholics and Jews in violation of the spirit of the charter of 1663. The Catholic disqualification was repealed in 1783 because of the assistance of Catholic France in our War of Independence. The Jewish restriction was removed in 1798.

Sephardic Jews, and Huguenots. In 1702, disgruntled Puritan leader Cotton Mather wrote that Rhode Island was a motley collection of all sects except Roman Catholics and true Christians (i.e., Congregationalists).

But has Rhode Island continued to practice what its founder preached? To a great extent, it has: never has freedom of worship been impaired within Rhode Island's borders. Such a record is truly commendable. And yet for nearly two centuries the spirit of Rhode Island's famed guarantee was violated because both colony and state imposed various civil disabilities and discriminatory policies upon religious minorities, especially Roman Catholics. After Williams passed from the scene, Rhode Island too often exemplified the condition lamented by the eighteenth-century Irish satirist Jonathan Swift: "We have just enough religion to make us hate," said Swift, "but not enough to make us love one another."

Rhode Island's religiously inspired litany of civil wrongs began in 1719, when the General Assembly enacted a code of laws containing a statute denying freemanship—the right to vote and hold office—to Catholics and non-Christians. Enacted during the frenzy over the possible return of the Catholic pretender James III to the English throne, this statute was reaffirmed by the General Assembly in the legal codifications of 1730, 1745, and 1767. (In 1756, when Catholic France was menacing the northern settlements during the French and Indian War, Rhode Island enacted a statute ordering an oath of allegiance and abjuration to be administered to suspicious persons and decreed that any who refused to subscribe be proceeded against as "popish recusants and have their goods confiscated.") Not until 1783, after the benevolent occupation of Rhode Island by Count Rochambeau and his French forces, was the arbitrary disqualification of Catholics removed.

The act that accomplished this, however, neglected to define the civil status of those professing the Jewish faith. The Rhode Island colony's refusal to naturalize Jews was another blemish on the charter's guarantee of religious equality. Although Jews enjoyed freedom of worship, none, however qualified or competent, was ever made a freeman of the colony. On the issue of naturalization, both the Superior Court and the General

Assembly, in 1761 and 1762 respectively, rejected the citizenship petitions of wealthy Newport merchants Aaron Lopez and Isaac Elizer because they were non-Christians.

In August 1790, when George Washington visited Rhode Island following its ratification of the Constitution, he was greeted by many well-wishers, including the congregation of Newport's Touro Synagogue. In a grateful response to his warm welcome from the Jewish community, the president later wrote the congregation a now-famous letter which prophesied that the new nation would provide the world with a model society where all people would enjoy liberty and the natural right to respect from their fellows. Washington also assured his Jewish audience that "happily the government of the United States, which gives to bigotry no sanction, to persecution no assistance, requires only that they who live under its protection should demean themselves as good citizens." Happily also, Rhode Island's legislature fulfilled Washington's aspirations in 1798 by passing "An Act Relative to Religious Freedom and the Maintenance of Ministers," which finally removed the civil disabilities imposed against Rhode Islanders of the Jewish faith.

An interior view of Newport's Touro Synagogue (1763), the oldest Jewish house of worship in North America. Touro was visited by George Washington in August 1790, after which he wrote his famous toleration letter to the Hebrew congregation.

Despite the abandonment of all religious qualifications by 1798, Rhode Islanders of a later generation developed such criteria as native birth to discriminate on religious grounds, much in the way that post-Civil War Southerners used grandfather clauses and literacy tests to circumvent the Fifteenth Amendment's ban on racial discrimination. Even in the land of Roger Williams, religious bigotry delayed the attainment by some Rhode Islanders of equal civil rights.

The "Sacred Right"

While "soul liberty" is Rhode Island's great contribution to the American litany of freedoms, trial by jury was nearly as sacred as religious freedom to early Rhode Islanders. In 1647 a General Assembly of the four original towns—Providence, Portsmouth, Newport, and Warwick—enacted the first colonywide system of laws. According to noted colonial historian Charles McLean Andrews, "the acts and orders of 1647 constitute one of the earliest programmes for a government and one of the earliest codes of law made by any body of men in America and the first to embody in all its parts the precedents set by the laws and statutes of England."

This landmark 1647 assembly, proceeding under the authority granted by the parliamentary patent of 1644 (the colony's first constitution), provided for administrative officers, a judicial process, a system of representation, and legislative procedures that contained provisions for both local initiative and popular referendum. Its remarkable code was an elaborate body of criminal and civil law prefaced by a brief statement of protections.

First and foremost among these was the assertion, derived from the Magna Carta, that "no person ... shall be taken or imprisoned or be disseized of his Lands or Liberties, or be Exiled, or molested ... or destroyed, but by the Lawfull judgment of his Peeres, or by some known Law, and according to the Letter of it, Ratified and confirmed by the major part of the Generall Assembly lawfully met and orderly managed."

According to the "laws and orders" of 1647, accused criminals were to be indicted by a grand jury of "twelve or sixteen honest and lawful men" and tried by a separate jury of twelve empowered to hear and determine all "controversies and differences... between partie and partie." The members of this petit jury were to receive "a solemn charge" from the trial's presiding officer, "upon the perill and penaltie" of the law, "to do justice between the parties contending, according to the evidence." At trial's end, that officer was to remind the jury of the "most material passages and arguments" brought by each side "without alteration or leaning to one party or another." Thereupon the jury were "to goe forth and do justice and right between their neighbors." It is important to note that in colonial times the right of trial by jury was regarded as a right belonging not only to the accused but also to the citizen as juror. In Rhode Island only freemen (i.e., voters) were eligible to serve on juries. Until 1827 these select citizens decided both the law and the facts in every case and exercised a strong popular check on judges, administrators, and lawmakers alike. Small wonder that the jury was such a revered institution!

This annotated edition of the famous 1647 code was edited and published by lawyer-historian William R. Staples on the occasion of the code's bicentennial in 1847.

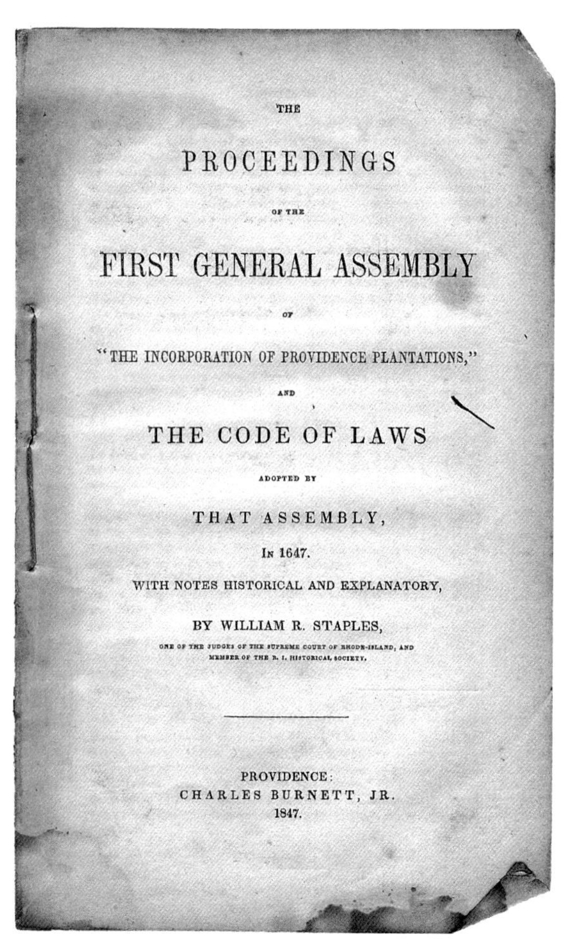
THE
PROCEEDINGS
OF THE
FIRST GENERAL ASSEMBLY
OF
"THE INCORPORATION OF PROVIDENCE PLANTATIONS,"
AND
THE CODE OF LAWS
ADOPTED BY
THAT ASSEMBLY,
IN 1647.
WITH NOTES HISTORICAL AND EXPLANATORY,
BY WILLIAM R. STAPLES,
ONE OF THE JUDGES OF THE SUPREME COURT OF RHODE-ISLAND, AND
MEMBER OF THE R. I. HISTORICAL SOCIETY.

PROVIDENCE:
CHARLES BURNETT, JR.
1847.

Under the Code of 1647, defendants in criminal trials were allowed preemptory challenges against as many as twenty prospective jurors. They could plead their own case, select a personal attorney to defend them, or "use the Attorney that belongs to the Court." The only caveat was that such "pleader or attorney" shall not "use any manner of deceit to beguile either Court or partie." Thus did the law of 1647 lay the groundwork for the Rhode Island bar and its canons of ethical conduct.

The early and emphatic origin of trial by jury in Rhode Island discouraged any internal abridgment of this right during the colonial period. Ironically, when a challenge finally came, England, the matrix of that liberty, posed the threat. After 1763, when Britain had successfully concluded its war for empire with France and Spain, the mother country sought revenue through a reorganization of its imperial system. Two early-ripened fruits of this new fiscal policy were the Sugar Act of 1764 and the Stamp Act of 1765. Both decreed that at the option of the informant or the prosecutor, juryless admiralty courts could try those who attempted to evade these revenue measures. Since Rhode Island's royal charter of 1663 (like many other colonial charters) decreed that inhabitants of the colony "shall have and enjoy all liberties and immunities of free and natural subjects... as if they... were born within the realm of England," admiralty jurisdiction raised an outcry. Violators of similar tax laws in Britain had benefit of trial by jury, so Rhode Islanders claimed deprivation of their "rights as Englishmen."

Whether rightly or wrongly, most Rhode Islanders and other colonials regarded the new taxes as unconstitutional, the Sugar Act because it was levied for revenue rather than regulation and the Stamp Act because it was internal. The use of existing admiralty courts, whose jurisdiction had been confined to maritime matters, compounded the violation of rights, for such tribunals would enforce unconstitutional taxes by unconstitutional means. Adding to colonial apprehension, Parliament also passed an order-in-council establishing a vice-admiralty court for all America, with both appellate and original jurisdiction, to be located in the new Royal Navy town of Halifax, Nova Scotia. Heretofore a Rhode Islander who refused to pay his taxes was subject to the jurisdiction of the colony court within his home county or vicinage and was tried by a jury of his peers; in 1765 his evasion of an internal stamp tax could subject him to a juryless trial in Nova Scotia.

Rhode Island's response to these measures was predictable. In October 1765 the colony took part in an organized protest called the Stamp Act Congress, and the General Assembly promptly ratified that body's declarations opposing both Parliament's claim to tax Americans and its effort to subvert their right of trial by jury.

Although the Stamp Act was repealed in 1766, admiralty jurisdiction continued. Three additional courts were established by the Townshend Acts of 1767, and these tribunals continued to function until repudiated by armed rebellion. As late as 1773 Benjamin Franklin, from his London residence, warned his fellow Englishmen that depriving Americans of trial by jury and subjecting them to arbitrary and venal admiralty judges was one of the "rules by which a Great Empire may be Reduced to a Small One."

Instructing its representatives to the General Assembly in August 1765, the Providence town meeting expressed this grievance well:

> With utmost Concern and Dread, we consider the Extension of the Powers of the Court of Admiralty; and must freely declare to the whole World, that we look upon our natural Rights to be diminished in the same Proportion as the Powers of that Court are extended; And in Particular we are unhappily distinguished from our Fellow-Subjects in *Britain*.

The remedy proposed by the townspeople of Providence was simple: Pass an act "declaring that the Courts of Common Law only, and not any Court of Admiralty, have, and ought to have jurisdiction in all Causes growing and arising in this Colony on Account of levying or collecting any internal taxes, or of any Matters relating thereto." Paraphrasing Blackstone, they noted that jury trial has "been usual and accustomed Time out of Mind." Then they threw down the gauntlet: "No Decree of any Court of Admiralty respecting these Matters shall be executed in this Colony."

Seven years later, in June 1772, after repeated incidents and confrontations over the revenue laws, these same Providence townspeople, in a daring nighttime raid on Narragansett Bay, burned the stranded British revenue schooner *Gaspee*, which had run aground chasing a suspected smuggler. A royal investigation of the affair yielded insufficient evidence to indict the prominent Providence perpetrators. These culprits were the beneficiaries of an artful public cover-up that shielded them despite a reward of up to one thousand pounds offered by King George himself for information leading to the conviction of the *Gaspee* raiders. The royal *Gaspee* inquiry intensified the establishment of legislative committees of correspondence by rebels throughout the colonies, a major step on the road to Revolution.

Of greatest alarm to Rhode Islanders was the position by the Crown's lawyers that the burning of the *Gaspee* was an act of high treason. This view —expressed by the earl of Dartmouth, secretary at state for the colonies, in a September 4, 1772, letter to Governor Joseph Wanton—had great legal ramifications. In 1768 Parliament had revived a sixteenth-century treason statute (35 Henry VII, c. 2), which provided that any treason committed outside the realm of England might be tried at Westminster before the King's Bench or in any English county by special commissioners appointed by the king. This ultimate coercion for acts of rebellion could lead to a faraway trial and punishment by execution in its most barbarous mode—by hanging, drawing, and quartering. Such a procedure ignored the colonials' right to trial by a jury of the vicinage or local area. Said a contemporary *Gaspee* balladeer of George III:

> For he's declared, in his passion,
> He'll have them tried [in] a new fashion.

This "new fashion," which could have dire consequences for an accused rebel, did have dire consequences for the king. Four years after the *Gaspee*'s embers cooled, Thomas Jefferson, in his famous Declaration, indicted George "for transporting us beyond seas to be tried for pretended offenses."

The final eighteenth-century threat to the right of trial by jury came from a most unexpected source—the Rhode Island General Assembly. During the nationwide economic depression of the mid 1780s, Rhode Island farmers groaned under the heavy land tax imposed upon them by the merchant-controlled General Assembly. Many lost their farms through tax foreclosure. Then, in early 1786, a harried South Kingstown tax collector named Jonathan Hazard led a rural taxpayers' revolt, and his ad hoc Country Party seized control of the powerful state legislature in the annual April elections. Immediately these agrarians passed debtor-relief measures, including the issuance of £100,000 of paper money that was to be loaned by the state to freeholders using their land as security. The currency was declared legal tender and could be used to pay both taxes and private debts. Merchants and creditors denounced the currency, however, and they resolutely resisted the scheme.

The Country Party met this opposition head-on. Its legislative majority first passed a forcing act in June 1786, which was designed to check the rapid depreciation of the paper bills. This statute stipulated that any person who refused to take these bills at par in exchange for any articles he offered for sale, or made any difference in the prices between silver and paper money in any sale or exchange, or attempted to depreciate or discourage the passing of these bills, would be fined one hundred pounds for the first offense. For the second violation he would be fined the same amount and rendered ineligible to vote or hold office in the state.

This penal law apparently failed to achieve its intended effect because of delays in meting out penalties to violators, so a specially convened August session of the legislature modified the law with an ill-advised amendment. The August act lessened the monetary penalty on those refusing the paper, but it provided for the immediate trial of violators by a special court.

This supplementary statute stated that if any person refused to receive paper according to the requirements of the previous law, the individual tendering the money could apply for relief to a justice of the Superior Court or to a judge of the Court of Common Pleas in the county where the offense was committed. The judge handling the complaint was then directed to summon the refusing party to appear before a *special* court within three days to stand trial, without benefit of jury. The judgment of this special court was to be final and conclusive; no appeal from its decision was allowed. If the accused were found guilty, he was to pay the assessed fine plus costs or be committed to the county jail "till sentence be performed."

Needless to say, this law provoked an uproar because of its disdain for procedural due process, and it was immediately defied. In Newport, where the anti-paper forces held a majority, John Weeden, a butcher, refused to accept the paper tender that John Trevett offered in payment for meat. Trevett, a Revolutionary War naval hero, entered a complaint against the recalcitrant butcher with the chief justice of the Superior Court, Paul Mumford, thus precipitating the case of *Trevett* v. *Weeden.*

Two of Rhode Island's ablest lawyers sprang to Weeden's defense—Henry Marchant, a former attorney general and a recent delegate to the Confederation Congress, and General James Mitchell Varnum, a member of Congress from Rhode Island. Despite provisions of the penalty law, the trial was conducted at a special *session* of the Superior Court of Judicature, Rhode Island's highest tribunal, in Newport on September 22, 1786, with Chief Justice Mumford presiding. The case was highlighted by Varnum's speech for the defense, a brief which indicates, perhaps better than any other document prior to the federal convention, the ideas on which reliance was placed in accepting the principle of judicial review of legislative enactments.

Varnum, a man of eloquence and imposing appearance, prayed at the outset that the court would not take cognizance of Trevett's complaint because of three major objections to the act under which the charge was brought. First, the defense counsel contended, the August act under which Weeden stood accused had expired ten days after the rising of the Assembly. Faulty draftsmanship of the penal statute by the legislature gave this technical allegation much merit.

Varnum informed the judges, however, that "we do not place our principal reliance upon this objection." He then embarked upon a more formidable avenue of attack: namely, that by the statute "special trials are instituted, incontroulable by the Supreme Judiciary Court of the State."

This was a gross violation of the long-standing principle that "the highest court of law, hath ... power to reverse erroneous judgments, given by inferior courts," and the duty to command, prohibit, and restrain "all inferior jurisdictions, whenever they attempt to exceed their authority, or refuse to exercise it for the public good."

Finally Varnum attacked the measure for its failure to provide the accused with a jury trial. His arguments on this point were most effective. He made several allusions to the charter of Charles II and listed two principal causes of colonial discontent on the eve of the Revolution in the process of developing his position. "Trial by jury," asserted Varnum, "was ever esteemed a first, a fundamental, and a most essential principle, in the English constitution." This "sacred right" was transferred from England to America by numerous royal charters, including Rhode Island's basic law of 1663. He cited the charter provision giving colonists the right to "have and enjoy all liberties and immunities of free and natural subjects" of England as proof of this contention. These privileges and immunities were abridged by the Stamp Act levy and by England's use of admiralty jurisdiction. In fact, contended the learned Revolutionary general, Parliament's attempts to deprive the colonists of trial by jury "were among the principal causes that united the colonies in a defensive war."

Now the Assembly had denied that long-cherished right of trial by jury, claimed Varnum. This was a clear usurpation, for the charter prohibited the legislature from making laws contrary and repugnant to the general system of laws that governed the realm of England at the time of the grant. The Revolution, said Varnum, had made "no change" in this limitation of legislative power. Trial by jury, he contended, "is a fundamental right, a part of our legal constitution," and one with which the Assembly cannot tamper.

Then, after references to Coke and other legal authorities, Varnum espoused the doctrine of judicial review in his learned and forceful summation:

> We have attempted to show, that the act, upon which the information is founded, has expired: That by the act special jurisdictions are erected, incontroulable by the Supreme Judiciary Court of the State: And that, by the act, this court is not authorized or empowered to impannel a jury to try the facts contained in the information: That the trial by jury is a fundamental, a constitutional right—ever claimed as such—ever ratified as such—ever held most dear and sacred: That the Legislature derives all its authority from the constitution—has no power of making laws but in subordination to it—can not infringe or violate it: That therefore the act is unconstitutional and void. That this Court has power to judge and determine what acts of the General Assembly are agreeable to the constitution; and, on the contrary, that this Court is under the most solemn obligations to execute the laws of the land, and therefore cannot, will not, consider this act as a law of the land.

Contrary to the generally accepted belief, Rhode Island's highest court did not, on the basis of Varnum's appeal, declare the penalty statute unconstitutional and void. It did, however, accede to Varnum's plea by denying jurisdiction over Trevett's complaint, for the court unanimously decided "that the said complaint does not come under the cognizance of the Justices here present, and... it is hereby dismissed." Presumably cognizance was denied because the justices heard the case in special session of the regular term and not as a special court as directed by the force act.

David Howell (1747–1824), a delegate to the Confederation Congress and a Superior (Supreme) Court justice, defied the General Assembly in the *Trevett* v. *Weeden* case and expressed his personal view that the force act was unconstitutional. He ended his career as a U.S. District Court judge for the District of Rhode Island (1812–1824).

In the commotion that followed the trial, knowledge of the specific decision was somehow distorted, for the infuriated Assembly in special session issued a summons requiring the immediate attendance of the judges of the Superior Court to render their reasons for adjudging "an act of the supreme legislature of this state to be unconstitutional, and so absolutely void." This may have been the justices' personal view, but it was not their formal decision.

In early October, after a two-week delay, Judges David Howell, Joseph Hazard, and Thomas Tillinghast appeared before the General Assembly to defend their course of action. Chief Justice Paul Mumford and Associate Justice Gilbert Devol were conveniently ill.

Both Tillinghast and Hazard (the latter a paper-money supporter) stoutly defended the judgment which they had rendered. Howell did likewise in a speech that was much lengthier and more fully preserved. He asserted that the justices were accountable only to God and their own consciences for their decision. It was beyond the power of the General Assembly to judge the propriety of the court's ruling, the angry Howell continued, for by such an act "the Legislature would become the supreme judiciary—a perversion of power totally subversive of civil liberty." Howell then contended for an independent judiciary so that judges would not be answerable for their opinion unless charged with criminality.

Showing little remorse or contrition for his act, Howell boldly informed the lawmakers that the legislature had assumed a fact in their summons to the judges that was not justified or warranted by the records. The plea of Weeden, he pointed out, mentioned the act of the General Assembly as unconstitutional, and so void, but the judgment of the court was simply that the information was not cognizable before it. Hence, chided Howell, it appeared that the plea had been mistaken for the judgment. His personal opinion, however, was that the act was indeed unconstitutional, had not the force of law, and could not be executed.

The retorts of the judges, especially Howell, did little to endear them to the agrarian-controlled General Assembly. Thus the legislature declared its dissatisfaction with this response, and a motion was made to dismiss the justices from office. Before the vote on this imprudent suggestion was taken, a memorial signed by the three judges was introduced and read. They had anticipated the plan to remove them, and they demanded as freemen and officers of the state the right of due process—"a hearing by counsel before some proper and legal tribunal, and an opportunity to answer to certain and specific charges... before any sentence or judgment be passed, injurious to any of their aforesaid rights and privileges." After the memorial was read, General Varnum addressed the House in defense of the court.

This determined show of resistance caused the Assembly to waver. A motion was passed directing that the opinion of the attorney general and other learned lawyers be obtained on the question of "whether constitutionally, and agreeably by law, the General Assembly could suspend, or remove from office the Judges of the Supreme Judiciary Court, without a previous charge and statement of criminality, due process, trial, and conviction thereon." Thus a case that began over a denial of a jury trial for John Weeden ended with the judges' demanding one for themselves.

Attorney General William Channing (father of the famed Unitarian minister) and others who were consulted denied such power to the General Assembly, an opinion that prompted a large majority of the legislators to agree that since "the judges of said superior court, etc., are not charged with criminality in giving judgment upon the information, John Trevett against John Weeden, they are therefore discharged from any further attendance upon this Assembly on that account" and could resume their judicial functions.

The forcing statute that sparked the dispute was repealed in December, but the Assembly gained some measure of satisfaction from the independent-minded court when it declined to reelect Howell, Hazard, Tillinghast, and Devol upon the expiration of their terms in May 1787. Chief Justice Mumford, who had failed to testify before the Assembly because of either illness or discretion, was surprisingly retained. Congressional delegate Varnum and Attorney General Channing were also ousted after their defiant stands, whereas Henry Goodwin, the state's counsel in the proceedings, was elevated by the Country Party to the position vacated by Channing.

The decision of the Rhode Island Superior Court in *Trevett* v. *Weeden* was not an authentic or technical precedent in the development of judicial review, nor did the action of the court prevent the implementation of the paper-money program. Further, the effect of the case upon Rhode Island's long-range judicial development was slight. *Trevett* v. *Weeden* was a cause célèbre that produced great temporary excitement but made little permanent impact upon the operations of Rhode Island's governmental system. After 1786 the legislature exerted as much control over the state's courts as before. The dominant party continued to elect judges annually, despite the periodic protests of reformers, until the establishment of a written state constitution in 1843. The Assembly still entertained petitions from individuals adversely affected by legal decisions and often honored such petitions by overturning the judgment of the Supreme Court in cases of insolvency and by authorizing new trials in civil suits. These practices were not terminated until 1856, when the state Supreme Court finally asserted its independence of the Assembly in the landmark case of *Taylor* v. *Place*. Until the *Taylor* decision, seventy years after *Trevett*, no state court dared challenge the Assembly; no Rhode Island justice gave official endorsement to the doctrine of judicial review.

The real significance of the *Trevett* v. *Weeden* episode lies not in the formal action of the court (which ducked the issue) but in the utterances of defense counsel James Mitchell Varnum and, to a lesser degree, in the personal observations of Justice David Howell. General Varnum's statement of the doctrine of judicial review was one of the most forceful and extensive arguments on that subject developed during this formative period.

No doubt Varnum was driven to seek relief from the bench because the force act, by eliminating the jury (which then judged law as well as fact), left the judiciary as the last guardian of minority rights against the unconstitutional action of a government controlled by the majority faction. Thus Varnum anticipated the judiciary's modern role.

The arguments of Varnum and Howell did not go unnoticed. On the eve of the 1787 general election, an anonymous correspondent in the *Providence Gazette* denounced the legislature's paper-money policies. "The Happiness of Individuals, as well as the public Safety, depend more ... on the Superior Court, than many People apprehend. They are a Shield, nay a Bulwark to their Fellow-Citizens, against all Kinds of Injustice and Oppression: It is not only their Duty to controul and restrain all inferior Courts and Tribunals, but to discern the Boundaries of the Power both of State and federal legislation."

The Providence town meeting went even further in stressing the importance of judicial review as the guardian of liberty. On April 28, 1787, this body of citizens declared:

> The General Assembly are restrained and limited, in all their legislative acts, by the constitution. They are, in fact, the creature of the constitution; they are brought into existence thereby, empowered to act agreeably thereto, for a certain term, and then sink back again into the mass of their fellow-citizens. All their acts are liable to examination and scrutiny by the people, that is by the Supreme Judiciary, their servants for this purpose; and those that militate with the fundamental laws, or impugn the principles of the constitution, are to be judicially set aside as void, and of no effect. Here is the safety of rich and poor; here is a rampart thrown up against arbitrary power....
>
> Precarious indeed would be the tenure of life, as well as of liberty and property, held at the mere will of a popular Assembly, sole judges of their own powers, of their own acts, and of the people's liberties.

Assuredly the views of James Mitchell Varnum were known not only to Rhode Islanders but also to the framers of the federal Constitution and to such supporters of that document as James Iredell and John Marshall. Varnum furnished his contemporaries and posterity with a full statement of his position by publishing it in pamphlet form together with an account of Weeden's trial and the judges' hearing before the Assembly. This work was widely disseminated and was even advertised for sale in the Philadelphia press during April and May 1787 as the delegates were entering that city to participate in the Grand Convention. Rhode Island's paper-money embroglio had an impact far beyond the confines of the butcher shop of John Weeden, for it enabled James Varnum, in defending the right of trial by jury, to make a significant contribution to the development of American constitutional thought.

"The First Liberty"

When one considers voting rights and the federal Constitution today, the Fifteenth, Nineteenth, and Twenty-sixth amendments come most readily to mind. The Bill of Rights is mute, because voting in pre-Civil War

America was left solely to colonial and then to state regulation. Yet any discussion of rights in early America must deal with the right to vote (or, as conservatives may call it, the privilege), because it was then considered to be "the first liberty," the "basis of civil liberty," and a key to the enjoyment of most other individual rights. In Rhode Island an eligible voter was in fact styled a "freeman." Under the charter of 1663 only a freeman had a right to hold office, to sit on juries, and to be a plaintiff in any suit. The freehold (i.e., the ownership of real property) was not only the prerequisite for suffrage and office-holding but the ticket of admittance into civil society as well.

Contrary to widely held opinion, Rhode Island's basic law of 1663 did not establish a specific suffrage requirement. It simply empowered the Assembly to "choose, nominate and appoint" freemen of the colony. However, both the framers and recipients of the charter apparently considered the franchise a privilege to be exercised only by those who had been elevated to the status of freemen, and indeed such was the practice both in the towns and in the colony prior to 1663. Thus, under the royal charter freemanship remained a prerequisite for voting, and the colonial legislature in 1664 declared "that none presume to vote... but such whome this Generall Assembly expressly by their writing shall admitt as freemen."

In 1665 visiting royal commissioners informed Rhode Islanders that it was "his Majestyes will and pleasure" that an oath of allegiance be taken by every householder in the colony and that "all men of competante estates and of civill conversation, who acknowledge and are obediante to the civill magistrate, though of differing judgments, may be admitted to be freemen, and have liberty to choose and to be chosen officers both civill and military." The Assembly promptly responded to the commissioners' suggestions by enacting a statute which enabled those of "competent estates" to become freemen of the colony after taking a prescribed oath. Those not admitted to colony freemanship could not vote for "publicke officers" (i.e., governor, deputy governor, and assistants) or deputies, nor could they hold colonial office themselves.

Because most freemen had dual status, many historians have failed to realize that a distinction existed between freemen of the towns and freemen of the colony. The town freeman was empowered to vote for local officials such as members of the town council, sergeant, constable, and treasurer, but the suffrage statute of 1665 withheld from one who was only a freeman of a town the privilege of selecting deputies to the colonial Assembly. This restriction was not permanently removed until 1723. In addition, a man who was merely a town freeman could not vote for general officers of the colony; an act of 1760 clearly stated that such votes were invalid and "shall be rejected and thrown out."

According to the statute of 1665, a person became a freeman of the colony either by direct application to the Assembly or through being proposed by the chief officer of the town in which he lived. In the early years some who petitioned the Assembly directly were not town freemen. A few (such as some Block Island petitioners of 1665) were inhabitants of unincorporated territory, while others held their land elsewhere in the colony than the town in which they resided. A person who was only a freeman of the colony was prohibited by statute from voting for local officials.

In the normal course of events, however, Rhode Islanders secured dual freemanship. After gaining the right of inhabitancy and acquiring a "competent estate" in the town where they had chosen to reside, they applied and were admitted to town freemanship by their fellow townsmen of that status, and then their names were proposed or "propounded" to the General Assembly for admittance as freemen of the colony by the town's chief officer or the town clerk. When town freemen were proposed to the Assembly in this manner, their acceptance as freemen of the colony was practically assured. Once they were approved, their names were entered in the records of the colony.

In 1719 a religious test was added to the property qualification. As previously noted, it denied freemanship to Roman Catholics and non-Christians. Such exclusions, though violating the spirit of the charter, remained in effect until 1783 for Catholics and until 1798 for Jews and other non-Christians.

In 1723 the Assembly passed a statute setting the first specific landed requirement for town freemanship. Since that status was the usual and nearly automatic prelude to colonial freemanship, the act is worthy of citation. This law stipulated that a person must be a "freeholder of lands, tenements, or hereditaments in such town where he shall be admitted free, of the value of one hundred pounds, or to the [rental] value of forty shillings per annum, or the eldest son of such a freeholder." In 1729 the General Assembly increased the real estate requirement to £200, raised it to £400 in 1746, and reduced it to £40 (ca. $134) by 1760. These drastic and erratic changes were more the result of inflationary and deflationary trends than of legislative stringency or fickleness.

The changes in land valuation requirements were often accompanied by provisions designed to eliminate fraud and election abuses. Since many people continued to vote after they had disposed of the property upon which they had been admitted, legislation was enacted in 1742 and 1746 to ban this practice and other types of chicanery.

The last reform and revision of the colonial franchise laws in 1762 attacked further irregularities by denying the vote to those who owned only houses or tenements, but not the title in fee simple to the land upon which the structure stood. It also denied the franchise in the right of a wife's dower. This law was the first to specifically acknowledge the reserved right of townsmen to reject a freeholder proposed and duly qualified according to law. Henceforth, property did not *ipso facto* carry with it the right of admission.

Freehold requirements and suffrage stipulations enacted by the legislature might cause the uncritical reader to assume that the franchise was a privilege enjoyed by a select minority. Such an inference would be erroneous. The real estate requirement for freemanship was not a measure of oppression or restriction in a rural, agrarian society where land tenure was widely dispersed. The suffrage statute of 1746 declared that the manner of admitting freemen was "lax" and the real estate qualification was "very low." Authoritative students of Rhode Island's colonial history estimate that 75 percent of the colony's white adult male population could meet the specific freehold requirements from the time of their imposition in 1723 to the outbreak of the Revolutionary War.

This fact, however, needs some qualification. Being allowed to vote and to hold office was not synonymous with exercising those privileges. Normally less than half the freemen bothered to vote, and those that did often elected to office men from the upper socioeconomic strata. To coin a phrase, Rhode Island democracy was one of indifference and deference, but a democracy it was.

Rhode Island's political antics (not to mention its autonomy) scandalized many a squeamish observer. In the eyes of conservative critics, the land of Roger Williams, even on the eve of revolt, was "dangerously democratic." Chief Justice Daniel Horsmanden of New York, in a 1773 report to the earl of Dartmouth during the *Gaspee* investigation, disdainfully described Rhode Island as a "downright democracy" whose governmental officials were "entirely controlled by the populace," and conservative Massachusetts governor Thomas Hutchinson lamented to George III that Rhode Island was "the nearest to a democracy of any of your colonies."

Because of such "democratic" conditions, the generation prior to the War for Independence saw no protests or reform measures indicating dissatisfaction with the suffrage requirements or with the charter-imposed system of legislative apportionment. Rhode Islanders of the Revolutionary generation and their individualistic forebears were ever mindful that they enjoyed near-autonomy within the empire and broad powers of self-government within their colony. They were also keenly aware that their self-determination flowed in large measure from the munificent charter of Charles II. Thus they harbored a passionate attachment for the document and defended it against all comers. They allowed it to weather the Revolutionary upheaval, and they retained it as the basic law of the state until 1843, a point far beyond its useful life.

The liberality of the seventeenth-century charter prompted Rhode Islanders to preserve and enshrine it—even, we may say, to embalm it—until the patent became, in the eyes of Thomas Wilson Dorr and other political reformers of the nineteenth century, a despised and reactionary relic of a bygone age. That such a font of freedom could become the source of real injustice is the cruel irony and the great tragedy of Rhode Island's constitutional history.

Land of the Free, Home of the Slave

It is sometimes said that the road to hell is paved with good intentions. So it was in colonial Rhode Island. In the first fifty years of the colony's existence, the lawmakers in Roger Williams's refuge from oppression passed two notable measures banning the enslavement of blacks and Indians. In 1652, during William Coddington's short-lived secession from the colony (he had secured a proprietorship over Conanicut, later Jamestown, and the Aquidneck Island settlements of Newport and Portsmouth), the remaining towns of Providence and Warwick passed a measure banning permanent black servitude. This law, called by American colonial historian Charles McLean Andrews "the first legislative act of emancipation in the history of the colonies," was probably the work of Samuel Gorton, for Williams was in England at the time securing a revocation of Coddington's proprietorship. Perhaps written in response to the purchase of blacks from the Dutch by Newporters, the law read as follows:

> Whereas there is a common course practiced among Englishmen, to buy negroes to the end that they may have them for service or slaves forever, for the preventing of such practices among us, let it be ordered that no black mankind, or white, being forced to covenant bond or otherwise, serve any man or his assigns longer than ten years, or until they come to be twenty-four years of age if they be taken under fourteen, for the time of their coming within the liberties of the Colony, and at the end or term of ten years to set them free as the manner is with English servants, and that man will not let them go free, or shall sell them away elsewhere, to that end that they may be enslaved to others for a longer time, he or they shall forfeit to the Colony forty pounds.

Rhode Island's Native Americans were also the beneficiaries of such good intentions. A subsidiary cause of Roger Williams's banishment from Massachusetts was his insistence that without Indian deeds the English colonists lacked valid title to their land. According to Williams, the king of England had no power to grant land owned by Native Americans. Williams's support of Indian property rights and his early missionary work among the local tribes prompted them to return his kindness. The Wampanoags under Chief Massasoit gave him shelter during the winter of 1635–36 following his banishment. Of Native American hospitality Williams later wrote:

> I've known them to leave their house and mat
> To lodge a friend or stranger
> When Jews and Christians oft have sent
> Christ Jesus to the manger.

In addition to his spiritual ministry to the Indians, Williams was concerned with their language and customs. On his return to England in 1643 to secure a patent to protect Providence, Portsmouth, and Newport from the encroachments of the neighboring colonies, Williams published his *Key into the Language of America*, the first English-language dictionary and ethnography of a Native American people.

Williams secured the lands upon which his Providence plantation was established between 1638 and 1659 by a series of deeds from the Narragansett tribe. Concerning the initial deed from chief sachems Canonicus and Miantonomi, Williams remarked that "Not a penny was demanded by either.... It was not price nor money that could have purchased Rhode Island. Rhode Island was purchased by love."

As late as March 1676, during a great Indian war, Rhode Island stood apart from its aggressive neighboring colonies by enacting a statute providing that "no Indian in this colony be a slave but only to pay their debts, or for their bringing up, or courtesy they have received, or to perform covenant as if they had been countrymen not in war." This curious language was designed to prevent the enslavement of Indian captives, a practice that began in New England when Connecticut colonists nearly exterminated the Pequot tribe in 1637.

So much for good intentions! Blacks lost their legislative protection against permanent enslavement in 1654 when the Rhode Island towns were reunited, thereby rendering the Providence-Warwick slave ban a dead letter. Indians lost their protection after the bitter and bloody King Philip's War (1675–76), the culmination of a four-decade decline of Indian-white relations in southern New England. Clashes in culture, the appropriation by whites of Indian land for their exclusive ownership, and a series of hostile incidents between the Wampanoag chief King Philip (Metacomet) and the aggressive government of Plymouth Colony resulted in this terrible colonial conflict. The natives' futile struggle to rid New England of the white man consumed the lives of several thousand Indians and more than six hundred whites and resulted in enormous property damage.

The Narragansetts, at first neutral, joined forces with the Wampanoags after a Plymouth force staged a sneak attack on the Narragansetts' principal village in the Great Swamp (South Kingstown) in December 1675. The Great Swamp Fight cost the lives of three hundred warriors and almost four hundred women and children. The Narragansetts regrouped and launched a vengeful offensive the following spring. On March 26 a large war party led by chief sachem Canonchet killed a company of approximately sixty-five Englishmen and twenty friendly Indians led by Captain Michael Pierce on the banks of the Blackstone in present-day Central Falls. Three days later the victorious Narragansetts descended upon defenseless Providence, burning most of the buildings in that town. For Roger Williams, who not only witnessed the event but saw his own home put to the torch, it represented the destruction of four decades of hard-earned progress.

But famine, disease, and wartime casualties soon decimated the ranks of the Narragansetts and their Wampanoag allies. The killing of King Philip in August 1676 by an Indian allied with the whites effectively ended the war. Remnants of the Narragansetts and Wampanoags, having lost most of their tribal land, sought refuge with the peaceful Niantics, who had remained neutral. This aggregate of remnant groups became the foundation of a new Indian community in Rhode Island that ultimately assumed the name Narragansett.

White retribution was harsh and cruel. The body of Philip was drawn and quartered and his head placed above the stockade at Plymouth as a warning to other potential rebels. Canonchet suffered a similar fate, and his head was sent to Hartford as a trophy of war. Some so-called "ringleaders" were executed for war crimes. Many Indians who survived fared little better. Philip's widow and nine-year-old son, along with other "dangerous" captives, were sold into permanent West Indian slavery. Two Providence trading companies were formed to engage in this exportation of human cargo. Other natives were sentenced to penal servitude for specified periods on local plantations in southern Rhode Island. A bitter and disillusioned Williams gave support to these retributions.

During the century following King Philip's War, slavery gained a strong foothold in Rhode Island, especially as a consequence of the development of the foreign slave trade after 1700. According to the census of 1708, the colony had 426 blacks out of a total population of 7,181. Nearly all came from Barbados, and a small percentage enjoyed free status. The black population peaked at 4,697 in the colonial census of 1755, a figure that was 11.62 percent of the total population, and it then declined (due to escapes and sales) to 3,668 by 1774. Native Americans numbered 1,479 in the latter census, and whites accounted for 54,560 inhabitants. These Rhode Island enumerations did not distinguish between free blacks and slaves, but best estimates place the slave population at about 3,000 on the eve of the Revolution.

A significant number of colonial Rhode Islanders were not free. Many blacks and Indians and their offspring of mixed blood were enslaved and labored on South County plantations or in the homes of wealthy merchants in Newport, Providence, and Bristol. Other colonists were indentured servants who were bound to work or serve as apprentices for a fixed number of years. Shown here is a copy of a 1760 indenture issued by the Providence Town Council binding pauper Phebe Smith and her infant to the service of Eleazer Green for a term of fifteen years and four months. The other illustration is a *Providence Gazette* advertisement for a runaway slave who escaped from the service of Mark Anthony D'Wolf of Bristol, a notorious slave trader.

PROVIDENCE, March 30, 1763.

RUN away from MARK ANTHONY D'WOLF, *of Bristol, a Negro Man named YORK, a very black looking Fellow, strait limb'd, well set, and speaks good English. He had on when he went away, a blue Broad-cloth Coat, a red great Coat, and a Pair of black Plush Breeches.——Whoever will take up said Negro, and deliver him to the Subscriber, in Providence, or otherwise secure him, so that his Master may have him again, shall have* FOUR DOLLARS *Reward, and all necessary Charges paid, by*

WILLIAM PROUD.

N. B. *He has been lately seen at Cranston, and other Country Places near Providence.*

Rhode Island merchants, especially Bristol's James De Wolf, dominated the eighteenth-century slave trade. In this contemporary sketch by Jens-Peter Kemmler, De Wolf, in command of the *Polly*, is depicted taking on a cargo of slaves at the Danish settlement on Africa's Guinea Coast.

Rhode Island slavery was concentrated in the commercial centers of Newport (the town with the largest slave population), Providence, and Bristol, and on the large farms of southern Rhode Island, especially those of South Kingstown, North Kingstown, and Charlestown. Mainly the stigma of Negro blood, either pure or mixed by liaisons with Indians or whites, it was enforced by a series of legislative enactments that cumulatively resembled the slave code of Virginia. Buttressed by Rhode Island's leadership role in the African slave trade, slavery was relatively more significant in Rhode Island than in any other northern colony.

The nefarious traffic in human chattel is the most serious blot on Rhode Island's libertarian reputation. Recounting the history of that trade in his book *The Notorious Triangle*, Jay Coughtry states that "Rhode Island was the principal American carrier" of slaves from Africa's Guinea Coast to the New World. On a typical voyage, a Newport, Bristol, or Providence merchant (e.g., Aaron Lopez, James De Wolf, or John Brown) sent rum and other items to Africa, traded these commodities for blacks, transported this human cargo along the brutal "middle passage" to the West Indies, and exchanged it for money, sugar, and molasses to make more rum. Some select blacks were retained by these slave traders for domestic or agricultural service in Rhode Island. For the period from 1709 (the year of the first Rhode Island voyage) to the end of 1807 (when Congress outlawed the traffic), Coughtry has documented 934 Rhode Island slaving expeditions carrying 106,544 Africans to bondage in the New World—and his figures are admittedly incomplete. "The trade," says Coughtry, "was a staple of Rhode Island commerce."

If there was a positive aspect to Rhode Island's slave system, it consisted in the fact that black slaves were not subjected to severer punishments than whites for the same offenses (as they were in some colonies), and they enjoyed the same legal protection that whites did for offenses against their persons. In addition, blacks could own real or personal property; and except for the period from 1822 to May 1843, there was no racial qualification for freemanship in Rhode Island.

As early as 1719, some leaders of Rhode Island's large and influential Quaker community began to publicly condemn the slave trade. Later, as more Friends embarked upon the crusade, they were joined by the Anglican Society for the Propagation of the Gospel in Foreign Parts and by such prominent Congregational ministers as the Reverend Samuel Hopkins. At first these moral exhortations were no match for economic realities, but by 1774 the state of public opinion about slavery had changed. In that year the Providence town meeting declined to accept six blacks that the town inherited when their master died intestate; "it is unbecoming the character of freemen to enslave the said negroes," that body declared. Then, upon the urging of Moses Brown and Stephen Hopkins, the town meeting memorialized the General Assembly as follows: "Whereas, the inhabitants of America are engaged in the preservation of their rights and liberties; and as personal liberty is an essential part of the rights of mankind, the deputies of the town are directed to use their endeavors to obtain an act of the General Assembly, prohibiting the importation of negro slaves into this colony; and that all negroes born in the colony should be free, after attaining to a certain age." This same momentous town meeting also called upon the legislature to appoint delegates to a continental congress, the first official act leading to a meeting of that revolutionary assemblage.

James De Wolf (1764–1837) was a slave trader, privateer, and, eventually, U.S. senator from Rhode Island. In 1837, after a full life as lawbreaker and lawmaker, De Wolf died on his elegant thousand-acre Bristol estate.

The legislature complied in part by approving a ban on the importation of slaves into the colony. After the outbreak of hostilities the revolution in race relations gained momentum. In 1778 the First Rhode Island Regiment of the Continental army recouped early losses by recruiting slaves (who were offered freedom for enlisting for the duration of the war) as well as free blacks, mulattoes, and Indians. This "colored" battalion fought with distinction at the Battle of Rhode Island (August 1778) and saw much bloody action later in the war.

The Quaker-led campaign against slavery advanced in October 1779, when the Assembly forbade the sale of Rhode Island slaves outside the state without their consent. The most significant of the Revolution-inspired statutes relating to blacks, however, was the Emancipation Act of 1784. With a preface invoking the sentiments of John Locke—namely, that "all men are entitled to life, liberty and property"—this gradual manumission measure gave freedom to all children born to slave mothers after March 1, 1784. Although the statute had obvious merits, it was not a complete abolition of slavery, for it failed to require the emancipation of those who were slaves at the time of its passage.

Three years later, as public debate on the merits of the new federal Constitution began, Rhode Island's increasing aversion to slavery intensified the state's Antifederalism. This attitude was strong among Rhode Island's sizable Quaker community, but it was shared by others as well, perhaps to atone for past sins. Opponents of slavery realized that the Philadelphia Convention had compromised on this issue, and they were aware that the Constitution thrice gave implied assent to the institution through the clauses on representation and taxation, fugitives, and the slave trade. In particular, the twenty-year prohibition on federal legislation banning the foreign slave traffic was a concession too great for many Rhode Islanders to accept.

Only five weeks after the adjournment of the Philadelphia conclave, the General Assembly passed an act, initiated by the influential and irrepressible Quakers, prohibiting any Rhode Island citizen from engaging in the slave trade. In vigorous language, this statute termed the nefarious traffic "inconsistent with justice, and the principles of humanity, as well as the laws of nature, and that more enlightened and civilized sense of freedom which has of late prevailed." A constitution that gave temporary protection to this trade was not an instrument to be warmly embraced.

Thus the state's antislavery contingent took refuge in Antifederalism, and during the critical year of 1790 this connection nearly thwarted ratification. Fortunately, however, there were some abolitionist leaders who began to see the difficulties inherent in Rhode Island's continued rejection of the Constitution. One such man was the influential Quaker Moses Brown of the famous mercantile family. Despite some initial misgivings, he actively embraced the Federalist cause by 1790. Early in this fateful year Brown and Daniel Howland toured the state, talking with Friends at the various monthly meetings in an attempt to overcome their opposition. Their campaign seems to have met with limited success, but the antislavery objections to the Constitution were by no means dispelled when the March session of the ratifying convention assembled.

Slavery engendered much discussion and debate at this South Kingstown meeting. In fact, the slave-trade provision of the Constitution provoked such opposition that an amendment (XVII) exhorting Congress to ban the traffic immediately was specifically proposed and approved. Rhode Island was the only state to suggest such an amendment to the federal Constitution during the ratification struggle.

Some local opponents of slavery doggedly maintained their Antifederalism until the end. When the Providence Abolition Society, founded in February 1789, received its charter from the state in June 1790, the list of incorporators included ten members of the May ratifying convention. The antislaveryites included President Daniel Owen and Antifederal floor leaders Joseph Stanton, Jr., and Job Comstock. Only three of these ten abolitionist delegates voted to accept the federal document on May 29.

Despite the successes of the abolitionists between 1774 and 1790, the first federal census in 1790 counted 948 slaves in a black population of 3,863. In 1810 there were 108 slaves in a black community that totaled 3,717, and as late as 1840 five blacks remained chattels. Not until the implementation of a written state constitution in May 1843 was slavery absolutely forbidden. In Rhode Island the "peculiar institution" died a lingering death.

Rights and Ratification

Concern for the preservation of individual liberty and the maintenance of states' rights profoundly influenced Rhode Island's reaction to the Constitution of 1787. The state's dogged Antifederalism was primarily rights-related. Rhode Island had a strong tradition of individualism, separatism, democracy, and liberty, both civil and religious. It harbored a long-standing distrust of government too far removed from the people, together with an attachment to popular control of government that one historian has termed "democratic localism." These principles were not endangered by the Articles of Confederation, to which the state readily assented. The Articles gave the people of a state—or, more precisely, their legislature—close control over delegates to Congress. Under the Confederation, members of Congress were annually appointed in a manner prescribed by the state legislature, they were subject to recall, and they were paid by their respective states. Under the Articles, as in Rhode Island, supreme governmental power was vested in the legislature.

In addition to these features, the Articles exalted state sovereignty. In all important civil matters Congress was dependent upon the voluntary compliance of the state legislatures to carry out its recommendations, and the approval of all the states was necessary to amend our inflexible first frame of government.

This system was rejected by the Constitution in ways too familiar to enumerate, and Rhode Island disapproved of the change. Some of its specific objections were contained in the eighteen amendments to the new federal document offered by the Rhode Island ratifying convention of March 1790. These amendments revealed a deep suspicion of the new central establishment, a suspicion that had been increased by the failure of the proposed Constitution to contain a bill of rights.

Rhode Island's first suggested amendment requested a guarantee to each state of its sovereignty and of every power not expressly delegated to the United States by the Constitution; Amendment II attempted to limit federal interference in a state's conduct of congressional elections; Amendment XII prohibited as "dangerous to liberty" standing armies in time of peace; Amendments XIII and XIV called for a two-thirds vote of those present in each house to borrow money on the credit of the United States or to declare war: Amendment XVIII subjected senators to recall and replacement by their state legislature. Rhode Island was so fearful that the newly created federal system would develop beyond control that it offered a unique amendment (IV) which would have required all changes in the Constitution after 1793 to receive the consent of eleven of the thirteen original states. Those congressionally advanced amendments that eventually became the Bill of Rights of course won the state's enthusiastic support, especially the Tenth Amendment.

In an official communication to Congress in September 1789, the General Assembly quite adequately and accurately expressed the ideological basis of the state's Antifederalism:

> The people of this State from its first settlement, have been accustomed and strongly attached to a democratic form of government. They have viewed in the new Constitution an approach, though perhaps but small, toward that form of government from which we have lately dissolved our connection at so much hazard and expense of life and treasure.... We are sensible of the extremes to which democratic governments are sometimes liable, something of which we have lately experienced, but we esteem them temporary and partial evils compared with the loss of liberty and the rights of a free people.

This was not mere rhetoric. Just as Rhode Islanders were quick to protest an alleged abridgment by England of their individual and collective freedom, so also did they resist an anticipated curtailment of their "liberty" and autonomy by the Founding Fathers. Self-determination in late eighteenth-century Rhode Island was a way of life, and no portion of it would be easily surrendered, as the contest over ratification dramatically revealed.

On May 29, 1790, nearly fifteen months after the new federal government began, Rhode Island grudgingly approved the Constitution by a vote of 34-32—the narrowest margin of any state. The formal certificate ratifying the Constitution also gave assent to eleven of the twelve amendments to the Constitution proposed by Congress and boldly offered twenty-one additional amendments, many of which had been previously proposed by the Virginia and New York ratifying conventions. On June 11, 1790, the General Assembly gave its necessary approval to the Bill of Rights, making Rhode Island the ninth state to take such action. Of the twelve proposed amendments, only number two, pertaining to congressional pay, was rejected.

Unfinished Business

Rhode Island was one of two original states (Connecticut was the other) to retain its royal charter rather than draft a new state constitution during the Revolutionary era. Since its 1663 basic law contained no procedure for amendment, newly enunciated rights could only be guaranteed by statute. The General Assembly enacted such a declaration in 1798, when it adopted the first compilation of the general laws since 1767. The most notable feature of this legal revision, called the *Digest of 1798,* was its statutory bill of rights. These "political axioms or truths," which were declared "to be of paramount obligation in all legislative, judicial and executive proceedings," were contained in ten provisions. They included the right of all to a legal remedy for injuries or wrongs to property and character, protection against unreasonable search and seizure, immunity from double jeopardy, protection from excessive bail and cruel and unusual punishment, the privilege of habeas corpus, a guarantee of procedural due process, the termination of imprisonment for debt once the debtor's estate had been delivered up for the benefit of his creditors, a ban on *ex post facto* laws, freedom from involuntary self-incrimination, and a presumption of innocence until guilt was proven.

Following this "Act Declaratory of Certain Rights of the People of this State" was another "Relative to Religious Freedom and the Maintenance of Ministers." This remarkable statute was as advanced as any drafted or conceived during this era of liberal religious declarations, but it was no more than an explicit rendering of the principles upon which Roger Williams founded his Providence plantation. The act itself declared that "no man shall be compelled to frequent or support any religious worship, place or ministry whatsoever; nor shall be enforced, restrained, molested, or bothered in his body or goods, nor shall otherwise suffer on account of his religious opinion or belief; but that all men shall be free to profess, and by argument to maintain, their opinions in matters of religion, and that the same shall in no wise diminish, enlarge or affect their civil capacities."

The act's preamble was even more emphatic. It condemned as "sinful and tyrannical" laws compelling a man to contribute money to support opinions in which he disbelieved and called forced contributions to support particular teachers of one's own religion a deprivation of liberty. It also claimed that civil rights were not dependent on religious opinions, so that barring any citizen from public office "unless he profess or renounce this or that religious opinion, is depriving him injuriously of those privileges and advantages to which, in common with his fellow citizens, he has a natural right." Such a proscription, the act concluded, tended "only to corrupt the principles of that religion it is meant to encourage, by bribing, with a monopoly of worldly honours and emoluments, those who will externally profess and conform to it."

This enlightened measure was a vigorous reaffirmation of Rhode Island's long-standing commitment to the principles of religious liberty and church-state separation. Roger Williams would have rejoiced at the enduring nature of his "lively experiment."

As the eighteenth century drew to a close, Rhode Island's government, its basic law, and the statutes which implemented that document still compared favorably with those of the other states. Although the retention of the colonial charter was unusual, few people were disturbed by its continued operation. Religious liberty continued to be as broad as it was anywhere, and the statute qualifying freemen was not unduly restrictive (such land qualifications were not uncommon at the turn of the century). In fact, there were no serious complaints except those occasioned by the charter's inequitable apportionment favoring the four original towns. But times and conditions were destined to change, and the inflexible charter could not.

Four decades later—with Rhode Island in the throes of economic and demographic change—limited suffrage, increasing malapportionment, the omnipotence and adamancy of the legislature, and the absence of a constitutional bill of rights became grievances severe enough to incite another crusade for equal rights, an upheaval that Rhode Islanders call the Dorr Rebellion.

This 1784 act providing for the gradual abolition of slavery in Rhode Island was an effect of the liberalizing tendencies of the American Revolution.

An ACT authorizing the Manumiſſion of Negroes, Mulattoes and others, and for the gradual Abolition of Slavery.

Act for the gradual Abolition of Slavery.

WHEREAS all Men are entitled to Life, Liberty, and the Purſuit of Happineſs, and the holding Mankind in a State of Slavery, as private Property, which has gradually obtained by unreſtrained Cuſtom and the Permiſſion of the Laws, is repugnant to this Principle, and ſubverſive of the Happineſs of Mankind, the great End of all civil Government:

BE it therefore Enacted by this General Aſſembly, and by the Authority thereof it is Enacted, That no Perſon or Perſons, whether Negroes, Mulattoes, or others, who ſhall be born within the Limits of this State, on or after the Firſt Day of *March*, A. D. 1784, ſhall be deemed or conſidered as Servants for Life, or Slaves; and that all Servitude for Life, or Slavery of Children, to be born as aforeſaid, in Conſequence of the Condition of their Mothers, be, and the ſame is hereby taken away, extinguiſhed and for ever aboliſhed.

AND whereas Humanity requires, that Children declared free as aforeſaid remain with their Mothers a convenient Time from and after their Birth; to enable therefore thoſe who claim the Services of ſuch Mothers to maintain and ſupport ſuch Children in a becoming Manner, *It is further Enacted by the Authority aforeſaid,* That ſuch Support and Maintenance be at the Expence of the reſpective Towns where thoſe reſide and are ſettled: *Provided however,* That the reſpective Town-Councils may bind out ſuch Children as Apprentices, or otherwiſe provide for their Support and Maintenance, at any Time after they arrive to the Age of One Year, and before they arrive to their reſpective Ages of Twenty-one, if Males, and Eighteen, if Females.

AND whereas it the earneſt Deſire of this Aſſembly, that ſuch Children be educated in the Principles of Morality and Religion, and inſtructed in Reading, Writing and Arithmetic: *Be it further Enacted by the Authority aforeſaid,* That due and adequate Satiſfaction be made as aforeſaid for ſuch Education and Inſtruction. And for aſcertaining the Allowance for ſuch Support, Maintenance, Education and Inſtruction, the reſpective Town-Councils are hereby required to adjuſt and ſettle the Accounts in this Behalf from Time to Time, as the ſame ſhall be exhibited to them: Which Settlement ſo made ſhall be final; and the reſpective Towns by Virtue thereof ſhall become liable to pay the Sums therein ſpecified and allowed.

AND be it further Enacted by the Authority aforeſaid, That all Perſons held in Servitude or Slavery, who ſhall be hereafter emancipated by thoſe who claim them, ſhall be ſupported as other Paupers, and not at the ſeparate Expence of the Claimants, if they become chargeable; provided they ſhall be between the Ages of Twenty-one Years, if Males, and Eighteen Years, if Females, and Forty Years, and are of ſound Body and Mind; which ſhall be judged of, and determined by the Town-Councils aforeſaid.

The BILL of RIGHTS, and AMENDMENTS to the CONSTITUTION OF THE UNITED STATES, as agreed to by the CONVENTION of the State of *Rhode-Iſland and Providence-Plantations*, at *South-Kingſtown*, in the County of *Waſhington*, on the Firſt *Monday* of *March*, A. D. 1790.

DECLARATION of RIGHTS.

1. THAT there are certain natural rights, of which men, when they form a ſocial compact, cannot deprive or diveſt their poſterity—among which are the enjoyment of life and liberty, with the means of acquiring, poſſeſſing and protecting property, and purſuing and obtaining happineſs and ſafety.

2. That all power is naturally veſted in and conſequently derived from the people: That magiſtrates, therefore, are their truſtees and agents, and at all times amenable to them.

3. That the powers of government may be reaſſumed by the people, whenſoever it ſhall become neceſſary to their happineſs:—That the rights of the States reſpectively to nominate and appoint all State officers, and every other power, juriſdiction and right, which is not by the ſaid Conſtitution clearly delegated to the Congreſs of the United States, or to the departments of government thereof, remain to the people of the ſeveral States, or their reſpective State governments, to whom they may have granted the ſame;—and that thoſe clauſes in the ſaid Conſtitution, which declare that Congreſs ſhall not have or exerciſe certain powers, do not imply, that Congreſs is entitled to any powers not given by the ſaid Conſtitution;—but ſuch clauſes are to be conſtrued, either as exceptions to certain ſpecified powers, or as inſerted merely for greater caution.

4. That religion, or the duty which we owe to our Creator, and the manner of diſcharging it, can be directed only by reaſon and conviction, not by force or violence—and therefore all men have an equal, natural and unalienable right to the free exerciſe of religion, according to the dictates of conſcience;—and that no particular religious ſect, or ſociety, ought to be favoured or eſtabliſhed by law, in preference to others.

5. That the legiſlative, executive and judiciary powers of government, ſhould be ſeparate and diſtinct;—and that the members of the two firſt may be reſtrained from oppreſſion, by feeling and participating the public burthens, they ſhould at fixed periods be reduced to a private ſtation, return into the maſs of the people, and the vacancies be ſupplied by certain and regular elections—in which all or any part of the former members to be eligible or ineligible, as the rules of the Conſtitution of government and the laws ſhall direct.

6. That elections of Repreſentatives in the Legiſlature ought to be free and frequent—and all men, having ſufficient evidence of permanent common intereſt with and attachment to the community, ought to have the right of ſuffrage: And no aid, charge, tax or fee, can be ſet, rated or levied upon the people, without their own conſent, or that of their Repreſentatives, ſo elected;—nor can they be bound by any law, to which they have not, in like manner, aſſented for the public good.

7. That all power of ſuſpending laws, or the execution of laws, by any authority, without the conſent of the Repreſentatives of the people in the Legiſlature, is injurious to their rights, and ought not to be exerciſed.

8. That in all capital and criminal proſecutions, a man hath a right to demand the cauſe and nature of his accuſation—to be confronted with the accuſers and witneſſes—to call for evidence, and be allowed counſel in his favour—and to a fair and ſpeedy trial by an impartial jury of his vicinage, without whoſe unanimous conſent he cannot be found guilty (except in the government of the land and naval forces) nor can he be compelled to give evidence againſt himſelf.

9. That no freeman ought to be taken, impriſoned, or diſſeized of his freehold, liberties, privileges or franchiſes, or outlawed, or exiled, or in any manner deſtroyed, or deprived of his life, liberty or property, but by the trial by jury, or by the law of the land.

10. That every freeman reſtrained of his liberty is entitled to a remedy, to enquire into the lawfulneſs thereof, and to remove the ſame, if unlawful;—and that ſuch remedy ought not to be denied or delayed.

11. That in controverſies reſpecting property, and in ſuits between man and man, the ancient trial by jury, as hath been exerciſed by us and our anceſtors, from the time whereof the memory of man is not to the contrary, is one of the greateſt ſecurities to the rights of the people, and ought to remain ſacred and inviolate.

12. That every freeman ought to obtain right and juſtice freely, and without ſale—completely, and without denial—promptly, and without delay—and that all eſtabliſhments or regulations, contravening theſe rights, are oppreſſive and unjuſt.

13. That exceſſive bail ought not to be required, nor exceſſive fines impoſed, nor cruel or unuſual puniſhments inflicted.

14. That every perſon has a right to be ſecure from all unreaſonable ſearches and ſeizures of his perſon, his papers, or his property;—and therefore that all warrants to ſearch ſuſpected places, or ſeize any perſon, his papers, or his property, without information upon oath, or affirmation of ſufficient cauſe, are grievous and oppreſſive;—and that all general warrants (or ſuch in which the place or perſon ſuſpected are not particularly deſignated) are dangerous, and ought not to be granted.

15. That the people have a right peaceably to aſſemble together, to conſult for their common good, or to inſtruct their Repreſentatives;—and that every perſon has a right to petition, or apply to the Legiſlature, for redreſs of grievances.

16. That the people have a right to freedom of ſpeech, and of writing and publiſhing their ſentiments:—That freedom of the preſs is one of the greateſt bulwarks of liberty, and ought not to be violated.

17. That the people have a right to keep and bear arms:—That a well regulated militia, including the body of the people capable of bearing arms, is the proper, natural and ſafe defence of a free State:—That the militia ſhall not be ſubject to martial law, except in time of war, rebellion or inſurrection:—That ſtanding armies in time of peace are dangerous to liberty, and ought not to be kept up, except in caſes of neceſſity;—and that at all times the military ſhould be under ſtrict ſubordination to the civil power:—That in time of peace no ſoldier ought to be quartered in any houſe without the conſent of the owner—and in time of war, only by the civil magiſtrate, in ſuch manner as the law directs.

18. That any perſon religiouſly ſcrupulous of bearing arms, ought to be exempted, upon payment of an equivalent to employ another to bear arms in his ſtead.

AMENDMENTS to the CONSTITUTION of the UNITED STATES.

1. THE United States ſhall guarantee to each State its ſovereignty, freedom and independence, and every power, juriſdiction and right, which is not by this Conſtitution expreſſly delegated to the United States.

2. That Congreſs ſhall not alter, modify or interfere, in the times, places and manner, of holding elections for Senators and Repreſentatives, or either of them, except when the Legiſlature of any State ſhall neglect, refuſe, or be diſabled, by invaſion or rebellion, to preſcribe the ſame;—or in caſe when the proviſion made by the States is ſo imperfect, as that no conſequent election is had;—and then only, until the Legiſlature of ſuch State ſhall make proviſion in the premiſes.

3. It is declared by the Convention, that the judicial power of the United States, in caſes in which a State may be a party, does not extend to criminal proſecutions, or to authorize any ſuit by any perſon againſt a State—but, to remove all doubts or controverſies reſpecting the ſame, that it be eſpecially expreſſed as a part of the Conſtitution of the United States, that Congreſs ſhall not, directly or indirectly, either by themſelves or through the judiciary, interfere with any one of the States in the redemption of paper money already emitted, and now in circulation, or in liquidating and diſcharging the public ſecurities of any one State:—That each and every State ſhall have the excluſive right of making ſuch laws and regulations for the before mentioned purpoſes, as they ſhall think proper.

4. That no amendments to the Conſtitution of the United States hereafter to be made, purſuant to the fifth article, ſhall take effect, or become a part of the Conſtitution of the United States, after the year 1793, without the conſent of eleven of the States heretofore united under one Confederation.

5. That the judicial powers of the United States ſhall extend to no poſſible caſe, where the cauſe of action ſhall have originated before the ratification of this Conſtitution, except in diſputes between States about their territory—diſputes between perſons claiming lands under grants of different States—and debts due to the United States.

6. That no perſon ſhall be compelled to do military duty, otherwiſe than by voluntary enliſtment, except in caſes of general invaſion; any thing in the ſecond paragraph of the ſixth article of the Conſtitution, or any law made under the Conſtitution, to the contrary notwithſtanding.

7. That no capitation or poll-tax ſhall ever be laid by Congreſs.

8. In caſes of direct taxes, Congreſs ſhall firſt make requiſitions on the ſeveral States, to aſſeſs, levy and pay, their reſpective proportions of ſuch requiſitions, in ſuch way and manner as the Legiſlatures of the ſeveral States ſhall judge beſt. And in caſe any State ſhall neglect or refuſe to pay its proportion, purſuant to ſuch requiſition, then Congreſs may aſſeſs and levy ſuch State's proportion, together with intereſt at the rate of ſix per cent. per annum, from the time preſcribed in ſuch requiſition.

9. That Congreſs ſhall lay no direct taxes, without the conſent of the Legiſlatures of three-fourths of the States in the Union.

10. That the journals of the proceedings of the Senate and Houſe of Repreſentatives ſhall be publiſhed, as ſoon as conveniently may be, at leaſt once in every year, except ſuch parts thereof, relating to treaties, alliances, or military operations, as in their judgment require ſecreſy.

11. That regular ſtatements of the receipts and expenditures of all public monies ſhall be publiſhed at leaſt once a year.

12. As ſtanding armies in time of peace are dangerous to liberty, and ought not to be kept up, except in caſes of neceſſity; and as at all times the military ſhould be under ſtrict ſubordination to the civil power——that therefore no ſtanding army, or regular troops, ſhall be raiſed or kept up in time of peace.

13. That no monies be borrowed on the credit of the United States, without the aſſent of two-thirds of the Senators and Repreſentatives preſent in each Houſe.

14. That the Congreſs ſhall not declare war, without the concurrence of two-thirds of the Senators and Repreſentatives preſent in each Houſe.

15. That the words "without the conſent of Congreſs," in the ſeventh clauſe, in the ninth ſection of the firſt article of the Conſtitution, be expunged.

16. That no Judge of the Supreme Court of the United States ſhall hold any other office under the United States, or any of them; nor ſhall any officer appointed by Congreſs be permitted to hold any office under the appointment of any of the States.

17. As a traffic tending to eſtabliſh or continue the ſlavery of any part of the human ſpecies, is diſgraceful to the cauſe of liberty and humanity—that Congreſs ſhall, as ſoon as may be, promote and eſtabliſh ſuch laws and regulations as may effectually prevent the importation of ſlaves of every deſcription into the United States.

18. And that the amendments propoſed by Congreſs, in March, A. D. 1789, be adopted by this Convention, except the ſecond article therein contained.

In CONVENTION, *March* 6, 1790.

VOTED, That the Bill of Rights and Amendments, propoſed to the Federal Conſtitution, be referred to the Freemen of the ſeveral towns, at their meetings on the Third Wedneſday of April next, for their conſideration: That one copy thereof be ſent to each Town-Clerk in this State, one to each Member of the Convention, and one to each Member of the Upper and Lower Houſes of Aſſembly; and that they be ſent to the Sheriffs of the ſeveral Counties, to be diſtributed.

The foregoing is a true Copy.

By Order of the Convention,

DANIEL UPDIKE, *Secretary.*

Rather than vote on the Constitution, the Antifederal-dominated March session of the ratifying convention boldly proposed a federal bill of rights and eighteen additional constitutional amendments.

BIOGRAPHICAL PROFILES

William Ellery, an ally of Governor Samuel Ward, replaced that deceased leader in May 1776 as Rhode Island's second delegate to the Continental Congress, and thus he gained the distinction (with Stephen Hopkins) of signing the Declaration of Independence. This Harvard-educated lawyer served in the national congress for nearly a decade, specializing in matters dealing with commerce and the navy. In the late 1780s Ellery became a leading supporter of the ratification of the Constitution. His advocacy of that successful cause earned him the lucrative collectorship of customs in Newport, a position he held for thirty years (1790–1820) until his death. Ellery had two illustrious grandchildren—writer and statesman Richard Henry Dana and Unitarian religious leader William Ellery Channing. William Fowler, Jr., has written an excellent life-and-times biography of the Signer entitled *William Ellery: A Rhode Island Politico and Lord of the Admiralty* (1973).

When the country towns took the lead in opposing the federal Constitution, Providence merchants and politicians labored for its ratification. Providence Federalists included lawyer Theodore Foster, for whom the Rhode Island town of Foster is named. Foster was a prominent representative in the General Assembly as well as the Providence town clerk from 1775 to 1787. His efforts in support of the Constitution, together with his advantageous marriage to the sister of Governor Arthur Fenner, gained him election as one of Rhode Island's first United States senators. He served in the Senate from 1790 until 1803, when he retired to engage in historical and scholarly activities. He died in 1828 at the age of seventy-five.

When many businessmen balked at accepting the paper money issued by the Country party in 1786, the General Assembly passed a "force act" imposing criminal penalties on anyone who refused this legal tender. This punishment was to be inflicted without the benefit of trial by jury. When Revolutionary War marine hero John Trevett tendered a bill to his Newport butcher John Weeden, and Weeden declined it, the stage was set for *Trevett* v. *Weeden*, the most important case in Rhode Island's judicial history. The cause was heard before the highest court in the state, and it concluded with the court's refusing jurisdiction and dismissing Trevett's complaint.

In the course of the trial, however, James Mitchell Varnum (right), one of Weeden's defense attorneys, advanced a learned and eloquent argument urging the court to exercise its hitherto unused power to review legislation and declare the force act unconstitutional. Although the court did not act on this plea, Varnum's printed brief was widely disseminated, and it probably influenced John Marshall in his famous formulation of the doctrine of judicial review.

Varnum, a distinguished Revolutionary War general and a founder of the Kentish Guards, left Rhode Island shortly after the trial to seek his fortune in the newly acquired Ohio Country. There he became United States judge for the Northwest Territory and assisted in drafting the first territorial code of laws. Although he was of powerful build and a physical culturist, his health failed in the frontier environment. On January 10, 1789, Varnum's death at the age of forty cut short his highly promising career.

Henry Marchant (1741–1796) was associated with General Varnum as counsel in *Trevett* v. *Weeden*. Marchant was a well-educated Newport intellectual and a protégé of Ezra Stiles. He was an ardent Son of Liberty during the Stamp Act protest and served as Rhode Island attorney general from 1771 to 1777. After the outbreak of the Revolution he was a Rhode Island delegate to the Continental Congress (1777–1779), and after the war he entered the General Assembly as a vigorous spokesman for the state's commercial interest (1784–1790).

In 1790, as a strong supporter of the new federal Constitution, Marchant introduced the successful bill for the call of a ratifying convention, at which he played a leading role. His efforts on behalf of Federalism were rewarded when George Washington appointed him Rhode Island's first federal judge, a post he held from July 1790 until his death in August 1796.

When the Revolution erupted, Marchant left Newport for his South County estate. Though he represented Newport in the General Assembly during the 1780s, he maintained a well-kept farm in South Kingstown until his death.

Part Two

From Statehood through the Nineteenth Century, 1790–1898: The Law as an Instrument of Change

12

The author of the following article, Donald W. Wyatt, has the distinction of being the successor of his pioneering subject, William Peck. Marshal Wyatt, a longtime confidant and political associate of United States senator John H. Chafee, demonstrates the continuing importance of party and patronage in the selection of a U.S. marshal since the time when Peck was identified to President Washington as "a true Federalist." Wyatt's competency in his eighteen-year stint as marshal was acknowledged when the new federal detention facility in Central Falls was named in his honor. Most recently he has served as chairman of the charter review commission in his home city of Warwick and as a member of the Rhode Island Lottery Commission.

William Peck did not fare as well as his biographer. His long tenure was followed by poverty and relative obscurity. Ironically, Peck's immediate successor, Ebenezer Knight Dexter (1773–1824), who assumed the marshal's post in 1810, was a wealthy Providence merchant and philanthropist about whom much more is known. In 1824, by the terms of his will, he bequeathed more than 2,275,000 square feet of land to the town. The largest tract, located off Hope Street, was given for use as a poor farm. An almshouse for paupers, called Dexter Asylum, was built there in 1830 from the designs of architect John Holden Greene. In accordance with Dexter's wishes, the thirty-eight-acre estate upon which the building stood was enclosed by a long stone wall, 8 feet high and 6,220 feet in length.

The property was purchased from the city by Brown University in 1957 for $1,000,777, a sum that was earmarked for poor relief as the Ebenezer Knight Dexter Trust Fund. Brown subsequently erected George V. Meehan Auditorium and a modern athletic complex on the asylum grounds. The Dexter Asylum building was demolished in 1958.

Another tract in his donation is the Dexter Training Grounds, a ten-acre parcel adjacent to the Cranston Street Armory. This land was designated by its grantor as a site for the training of militia. Smaller parcels in Dexter's bequest bring the total land currently in his donation to 584,414 square feet. Both the land and the financial proceeds from Dexter's bequest are managed by the commissioners of the Dexter Donation, a permanent five-member agency chaired by the mayor of Providence.

William Peck—Rhode Island's First U.S. Marshal

By Donald W. Wyatt

In 1790 a thirty-four-year-old Rhode Islander, a veteran of the Revolution, wrote to President George Washington seeking appointment as naval officer for Providence. Although the president did not grant the request, he shortly afterwards named the applicant to another position—that of United States marshal for Rhode Island. Thus William Peck attained the distinction of becoming the first man to serve in that post.

Peck was born in Lyme, Connecticut, on December 15, 1755, and graduated from Yale College in 1775. Joining the Continental Army, he rose through the ranks to become an aide to General Joseph Spencer. When Spencer was assigned to Rhode Island, Peck accompanied him and eventually became assistant adjutant general for the state. In 1779 he married Eunice Corliss in Providence.

Marquis de Chastellux, one of the French officers fighting with the Americans, wrote of Peck in November 1780:

> The 13th I breakfasted with Colonel Peck: He is an amiable and polite young man, who passed the summer with General Heath at Newport. He received me in a charming small house, where he lived with his wife, who is young also, and has a pleasing countenance, but without anything striking. This little establishment, where comfort and simplicty reign, gave an idea of that sweet and serene state of happiness which appears to have taken refuge in the New World, after compounding it with pleasure, to which it has left the Old.

Peck retired from military service in 1781. In 1784 his wife died, leaving him with two sons and a daughter, and on January 25, 1786, he married Abigail Mathewson. It was in the spring of 1790 that he wrote to President Washington to ask for appointment as naval officer for Providence.

Peck was involved at the time in what he described as "mercantile pursuits," but he was on the brink of bankruptcy. Support for his job quest came from William Greene, who informed the president that Peck "was very active and firm in the defense of his country, since obtaining our Independence hath been a true Federalist and is a man of integrity and ability." William Arnold wrote that Peck had a "young and growing" family.

While he did not obtain the desired position, Peck became part of the state's history when Washington appointed him Rhode Island's first United States marshal on July 3, 1790. The nation's first twelve marshals had already been named under provisions of the first Judiciary Act, signed on September 24, 1789, but Rhode Island did not ratify the U.S. Constitution until May 29, 1790, and thus was not part of the Union until that date. Appointed with Peck was U.S. District Court Judge Henry Marchant, who presided at the first

The first census, taken in 1790–91 under the direction of U.S. marshals, listed Americans in five categories and totaled the nation's population at nearly four million. Of that number Marshal Peck counted 68,825 Rhode Islanders, of whom 948 were still slaves. Not until 1907, however, did Congress appropriate funds to publish the manuscript schedules.

DEPARTMENT OF COMMERCE AND LABOR
BUREAU OF THE CENSUS
S. N. D. NORTH, DIRECTOR

HEADS OF FAMILIES
AT THE FIRST CENSUS OF THE
UNITED STATES TAKEN
IN THE YEAR
1790

RHODE ISLAND

WASHINGTON
GOVERNMENT PRINTING OFFICE
1908

federal court session in Newport's Colony House in August 1790. It was on that occasion that Peck chose James Champlin as his deputy.

Marshals originally were given two basic duties: they were to attend District and Circuit Courts and the Supreme Court when it was sitting in their districts, and they were to execute all lawful precepts under authority of the United States. Each marshal was required to post a $20,000 performance bond.

One of Marshal Peck's first needs was a facility to house federal prisoners, and in 1790 the General Assembly passed "An Act for the Safe Keeping in the Gaols of this State, of Prisoners in the Custody of the Marshal of the United States."

Since there was no federal bureaucracy, U.S. marshals became the principal representatives of the national government, and they quickly took on a wide range of duties. One of the most important of these was conducting the census of 1790, which was taken to determine allocation of seats in the U.S. House of Representatives.

While it is not known what Peck was paid for this assignment, it probably was $200, as that was the amount received by the marshal in Connecticut. Marshals were authorized to appoint "assistant marshals" for the census, and these were paid $1 for every 150 persons counted in the country or $1 for each 300 counted in a city or town over 5,000 in population. The cost of the entire census (which showed a national population of nearly 4,000,000) was $45,000.

Because roads were nonexistent in many areas of the young country and the only means of transportation was by horseback, taking the census was an arduous task. There was tremendous pressure to do the job correctly, since a marshal filing a false count could be fined $800.

Other duties of a marshal included receiving and executing precepts from French consuls, executing courts martial, taking custody of vessels and goods seized by revenue officers, selling lands for the federal government, serving as fiscal agents for the courts, and enforcing the Alien Acts of 1798. Among a marshal's more unusual responsibilities, he was to assure that animals in transit were watered and fed at least once every twenty-four hours.

Ebenezer Knight Dexter (1773–1824), a prominent Providence merchant and philanthropist, succeeded William Peck as Rhode Island's U.S. marshal.

Peck served for twenty years, the longest tenure of any of the first generation of marshals. He was succeeded in 1810 by Ebenezer Knight Dexter, a prominent Providence landholder, businessman, and philanthropist.

After retiring, Peck again had difficulty earning a living. In 1818 he wrote to Judge David Howell requesting benefits under an act of Congress granting pensions to indigent Revolutionary War veterans. He informed the judge that he was more than sixty years old, that he was indigent, and that he had "an amiable wife and family" dependent on him for support. His means were scanty, he said, and while early in life he was accustomed to enjoyment of all reasonable and necessary comforts, his present reduced situation obliged him, painful as it was, to apply for assistance. His sworn statement on April 23, 1818, said that he was not in any business, "nor has he been for some time past"; that he could not support himself, his fifty-six-year-old wife, or his two daughters; and that he was in debt for several hundred dollars. Records are silent on whether he was granted a pension.

Rhode Island's first U.S. marshal died on May 19, 1832, at his home on Westminster Street, Providence. He is interred in the North Burial Ground, where his grave is marked by a stone erected by the Society of the Cincinnati. There is no indication where his wife Abigail is buried, but a daughter, Abby E. Peck, rests nearby.

Providence Probate Court records show that Peck left an estate of $136.55 and debts of $156.28. It was necessary for his widow and daughters to pay $19.73 after all his goods had been auctioned.

In all, twenty-six men have served as U.S. marshal in the 195-year history of this federal judicial district [through 1986], but William Peck forever holds the distinction of having been the first. Little did he know when he accepted the appointment from President Washington that he was pioneering in a law enforcement organization which nearly two centuries later would have personnel on duty in ninety-four judicial districts from the Mariana Islands in the Pacific to Puerto Rico in the Atlantic Ocean.

Known today as the United States Marshals Service, a bureau within the Department of Justice, the organization carries out a potpourri of duties, which include providing security for the courts, apprehending fugitives, transporting prisoners, and administering both the Witness Security Program and the National Asset Seizure and Forfeiture Act.

Unlike some later U.S. marshals, William Peck did not end up on Boot Hill. His gravestone is located in Providence's North Burial Ground.

13

James Mitchell Varnum's argument in the 1786 case of *Trevett* v. *Weeden* (discussed in a preceding essay) and the U.S. Circuit Court's ruling in the 1792 case of *Champion and Dickason* v. *Casey* are the two Rhode Island encounters with the doctrine of judicial review prior to John Marshall's invocation of that power in the landmark case of *Marbury* v. *Madison* (1803).

The federal circuit court that decided the *Champion* case differed in composition and function from today's Circuit Court of Appeals. The Constitution created the Supreme Court and enumerated the classes of cases in which the jurisdiction of that court should be original, but it left Congress to determine the jurisdiction of whatever inferior courts might be created and to fix conditions governing appeals. Congress responded to this invitation by passing the Judiciary Act of 1789. This seminal measure determined that the original Supreme Court should have six justices—a chief justice and five associates—and that this court should hold two sessions each year. Thirteen inferior tribunals, called district courts, were created, one for each of the eleven states that had thus far ratified the Constitution plus one each for the Maine district of Massachusetts and the Kentucky district of Virginia. When North Carolina and Rhode Island joined the Union (in November 1789 and May 1790 respectively), each got its own federal district.

The Judiciary Act provided a single judge for each district court and grouped these courts into three circuits, for which there were no specifically designated judges. A session of the federal circuit court was held, in rotation, in each district of the circuit. This court (like the one in the *Champion* case) was composed of the district judge and two justices of the Supreme Court. As few cases were expected to come before the nation's highest tribunal because of its limited original jurisdiction, the main task of each Supreme Court justice was to "ride circuit," or make the rounds in one judicial circuit annually. This procedure explains why such eminent jurists and legal scholars as Chief Justice John Jay and Associate Justice James Wilson came to Rhode Island to preside in the Champion controversy.

One is amazed at the identity of the attorneys who supported Casey's effort to uphold a state stay law in the face of the contract clause of the federal Constitution. Not only had William Bradford of Bristol and Benjamin Bourne of Providence and Bristol been close allies of federal district judge Henry Marchant in the battle against states' rights opponents of the Constitution; Bourne was also the incumbent United States congressman from Rhode Island and a future federal district judge!

Patrick T. Conley, Jr., who brought this interesting case to light, was a history major at Providence College and now serves as a volunteer for several local historical organizations and projects. Professionally he is a practicing attorney in Providence and an assistant Providence city solicitor.

The First Judicial Review of State Legislation: An Analysis of the Rhode Island Case of *Champion and Dickason* v. *Casey* (1792)

Patrick T. Conley, Jr.

In this, the year of the bicentennial of the Constitution of the United States, it is fitting that attention be called to those cases and doctrines which have given substance and meaning to the blueprint of government drafted by the Founding Fathers in Philadelphia in 1787. The Constitution, by its nature, necessitated and continues to require interpretation and analysis in order for it to evolve from a static document into a vital, adaptable plan of government. This interpretative power falls within the province of the courts.

In the exercise of its interpretative function, the duty of the court is to examine enactments by the legislature properly brought before it and to determine whether such acts are in conformity with the manifest tenor of the Constitution. If the court finds they are not, such acts must be declared void. "The courts were designed to be an intermediate body between the people and the legislature, in order, among other things, to keep the latter within the limits assigned to their authority," wrote Alexander Hamilton in one of the *Federalist* papers. This power of judicial review of legislative enactments has been the tool which has enabled the courts to play a major role in determining how the Constitution is to be applied to American culture and society.

In its application, the doctrine of judicial review resulted in two important developments during the period immediately following the ratification of the Constitution. First, it confirmed the Supreme Court's role as an equal branch of the federal government by enabling the Court to render acts of Congress which were violative of the Constitution void. Second, through a number of decisions by both the Supreme Court and the inferior federal courts, judicial review served to establish the nationalistic governmental system anticipated by many of those at the Philadelphia convention by enabling federal courts to strike down state statutes which contravened the federal Constitution.

The establishment of the Supreme Court as an equal branch of the federal government was accomplished through the landmark case of *Marbury* v. *Madison*. Here, Chief Justice John Marshall, writing for the Court, propounded for the first time the proposition that the Supreme Court had the authority and the duty to declare an act of Congress unconstitutional and therefore unenforceable. Basic to Marshall's opinion were the assumptions that the Constitution is paramount to any legislative enactment and that it is the province and duty of the courts to determine what the law is and whether the law is in conflict with the Constitution.

The exercise of the doctrine of judicial review also enhanced the power of the national government. Implicit in enabling the federal courts to strike down enactments of state legislatures as violative of the federal Constitution was the primacy of the federal government and, conversely, the subservient, dependent status of the states.

Contrary to many authoritative works dealing with federal court disallowance of state statutes, the first case in which a federal court struck down a state act as contrary to the United States Constitution was the Rhode Island case of *Alexander Champion and Thomas Dickason* v. *Silas Casey*. Before this landmark decision is discussed, however, it is necessary to consider briefly those cases previously heralded by legal historians as the first such instance of judicial veto.

The decision most often cited as the first in which a federal court held a state act void is the 1795 case of *Vanhorne's Lessee* v. *Dorrance*. The case was decided in the Circuit Court of the United States for the Pennsylvania District with Justice William Paterson presiding. The court struck down the "Quieting and Confirming Act" passed by the Pennsylvania Assembly (an act which dealt with conflicting titles in Pennsylvania's Wyoming Valley lands) on the grounds that it violated the inalienable right of private property and was, therefore, inconsistent with the Constitution. The case, however, is perhaps most noted for Justice Paterson's impassioned charge to the jury, in which he stated:

> I take it to be a clear position; that if a legislative act oppugns a constitutional principle, the former must give way, and be rejected on the score of repugnance. I hold it to be a position equally clear and sound, that, in such case, it will be the duty of the Court to adhere to the Constitution, and to declare the act null and void. The Constitution is the basis of legislative authority; it lies at the foundation of all law, and is a rule and commission by which both legislator and judges are to proceed. It is an important principle, which, in the discussion of questions of the present kind, ought never to be lost sight of, that the judiciary in this country is not a subordinate but a coordinate branch of government.

Another case which has been held to be the first instance of a federal court holding a state statute void is the 1794 case of *Skinner* v. *May*. The case, decided by the United States Circuit Court for the Massachusetts District, held that a Massachusetts act of 1788 attempting to restrain the slave trade was repealed by Article I, §8, of the Constitution and that the Massachusetts legislature had no right or authority to make penal laws to regulate the conduct of citizens or aliens abroad.

In addition, two Supreme Court cases which held state acts unconstitutional have been also cited as the first such instances of judicial review of state law. In *United States* v. *Peters*, the Court held that a Pennsylvania statute prohibiting the execution of any process issued to enforce a certain sentence of a federal court, on the ground that the federal court lacked jurisdiction in the case, could not defeat the federal court's jurisdiction. In *Peters*, a state statute purporting to annul the judgment of a court of the United States and to destroy rights acquired thereunder was determined to be without legal foundation.

South County merchant and farmer Silas Casey (1734–1814) used his political influence to secure the passage by the General Assembly of a stay law impeding his creditors from attaching his property.

In *Fletcher* v. *Peck*, a Georgia statute annulling conveyances of public lands in the Yazoo River area that were authorized by a prior enactment was ruled violative of the obligation of contracts clause Article I, §10, of the Constitution.

Despite the pretensions of the aforementioned cases, the 1792 case of *Champion and Dickason* v. *Casey* antedates *Vanhorne's Lessee* v. *Dorrance* by three years, *Skinner* v. *May* by two years, and the others by nearly two decades, making it the first case where a federal court deemed a state statute void as contrary to the provisions of the Constitution of the United States. Though never explicitly followed, it was the decision in *Casey* that helped to pave the way for those later decisions that firmly asserted the supremacy of the federal Constitution over state acts and state constitutions and, therefore, the supremacy of the federal government over the governments of the individual states.

An understanding of the facts from which the case arose is necessary to completely understand the federal court's ruling. The defendant, Silas Casey, was a prominent Rhode Islander. By the time of the American Revolution he was one of the most successful merchants and shipowners of Narragansett Bay. In addition to his enterpreneurial achievements, Casey had been elected justice of the peace for the town of Warwick by the Rhode Island General Assembly for three consecutive years, 1769–1771.

While his prosperity and reputation were at their height, the American Revolution came. During the course of the war Casey's mercantile activity ceased and four of his privateering vessels were lost, and he was thereby deprived of much of his wealth and business opportunity.

In the years following the Revolution, Casey's financial position worsened. He became further indebted to a number of merchants, among them Alexander Champion and Thomas Dickason of London, with whom Casey had conducted business over the course of several years.

Realizing his plight, Casey petitioned the Rhode Island General Assembly for a reprieve. His petition was presented to the Assembly in its January 1790 session and granted in February 1791. Casey's plea for relief set out the following request:

> Your Petitioner from repeated heavy losses at sea, and other unexpected disappointments in a long course of very extensive mercantile transactions finds his affairs extremely embarrassed, and himself unable to do that justice to his creditors which his former prompt payment gave them reason to expect, he hath for some time past been arranging his books and papers and preparing them for a settlement, but he finds his account so extensive and his credits so peculiarly situated that it will require great attention, application and time to bring them to a close with advantage to himself and creditors, be impossible ever to complete that object, while he is subject to the demands which in apprehension of a change in his circumstances naturally urge, unless therefore he can obtain indulgence from your Honors to attend the settlement of his accounts without interruption, himself and family will not only be greatly distressed, but his creditors lose many advantages which such an opportunity would afford, he

> therefore most respectfully solicits the interposition of this Honorable Assembly, and that they would extend to him the term of three years for the above purpose, and that in the meantime he be exempted from all arrests and attachments.

Despite the passage of the resolution by the General Assembly, Champion and Dickason brought suit in the Circuit Court pursuant to §11 of the Judiciary Act of 1789 to recover the amount of the debt. In his defense Casey enlisted the legal counsel of Benjamin Bourne and William Bradford, both of whom had been leading Federalists in the recent battle over Rhode Island ratification of the United States Constitution. Casey interposed the resolution of the General Assembly as a defense and claimed that according to its provisions he could not be sued on the debt owed to Champion and Dickason for a period of three years.

The case was first heard by the United States Circuit Court for the Rhode Island District sitting at Newport. John Jay (1745–1829), Chief Justice of the United States Supreme Court, was the Presiding Justice. He was joined by William Cushing, Associate Justice of the Supreme Court, and Henry Marchant, United States District Judge. After hearing the arguments, the court ruled that the Assembly's resolution was insufficient to defeat the claim of the plaintiffs and found in favor of Champion and Dickason. Though no written opinion was filed for the decision, the local papers provided ample insight into the court's rationale. One paper reported:

> At the Circuit Court of the United States, sitting at Newport on Monday last, a decision was given in a case of importance. Two merchants, of London, in company, commenced an action against a citizen of this state for the recovery of monies due. The defendant's counsel pleaded a resolution of the legislature of this state in bar of the action—by which he was allowed three years to pay his debts—and during which time he was to be free from arrests on that account. The Judges were unanimously of opinion, that, as by the Constitution of the United States, the individual states are prohibited from making laws which shall impair the obligation of contracts—and as the resolution in question, if operative, would impair the obligation of the contract in question—therefore it could not be admitted to bar the action.

Another paper said:

> The Court also determined in the case of Champion and Dickason against Silas Casey that the legislature of a state has no right to make a law to exempt an individual from arrests and his estates from attachments, for his private debts, for any term of time, it being clearly a law impairing the obligation of contracts and therefore contrary to the Constitution of the United States.

Despite the apparent disposition of the case in this June term, the Circuit Court records indicate that the case was continued by agreement of the parties to the November 1792 term. The purpose for the continuance by agreement is not apparent from a review of the records. It appears, however, that the judges expressed their opinions

Riding circuit in New England, John Jay (1745–1829), the first chief justice, presided over the three-judge federal panel that considered the constitutionality of the Rhode Island statute.

Justice James Wilson (1742–1798), a leading member of the Philadelphia Convention, headed the second federal circuit panel to review Casey's exemption.

on the substantive arguments in the June term but for some reason delayed giving judgment.

The November court session was convened in Providence by Associate Justice James Wilson, Associate Justice James Iredell, and District Judge Henry Marchant. The case was reargued and the court again ruled in favor of Champion and Dickason, wholly adopting the June term's substantive conclusions. At this November term final judgment was entered by the court.

The decision given by the justices sitting for both terms, though important as a practical application of the doctrine of judicial review as an instrument of national supremacy, did not significantly enlarge what the majority of early judges already felt about the power of judicial review. Jay, Cushing, Wilson, and Iredell were all Federalist appointees of President Washington, whose views on judicial review were well known prior to the decision. Moreover, Marchant, a strong nationalist, had helped to lead the Federalist cause in Rhode Island by advocating a state ratifying convention in 1790. The landmark decision, therefore, was predictable.

Though it is important from an historical perspective to learn that *Champion and Dickason* v. *Casey* was the first case in which a federal court rendered a state statute void, it is equally important to examine an interesting fact which arises from an analysis of the case and its aftermath—the fact that the decision met little resistance and aroused scant interest within Rhode Island. The General Assembly, pursuant to the holding of the court, passed a resolution forbidding the passage of any act which would exempt an individual from arrests or attachments for private debts, thereby readily acquiescing.

Such compliance and lack of popular outcry is enigmatic because of Rhode Island's stout defiance towards the federal Constitution from 1787 to 1790. It is well known that Rhode Island was the last of the thirteen original states to ratify the Constitution of the United States. In fact, its ratification did not occur until nearly fifteen months after the new government had been put into place.

"The motives behind Rhode Island's long-term opposition and then grudging acceptance of the Constitution are multiple and complex," one historian has noted. However, among the reasons were the controversy over paper money, the fear of heavy federal direct taxes on land, and, perhaps most importantly, the reluctance of Rhode Island to relinquish the near autonomous status it had enjoyed under its Charter of 1663. It is therefore puzzling to learn of Rhode Island's acquiescence after it had become the first state to feel the constraints of the federal Constitution.

A possible explanation for this passive acceptance of the judgment may lie in the innocuous nature of the statute declared unconstitutional. That stay law was a private act; its nature was such that it did not involve a partisan political issue nor did it affect many people. "A careful study of the history of the periods from 1789–1819, from 1845–1860, and from 1865–1871," observed noted Supreme Court historian Charles Warren, "will show that each political party... upheld the power of the court when the court's decision, whether in favor of or against the validity of the statute, coincided with the political views of that party on the question involved in the case; and each challenged the court's power on many occasions when its decision was contrary to those political views." In short, acceptance or rejection of the doctrine of judicial review was largely dependent upon how the result of a decision affected political interests. *Champion and Dickason* v. *Casey* did not involve a statute with overriding or easily apparent political ramifications; therefore no political interests were directly affected and no concerted protest resulted from the decision.

Perhaps the most compelling question arising from consideration of the case, however, is why it has not received the attention it deserves. Though it is impossible to explain this neglect with absolute certainty, several factors may serve to explain why *Champion and Dickason* v. *Casey* has spent so many years in virtual obscurity.

First, the decision is an unreported one. In order to find any official reference to the case, it is necessary to peruse the minute books and records of the Circuit Court, a resource not readily available. Second, the court filed no written opinion explaining its decision. In order to discern the court's rationale, it is necessary to consult the local newspapers. Third, the decision involved a private act which affected only Silas Casey. There was no partisan political interest at stake, nor was there any sizable portion of the population directly affected by the act. Last, the case was decided in the smallest state in the new federal union, and this in itself limited its impact.

In contrast, *Vanhorne's Lessee* v. *Dorrance*, the case most often cited as the first instance in which a federal court held a state act invalid, was reported, produced a well-reasoned opinion, involved an act affecting the public at large, and was decided in America's largest city, Philadelphia. Further, Justice Paterson's jury charge was published in pamphlet form and distributed nationwide. In view of these differences it is not surprising to learn that *Vanhorne's Lessee* has received the attention of legal historians, while *Champion and Dickason* has been largely ignored.

Now that the case of *Champion and Dickason* has been given as full a treatment as its scanty remains allow, perhaps it can take its rightful place in the history of American jurisprudence. This Rhode Island ruling was the first instance of a federal court holding a state statute void as violative of the Constitution of the United States. It set the stage for the implementation of the federal plan of union embodied in the Constitution, and its legacy is strongly felt, even to the present day.

Although Casey lost his state statutory protection, he did not lose the farm. It survives today on Boston Neck Road in North Kingstown as a working farm, open to visitors who wish a glimpse of eighteenth-century rural elegance. Architect Edward Pearce Casey gave the 300-acre estate to the Society for the Preservation of New England Antiquities in 1940.

14

This survey of divorce in Providence County begins in 1749, when the General Assembly enacted a comprehensive and liberal divorce statute entitled "An Act against Adultery, Polygamy, and unlawfully marrying Persons; and for the Relief of such Persons as are injured by the Breach of Marriage Covenants." Prior to that year, local divorce procedure followed the common law and was granted only by the General Assembly upon petition. The 1749 act was amended in 1754 and repromulgated with further revisions in the first digest of the laws issued by the new state of Rhode Island in 1798.

The initial statute gave the court power to grant an absolute divorce on proof that the object of the complaint "hath wilfully and wickedly broken and violated the marriage covenant, either by any act done and committed, or by a continual absence from his or her husband or wife, without any just cause, by the space of seven years." The court was left to decide for itself what acts constituted willful and wicked breaches. Since the Assembly came to believe that too much had been left to judicial discretion, it established more specific grounds in 1798. Under the amended law, divorces were to be granted where the marriages were originally void, as well as "for impotency, adultery, extreme cruelty, wilful desertion for five years of either of the parties, and also for neglect or refusal on the part of the husband, being of sufficient ability, to provide necessaries for the subsistence of his wife, and also for any other gross misbehavior or wickedness in either of the parties, repugnant to or in violation of the marriage covenant."

Historian Sheldon S. Cohen was a professor of history at Loyola University, Chicago, in 1985 when this article appeared in *Rhode Island History*. His comparisons between Providence County and the state of Connecticut are based upon his previously published research into the issue of divorce in that colony and state. Like Catherine Osborne DeCesare, author of a preceding article on women in Rhode Island colonial courts, Professor Cohen has mined the manuscript records of the state judicial system. During the period of his research, these records were in the temporary custody of Providence College, where they were being arranged and cataloged under the direction of college archivist Matthew J. Smith, who would later become state court administrator, clerk of the Rhode Island Supreme Court, and a founder of the Rhode Island Judicial Records Center.

Cohen's reference to the Superior Court of Providence County is imprecise. Until 1798 the "Superior Court" was the state's highest tribunal; throughout the period of Cohen's study the intermediate county court that handled divorce proceedings was known as the Inferior Court of Common Pleas (1730–1789) and the Court of Common Pleas (1789–1893). However, both functioned in a manner similar to the Superior and Family courts of the present day.

Legal historian David A. Flaherty, in an article entitled "The Use of Early American Court Records in Historical Research" (*Law Library Journal* 69, August 1976), has argued that "these court records ... constitute the single most important source for the social, economic, and legal history" of early America. In utilizing these primary documents, Cohen has written a "grass-roots" account that is typical of what scholars term "the new social history." Such tightly focused monographic studies often proceed inductively to produce and validate significant generalizations about the American experience. For example, Cohen regards the precipitous increase in divorce litigation after 1783 as an effect of the liberal and egalitarian impulses of the American Revolution on the role and status of women.

Such a conclusion is consistent with the much more general thesis advanced by Brown University professor Gordon Wood in his Pulitzer Prize-winning book *The Radicalism of the American Revolution* (1992). Wood's belief that the Revolution was radical and produced a society that was free and democratic far beyond anything thought either possible or desirable by the Founding Fathers extends to his analysis of marriage and divorce. According to Wood, "the Revolution's assault on patriarchy inevitably affected relationships within the family.... With the Revolution men lost some of their earlier patriarchal control over their wives and property. Although wives continued to remain dependent on their husbands, they did gain greater autonomy and some legal recognition of their rights to hold property separately, to divorce, and to make contracts and do business in the absence of their husbands. In the colonial period only New Englanders had recognized the absolute right to divorce, but after the Revolution all the states except South Carolina developed new liberal laws on divorce."

The Broken Bond: Divorce in Providence County, 1749–1809

Sheldon S. Cohen

The high incidence of divorce in American society has recently been the focus of much attention. Contemporary media coverage of the various aspects of this subject has indeed been substantial and widespread. And despite a decline in the nationwide divorce rate from 5.4 per 1,000 population in 1980 to 5.2 in 1982, there remains concern that in future years such high percentages could completely alter the family structure.

The principal focus of this study, however, is not on the ramifications of contemporary or future divorce trends, nor even on the origins of a social institution that reaches back to the ancient Sumerians. Rather, it concentrates on the historical implications of 293 divorce petitions that were submitted to the Superior Court of Providence County between 1749 and 1809. These manuscript records are the only ones of Rhode Island's five county superior courts for this period that are legible and are already catalogued. However, since Providence was Rhode Island's largest county in size and population and also contained its greatest economic diversity, the manuscript records for this locale alone merit examination and analysis.

Providence County experienced significant changes during these sixty years. At the time of the superior court's first session in 1749, the county included approximately 11,600 inhabitants, most of whom were engaged in agricultural pursuits. Its largest settlement, Providence, with about 3,500 residents, had some commercial and other small enterprises, yet in such economic endeavors it still lagged behind the larger, more cosmopolitan, overbearing, and prosperous community of Newport. Yet subsequent decades produced new developments that altered the county's quiescent colonial environment.

The Old State House in Providence, erected in 1762, was the setting for most of the cases described in this essay. The building was in many ways Rhode Island's "Freedom Hall." Here the colony renounced allegiance to the king (1776), restored civil rights to Catholics (1783), and set in motion the demise of slavery (1784).

By 1809, as Thomas Jefferson prepared to relinquish his executive office and the nation was poised to experience profound changes in its economic and social order, Providence County contained almost thirty thousand residents. Providence town comprised a third of this number. Providence County's population was double that of Newport County, and the town of Newport, with only seven thousand inhabitants, had clearly been eclipsed as the foremost urban community in Rhode Island by its rival at the other end of Narragansett Bay.

This general framework of social, economic, and political change provides the background for consideration of the almost three hundred divorce petitions submitted to Providence County's superior court. The petitioners represented exceptions to traditional New England marital ideals of provident and faithful husbands bound to loyal, caring, obedient wives. In another respect, they also represented quite varied social levels within the county. Thus the petitioners included

Mary Cooke Bowen, who sought a divorce for desertion from Oliver Bowen, a successful Providence merchant, as well as Pink Arnold, a destitute black mother who obtained a legal separation from her husband, Prime, as a result of his alleged cruelty, adultery, and desertion.

These Providence County divorce records offer valuable insights into prevailing social mores in late eighteenth- and early nineteenth-century New England. By analyzing their records, we can relate the various circumstances of marital disruption to existing social customs and family life. And the legal proceedings themselves also serve as indicators of attitudinal changes toward marriage and marital responsibilities in pre- and post-Revolutionary America. The substantial increase of Providence County divorce petitions filed by wives in the years after the War for Independence supports the growing body of evidence regarding the influences of Revolutionary ideology on American women.

Marital separation occurred in Rhode Island almost from its beginnings. Indeed, in 1644 John Hicks requested Newport officials to grant him a separation from his wife, Horrod (Hardwood), on the grounds of adultery. Six years later the colony's General Assembly enacted legislation rejecting divorce requests "for any other case but that of Adulterie," reserving to itself jurisdiction in all such cases. However, in 1655 the legislature permitted "a general or town magistrate to grant a bill of divorce" in case of adultery, and by implication allowed the General Court to consider other grounds. A half-dozen divorce actions had been initiated in the colony before Providence County experienced its first case in 1667. About this same time, jurisdiction over divorce shifted to the Court of Trials, composed of the governor and his council, which maintained this authority until 1747 when supervision was delegated to each county's superior court. Afterward the General Assembly might still receive such petitions, but was involved only in exceptional cases. Desertion had already been added to adultery as an official ground for marital dissolution. The colony and county courts continued to grant divorces for other grounds prior to 1798 when a revised law code specifically added "impotency, extreme cruelty," and "gross misbehavior and wickedness in either of the parties, repugnant to and in violation of the marriage covenant."

These Rhode Island legal practices were more liberal than those of England and the southern colonies, which permitted only separation from bed and board, denying complete divorce from legally constituted marriages. Rhode Island's practices were also somewhat more liberal than those procedures in neighboring Massachusetts where, until 1786, the grounds for divorce were not codified and the governor and his council still made final decisions. Connecticut, which had codified its causes for divorce in 1667 and by the early eighteenth century allowed its superior courts to grant divorce, most closely approximated Rhode Island's legal convention.

But what of the almost three hundred men and women from Providence County who, between 1749 and 1809, felt sufficiently wronged to seek divorce and endure the social stigma that accompanied permanent dissolution of one's marital bonds? Their petitions to the superior court followed a generally similar pattern. The claimant normally began with a statement listing the date of the marriage, citing a specific grievance or grievances against the mate (often including, in the case of female petitioners, personal distress), and concluding with a plea that he or she be granted a divorce based on the alleged violations of the marriage contract. The court had the right to summon an accused spouse, though often, as in the case of desertion, no such attempt was made. However, when the respondent was notified of the action and appeared in court, a hearing usually took place in which both parties could present their arguments. And, similar to existing practices in Connecticut, cases could be referred to the General Assembly.

Petitioners to Providence County's superior court most often cited desertion as the primary cause of their actions. This reason appeared as the fundamental complaint in thirty-nine percent (114) of the 293 cases examined. Several of these actions also alluded to physical or mental maltreatment, but these were incidental addenda to the overriding claims of wanton abandonment. A majority of desertion-related divorce suits noted that the absent spouse had departed after several years of marriage and the birth of several children. Thus, in 1794, Deborah Baker of Glocester declared that her husband, Stephen, had deserted her after twenty-one years of marriage and five children, while that same year Thomas Eddy of Johnston noted that his wife, Ann, had left him and their children after twenty-three years of marriage. Conversely, a significant minority of such petitioners claimed that their spouses had fled within a short time after their nuptials. Lydia Sylvester of Scituate declared that her husband, Amos, deserted "immediately" after their wedding ceremony, while Samuel Johnson asserted that his wife, Nancy, had fled to unknown locales only one day after exchanging wedding vows.

A significant number of these petitions cited the absent respondent's whereabouts; most reported places within other American colonies or states, principally in neighboring New England. Thus James Prince of North Providence asserted that his wife, Eunice, had deserted to Plymouth, Massachusetts, while Lillis Inman of Smithfield declared that her laborer husband, Joseph, had departed to Maine. Errant spouses allegedly had fled to the Middle Atlantic and southern states and the Northwest territories as well. And a few petitioners (all female) listed places outside America where their absent husbands reportedly resided. Hence Dinah Row of Cranston stated that her husband, John, had gone to France after leaving her; Freelove Tweedy reported that her husband, an apothecary, was refusing to return from St. Croix in the Danish West Indies; and the greatest distance-setter, Jane Todd, proclaimed that her mate, Joseph, a former Providence bookseller, had declined to return from Buenos Aires.

Men were cited more often as the offending party in these abandonment cases. Indeed, male deserters accounted for 78 of the 114 or almost seventy percent of the abandonment cases. Of course, several Providence County wives deserted their husbands, too, and the memorials revealed their whereabouts more frequently than those concerning absent males. Many of the departed wives sought shelter among family or other supportive groups. For example, Daniel Barnes, a Glocester yeoman, claimed that his wife,

Hope, had behaved in an "incorrigible and undutiful manner" after their marriage the previous year. Daniel added that two months prior to his petition, Hope had left in the company of her father and brothers, who had also helped themselves to furniture and other goods. Stephen Page, Paul Smith, David Darling, and Robert Potter all protested that their wives had left them for the sanctuary of their parents' homes. Marcy Brown of Glocester and Chloe Edely of Providence found other refuges; their husbands claimed that these women had deserted them after lengthy marriages and raising children in order to join the Shaker religious sect.

Petitioners who knew the whereabouts of absent spouses ordinarily sought their return. Such endeavors came in the form of letters or personal appeals by the claimant or supplications of friends, relatives, clergymen, and, in a few instances, local magistrates. However, these attempts were fruitless. Sarah Wood, for example, declared in 1786 that her absent husband, Zephaniah, had written her from Massachusetts: "I intend to travel for the future. Get married as quick as you please." Two years later, Jeremiah Williams of Scituate declared that his wife Suze had left him for her parents' home and, despite his pleas for reconciliation, declared that "she wished him to get clear of her." And Mary Potter of Smithfield was even more defiant; she allegedly told her husband, Christopher, that "she did not love him, and she would rather cut her throat than return again."

The second most frequently cited cause for divorce combined adultery and desertion. There were ninety-one such actions in this category, approximately thirty-one percent of the total petitions. And like the classification for desertion alone, males formed the majority (sixty-six percent) of the respondents for these offenses. Irrespective of the offending party's gender, these adultery-desertion cases obviously manifested drastic breaches of conjugal harmony. Indeed, the first divorce petition presented to the Providence Superior Court fell within this classification. In 1749 Marcy Olney of Providence declared to the justices that her husband, Nedabiah: "Several years past left her and a large family of Children in poor Circumstances, and he has since married another woman in the Province of Pennsylvania."

Subsequent actions within this group reveal similar particulars of abandonment and betrayal. Thus, Mary Manchester of Scituate received a divorce in 1758 after claiming that her husband, Bage, who had deserted her sixteen years before, had committed adultery with Mehitable Eddy and now planned to marry her. Ephriam Baker, also of Scituate, stated in his petition that his wife, Hannah, had "behaved herself most inconsistent with the *Marriage Contract* by leaving him the previous November and committing adultery with one Edward Clifford, "a transient man." Phebe Peck of Cumberland declared in her successful action that her husband, Steven, had left her and their seven children, and had committed adultery with Phebe Ballou. He went to Maine, where he subsequently married Miss Ballou. Not surprisingly, the offenders within this category included several of the county's mariners. Sarah Jones, wife of Providence sailor George Jones, declared to the justices that he had left on a voyage shortly after their marriage and now lived with another woman in Norfolk, Virginia.

Many of the adultery-desertion proceedings included allegations of ignominious indignities endured by the petitioners, especially the wives.

Rebecca Thayer, for example, received a divorce from her absent and unfaithful husband, David, after declaring that she had borne his cruel treatment and his blatant infidelities—even those with the housemaids. One deponent testified that David had boasted to him that "he would not trier [*sic*] no maid except they would have do with him." Patience Dolbe of Scituate sought a divorce from her husband, John, not only for his desertion and illicit affairs, but because he had once attempted to rape her mother. In 1800 Mary Smith alleged that she "had to get wood in the snow and take care of cattle wast John [her husband] was sporting" with Vine Herendeen of Smithfield. Some petitioners also added accusations of drunkenness and cruelty to their principal charges of desertion and adultery. But the single additional charge most often entered by the woman petitioner was that the unfaithful spouse had left her destitute. Many of these women received succor from family or friends, but some, like Phebe Lawrance and her two children, had to be supported by Providence's Overseers of the Poor.

Destitution was not cited by the husbands who submitted petitions involving desertion and adultery or simply adultery. A few male petitioners within these groups added general charges of wifely neglect or contentiousness, and in one instance farmer Joseph Burlingame asserted that his wife, Sarah, had even stolen his horse and saddle when she eloped with her younger paramour. Perhaps Timothy Vincent presented the most ignominious allegation. He claimed that his wife, Harriet, had "often for long periods of time been [an] inmate of brothels and houses of ill fame."

The third most prevalent class of divorce memorials cited only adultery as the fundamental complaint. Fifty-one such petitions, or seventeen percent of the total, were submitted to the superior court during this period and the majority (twenty-seven) were filed by men. The preponderance of these accusations did not mean that men were more faithful, but rather suggests their greater ability to hide indiscretions. It was also indicative of the fact that prior to the American Revolution, wives were less inclined to sue on the basis of adultery alone. Actually, a woman filed only one of nine such suits prior to 1776. Providence County males, however, were not so reluctant to overlook their wives' adultery, and they generally instituted divorce proceedings more quickly once they discovered evidence of their spouses' infidelity.

These male petitioners and their supporting depositions depict a variety of circumstances surrounding the adultery. Thus in 1758 John Clemence of Providence and Noah Smith of Smithfield obtained divorces after claiming that their wives had conceived illegitimate offspring following their infidelities. Providence's Amasa Killiam lacked such damning evidence; his petition included only unspecified charges that his wife, Hannah, had committed adultery "over diverse years." Glocester's William Peters alleged that his wife, Sarah, had committed her indiscretions in her own home. Foster's Benjamin Dexter divorced his wife, Sarah, in 1796 after citing her liaisons with fellow townsman Joseph Hopkins. Benjamin supported his petition with six depositions including one from Joseph's wife, Mary. While most of these particular male-instituted proceedings occurred after relatively short marital spans, some were submitted after long marriage. For example, William Bowen and James Briggs, both of whom had spouses significantly named Freelove, were among several males whose marriages of over fifteen years dissolved on charges of adultery.

Many Providence County males learned that *their* absences had not made their spouses' hearts grow fonder. Merchant Noah Smith's memorial, for instance, revealed that a month before he returned from a seventeen-month business venture in the Middle Colonies, "his said wife [Anne] was delivered of a child in said Smithfield." Mariners, who often left the region for quite lengthy periods, offered similar testimony. Providence County sailors including William Young, Benjamin Coleman, Samuel Morgan, and Robert Norris all declared their shock and dismay on returning home from long sea voyages to discover their wives with newborn infants.

Eighteenth-century Boston engraver Nathanael Hurd offered this humorous rhyme and illustration to warn of the perils of marriage.

Petitions and substantiating depositions filed by wives primarily alleging adultery reveal widely varying circumstances. In September 1753, Sylvia Whipple of Smithfield received a divorce from her husband, Ephraim, based upon his adulterous conduct with Sarah Staples of nearby Cumberland. Although Ephraim denied any misconduct before the justices, accounts by four sworn witnesses to his infidelity, including Sarah Staples's mother, evidently swayed them. Elizabeth Maloney also provided testimonies of informants when she received a divorce from her husband, a Providence barber, for his assignations with "a certain Negro or Mulatto girl." Prudence Austin had nine children during her thirty-four-year marriage, but these marital bonds were severed in 1787 after she charged her husband, Gideon, with adultery over a twenty-year span. It was Providence's Nancy Smith, though, who seemed the most humiliated when she successfully argued to the county justices in 1808 that her husband, John, had repeatedly flaunted his infidelities as well as his drunkenness before her and their eight children.

One of the most revealing and recurrent aspects contained within the depositions accompanying these adultery-related actions was the manner in which the alleged indiscretions occurred. Though New Englanders of the late eighteenth century may have sought privacy, in fact a considerable lack of such privacy existed in daily life. Many of the deponents in divorce actions testified to overhearing the respondents mentioning their infidelities, but many others actually witnessed acts of adultery. Ruth Bartlett of Cumberland, for example, declared that during a winter evening in 1752–53 she was in bed with Sarah Staples when Ephraim Whipple "climbed into the other side" and "had Carnel Knowledge of the body of ye said Sarah." Ruth's fourteen-year-old brother, John, swore that he had once seen Ephraim and Sarah "both in motion on the ground." In September 1773 Stephen Herendeen of Douglas, Massachusetts, declared that he had lodged in the same room the previous year with his fellow townsman David Brown, and also Hannah Ross, a married Glocester woman. He added that "I used to see them strip and go to bed together, and I think other ways behave themselves like Man & Wife—." And in 1800 Elliot Marshall swore that he and Elizabeth Olney, married to Stephen Olney of Providence, were among six men and women in Olney's home who had "all slept promiscuously in the same bed together at which time the said Stephen was absent." Elliot also noted that Stephen's brother Peter participated in this frolic.

The least frequent of the categories for which these divorce actions were instigated involved cruelty, gross misbehavior, wickedness, fraudulent contract (i.e., impotency, bigamy), and lengthy absence at sea. Only thirty-seven such cases, less than thirteen percent of the total, fell within this grouping. Over half of these cases occurred in the decade after 1798 when the revised law code, as previously noted, recognized officially the above-mentioned causes as grounds for marital dissolution. Furthermore, only two memorials during the entire period cited lengthy absences as the cause for their action. No doubt this low figure stemmed from the fact that wives of missing sailors could obtain divorces on the grounds of desertion, or if their absent husbands were declared legally dead, they were not obliged to sue for divorce in order to remarry.

Thirty petitions citing cruelty or gross misbehavior comprised the majority written in this last category and, as might be expected, wives initiated three quarters, or twenty-three, of the complaints. Some of these women reported the maltreatment that their husbands inflicted upon them in general terms or merely focused on verbal abuse. More often, these women spoke of physical as well as emotional ill-treatment. Hannah Blanchard of Smithfield claimed that her husband, Joseph, had refused to allow a physician to attend her during an illness and later forcibly turned her out of their home. Mary Brown of North Providence augmented her petition with a deposition from Ezra Hubbard alleging that her husband, Jeremiah, had "bit part of her finger off," and also swore that "he would split her damn brains with an axe." Mary Miller asserted that her sailor husband, Ebenezer, while beating her "with many stripes," had "threatened to take her life and has frequently armed himself and laid wait for that purpose." And in 1799, Anna Nichols of Providence described quite graphically how she endured her husband, Fortune's, beatings with "whips, fists, a shovel, and Tongs."

Few of these memorials portrayed the contemporary, albeit little publicized, phenomenon of "battered" husbands. Though infrequent, such complaints did occur. For example, in 1795 farmer Andrew Stone of Cranston sought a divorce from his wife, Mary, for gross misbehavior and cruelty. According to some of Andrew's six deponents, his spouse of fourteen years had thrown objects at him and beat him with a broom and birch rod. Later, in 1804, Peter Brown, a Providence laborer, declared that during his twenty-year marriage to his wife, Phebe, she "hath many times driven him from his house with force & violence, shamefully beating & bruizing him in a cruel manner & threatening his life." Peter, however, submitted no depositions to substantiate these and other claims of gross misbehavior. And

This advertisement in the *Providence Gazette* was placed by a frustrated husband to warn those who would support his newly liberated wife.

WHEREAS SYLVIA, the Wife of me the Subſcriber, hath left my Bed and Board, and endeavoured to ſell all my Furniture and wearing Apparel: This is to forbid all Perſons harbouring or truſting her on my Account, as I will not pay any Debts of her contracting from this Date. EZEKIEL BALLOU.
Providence, Auguſt 29, 1795.

in February 1807 Nathan Walker, a Scituate gentleman, declared that his wife, Mary, had wasted his property and threatened violence against him and their children. While there may have been other physically abused husbands, such charges, if accurate, were still exceptions in this male-dominated society. Most men who did cite cruelty in their petitions used complaints similar to those of female plaintiffs. However, terms such as "neglectful of wifely duties" and failure to prepare necessary food indicate a specific gender connotation.

A few cases within this last classification fell within the category of fraudulent contract or deceitful conduct involving one of the marital partners. Stephen Day of Smithfield, Benjamin Spooner of Providence, and Weaver Hopkins of Scituate all claimed that they had been tricked into marrying their wives after false accusations that they were the fathers of expected offspring. Day and Spooner submitted depositions in their successful actions alleging the actual fathers; Hopkins, who claimed that he had been forced to marry his wife, Urania, or go to jail, submitted depositions, including one from a physician, to prove that he had been working in upstate New York when Urania had become pregnant. Women, too, had their own versions of fraudulent contract. Mary Blackman and Martha Bishop, both widows, asserted that their new husbands deliberately tried to cheat them out of their estates. Martha alleged that her merchant husband, John, took all of her personal estate "except for one bed and a few other trifling articles." Yet, regardless of gender, the plaintiffs in fraudulent contract cases appeared most obliged to submit depositions that supported their contentions.

The Superior Court of Providence County granted seventy-one percent of the initial divorce petitions submitted during this time. As might be expected, the petitioners showing desertion or adultery-desertion over a considerable duration had the easiest time obtaining approval of their cases. Reasons cited by those who failed to receive approval for their initial petitions were that court citations were being issued; the case was being filed or continued; the case was withdrawn, dismissed, or referred to another court; or, lastly, that the case was being contested.

Contested divorce actions included varying details and results. Sarah Lyndsay of Providence challenged her husband, Thomas, when he sought a divorce from her alleging periodic desertion and adultery with Thomas Taylor on Hope Island. A divorce was granted by mutual agreement, but only after Sarah denied his charges as "malicious, false willed, and groundless" and accused her husband of constantly displaying a "morose Temper & Bitterness of Heart towards her." Later, in 1787, Esther Brown of Cumberland, married for thirty-one years, contested a petition from her husband, Christopher, in which he alleged desertion and adultery. The court sought citations after Esther submitted a deposition signed by twelve individuals declaring Christopher's accusations groundless, and she eloquently offered to defend her innocence in a "faire tryall." And during the September 1807 session, the court dismissed farmer Stephen Sheldon's memorial seeking divorce from his wife, Lydia, for assertedly threatening him, refusing to carry out her marriage vows, and reneging on a substantial cash agreement for a separation. Lydia's countercharges accused Stephen of insanity and also of forcing her to sign under duress the separation agreement.

The Revolution, which bisects these first six decades of Providence court records, caused significant social changes within the United States. War-related petitions deserve perhaps the most immediate notice. Although Newport County suffered more severe wartime dislocations, including lengthy British occupation, and perhaps had more marital problems, Providence County families were not unaffected by the conflict. Thus Elizabeth Sanford of Providence received a divorce from her husband, Robert, after alleging that he had deserted her in 1775 to join the service of King George and had later committed bigamy in Great Britain. Elizabeth Smith's wartime marriage ended after assertions that her spouse, John, had failed to support her or their child during his Continental Army service, and that he was also guilty of adultery. Among the male plaintiffs, Israel Bryon claimed that his wife, Robe, had sexual relations with both a patriot volunteer and a British deserter from Newport. Providence laborer Edward Vose obtained a separation from his wife, Dorothy, after being cuckolded by a Hessian officer.

Yet the Revolution had less direct though far more significant effects on marital patterns. Linda Kerber and Mary Beth Norton's studies of the status of women during the colonial and post Revolutionary eras suggest that the latter decades transformed the standing of American women. Both of their studies demonstrate that colonial wives in fact did not experience a "golden age" of respect, freedom, and domestic equality, but rather an age of debasement and inferiority in relationship to their male counterparts. The struggle for independence, however, altered this situation as women enjoyed new feelings of individualism, self-confidence, and self-assertion. Marital patterns reveal allegedly some of the effects of these emergent sentiments: women resist male monopolization in family matters, reject their husbands' denigration of their characters, and declare themselves openly in the event of abuse or dissatisfaction in marriage. The increasing prevalence of post-war divorce petitions and their wordings can thus be seen as indicators of such social changes.

Statistics from these Rhode Island litigations offer part of the evidence of transformation. A computation of divorce petitions during each of the six decades after 1749 shows that, as in Connecticut and Massachusetts, the frequency of such litigations was extremely small prior to the American Revolution (see Appendix). For the decades 1749–58 and 1759–68, the figures averaged .066 and .053 per 1000 population, and .097 per 1000 population for the pre-Revolutionary period from 1749 through 1774. Such inconsiderable numbers compared to those of Connecticut for these same periods. During the Revolution (April 1775–September 1783) there were only fifteen divorce memorials presented to Providence Superior Court, a frequency rate of about .095 per 1000 population—slightly higher than that for Connecticut. After the Revolution, the average frequency rate for Providence County climbed dramatically, reaching .310 for the decade 1789–98, .485 for the decade 1799–1808, and an overall average frequency of .380 during the quarter-century after September 1783. Such numbers are considerably higher than Connecticut's growth of .170 for the postwar years 1786 through 1797. Connecticut as a whole, however, was more isolated than Providence County, and its continued Congregational Church establishment probably hindered a comparative upsurge in divorce actions.

The wording of female divorce petitions after 1783 offers a barometer of shifting circumstances. Their phraseology clearly displays a greater emphasis on wifely expectations of obtaining future lives of happiness and peace on a more equal or cooperative basis with their husbands. Less prevalent are complacent declarations such as that of Sarah Lyndsay, who in 1769 replied to her husband's accusation of adultery that "she hath managed her Domestic affairs with Industry & frugality & in all things acted as a prudent, obedient & good wife ought to do toward her Husband." Wives also became less reticent about seeking legal separation on the grounds of cruelty and nonsupport. Providence's Mary Smith exemplified this new spirit. She declared to the justices in March 1805 that despite her own destitution and need to support six children, "she did not find it her duty to struggle any longer with her aflictions," and had therefore left her drunken and abusive husband.

Other statements or actions by wives in post-Revolutionary Providence County were equally explicit. Smithfield's Mary Potter swore to her husband, Christopher, that "she would rather cut her throat" than reconcile with him. Elizabeth Peck of North Providence deserted her husband, Benjamin, shortly after their marriage in November 1791 and afterwards bluntly advised him, "if he wished for a wife to seek for and obtain another." Stephen Mathewson's petition and supporting depositions declared that not only had his wife, Sarah, deserted him and gone back to her mother, but she was obstinately refusing him any visits to their children. And Providence ropemaker George Dunkin asserted that his wife, Patience, had not only left him, taking their furniture, but had subsequently answered his entreaties to return only with threats and curses. Robert Brettun's divorce petition of 1799 offers another representative example of this emergent female individualism. Brettun claimed that his wife, Sarah, whose parents had induced her to marry him, had left him the previous year and "openly declared she will never cohabit with him."

The precipitous increase in divorce litigations after 1783 did not signal the destruction of family life in Providence County. Despite the fact that the frequency of postwar divorce cases was considerably higher than that of Connecticut, marital separation remained infrequent and socially unacceptable in the region. Furthermore, even the .485 frequency rate per 1000 for the period 1799–1808 was almost eight times lower than all divorces granted in the county during 1980.

Nevertheless, examination and analysis of these 293 cases does offer further significant substantiation for Kerber and Norton's portrayal of post-Revolutionary feminine awareness. For it is apparent in the memorials after 1783 that many Providence County women had come to regard their marital bonds in a new perspective. While their suits still acknowledged the need to carry out the sacred precepts of the marriage contract, these women were reexamining and demanding more from marital bonds. In growing numbers after the War of Independence, wives, and also husbands, repudiated earlier tenets that they should endure the afflictions of unhappy wedlock, and they sought instead marital relationships based upon more modern concepts of romantic affection and mutual respect. Indications of such changing feelings can be observed in this county's sharp postwar increase in the number of litigations involving desertion, adultery, or cruelty; the growing expectation of mutual cooperation in marriage; and the tendency of wives to institute divorce proceedings as soon as possible after their spouse's alleged indiscretions. And finally, most of the new feminist sensitivity can be traced to the Revolution itself. I believe that the unprecedented wartime involvement and responsibilities of Providence County women, and their varying contacts with liberative Revolutionary ideology, gave many of them their own particular framework of independence.

Certainly many aspects of the subject and implications of divorce in early America remain to be explored. Classification of the Newport County Superior Court records should offer a valuable comparison to the broken marital bonds of Providence County. Moreover, such matters as child custody practices, alimony and property settlements, and the average marital spans of divorce petitioners remain open for research and exposition. Naturally, no accurate gauge can measure the acrimony, stress, and heartache involved in failed marriages of the eighteenth century. But these weathered Providence County divorce petitions offer opportunities for new insights into the social history and family relationships of early America.

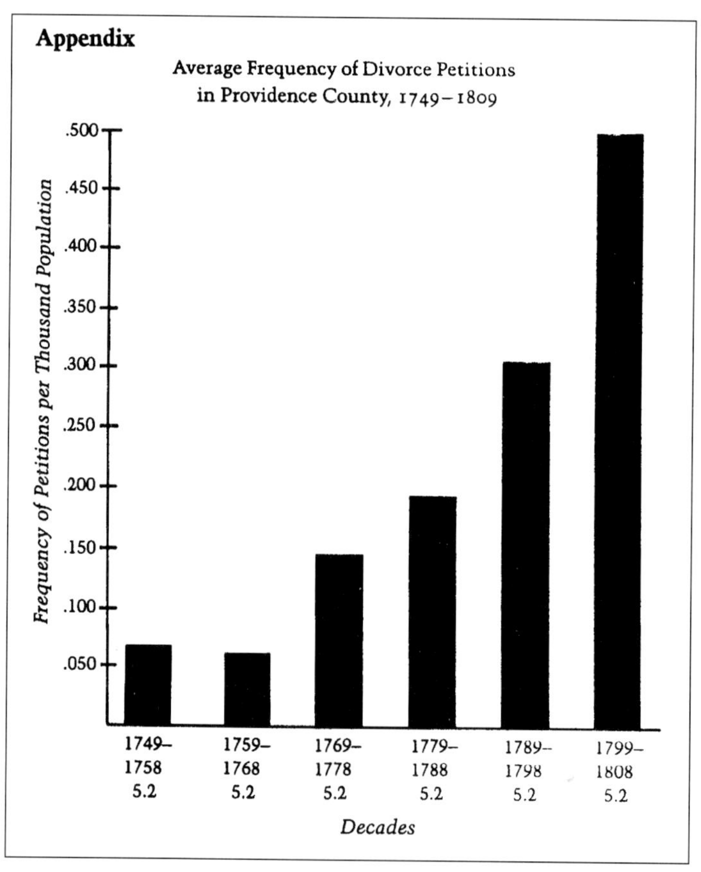

An ACT against Adultery, Polygamy, and unlawfully marrying Persons; and for the Relief of such Persons as are injured by the Breach of Marriage Covenants.

BE IT ENACTED *by the General Assembly, and by the Authority thereof, It is Enacted,* That if any Man or Woman in this Colony, shall commit the Crime of Adultery, and be thereof lawfully convicted before the Court of Assize in the County where the Crime shall be committed, every such Person shall be punished, by being set publickly on the Gallows in the Day-time, with a Rope about his or her Neck, for the Space of one Hour; and in his or her Return from the Gallows to the Goal, shall be publickly whipped on his or her naked Body, not exceeding thirty Stripes; and that such Person or Persons shall stand committed to the Goal of the County wherein convicted, until he or she shall pay all Costs of Prosecution.

And be it further Enacted by the Authority aforesaid, That if any Man or Woman in this Colony, having a Husband or Wife alive, shall marry another Woman or Man, and be thereof lawfully convicted, in Manner as abovesaid, the Person or Persons so offending, shall suffer the same Pains and Punishment, as in case of Adultery.

And be it further Enacted by the Authority aforesaid, That if any Officer or Minister in this Colony, having lawful Authority to marry, shall presume to marry any Man or Woman that he knows hath a Wife or Husband living, or hath had a Wife or Husband within his Knowledge, and doth not know that said Husband or Wife is dead, or that the Person offering to be married, hath been lawfully divorced, such Officer or Minister so offending, and being thereof lawfully convicted before said Court of Assize, shall pay as a Fine to and for the Use of the Colony, the Sum of Five Hundred Pounds, lawful Money of said Colony, and be rendered utterly incapable of sustaining any Office in this Colony.

And be it further Enacted by the Authority aforesaid, That the Justices or Judges of the Superior Court of Judicature, Court of Assize, and General Goal Delivery, of this Colony, are hereby authorized and fully impowered to hear and determine all Matters and Causes relating to, or concerning the Breach of the Marriage-Covenant, by any Person whatsoever, that is in a married State in this Colony; and upon due Proof thereof, made against any married Man or Woman, that he or she do, or hath wilfully and wickedly broken and violated the Marriage-Covenant, either by any Act done and committed, or by a continual Absence from his or her Husband or Wife, without any just Cause, by the space of seven Years, then, and in every such Case, to pronounce Sentence of Divorce, in Favour of such Man or Woman who shall be injured by such Violation of the Marriage-Covenant; which Sentence of Divorce, so lawfully made and published by the said Justices, or Judges, shall be Good and Valid, and shall absolutely dissolve the Marriage of the Persons so divorced.

This is Rhode Island's original divorce statute as it appeared in the *Schedules* of the General Assembly for 1749.

15

Just as lawyer-jurist Stephen Hopkins was the preeminent Rhode Islander of the eighteenth century, attorney-reformer Thomas Wilson Dorr was the most significant Rhode Islander of the nineteenth century. Despite their importance, locally and nationally, neither man has been the subject of a full-length scholarly biography. The two most extensive sketches of Dorr's life and career are Dr. Dan King's *The Life and Times of Thomas Wilson Dorr* (1859), published privately by Dorr's colleague and supporter, and Amasa M. Eaton's "Thomas Wilson Dorr and the Dorr War," in William Draper Lewis (ed.), *Great American Lawyers* (1908). Eaton, a constitutional reformer in his own right, was a lawyer rather than a trained historian, and his long essay is undocumented and uncritical.

Excellent brief glimpses into Dorr's complex personality are C. Peter Magrath, "Optimistic Democrat: Thomas W. Dorr and the Case of *Luther* v. *Borden*," *Rhode Island History* 29 (1970), 94–112, and Chilton Williamson, "The Disenchantment of Thomas W. Dorr," *Rhode Island History* 17 (1958), 97–108.

The following sketch by historian Patrick Conley, like all of the aforementioned works, is very sympathetic to Dorr. It has been written as an entry in the forthcoming multivolume *American National Biography* and as an outline for a future book-length biography.

The Sullivan Dorr house on Benefit Street in Providence, where the unmarried Thomas lived and died, has been preserved and remains in the possession of Sullivan Dorr's descendants.

Attorney Thomas Dorr: Rhode Island's Foremost Political Reformer

Patrick T. Conley

Thomas Wilson Dorr (November 5, 1805–December 27, 1854), a political and social reformer of national significance, was born in Providence, Rhode Island, the son of Sullivan Dorr, a wealthy merchant and business leader, and Lydia (Allen) Dorr, a prominent socialite and sister of noted inventor Zechariah Allen and Rhode Island governor and U.S. senator Philip Allen.

Dorr is best known to American historians as the determined leader of the Dorr Rebellion (1841–43), Rhode Island's crisis in constitutionalism. But he was much more than merely a "rebel" or a political reformer. Dorr was in fact a man of quality education, high social standing, and diverse intellectual and social interests.

Sullivan Dorr, prominent China merchant and longtime president (1838–1858) of the Providence-Washington Insurance Company, was the husband of Lydia Allen, the father of Thomas Wilson Dorr, and the father-in-law of Chief Justice Samuel Ames. Sullivan's portrait is by Charles Loring Elliot.

Some American historians have suggested the name "Age of Egalitarianism" for the period of American history extending from the mid-1820s to the mid-1850s, when a passion for equality of opportunity was the overriding theme of political, social, and economic activists. A more broadly based democracy, an assault on neomercantilism and government- granted privilege, and a crusade for a more just, humane, and upwardly mobile social order were hallmarks of the era. This was the first great age of American reform, and Thomas Dorr was in the midst of it as an archetypical Equal Rights proponent.

Studious and dutiful as a youth, Dorr graduated with honors from Harvard, the second-ranking pupil in his class. He then studied law in New York City under Chancellor James Kent. After passing the bar, he toured the country, practiced law for a time in New York, and returned to Providence in 1833 to begin a life of public service.

As a Whig state legislator (1834–37), a Democratic state chairman (1840–41), a political insurrectionary (1842), and the leader of the Equal Rights wing of the Rhode Island Democratic party (1842–54), Dorr was the catalyst that hastened the demise of Rhode Island's royal charter of 1663 and the adoption of a written state constitution.

Chancellor James Kent of New York (1763–1847) was a noted jurist and legal scholar under whom Dorr studied in the 1820s. Kent is depicted in an engraving by Asher Durand from a painting by Frederick R. Spenser.

Ironically, neither document met with his approval; his egalitarian philosophy was best expressed, rather, in the so-called People's Constitution, of which he was the principal draftsman. It was Dorr's attempt to put this constitution into effect by invoking his version of the Lockean doctrine of popular constituent sovereignty that precipitated the Dorr War in 1842. Although Dorr's political goals—"free suffrage" (with no discrimination against the foreign-born), "one man, one vote," an independent judiciary, a more powerful and dynamic executive, the secret ballot—were not permanently achieved in Rhode Island during his lifetime, they placed him in the front rank of the political reformers of Jacksonian America.

Late in December 1841 the progressive People's Constitution was approved in a three-day referendum by a majority of Rhode Island's free

Dorr as he appeared in 1842 as the "People's Governor," from a Daguerreotype.

white adult males acting in defiance of the existing state authorities. In April 1842 Dorr was elected the "People's governor" under this new regime, and the state was confronted with two rival governments.

Generally, urban Whigs and rural Democrats opposed the Dorrites and united to form the Law and Order party. These conservatives prevailed, and after surrendering to them Dorr was tried, convicted, and imprisoned for treason against the state. The Whig-led Law and Order coalition dominated state politics for the remainder of the decade, despite a brief intraparty dispute in 1845 over whether or not to liberate Dorr.

Counting the time he spent awaiting trial, the vanquished reformer was actually confined to state prison for a total of twenty months, an ordeal that shattered his fragile health and contributed to his political and physical demise. His liberation, finally achieved on June 27, 1845, stirred national interest and was a Democratic issue in the 1844 presidential campaign, as evidenced by the slogan "Polk, Dallas, and Dorr."

Dorr's rebellion was no tempest in a teapot; it had national repercussions and has enduring significance. The most important and controversial domestic occurrence of the Tyler administration, it eventually involved the president, both houses of Congress, and the Supreme Court. Of even greater significance, the Rhode Island upheaval inspired substantial contributions to the theories of suffrage, majority rule, minority rights, and constitutional government by John C. Calhoun, John L. O'Sullivan, Orestes Brownson, Joseph Story, Daniel Webster, Horace Greeley, Benjamin Hallett, and others of similar stature.

Much less known but no less significant were Dorr's economic and social concerns. Despite his patrician status, Dorr gradually evolved into a laissez-faire Democrat with a deep aversion toward economic privilege. As a young state legislator he sponsored the first comprehensive statute regulating state banks in 1836, a measure that led to his break with the local Whig party. The People's Constitution was permeated with equal rights (Locofoco) economic doctrine that sought to curb the abuses of special corporate "privilege" and monopoly grants from government.

Dorr was also a pioneer of free public education, and his People's Constitution made education a fundamental right. As a member, and then chairman, of the Providence School Committee (1836–1842), Dorr established that city's secondary school system and made significant improvements in teacher education, recruitment and certification, administrative reorganization, and physical facilities. When the famed educational innovator Henry Barnard came to Rhode Island in 1843 and observed the workings of the Providence school system, he announced that his goal as state commissioner was to bring the schools in the other towns up to the standards established by Dorr in the city of Providence.

Dorr was intensely concerned with the status of minorities. His support of equal voting rights for Irish Catholic immigrants was exploited by his opponents and led to the breakup of his reform coalition. Though not an abolitionist, Dorr actively opposed slavery, urged civil rights for blacks, and worked with the leaders of the American Anti-Slavery Society as a delegate to that group's national convention. Dorr, a bachelor, worked well with local women's leaders, and they played a major role in the agitation leading to his liberation from prison.

Beginning in 1851, Dorr's uncle, Philip Allen, the new leader of Rhode Island's reform Democrats, captured the governorship for three successive years because of the defection of the rural Democrats from the Law and Order party. When the Allen faction (called "Dorr Democrats") pardoned Dorr, reversed his treason conviction, and attempted to reenact the People's Constitution, the agrarians again defected. At this juncture, Know-Nothingism and the rise of the Republican party produced a major political realignment in Rhode Island.

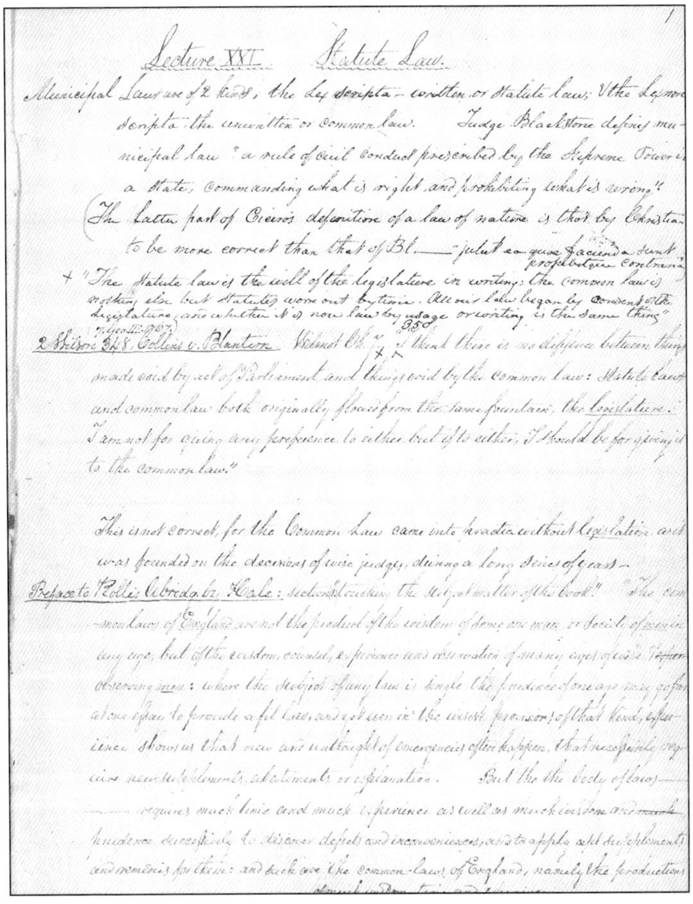
Lecture XVI. Statute Law.

Municipal Laws are of 2 kinds, the Lex scripta – written or statute law; & the Lex non scripta the unwritten or common law. Judge Blackstone defines municipal law "a rule of civil conduct prescribed by the Supreme Power in a State, commanding what is right, and prohibiting what is wrong."

(The latter part of Cicero's definition of a law of nature is thot by Christian to be more correct than that of Bl.— "jubet ea quae facienda sunt prohibetque contraria"

+ "The statute law is the will of the legislature in writing: the common law is nothing else but statutes worn out by time. All our law began by consent of the legislature, and whether it is now law by usage or writing is the same thing" 7. Geo. III. 1767.

2 Wilson 348, Collins v. Blanton. Wilmot Ch. J. 350 "I think there is no difference between things made void by act of Parliament and things void by the common law: Statute law and common law both originally flowed from the same fountain, the legislature. I am not for giving any preference to either but if to either, I should be for giving it to the common law."

This is not correct, for the Common Law came into practice without legislation and was founded on the decisions of wise judges, during a long series of years –

A page on "Statute Law" from Dorr's student notebook (1824), in the possession of the author.

Dorr participated in the equal-rights resurgence of the early 1850s as a political strategist and advisor to his popular uncle. In December 1854, as the tide of reform began to ebb, Dorr died at the age of forty-nine.

By the end of this turbulent political decade, the Republicans, who had revived the Law and Order coalition, dominated state politics (and would continue to do so until the New Deal). The urban wing of the Democratic party, appealing mainly to equal-rights advocates and Irish Catholics, was consigned to minority status until well into the twentieth century. During this time the party enshrined Dorr as their hero. In 1935, when the state's Democrats finally gained control of the governorship and both houses of the General Assembly via the "Bloodless Revolution" for the first time since 1854, Governor Theodore Francis Green justified the coup by telling a statewide radio audience that his party's success was inspired by "the spiritual presence of the patron saint of the Democratic Party in Rhode Island—Thomas Wilson Dorr!"

16

Since the author of the following essay doubles as editor of this anthology, an extensive introduction to this piece could prove redundant. Conley's article is adapted from *Democracy in Decline: Rhode Island's Constitutional Development, 1776–1841* (1977), a detailed and heavily documented study of the coming of Dorr's rebellion, its course, and its effects.

The Dorr War has long fascinated historians and students of Rhode Island history, so a review of the best writing on this colorful topic may serve as the most useful introduction to it. All credible accounts draw, at least in part, upon primary documents. The extensive Dorr Papers and Correspondence are housed at the John Hay Library of Brown University, and many of Dorr's letters survive in other depositories, especially the Rhode Island Historical Society Library.

Arthur May Mowry, *The Dorr War* (Providence, 1901), the first full-length analysis of the rebellion, is written from the conservative viewpoint and upholds the position of the Law and Order party; Marvin E. Gettleman, *The Dorr Rebellion: A Study in American Radicalism* (New York, 1973), interprets the Rhode Island reform movement from a New Left perspective as an episode in American radicalism; and George M. Dennison, *The Dorr War: Republicanism on Trial, 1831–1861* (Lexington, Ky., 1976), analyzes the impact of Dorr's movement on the development of American republican theory.

Two extensive and valuable accounts are unpublished and therefore relatively inaccessible: Anne Mary Newton, "Rebellion in Rhode Island: The Story of the Dorr War" (master's thesis, Columbia University, 1947), is condescending towards the reformers; Sidney S. Rider, "The Development of Constitutional Government in Rhode Island...," a manuscript bound in twenty-seven scrapbooks at the Rhode Island Historical Society Library, is meticulously researched, detailed, and sympathetic to the reform cause.

The presidential campaign of 1840 greatly popularized the use of political paraphernalia like badges, buttons, and banners and such techniques for mobilizing the electorate as mass meetings, torchlight processions, oxen roasts, and bonfires. In the aftermath of that election, Rhode Island constitutional reformers reasoned that they could use these devices to incite the state's second-class citizens to vigorous action. This Ward 2 banner, made by Providence suffragists in 1841 and carried to numerous rallies, depicts liberty as an American eagle clasping the nation's flag in its talons.

Of the extended accounts of the rebellion in general histories, the most useful are "Minorities and Majorities" in Arthur M. Schlesinger's Pulitzer Prize-winning *The Age of Jackson* (1945), pp. 401–421; "Spirit of the Laws" in Joseph Brennan, *Social Conditions in Industrial Rhode Island, 1820–1860* (1940), pp. 147–178; "The Rhode Island Explosion" in Chilton Williamson, *American Suffrage from Property to Democracy, 1760–1860* (1960), pp. 242–259; "Society and Politics" in Peter J. Coleman, *The Transformation of Rhode Island, 1790–1860* (1963), pp. 218–294; "Voting Rights in the Pre-Intervention Period, 1776–1868," in Ward E. Y. Elliott, *The Rise of Guardian Democracy: The Supreme Court's Role in Voting Rights Disputes, 1845–1969* (1974), pp. 34–54; and "Domestic Violence" and "*Luther* v. *Borden*" in William M. Wiecek, *The Guarantee Clause of the U.S. Constitution* (1972), pp. 78–129. Of these studies, Schlesinger, Williamson, Coleman, and Elliott are supportive of the Dorrites, while Wiecek gives an impressive analysis and defense of the Law and Order party's constitutional theory, which he later supplements in "Popular Sovereignty in the Dorr War—Conservative Counterblast," *Rhode Island History* 32 (1973), 35–51, and "'A Peculiar Conservatism' and the Dorr Rebellion: Constitutional Clash in Jacksonian America," *American Journal of Legal History* 22 (1978), 237–253.

Among the several analyses of *Luther* v. *Borden*, the most interesting from a Rhode Island perspective is John S. Schuchman, "The Political Background of the Political Question Doctrine: The Judges and the Dorr War," *American Journal of Legal History* 16 (1972), 111–125, which examines the highly partisan conduct of the Rhode Island judiciary during and after the rebellion.

The Dorr Rebellion and American Constitutional Theory: Popular Constituent Sovereignty, Political Questions, and *Luther* v. *Borden*

Patrick T. Conley

This badge was worn at a suffrage rally at the Dexter Training Grounds in Providence on July 5, 1841. At this gathering the reformers decided to invoke the doctrine of popular constituent sovereignty by calling a "People's Convention." They were urged on by such speakers as the Reverend William Balch, who asked rhetorically: "Call it a revolution that we say virtue, honor, patriotism makes the man and not dirt and primogeniture? Call it a revolution that we level every false distinction, every grade not based on talent or moral worth, and proclaim liberty and rights to the people?"

On 5 July 1841, frustrated members of the fifteen-month-old Rhode Island Suffrage Association irrevocably embraced the doctrine of popular constituent sovereignty in a mass meeting at the Dexter Training Grounds in Providence. This theory held that "the people" in their primary capacity could call a constitutional convention and draft a new basic law without the authorization of the existing government if that government was unresponsive to the urgent need for political and constitutional reform. The association was driven to embrace this radical concept because those Rhode Islanders in power, regardless of party affiliation, had resolutely resisted or deflected constitutional reform for nearly a quarter century.

Since 1818, when Connecticut drafted a written constitution, Rhode Island had been the only state to be governed by a royal charter; since 1830, when Virginia relented, Rhode Island had been the only state to impose a general real estate requirement for voting and officeholding. The state's basic law, the colonial charter of 1663, was unamendable, and it contained no separation of powers, no bill of rights, and no provision for reapportioning seats in the legislature. Under this archaic document the General Assembly was supreme, and that body was dominated by conservative, landholding white males who saw no need to share their power with those less favorably situated.

A reform effort that began in 1817, during a period of national constitutional ferment, culminated in the call of Rhode Island's first constitutional convention in 1824, but even the conservative document drafted by that convention—whose delegates were chosen according to the same apportionment scheme as the legislature—was rejected by the state's freemen. In 1834, after five years of reform agitation, the legislature authorized another, similarly composed constitutional convention, but this second gathering adjourned without producing a final draft for voter approval, and the reform movement, led by Providence attorney Thomas Wilson Dorr, evaporated during the economic depression of 1837.

The hectic "Log Cabin and Hard Cider" presidential campaign of 1840, which appealed to the simple values of the common man, resurrected the reform cause and precipitated the rise of the radical Rhode Island Suffrage Association. With the previous litany of frustrations in mind, many advocates of suffrage extension became convinced that only revolutionary measures would achieve their desired reforms. Emulating the novel political techniques used with such success by "Tippecanoe and Tyler too"—parades, mass meetings, torchlight processions—the association launched a vigorous and spirited campaign to eliminate Rhode Island's governmental abuses.

Like the movement of the 1830s, this militant suffrage movement was at least technically nonpartisan. It differed from its predecessor, however, in several respects: its membership was drawn overwhelmingly from the ranks of the Democratic party; its rank and file was composed mainly of nonfreeholders; it advocated universal manhood suffrage and denounced real and personal property qualifications for voting on political (but not financial) questions; and it was willing to utilize extralegal methods to achieve reform by ignoring or intimidating the legally constituted charter government. The responsibility for the creation of this revolutionary association rested in part with the landed oligarchy, irrespective of party affiliation and including propertied Democrats, because of that oligarchy's reactionary and obdurate refusal to amend or replace the antiquated charter. Its stand demonstrated the peril of unreasonably blocking change.

Once again reformist agitation prompted the General Assembly to authorize a constitutional convention, this one scheduled for November 1841. The agitators correctly assumed, however, that the Assembly's act was insincere and opportunistic, designed merely to sap vitality from the association's cause and no more intended to be the vehicle of change than the

STATE CONSTITUTION.

A CALL

To the People of Rhode-Island

TO ASSEMBLE IN CONVENTION.

At a Mass Convention of the friends of Equal Rights and of a WRITTEN REPUBLICAN CONSTITUTION for this State, held at Newport, on the 5th day of May, 1841, the following persons were appointed a STATE COMMITTEE for the furtherance of the cause, which the Convention had assembled to promote,—viz:—for

NEWPORT COUNTY, CHARLES COLLINS, DUTEE J. PEARCE, SILAS SISSON.
PROVIDENCE, SAMUEL H. WALES, BENJ. ARNOLD, JR. WELCOME B. SAYLES, HENRY L. WEBSTER, PHILIP B. STINESS, METCALF MARSH.
BRISTOL COUNTY, BENJ. M. BOSWORTH, SAMUEL S. ALLEN, ABIJAH LUCE.
KENT, EMANUEL RICE, SILAS WEAVER, JOHN B. SHELDON.
WASHINGTON, SYLVESTER HIMES, WAGER WEEDEN, CHARLES ALLEN.

The State Committee were directed "to carry forward the cause of Reform and Equal Rights, and to call a Convention of Delegates to draft a Constitution at as early a day as possible."

At an adjourned meeting of said Mass Convention held at Providence, on the 5th day of July, the instructions before given were reaffirmed; and the committee were directed to call a Convention of the People, on the basis of the Resolutions passed at Newport, "at an early day, for the formation of a CONSTITUTION."

Pursuing these instructions, the Committee held a meeting at Providence, on the 20th of July, and in conformity with the Eleventh Resolution adopted at Newport, which prescribes the call of a Convention of the People at large, to be represented in PROPORTION TO POPULATION, passed unanimously the following Resolutions, for the CALL of a POPULAR CONVENTION.

Voted, That we proceed to issue a CALL for the election of DELEGATES, to take place on the LAST SATURDAY in August, (the 28th day,) to attend a CONVENTION to be holden at the STATE HOUSE in PROVIDENCE, on the FIRST MONDAY in OCTOBER, (the 4th day,) for framing a CONSTITUTION to be laid before the People for their adoption.

Voted, That every American male citizen, twenty-one years of age and upwards, who has resided in this State one year, preceding the election of delegates, shall vote for Delegates to the Convention, called by the State Committee to be held at the State House in Providence on the first Monday in October next.

Voted, That every meeting holden for the election of Delegates to the State Convention shall be organized by the election of a Chairman and Secretary, whose certificate shall be the authority required of the Delegates.

Voted, That each Town of *one thousand* inhabitants, or less, shall be entitled to one delegate, and for every additional thousand, one delegate shall be appointed; and the city of Providence shall elect three delegates from each Ward in the city.

Voted, That the Chairman and Secretary be directed to cause one thousand hand-bills to be printed and distributed through the State, containing the call for a Convention of Delegates.

Voted, That the proceedings of this meeting be signed by the Chairman and Secretary, and be published.

On motion, *Voted*, That this meeting stand adjourned to meet at this place on the first day of September, at 11 o'clock A. M.

FELLOW CITIZENS—We have discharged our duty in the call of a CONVENTION of the WHOLE PEOPLE, to provide for the attainment and security of those invaluable rights, which have so long been withheld from them, and without which they are but subjects and slaves in a State only nominally Republican.

Depend upon it that a spirit has been awakened in this State, which cannot be intimidated nor repressed—which has suffered long, until patience has ceased to be a virtue, and which, regarding the Republican institutions every where else enjoyed but here, and prompted by the memory of our venerable and patriotic ancestors, the first to assert the true principles of Religious and Political freedom, will brook no farther delay, and which cannot be more appropriately expressed than when we say, in behalf of the great majority of the PEOPLE,

GIVE US OUR RIGHTS, or *WE WILL TAKE THEM.*

We ask for nothing that is not clearly right, and we are determined to submit to nothing so manifestly wrong as the corrupt and anti-republican system of government which has so long subsisted in Rhode Island by the forbearance of the People.

Bear in mind, that there is no CONSTITUTIONAL MODE OF AMENDING our government, except by the People at large, in whom, as the successors to the King of England, the sovereign power resides, and remains unimpaired by any lapse of time, or toleration of past abuses.

That there is no BILL OF RIGHTS in this State, except that *granted* by the Legislature, and which they can at any moment resume and annul.

That the General Assembly is a body irresponsible to the majority of the People, restricted by no constitutional rule of action, virtually omnipotent—making and unmaking the People, doing and undoing what it pleases, according to its "especial grace, certain knowedge and mere motion," in imitation, upon a smaller scale, of the Monarchy of Great Britain.

That the SYSTEM of representation to this Assembly is also the ROTTEN-BOROUGH system of Great Britain now partially reformed; by which system, in this State, a *third* of the *freemen*, and one *ninth* of the *People* command the House of Representatives.—

That, by reason of a landed qualification, which it is impossible for the great majority to obtain, *two thirds* of the people are ousted of the birthright acquired for them by their fathers, and are governed, taxed, compelled to do military duty, and subjected in all respects to the will and pleasure of *one third*, with the sole restriction, imposed by the Constitution of the United States.

Instead of enumerating other particulars, we only say—look at the history of Rhode Island legislation.

Fellow Citizens—It is these evils to which the great unenfranchised majority, acting in their *original, sovereign capacity*, propose and intend to apply an effectual remedy. We ask your aid and assistance in this good work. We respectfully urge upon you to assist in the election of delegates to the Popular Convention to be held in October next, not as the friends or opponents of any political party now existing in this State, but as the friends of Justice, of Humanity, of Liberty, of Equal Rights, of well regulated Constitutional Government.

Do not be deceived by the Freeholders Convention called for November next. It is a gross fraud upon the people. The design of its originators was to crystalize in a stronger form the present statute provisions relating to suffrage, and to place them beyond the reach of amendment except by the hand of force.

Once more, we say to the unenfranchised mass of our brethren and fellow-citizens—your rights are in your own hands. Assert and vindicate them like men determined to be free. See to it that a meeting for the choice of delegates is duly held in every town, and that its proportional number is regularly elected. Summon your friends and neighbors to the work—and rely upon it that a CONSTITUTION framed by such a Convention, and SIGNED by a MAJORITY of the people, will be promptly acquiesced in by the MINORITY—will be vigorously sustained, and will become without delay, the undisputed, paramount law of our State.

Providence, July 24th, 1841.

By order and in behalf of the State Committee.

SAMUEL H. WALES, Chairman.

BENJAMIN ARNOLD, JR., *Secretary*.

After the July 5 rally, the state committee of the Rhode Island Suffrage Association issued this formal call for a People's Convention. The delegates to the proposed gathering were to be apportioned according to population and chosen by universal male suffrage in town elections on August 28. The revolutionary body was to convene on October 4, 1841, a month prior to the convention authorized by the General Assembly in which only white male landowners could be delegates. This appeal for the citizens of Rhode Island to exercise their popular constituent sovereignty finally brought Dorr into the public arena again. Contrary to the general opinion of historians, Dorr had played no role in the genesis of the Suffrage Association, but when agitators approached him in August to serve as a delegate to the People's Convention, the once-apprehensive patrician immediately declared that his services would "be very cheerfully rendered."

previous "do-nothing" conventions summoned to appease the disfranchised in 1824 and 1834. As a result of this assumption, members of the Suffrage Association decided upon an extralegal course to attain their ends. Drafting Thomas Dorr to lead them, they exhorted the adult male citizenry to disregard the landholding qualifications and go to the polls to elect delegates to a "People's Convention," which would meet in October 1841. The elections were duly held late in August, and within six weeks the reformers' convention presented the fruit of its deliberations to the white male populace of Rhode Island for ratification. Meanwhile, the legally authorized Landholders' Convention met and adjourned without producing a new basic law.

The "People's Constitution," of which Dorr was the principal author, remedied many abuses that had persisted under the charter regime. The most notable and controversial departure from the charter system was in the area of suffrage: the statutory $134 freehold requirement was repudiated by a clause that extended suffrage to adult white male citizens with one year's residence in the state.

Other significant features of the People's Constitution were its reapportionment provision, which increased the representation of Providence and other urbanized centers in the Assembly's House of Representatives; a secret-ballot clause; a bill of rights; and a general diminution of the power of the legislature through the establishment of clear separation of powers on the principle of three-branch government. The conservative aspects of the document were its denial of a number of important public offices, including those of mayor and councilman, to nontaxed citizens and its provision whereby no person was allowed to vote on any financial question in the cities or towns unless he was a taxpayer or the owner of ratable property (real or personal) of at least $150 in value.

Beginning on 27 December 1841, a three-day popular referendum was held to decide on this proposed constitution. With no landholding requirements for participation, the turnout of voters approached 14,000. Only 52 votes were cast against the People's Constitution, since charter adherents boycotted the election. Because 13,944 of the state's estimated 23,142 white

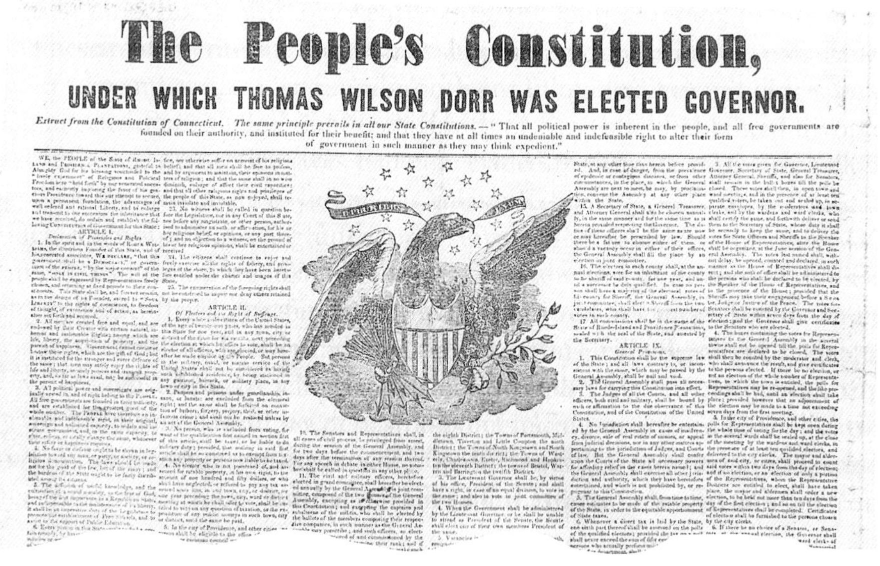

The People's Constitution,

UNDER WHICH THOMAS WILSON DORR WAS ELECTED GOVERNOR.

Extract from the Constitution of Connecticut. The same principle prevails in all our State Constitutions. — "That all political power is inherent in the people, and all free governments are founded on their authority, and instituted for their benefit; and that they have at all times an undeniable and indefeasible right to alter their form of government in such manner as they may think expedient."

The People's Constitution, with Dorr as its principal draftsman, was permeated with the ideology of equal rights. It was therefore denounced by its critics as "unadulterated Locofocoism"—a reference to the Equal Rights, working-class wing of New York's Democratic party. That group had influenced the course of reform in Rhode Island from the late 1830s onward, and Dorr embraced most of its principles. This ideology of equal rights has been described as an amalgam of Lockean theories of freedom, laissez-faire economics, Calvinistic moral scruples, hostility towards "aristocratic" privilege, and a belief in the negative state.

adult males had voted to approve the document, as had 4,960 of the state's 9,590 freemen, Dorr declared that the constitution had been duly ratified. The possibility of fraudulent voting was high (as for any election in that age), and undoubtedly a number of bogus ballots were cast, but when the results were tabulated and certified on 13 January, the reformers insisted that the People's Constitution had supplanted the charter as the paramount law of the state. Popular constituent sovereignty had triumphed, or so it seemed!

Ironically, the suffragists relinquished their momentum in January 1842 at the peak of their campaign. The very orderly and peaceful nature of their revolution impaired its decisiveness, for they had decreed in the People's Constitution that the charter government "shall exercise all the powers with which it is now clothed, until the said first Tuesday of May 1842, and until their successors, under this constitution, shall be duly elected and qualified." This clause (overlooked by most historians) gave the charterites nearly four months to devise an official counteroffensive to prevent the People's Constitution from taking effect. Seldom have revolutionaries been so obliging or respectful toward an existing government.

Too much was at stake for the long-entrenched establishment to acquiesce without a fight, but its forceful countereffort was not anticipated by most reformers, especially those who naively believed that the December referendum would be legally and morally binding on all Rhode Islanders. They were warned of the impending crisis in January at the height of their success by Henry Dorr, Thomas's younger but more conservative brother, who challenged the validity of the People's Convention and predicted that most people would bow before "constituted authority." If the suffragists persisted, he admonished, they "would be like the Chartists of England with a few leaders, and those not the right men to head such an enterprise—and no people on which you can depend to support you at all risks." The younger Dorr indeed proved to be a prophet.

Many reasons explain the charterites' resistance towards the People's Constitution—its radical doctrine of popular constituent sovereignty, its anticorporate ideology of equal rights, its impact on the "agrarian interest" through reapportionment, and its enfranchisement of the "low Irish"—but undoubtedly it was the never-articulated urge for political self-preservation that was the underlying motive animating leaders of the Law and Order coalition that formed to defend the existing regime. The proposed changes simply made retention of their power more imperative.

Dorr's opposition—mainly politically dominant urban Whigs associated with the commercial-business-industrial complex, and rural Democrats from South County and the western hill towns—had every intention of asserting their legal authority, and in January 1842 they launched a determined bid to undermine the revolutionaries' position. Their attack on the Dorrites was multifaceted. The prestigious judiciary spearheaded one thrust; during the winter and early spring of 1842, federal district judge John Pitman and state Supreme Court chief justice Job Durfee descended from their neutral benches to attack the People's Constitution openly on theoretical and legal grounds. Pitman, a former supporter of suffrage extension, penned a January address *To the Members of the General Assembly of Rhode Island*, which attacked the extralegal methods of the suffragists and urged that their criminal "revolutionary movement" be immediately suppressed. Pitman also corresponded with United States Supreme Court justice Joseph Story, then riding the New England circuit. The conservative Story—who would later preside over several cases arising from the Dorr Rebellion—was equally partisan. "If ever there was a case that called upon a judge to write and speak openly and publicly, it was the very case then before you," he advised Pitman.

According to Story's Whig view, "the Constitution of Rhode Island was to be overturned by a self-created body," and there was "no duty more sacred in every citizen than upon such an emergency to come forth and resist, by all the just and moral means in his power, such proceedings." Job Durfee agreed with this extreme judicial activism. In early March his three-judge court (which included William R. Staples and Levi Haile, a leader of the Constitutional party of the 1830s) issued a public letter asserting the illegality of the People's Constitution and contending that any attempt to carry it into effect would be "treason against this State."

Justice Durfee—erstwhile poet, former congressman, and formidable orator—was not content with a single swipe at the "mobocratic" suffragists. On 15 March he delivered a charge to a Bristol grand jury, which it subsequently published, reaffirming his belief that support of the People's Constitution was treasonous and expounding a persuasive and logical refutation of popular constituent sovereignty.

In attempting to define "the people," Durfee distinguished between the "natural people," or the entire human population regardless of age, sex, color, citizenship, or legal or mental status, and the "corporate people," or the legal voters in whom alone sovereignty resides. For him, sovereignty was not some vague primal right in the hands of a majority of natural people but a carefully defined, limited power to be exercised by the people's representatives under established, legitimate modes. Durfee's distinction was followed by other Law and Order apologists, including John Whipple and Daniel Webster when they defended the charter regime before the United States Supreme Court in the case of *Luther* v. *Borden* (1849). These conservatives, in the tradition of Hamilton, stressed the primacy of order and authority, while Dorrites argued in Jeffersonian fashion that order was not possible without liberty and that liberty was possible only when the people controlled their government.

In another extremely potent maneuver, charter adherents appealed to the class, sectional, occupational, and ethnoreligious sentiments of Rhode Islanders in an inconsistent but effective propaganda campaign waged against the People's Constitution in broadsides, pamphlets, and the pages of the *Providence Journal.* Conservatives warned well-to-do urbanites and farmers that the proposed basic law would bring the city under the domination of the idle, ignorant, and poorer class; they alarmed farmers by contending that the document's reapportionment plan would place the agrarian interest at the mercy of the industrial and shift the basis of taxa-

COMPARISON.

The following is a fair comparison of some of the most prominent points in the two Constitutions:

Constitution of the Regular Convention.	*People's Constitution.*
The declaration of Rights does not contain the express statement that all men are created free and equal, or that the government shall be a democracy.	The declaration of Rights sets forth that all men are created equal, and that the government shall be a democracy.

In both Constitutions, however, about the same doctrines are contained, so that there is no more equality or democracy in the People's Constitution, than in the other.

The civil capacity of a man is not to be affected by his religious opinions.	No person is to be questioned in court, nor by a magistrate, nor his oath or testimony to be rejected on account of his religious opinions.

Both these provisions amount to the same thing; because to reject a man's oath or testimony, is to affect his civil capacity.

SUFFRAGE.

Freeholders, and others now qualified, to be still allowed to vote.—Also, all native born white male citizens, resident two years in the State, and six months in the town. Also, naturalized foreigners, resident three years in the State after naturalization, and six months in the town, with a freehold of $134. The General Assembly may also enact laws to admit other native citizens, white or colored. All voters to be at least twenty-one years of age.	Every white male citizen, resident one year in the State, and six months in the town, foreigners naturalized, as well as native born, is allowed to vote. To be twenty-one years of age, and upwards.

The principal difference in these two provisions, is, that the People's Constitution admits naturalized foreigners on the same conditions as native citizens, and the other does not—That the People's constitution requires a residence of only one year in the State, while the other requires a residence of three years for naturalized foreigners, and two years for native citizens. Also that the People's Constitution excludes colored people, so that they cannot be permitted to vote without an amendment of the Constitution; while, by the other, the Legislature may admit them. In a State like ours, in which so many transient persons are employed in comparison with our permanent population, we believe the residence of two years, to be far preferable to one year; as by it, our voters become more permanently incorporated among the people, more directly interested in the welfare of the State, and our institutions subject to far less fluctuation and instability.

As to foreigners, we consider they have no direct claims on any State to be admitted to the ballot box; and that such admission is an act of clemency in a State government; as the act of naturalization only makes a foreigner a citizen of the United States, and not of any particular State, and lays no State under any obligation to receive him as such: especially while a State Constitution excludes native citizens merely on account of color. We consider also, that, with the great influx of foreigners into our country, our government, and the interests of our State, would be unsafe, considering the great facilities for becoming naturalized, should they be admitted to vote without some farther evidence of their worth, and of their attachment to our State and its laws, than a mere residence.

By the People's Constitution, should it go into operation, a large body of foreigners already in the State, would be brought immediately to the polls. Additional encouragement would be held out to others to come into the State, and augment the number. Thereby our native mechanics and workingmen would suffer by the competition, for labor; and the balance of political and civil power would inevitably be placed in the hands of emigrants from foreign countries, who would, either directly, or indirectly, control the State. Let native American citizens pause and reflect, and honestly decide, if they are or are not willing to become subject to such control; and then act accordingly.

REPRESENTATIVES.

The Representative apportionment gives to the city of Providence, eight Representatives, to be elected by general ticket; which number cannot be increased or diminished. No town, however small, can have less than two; and, for other towns, they are to be increased or diminished, as the population may increase or diminish, in a given ratio. The whole number of Representatives is seventy-seven, at present.	The Representative apportionment, as fixed, gives a certain number of Representatives to a town or city, which number, however the population may be increased or diminished, cannot be changed without an amendment of the Constitution. To the city of Providence, are given twelve Representatives—the city to be divided into six districts, and each district to elect two Representatives. Jamestown, Middletown, and Barrington, are to elect one Representative each. The Whole number is eighty.

The principal differences in these provisions are as follows—1st. By the People's Constitution, Providence, as a city, has no Representative; and elects twelve, who are only the delegates of wards. By the other Constitution, Providence, as a CITY, and not as wards, has her undivided influence in the persons of eight men chosen by a majority of all the electors, whereas by the districting system, a minority of the electors may elect a majority of the Representatives. 2d. The People's Constitution gives to Smithfield 5 Representatives, and the other gives 4. It gives to Newport 5, and the other gives 4. It gives to Middletown, Jamestown and Barrington 1 each, and the other gives them two each. These differences, for all practical purposes, are mere trifles; except for Providence, which by the districting system in the People's Constitution, is deprived of all corporate representation.

But, a very material difference is, that the People's Constitution adopts the *rotten borough* system, making the present apportionment permanent, and unalterable by law, so that it can never become more equal; while by the other Constitution, in all towns, the representation can be changed to correspond with important changes that may occur in population. By the People's Constitution, Providence County has 36 Representatives, by the other, it has 31; by the People's, Newport County has 15, Bristol 5, Kent 10, and Washington 14. By the other, Newport has 16, and Bristol 6; the other counties are alike in both. From these facts, it is believed every unprejudiced and intelligent mind, must give the preference to what is called the Landholders' Constitution, as to Representation.

SENATORS.

The Senate is to consist of nineteen Senators, as follows, in respect to counties:—Providence, 6; Newport, 4; Bristol, 2; Kent, 3; Washington, 4.	The Senate is to consist of twelve Senators, as follows:—Providence, 5; Newport, 2; Bristol, 1; Kent, 2; Washington, 2.

The difference in these provisions is, that the People's Constitution provides for twelve Senators, and the other for nineteen; and that the apportionment is somewhat different. It is complained by those friendly to the People's Constitution, that the apportionment of Senators is unequal, and gives an undue preponderance of one portion of the State over another. The Senate in the Landholders' Constitution, so called, is based on a conservative principle common to all representative governments, to protect the rights of the minority against the majority power. In this case, it is believed, the conservative principle is not carried beyond proper bounds. The great fear expressed, is for the interest of Providence county. But it will be seen, that with the six Senators in this county, it will require the union of Newport and Washington, Washington and Kent, or Newport and Kent, to outvote the county of Providence, in the Senate; and we do not believe the true interests of the county of Providence, or any other county in the State, will ever suffer by means of such a combination. To attempt to form a government with the necessary checks and balances, without the conservative power somewhere to protect the minority, is perfectly idle, and we believe this provision is right. On the other basis, Providence County can outvote any two counties in the State, and will tie all the other counties, except one; so that she can never be outvoted, except by the union of at least three others.

There are some other differences between many other articles, most of them of comparativly little importance, that may be attended to hereafter. A careful and candid perusal of the foregoing, by every American in the State, and an honest decision in the exercise of a sober and unbiassed judgment, is respectfully solicited.

This "Comparison," published by supporters of the Freemen's Constitution, exploited the difference between the suffrage clauses of the two basic laws.

tion from business to land; and they excited entrepreneurs by emphasizing the reformers' anticorporate philosophy of equal rights. Propagandists—especially Henry Bowen Anthony and Professor William G. Goddard—played upon the fears of native-born Protestants, warning them that the liberal suffrage clause of the People's Constitution would pave the way for the political ascendancy of those Irish Catholic immigrants who were swarming into the state in ever-increasing numbers.

Political nativism, a potent weapon in the arsenal of the Law and Order conservatives, was especially evident in the final draft of the Freemen's (or Landholders') Constitution, produced in February 1842 by the reconvened session of the Landholders' Convention. This Law and Order body drafted a compromise document designed to wean moderates from their adherence to the extralegal People's Constitution. The tactic was highly successful. The Freemen's Constitution contained no lofty appeals to the doctrine of popular constituent sovereignty and no traces of the ideology of equal rights. It reapportioned the legislature, but less drastically than Dorr's document, especially in the upper house, where it gave great security to the farming interest by allocating 60 percent of the Senate's nineteen seats to rural areas. Although it slightly reduced the power of the legislature, it allowed it to retain all its judicial functions and denied the governor a veto. The freemen's bill of rights, however, was quite progressive, and perhaps even modeled upon that of the People's Constitution.

The most exploitable difference between the two documents appeared in the area of suffrage. The Freemen's Constitution gave the franchise to those white, male, *native-born* citizens who met age and residency requirements, but it retained the real estate requirement for naturalized citizens, for whom it actually lengthened the state residency qualification from one year to three years after naturalization. By resolution of the General Assembly, all those who would be enfranchised by the Freemen's Constitution were allowed to vote upon its ratification in a three-day referendum scheduled for 21–23 March.

These concessions—especially that of suffrage to the native-born—stole the thunder from the Dorrite cause and drove a wedge between extreme and moderate reformers. The *Providence Journal*, the leading organ of the Law and Order faction, told natives that the freemen's basic law "extends suffrage for which you originally contended," whereas "foreign elements in the other constitution would neutralize your power and effectiveness." As editor Henry Anthony admonished: "The great difference between the two constitutions lies in the provision respecting foreigners. Everything else is nothing to this."

Nativistic rhetoric became increasingly inflammatory in the March campaign over ratification. One broadside warned men of Rhode Island stock that the People's Constitution would "place your government, your civil and political institutions, your PUBLIC SCHOOLS, and perhaps your RELIGIOUS PRIVILEGES, under the control of the POPE of ROME, through the medium of thousands of NATURALIZED FOREIGN CATHOLICS." This widely disseminated leaflet further advised that support of the Freemen's Constitution was essential unless natives were "prepared to see a Catholic Bishop, at the head of a posse of Catholic Priests, and a band of their servile dependents, take the field to subvert your institutions, under the sanction of a State Constitution."

NATIVE AMERICAN CITIZENS!

READ AND TAKE WARNING!

A SHORT SERMON.

LET EVERY SOUL BE SUBJECT TO THE HIGHER POWERS. *Romans*, 13, 1.

Christians, like all other men, have the right to protect themselves against oppression. They have also the right to aid in the protection of others, but our Savior said, "MY KINGDOM IS NOT OF THIS WORLD," and thus taught his followers that it was inconsistent with their duty to him, and with their respect for his doctrines, to mingle in the strife for power. Paul, in the above quoted text, did not intend to teach his brethren that they should submit, with degrading servility, to tyranny, cruelty, and oppression, when they could remove the evil without producing another equally great. But his frequent exhortations, as well as those of his DIVINE MASTER, fully show that they considered it the indispensable duty of CHRISTIANS to submit to existing governments for the sake of peace, until oppression became too cruel to be borne, or until the evil could be remedied without unnecessary violence; and that, in ALL CASES, for the HONOR of the CHURCH, the SUCCESS of the GOSPEL, and the PEACE of the COMMUNITY, CHRISTIANS should "be subject to the HIGHER POWERS," as *long as forbearance would be a virtue.*

CHRISTIAN PROFESSORS OF RHODE ISLAND, I put to you a plain question—Will you answer it as on the ALTAR of GOD, to HIM AND YOUR OWN CONSCIENCES? Does it appear that the Constitution to be voted on for adoption or rejection, on the 21st, 22d, and 23d, inst. is of such a character as to threaten danger to your rights and privileges, or those of others? Is it oppressive in its provisions or bearings? Would you be justified in rejecting it, and in adoptiong another which will place your government, your civil and political institutions, your PUBLIC SCHOOLS, and perhaps your RELIGIOUS PRIVILEGES, under the control of the POPE of ROME, through the medium of THOUSANDS of NATURALIZED FOREIGN CATHOLICS? Does the honor and prosperity of the church require it? Do the peace, welfare, and prosperity, of the State require it? Yet, reject the Constitution now presented to you, and you show your preference for another, which, *should it ever be adopted*, WILL PLACE THE BALLANCE OF POWER IN THE STATE, IN THE HANDS OF THOSE PEOPLE. The event can readily be predicted. Would you defend yourselves and your church against the operations and predominance of such a power, and preserve the State from anarchy and ruin? Would you preserve peace, and thereby avoid violence and bloodshed? Would you pay that respect to the CONSTITUTED AUTHORITIES WHICH THE GOSPEL DEMANDS? Would you keep a conscience pure and undefiled, by pursuing a course on which you can hereafter look with approbation, and for the correctness of which, you can CONFIDENTLY APPEAL TO HEAVEN IN THE HOUR OF DEATH, AND AT THE DREAD TRIBUNAL HEREAFTER? Then, and I must suppose such to be your wish, array yourselves on the side of the "HIGHER POWERS," in a quiet and peaceable manner, GIVE YOUR VOTES FOR THE CONSTITUTION ON MONDAY NEXT. Show those who act in the opposition only to carry out their will, that you value too highly your CHRISTIAN PROFESSION, your CHRISTIAN CHARACTER, and your CHRISTIAN PRINCIPLE, to countenance sedition, and to endanger the peace of an entire community, only to defeat the benevolent object of the existing government, and to give encouragement and support to a spirit of violence and disorder. Tell those who would allure you to aid them in the work of strife.

'WE HAVE NOT SO LEARNED CHRIST.'

REV. WILLIAM S. BALCH.

The above gentleman, late Pastor of the First Universalist Church in this city, and who, while *here, did much for the party* which have made and voted for the "*People's Constitution*," was requested by that party to lecture during his visit here this week from New York. He very properly refused to do so; and said he *would not were he now a resident here*; for the reason, that the *party have carried the thing too far*, and are *now* making a *political affair of it, and he would have nothing to do with it.* This is valuable testimony from one of the *ablest* and *fastest friends of the suffrage cause.*

AN EXAMPLE.

In a "Short Sermon" puplished in our extra sheet, the writer alluded to the possibility that, should a constitution like that called the "People's Constitution" be adopted, the naturalized foreign Chatholics might exercise a pernicious influence on our political, civil, and religions institutions, and on our public schools. We have a case in point. The CATHOLIC BISHOP HUGHES, of New York, at the last election in that city, ARRAYED UNDER HIS CONTROL, some THREE THOUSAND FOREIGN CATHOLIC VOTERS, after an effort of a few days, to sustain at the BALLOT BOX his own views on the question of public schools, for the purpose of diverting to the use of the CATHOLIC CHURCH, a portion of the common school fund of the State. With a longer period for the purpose, it is probable a body of foreign naturalized Catholics might have been organized, and will hereafter be organized, in that city and State, under PAPAL ECCLESIASTICAL INFLUENCE, *to carry out their views.* The excitement on the question still continues. The Bishop and his party are determined to succeed in their efforts. The native citizens have become alarmed. And meetings have been held to prevent the abhorred attempt from becoming successful.

On Wednesday last, a meeting was held in the Park, New York city, on the question. And during the procedidgs, a band of foreigners broke in upon the assemblage, and by means of violence, broke up the meeting. A New York paper says,

"Our cheeks are suffused with shame and indignation as we write about this matter; for so gross an insult to our rights as Americans, we have never seen or heard of before. Bands of filthy wretches, whose every touch was offensive to a decent man, drunken loafers; scoundrels who the police and criminal courts would be ashamed to receive in their walls; coarse, blustering rowdies; blear eyed and bloated offscourings from the stews, blind alleys and rear lanes; disgusting objects bearing the form human, but whom the sow in the mire might almost object to as companions—these were they who broke into the midst of a peaceful body of American citizens—struck and insulted the chosen officers of the assemblage, and with shrieks, loud blasphemy, and howling in their hideous native tongue, prevented the continuance of the customary routine. We saw Irish priests there—sly, false, deceitful villains—looking on and evidently encouraging the gang who created the tumult. We noticed two or three tavern bullies strike on the head a presiding officer—one of the most aged and respectable men of our city. We beheld the whole body of those officers forced, at length, from their seats, and driven, with jibes and blows, from the stage. And these officers were native Americans—men with grey heads—men known for long years among us, as gentlemen of reputation, philanthropy and exalted worth!

And is New York to utter no loud voice of abhorrence towords this transaction? Is this hypocritical scoundrel Hughes, and his minions, to drill ranks of ignorant and vindictive followers—and send them forth to act as those wretches acted—and shall no note be taken of it? It is a blot and an insolent violation of our dearest and most glorious privileges. The whole city—the whole state—ought to rise up as one man, and let these jesuitical knaves, and their apt satellities, know what it is to feel the blast from an injured and outraged country."

RHODE-ISLANDERS—Read this. Ponder seriously on it. Say—are you prepared to witness such scenes enacted in your little, and hitherto peaceful and prosperous State? Are you prepared to see a Catholic Bishop, at the head of a posse of Catholic Priests, and a band of their servile dependents, take the field to subvert your institutions, under the sanction of a State Constitution. If not, vote for the Constitution now presented to you, which is well calculated to protect you from such abuses. ROGER WILLIAMS.

The Law and Order advocates of the Freemen's Constitution attempted to gain support for the document in the March 1842 referendum by appealing to anti-Irish Catholic prejudice, as they did in this broadside. They warned that the People's Constitution placed the naturalized citizen on an equal footing with the native-born, thus paving the way for an Irish Catholic political ascendancy in Rhode Island. If the real estate requirement for naturalized citizens was not maintained, the *Providence Journal* later exclaimed, Rhode Island "will become a province of Ireland: St. Patrick will take the place of Roger Williams, and the shamrock will supersede the anchor and Hope!"

Suffragist Joshua B. Rathbun wrote Dorr from Tiverton that "this right to exclude naturalized citizens is strongly insisted upon here and has perhaps operated against us more than anything else. Men were called upon not to vote for a constitution but to vote against Irishmen." Providence Brahmin John Carter Brown privately urged reformer Walter R. Danforth to accept the Freemen's Constitution. "Perhaps you can influence Colonel [Franklin] Cooley to hammer away on the right side, seeing that suffrage is extended to everybody of native growth," Brown told the suffragist leader. "The Colonel would hardly desire to be governed by the Catholic priesthood." Contemporary broadsides played upon this xenophobia; one expressed the exaggerated opinion that "every Roman Catholic Irishman in Rhode Island is a Dorrite."

The *Journal* utilized the acid pens of Henry Anthony and William Goddard on the eve of the referendum to succinctly state its case:

> The balance of power in the Legal [i.e., Freemen's] Constitution resides in the Senators from those portions of the State engaged in agriculture....
>
> Where is the balance of power left in the instrument manufactured by Messrs. Dorr, Brown & Co.? Where, but among the twenty-five hundred foreigners, who are already in the State, and the hundreds more who will be imported?...These are the men, leagued together as they are in one band, who will hold the rod of political power over our native citizens, and usurp the seat of political justice. Their priests and leaders will say here to a political party, as they say in New York City, give us by law, every opportunity to perpetuate our spiritual despotism...and we will assist you to a man; we will give you power.... At the feet of these men, may you lay down your boasted freedom of thought and political independence.
>
> ...Wherever he [the foreigner] wanders, he still sings songs of his early home. The arms of his mother church embrace him,—he still bows down to her rituals, worships the host, obeys and craves absolution from his priests.... He cannot associate freely, with the independent sons of our free land, and cannot assimilate himself to our institutions....
>
> Now is the time to choose between these two systems. Where will you place the great conservative check in our government? With foreigners responsible only to their priests, or with intelligent Rhode Island farmers?

Conversely, the American Irish press lined up with Dorr. "It is our own Home Rule question in Rhode Island," asserted the *Truth Teller* (New York) in an article upholding the Dorrites' cause. Clearly the Irish Catholic issue was an essential aspect of the 1842 controversy, both as a scare tactic and as a genuine apprehension.

Moved more by principle than by a quest for power, Dorr and his leading associates exhorted "the people" to vote down the handiwork of the Landholders' Convention. The electorate responded to this appeal, despite the vote-buying tactics of freeholders, and the Freemen's Constitution was defeated by the ominously narrow margin of 8,689 to 8,013 in a turnout that exceeded the record-breaking December referendum. Ironically, it was the negative stance of the ultraconservative faction of the Law and Order party, those opposing any reform whatsoever, that saved the day for the Dorrites; the vote of the reformers alone (with naturalized Irish excluded from the referendum) would not have been sufficient to defeat the Freemen's Constitution. Nonetheless, suffragists hailed the election as a vindication of the "sovereignty of the people" over the alleged "sovereignty of corporations."

As the charter government prepared for the annual April elections, it took other decisive steps to reverse the suffragists' momentum. One such tactic was the mobilization of the state militia companies by an executive order commanding them to be ready to appear armed and equipped at thirty minutes' notice. On 2 April the Assembly passed its "Algerine Law" (so-called by Dorrites because they equated its harshness with the arbitrary rule of the dey of Algiers). This menacing statute imposed severe penalties against those who participated in the upcoming "People's" election and declared that anyone who assumed state office under the People's Constitution was guilty of treason against the state and subject to life imprisonment. On 7 April Judge John Pitman advised Justice Story that "we are not idle. Full power has been given to the governor to meet the exigency of the crisis and he is doing all he can to put the state in military array."

The charterites also began to appease Rhode Island's black community. Although the Freemen's Constitution had denied the vote to Afro-Americans, some conservatives were now willing to grant that concession in return for black assistance against the suffragists.

The apparent "unreliability" of the regular state militia, many of whose members supported Dorr, prompted Governor Samuel Ward King to apply to President John Tyler with the request that "such precautionary measures ... be taken by the Government of the United States" as might afford the charter government the protection against domestic violence required by the United States Constitution. On 4 April, at the instigation of Judge Pitman, King sent a three-man delegation to confer with Tyler, this delegation consisting of conservative rural Democrats Elisha Potter, Jr., and John Brown Francis and Whig attorney John Whipple, in whose office Dorr had clerked. One week later, after some ambivalence, the states' rights Virginian president "assured" King that "should the time arrive, when an insurrection shall exist *against the government of Rhode Island*, and a requisition shall be made upon the Executive of the United States to furnish that protection which is guaranteed to each by the constitution and laws, I shall not be found to shrink from the performance of a duty." Tyler then added a provision that gave a lift to the Law and Order cause: "In such a contingency, the Executive could not look into real or supposed defects of the existing government"; on the contrary, it was his duty to continue "to respect the requisitions of that government which has been recognized as the existing government of the State through all time past" until such time as he should be "advised in a regular manner that it has been altered and abolished and

Samuel Ward King (1786–1851) of Johnston was elected governor of Rhode Island on the Whig ticket in 1840. He was reelected annually in 1841 and 1842, and thus he was the incumbent during the rise of reform agitation leading to the Dorr Rebellion. A physician by profession, the Law and Order governor had served as a surgeon in the War of 1812 and had attended mortally wounded Captain James Lawrence as that naval hero uttered his famous injunction, "Don't give up the ship," during the battle between the USS *Chesapeake* and the HMS *Shannon*. In 1842 King took Lawrence's advice.

another substituted in its place by legal and peaceable proceedings adopted and pursued by the authorities and people of the state."

With their counteroffensive in full swing, Law and Order forces looked towards the regular annual election on 20 April to sustain themselves in power until the Dorrites' challenge was overcome. Though now on the defensive, the suffragists, for their part, were not idle. In February and March they held rallies in various mill villages, and they counteracted the legal challenge to popular constituent sovereignty posed by Durfee and Pitman by drafting the impressive *Nine Lawyers' Opinion*, the most cogent and persuasive statement of suffrage ideology. On 5 April they dispatched reform editor Dr. John A. Brown (who proved to be a naive emissary) to confer with Tyler and leading Democratic congressmen to forestall federal intervention, and on 18 April they fielded a full slate of state officers in defiance of the Algerine Law. Thomas Dorr was their reluctant but courageous candidate for governor (after both Democrat Thomas F. Carpenter and Whig Wager Weeden had declined the nomination), despite a plea from his prestigious parents to save them "from that shame and disgrace which will attend us if you persist, and which will hurry us sorrowing to the grave."

The April elections brought the crisis to a head. When the balloting was done on 18 April, Dorr had polled 6,359 votes to become the "People's governor." Two days later incumbent Whig Samuel Ward King defeated Democratic suffragist Thomas Carpenter by a margin of 4,864 to 2,211. Although Dorr's election under the People's Constitution was unopposed and a fierce storm dampened the contest, the turnout was still disappointing; Dorr's total was 2,330 less than the vote against the Freemen's document and 7,585 less than the vote in favor of the People's Constitution three and a half months earlier. Further, the 4,864 votes cast by freeholders for King in the regular election represented a majority of the total number of freemen (9,590). Dorrites had claimed this majority in January when they tallied the votes on the People's Constitution, but on 20 April most freeholders allied with the forces of Law and Order.

Suffragist support was clearly on the wane, especially in southerly rural areas, and several prominent Rhode Islanders had publicly switched sides. Notable among the defectors were wealthy industrialist and political chameleon William Sprague, who received a United States senatorship in February 1842 for his change of heart, and Jacob Frieze, a historian of Rhode Island suffrage reform. Even state representative Samuel Atwell of Glocester, the leading suffrage spokesman in the General Assembly, wavered after enactment of the Algerine Law.

Emboldened by reform's ebbing tide, the charterites added new tactics to their counteroffensive in the aftermath of the April balloting. Governor King called a special session of the Assembly that strengthened governmental prerogatives under the riot act, authorized armed volunteer "police companies" in Providence, and created a Board of Councillors "to advise

The Paddy's Lament for Tom Dorr.

Air—Widow Malone.

'TWAS that swate little lump of Tom Dorr,
That so nately could break through the law,
And could raise such a row
By the wag of his pow,
And such crowds at his heels he could draw
With his jaw,
Och a swate chap was Governor Dorr.

He knew how to govern a state
In a way that was new and first-rate,
And the votes in his day
Were all our own way,
And the way we did brag was so great,
Och t'was swate,
When we and Tom Dorr ruled the state.

And to please the dear people—that's us—
He kicked up a beautiful fuss,
Och we'd plenty of mobs
And some swate little jobs
To rob Algerines in the muss,
And no worse,
Though for law we did not care a curse.

Then he mustered us all in his ranks,
And promised us "beauty and banks,"
But Algerines came
With guns, swords and flame,
And our hero he took to his shanks,—
Small thanks
Did we get 'stead of "beauty and banks."

Still Tom is a hero full grown,
And dear to the hearts of his own,
He's been true as steel,
As we all of us feel,
For when he was balked of his fun—
Why he run,
Just as any of us would have done.

Shure Tom is a broth of a boy,
The Spartans and Buttenders joy
And we'll flog him gentailly
With fist or shillala,
Who finds in his doings a flaw,
Then hurrah!
For our jewel is Governor Dorr.

Through historians of the Dorr Rebellion have ignored or slighted the importance of anti-Irish Catholic sentiment throughout the controversy, the evidence is overwhelming that nativism was a decisive aspect of the constitutional drama. The connection between Dorr and the small but rapidly growing Irish Catholic community is satirized in this poem. Nationally the Irish American press lined up with Dorr; "It is our own Home Rule question in Rhode Island," asserted the *Truth Teller* (New York City) in an article upholding the reform cause.

with the Governor as to the executive measures proper to be taken in the present emergency of the State." This "council of war" consisted of six prominent Whigs and conservative James Fenner, a former Democratic governor. After vigorous debate, a proposition to call a third constitutional convention was deferred to the next session of the Assembly by a vote of 45 to 12. Shortly after the special session adjourned, there came another move fraught with ominous implications for the suffragists: on 2 May the Tyler administration decided to reinforce the garrison at Fort Adams in Newport by increasing its regular complement of 119 to a total of 302 officers and enlisted men.

As the rival governments prepared to assume power on 3–4 May under their respective basic laws, a clash appeared imminent. On 3 May the suffragists prefaced their accession to office by staging a colorful parade in Providence from the Hoyle Tavern in the West End to the State House on North Main Street. The entourage featured the Providence Brass Band, members of the People's government, and a strong military contingent that included the sixty-member Dorr Troop of Horse, the governor's personal guard. Only the eventual setting for the People's legislature diminished the luster and triumph of the occasion. Since the charterites had locked the State House, which contained the state's seal, archives, and other symbols of sovereignty, the suffragists retreated to a preselected alternative site, an unfinished foundry building on Eddy Street near Dorrance, to conduct their legislative deliberations.

Dorr unsuccessfully opposed such timid acquiescence. Later he ruefully observed "that it was here that the cause was defeated, if not lost." In chiding his more moderate associates, Dorr contended that "the period for decided action had now arrived." A valid government, he said, "was entitled to sit in the usual places of legislation, to possess and control the public property, and to exercise all the functions with which it was constitutionally invested. A government without power, appealing to voluntary support, destitute of the ability or disposition to enforce its lawful requisitions, was no government at all and was destined to extinction." Had the State House been seized, lamented Dorr, "right would have been confirmed by possession, the law and the fact would have been conjoined, and the new order of things would have been acquiesced in by all but a minority" of powerless reactionaries.

But the Foundry Legislature, intimidated by the Algerine Law and the threat of federal intervention, preferred ritual to what Dorr termed "the moderate degree of force which was necessary at this critical point of affairs." With sixty-six of eighty representatives and nine of twelve senators present, the gathering met for two days, chose officers and committees, abrogated the Algerine Law and the Board of Councillors, passed several statutes regulating elections and the selection of militia officers, and chartered the Glocester and Burrillville Greene Artillery Company. Curiously, it did not remove the incumbent and hostile state judiciary, an omission that Dorr later termed "a remarkable oversight." Before adjourning, the legislature passed without dissent an act requiring all persons to deliver to the People's government any public property held by them (e.g., the state armory), relegating the execution of this mandate, with the other laws and resolutions, to the future attention of the People's governor. Then, showing more patriotism than pragmatism, the assembly adjourned until the Fourth of July, leaving Dorr to sustain these quasi-symbolic pronouncements in whatever manner he could. Even the critical study of the rebellion by Arthur May Mowry asserts that such "hasty adjournment threw the whole brunt of the battle upon Governor Dorr."

Apprehensive moderates in the Foundry Legislature authorized dispatch of a commission to Washington to inform President Tyler that the people of Rhode Island "have formed a written constitution, elected officers, and peaceably organized the government now in full operation." Dorr, a confirmed states' rightist, was unenthusiastic about sending a delegation, but when his allies Burrington Anthony and Dutee Pearce departed for the Potomac, he reluctantly followed, having received resolutions passed by an informal assemblage of suffragists urging him to personally present his case in Washington. Dorr made the trip primarily to avert federal intervention and to show moderate suffragists that "the only hope for success lay in vigorous action within Rhode Island." He left the state convinced that the suffragists must implement the will of the people by creating a government of fact as well as right, and he returned to the state strengthened in that conclusion.

Dorr's sojourn southward left the reform movement leaderless and in disarray, but it was an interesting and eventful excursion. On 10 May he gained an inconclusive audience with President Tyler, who was firm yet "pleasant." In a judgment both partisan and unfair, Dorr found the president lacking in principle and dominated by his conservative secretary of state, Daniel Webster. Tyler's dilemma may have eluded the suspicious Dorr: though the president was a states' rights Virginian, his acquiescence in a local majoritarian revolt would have been a dangerous precedent that could menace the southern slave system. According to Elisha Potter, Jr., Tyler accepted the premise, suggested to him by the charterites, that the federal government must uphold "legitimate" state governments "to prevent Negroes [from] revolutionizing the South." According to Senator Sprague, the president told Dorr, Pearce, and Burrington Anthony that "their proceedings were treasonable against the state and if they committed an overt act and resisted the force of the United States, they would commit treason against the United States" as well.

A movement to bring the alleged validity of the People's Constitution before the United States Senate, initiated by Dr. John Brown during his Washington trip in early April, was also checked by mid-May. In response to an appeal from the suffragists, five prominent northern Democratic senators—Perry Smith (Connecticut), Levi Woodbury (New Hampshire), William Allen (Ohio), Thomas Hart Benton (Missouri), and Silas Wright, Jr. (New York)—wrote letters of encouragement but counseled caution and moderation. Benton assured Dorr that "the Democracy [i.e., Democratic party] fully admit the validity of the constitutional movement of the people in Rhode Island," but he urged that violence be avoided because "this is not the age, nor the country, in which to settle political questions by the sword."

Senator Allen, an ardent Ohio expansionist, was sufficiently inspired by principle and partisanship to try to impede possible intervention by Tyler in the Rhode Island imbroglio. On 18 April, the day of Dorr's election, Allen introduced a Senate resolution which in substance demanded that the president reveal all the information upon which he was acting in the Rhode Island situation and all the orders and instructions that he had issued to such subordinates as the secretary of war. The resolution was read, printed, taken up again two days later, and passed over informally. On 22 April it was tabled by a vote of 24 to 13.

Five additional attempts were made by Allen and his associates to gain consideration of the resolution, but all these efforts failed. William Sprague informed John Brown Francis that many senators were "indignant" over Allen's action and that a Virginia senator remarked that the Rhode Island rebels "ought to be hung!" Despite such opposition the persistent Allen (nicknamed "the Ohio foghorn") presented new resolutions against interference by the president and urged their passage in a long speech on 17 May, declaring that there were two governments in operation in Rhode Island and that Tyler should not assume to himself the power to decide between them. Whig James Fowler Simmons, Rhode Island's other senator, answered Allen by upholding the position of the charter government. On the following day the resolutions were tabled, never to be reintroduced. With the issue squarely before it, the Senate, by inaction, thus refused to accept the view that the president had no authority to act, or that in acting he was doing so unwisely. In the same session the upper house also refused to receive a letter from Dorr in which he claimed to be the governor of Rhode Island.

The successful senatorial opposition to Allen and Dorr was led by an incongruous coalition that included northern Whigs such as Simmons of Rhode Island and Jabez Huntington of Connecticut; Nathaniel Tallmadge of New York, a conservative agrarian Democrat who often aligned himself with the Whigs; and southern nullifiers, especially William C. Preston and John C. Calhoun of South Carolina. By their action the Whigs gave partisan endorsement to the regime of Samuel Ward King, Tallmadge continued his war against the Locofoco or Equal Rights wing of the New York Democratic party, and Preston and Calhoun sought to repudiate the majoritarian right of revolution and to provide support for incumbent state governments. Dorr acknowledged that most southerners rejected suffragist principles because "they might be construed to take in the southern blacks and to aid the abolitionists."

A year after the controversy had subsided, Calhoun justified his vote in an important public letter wherein he expressed sympathy for the suffrage party's quest to enlarge the franchise and denied the propriety of federal intervention so long as the controversy was confined to discussion and agitation. But after an incisive survey of constitutional precedents, this zealous defender of minority rights declared that it would be the "deathblow of constitutional democracy to admit the right of the numerical majority to alter or abolish constitutions at pleasure" by resort to extraconstitutional means. He also asserted that if the federal government possessed "the right to establish its own abstract standard" of what constitutes a republican form of government, "it would be made absolute master of the States."

Back in Rhode Island, the Law and Order response to the maneuvers of the People's government was accelerated mobilization and increasingly strong opposition. The charter Assembly, convened on 4 May for a two-day session at Newport, declared that there existed "an insurrection against the laws and constituted authorities" of Rhode Island and made a requisition upon Tyler "to interpose the authority and power of the United States to suppress such insurrectionary and lawless assemblages, to support the existing government and laws, and protect the State from domestic violence." Governor King immediately dispatched Democratic state senator Elisha R. Potter, Jr., and state representative Richard K. Randolph to carry the resolution and a personal letter to Tyler. Randolph was an appropriate emissary, being speaker of the House and a former Virginia Whig who had made the resort town of Newport his permanent home.

King's request for federal troops, received by the president on 6 May, annoyed Webster and placed Tyler in a precarious situation. If the president acceded to King's plea, he would have to deny the legality of the popular movement in Rhode Island; if he refused assistance, he would be vulnerable to charges of timidly acquiescing in rebellion. Tyler replied to the Law and Order governor in a fair and prudent manner, expressing great reluctance to employ the military power of the federal government. Assistance could be given not to prevent but only to suppress an insurrection, and it could not be rendered until actual violence had been committed by the suffragists. But "if resistance is made to the execution of the laws of Rhode Island by such force as the civil power shall be unable to overcome, it will be the duty of this government to enforce the constitutional guaranty" against domestic violence, asserted Tyler.

Two days later, on 9 May, Tyler proposed "measures of conciliation" to the desperate King: "*I am well advised*, if the General Assembly would authorize you to announce a general amnesty and pardon for the past, without making any exception, upon the condition of a return to allegiance, and follow it up by a call for a new convention upon somewhat liberal principles, that all difficulty would at once cease.... A resort to force, on the contrary, will engender for years to come feelings of animosity."

After the regular General Assembly reconvened on 11 May, Potter informed the president that "the subject of calling a convention immediately, and upon a liberal basis was seriously agitated amongst us," and "the only objection made was that they did not wish to concede while the people's party continued their threats." Potter's solution to this impasse was for Dorr to "allow himself to be arrested peaceably and give bail." On 12 May, King promised pardon to those "engaged in treasonable or revolutionary designs against the state ... on the condition only that they withdraw themselves from such enterprise and signify their return to their allegiance to the government." In essence, both the moderate Potter and the hard-nosed King were requesting that Dorr and the People's government capitulate.

A last-ditch attempt to avert forceful confrontation was made on 14 May at a secret New York City conference, at which Daniel Webster presided. Burrington Anthony, Dutee Pearce, and John S. Harris represented the suffragists, and John Whipple attended as an unofficial spokesman for Law and Order, though he thought Governor King's conduct too inflexible. Dorr participated reluctantly because he believed, like King, that disbanding the opposition government was the only acceptable solution.

Whipple proposed that the United States Circuit Court promptly decide the validity of the People's Constitution, with the "facts to be first ascertained by a suitable committee, to be chosen by agreement of the parties." The Algerine Law would be suspended in the interim, but the charter government would "remain in the full exercise of their authority and the persons claiming to exercise authority under the People's Constitution [would] omit such exercise altogether." For Dorr to accept any such proposals for judicial determination of the dispute would have been tantamount to surrender; Dorr and his opponents were well aware of the verdict to be expected from Job Durfee or John Pitman or from Justice Joseph Story, who would preside in circuit court if Whipple's compromise was accepted.

As the New York peace parley collapsed, chieftains of New York's Democratic machine, Tammany Hall, called councils of war. Tammany leaders warmly received the People's governor during his three-day sojourn in the metropolis. William Cullen Bryant's influential *Evening Post* supported his cause, and the New York Democracy staged a huge mass meeting and a colorful parade in his honor, attended by *Democratic Review* editor John L. O'Sullivan, *New Era* editor Levi Slamm, and such prominent politicians as Samuel J. Tilden, Elijah F. Purdy, and Ely Moore.

The enthusiasm shown for the reform cause by Tammany, the promise of armed assistance from several units of New York militia, the urging of well-intentioned zealots, and the support of such Irish American militants as Big Mike Walsh's "Spartan Band" fortified Dorr for the task ahead. He had recommended modest force at the State House on 3 May; en route to

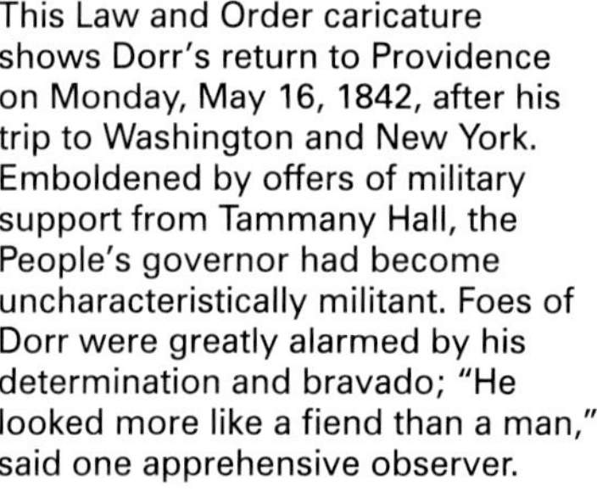

This Law and Order caricature shows Dorr's return to Providence on Monday, May 16, 1842, after his trip to Washington and New York. Emboldened by offers of military support from Tammany Hall, the People's governor had become uncharacteristically militant. Foes of Dorr were greatly alarmed by his determination and bravado; "He looked more like a fiend than a man," said one apprehensive observer.

Washington on 8 May he had written that "it may be expedient to strike a blow as soon as I return"; and upon his arrival in New York on 12 May he had written his trusted confidants Aaron White and Walter S. Burges that he would make "personal application for military aid" in the event of federal intervention and that he would "return to Providence as soon as possible, and... forthwith call on the military to protect me and others from arrest under the Algerine Law." His New York reception convinced Dorr that his anticipated use of force would enable the People's government to prevail.

It is most important to note that Dorr spoke of military action mainly in defensive terms. He sought outside aid only in response to outside intervention by federal troops, and he spoke of using his local militia primarily to protect himself and his associates from what he regarded as the unauthorized and invalid aggression of the defunct charter government operating under the Algerine Law, which had been repealed by the Foundry Legislature.

Specifically, Dorr was reacting to a series of arrests perpetrated by charter officials against members of his government. The first victim was Daniel Brown, a People's representative from Newport, who was served a warrant for treason under the Algerine act on 4 May and then released under a $5,000 bail bond restraining him from further illegal acts. On two succeeding days Dutee Pearce and Burrington Anthony suffered an identical fate, giving even greater urgency to their Washington mission. Others charged under the Algerine act included People's Attorney General Jonah Titus, General Treasurer Joseph Joslin, and House Speaker Welcome B. Sayles. A warrant was issued for Dorr himself, but Sheriff Roger Potter was unable to serve the People's governor prior to Dorr's departure for Washington.

Such bold and vigorous prosecution of the Algerine Law by the charterites during Dorr's absence caused many moderate or timid suffragists to abandon the cause and resign their offices. Dorr was kept informed of these developments, and he knew that forceful countermeasures were essential upon his return if his government was to survive. Sincerely convinced beyond doubt that he was the legitimate governor, Dorr decided that a good offense was the best defense against the stubborn charter regime.

After a rousing Tammany send-off, and with promises of armed support ringing in his ears, Thomas Dorr traveled by boat to Stonington, Connecticut, and then proceeded overland by special train to Providence. Arriving at 10:00 a.m. Monday, 16 May, he entered a waiting coach-and-four and rode triumphantly in a procession of twelve hundred cheering men, one-fifth of them armed, to the home of Burrington Anthony on a rise of land called Federal Hill in the west side of the city. Here, "fatigued and covered with dust," as one account reported, Dorr addressed the crowd. Brandishing a sword in the course of his speech, he warned against the consequences of federal interference with his government and vowed that he was willing to die with his sword in hand if need be to sustain the People's Constitution. Then, having established a headquarters at the Anthony house, he began to formulate plans to ensure the supremacy of his government. In a proclamation, he promised his followers massive outside support in the event of federal intervention; "they who have been first to ask assistance from abroad," it declared, "can have no reason to complain of any consequences which may ensue." Vowing that "no further arrests under the law of pains and penalties [the Algerine Law] will be permitted," he directed his militia to prevent enforcement of this "detestable" measure.

Foes of Dorr were greatly alarmed by his determination and bravado; "he looked more like a fiend than a man," said one apprehensive observer. Excitement and tension reached a fever pitch on the following day when more than sixty armed Dorrites raided the Providence armory of the United Train of Artillery and seized with no resistance two Revolutionary War cannons that had been confiscated from Burgoyne at Saratoga. The fieldpieces (minus their ammunition) were transported to Federal Hill, where Dorr and his most radical adherents were formulating plans to capture the state arsenal on Cranston Street adjacent to the Dexter Training Grounds. Despite strenuous objections from more moderate and genteel suffragist professionals and tradesmen, many of the lower-class members of the suffrage party—farmers, housewrights, shoemakers, blacksmiths, stonemasons, and factory hands—were now ready to fight for the equal political rights that they had loudly demanded. Dorr later justified his violent course by explaining that "to submit to an arrest, and to the breakup of the government, without an effort in its behalf... would have been in the general opinion and in fact a dishonorable abandonment of the means apparently placed at my disposal, to maintain my own, and the rights entrusted to my keeping."

Early on the evening of 17 May a council of war presided over by Dorr decided to attack the arsenal, despite the admonitions of several insurgents. At two o'clock the following morning the rebels arrived with the two cannons at the Cranston Street Armory, which they found garrisoned by two hundred men. Colonel John Wheeler, the Dorrites' field commander (whose force had dwindled to 234 by the zero hour), demanded the surrender of the armory in the name of the People's governor. When Colonel Blodget of the charter militia issued an adamant refusal, Dorr audaciously ordered his cannons to be discharged. Fortunately the fog-dampened powder caused the old relics to misfire. When the cannons failed, the besiegers quickly dispersed, and Dorr, with a mere handful of staunch adherents, retreated to Federal Hill. Arriving at his headquarters, he received an additional jolt: eleven of his legislators had resigned because of his resort to violence. Shortly thereafter, with charter forces in close pursuit, Dorr fled across the state line into exile.

The arsenal fiasco was the death knell of the Dorrite cause, but Dorr refused to accept the inevitable. From New York he wrote that the People's Constitution, "being founded in right and justice, cannot be overthrown by a failure of arms, or by the resignation of those elected to office under... the duty to maintain it." Less than a week after the arsenal raid, former president Andrew Jackson sided with Dorr: "The people are the sovereign power and agreeable to our system, they have a right to alter and amend their system of Government when a majority wills it, as a majority have a right to rule."

On 25 May, Dorr's close associate Aaron White conveyed to the stubborn People's governor a more realistic message: "Your idea of using force must be abandoned entirely; there is no hope in that remedy now. I verily believe that if you were to come on with 1,000 men to aid the Suffrage Party just now, you would have to fight suffrage men, just so completely have the minds of many been turned by recent misfortunes.... I can hardly find a suffrage man in the city with whom to advise or consult, so completely have we been defeated."

Governor King and his advisers now felt that they must exercise constant vigilance to preclude another Dorrite challenge to the Law and Order government. Moderates on both sides firmly believed that timely concessions in the form of a new constitution could defuse the Rhode Island powder keg: "We must have free suffrage or civil war," John Brown Francis observed, and John Whipple, Richard Randolph, William Sprague, and other leading politicians agreed. During late May and June 1842, vigorous suppression of radicalism and modest concessions to reform became the strategy of King's administration. Arrests of defiant suffragists under the Algerine Law continued; appeals were made to neighboring governors for Dorr's apprehension and rendition, and a reward of one thousand dollars was offered for his capture; new militia companies were chartered and drilled, many loyal units were given generous funding, and suspect companies were purged or disarmed (two had their charters vacated). Meanwhile, several further appeals were made to President Tyler for protection.

The repeated requests for federal intervention were prompted by overreaction to the bluster of local radicals and King's acceptance of exaggerated rumors about Dorr's plans and movements. On 27 May, Senator Sprague erroneously reported from Washington that "Dorr is organizing an army to... pillage Providence." Ten days later he mistakenly contended that "there is an effort by Dorr and by a large number of desperate men out of the state to invade it and to take possession of it at all hazards."

On 28 May, Tyler confessed he was "slow to believe" the imminence of armed invasion in Rhode Island, but he directed Fort Adams commandant Colonel James Bankhead, Secretary of War John C. Spencer, and Daniel Webster to investigate the situation. An anonymous emissary sent by Webster to Rhode Island reported on 3 June that "Governor King and his council alone of all intelligent persons with whom I consulted, fear an eruption upon them of an armed force to be collected in other states.... The supposition that Rhode Island is to be invaded by a foreign force, when that force would neither be led nor followed by any considerable number of the people of the State, does not seem, to say the least, a very reasonable one." This report prevented issuance of a prepared presidential proclamation commanding "all insurgents, and all persons connected with such insurrection to disperse," and it led to a reduction in the garrison at Fort Adams from 302 to 190 on 17 June. Nevertheless, fear and apprehension persisted throughout the month of June, for Dorr had indeed determined to return—not to fight, but to reconvene the People's legislature on 4 July.

* * *

For his assembly session Dorr chose Chepachet, a village in the northwestern town of Glocester, handy to the Connecticut border and accessible to the friendly mill villages in Smithfield and Cumberland, where working-class supporters of reform could still be relied upon to defend the People's government. The basis of rebel power had shifted northward by June, and the remaining suffragist leadership was more plebeian in character.

Dorr moved with ease through adjacent Connecticut in the days preceding his return, freely visiting Norwich, Killingly, and other towns, since Democratic governor Chauncey Cleveland was sympathetic to the rebel cause. In the eyes of Law and Order men, Cleveland had made Connecticut "the Texas of New England."

In anticipation of the arrival of the People's governor on 25 June, pro-Dorr rallies were held at various points in northern Rhode Island from Chepachet to Woonsocket to Diamond Hill. New militia units formed, bearing names that often reflected the mentality of their organizers—Dorr's Invincibles, Johnston Savages, Pascoag Ripguts, Glocester Volunteers, Pawtucket Invincibles, Diamond Hill Volunteers, and Harmonious Reptiles. Suffragists held military drills and stockpiled supplies. Armed night patrols roamed the northern highways, attempted raids on charter munition depots in Warren and Providence, and threatened another confrontation.

The charter government had prepared well for Dorr's return, politically and militarily. In response to several town petitions and town meeting resolves, on 23 June the General Assembly debated, amended, and approved a resolution, presented two days earlier by David Daniels, calling for a new constitutional convention to convene at Newport on the second Monday of September 1842. Voters would choose delegates in a ratio similar to that which the Assembly had conceded in May 1841 for apportionment of the Landholders' Convention—a procedure much more equitable than the charter's allocation but far short of the "one man, one vote" stan-

Henry Lord, who was arrested after the invocation of martial law, drew this sketch of the so-called Battle of Acote's Hill. Actually the Dorr War was nearly bloodless. Only two rather bizarre fatalities were recorded during the uprising's various episodes: Alexander Kelby of Pawtucket, Massachusetts, an innocent bystander, was shot on his own side of the state boundary by a tense and harassed militiaman who had earlier been confronted by a rock-throwing crowd while guarding the Pawtucket Bridge, and a member of a militia company from Westerly "became insane through excitement" en route to Chepachet (according to his commander) and shot and killed his brother.

dard. Providence and expanding towns would still be underrepresented. But unlike the Landholders' Convention, which was limited to freemen, this convention would allow participation by most adult males: all those who were qualified to vote for general officers under existing laws, plus "all native male citizens of the United States of the age of twenty-one years and upwards" who had lived in Rhode Island for three years, could vote for delegates. Excluded were naturalized citizens lacking the freehold and Narragansett Indians; included—as a reward for their military alliance with the forces of Law and Order—were blacks. Although some opposed this concession, "there is not so much scolding about letting the blacks vote as was expected," observed the perceptive Elisha Potter; "they would rather have the negroes vote than the d——d Irish."

This convention call was a conciliatory maneuver that appeased most suffragists, especially those middle-class reformers whom Dorr derisively called "no-force constitutionalists." Quite understandably, few would go to the barricades for abstract issues of equal rights or popular constituent sovereignty, and fewer still would fight for the political rights of naturalized but landless Irish Catholics.

Even Dorr's close friend and confidant Walter S. Burges copublished a broadside in support of the proposed convention. "Law and Order, justice and political equality are no longer enemies," exclaimed Burges and other suffragists. "Who will fight for *any form*, when the substance can be gained by peace?" was their rhetorical query. Although it proved naive, this expectation of justice and genuine reform from King and his councillors dashed any chance for reconvening the People's legislature in the inauspicious setting of Chepachet.

The charter government's military preparations were equally effective. As Dorrite activity increased during mid-June, the *Providence Journal* spread the unfounded rumor that the rebels intended to attack Providence, raid its banks and stores, and loot its homes. The paranoiac Governor King

fell victim to this propaganda. Alluding to recent Dorrite maneuvers—the theft of armaments, the establishment of "a kind of martial law" in Chepachet and Woonsocket, the seizure and detention of four charter scouts "under pretense of being spies," and the imminent arrival of Dorr—King, in a letter hand-carried to Tyler by Senator Sprague, contended that such "open violence" made federal military aid "imperatively required." Despite corroboration of these assertions by Providence mayor Thomas Burgess and Colonel Bankhead of Fort Adams, Tyler deftly sidestepped the appeal on 25 June, using a technical excuse. Citing a 1795 federal statute, he informed King that the request for aid must "be made by the legislature if in session" rather than by the governor. This evasion prompted an additional plea on 27 June from Senators Sprague and Simmons and Rhode Island congressman Joseph L. Tillinghast. By the time Tyler finally dispatched Secretary of War John Spencer to Rhode Island on 29 June with discretionary power to promulgate the suspended cease-and-desist proclamation, summon militia from Massachusetts and Connecticut, and employ federal troops to defend Providence, the crisis had passed.

King and his military advisers were in fact equal to their task, for the threat from Dorr was greatly exaggerated. On 23 June the charter governor issued orders for military mobilization that directed the state's southern militia companies and selected independent commands to assemble at Providence. West Pointer William Gibbs McNeill (an army engineer and a builder of the Providence and Stonington Railroad) arrived from his home in Stonington to assume command of this force, which was specially formed to do battle with Dorr. In creating the new army, King and his council disregarded the existing state militia division, much of which was poorly organized and whose largest component—the second brigade of Providence County—contained many Dorr sympathizers. Major General McNeill's force consisted of loyal militia units from the southern counties, several efficient chartered commands, and some newly created volunteer companies. Elisha Dyer was its adjutant general and Dorr's brother-in-law, Samuel Ames, its quartermaster. By Saturday, 25 June, when the General Assembly proclaimed martial law throughout the state, between 2,500 and 3,000 troops had assembled in Providence.

While this rapid and efficient mobilization was transpiring in Providence, the suffragists, commanded by Colonel Henry D'Wolf, hastened to defend Chepachet by fortifying Acote's Hill, an eighty-foot rise of land at the southeastern end of the village overlooking the road from Providence. At 2:00 a.m. on 25 June, Dorr appeared with Big Mike Walsh of New York and approximately a dozen members of Walsh's "Spartan Band," a political gang of militants and rowdies from New York's notorious Five Points ghetto. The People's governor soon established headquarters at Sprague's Hotel, reviewed the troops, conducted an inventory of supplies (some of which had come from New York, Connecticut, and Massachusetts), and issued a call for reconvening his General Assembly on 4 July.

Estimates of the size of the force that greeted Dorr at Chepachet vary, ranging as high as 1,000 men. Of this number many were merely spectators, villagers, or unarmed sympathizers. Others who came with arms dispersed when news of King's massive mobilization filtered into Chepachet. By Monday, 27 June, only 225 courageous diehards remained, and no legislators had heeded Dorr's call. At this juncture, urged by such visitors as his father and Dutee Pearce, Dorr decided to disband his small, underprovisioned military guard, and at 4:00 p.m. he sent a copy of the dispersal order to Walter S. Burges with instructions to print it in the *Providence Express*, the suffrage daily. Early that evening Dorr bade good-bye to his supporters and went into exile for the second and final time. He spent that night in nearby Thompson, Connecticut, at the Vernon Stiles Inn. Ultimately, with the price on his head raised to five thousand dollars, he found refuge in New Hampshire under the protective care of Democratic governor Henry Hubbard and Congressman Edmund Burke.

By the time of Dorr's departure, General McNeill had organized and equipped his force, now totaling over 3,500. Several advance units marched toward the enemy with plans to confront Dorr at Chepachet, occupy Woonsocket, and cut off any retreat into Massachusetts or Connecticut. To prevent Dorr's Massachusetts sympathizers from reinforcing his Chepachet garrison, the Kentish Guards of Warwick and East Greenwich deployed at the Pawtucket Bridge over the Blackstone River, where they joined the Pawtucket and Central Falls Volunteers, and some City Guards defended the India Point Bridge over the Seekonk. To deter potential Connecticut interlopers, the Westerly Infantry patrolled the state's southwestern border along the Pawcatuck River.

Colonel William Brown's main strike force had encamped at Greenville in Smithfield, midway between Providence and Chepachet, when a charter patrol apprehended the messenger carrying Dorr's order to disband and the accompanying letter to Walter Burges. Colonel Edwin Hazard brought them to Burges, who read his friend's parting missive: "Believing that a majority of the people who voted for the constitution are opposed to its further support by military means," Dorr had written, "I have directed that the military here assembled be dismissed"; hopefully, he had added, "no impediments will be thrown in the way of the return of our men to their homes." Hazard then carried the order—meant for publication in the *Express*—to General McNeill, who conferred with King, his councillors, Mayor Burgess, and Colonel Bankhead. These men decided to delay publication until Colonel Brown's force could "capture" Dorr's fort and apprehend as many "combatants" as possible. Such a daring victory, they reasoned, would discourage any future forceful effort against the charter government. They ordered Brown to advance swiftly the same evening, but a severe rainstorm delayed him until 6:00 a.m. on 28 June, when he moved out in company with some federal officials and other dignitaries, including Whig potentate Thurlow Weed, an adviser to New York governor William Seward.

Several suffragists heading back to Providence, North Providence, or Johnston were seized by the Law and Order army en route to Chepachet. Then, according to Colonel Brown's report, charter troops "stormed the insurgent fortification" on Acote's Hill at 7:45 a.m., sustaining no casualties. Jubilant and rowdy militiamen searched and looted homes and stores in and around the village, ransacked Sprague's Hotel, forayed through the adjacent countryside, and took a total of a hundred prisoners, whom they suspected of disloyalty. These captives and others seized elsewhere were harshly treated, harassed, incarcerated in crowded, unsanitary, and poorly ventilated cells, and denied their civil rights.

By 2 July all of McNeill's troops had returned home and resumed civilian pursuits. On 4 July—the date scheduled for reconvening the extinct People's legislature—Providence militiamen turned out in a massive parade to celebrate their victory. On the following day General Winfield Scott, the nation's highest-ranking military officer, congratulated General McNeill for such "admirable success, without federal aid, in the suppression of domestic violence. Rhode Island has covered herself with glory, and may well be termed the great conservatrix of law and order." Though martial law continued until 8 August and over three hundred indiscriminate arrests and irregular interrogations occurred during its operation, the Dorr War had ended; the freemen had prevailed.

In late 1842, after Dorr's second flight, the triumphant Law and Order party convened another constitutional convention. This was the gathering that framed the present state constitution. To a degree the demands of reformers were met; the new document contained a bill of rights, paved the way for eventual establishment of an independent judiciary, slightly diminished the power of the Assembly, and provided for a fairly equitable apportionment of its House of Representatives.

Arthur May Mowry, the first major historian of the Dorr War, calls this instrument "liberal and well-adapted to the needs of the state," but his appraisal neglects one important item: the 1842 constitution established a $134 freehold suffrage qualification for naturalized citizens, and this restriction, not removed until 1888, was the most blatant instance of political nativism found in any state constitution in the land. This fact cannot be overemphasized. It furnishes the central theme in Rhode Island political history from 1842 until the passage of the twentieth amendment to the state constitution in 1928. The stranglehold on the state Senate (one senator from each town regardless of its population) that the 1842 document gave to the rural towns is also a fact of paramount importance, and it remained so at least until the "Bloodless Revolution" in 1935.

The new constitution was overwhelmingly ratified in November 1842 by a tally of 7,024 to 51, and it became effective in May 1843. Despite the margin of victory, the turnout was meager, for there were more than 23,000 adult male citizens in the state. That the opposition, in mute protest, refrained from balloting explains in part the constitution's apathetic reception and the lopsided vote.

His spirit crushed by the adoption of the nativistic suffrage clause and the gubernatorial triumph of James Fenner, his archrival and a conservative old-line Democrat, Dorr returned to Providence in October 1843 to surrender. Immediately arrested and jailed until February 1844, he was prosecuted under the Algerine Law for treason against the state. In a trial of less than two weeks he was found guilty by a jury composed entirely of political opponents. Denied a new trial, he was sentenced to hard labor in solitary confinement for life. Dorr served one year of this sentence before Governor Charles Jackson—elected on a "liberation" platform—authorized his release.

The verdict and, especially, the sentence against Thomas Dorr outraged his supporters and troubled his more moderate opponents, some of whom were motivated by humane feelings and others by fear of political repercussions. As early as 22 May 1842 John Brown Francis had asked rhetorically, "Why make a martyr of this patricide?" The wisdom of that question would soon become painfully evident to the forces of law and order.

The reaction to Dorr's imprisonment was quite predictable, for during the rebellion itself the national press had distorted the nature of the conflict for partisan gain. Whig papers throughout the country had praised Governor King's administration for its courageous stand against radicalism and anarchy, while the northern Democratic organs simplistically depicted the struggle as one between progressive, enlightened Democrats led by Dorr and reactionary Whigs. The substantial Democratic contribution to the cause of law and order, which had been supported by extremists such as those of the Arthur Fenner-William Gibbs clique and by moderates like Sprague, Francis, and Potter, was ignored. As Francis remarked in 1842, "The course of all the papers has been infamous—coining political capital out of our blood." Most notable and enduring of these national fulminations was the epic debate on political theory waged in the pages of the *Democratic Review* during 1842–43 between former suffrage agitator Orestes Brownson, who defended the minoritarian principles of law and order, and the *Review*'s editor, John L. O'Sullivan, a longtime friend of Dorr who supported the majoritarian doctrine of popular constituent sovereignty.

The bitterness of the liberation issue was graphically depicted in this election broadside as Law and Order regulars branded Dorr's temporary Whig allies "four traitors" because of the way they engineered his freedom. Charles Jackson, a lawyer and prominent industrialist, was the grandson of Stephen Jackson (1700–1765), an Irish tutor who immigrated from Kilkenny in the early eighteenth century.

In 1844, a presidential election year, Dorr's plight again became grist for the political mill under the banner of "Polk, Dallas, and Dorr." Even before Dorr's trial the propaganda value of the episode became apparent to Democrats in Rhode Island and elsewhere. On 1 February 1844 the General Assembly's twenty-six-member Democratic minority—seven senators and eighteen representatives from seven towns in Providence County and the senator from Jamestown—sent a memorial to the United States House of Representatives requesting Congress to inquire into the "interference" by Tyler in Rhode Island affairs from April through June 1842. Local Dorrites also challenged the right of Representatives Henry Cranston and Elisha Potter, Jr., to their seats in Congress and requested that the House apply the federal guarantee clause relating to a "republican form of government" (Article IV, Section 4) in favor of the legitimacy of the People's Constitution.

On 19 February, Dorr's New Hampshire protector, Congressman Edmund Burke, presented the Rhode Island memorial to the Democratic-controlled House, where it

Benjamin F. Hallett (1797–1862), a native of Cape Cod, became a newspaper editor in Providence during the 1820s and was an early advocate of suffrage expansion. He helped to compile *Burke's Report* for the House of Representatives in 1844 and defended the Dorrite cause before the U.S. Supreme Court in the case of *Luther* v. *Borden*. His argument, an eloquent defense of popular constituent sovereignty, was published as *The Right of the People to Establish Forms of Government*.

was debated at length and then printed and referred to a five-man committee chaired by Burke himself. After seventeen sessions a majority report was prepared and adopted by the three Democrats on the panel, Burke, George Rathbun (New York) and John A. McClernand (Illinois). Slave-state Whigs Jacob Preston and John Causin, both of Maryland, subsequently compiled a minority report vindicating Tyler and the Law and Order party, a course of action recommended by William Goddard even before the Burke committee had begun its investigation, because Goddard knew that the sponsors of the memorial hoped "to make the Rhode Island Question one of the main issues in the approaching presidential election."

Burke's Report, as the majority brief was called, was far from neutral; its first printed page, the frontispiece, displayed an engraved daguerreotype of "T. W. Dorr, Inaugurated Governor of Rhode Island, May 3, 1842." From that point onward, through eighty-six pages of formal conclusions and nearly a thousand more of documents, depositions, court records, and voting lists, the report upheld the philosophy of Dorrism, censured Whig president John Tyler for "interfering," and criticized Rhode Island "Algerines" for their forceful resistance to popular constituent sovereignty. Dorr and his associates furnished Burke with his documentary evidence, and former Rhode Island suffragist editor Benjamin F. Hallett obtained depositions from witnesses to the events of 1841–42. Devotees of law and order, alleging unfounded congressional intermeddling, were uncooperative. Law and Order governor James Fenner caustically observed that "a more villainous business never was entertained by the House."

Burke unquestionably made a sincere attempt to vindicate the philosophy of equal rights, which he himself espoused; just as surely, both Burke and Dorr intended and timed the report—five thousand copies were printed in June 1844—to discredit Whiggery and bolster the Democratic cause in the presidential election of 1844. *Burke's Report* is still the most valuable published source on the Dorr Rebellion, but it was also a political campaign document. Once the election had passed, the report became of interest primarily to historians, and apart from printing a second edition in early 1845 and engaging in brief desultory debate, the House took no action on Burke's findings.

While the House conducted its investigation, affairs in Rhode Island continued tranquil, except for a petition circulated by Irish leader Henry J. Duff and other naturalized Rhode Islanders and sent to Congress in April 1844. This petition alleged that the state's new suffrage law deprived the petitioners of their proper privileges as citizens of the United States because it required that naturalized citizens own real estate in order to vote but imposed no such standard on the native-born.

Describing Duff as a "rabid Dorrite," Samuel Ames thought the petition might gain the support of southerners appalled that "a white foreigner is required by our constitution to have a higher qualification to vote than a native Negro." Ames's apprehensions proved unfounded. Duff got no relief from Congress, and when he turned to the General Assembly in May 1846, his petition was referred to committee, studied, then flatly denied in a report that defended the voting discrimination, lectured Duff's Irish signatories that "they must not expect to be placed on a perfect equality with native citizens," and asserted that the request would "lead to acrimonious debate and serve to increase the ill feeling and prejudice which the petitioners complain now exist between them and native citizens."

Despite Dorr's observation in February 1843 that appeals to Congress or the Supreme Court are "delusive and frail," he eventually grasped at both these remaining straws to vindicate his cause. While Burke investigated and liberationists agitated, Dorr, Burges, Atwell, George Turner, and Benjamin Hallett moved to place the People's Constitution before the United States Supreme Court for a test of its validity and for the ultimate vindication of the People's cause. The agent for this appeal to the nation's highest tribunal was Martin Luther, one of approximately three dozen suffragists formally indicted and jailed for violation of the Algerine Law. Instead of accepting this fate passively, Luther and his mother, Rachel, waged a legal counterattack in the form of suits for trespass. His $5,000 damage claim arose from the invasion of his Warren home by a group of nine armed charter militiamen acting under their government's declaration of martial law.

On 29 June 1842 this charter force, led by Luther M. Borden, had broken into Martin Luther's private dwelling, roused and rousted his elderly mother, and conducted a search for Luther, a Warren town moderator serving under the People's Constitution. The search was fruitless; Luther had fled to the adjacent town of Swansea, Massachusetts, and there he established residence and eventually filed suit against Borden and the other militiamen in United States Circuit Court, using diversity of citizenship to secure federal jurisdiction in the case.

This claim was a routine trespass action in form, but in reality it raised profound issues relating to the guarantee clause of the federal Constitution, the doctrine of political questions, and the exercise of martial law. Luther's case was potentially a vehicle whereby the Supreme Court would be called upon to decide between the legal claims of the People's government and the charter government.

According to the Dorrites, the People's Constitution had replaced the charter on 3 May 1842. If this assertion was legally valid, then Luther had acted properly as an official in the new regime and Borden had committed actionable trespass, having taken orders from a defunct government that had no power to proclaim martial law: it was Borden, not Luther, who was the insurrectionist.

When Luther finally returned to Rhode Island, he was tried, fined, and imprisoned for six months for violating the Algerine Law. From jail he wrote to Dorr, who was also incarcerated awaiting trial. By late 1844 the People's governor had become convinced that "the great question of sovereignty" could not be developed clearly in his treason case (*State* v. *Dorr*), but it could be "fully and perfectly presented in the case of Luther"; "for God's sake," Dorr pleaded to his legal colleague Walter Burges, "do not let that case fall through."

While he was writing to Burges, the issue was being docketed with the Supreme Court, having been expeditiously disposed of in the lower federal court during its November 1843 term by those twin legal nemeses of Dorrism, John Pitman and Joseph Story. Their strategy, agreed to by Dorr's attorney, Benjamin Hallett, was to use a pro forma decision to construct grounds for an appeal to the high court because of the momentous issues at stake. Rachel Luther's action for personal trespass, raising questions posed by Aaron White and others concerning the validity of the charter government's declaration and use of martial law, also went to the high court as a companion suit. In addition, Dorr's own appeal for a writ of error on his treason conviction (*Thomas W. Dorr* v. *Rhode Island*) was filed on 7 February 1845 as a parallel case.

Dorr's letters and memoranda indicate that he stage-managed the Luther litigation to its bitter conclusion in 1849. He was assisted by two nationally known attorneys, both members of the Democratic administration of James Knox Polk—crafty Robert J. Walker, secretary of the treasury, and learned Nathan Clifford of Maine, attorney general and future Supreme Court justice (1858–1881). With such top-level assistance before a high court composed mainly of Jacksonian jurists, Dorr entertained strong expectations for a retroactive vindication of his cause. Aaron White and Benjamin Hallett were pessimistic, however, especially after Daniel Webster agreed to join John Whipple in defending law and order.

After several exasperating delays, oral arguments were presented in the Luther litigation for six days in early 1848. Hallett and Clifford eloquently sought judicial approval for the doctrine of popular constituent sovereignty, upon which, according to Dorr, there were only two federal constitutional limitations: the constitution drafted by the people must be republican, and the people must proceed without domestic violence. The People's Constitution was prima facie evidence that the first requirement had been met, and events up to 3 May 1842 were certainly nonviolent. Thereafter, asserted the plaintiffs, the charter adherents became the insurrectionaries by refusing to acquiesce peacefully in the will of the majority.

The appellants' basic claim was that the People's Constitution superseded the charter, since it had been adopted by a majority of the state's adult male voters. They refrained, however, from demanding that the Court issue a decision that would retroactively install the People's government, realizing that such a request would doom their appeal and produce political chaos. They therefore contended that the people of Rhode Island had "permitted" the establishment of a valid government in May 1843 under a new written state constitution that superseded the Dorrite document.

Webster and Whipple countered with an impressive defense of King and the charter government. In accord with the judicial and extrajudicial opinions of Pitman and Durfee, the eloquent Webster admitted that the people were indeed sovereign, but he persuasively argued that this sovereignty had to assert itself through the forms of law and the mechanics of representation. The foremost prerequisite for change was consent of the existing government. He further argued that federal authorities had recognized the legitimacy of the charter regime: Tyler had promised it support in the event of insurrection, and Congress had continued to seat its senators and representatives with no serious challenge from the Dorrites. Further, the Supreme Court of Rhode Island, in the trials of Dorr and his leading associates, had confirmed the illegitimacy of the People's Constitution. The United States Supreme Court was not the proper authority to conduct a detailed retroactive investigation of the rival claims to sovereignty, Webster concluded. That determination belonged to the political branches of the government—Congress and the president—and by their actions they had decided in favor of law and order.

In a 5-to-1 opinion handed down in January 1849, when the national election fever of 1848 had subsided, Chief Justice Roger Taney accepted the main points of Webster's argument. The Luthers had presented "a political question" that was not justiciable, said Taney in a conclusion influenced by expedience and practicality. Responsibility for deciding questions of disputed sovereignty was vested not with the Court but rather with the political branches—Congress and the president, state legislatures, and governors. In response to the Dorrite request that Taney apply the guarantee clause to the Rhode Island situation, the Maryland jurist insisted that

> Congress must necessarily decide what government is established in the State before it can determine whether it is republican or not. And when the senators and representatives of a state are admitted into the councils of the Union, the authority of the government under which they are appointed, as well as its republican character, is recognized by the proper constitutional authority. And its decision is binding on every other department of the government, and could not be questioned in a judicial tribunal.

Congressional acceptance of the charter delegation and Dorr's failure to send rival congressmen could be construed as implicit recognition of the Law and Order government. Further, Tyler's mere promise of federal support to King under the power delegated to the president by Congress to protect states from domestic violence or invasion was "as effectual as if the militia had been assembled under his orders" to suppress the Dorrites. The high court would abide by the implicit and explicit actions of the political branches and by the determination of Judge Durfee's court, said Taney.

Levi Woodbury of New Hampshire, a Dorr sympathizer in 1842, filed the lone dissent, but he confined his objection to a learned discussion of martial law. His detailed and well-researched opinion that the charter forces used this power arbitrarily, extravagantly, and unconstitutionally failed to dissuade the majority from its belief that "the established government resorted to the rights and usages of war to maintain itself and to overcome unlawful opposition." With such a rude dismissal, the Dorr Rebellion ceased to vex the federal government.

The Dorr Rebellion was no tempest in a teapot; it had national repercussions and enduring significance. The most important and controversial domestic event of the Tyler administration, it eventually involved the president, both houses of Congress, the U.S. Supreme Court, and the lower federal judiciary. Of even greater significance, the Rhode Island controversy inspired substantial contributions to theories of suffrage, majority rule, minority rights, and constitutional government by John C. Calhoun, Henry Clay, John L. O'Sullivan, Orestes Brownson, John Quincy Adams, Daniel Webster, Horace Greeley, Benjamin F. Hallett, George Bancroft, and others of similar stature.

The underlying political philosophy of the insurgents—their doctrine of popular constituent sovereignty—was to them a reaffirmation of the principles of 1776. This theory asserted the preeminent right of the people at large to draft constitutions. Conventions for such a purpose, Dorr and his associates claimed, were expressions of public will and did not depend on prior legislative authorization; "the doctrine of a necessary permission, authority, or request from the General Assembly to the People before they can rightfully proceed to form a constitution... has no application in this country, where the sovereignty resides in the people." According to Dorr, "the people" were entitled to draft constitutions not only in Rhode Island, where the charter provided no established mode of constitutional change or amendment; they could "rightfully proceed in the mode and manner which they deem most proper" even where such provisions existed.

In 1841 the Rhode Island Suffrage Association insisted that a state constitution be drafted "by the people in their primary capacity," not by the secondary power of the General Assembly. The association was asserting what one historian has termed a "domesticated" right of revolution—a natural right, exercisable in an orderly way within society, to act outside the law. Its demand seemed consistent with the theory of "the people as constituent power," which Professor Robert R. Palmer has called America's unique contribution to the eighteenth-century "Democratic Revolution." When Dorrites applied this doctrine, hallowed by the American Revolutionary experience, the conclusion seemed inescapable: the framing and the adoption of the People's Constitution were completely consistent with America's revolutionary past. The reformers failed to recognize, however, that this cherished principle of popular constituent sovereignty was a minority position held only by extreme democrats of the Revolutionary generation.

Dorr's conservative opponents, led by Chief Justice Job Durfee and federal district judge John Pitman, dismissed as "preposterous" the idea that in 1776 there had been a lapse into a state of nature, a dissolution of the social contract, that had transferred sovereignty directly to the people, allowing them to create new constitutions and new political communities by whim and will. Conservatives like Durfee contended that the state was a continuous entity and that the American Revolution was so great an achievement, and the society it fostered so excellent, that no further need for revolutionary measures existed. America's revolution was finished! Durfee further asserted that there was no grievance great enough in Rhode Island to justify Dorr's course of action, and he challenged the reformers where their ideology was most ambiguous and vulnerable—on the question of whether force would be necessary to achieve their ends. Ironically, this Law and Order position was ultimately sustained not only by logic and the weight of tradition but by superior force, causing one of Dorr's defenders to depict the struggle in terms of "might versus right."

Despite his defeat and the repudiation of his revolutionary doctrine of popular constituent sovereignty, Thomas Wilson Dorr, the rebellion's central figure, must be ranked among the greatest American reformers. He was a man of integrity, intelligence, and lofty ideals. His rash act at the arsenal should not obscure his many positive contributions to his fellow men: he was a champion of educational reform, an outspoken foe of slavery, and an initiator of notable banking reforms, and he made the cause of the immigrant his own. He was a lawyer, an influential political theorist, and a keen student of politics. The list of those men with whom he corresponded is like a who's who of the Jacksonian era. His letters reveal that he had a working knowledge of several foreign languages and a searching and inquiring mind that ranged with facility through the fields of theology, literature, economics, science, and, of course, history.

By his action Dorr revived and reaffirmed some of the revolutionary principles upon which his nation and his state were founded, and he came to personify for his own and future generations the cause of equal rights. Thomas Wilson Dorr, the much-maligned and misunderstood rebel who devoted his life to the unprofitable and thankless task of human betterment, was one of the most remarkable Rhode Islanders of his or any century.

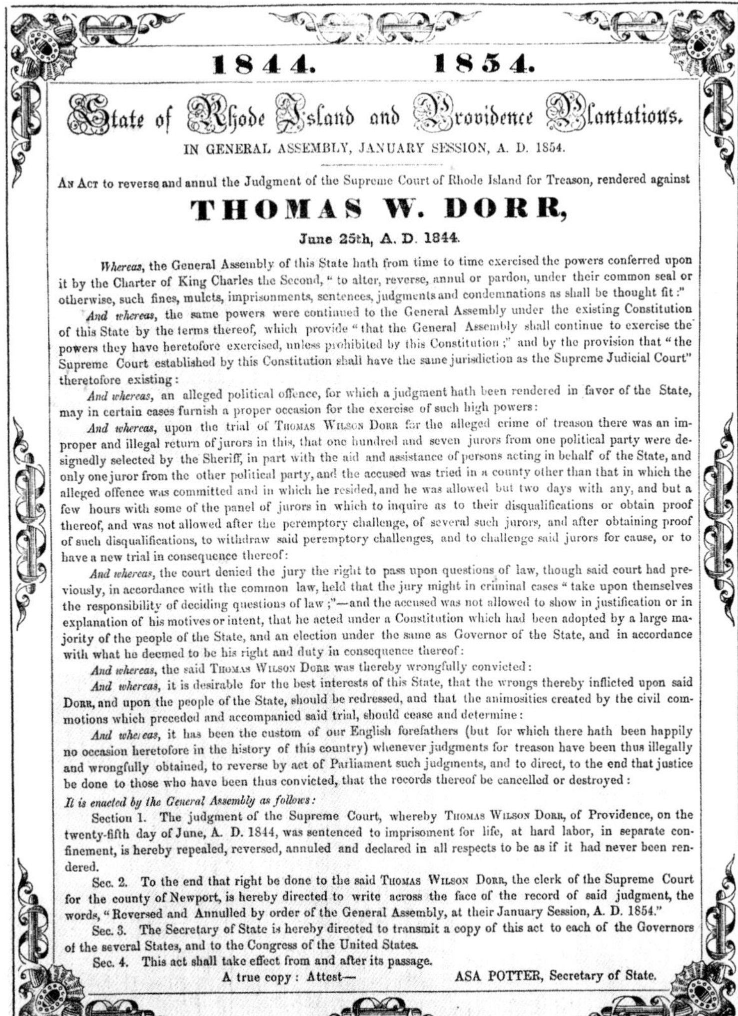

1844. 1854.

State of Rhode Island and Providence Plantations.

IN GENERAL ASSEMBLY, JANUARY SESSION, A. D. 1854.

AN ACT to reverse and annul the Judgment of the Supreme Court of Rhode Island for Treason, rendered against

THOMAS W. DORR,

June 25th, A. D. 1844.

Whereas, the General Assembly of this State hath from time to time exercised the powers conferred upon it by the Charter of King Charles the Second, "to alter, reverse, annul or pardon, under their common seal or otherwise, such fines, mulcts, imprisonments, sentences, judgments and condemnations as shall be thought fit:"

And whereas, the same powers were continued to the General Assembly under the existing Constitution of this State by the terms thereof, which provide "that the General Assembly shall continue to exercise the powers they have heretofore exercised, unless prohibited by this Constitution;" and by the provision that "the Supreme Court established by this Constitution shall have the same jurisdiction as the Supreme Judicial Court" theretofore existing:

And whereas, an alleged political offence, for which a judgment hath been rendered in favor of the State, may in certain cases furnish a proper occasion for the exercise of such high powers:

And whereas, upon the trial of THOMAS WILSON DORR for the alleged crime of treason there was an improper and illegal return of jurors in this, that one hundred and seven jurors from one political party were designedly selected by the Sheriff, in part with the aid and assistance of persons acting in behalf of the State, and only one juror from the other political party, and the accused was tried in a county other than that in which the alleged offence was committed and in which he resided, and he was allowed but two days with any, and but a few hours with some of the panel of jurors in which to inquire as to their disqualifications or obtain proof thereof, and was not allowed after the peremptory challenge, of several such jurors, and after obtaining proof of such disqualifications, to withdraw said peremptory challenges, and to challenge said jurors for cause, or to have a new trial in consequence thereof:

And whereas, the court denied the jury the right to pass upon questions of law, though said court had previously, in accordance with the common law, held that the jury might in criminal cases "take upon themselves the responsibility of deciding questions of law;"—and the accused was not allowed to show in justification or in explanation of his motives or intent, that he acted under a Constitution which had been adopted by a large majority of the people of the State, and an election under the same as Governor of the State, and in accordance with what he deemed to be his right and duty in consequence thereof:

And whereas, the said THOMAS WILSON DORR was thereby wrongfully convicted:

And whereas, it is desirable for the best interests of this State, that the wrongs thereby inflicted upon said DORR, and upon the people of the State, should be redressed, and that the animosities created by the civil commotions which preceded and accompanied said trial, should cease and determine:

And whereas, it has been the custom of our English forefathers (but for which there hath been happily no occasion heretofore in the history of this country) whenever judgments for treason have been thus illegally and wrongfully obtained, to reverse by act of Parliament such judgments, and to direct, to the end that justice be done to those who have been thus convicted, that the records thereof be cancelled or destroyed:

It is enacted by the General Assembly as follows:

Section 1. The judgment of the Supreme Court, whereby THOMAS WILSON DORR, of Providence, on the twenty-fifth day of June, A. D. 1844, was sentenced to imprisoment for life, at hard labor, in separate confinement, is hereby repealed, reversed, annuled and declared in all respects to be as if it had never been rendered.

Sec. 2. To the end that right be done to the said THOMAS WILSON DORR, the clerk of the Supreme Court for the county of Newport, is hereby directed to write across the face of the record of said judgment, the words, "Reversed and Annulled by order of the General Assembly, at their January Session, A. D. 1854."

Sec. 3. The Secretary of State is hereby directed to transmit a copy of this act to each of the Governors of the several States, and to the Congress of the United States.

Sec. 4. This act shall take effect from and after its passage.

A true copy: Attest— ASA POTTER, Secretary of State.

In 1854, during the administration of Dorr's supportive uncle Governor Philip Allen, a Democratic-controlled General Assembly reversed and annulled Dorr's treason conviction. A tinge of irony marked this act, since Dorr had fought to free the judiciary from the control of the powerful legislature. In a further twist of fate, the conservative state Supreme Court vindicated Dorr's view by issuing an opinion to the legislature that the resolution was unconstitutional and "a mutilation of the record."

17

Eighty years before the infamous Massachusetts saga of Sacco and Vanzetti, Rhode Island experienced its own inglorious version of blind justice—the Gordon murder trial. Similarities between the two cases abound. In both, the defendants were recent immigrant arrivals, Catholic in religion (at least nominally), members of the working class, and supporters of unpopular political views. In both, nativism, prejudice, and a repressive legal system elevated circumstantial evidence beyond the realm of reasonable doubt. In both, the alleged perpetrators were denied post-conviction relief or governmental clemency and were executed. In both, sober reflection produced widespread skepticism about actual guilt and led many to question the wisdom of capital punishment.

The following 1986 article by Patrick Conley, which won the first annual writing award from the *Rhode Island Bar Journal*, was the first account of the Gordon trial to connect this cause célèbre with the nativistic impulses that inspired many opponents of the Dorr Rebellion, as well as the first to link the Dorrites to John Gordon's defense. Since its publication the Gordon trial received its first book-length treatment in 1993 with *Brotherly Love: Murder and the Politics of Prejudice in Nineteenth-Century Rhode Island*, by Charles and Tess Hoffman. These authors, both professors of English by trade and training, go far beyond mere doubt in their detailed analysis of the murder of Cranston industrialist Amasa Sprague. With poetic license and subjectivism forbidden to historians, they not only exonerate the Gordons but also implicate U.S. senator William Sprague in the murder of his brother and business partner, Amasa.

The Hoffmans make full use of the secondary literature pertaining to their subject but neglect unpublished court records and manuscript accounts that might have yielded more detail. They accept my conclusions regarding the strong nexus between anti-Irish Catholic nativism and the Dorr Rebellion and note the interaction between Dorrite leaders and the Gordons. They are probably correct in exonerating John Gordon, but their indictment of ambitious and grasping Senator William Sprague for conspiracy to commit fratricide is based on even flimsier circumstantial evidence. The defense, with similar resourcefulness, tried to cast suspicion on "Big Peter," a shadowy mill worker who had strong resentments against Amasa and permanently disappeared from the village immediately after the murder.

We will never know who killed Amasa Sprague. We do know that as soon as the Dorrites gained brief control over state government in 1852, they joined with members of the antigallows movement to abolish capital punishment—undoubtedly with John Gordon in mind.

The 1920s case of Sacco and Vanzetti has also continued to merit restudy. The most recent analysis—*The Verdict of History: Sacco and Vanzetti* (1997)—should be of particular interest to Rhode Islanders. Written by North Providence physician Frank M. D'Alessandro, it exonerates the defendants and persuasively implicates the Providence-based Joe Morelli gang in the South Braintree, Massachusetts, murders for which Sacco and Vanzetti were electrocuted.

The Rhode Island state prison was located in Providence on the northwest shore of the old cove. Thomas Dorr and John Gordon were confined there when this sketch was made in 1845. The site is now occupied by the Providence Place Mall.

Death Knell for the Death Penalty: The Gordon Murder Trial and Rhode Island's Abolition of Capital Punishment

Patrick T. Conley

On February 19, 1979, in the companion cases of *State* v. *Cline* and *State* v. *Anthony* (121 R.I. 299), the Rhode Island Supreme Court struck down the state's last remaining vestige of capital punishment, thus writing what may be the concluding chapter of a process that began in the decade of the 1830s. The death penalty invalidated by the court was contained in G.L. 1956, § 11-23-2, a 1973 statute which provided that every person who shall commit murder while serving a jail sentence in the Adult Correctional Institutions or the reformatory for women shall be put to death by lethal gas. In the court's opinion, this law's mandatory sentence "amounted to cruel and unusual punishment in violation of the Eighth Amendment by reason of its failure to provide for consideration of any mitigating factors" by the sentencing authority. In so ruling, our high tribunal followed a line of recent United States Supreme Court decisions, extending from *Furman* (1972) through *Woodson* (1976), *Roberts* (1977), and *Lockett* (1978).

The General Assembly had passed the nullified law during a nationwide epidemic of prison revolts, specifically in response to a series of disturbances at the ACI that culminated in the killing of a prison guard. The 1973 penal measure replaced a one-hundred-year-old statute that limited the penalty of death by hanging to a person who committed "murder while under the sentence of imprisonment for life."

Though significant, the recent controversy over capital punishment is bland in comparison with the mid-nineteenth-century campaign called the anti-gallows movement. According to historians, the three decades from the mid-1820s to the mid-1850s constitute the first great era of American reform. This "Age of Egalitarianism" witnessed political innovations such as the national nominating convention, the choosing of presidential electors by popular vote, the proliferation of elective offices (including judgeships), the development of populistic political campaign techniques, and the removal of personal property qualifications for voting and officeholding. In the economic realm, neomercantilism gave way to laissez-faire, a transition symbolized by Andrew Jackson's successful war against the monopolistic Bank of the United States.

But it was the social order that experienced the most variegated demand for change, with causes that included antislavery, temperance, free public education, pacifism, women's rights, and communitarianism, as well as institutional and legal reform. Ralph Waldo Emerson, the era's most noted philosopher of change, observed in 1841 that America was conducting "a general inquisition into abuses." He then believed that "in the history of the world the doctrine of Reform had never such a scope as at the present hour." In seemed to Emerson that every human institution was being questioned—"Christianity, the laws, commerce, school, the farm, the laboratory"—and that there was not a "statute, rite, calling, man, or woman, but is not threatened with the new spirit." Indeed, "the demon of reform" roamed the land—moralistic and comprehensive—optimistically seeking the liberation and perfection of the individual in a truly egalitarian society.

The reform impulse affected Rhode Island's legal system in a variety of ways. In 1827 the state legislature upgraded the Supreme Court in both personnel and procedure, passing a restructuring act that reduced the size of the court from five to three and more than doubled the salaries of the justices. It was the intention of the act's sponsors that the Assembly would henceforth appoint distinguished men with legal training and experience and refrain from the common practice of elevating nonlawyers to Supreme Court judgeships. In anticipation of qualified appointees, the reconstituted high court (which was a trial court until the reoganization of 1905) was commissioned "to instruct the grand juries in the law relating to crimes and offenses cognizable" by the Supreme Court and "to instruct the petit jury in the law that may be applicable to each case by them tried...before they retire to consider their verdict." Prior to this reform the jury could decide both the facts and the law to be applied.

Other Rhode Island legal innovations of the age included abolition of imprisonment for debt and a mechanics' lien law. In addition, inspired by New Yorker Edward Livingston's code of penal law and discipline, in the mid-1830s the state constructed a new prison in Providence on the northwest shore of the saltwater cove that once occupied the site of the new Capital Center.

Rhode Island also played a leading role during this time in the antigallows movement, a humanitarian effort to abolish capital punishment. In 1647, when the colony enacted its first legal code, the legislature decreed the death penalty for nine crimes: treason, murder, manslaughter, burglary (except for those who "steal for hunger" and "fools"), arson of dwelling houses and barns filled with corn, robbery, witchcraft, rape, and "buggery" (as sodomy was then called). During the eighteenth century, witchcraft was permanently deleted from the list of capital offenses, while arson and rape were omitted temporarily.

In the famous digest of 1798, the state's first legal code, manslaughter and treason were also removed from the roster of capital crimes, but arson and rape were restored. Until the 1830s such penalties evoked little interest, in part, perhaps, because no hangings occurred from 1798 until June 1832, when a series of three executions were performed within a span of nineteen months. Ironically, this wave of hangings had one salutary result—it prompted the General Assembly in June 1833 to ban public executions, making Rhode Island the first state in the union to abolish this macabre spectacle.

In 1838 a state legislative study committee appointed to revise the penal code urged complete abolition of the death penalty. Judge William R. Staples, Rhode Island's most noted lawyer-historian, and Samuel Y. Atwell, a lawyer and legislator from Glocester, spearheaded this anti-gallows effort. In a two-page report justifying their recommendation, Staples and Atwell urged Rhode Island to take the lead in this matter. Since the state was founded by innovators, said the reformers, they hoped that the legislature would not succumb to the spurious claim that the abolition of hanging would be a dangerous change. During the ensuing public discussion a letter to the editor of the *Providence Journal* made a more eloquent appeal to the state's reforming spirit: "Let the little republic of Rhode Island emulate the fame of its founders and fairly test by experience whether its citizens may not be governed with the halter [noose], as well as truly worship God without resort to sword or faggot."

When the General Assembly considered the proposed revisions during its January session of 1838, the legislators, in a close vote, retained capital punishment for two crimes—murder and arson. In the wake of this limited victory for leniency, local anti-gallows agitation subsided until the 1844 murder trial of John and William Gordon, a *cause célèbre* that can be best understood when viewed within the context of the Dorr Rebellion and the nativistic surge that this disturbance spawned.

From 1841 to 1843 Rhode Island was convulsed by a popular crusade for political change known as the Dorr Rebellion. The principal figure in the uprising was Thomas Wilson Dorr, a reform-oriented attorney from a distinguished Providence family. The so-called rebellion stemmed from forceful and extralegal attempts by Dorr and his associates to modernize and democratize the reactionary government of Rhode Island via a People's Convention unauthorized by the General Assembly. As their principal improvement, the Dorrites sought to broaden the suffrage by removing the prevailing real estate qualification, a change which would have allowed newly arrived Irish Catholic immigrants the vote once they had gained citizenship.

The faction of urban Whigs and rural Democrats that opposed reform, the so-called Law and Order party, turned many native Rhode Islanders against Dorr by alleging that suffrage expansion would result in Irish Catholic political control of the state. This tactic and several other maneuvers by the Law and Order men produced many defections from the ranks of the Dorrites, and eventually Dorr was overcome by his opponents, subjected to a farcical trial, and sentenced to jail for treason against the state. Although his reform agitation did pressure the conservatives to draft the present state constitution, when the document went into effect in May 1843 it contained a voting provision which severely discriminated against Irish Catholic immigrants. The native-born got "free suffrage," but naturalized citizens were still required to own land in order to vote or hold office. This clause was a manifestation of the intense anti-Catholic nativism generated by the Dorr Rebellion.

On December 31, 1843, before the nativistic tide had receded, Amasa Sprague was brutally bludgeoned to death. This gory incident touched off the Gordon murder trial, an event which became the Rhode Island version of the Sacco-Vanzetti case—but here the defendants were Irish Catholic immigrants rather than Italians.

Prominent textile magnate Amasa Sprague (1798–1843) was the victim in Rhode Island's most notorious murder.

Amasa Sprague was a powerful, wealthy, and influential man. He was administrator of the A. & W. Sprague industrial empire, a portion of which was based in Cranston. He personally supervised the Cranston complex at Sprague's Village (near the present Cranston Print Works) in the manner of a feudal baron, with several hundred Irish men, women, and children in his employ. Amasa and his brother William, the United States senator from Rhode Island and a former governor, arrayed themselves with the Law and Order faction during the Dorr Rebellion.

The Spragues had a disdain for those recent immigrants called the " low Irish," but not to the extent of penalizing their own interests, and thus they drew no ethnic barrier against the willing and hardworking Celts who toiled for meager wages in their textile mills.

Amasa was a strong and forceful personality. Sprague's Village was his. He owned the plant, the company houses, the company store, and the farm which supplied that store. He even owned the church where the Protestant workers worshiped.

On that fateful Sunday afternoon in late December, the forty-six-year-old Amasa left his mansion adjacent to his factory and began to walk northwestward to a large farm he owned in the neighboring town of Johnston, a mile and a half distant, using a shortcut through fields and meadows.

Between dusk and darkness of that day, Michael Costello, a handyman in the Sprague household, took the same route and came upon Sprague's bloodied body. He had been shot in the right forearm and then brutally beaten to death. The sixty dollars found in the victim's pocket seemed to eliminate robbery as a motive, making the murder appear to be one of hatred or revenge.

Suspicion immediately centered on the Gordon family, a clan of Irish immigrants who were particularly hostile towards the strong-willed Yankee industrialist. Nicholas Gordon, the family's earliest arrival, had emigrated from Ireland sometime in the mid-1830s, settled in Cranston, and opened a small store near Sprague's Village, where he sold groceries, notions, and miscellaneous items. He then expanded his business by obtaining a license to sell liquor from Cranston town officials. This new commodity proved so popular in the dreary mill village that in 1843 Nicholas was able to finance the migration of his family—his aged mother; his sister; three brothers, John, William, and Robert; and a niece—from Ireland to America.

But Gordon's liquor sales also produced a confrontation with Amasa Sprague, who felt the intoxicating brew was adversely affecting the productive capacity of his factory hands. Thus Sprague used his considerable political weight in June 1843 to block a renewal of Nicholas Gordon's liquor license.

Tempers had flared and harsh words had been exchanged because of this incident, and consequently the Gordon brothers became prime suspects in Amasa Sprague's murder. One might say that public opinion convicted them immediately, as it appeared to many that this heinous crime

General Thomas F. Carpenter, a leading member of the bar, joined with Samuel Y. Atwell in defense of the Gordons. Carpenter, an ally of Thomas Dorr, had been the unsuccessful Democratic candidate for governor in 1840 and 1843. His Catholic sympathies led to his conversion to that faith in 1850.

was another instance of the infamous "Whiteboy" outrages which Irish peasants had visited upon their opponents throughout the early nineteenth century.

Three Gordon brothers were promptly indicted on circumstantial evidence—John and William for murder, Nicholas for being an accessory before the fact, the implication being that Nicholas had instigated his brothers to commit the murder in revenge and had even imported them for that purpose. Nicholas received the lesser charge because an investigation proved he was in Providence on the day of the murder, first at Mass and later at a christening.

The Irish communities in Providence and Cranston rallied to the support of the Gordons and raised money to employ able counsel. Several colleagues of Thomas Dorr accepted the challenge to defend the accused Irishmen and did so without fee. One was John P. Knowles, a suffrage reformer; another was General Thomas F. Carpenter, three times an unsuccessful Democratic candidate for governor (in 1840, 1842, and 1843) and a leading member of the Rhode Island bar. The Catholic sympathies which would lead to Carpenter's conversion in 1850 were already in evidence.

A third attorney assisting the Gordons was the legislator and anti-gallows reformer Samuel Y. Atwell, who later in the year would serve as chief defense counsel for Dorr in his trial for treason. The Yankee community was far from monolithic in its intolerance, as Dorr, Carpenter, Knowles and Atwell illustrated, but the climate of native opinion in this year of the bloody Philadelphia religious riots was decidedly anti-Catholic and anti-Irish. John Gordon would feel its oppressive weight.

The trial of John and William was conducted at the spring 1844 term of the Supreme Court before a twelve-man jury devoid of Irish Catholics. With Chief Justice Job Durfee presiding, the ordeal lasted from April 8 to April 17. At the outset William definitely established that he was elsewhere when the crime was committed, so Attorney General Joseph M. Blake and prosecutor William H. Potter zeroed in on the hapless twenty-one-year-old John, who could not prove his whereabouts.

The evidence, which was entirely circumstantial and conflicting, consisted primarily of the fact that the murderer had a shoe size and a stride similar to John's, that a broken gun was found which allegedly belonged to Nicholas (though Nicholas produced a gun he said was his), and that a blood-stained coat belonging to the Gordons was found in the vicinity of the crime (the "blood" was later proven to be madder dye used in coloring textiles).

The Gordons proclaimed their innocence, and the defense suggested that another laborer, called "Big Peter," was the real culprit. Peter disappeared from the village immediately after the killing, and no serious attempt was made by the state to determine his whereabouts.

When the testimony concluded, Chief Justice Durfee (who was soon to preside in a partisan fashion over the treason trial of Dorr) gave a charge to the jury in which he called the killing the "most atrocious" crime that ever came to his attention and one that "has no parallel in the annals of the state" or "in the annals of any one of the United States." In the aftermath of such obvious hyperbole, Durfee drew a distinction between the testimony of native-born witnesses and that of the Gordons' "countrymen," implying that the latter was less credible.

The jury apparently took Durfee's injudicious advice; leaving the box at 6:30 on the night of April 17 and returning one hour and fifteen minutes later, it announced a verdict of guilty for John Gordon and freedom for William. John was then sentenced to death even before the trial of his brother Nicholas for a related offense.

John Gordon's attorneys made an appeal to the October session of the court, but the justices rejected it. Then Gordon petitioned the General Assembly for a reprieve and a commutation of sentence. The House debated this petition on January 14, 1845, with Law and Order chieftain Wilkins Updike of South Kingstown vigorously leading the opposition. By a vote of 36 to 27 the Irishman's plea was rejected, but the narrowness of the margin indicated growing doubts concerning the fairness of the trial.

Chief Justice Job Durfee (1790–1847), a highly partisan jurist, presided over the Gordon trial. Until 1905 the Supreme Court was both a trial and an appellate court. Durfee was a versatile man—lawyer, poet, amateur historian, legislator, Speaker of the Rhode Island House (1827–1829), and United States congressman (1821–1825).

Time was running out for John Gordon, and Governor James Fenner, Dorr's archrival, was not sympathetic to the convict's plight. When no reprieve was granted, John Gordon was hanged on February 14, 1845, in the yard of the state prison, where Dorr was also an inmate. The young immigrant devoutly maintained his innocence to the end. In those final moments Father John Brady, who attended Gordon, tried to console him: "Have courage, John," said his confessor, "you are going to join the noble band of martyrs of your countrymen who have suffered before at the shrine of bigotry and prejudice."

The funeral of John Gordon was attended by Irish from miles around, some journeying from Massachusetts and Connecticut. According to observers, mourners in the procession took thirty minutes to pass a given spot.

The controversial trial left many questions unanswered, but the compelling attitude, which even some of those who thought John guilty came to share, was that the young Irishman had been convicted on insufficient and unsatisfactory evidence which fell far short of the required standard of reasonable doubt.

Nicholas Gordon was later freed after two juries deadlocked on the question of his guilt, but he never recovered from the personal calamity of his younger brother's death or from his own confinement in the damp coveside prison. Broken in health, he took to excessive drink and suffered a premature death.

In the immediate aftermath of John Gordon's execution, numerous mass meetings were held in Providence to protest the continuance of the death penalty. Several nationally prominent anti-gallows campaigners attended these demonstrations. Dorrites such as the Reverend Martin Cheyney, a Free-Will Baptist minister from Olneyville, and Samuel H. Wales, a watchmaker and delegate to the People's Convention of 1841, were prominent speakers at these gatherings, but they effected no change in Rhode Island's law. Undaunted, local reformers persisted in their abolition effort. In January 1846 Reverend Edward B. Hall, pastor of Providence's First Unitarian Church, published an anti-gallows essay in the prestigious and influential *North American Review*. In that same month Smithfield representative Thomas Buffum, a Quaker, sponsored an abolition bill in the House; initially tabled, the bill was revived on the last day of the session, only to be returned to the table by a vote of 53 to 9. The conservative Law and Order party that controlled state government in the decade of the 1840s simply turned a deaf ear to the reformers' pleas.

Historian Philip E. Mackey, the leading authority on the national anti-gallows movement of the mid-nineteenth century, discounted the impact of John Gordon's execution on the demise of Rhode Island's death penalty because the statute abolishing capital punishment was not enacted until 1852. Then, according to Mackey, "with little warning, reformers reappeared...stronger than before and—with comparative ease—persuaded the legislature to abolish capital punishment completely in a scant four weeks." Mackey's surprise would have been lessened had he recognized the temporary political realignment that occurred in Rhode Island from 1851 to 1853. During those years the Law and Order party split, with that faction's rural members briefly returning to the Democratic fold. Their earlier defection during the Dorr Rebellion, however, had placed Thomas Dorr and his reform contingent in control of Democratic organization and policy.

The Gordon trial was such a cause célèbre that the court report of the proceedings was published and widely distributed.

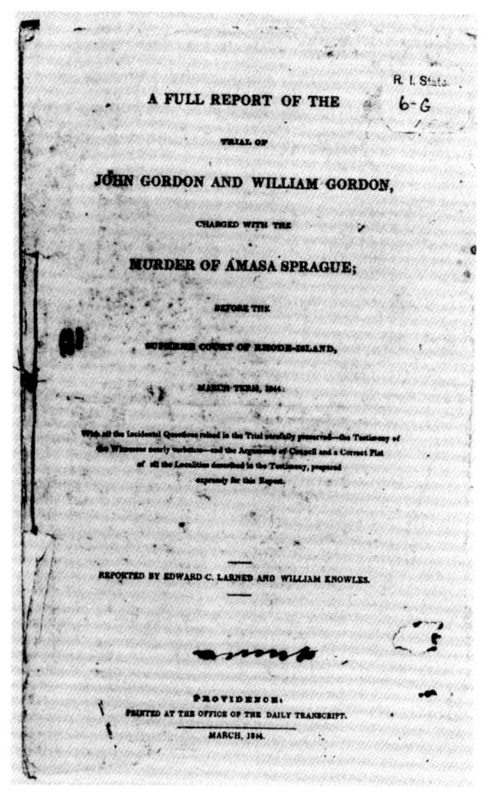
A FULL REPORT OF THE

TRIAL OF

JOHN GORDON AND WILLIAM GORDON,

CHARGED WITH THE

MURDER OF AMASA SPRAGUE;

BEFORE THE

SUPREME COURT OF RHODE-ISLAND,

MARCH TERM, 1844:

With all the Incidental Questions raised in the Trial carefully preserved—the Testimony of the Witnesses nearly verbatim—and the Arguments of Council and a Correct Plat of all the Localities described in the Testimony, prepared expressly for this Report.

REPORTED BY EDWARD C. LARNED AND WILLIAM KNOWLES.

PROVIDENCE:
PRINTED AT THE OFFICE OF THE DAILY TRANSCRIPT.

MARCH, 1844.

In the state elections of 1851, 1852, and 1853 (governors and state legislators then had one-year terms), Providence humanitarian and industrialist Philip Allen, uncle and ally of Dorr, won the governorship. Many reform-minded Dorr Democrats were also successful in Assembly races. The influence of these progressives on legislation from May 1851 to April 1854 accounts not only for the abolition of the death penalty but for numerous other innovations, including a secret-ballot law and the first three amendments to the state constitution. These zealots even passed a measure reversing and annulling Dorr's conviction for treason against the state.

Clearly these Dorr supporters, who had vainly defended John Gordon, used their newly won political power to prevent others from experiencing his fate. On January 23, 1852, a Senate committee chaired by People's Convention delegate and longtime Dorr ally Ariel Ballou of Cumberland issued a forty-three-page report containing a proposed bill to ban capital punishment. This document concluded that "the spirit of the age in which we live, the sublime principles of Christianity, as well as the ends of justice, demand the abolition of death as a penalty for crime." In less than two weeks the Senate passed the committee's bill by a 17 to 13 vote. On February 11 the campaign shifted to the House, where Dublin-born Protestant Thomas Davis (who owned the Providence estate upon which Veterans' Hospital and Davis Park now stand) led the fight for passage. By a decisive 44 to 20 margin, the House made Rhode Island the second state (Michigan in 1846 was first) to abolish capital punishment. In its stead the maximum criminal penalty became life imprisonment and a loss of all civil rights.

Though weak on the reform role of the Dorr Democrats, Professor Mackey's analysis of the 1852 abolition effort is otherwise commendable, especially in its disclosure of the prominent role played by Thomas Robinson Hazard, a wealthy reformer, in drafting not only the Ballou Committee's report but also the publicly circulated abolition petition that prompted it, as well as numerous newspaper articles that justified the anti-gallows movement on Christian principles.

Also important, Mackey shows, was "the state's unique religious composition, for in the nineteenth century one's views about capital punishment were closely bound up with one's sectarian orientation." Orthodox Calvinists tended to take Genesis 9:6 literally ("Who so sheddeth man's blood, by man shall his blood be shed"), while so-called liberal Protestants—Unitarians, Universalists, and Quakers—embraced a more humane view. In Rhode Island, adherents of these liberal sects were numerous, outspoken, and influential.

Despite many attempts, a general death penalty was never reinstated in Rhode Island. In 1872 the legislature did authorize capital punishment for a prisoner who committed murder while under life sentence, but that crime never occurred. In 1973 a broader capital penalty for convicts was enacted, only to be invalidated six years later by the state Supreme Court in the decision described at the outset of this essay. Thus John Gordon remains the last Rhode Islander to suffer the fate of execution.

Notwithstanding other influences, the ordeal of John Gordon had a permanent impact on Rhode Island law and politics, and it stands today as one of the darker episodes in Rhode Island history. Seldom before or since has the cause of justice or the spirit of religious toleration implanted here by Roger Williams received such a severe jolt as it did on the day John Gordon died.

Thomas Robinson Hazard (1797–1886), shown here with his family, was a South County agriculturist, manufacturer, author, and social reformer. "Shepherd Tom," as he was affectionately called, served as vice president of the American Colonization Society, an organization to relocate freed blacks; he wrote an influential state-sponsored report on the poor and insane in 1851 that prompted several institutional reforms; he undertook relief efforts to aid the Irish victims of the Great Famine; and he led the successful 1852 fight for the abolition of capital punishment in Rhode Island.

18

In the nineteenth century, Rhode Island boasted two nationally renowned legal writers: Henry Wheaton (1785–1848), a noted commentator on international law, and the versatile James K. Angell (1794–1857), the nation's leading authority on tidewaters, riparian rights, and the law relating to carriers of goods and passengers by land and water.

In addition to his scholarly pursuits, Angell was an activist in the constitutional reform movement of the 1830s and 1840s. He collaborated with Thomas Wilson Dorr in the authorship of two leading reformist tracts—the *Address to the People of Rhode Island* (1834), which served as the bible of the Constitutional party of the 1830s, and *The Nine Lawyers' Opinion* (1842), the most cogent and persuasive statement of Dorrite political theory.

Sidney S. Rider (1833–1917), the author of the following profile of Angell, was also a remarkable figure in Rhode Island legal and constitutional history. A Providence curmudgeon, for thirty-three years (1883–1916) he published an eight-page biweekly pamphlet called *Book Notes* from his Almy Street office. Though his focus was historical and literary, and he was considered a crank by some, he spoke out on the major political and social issues of the day as they affected both the city and the state. The most knowledgeable local historian of his generation, Rider had a running feud with "Boss" Brayton, who, he felt, caused the suicide of his brother Frederic Rider in 1881, when both were officials of the Providence post office.

As a typical middle-class progressive, Rider championed the cause of the consumer against the New Haven Railroad, the Rhode Island Company, the utilities, and other monopolies, and he espoused "good government" reforms. However, his observations revealed him to be a nativist who was cool towards Catholicism and condescending towards the new immigrants arriving in Providence during the early years of the twentieth century.

In addition to *Book Notes*, Rider published a series of volumes called *Rhode Island Historical Tracts*, which included such law-related items as this profile of Angell, *The Nine Lawyers' Opinion*, a biography of Stephen Hopkins, a legal defense of Samuel Gorton, and Judge Thomas Durfee's *Gleanings from the Judicial History of Rhode Island*. Rider also wrote (but could not publish) an extensive constitutional history of Rhode Island, which was alluded to in a previous introductory essay.

Artist James Calvert Smith did this oil painting to re-create a typical law school lecture. Tapping Reeve is depicted answering a question posed by the student standing—John C. Calhoun, class of 1805.

Joseph K. Angell, Law Writer

Sidney S. Rider

Joseph Kinnicutt Angell, the only son of Nathan and Amey [Kinnicutt] Angell, was born in Providence, Rhode Island, on April 30, 1794. He was descended from Thomas Angell, one of the five companions of Roger Williams in the settlement of Providence. Others soon joined these first comers, and the little band so increased became the thirteen original proprietors.

Young Angell early betrayed a fondness for study, and his parents determined to provide him with the opportunities of obtaining a good education. By whom he was prepared for college is not now known. He entered Brown University as a student in his fifteenth year. Among his classmates were Job Durfee, afterwards Chief Justice, and Romeo Elton, afterwards Professor, two friends filled with the spirit of Rhode Island History, and both of whom left enduring literary monuments to perpetuate it.

Joseph K. Angell (1794–1857) was one of several early Rhode Island attorneys to attend the Litchfield Law School—America's first—established in 1784 in Litchfield, Connecticut, by Judge Tapping Reeve. The school, which operated until 1833, was housed in this one-room building, seen below in its restored state. Similar private law schools were set up in the early nineteenth century and were the chief source of formal instruction in the law prior to the 1830s. Chief Justices Richard Ward Greene, George A. Brayton, and Samuel Ames also attended Litchfield, and Governor John Brown Francis was Angell's classmate in 1813 at the Connecticut academy. No likeness of Angell has been located, although his portrait was allegedly donated by a group of his admirers to Brown University in the late nineteenth century.

After his graduation from Brown University in 1813, Mr. Angell was sent to the Law School at Litchfield, Conn.; justly considered the best school of its kind then in the country. It was conducted at the time by Tapping Reeve, assisted by James Gould, both gentlemen of distinguished ability as lecturers, and both authors of treatises which for many years and even to this time are cited as books of authority. At this school Mr. Angell formed acquaintances with young men which ripened into life-long friendships, and which were of the greatest use to him in after years. Among these friends was John Brown Francis, subsequently Governor and United States Senator for Rhode Island.

After leaving the law school at Litchfield, Mr. Angell entered as a student the law office of Thomas Burgess in Providence, who subsequently and for many years held the office of Probate Judge for that city. Burgess was never an advocate, but he was a prudent and discreet counsellor, and was the confidential law advisor of many merchants. How long Mr. Angell read law in the office of Mr. Burgess is not now known. Of the three years which had elapsed since his graduation at Brown University, and previous to his admission to the Bar, it is probable that one year was passed at Litchfield and the remaining two years with Mr. Burgess. What influence on the formation of his character this connection with Mr. Burgess exerted it is difficult now to determine; but it is certain that peculiarities of thought and action were common to both.

At the March term of the Supreme Court, 1816, Mr. Angell, in company with Charles F. Tillinghast and Charles H. Bruce, was proposed for admission to the Rhode Island Bar by Nathaniel Searle, a man described by Judge Story as one "whose arguments were characterized by exact learning and clear reasoning, and whose elocution was rapid, clear and affluent almost beyond example." This Bar was just then entering upon a glorious period of its history. May not a slight digression be excusable that mention may be made of some of the distinguished contemporaries of Mr. Angell. The great change which has since taken place in the structure, power, and method of procedure in our courts was but just beginning. For many of these wise changes the State is indebted to James Burrill, Jr., who was elected to fill the seat of Chief Justice in 1816. He held the office but a single year, when he was sent to the Senate of the United States from Rhode Island. He was succeeded by Tristam Burges. Before the elevation of Mr. Burrill to the bench, he had held the position of Attorney General for upwards of sixteen years. Both of these gentlemen were distinguished advocates. Succeeding them, and no less distinguished, came John Whipple, Samuel Y. Atwell and Nathaniel Searle, all men of very great power. Samuel W. Bridgham, the first mayor of Providence, and Walter R. Danforth, who held the same office at a later period, were members of the same Bar.

William R. Staples, Richard W. Greene, and Samuel Ames, who all became Chief Justices of the Supreme Court, or Supreme Judicial Court, as it was once called; Charles F. Tillinghast, William E. Richmond, and Thomas Burgess, who were Counsellors at Law in the highest meaning of the term; John Pitman, who was for many years Judge of the United States District Court for this State; Henry Bowen, who for thirty years was the Secretary of State of Rhode Island, and Albert C. Greene, who for eighteen years was the Attorney General, and afterwards a United States Senator; Benjamin Hazard, who was sixty-two successive times elected a member of the Geueral Assembly from Newport; Job Durfee, whose father was a Judge, who himself became Chief Justice, and whose son now occupies the seat of his father; Thomas F. Carpenter, whose name should have a place in our list of advocates; Elisha R. Potter, whose name was the synonym of power in the southern counties for a third of a century; and many others, whose names will at once occur to those familiar with the history of the Rhode Island Bar in those its palmiest days. Names upon names rise before us, but this is neither the time nor the place to call the roll of its members.

Williams and his companions planted the colony, and laid the foundations of a State. May it not with justice be said that these are the men who nourished it in its youth, who formulated its laws, and by whose earnest and honest efforts strength was imparted to its every part.

Mr. Angell now entered upon the practice of his profession. He was by nature far better fitted for a counsellor than for an advocate, and his name would not have been found in a list of Rhode Island advocates. He was a sound theoretical lawyer, and an admirable advisor. His practice before the courts must have been of short duration. An event soon occurred which turned the whole current of his life. In 1819, he received a letter from Mr. Chalmers, counsellor at law, living in London, England, informing him that there was then before the courts of chancery of England, an immense estate looking for an heir to inherit it, and expressing the belief that he was the legal heir. Counsel was taken of the friends of Mr. Angell in Providence, and it was decided to send him to England to look after his interest in this vast estate, which lay in some of the most fertile counties in the kingdom.

Early in February, he left Providence and journeyed by stage to New York. He reached the latter city, as he details in a letter to his mother, at eight o'clock in the morning of Wednesday, the 9th of February, having passed two sleepless nights upon the road, and being necessarily much fatigued. He immediately entered upon the search for a ship bound for England, and soon found one—the ship *Amity*, which was to sail the following morning. In this vessel Mr. Angell took passage for Liverpool, which city he reached after a pleasant voyage of twenty-six days. Here however he tarried not, but made the best of his way to London. From letters written to his mother and to his sister may be gathered the impressions upon his mind of the scenery through which he passed. He speaks with mortification of the fact that Shakspeare's house at Stratford was then in use as a butcher's shop. At Oxford he spends much of his time in the libraries, the like of which he had never seen before. Of these, and of the chapels, halls and paintings, he writes to his mother an admirable account. He finally reached London, where he resided at Richards's Coffee House, in Fleet street, near Temple Bar, a central position for the business upon which he went, and near by the men whom he delighted to meet. He entered at once and vigorously upon the work which he had undertaken, and his letters, while keeping his friends fully informed of his progress in that business, are also filled with descriptions of the things which he saw and the events which occurred and which interested him.

By the will of John Angell, made in 1774, he "gave and devised to the heirs male, if any such there were, of William Angell, the first purchaser at Crowhurst, and father of his great grandfather, John Angell, Esq., and their male heirs forever, all his lands and estates both real and personal, in Surrey, Kent, and Sussex, nevertheless subject and liable to such conditions as should be thereafter mentioned, and should not be otherwise disposed of and given; and if there should be no male heirs or descendants of the same William or the first Angell of Northamptonshire, in order as they should be found or made apparent, and if there should be none of those in being, or that should be apparent and plainly and legally make themselves out to be Angells and so related and descended, he then gave all his estates whatsoever, both real and personal, to William Browne, Esquire, grandson to Mrs. Frances, the wife of Benedict Browne, Esquire, who was an Angell, and his male heirs forever."

The claim of Mr. Angell was, that notwithstanding there were many Angells living in England, none were male heirs of the body of William Angell, the first purchaser of Crowhurst, nor were there any such heirs in existence; that he was the male heir by collateral descent, tracing his descent from the only brother of William Angell, the aforesaid Thomas Angell, who first came with Roger Williams to plant the town of Providence. In the prosecution of his search, Mr. Angell exhibited great patience and perseverance. He personally examined the register of every parish church in London in his pursuit of evidence, and having obtained a vast amount, which could not then well be transmitted by reason of the slow progress of the mails, he determined to return with it to Providence, lay it before his friends, take advice, and start afresh.

He reached New York on the 22d of October, 1820, and repaired at once to Providence. Having laid the case fully before his friends, it was determined that he should return to England and press the claim. With this end in view, he sailed from Boston in the ship *Parthian*, on the 5th of July, 1821, and reached Liverpool on the 1st of August. He entered immediately with renewed vigor upon the business which called him again to England. In the course of it, it became necessary to visit many of the towns and counties in the interior. In this way he saw much of the rural life of the people, which filled him with pleasure and his letters with charming descriptions. Having with much labor prepared his case in the spring of 1822, he filed a bill in the Court of Chancery. This bill prayed for a commission to examine witnesses abroad and to perpetuate their testimony. The Vice Chancellor refused to grant the commission, because there was no action pending, and nothing had been exhibited to show that an action could not be brought. Thus ended the pursuit of this property by Mr. Angell, who did not indeed wait for the decision, but returned to Rhode Island before it had been rendered, fully persuaded with the belief that "the longer he was absent from home the more he became sensible of the strength of those ties which bound him to his native soil, and which are so natural and interwoven with the heart, that it is impossible to utterly destroy them without destroying the heart itself."

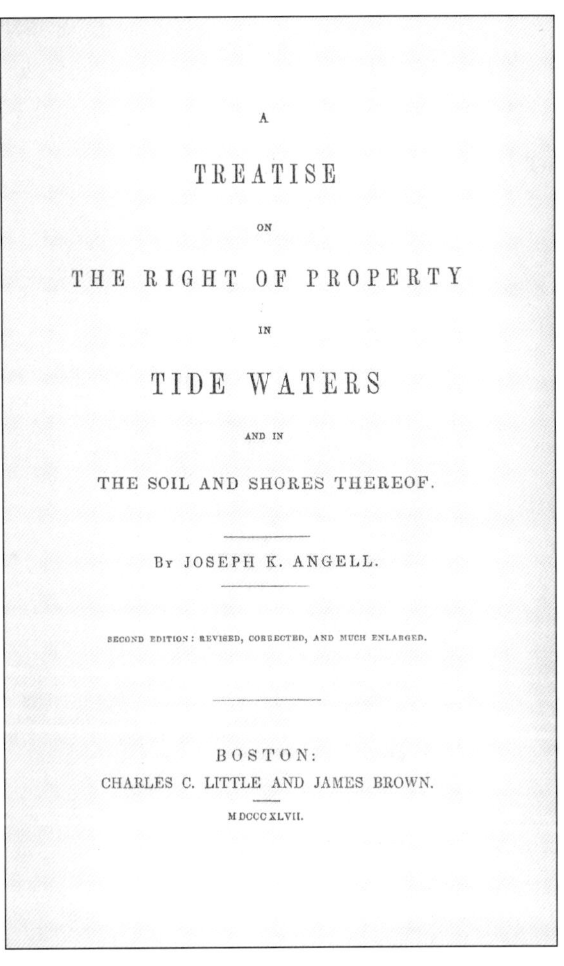

A

TREATISE

ON

THE RIGHT OF PROPERTY

IN

TIDE WATERS

AND IN

THE SOIL AND SHORES THEREOF.

By JOSEPH K. ANGELL.

SECOND EDITION: REVISED, CORRECTED, AND MUCH ENLARGED.

BOSTON:
CHARLES C. LITTLE AND JAMES BROWN.
MDCCCXLVII.

Angell's treatise *On Tide Waters* is still a valuable legal reference.

Mr. Angell returned to Rhode Island without having reached that success for which he had hoped in the business upon which he went abroad, but an idea had occurred to him while there which resulted in a splendid success. He resolved to devote himself to the profession of a law writer, a branch of the profession far more consonant to his tastes than that of an advocate or a counsellor, and which he had seen carried to such an extent in England. At the period of his return, the business interests in Rhode Island were in process of transformation from a commercial to a manufacturing industry; mills for the manufacture of cotton into cloth were being erected upon every stream where water power could be found. Naturally, therefore, was the attention of Mr. Angell called to the subject of the law relating to water courses, and he chose that subject for the title of his first work. It appeared in 1824, since which time many editions have appeared, and more than twelve thousand copies have been sold. The work has been very much enlarged at each successive revision, and is still a leading authority upon the subject. While engaged upon this work, the attention of Mr. Angell was called naturally to the title which he selected for his second work, *The Right of Property in Tide Waters and in the Soil and Shores Thereof*, which work appeared in 1826. A second and much enlarged edition was published in 1847. Both works met with a favorable reception from the bench and from the bar. Chancellor James Kent said of them, that "they were works which no intelligent lawyer could well practice without."

Early in 1837, Mr. Angell published his third work. It was entitled, *An Inquiry into the Rule of Law which creates a Right to an Incorporeal Hereditament by an Adverse Enjoyment of twenty years, with remarks on the application of the rule to Light, and in certain cases to a Water Privilege.* This essay was not at first intended for publication, but the interest in the subject induced the author to publish it. Its object was to investigate the original establishment of the rule and to trace its progress, to explain the qualifications to which it is subject, and develop the principle and policy on which it is founded. It is a small octavo volume of one hundred and seventeen pages.

Following this came in the same year, *An Essay on the Right of a State to Tax a Body Corporate considered in relation to the Bank Tax in Rhode Island.* This was a pamphlet of forty-four pages, and was called out by the exigency of the times. The General Assembly of Rhode Island had assumed tbe power to tax banks incorporated by charters granted by this same honorable body, but the charters of which contained no reservation of power to tax. Neither of these essays were ever reprinted.

With the beginning of the year 1829, Mr. Angell began the publication at Providence of the *United States Law Intelligencer and Review.* The periodical, for it was issued monthly, was to be a synopsis or abridged record of the changes and progress of the Law. The first volume only was published in Providence. The work was disposed of to Philadelphia parties, and the office of publication removed to that city. Mr. Angell continued its editor two years. It had but a short life after he left it, three volumes only having been issued. It was a great advance upon any similar journal issued before it in this country, and it pointed the way for other similar enterprises.

During this same year, 1829, Mr. Angell published *A Treatise on the Limitations of Actions at Law and Suits in Equity*, a volume of upwards of five hundred pages. In 1846 appeared the second edition of the same work, much enlarged, and with many of the errors in the former edition corrected. In the first edition was reprinted, *The Reading upon the Statute of Limitations* of that famous Lawyer, Sir Robert Brook, Kt., from the London edition of 1647. This reprint was omitted in the second edition. This work Mr. Angell dedicated to his lifelong friend, John Brown Francis, late Governor of Rhode Island. It was at once favorably received by the profession generally, and by no one more so than by Chancellor Kent. The copy before us is filled with his manuscript memoranda. Soon after the publication of the first edition, the author sent a copy as a present to Brougham, then Lord Chancellor of England. In acknowledging its receipt, Lord Brougham used the following language: "Lord Brougham begs Mr. A. would kindly communicate to Mr. Angell, his very grateful sense of the favor done him by the valuable present of Mr. A.'s work. Lord B. has already consulted it, and found it to be by much the best treatise on this very important subject." Unfortunately, this letter is now lost, and this short extract is all that remains of a manuscript which Mr. Angell cherished as among the choicest of his earthly treasures. It may be doubted whether any event in the literary life of Mr. Angell ever gave him so much pleasure as this letter, which he exhibited with delight to his friends. Of this treatise six editions, comprising in the aggregate more than eight thousand copies have been issued.

In 1832, Mr. Angell, in connection with Samuel Ames, issued a *Treatise on the Law of Private Corporations Aggregate*. This work needs no other commendation than an enumeration of its editions, numbering ten, and a statement of the numbers which have been sold, exceeding twelve thousand copies. His next work in order of time was the *Practical Summary of the Law of Assignments in Trust for the Benefit of Creditors*. This work appeared in 1835. It was a duodecimo volume of upwards of two hundred and twenty pages. Notwithstanding the high commendation bestowed upon it, but one edition was ever published, and the book is now scarce and much sought for.

From this time until 1849, Mr. Angell undertook the publication of no new work, but revised and edited the successive new editions of his former works. In this year he published his treatise on the *Law of Carriers of Goods and Passengers by Land and Water*. It was a stout octavo of upwards of eight hundred pages. A second edition followed in 1851, a third in 1857, and others have succeeded. More than seven thousand copies have been sold, and the book is still the leading authority. It was dedicated to his life-long friend, John Carter Brown. The various editions of Mr. Angell's books vary in several ways which have not been mentioned in this memoir. For instance, in the case of the third edition of this work, which contains the United States laws relating to steamboats, and sundry forms of pleadings. These were omitted in subsequent editions and other material substituted. In the first edition were incorporated in the appendix certain leading cases which found no place in subsequent editions. This has been the case, although not perhaps to the extent, with the other works of Mr. Angell.

It was provided in the act organizing the courts of Rhode Island, after the adoption of the constitution in 1842, that a reporter of the decisions of the Supreme Court should be appointed. The law was subsequently modified, directing the Supreme Court to appoint the reporter, who was to be a person not a member of the court, and further directing the election to be made at the March term, 1845. The reporter was to publish his reports annually. He was to be paid one hundred dollars by the State for his services, and was at liberty to make or lose as much money as might happen, he assuming all risk of publication, the State agreeing to purchase one hundred and twenty-five copies for distribution. A worse arrangement for the eporter could not well be devised, the purchase by the State practically destroying all chances of sale to other parties. The reports were first issued in pamphlet form. The first of these pamphlets appeared in July, 1847. It contained seventy-one pages, and consisted entirely of opinions given long before the date of its publication. The second number soon followed. This also was prepared by Mr. Angell, and was the last prepared by him. He resigned the office of reporter at the September term of the court, 1849. Thomas Durfee was elected to succeed him; and by Mr. Durfee was prepared the third and concluding and by much the larger part of the first volume.

In 1854, was published a *Treatise on the Law of Fire and Life Insurance*. The following year a second edition was called for, since which time no further issue has been required, other authors having occupied the field. In 1857, appeared a *Treatise on the Law of Highways*. This work was begun by

Mr. Angell, and was in process of publication at the time of his death. It was the last of his literary labors. The first, second, and a portion of the fourth chapters were the work of Mr. Angell; the remainder was the work of Thomas Durfee. The following year a second edition was required, and the work still continues to be a leading authority upon the subject.

Here ends the list of books which contain the writings of Mr. Angell. Many of them are still the most valuable treatises upon the subjects of which they treat, and are constantly kept upon the market, which has already absorbed in the aggregate more than fifty thousand copies. On a list, received while printing these sheets, of law books for sale by a prominent firm of law booksellers in London, the first five titles offered were the leading books of Mr. Angell.

Mr. Angell was one of the signers of the famous *Nine Lawyers' Opinion*. It was upon the right of the people to form a constitution. It was published in 1842, a time of unprecedented political excitement in Rhode Island. It claimed that the power to prescribe a form of government rested with the people; that the legislature was the creature of the people, and was not superior to its creator; that before the Revolution the sovereign power was in the King of England; that by the Revolution the sovereign power was divested from the King and passed to the people, the whole people, of the colony, and which became the State; that the charter contained within itself no power of amendment or of change, and that since the Revolution, no way had existed for amending the form of government; that the legislature being the creature of the people, possessed no power to enforce the people to change their form of government—their utmost power was to request them to change it; that the Freeholders' Constitution rested on the request of the General Assembly, while the Peoples' Constitution rested on the request of the people themselves, and therefore rested on the firmest possible basis. Such in a general way is the tenor of this famous document. It was published only in the *Daily Express*, a newspaper published in Providence, on the 16th of March, 1842.

As a writer, the style of Mr. Angell is simple and direct, with little or no effort at ornament or illustration; to quickly reach the point of a decision and clearly state it was his aim as a writer; he presents the law as he finds it, with no tint or shade of coloring imparted by his own opinions. Doubtless it is these excellencies which lend permanence to his works.

Rosina, the sister of Mr. Angell, died in 1831, leaving him no near relative. He was never married. He died suddenly, in Boston, May 1, 1857, whither he had gone on business. He died as he had lived, without an enemy; distinguished through life by the simplicity of his character, by his kindly feeling towards all around him, by his attachment to his friends, by his freedom from prejudice, and by the total absence of all malevolence of spirit. His amiable qualities had won for him many valuable friends who throughout his life remained strongly attached to him, and after his death provided his body with a resting place, and adorned the walls of Rhode Island Hall at Brown University with his portrait.

Angell's biographer, Sidney S. Rider (1833–1917), was a publisher, an antiquariarian, and Rhode Island's leading nineteenth-century constitutional historian.

BOOK NOTES

HISTORICAL, LITERARY AND CRITICAL.

CONDUCTED BY

SIDNEY S. RIDER,

73 ALMY STREET, - - - - - - - - *PROVIDENCE, R. I.*

Entered as Second class Matter, at the Providence, R. I. Post Office.

50 Cents per annum. Fortnightly. Single Copy 5 Cents. | SATURDAY, APRIL 29, 1911. | Vol 28 No. 9.

DE MORTUIS NIL NISI BONUM.

CHARLES R. BRAYTON,
Dead 23 September, 1910.

PAPER NUMBER 2.

The time to write History is after men have ceased to make it. The time to write an account of Brayton's connection with the History of Rhode Island is after he has ceased to manipulate it. Shall such *Black* work be written in letters of *Gold*; or in good Black ink. I would not knowingly wrong any man nor will I ever submit, that any man shall prevent me from writing and printing the truth of History as I find it; for the Truth is an Almighty Power, against which no man living nor dead can stand. I will continue my work.

—

... ecuted it. Frederick C. Rider under Brayton was Superintendent of Carrier Work, during the years 1878, 1879, 1880 and 1881, until 8:30 o'clock of the morning of July 6th. At that moment he was dead. Brayton's great robbery of the Post Office money was not discovered until the 17th of January, 1880. My brother was Superintendent of Carriers when Brayton fled, or had been reported as having fled from the State. In 1879. Brayton published "A Handy Book of the Postal Service of the Providence (R. I.), Post Office 1879. C. R. Brayton, Post Master. This work was prepared for Brayton by Frederic C. Rider. My brother was taken by Senator Henry B. Anthony, to Newport, in August 1879, to be used before the Butler Committee; but he was not called to testify. Exact-

Rider's *Book Notes*—a series of literary, political, and historical booklets published "fortnightly" (i.e., every two weeks) from 1883 to 1916—contained many authoritative legal and historical essays. This issue notes the death of Charles R. "Boss" Brayton.

19

This essay by attorney John Robinson compares the cases contained in the first volume of *Rhode Island Reports*, covering the period from 1828 to 1851, with those mid-1880s cases reported in volume 15. The most significant contrasts are in the type of cases—the 1880s decisions showing the impact of industrialization and mechinized transportation—and the reliance on precedents and published authorities by the 1885 tribunal.

In a chapter entitled "The Struggle for Judicial Supremacy" that appeared in 1902 as part of Edward Field's cooperative history of Rhode Island, Chief Justice Edward C. Stiness commented upon the slowness of Rhode Island in preparing published court decisions. Stiness attributed this delay to a system whereby the Rhode Island jury determined both the facts of a case and the law to be applied. This method endured until 1827, when the legislature established the modern procedure. Under the old system, said Stiness, "there was, therefore, nothing to report—no need of precedents where each case could be decided according to the light which an individual jury might or might not possess."

Judge Stiness then proceeded to chronicle the first halting steps towards the establishment of the *Rhode Island Reports*:

> The few early cases found in the first volume of the *Reports* are merely charges of the court to the jury in the rare cases when charges were made. When the act was passed providing for a reporter of the decisions of the Supreme Court, Charles F. Tillinghast was appointed, but declined to accept. It was then offered to the late Abraham Payne.... Mr. Payne, in turn, declined the office. It was finally accepted by Joseph K. Angell, a pioneer among writers of legal text books in this country. The *Reports* were first issued in pamphlet form. The first of these pamphlets appeared in 1847. It contained seventy-one pages and consisted entirely of opinions given long before the date of its publication. The second number soon followed. This also was prepared by Mr. Angell, and was the last prepared by him. He resigned in 1849, and Thomas Durfee was elected his successor.

The fact that the first case recorded in the *Rhode Island Reports* was decided in 1827 is not mere happenstance, for that was the year of major judicial reform. Prodded by the local press and influenced by the spirited debate on the composition of the judiciary during Rhode Island's first constitutional convention in 1824, the General Assembly enacted a statute in its January 1827 session that upgraded the state Supreme Court in both personnel and procedure. The provisions of this restructuring act reduced the size of the court from five members to three and more than doubled the justices' salaries. The sponsors of the act intended that the Assembly would henceforth appoint distinguished men with legal training and experience and refrain from the common practice of elevating nonlawyers to such an exalted judicial post.

In anticipation of qualified appointees, the reconstituted high court was commissioned "to instruct the Grand Juries in the law relating to crimes and offenses cognizable" by the Supreme Court and "to instruct the Petit Jury in the law that may be applicable to each case by them tried, by giving them publicly in charge, before they retire to consider their verdict, the opinion of the Court upon the law." Prior to this change, the jury could decide both law and fact.

The court-reform statute became effective in May 1827 over the strong objections of those incumbent justices who were replaced, and the able Samuel Eddy, distinguished advocate and former congressman, was chosen chief justice. Eddy, who succeeded Isaac Wilbour, a farmer-politician with no formal legal training, has been called by one student of Rhode Island judicial development "the first of the new regime." Although the Assembly retained the power to appoint Supreme Court justices annually, the caliber of the new tribunal henceforth discouraged interference with the judiciary.

John R. Robinson wrote his essay in 1976 while studying for a master's degree in legal history. He is a former U.S. attorney for the Southern District of New York and a member of the historic Hazard family of South Kingstown. Robinson's article has been altered slightly for republication.

Rhode Island Reports—1828–1885

John R. Robinson

The nineteenth century in Rhode Island reflected a period of change for the law and for those who administered it. The types of cases that were reported remained similar between 1830 and 1850. However, by 1885 the cases became more numerous and were decided on a more intellectual basis. Industrial development and the ensuing litigation that accompanied that development changed the type of case and legal practice before the Supreme Court of Rhode Island.

In the early 1800's, Rhode Island was recovering from the Revolution and the War of 1812 and reorganizing its judiciary and its government. Prior to the Revolution the General Assembly exercised judicial power with the courts deciding the other cases left to them in the vacuum. Upon the completion of a trial, many matters were simply appealed to the General Assembly if a litigant felt that a fair trial had not been received. It was not until 1843 that the state adopted its new constitution. The General Assembly had the last word on every case of importance. Several trials could be had of the same subject matter with the same parties.

In the early days after the Revolution, one form of entertainment was the courtroom if there was a particularly good spectacle in the offing. The lawyers of the day rose to the occasion and many would argue for each side. The Rhode Island court rules in the early part of the nineteenth century seem to be based more upon the conditions of the times than upon the certain administration of justice. The judges would ride circuit between the courts in Washington, Kent, Newport, Bristol, and Providence Counties, spending at least a week in the various jurisdictions, making a social occasion of the visit. Consequently, they became acquainted with local problems and people of the locality. As the industrialization and railroads of the state increased, the habits of the judges changed, giving them a greater opportunity to exchange views and opinions on the increasingly more complex issues of the business world.

If a close examination is made of volume one of the *Rhode Island Reports,* one finds that in physical appearance it resembles any other report of its day. However, the edition appears to be a reprint of the earlier cases, and one wonders how much has been left out and how much was deemed worthy of printing.

Sidney S. Rider, the reporter, in his preface to the first volume of *Rhode Island Reports* lauds the work of Joseph K. Angell, the first reporter of the Supreme Court of Rhode Island who was appointed about 1847. The preface cites many of the treatises of Mr. Angell and is valuable for the insight it gives into the works used by the lawyers and the

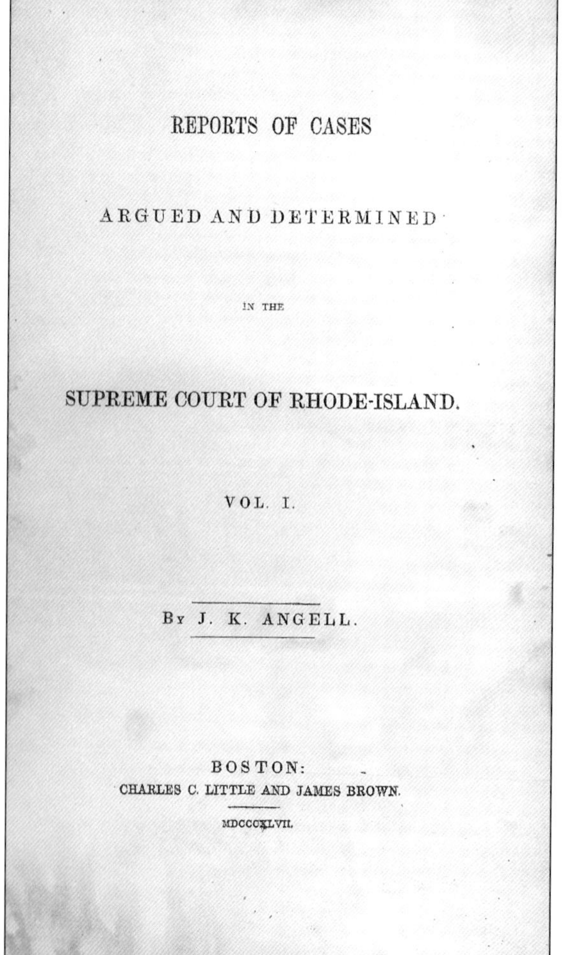

REPORTS OF CASES

ARGUED AND DETERMINED

IN THE

SUPREME COURT OF RHODE-ISLAND.

VOL. I.

By J. K. ANGELL.

BOSTON:
CHARLES C. LITTLE AND JAMES BROWN.
MDCCCXLVII.

The title page from volume 1 of the *Rhode Island Reports*, prepared by Joseph K. Angell and published in Boston by Little, Brown in 1847. The series extended through 122 volumes before it was absorbed by the *Atlantic Reporter* in 1980.

judges of the times. It points out that the recorded history of the court in the early nineteenth century was a haphazard affair with the records being scattered in the local town halls or in the minds of the judges. J. K. Angell was the scholar of Rhode Island history. The well-known treatises by Angell include first in 1824 *Law Relating to Water Courses*, then in 1826 *The Right of Property in Tide Waters and the Soil and Shores Thereof*, a second edition appearing in 1847. Chancellor James Kent of New York said of them that, "they were works which no intelligent lawyer could practice without." During the ensuing years Angell published many other well-regarded treatises on a variety of legal topics.

The learned Mr. Angell, who took over the duties of court reporter in 1845, the beginning years of this study, alas had little effect on the thinking of the courts of his native state during those years. What is missing from the introduction by the twentieth century reporter is the fact that in all of the first volume of the *Rhode Island Reports*, Angell is cited only a few times in approximately 200 cases. In fact, very few authorities are cited in the cases, which range from the March term in 1828 to the March term of 1851.

A good example of the lack of citations appears in the cases involving the right of "common seaweed." The right of common seaweed was due the owner of land. The seaweed was taken from the "common lot" situate in the town every year and at all times a year. The defendant had appropriated to himself one hundred loads of seaweed and sea manure which had been put there by the sea. *Kenyon* v. *Nichols, Jr.*, 1 R. I. 106 (March term 1848, Washington County, Haile, J.). The court rests its decision in part on Angell on Tide Waters. This case is unique in that various precedents are used which have been previously decided by the court but which are not available in the reports. Interestingly enough, the cited case used by the court for precedent, *Knowles* v. *Nichols*, is not reported nor is the term of the court in 1846 reported. In the case of *Peleg Bailey et al.* v. *Lemuel Sisson et al.*, 1 R. I. 233, decided in the August term of 1849 by Greene, C. J., the court is totally unaware of the previous decision in *Kenyon* v. *Nichols*, supra, and in its decision the court does not cite Angell or any other treatise of the time.

Chief Justice Richard Greene had a short memory, for in the February term of the court in Washington County in 1851 again appears another similar case, *Nathan G. Kenyon* v. *Jonathan Nichols*, 1 R. I. 412. Chief Justice Greene does not refer to either of the previous decisions of the court on the right of "common seaweed," even though both of the Kenyon cases were "actions on the case for an injury to the plaintiff's rights of common seaweed." The authority, Angell on Tide Waters, is not considered nor is it used for purposes of argument. Prior cases decided by the Rhode Island court do not appear in the decisions. A lack of references to the prior cases can be in part explained by the fact that the compilation in the appendix is confusing and misleading.

In criminal cases little authority is cited in support of the court's position, other than the general learning of the judge. In one case of "trespass for breaking and entering the close of the plaintiff and throwing down his fences and subverting his soil," the court dismissed the case against the town surveyor with passing reference to three somewhat similar cases, one

The lack of a legally trained judiciary prior to 1827 and legislative dominance over the courts until 1856 prompted Rhode Island litigants to forum-shop. Many continued to bring their cases to the federal circuit court where the renowned Justice Joseph Story (1779–1845) presided. Story rode the first federal circuit (which included Rhode Island) as part of his Supreme Court duties. His impact on both American and Rhode Island law was considerable.

of which came from nearby Connecticut: *Simmons* v. *Cornell*, 1 R. I. 519. In the case of *Humes* v. *Tabor et al.*, 1 R. I. 464, the plaintiff petitioned for a new trial. The court's decision turned upon whether or not the search of the premises for the stolen goods was conducted in a lawful manner, which in turn depended upon the search warrant, which in turn depended upon the sufficiency of the complaint. The court, Greene, C. J. presiding, cast aside the arguments of counsel and, without referring to one citation, made his decision upholding the sufficiency of the complaint and the correctness of the search. In *Albert W. Snow, Ex Parte*, R. I. 360, defendant was charged with embezzling $100,000, a huge sum for the time. The issue before the court was the amount of bail. The only legal reference in the case was cited by counsel for petitioner, *Chitty's Criminal Law*, which said that "the bail should be apportioned to the pecuniary ability of the accused and to the penalty with which the crime of which he is accused is punished." The court in its opinion, per curiam, stated, "If you look only to the fine (five thousand dollars) and determine the bail, the defaulter for fifty thousand dollars has only to pay over his five thousand and escape with the remaining forty-five thousand. The bail required ought to be such as will afford a reasonable security that the prisoner will abide the sentence of the court, should he be found guilty." 1 R. I. 363.

Other reported cases involve breach of promise to marry, will construction, land partition, mortgage redemption, as well as divorce, residence of paupers, and the sale of liquor without a license. The literary quality is poor, as is the reasoning. It is interesting to note that there is only one major case involving an industrial issue. At this time mills were appearing on Rhode Island waterways, and yet there seems to be no litigation on the subject.

The one major industrial case which appears is *Hodges* v. *New England Screw Company*, 1 R. I. 321. In this case the court, Chief Justice Greene presiding, is sitting in Providence; the array of counsel is formidable. There are three lawyers for plaintiff and two for defendant. Samuel Ames, for the plaintiff, is later to become Chief Justice, succeeded in that position by Charles Bradley, who represents defendant. The briefs of the lawyers are excellent and are reprinted fully in the *Reports*. A scholarly aspect envelops Chief Justice Greene, who cites Angell and Ames on Corporations, in support of the proposition that, "If the corporation is under the control of the guilty directors, the stockholders may sue for a fraudulent breach of trust." Earlier in the opinion Greene states that the directors are "liable in equity as trustees for a fraudulent breach of trust." After these two statements, he returns to his usual form and holds that, "This power over corporations, not being vested in this court by law, we think it far better and safer that the General Assembly should confer it, if it be thought for the public good, rather than that we should assume it." Although there are other cases involving banks and businesses, this is the only major case involving a substantial amount of money. Curiosity leads one to suspect that there must have been other interests that became involved with the courts, but for some reason were not reported.

Research of a most limited nature reveals that at this time the Federal Circuit Court had as its presiding judge, Justice Joseph Story. Apparently, plaintiffs would contrive to obtain diversity of citizenship by moving to Connecticut and bringing their cases before Judge Story, who was "learned in the law" and was the leading figure of the period between 1812 and 1845 in Rhode Island area courts.

Chief Justice Thomas Durfee of Tiverton (1826–1901), son of Chief Justice Job Durfee, served as the court reporter following Angell's resignation in 1849. By the time volume 15 was prepared, the younger Durfee had become chief justice. Durfee was the author of *Gleanings from the Judicial History of Rhode Island*, published in 1883 by Sidney Rider.

Another reason for the diverse jurisprudence in the reported cases is due to the fact that the Rhode Island constitution was adopted in 1843 and for the first time exclusive judicial power was vested in the Supreme Court of the state and in such inferior courts as from time to time may be ordained and established by the General Assembly. It was not until 1854, though, that the independence of the court from the Assembly was tested. In January of 1854, a bill was passed by the Assembly reversing and annulling the sentence of Thomas W. Dorr for treason, and directing the clerk of the Supreme Court to write across the record of judgment the words, "Reversed and annulled by the order of the General Assembly at their January session A. D. 1854." Soon after this bill was passed there was a change of administrations; the new officials requested an advisory opinion from the court as to the constitutionality of the act. The justices found it unconstitutional. In the case of *Taylor* v. *Place*, 4 R. I., 324 (1856), Chief Justice Ames finally settled the question by denying all judicial power of the Assembly.

During this period in time, judges were appointed by the legislature and not by general election from the public at large. The justices of the court now consisted of a Chief Judge and three associate judges.

The change that took place over the intervening fifty years is best described by Chief Justice Thomas Durfee writing in 1883:

> Of course many kinds of cases familiar a century ago, are familiar still; but there are kinds, familiar then, which have ceased to be familiar now and kinds unfamiliar then, which have become familiar now; as there are also cases, now continually in court, of a kind that was then unknown. Cases in constitutional law are of the kind last named. Cases in the law of fire or life insurance, so frequent now were very rare fifty years ago. The Law of Railroads which is now a study in itself has grown up within less than fifty years. The law of corporations, though an old head of the law, has greatly expanded within the same period, developing new doctrines and distinctions. A similar remark may be made of the law of equitable estoppel and trade marks. The law under which cities and towns have become civilly liable for their neglects of municipal duty, is a creation of the present century.

In spite of Justice Durfee's pronouncements, the case of *Carroll* v. *Rigney*, 15 R. I. 81, (1885) is a typical 1830 type case concerning trespass for injuries to the plaintiff's barn, caused by a horse kicking down a stall, with the defendant contending that the horse being seized by the colic, rolled about while in great pain and kicked down the stall. Instead of general reasoning of Chief Justice Greene, there are now case citations from New York and South Carolina as well as references to *Addison on Torts* and *Greenleaf on Evidence*, a standby of the 1830's. There are now appeals taken from the court of common pleas; municipalities are being sued for defects in their highways and new treatises, such as *Dillon on Municipal Corporations*, are cited as authority along with cases from Kansas, Vermont, New Hampshire, Missouri, Illinois, Connecticut, Indiana, England, and upper Canada, *Hampson* v. *Taylor*, 15 R. I. 83. New among the cases are appeals from the probate courts of the various towns; previously the town officials functioned as probate courts, *Johnson* v. *Johnson*, 15 R. I. 109.

Although advisory opinions were occasionally requested from the Supreme Court, few were reported in Rhode Island. Fifty years later there are numerous requests for advisory opinions from the court concerning such matters as the legal election of town officials for the town of Cranston, *Budlong et al.*, petitioners, 15 R. I. 332, and the constitutionality of a statute forbidding the sale of liquor on the sabbath, *State* v. *Hattie Clark*, 15 R. I. 383. In addition opinions were requested from the court on the legality of the appointment of the superintendent of the census, in re *The Census Superintendent*, 15 R. I., 615; on the question of a plurality of electors, in re *The Plurality Elections*, 15 R. I. 617, as well as in cases involving the election of a representative to the Congress of the United States, in re *The Congressional Election*, 15 R. I. 624. The court through its decisions now had a decisive input into the election and political process. This was a full circle from the position where the Assembly exercised judicial power before the constitution of 1843.

True to Durfee's description, there is considerably more litigation involving corporations and insurance companies. The court is more sophisticated and its opinions are solidly researched with emphasis on prior Rhode Island decisions. By 1885, the railroad enables the judges to travel to the different county courts and to return in one day. No longer are the judges isolated from one another in the country inns and friends' homes for weeks and perhaps a month or more at a time while they hold court. The railroad has brought not only a physical presence to Rhode Island, it has caused a more cohesive intellectual presence to form in Providence. The opinions are more uniform and there is a more organized bar.

One of the interesting aspects is the requirement for admission to the bar in the 1830's as compared with the requirements in 1885. In 1837 to be admitted to the bar one had to have received a classical education plus two years of study with a member of the Rhode Island Bar, or if the applicant had not received a classical education, he had to have studied three years with a member of the Rhode Island Bar, plus in all cases have a good moral character. No mention was made of attorneys from other jurisdictions. In 1885 the requirements are good moral character, attainment of 21 years of age, a classical education, and study in a law office for two years without practicing law or having other employment. Two years of study in a law school of "the country" plus a six months internship was also acceptable.

The lack of a classical education still meant three years of law study. In all cases the applicant now had to "sustain a satisfactory examination by an examining committee appointed by the Supreme Court." For the first time there is provision for admitting attorneys from other states. These attorneys could not be admitted unless they had been in practice for three years, studied for the required length of time for Rhode Island attorneys, and in addition, they had to sustain a satisfactory examination by the examining committee. Only those with more than ten years of practice could be admitted on motion, without examination. The rules of the court also included a new provision: attorneys may not, upon the "pain of being struck from the roll, become bail in any cause depending in, or surety in any recognizance taken by the Supreme Court or Court of Common Pleas."

The sophistication of the court is apparent and its upgrading is due in all likelihood to the higher qualifications it required of the attorneys who practiced before it. Commercial litigation involving actions against railroads and other corporations, along with the cases involving company against company, must have proved more lucrative for the attorneys. Judge Durfee laments: "Latterly the gains of successful civil business are so large that the ambitious young lawyer has become ambitious of money more than of fame, and disdains a practice in which the profits are precarious. The effect of this on the administration of justice is probably not a matter for regret; for, in consequence of it, guilt is surer of its desert and innocence, now that it has acquired the privilege of testifying in its own behalf, seldom stands in any serious jeopardy."

In these fifty or so years, the development of the law in Rhode Island was influenced by Chancellor Kent and J. K. Angell; however, it was the industrialization of the state that brought the lawyers and judges into closer contact. Untouched by the Civil War, its cities whole and unscarred, the Rhode Island court system continued on its path to legal excellence and scholarly opinions. In these few short years, the Supreme Court became a powerful influence rightfully taking its influential place in Rhode Island government.

20

The career of Samuel Ames illustrates the incestuous nature of Rhode Island politics and the ironies that often flow from what political scientist Duane Lockard once termed our "politics of intimacy." During the Dorr Rebellion Ames was a leading pundit and pamphleteer for the Law and Order party. He was also a leader of the state militia during its defense of the arsenal at the Dexter Training Grounds when that facility was menaced in May 1842 by a force under People's Governor Thomas Wilson Dorr. Yet Dorr and Ames had been schoolmates at Phillips Academy (Andover) and allies in the formation of the reform-oriented Constitutional party in 1834. In 1839 Ames had married Mary Throop Dorr, the famed rebel's younger sister.

During the rebellion that Dorr led and Ames opposed, the establishment of an independent judiciary had been a leading goal of the reformers. The People's Constitution, mainly drafted by Dorr, diminished the power of the General Assembly by providing for a clear and strict separation of powers according to the three-branch principle (Article III), barred the Assembly from exercising its traditional judicial functions (Article IX, 4), and gave stronger tenure to the judiciary (Article XI, 3). The Whiggish Law and Order constitution that was eventually adopted did not embrace the doctrine of strict separation of powers, and it was much less decisive in its approach to separation of powers and judicial independence, so the opinion by Ames in *Taylor* v. *Place* (1856) had less explicit constitutional support than if the People's Constitution had been the basic law of the state.

Actually, the high court had moved towards *Taylor* in 1854, two years prior to Ames's accession. In an advisory opinion to the Senate and House of Representatives (3 R.I. 299), the Supreme Court under Chief Justice Richard Ward Greene vindicated Dorr's position on judicial independence while delivering a setback to Dorr's legal rehabilitation. This incongruity occurred because the act of the Assembly the court found unconstitutional was an 1854 Democratic-sponsored measure reversing and annulling the verdict in the Rhode Island Supreme Court treason trial of 1844 that sent Dorr to prison.

When the following article was published in 1965, C. Peter Magrath was a professor of political science at Brown University. He subsequently left Rhode Island for other teaching assignments and eventually became president of the University of Missouri. His most significant work in legal history is *Yazoo: Law and Politics in the New Republic, The Case of Fletcher v. Peck*, published in 1966.

Samuel Ames, the "Great Chief Justice."

Samuel Ames: The Great Chief Justice of Rhode Island

C. Peter Magrath

Nineteen sixty-five is the hundredth anniversary of the death of Samuel Ames, chief justice of the Supreme Court of Rhode Island. It provides an appropriate occasion to re-examine his life and achievements which today are buried, half-forgotten, in dusty law reports. There is another reason, however, why Samuel Ames deserves our serious consideration: he is an outstanding representative of a remarkable group of state judges who too long have been neglected by lawyers, historians, and students of our legal system. Too long we have emphasized only the United States Supreme Court, as if all the significant law and the history of its development could be found in the *United States Reports*, with perhaps a short bow being made to Chancellor James Kent of New York. In fact, the decisions and opinions of such nineteenth-century state judges as Cooley in Michigan, Doe in New Hampshire, Gibson and Tilghman in Pennsylvania, Roane in Virginia, Ruffin in North Carolina, Parsons and Shaw in Massachusetts—and Samuel Ames in Rhode Island—are at least as significant as the better publicized decisions of Marshall, Story, Taney, and Waite on the federal Supreme Court.

Ames clerked under the supervision of attorney Samuel W. Bridgham (1774–1840), who became the first mayor of Providence in 1832 under the initial city charter. Bridgham, state attorney general from 1813 to 1817, was a reformer who advocated free public education, temperance, and relief for the poor as means to combat the urban disorder that had prompted Providence to adopt a mayor-council form of government.

Samuel Ames was born in Providence on September 6, 1806, the son of Samuel Ames, Sr., and Anne Becker Checkley, a well-established colonial family. Samuel's father was a merchant, and he was able to provide his son with an excellent education. Samuel first studied in the Providence public schools and later at Phillips Academy in Andover, Massachusetts. He entered Brown University in 1819, at the age of thirteen, and was graduated in 1823. Young Samuel Ames then studied law. He read law for two years in the office of General Samuel W. Bridgham, one of the finest lawyers in the state during the early nineteenth century. He studied also for a year at the nation's first law school, the famous Litchfield Law School in Connecticut, established by Judge Tapping Reeve in 1784.

In 1826 Samuel Ames was admitted to the Rhode Island Bar and quickly established his credentials as one of the state's ablest attorneys. One measure of the success which Ames attained was his large practice; eventually the demand for his services compelled Ames to open a branch office in Boston. By the 1840s Ames was a leader of the Rhode Island Bar, and he frequently appeared before the United States Supreme Court. Another measure of his success is that at the age of twenty-six he was asked by the distinguished legal scholar, Joseph K. Angell, to co-author the book *Treatise on the Law of Private Corporations Aggregate*, which made its first appearance in 1832. The title may seem ponderous, but Angell and Ames on Corporations became a standard authority on every aspect of the law governing private corporations; it went through ten editions and sold 12,000 copies—a large figure in those days.

As might be expected, Samuel Ames rooted himself deeply in the city of Providence. He was an Episcopalian and one of the founders of St. Stephen's Church. He served for many years as a vestryman and as a teacher of its Sunday School. There is, in fact, a vivid sketch of Ames on his way to teach Sunday School that has been preserved in a description given by his early partner, Abraham Payne. As he started off to the Sunday School at St. Stephen's Church, Payne recalled,

> in his heavy lion's skin overcoat with his Bible under his arm, for his duties at the school, he reminded me of those churchmen of the middle age who, though not unmindful of the duties to which they were especially consecrated, were yet more at home when intrusted with the command of armies.

In Providence, too, Samuel Ames established his family. In 1838 he married Mary Throop Dorr, the sister of one Thomas Wilson Dorr, a fact, as we shall see, that makes for what our newspapers like to call a human interest story. Ames was thoroughly devoted to his wife and she was to him; they gave birth to a daughter Mary and to four sons—Sullivan, William, Edward, and Samuel.

According to the labels commonly (and too casually) thrown about today, Ames would probably be called a conservative. But perhaps it is best simply to refer to him as he was, as a partisan of the Whig Party in the days when the flamboyant Henry Clay was the idol of many millions of Americans. Ames was a man of property and substance, and in an age of emerging capitalism much of his practice quite naturally was geared to the service of business needs. His clientele, for example, included that ultimate symbol of nineteenth-century American capitalism, the railroad. Perhaps the most revealing glimpse of how well acclimated Samuel Ames was to the capitalist environment occurs in a passage in the treatise he and Joseph Angell prepared on corporations. There, in a section defining the word *corporation*, we are told that "the *United States* may be termed a corporation" because "they are a collective invisible body, which can act and be seen only in the acts of those who administer the affairs of the government, and also their agents duly appointed."

In the days of Ames partisan political participation was regarded as a civic duty to be undertaken by those who had social and economic stature. Samuel Ames exemplifies this ideal. He served in the Providence City Council; from 1841 to 1851 he sat as a Whig representative in the state House of Representatives; in 1845 and 1846 he was Speaker of the House. During the 1850s Ames served on a number of state commissions. He was a member of a commission which revised the Massachusetts-Rhode Island boundary, chairman of an important commission which revised the state's statutory laws, and, in 1861, a delegate to the Washington Peace Conference, a conference which failed to repress the irrepressible conflict.

There is much that could be said about the political career of Samuel Ames. I will, however, confine myself to discussing briefly his behavior during those exciting events which, with some exaggeration, we call the "Dorr War." I say "with some exaggeration" because, if we are to have wars, the Dorr War represents my favorite kind of war—soldiers marched and paraded but fortunately only one person lost his life.

An excellent study by Professor Peter J. Coleman of the University of Wisconsin has shown that the issues underlying the Dorr War were more complex than is commonly supposed. It was not only a matter of conflict between oppressed workers, foreign-born Catholics, townsmen, and Democratic Party members on one side, and rich employers, native-born Protestants, farmers, and Whig Party members on the other side. This was part of the story, but only a part. The issues that led to the Dorr War cut across class, ethnic, religious, geographic, party and, indeed, family lines.

Dorr himself was a moderate—a reformer, not a radical—and the objectives of his movement undoubtedly strike most of us as eminently reasonable ones. He sought a reapportionment of the legislature to give the growing cities more equitable representation, an expanded suffrage that would eliminate the freehold requirement written into the statute books, a bill of rights, and an independent judiciary. In the short run the reform movement failed; the Dorr rebellion collapsed harmlessly. In the long run, however, the objectives of the reformers prevailed. Certainly Dorr's opponents felt the pressure that he and his supporters generated. In sponsoring the Constitution of 1843, the Law and Order Party made possible an expansion of the suffrage which eventually stimulated democratic reforms.

What, in any event, was the relationship of Samuel Ames to the reform movement? He opposed it, though he apparently was not a die-hard old Charter man, for he supported the changes adopted in the Constitution of 1843. Despite the fact that his wife was the sister of Thomas Dorr and that his friend, Joseph Angell, was prominently identified with the reform movement, Ames stood firmly with the Law and Order Party. Under the pen name *Town Borne* he wrote scores of articles for the *Providence Journal* in 1841 and 1842, which deftly ridiculed the suffrage reformers. (These articles are collected in a specially bound volume located in the John D. Rockefeller Library of Brown University; the volume includes a miscellany of newspaper clippings on events in which Ames played a part. Most of the items concern the Dorr War.) He voted with the Law and Order Party in the state legislature. During the disturbances in the spring of 1842 he served as quartermaster general with the loyal state militia. Ames, in fact, was in command inside the state arsenal in Providence on the night of May 17–18, 1842, when Dorr's rag-tag army made its half-hearted and completely unsuccessful attack on the arsenal.

Samuel Ames knew how to speak effectively, and he could hit hard. Consider this excerpt from a General Assembly debate in 1841. Ames was rebutting the arguments of Samuel Y. Atwell, a strong Dorr supporter. Atwell had said that if the suffrage were not reformed, a violent revolution might follow, even though he would deplore it and would

To commemorate the victory of the Law and Order party in the Dorr Rebellion, Ames and others composed a satirical epic poem called "The Dorriad," which ridiculed the reform effort. Among those assisting Ames in writing the spoof were *Providence Journal* editor Henry Bowen Anthony and prominent attorney and future U.S. congressman Thomas A. Jenckes.

The Dorriad.

THE ATTACK ON THE ARSENAL.

TH' impatient chief[1] looked on with ire,
Blanched was his cheek, but tenfold fire
Was flashing in his eye.
He threw his martial cloak aside,
And, *waddling* up—he meant to *stride*—
"Give me the torch," with fury cried,
"And, d—— it, let me try!"
He seized the match with eager hand,
While backward his brave soldiers stand;
Three times he waved it in the air,
The cursed Algerines to scare,
And bid them all for death prepare;
Then down the glowing match-rope thrust,
As though he'd have the cannon burst.

2

side with the constituted authorities. Ames responded to Atwell's statement with this comment:

> As to revolution and fear of revolution, which the gentleman suggested, and said that he would resist with all his might; he gave me great encouragement. He will be with us if such a time comes; he will fight on our side. And he will be of great assistance. He is a gentleman of great influence in this State; he has held a high military office under this General Assembly. Aye, Mr. Speaker, he has fought shoulder to shoulder in our militia with the gentleman who is now sleeping by your side. (The Attorney General was nodding at the time in his chair beside the Speaker, but was aroused by the peals of laughter which followed this allusion.)

Or, consider another example. During the Dorr War Ames and his friends put together a number of satirical pamphlets, most notably *The Dorriad* and *The Great Slocum Dinner*, which roundly mocked Thomes W. Dorr. In one piece of doggerel Dorr is labeled as *The Caesar of Rhode Island* in verses that read:

> The quick, decisive mind of Dorr,
> No chains of custom hampered,
> Like Caesar's, short his tale of war,
> HE CAME, HE SAW, HE SCAMPERED.

The testimony of his contemporaries suggests also that Ames was a positive and strong man. Prominent in politics and law and well-read in literature and theology, Ames was not blessed with the virtue of being able to suffer fools gladly. "His consciousness of his own great powers," one fellow lawyer recalled, "made him frequently impatient in dealing with men of less capacity." This, no doubt, was a flaw in his personality, but it was made tolerable by the fact that Samuel Ames was intellectually powerful. Conceit rooted in ability is tolerable; conceit rooted in mediocrity is insufferable.

Ames, fortunately, had the saving quality of a sense of humor. On Christmas morning, 1856, he sent a letter to his son, Sullivan Dorr Ames. Sully, as the family called him, was then a first-year cadet at the United States Naval Academy. "I wish you a merry Christmas," he wrote,

> and send two dollars pasted above, from your uncle Sullivan—sent with other money to the *children* without distinction; and so we send to you your share. If not a *child* send it back for the others. We do not see how you can lawfully spend so much pocket money—some 40 dollars in 14 weeks. You must be more careful if you would have a penny in hand.

He was, too, a man of sensitive emotions. The reports of a number of incidents involving Ames bring this out, but the most conclusive proof is contained in his own writings. Apparently, although the reasons are not clear, Ames suffered business losses and personal embarrassments from former friends in the years between 1854 and 1856. He became depressed and felt alienated from the world. To escape from his gloom, he gave his spare hours to writing a thoroughly romantic novel. Its purpose, he declared in a preface addressed to his wife, was "to create an ideal world... in which the men and women should be and do just as I would have them." This he did. His unpublished book of sixteen manuscript chapters is called "Arthur Ledgeley or Some Passages in the Life of a Lawyer." He subtitled it, "A Love Story," and, appropriately enough, his heroes lived happily ever after. Ames idealized love "in its best and purest form," and he asked his wife not to "think lightly of me for this endeavor to regain my youth of heart by depicting the 'great'-heaven-ordained passion...."

On June 26, 1856, the Grand Committee of the General Assembly elected Samuel Ames to be chief justice of the Supreme Court; undoubtedly his former service in the state legislature was not a liability. The salary provided for Chief Justice Ames was $2,500. To ease his financial sacrifice in giving up his law practice, he was also appointed reporter of the Court's decisions—for another $500 a year. Interestingly, the state's two leading newspapers, one Democratic and the other Republican, favored his election. The Democratic *Providence Post* declared that the selection of Ames gives "satisfaction to nearly all classes of people"; the Republican *Providence Journal* commented that the state judiciary would be strengthened by his appointment.

Why did Ames go on the bench and thus abandon his lucrative practice? I think we can safely believe the answer he gave to a friend who asked him this question:

> I never designed to continue at the Bar all my days. If I continued practice to the age of fifty years, I did not design to continue it longer. I do not like to be at the Bar. I do not desire to be compelled to make the worse appear the better reason.

Samuel Ames served as chief justice of the Rhode Island Supreme Court for a comparatively short period, from 1856 to 1865, which makes his accomplishments all the more remarkable. As late as the 1840s some of the state's judges refused to publish their opinions, claiming that oral statements from the bench were adequate. Chief Justice Ames, believing that reasoned judicial opinions were an essential part of a civilized legal system, set an example for all of the state's judges. He saw to it that he and his associates wrote full opinions on all the legal questions argued before the Supreme Court. Equally important, as reporter he placed the reporting of the Court's decisions on a thoroughly professional plane, carefully reporting both the essential arguments of opposing counsel and the factual circumstances of the case. As one of Ames's successors as chief justice, John Henry Stiness, has written, a comparison of his reports in volumes four through part of eight of the *Rhode Island Reports* "with the preceding three volumes and indeed with other reports of that period, show that his were compiled by a masterhand." In addition, he introduced new and more orderly procedural rules of practice. The influence of Ames on the quality of the Supreme Court was quickly reflected in a sharp rise in its case load. During the first half of the last century, partly because federal Supreme Court Justice Joseph Story presided in this judicial circuit and partly because our state supreme court lacked distinction, most litigants maneuvered to have their equity and commercial suits tried in the federal court. After Ames's accession the imbalance ended, and there was a marked rise in the number of cases tried in the state courts.

None of these accomplishments, important as they are, ultimately account for the greatness of Samuel Ames. It is rather to a case, *Taylor* v. *Place* (1856), that we must turn in order to understand why the chief justice deserves to be ranked as one of our most significant judicial figures. For until Ames became chief justice of the state, the Rhode Island judiciary was not truly independent of the legislature. The reasons extend back into our colonial history when the judicial and legislative powers were freely mingled and jointly exercised by the General Assembly. Well into the 1840s the judiciary was subservient to the legislature. The legislature granted divorces, passed probate and bankruptcy laws, annulled criminal convictions, and in effect over-ruled the state courts by authorizing new trials in civil suits. Indeed, John Whipple, a well-known lawyer of the state, in 1829 boasted that the Rhode Island General Assembly was "the best chancery court in the world" while arguing before the Supreme Court of the United States in *Wilkinson* v. *Leland*.

Within his first term on the Court Chief Justice Ames and his three associates were squarely presented with the question of the judiciary's relation to the legislature. The case was *Taylor* v. *Place*. The G. and D. Taylor Company initiated two suits against a manufacturing company in the Providence County Court of Common Pleas for a recovery of debts. Two men by the name of Place, who were acting as garnishees for the debtor, filed affidavits disclosing that they held certain properties of the manufacturing company. As a consequence, Taylor began an action against Place to recover the sum which the affidavits had revealed to be in the hands of the garnishees. Taylor won a verdict and a financial award. At this point, Place, as had often been done in the past, successfully appealed to the General Assembly for a law ordering a new trial and authorizing the court to receive new affidavits; the garnishees claimed that their original affidavits had been mistaken. The Court of Common Pleas complied with the law, and on a retrial issued a judgment in favor of Place.

Now it was Taylor who was aggrieved, and he appealed to the Supreme Court of Chief Justice Ames. The legal dispute was really quite simple. Could the legislature constitutionally pass laws which upset the verdicts of courts? Under the Constitution of 1843 the executive, legislative, and judicial powers are distributed among three separate branches of government; the judicial power, for example, is vested in the supreme and inferior courts. But the Constitution also contains a provision stating that "the general assembly shall continue to exercise the powers they have heretofore exercised, unless prohibited in this constitution." Since the Assembly had often exercised its powers in such a way as to upset court orders, was the law that decreed a new trial in the case of Taylor and Place, a law prohibited by the Constitution of 1843? This question, while simple, raised a momentous issue. Taylor and Place were not the only parties involved. Standing behind them were the real parties to the case—the legislative and the judicial branches of the state government. Between these two parties the issue was a profound one: was the judiciary to be a co-equal and independent branch of government, or was it to be, ultimately, subservient to the legislature?

Speaking on behalf of a unanimous court, Chief Justice Ames declared that the Assembly's law decreeing a new trial was unconstitutional. Although the legislature had traditionally interfered with the decisions of courts, he skillfully drew on various provisions of the Constitution to build a powerful argument that the judicial power was to be exercised by courts alone. It was not to be exercised by the courts and the legislature together—with the General Assembly sitting as a sort of super supreme court. Nor was the chief justice impressed by the fact that, despite the provisions of the Constitution, the legislature had continued to exercise judicial power:

> ...our short and true reply is, that the exercise of judicial, and especially of chancery powers, *is* prohibited to them by the constitution; and that we must be false to history, right reason, the settled rules of judicial exposition, the established meaning of the language of the constitution as given unvaryingly by the highest authorities, and with that meaning adopted by the people in adopting the constitution, and so false both to the people and the constitution, if we come to any other conclusion.

The Ames opinion in *Taylor* v. *Place* is distinguished by its masterful analysis of the nature of the judicial power. The chief justice wisely noted that "it is difficult to draw and apply the precise line separating the different powers of government." He realized that in performing their own distinctive functions each branch of government inescapably exercised some of the power characteristic of its fellow departments. But, he wrote, "to hear and decide adversary suits at law and in equity, with the power of rendering judgments and entering up decrees according to the decision, to be executed by the process and power of the tribunal deciding... *is* the exercise of the *judicial* power, in the constitutional sense." And this power he reserved exclusively for the courts.

While *Taylor* v. *Place* deserves admiration for the soundness of its reasoning, it also deserves recognition as a shrewd assertion of judicial power. In many ways it is reminiscent of the performance of Chief Justice John Marshall in that landmark case of our federal constitutional law, *Marbury* v. *Madison*. Like Marshall, Chief Justice Ames asserted in uncompromising terms the independence of the judiciary and its power to void unconstitutional legislative acts. Like Marshall in *Marbury* v. *Madison*, he did so in a case where the assertion of judicial power would be most logical and least controversial. The context of *Taylor* v. *Place*, after all, was a legislative interference in a *judicial* case.

Naturally enough, Ames's decision provoked some muttering. One newspaper editorial called it "ridiculously unsound," and said that it wrongly deprived the Assembly of its traditional "judicial and *quasi* judicial powers." The same editorial went so far as to condemn the opinion as extra-judicial! There was resistance in the legislature, but there were also allies of the judiciary in the General Assembly. In 1859 an attempt was made to pass a law reversing a controversial decision of the Supreme Court, but it was beaten back, and the failure of this bill indirectly confirmed the ruling in *Taylor* v. *Place*. The case was *Ives* v. *Hazard*, 4 R.I. 14 (1856), in which the Court ruled that Charles T. Hazard was obligated to carry out the terms of a contract for the sale of a piece of land to Robert H. Ives. Although the Ives case was decided before Ames became chief justice, he was deeply involved in the prolonged Ives-Hazard dispute. He had served as counsel for Ives in his successful appeal to the Supreme Court in 1856, and subsequently, as the Court's reporter, he reported the *Ives* v. *Hazard* case. This led Hazard to claim that there had been irregularities in Ames's reporting of the case; indeed, he charged that the chief justice had libeled him. After a good deal of pamphleteering and an investigation by a joint committee of the General Assembly, Ames was wholly exonerated of all charges of impropriety.

When Ames died a few years later there was no longer any dissent from the conclusion of the *Providence Journal* that his decision in the case of Taylor and Place, by freeing the judiciary from legislative control, built a "bulwark" for the liberties of the citizens of Rhode Island. Ironically, then, the man who opposed Thomas W. Dorr became the judge who furthered one of Dorr's objectives—judicial independence.

Although Chief Justice Ames strongly asserted judicial power, he believed that the judiciary should use its power sparingly whenever it evaluated the constitutionality of legislative acts. I refer here to such judicial gems as *In the Matter of Dorrance Street* (1856), *State* v. *Paul* (1858), and *State* v. *Keeran* (1858). Ames believed, in other words, that courts should uphold the validity of controversial legislation unless it could be shown that the laws violated specific constitutional guarantees. In particular he rejected the arguments of business attorneys, which were already becoming a commonplace in the 1850s, that the regulation of private property could often be voided on the vague ground that it violated "due process of law." The rights of property, Ames believed, were not absolute and unqualified; subject to explicit constitutional prohibition, property rights were open to legislative restriction in the name of "the greater right of the community, to have them so exercised within it as to be compatible with its well-being. As he put it in a pungent example in a decision upholding the constitutionality of a confiscatory prohibition law, a person cannot "use his pick for burglary, or his sword for murder, merely because they are his."

Not only did Chief Justice Ames refuse to use vague constitutional provisions to place limits on the state police power, but he insisted that the best guard against unwise legislation lay in the vigilance of the people in electing wise legislators. "In a popular government, as in all governments," he declared in *State* v. *Keeran*, "power must be reposed somewhere; and he does not take in its theory who does not see, that in the power of the people at short intervals to change their rulers and agents, consists their main security against the dangerous and excessive exercise of the powers necessarily vested in them." Ironically, again, the man who opposed the popular party of Thomas W. Dorr became the judge who spoke for another of

Dorr's grand objectives—popular sovereignty. Those who think that the behavior of judges is easily deduced from their earlier social and political associations would do well to ponder the career of Samuel Ames as politician and Samuel Ames as judge.

In 1865 Ames's health became poor. He resigned from the Supreme Court on November 15, and he died a few weeks later, on December 20, 1865. Samuel Ames was called by his generation "The Great Chief Justice," a tribute no doubt intended to compare him favorably with perhaps the greatest American Chief Justice of all—John Marshall. Historians delight in revising the judgment of earlier generations, but in the case of Samuel Ames I think we are compelled to confirm the judgment of those who knew him: Samuel Ames was the Great Chief Justice of Rhode Island. He has, moreover, left us with a valuable legacy. By contributing to the construction of a strong and independent judiciary, Chief Justice Ames helped create a system of law—of ordered liberty—that is well worthy of the respect and obedience of our citizens.

As for Samuel Ames, he unwittingly wrote his own epitaph in a decision where he said:

> For once, and for all, and everywhere, we desire it to be understood, that we look upon the highest judicial station as a station of infamy and disgrace, if it does not elevate us above every fear but that of doing wrong, and above every inclination but that of doing right.

Chief Justice Ames fulfilled his own high standards—he pursued "the better reason"—and this is the basis of his greatness.

The attempt on the Arsenal on the night of May 17th

Upper room of the Arsenal, on the night of the 17th of May.

The quartermaster general of the Rhode Island militia, Ames was one of the leading defenders of the state arsenal at the Dexter Training Grounds in Providence when his brother-in-law Thomas Dorr attempted to seize it on the night of May 17, 1842.

21

In this excerpt from his anecdotal *Reminiscences of the Rhode Island Bar*, attorney Abraham Payne noted the vast changes that had occurred in the legal profession during that span of years from 1840 to the mid-1880s when he practiced law in Providence. Payne, according to one reviewer, wrote legal profiles "in a charming gossipy style" that "present pictures of contemporary life that are unsurpassed by any other literary memorials emanating from a Rhode Island pen. Anecdotes of leading members of the bar are told, with incidents about peculiar cases, while allusions to political events and to well known men are frequent."

Payne himself was an important figure in nineteenth-century local law and politics. He held various positions in Providence city government, served a term as state attorney general in 1863–64, was one of the commissioners who prepared the 1872 digest of state laws, and sat in the state legislature as a representative from Providence. In addition to his legal and political achievements, he was known as an orator and delivered the principal address upon the dedication of Providence City Hall in 1878. A loyal graduate of Brown, Payne served as president of that university's alumni association in the early 1880s.

Payne's obvious hero among Rhode Island's mid-nineteenth-century attorneys was General Thomas F. Carpenter. A former adjutant general, an ally of Thomas Wilson Dorr, and a Democrat in politics, Carpenter was his party's unsuccessful candidate for governor in 1840, 1842, and 1843. Carpenter joined in *The Nine Lawyers' Opinion* in defending the legitimacy of the People's Constitution, and in 1844 he volunteered his services as co-counsel for the Gordons in their trial for murder. In 1850 he created a major stir among his colleagues at the bar by converting to Roman Catholicism.

Among the other lawyers mentioned by Payne, perhaps the most talented and respected was John Whipple, a prominent Whig in whose Providence law office young Thomas Dorr performed his clerkship. Whipple was a leading light in the successful Law and Order campaign to repudiate the

People's Constitution; he was a close associate of Justice Joseph Story; and he joined with Daniel Webster to defeat the Dorrite claims in the case of *Luther* v. *Borden* (1849). According to Payne, Whipple "was a student of history and a profound thinker on all social, moral, and political questions." Payne also recalled that a "very good judge, who had heard the arguments of Mr. Whipple and Mr. Webster in a celebrated case in this State, told me that he thought Mr. Whipple was quite the equal of his great antagonist, and Mr. Webster is reputed to have said that John Whipple and Jeremiah Mason [of New Hampshire] were the two ablest opponents he had ever met at the bar."

Reminiscences of the Rhode Island Bar [1840-1883]

Abraham Payne

On the fourteenth day of September, 1840, I entered the office of General Thomas F. Carpenter as a student at law. On this fifteenth day of December, 1883, I commence what I intend to make a record of some of my reminiscences of law and lawyers in Rhode Island.

The office of General Carpenter was a single large room, up one short flight of stairs, in the building at the junction of Westminster and Weybosset streets, known as the "Turk's Head." The room was uncarpeted, it contained a moderate bookcase with a small collection of law books, an old-fashioned desk and a very limited supply of pigeon holes, a large table covered with green baize cloth, an old-fashioned cylinder stove, a few common chairs and a long wooden settee. At one end of the room was a coal bin, and there was a small safe. I may mention as illustrating a change in the habits of law students that during the two years while I remained a student with General Carpenter, I swept the office and made the fires, and did all the errands now usually expected of an office boy, and this without compensation except that I was charged nothing for my tuition.

I had no previous acquaintance with General Carpenter, although I had often seen him upon the street. At the request of my friend, Edward D. Pearce, Esq., he had consented to receive me as a student, and found me at his office at the close of a busy day in court. He came in, and laying down his green satchel upon the table, greeted me with much dignity and courtesy, and asking me to be seated, commenced conversation by explaining to me that a lawyer should make himself familiar with the Bible, and taking the book, read some passages in confirmation of this advice. He said that it was his daily habit to read a chapter in the original Greek in his house every morning. He then proceeded to impress upon me the importance of treating everything that should pass in the office as strictly confidential, remarking that in his safe there were wills and conveyances which if known would startle the community.

Quite a number of people have tried their hands at a description of General Carpenter, and an analysis of his character. I shall attempt nothing of the kind, but content myself with recalling some of the circumstances which have fastened themselves upon my memory. He was of middle height, had a very large head, and uniformly wore a blue coat with brass buttons, black pantaloons, black satin vest, ruffled shirt, and black cravat. His manners were dignified, but affable. In his intercourse with clients, with his students, and with his brethren of the bar, he was always courteous, and when appearing before the courts, he was a model of dignity and deference to the tribunal. So much for the outward man. In his temper there was a mixture of kindness and prejudice. I think he was never rude in the presence of any human being, but he knew how to make known what was his real opinion, and those whom he met in daily intercourse knew very well for what individuals, and what classes of people, he entertained feelings of hostility or of contempt. While I was in his office, he rarely looked into a law book, and yet he was in one sense the best lawyer I have ever known. In his early life, he must have been a careful student of the common law, and somehow he attained a competent acquaintance with equity jurisprudence, the practice of which was then recent in the courts of Rhode Island. He never gave any bad advice. Nobody got into a foolish lawsuit who consulted General Carpenter. It was his custom to say to a client, who was anxious to get his grievances into court: "No doubt you have a perfectly good case, but there are some technical difficulties in your way, and I think it is for your interest to make a settlement." In this way he seldom lost a cause in which he appeared in court, and the reputation of success largely increased the number of his clients.

I must now ask the reader to go with me to the old court-house, at the September term of the Supreme Court, 1840. On the bench are Job Durfee, chief justice, and William R. Staples and Levi Haile, associates. Within the bar, around one large table, are seated Samuel Y. Atwell, Thomas F. Carpenter, Samuel Ames, Albert C. Greene, attorney general; and among younger men, William H. Potter, Samuel Currey, John P. Knowles, George Rivers, and Edward H. Hazard. From Woonsocket are Christopher Robinson and Judge David Daniels. From Scituate, Jonah Titus. From Pawtucket, John H. Weeden. John Whipple and Richard Ward Greene are not present. They alone, among the leading members of the bar, have adopted the practice of coming to the court-house only when one of their cases is in order for trial.

The docket has been called, and Mr. Atwell, whose home is in Chepachet, and who spends much of his time when he is in the city in the court-house, rises and addresses the court: "May it please your honors: if the court are not engaged, I would like to call attention to the fact that most of those persons who hang about the court-house for the purpose of being taken up on venire are now present, and I presume would be glad to know whether their services will be wanted." Thereupon several well-known parties are quietly leaving their seats and making their way to the door. I shall have much to say of Mr. Atwell, but this was his way of calling the attention of the court to a great nuisance.

Let us now attend the opening of the December term of the Court of Common Pleas. It is the same room in which the Supreme Court was held. The different courts and terms did not interfere with each other. The September term of the Supreme Court was over in time for the December term of the Court of Common Pleas. The Common Pleas made way for the General Assembly, and the General Assembly adjourned, and left time for the Supreme Court at its March term. The different courts had ample room and time in thc other counties without interfering with each other. There never was more than one court in session at the same time, and the attorney general,

Samuel Y. Atwell (1796–1844) of Glocester was a legislative leader (Speaker of the House, 1836–1837), an able attorney, a leading Dorrite, and counsel for Dorr and John Gordon in their celebrated trials. Depicted here is his spacious Chepachet home on Putnam Pike, a house befitting Glocester's most prominent citizen. After Atwell's death in 1844 at the age of forty-eight, his residence became the Chepachet Inn and a setting for court trials, town meetings, and other public gatherings. Fire leveled the historic structure in 1913. According to Payne, Atwell was characterized by the great John Whipple, under whom he studied, as "the ablest antagonist he ever met at the bar." Payne himself observed that "as an orator Mr. Atwell had few rivals and no superior." No likeness of Atwell has survived.

without assistance, attended all the courrts and the General Assembly, and found time to conduct a large private business.

I have heard the causes of the change that has come over the State, in this respect, explained in various ways, some of them very philosophical and profound; but some of these causes lie on the surface. The courts met early in the morning, and sat, with a short recess, until long after candle-light in the evening. Neither parties nor interested witnesses could be heard in evidence. No one of the prominent lawyers, as I remember, spent much time in cross-examining the witnesses of his opponents. There were no stenographic reporters. There were no printed reports of the cases, and very seldom written opinions delivered by the court. Cases were seldom held for advisement for a long time, and exceptions and rehearings were very rare.

When the act was passed, providing for a reporter of the decisions of the Supreme Court, Charles F. Tillinghast was appointed, but declined to accept the office. It was then offered to me. I called upon Judge Staples to consult him about the matter, and I well remember his voice and manner as he said: "You can take the office if you choose, but we shall make you all the trouble we can. We shall give you no written opinions, unless we are compelled to do so. We don't want any reporter or any reports. We mean to decide cases rightly, but we don't want to be hampered by rules, the effect of which would be to defeat justice. We had a petition for a new trial before us in Newport county, last term; there was no rule or authority by which we could grant it; but we saw that if we did not grant it, an honest farmer would be cheated out of his farm, and we granted it without giving any reasons for doing so." I declined the office, and it has been held by able men until the number of volumes is quite respectable, and I have not observed that any evil consequences have followed, and I quite agree with those of my brethren who think that judges should give reasons for their decisions.

John Whipple (1784–1866) was the acknowledged leader of the Rhode Island Bar during the second quarter of the nineteenth century. Thomas Dorr clerked in his office. In the Supreme Court case of *Wilkinson* v. *Leland* (1829), Whipple bested Daniel Webster while defending the plenary power of the Rhode Island legislature. Two decades later he was joined by Webster as the two successfully defended the Law and Order government in the landmark case of *Luther* v. *Borden* (1849).

But I wander, and the Common Pleas is open and waiting. Chief Justice Thomas Burgess, a grave and distinguished magistrate, is on the bench; on his left sit Judges Potter and Armstrong; on his right, Judges Howard and Westcott; a motion for continuance is argued; John H. Weeden, of Pawtucket, opens the motion. Probably some of my readers may remember his deliberate style. He states the name of the absent witness; recites, much in detail, what he expects to prove by him, shows that his testimony would be very material, and repeats the means that have been taken to procure his attendance and their failure. General Carpenter resists the motion; he does not see that the witness, if present, could give any material testimony, and is quite sure that if proper diligence had been used, the attendance of the witness might have been secured. Mr. Whipple follows on the same side, and after speaking very slightingly of the materiality of the absent witness, ridicules the pretense that any proper diligence has been used, winding up with: "May it please your honors: there is nothing diligent about this case except the grave face of my brother Weeden, which always *looks* diligent." Then Richard Ward Greene rises to close the motion; he rebukes Mr. Whipple for his flippant remark about Mr. Weeden, and is astonished that his learned brothers Carpenter and Whipple should have the face to oppose so reasonable a motion, and gets very earnest over the consequences to his client of being compelled to go on with the trial in the absence of the witness. The judges then consult together, and presently the chief justice announces that the majority of the court are of the opinion that the motion must be denied. It is quite evident that Judges Westcott, Howard and Potter have seen through the motion and have overruled the chief justice and Armstrong. This will give a correct notion of the mode in which business was transacted in court at that time. In every cause, there were two counsel on each side, and all the incidental motions were regularly argued in the manner above described, and these arguments did not occupy so much time as I have frequently seen consumed by two young lawyers, one on each side of a case, and talking alternately until the court, weary of their repetitions and contradictions of each other, stops the discussion, and sometimes decides the motion and sometimes holds it for advisement.

Charles S. Bradley (1819–1888), to whom Payne dedicated his *Reminiscences*, entered the practice of law in 1840, the same year as Payne. Bradley's keen analytical mind propelled him to the chief justiceship of the Supreme Court by 1866. According to Payne's dedicatory note to Bradley, "you...were early elected...by the unanimous vote of the Legislature, when largely composed of men differing from you in political opinions." Bradley, a Democrat, resigned from the high court in 1868 and later became a professor of law at Harvard University (1876–1879). In 1885, the year Payne published his *Reminiscences*, Bradley wrote an impressive treatise entitled *The Methods of Changing the Constitutions of the States, Especially That of Rhode Island*, a work that rebutted the controversial 1883 advisory opinion of the Rhode Island Supreme Court which had held that the General Assembly had no power to call a state constitutional convention. The essay prompted a vigorous rebuttal by Chief Justice Thomas Durfee. In 1935 the Supreme Court vindicated Bradley's position.

While I was a student, I had very little personal acquaintance with members of the bar, but I attended court when any trial of importance was held, and so became familiar with the lawyers who conducted these trials. It is difficult, perhaps, to separate the impressions made upon me at that time from the knowledge afterwards acquired when I was a member of the bar, but I shall do it as well as I can. These trials were conducted for the most part by John Whipple, Samuel Y. Atwell, Albert C. Greene, Richard Ward Greene, Thomas F. Carpenter and Samuel Ames. Occasionally Judge Daniels, Christopher Robinson, John H. Weeden or John P. Knowles would be associated with some one of the gentlemen above named, and in the year 1840, Charles S. Bradley and Thomas A. Jenckes were admitted to the bar, and soon became prominent in the trial of causes.

Members of the bar who in these days notice that important causes are frequently tried in an empty court-room, no one being present but the judges, counsel, witnesses, and sometimes officers of the court, and sometimes parties in the case, will hardly realize the change that has taken place. When I was a student, almost always there was a large attendance of spectators in court, and when it was known that Mr. Whipple, or Mr. Atwell, or General Greene was to speak, the court-house would be crowded, many prominent citizens of Providence being present. Probably the presence of an audience had some effect upon the speakers. Chief Justice John Marshall said that "when Mr. Pinckney was on his feet, he could tell when ladies entered the court-room without raising his eyes by the change in Mr. Pinckney's style of speaking." Within a year or two, I have seen a letter published by a Justice of the Supreme Court of the United States, in which he says that the days of eloquence at the bar are gone by. This, I think, is a

Walter Snow Burges (1808–1892) was a close associate of Thomas Wilson Dorr. His career subsequent to the rebellion is most interesting. Burges became federal district attorney for Rhode Island under Democratic president James K. Polk (1845–1849), state attorney general (1851–1854 and 1860–1863), and the selection of a Republican-controlled General Assembly for associate justice of the Rhode Island Supreme Court (1868–1881). It was to Burges that Dorr left his voluminous papers and correspondence. Burges entrusted these manuscripts to historian Sidney Rider, who eventually donated them to Brown University.

mistake; there will always be eloquence where there is the man, the subject and the occasion. But there has been a great change in the mode of arguing cases in the State since I was a student-at-law. Attorney General Greene, for instance, never addressed court or jury without consulting propriety in every detail. Cicero was not more careful in the arrangement of his robes than was General Greene to appear in appropriate costume. There was nothing rude or slip-shod in his manner. His voice was carefully modulated, and his whole bearing was dignified and persuasive. General Greene was a thoroughly instructed lawyer, a skillful and successful advocate, but he was first of all and always a gentleman. When Samuel Y. Atwell was to speak, all eyes were fastened upon him, and all ears were compelled to listen. He was a natural orator and a profound lawyer.

John Whipple was not so uniformly eloquent as Mr. Atwell, but he had a powerful mind, fully conscious of its own strength, and, when speaking, secured the close attention of court, jury, and audience. Though a great lawyer, he did not always confine himself strictly to the case in hand, and everybody was on the watch to hear what striking or brilliant thing he would say next.

Richard Ward Greene, though not an eloquent, was often a convincing speaker. He always came to his argument fully prepared, and I think his brethren of the bar felt that he was a "foeman worthy of their steel."

I did not have the benefit of instruction at a law school, but I think the loss was, in great part, made up to me by listening to these men while I was a student.

I do not think that I was what is called a hard student. Mr. Whipple said that the true test, whether a young man was fit to be a lawyer or not, was whether or not he could keep himself warm, on a cold day in December, without a fire, by reading *Fearne on Contingent Remainders*. I do not think I could have stood that test. Mr. Currey was often heard to say that, while a student, he spent fourteen hours a day for three months in the study of the first volume of *Chitty on Pleading*. I never spent so much time on any book. But I was not idle. I occupied a good many hours every day in reading law. I did most of the conveyancing in General Carpenter's office, but that was not much. I drew most of the declarations in actions which he commenced, but they were mostly formal. In contracts, or other papers of much delicacy or difficulty, and in cases where special declarations were required, he had associates, and the work was done out of the office.

I found plenty of time for pleasant intercourse with Charles Congdon, Walter Updike and Benjamin Latham. When I entered the office [in 1840], the singing campaign of the Whigs was at its height, and we were all Democrats, including John P. Knowles and James C. Hidden, who had offices on the same floor. Soon after the election of General William Henry Harrison, the movement for the extension of suffrage was set on foot. In the following spring, the death of General Harrison, and what the Whigs called the treachery of Tyler, deprived them of all the fruits of victory. The mass meetings, the political conventions and the Dorr war followed, and occupied much of my attention. Of these matters I propose to write, but not now.

Attorney Thomas A. Jenckes (1818–1875) began his legal career as secretary of both 1842 Law and Order constitutional conventions. As a leader of the Republican party from its formation in 1854, he served four terms as U.S. congressman (1863–1871). In Washington he became one of the earliest proponents of civil service reform based on "merit," helped rewrite the federal bankruptcy law, and initiated competitive examinations for admission to West Point. His specialty was patent law.

If we do not inquire wisely when we ask why the former days were better than these, it is still lawful to note some points of difference between the past and the present times. When I came to the bar only one lawyer had ventured to take an office on the third floor of a building, and this was Richard Ward Greene, whose standing was such that his clients would follow him wherever he might go. I am writing in the fourth story of a building, and look across the street upon the office of my classmate, George H. Browne, on a level with me in another building. At this time, General Carpenter added a small consultation room to his office and covered its floor with an ingrain carpet. This event made some talk, and when soon after Hazard & Jenckes fitted up their office with a Brussels carpet and expensive furniture, it was visited for some time as a curiosity.

To-day the offices of many of the profession are handsome and well-furnished rooms. Then every lawyer did his own errands or had them done for him by his students; now, many of the profession converse with each other, and with the officers at the court-house, by telephone. Then the headquarters of the profession were in the old wooden building at the corner of College and South Main streets; now lawyers are to be found in large numbers in many buildings in different parts of the city. Then at the call of the docket nearly the whole bar would be present in a room of moderate size, and from the youngest to the oldest all knew each other. When I last attended the call of the docket in the Supreme Court, the large room was crowded with lawyers, only three or four of whom started with me in the profession, and the greater number of whom were the rising men of a new generation.

When I first took an office in College street, across the way, in Whipple's building, were John Whipple, Edward H. Hazard, Thomas A. Jenckes, Henry L. Bowen, Charles Holden, Walter S. Burges, John B. Snow, George F. Mann, Samuel W. Peckham and William J. Pabodie. On the same floor of the building, just above, were Albert C. Greene and William H. Potter, Peter Pratt and Edward D. Pearce. In the little building next again above, which for many years had been occupied by Thomas Burgess, was John M. Mackie, who soon after left the law for the more congenial pursuits of literature and fancy farming at Great Barrington, Mass. On the corner of South Main street and Market square, were Levi C. Eaton, Peres Simmons, Gamaliel L. Dwight and Levi Salisbury. In the Mallett building, on South Main street, were Richard Ward Greene and James M. Clarke. In the old building where the Merchants Bank now stands, were Charles F. Tillinghast and Charles S. Bradley. John P. Knowles was then with General Carpenter, at the "Turk's Head." I think Mr. Atwell had then no office in the city, but soon after took one on College street. There were other lawyers, as Samuel Ashley and Samuel Currey, whose offices I cannot now locate, and still others, whose names even I do not now recollect. I have been told that not many years before I came to the bar, it was the custom of the lawyers to have a supper together at the house of some one of their number, once or twice in the year, but the members of the bar are now too numerous for such gatherings.

Abraham Payne (1818–1886), the author of this memoir, was himself a prominent attorney and civic leader.

Payne's book of recollections was influenced by Wilkins Updike (1784–1867), a South County historian, lawyer, and politician, whose *Memoirs of the Rhode Island Bar* (1842) is a detailed account of law and lawyers in early-nineteenth-century Rhode Island.

This is the first Providence County courthouse erected exclusively for court use. Built of brick, brownstone, and granite, the edifice was designed by Providence architects Stone and Carpenter and dedicated on December 18, 1877. The French Gothic structure stood on the present site of the Licht Judicial Complex, on a lot earlier occupied by the Old Town House. Here the Supreme and Superior courts were quartered until the building was demolished in 1930 to make way for the present courthouse.

22

The Sprague family, which had been at the center of nineteenth-century Rhode Island's most famous criminal trial, was also at the center of the state's most sensational civil litigation. Such notoriety was not surprising, because the Spragues were Kennedyesque. They boasted U.S. senators, congressmen, governors, multimillionaires, bold entrepreneurs, a military hero, at least one very glamorous woman, and a murder victim. Their successes and scandals inspired envy and enmity among Rhode Islanders great and small.

The A. & W. Sprague Company spanned three generations, beginning with William Sprague II, who built his first mill in Cranston in 1808. His sons Amasa I (the murder victim in the John Gordon case) and William III (U.S. senator, 1842–1844) took over the enterprise in 1836 at the death of its founder. After 1843 William III ran the company alone, expanding control to nine mill villages before his death in 1856. At that point his nephew, Amasa II, and his son, William IV (U.S. senator, 1863–1875), jointly took command. During their tenure the Panic of 1873 triggered the fall of the Sprague empire and the litany of litigation described by lawyer-historian Charles Carroll in the following essay.

When the crash of '73 occurred, the Sprague holdings had grown to at least $19 million, making this family the most powerful and wealthy in Rhode Island. Sprague investments extended far beyond the original cotton textile holdings and far beyond the borders of Rhode Island: there was lumber in Maine, mill sites in the South, agricultural land in Kansas, steamboats in New York, and coal and oil in Pennsylvania.

By entering politics, William IV (1830–1915) made powerful enemies. In 1860 he became governor at the age of twenty-nine by spending $125,000 to get himself elected—a fantastic sum for that time. In 1861 the "boy governor" outfitted and led one of the first volunteer Northern regiments to do battle with the Confederates. In 1863 this war hero used his financial clout to persuade the General Assembly to send him to the U. S. Senate.

Meanwhile, the powerful Republican machine, known as the Journal Ring because it was led by *Providence Journal* publisher Henry Bowen Anthony, grew increasingly resentful of Sprague's power, independence, and flamboyance. Flaunting his wealth and prestige, Sprague constructed a great mansion, which he called Canonchet, at Narragansett Pier, built a track there for trotting horses, and hosted gala parties with his beautiful bride, Kate Chase Sprague, daughter of the chief justice of the United States Supreme Court and the belle of Washington society.

Such power, glamor, and ostentation begat envy. In addition to the politicos of the Journal Ring, Sprague antagonized their allies, the powerful Providence industrial firm of Brown, Goddard, and Ives, which waited for him to overreach himself. In the late 1860s Sprague's far-flung speculations exceeded his liquid capital, forcing him to borrow at high rates of interest. When he tried to gain additional credit from local banks after the onset of the panic, the Browns and the Goddards used their influence to block his credit, and the Sprague empire was forced into receivership.

Rhode Island historian William McLoughlin, in his sprightly survey *Rhode Island: A History* (1978), recounts Sprague's economic and legal bind with a candor and criticism best expressed in his own words:

> The economic shock to the state was enormous. Few banks were not involved in some way, and thousands of small and large investors and creditors faced ruin. In addition, with 25 percent of the state's textile industry and 12,000 of its operatives tied up in the firm, it appeared that Sprague's ruin might drag countless others with him. His creditors consequently took steps to alleviate the situation. Although Sprague was in debt to the tune of $11 million, his assets were worth $19 million. With careful manipulation, the creditors might yet get their money returned. They joined together and appointed a trustee for the Sprague Company, a Providence ironmonger named Zechariah Chafee. Chafee was given the power to take charge of all Sprague's enterprises and agreed to continue to run them. Their profits were to be turned over to the creditors each year until all were paid off. Chafee was given four years to work out the firm's financial problems.
>
> However, Chafee was incompetent, if not crooked. He betrayed his trust and enriched himself by defrauding both the Sprague family and the creditors who appointed him. Almost $14 million of the Sprague assets were lost before the creditors discovered what Chafee was up to. Not even Nelson Aldrich could straighten out the mess, though he tried his best. The case went to court and dragged on until 1882. But Chafee, by clever legal maneuvers and special favors, managed to save himself from indictment. The creditors finally permitted Chafee to sell off the firms' remaining assets one by one. They were bought for a fraction of their value by competing firms, and Chafee emerged a rich man.

Professor McLoughlin rendered his harsh judgment of Chafee's stewardship despite an apologetic defense by famed Harvard law professor Zechariah Chafee, Jr., written in 1940 to exonerate his grandfather, the Sprague trustee. Published as *Weathering the Panic of '73: An Episode in Rhode Island Business History*, this treatise claimed that the elder Chafee was a man of integrity who may have made errors in judgment because of the complexity of the case and his lack of experience as a trustee.

The Sprague litigation dragged on for years. Trustee Chafee died in March 1889, but the final court decree in this case was not made until thirty-eight years later, in 1927, when the second substituted trustee was told by the court to destroy all the Sprague books by fire, and was then discharged. The Sprague litigation outlived its main subject by a dozen years. The erratic William Sprague IV died in Paris in 1915.

The threat to Canonchet and Sprague's personal estate, described in the following essay, prompts a final introductory observation. In his classic study *American Business Corporations until 1860* (Harvard, 1954), Professor Edwin Merrick Dodd has shown that Rhode Island "was the last of the industrial states to adopt a friendly attitude towards petitions for the incorporation of manufacturing companies, the last to include limited liability in the privileges granted to such companies, and the last to permit incorporation by general act [in 1893]." Such backwardness in developing the modern corporate forms of business organization is quite surprising in view of the fact that Rhode Island was the first urban-industrial state. The absence of limited liability was one of the many problems confronting the beleaguered Spragues.

The Sprague Cases

Charles Carroll

The panic of 1873, the failure of the A. & W. Sprague Manufacturing Company and other Rhode Island corporations, partnerships and individuals, precipitated litigation that engaged the attention of Rhode Island courts for years after 1873. The panic opened with the bankruptcy in September, 1873, of Jay Cooke & Company of Philadelphia. Hoyt, Sprague and Company of New York, buying and selling agents for the A. & W. Sprague Manufacturing Company, failed with Jay Cooke.

The A. & W. Sprague Manufacturing Company sought loans and extensions of credit to avoid suspension, but yielded in October to a suspension that had become almost inevitable. An unsuccessful effort was made to obtain loans from Rhode Island banks which were not already embarrassed—as were two savings banks and three national banks—by holding excessive amounts of Sprague notes. Banks which had available more than the $3,000,000 which *might* have carried the Spragues through the crisis could not be persuaded that the credit was warranted by the financial condition of the Sprague companies and the prospects for an immediate return of prosperity throughout the country, following what had been one of the worst panics in American history.

With respect to this phase of the Sprague failure a marked difference of opinion persisted in Rhode Island among persons who were acquainted with the facts, and remains as a tradition. The refusal to extend credit was characterized by friends of the Sprague family as approaching financial freebooting. The charge of piracy rested upon an assumption that jealousy of rival and competing manufacturers had ripened into ill-feeling, which prompted measures to remove the Spragues from their position of prestige and influence in Rhode Island. Resentment because of Senator William Sprague's scathing speeches in the Senate of the United States suggested an additional provocation or motive. The Senator entertained and expressed views on the monetary problems of the period following the Civil War, which startled his conservative colleagues in the Senate, and passed so far beyond the boundary line between orthodox and heterodox and between conventional and unconventional as to be considered inflammatory and radical.

Speaking in 1869 in the Senate discussion of the currency precipitated by the bill "to strengthen public credit and relating to contracts for the payment of coin," Senator Sprague, advocating relief for manufacturers with small ready money capital and limited bank credit, proposed a national bureau to loan money on credit. The *Providence Journal*, in an editorial treating Senator Sprague's remarks as Pickwickian, said: "The Senator's intense application to his official duties and to his extensive private interests, we fear, cause him to take too gloomy a view of the situation."

At the time interest rates were high, and money was scarce; Senator Sprague had been experiencing difficulty in obtaining extended credit for his various enterprises, including the actual money needed for payrolls and other cash payments. He was sensitive, and construed the *Journal* editorial as an attempt inspired by [the rival firm of] Brown & Ives to injure his credit with the purpose of accomplishing his ruin. He made another speech, in the course of which he declared: "There is in my state a great capital centered in one family, and that family has a newspaper organ, and that newspaper organ is conducted by my colleague. There are throughout the state those who receive or expect to receive, stipends at the hands of that family, or whose business rests on its favor. They and their agents are in possession of most of the moneyed institutions of the state, and when they sneeze there is a great deal of sneezing from one end of the state to the other." The references were to the firm of Brown & Ives, which controlled the most extensive textile manufacturing corporations competing with the Spragues and which was associated with the strongest financial interests in Rhode Island; to the *Providence Journal*, and to Senator Henry Bowen Anthony, as editor of the *Journal*.

Senator Sprague alleged further that an agent of Brown & Ives had approached him in 1857, during the business depression in that year, with a proposition substantially as follows: "Let us join forces, prevent a suspension of specie payments, break down those who are our rivals in business or otherwise, and buy up their property. At that time," the Senator continued, "I had no debts whatever pressing me. But did I unite with them in carrying into effect their vicious and pernicious wishes? Sir, I did not. I repudiated and spurned his proposal." So serious a statement, made in the Congress of the United States, was privileged in the sense that a member of Congress may not be sued for slander occurring in debate, and Brown & Ives had neither effective legal remedy by suit for damages nor recourse to any tribunal for vindication. Senator Anthony, by adroit parliamentary practice, read into the record of the United States Senate a specific denial by Brown & Ives that any proposition of the sort had been made by them, or on their behalf, to William Sprague in 1857. There had been a difference of opinion in Rhode Island in 1857 as to the necessity for or desirability of suspension; it appears in the facts (1) that twelve of thirty-three banks in conference were not in favor of suspending specie payments, and (2) that six strong banks ignored altogether an invitation to send representatives to the conference called to discuss suspension.

William Sprague (1830–1915) was a textile magnate, Union officer, Rhode Island governor (1860–1863), U.S. senator (1863–1875), and a financial casualty of the Panic of 1873, which destroyed his textile empire. Despite his achievements he was eccentric and erratic in behavior. His public life ended in 1883 after an unsuccessful run for another term as governor. He died in Paris in 1915.

Senator Sprague followed his attacks upon Brown & Ives and the *Journal* by others—upon General Ambrose Burnside, the First Rhode Island Regiment because of alleged cowardice at Bull Run, upon conditions in Rhode Island and in the country generally. Occasionally he attacked a colleague in the Senate, among them Senator Simon Cameron, whom he accused of tempting him to drink: "He would take me down to his committee room and set out champagne and ask me to drink. Finally I said to him: 'Cameron, you are a vicious old fellow. I am a young man and you are an old sinner, and you are always putting temptation in my way.'" An attack on Senator Abbott of North Carolina threatened to result in a duel. Some there were who circulated a story that Senator Sprague was insane. Distracted from time to time to other men and other subjects, Senator Sprague invariably returned to denunciation of the "money power." Thus he was approaching that day in which, his argosies failing, like Antonio he must pay forfeit to Shylock.

Contrary to the view that Senator Sprague's political, business and financial enemies united in 1873 to accomplish his destruction, one fact is outstanding and decisive: The suspension of the A. & W. Sprague Manufacturing Company, and the assignment for the benefit of creditors were not made a pretext for forcing the Spragues into bankruptcy under the national bankruptcy act; instead, the Spragues were permitted to negotiate with a committee of their creditors a three-year moratorium.

But the difference of opinion noted above is not related to restraint from action that would have precipitated liquidation in bankruptcy so much as the refusal of strong financial interests in Rhode Island to loan additional money. For this conservative attitude several reasons were assigned, among them (1) that the financial embarrassment of the Spragues was not sudden and momentary so much as chronic over a long period preceding 1873; (2) that Senator Sprague's altogether radical views on economic questions did not accord with financial soundness; (3) that the Sprague family, and particularly Senator Sprague's own immediate branch, had become extravagant; (4) that the Sprague enterprises, including the steamboat line to New York, had suffered excessive disasters; (5) that there was reasonable doubt that the Sprague investments of borrowed money in property for development were not rather highly speculative; and (6) that the rigid examination of the Sprague business in 1873 did not yield an assurance that additional credit would solve the problems. Briefly, the Sprague enterprises had passed the line at which bankers distinguished safety from danger in making loans.

The Sprague factories in Rhode Island, Connecticut and Maine in 1873 provided employment for 10,000 to 12,000 operatives at 280,000 spindles and twenty-eight printing machines, the output of which exceeded 1,000,000 pieces of cloth annually. The Spragues were enterprising, and members of the family had invented and introduced improvements on calico printing presses, and in dyeing and printing processes. Their iron factories made and marketed the Sprague mowing machine, horseshoes made by a new process, as well as nails of new design. They owned and operated the street railway in Providence, as well as a line of freight and passenger steamers between Providence and New York, and they held large blocks of shares in steam railroads, including the Providence and Fishkill, the line of which had been constructed to pass through one of their factory villages. They were interested by investment and stockholding in a great variety of manufacturing and other corporations. They owned real estate in almost every town in Rhode Island, additional to factories, factory sites, water rights and factory villages.

In Maine, besides a factory operating 34,000 spindles and a water right at Augusta on the Kennebec River, they held land as sites for other factories, and vast areas of timber lands with sawmills as part of a project for a lumber company. Westward their holdings of land extended to Kansas and Texas; their purchase of a water right and land at Columbia, South Carolina, suggests that they had grasped the possibility of manufacturing cotton cloth in the South as supply for their vast converting factories in Rhode Island and Connecticut. The conception of expansion was gigantic, and the Spragues through years of uninterrupted success had become convinced of their own invincibility. The house had risen because of the tremendous ability of the family for several generations.

Failing to obtain fresh loans or more favorable terms, members of the Sprague family, as individuals and as stockholders and owners of the Sprague factories, executed a trust mortgage on November 1, 1873, to secure the payment of 16,500 promissory notes, amounting to $14,000,000. The execution of the trust mortgage followed a meeting of creditors, at which the controlling motive for the composition accepted was avoidance of the expenses of bankruptcy. Zechariah Chafee became trustee. The notes were new, and were issued on surrender of outstanding claims; they were to run for three years and carry interest at 7.3 per cent. annually. The trust mortgage witnessed what was practically an agreement for a moratorium of three years. Its purposes were avoidance of forced liquidation and the immediate sale of the Sprague properties.

The mortgage itself was an act of bankruptcy, as an assignment, but it was expected that creditors would accept it and waive bankruptcy proceedings. The National Bank of Commerce filed a petition for involuntary bankruptcy a few hours before the time at which the right would expire by limitation, but withdrew the petition after there had been excitement and demonstration of opposition, suggesting the possibility of violence. The house of Sprague was still popular in Providence, and the people had confidence in the Spragues, even if the banks and bankers had not. Besides that, a resort to bankruptcy was considered hostile to the interests of creditors who were friendly to the three-year agreement. Thus the tragedy was postponed, and a comedy of errors lasting ten years began.

While the trust mortgage was assailed in subsequent litigation as fraudulent in fact and in purpose, there was a disposition in the period immediately following the assignment to carry the agreement into effect. The Spragues, at the request of the trustee, turned over to him additional property, including stock in the Quidnick Company not included in the trust mortgage, thus to facilitate the plans for continuing the operation of factories, and Chafee became treasurer of the Quidnick Company.

A contract was made by and between the Quidnick Company, which was owned by the Spragues and which was solvent, and the A. & W. Sprague Manufacturing Company, under the provisions of which the Quidnick Company was to manufacture and supply gray cotton cloth for printing, thus to keep the Sprague corporation operating. The Quidnick Company agreed to furnish "the necessary means, stock and supplies for running their mills and printworks," the stock and supplies to remain the property of the Quidnick Company until sold for the benefit of the Quidnick Company, and the Sprague corporation to have the profits of sales over and above a commission of one-quarter of one per cent., which was to be paid to the Quidnick Company.

Supreme Court justice Elisha R. Potter, Jr. (1811–1882) generally cast his dissenting vote in favor of the Sprague interests during the protracted litigation stemming from the company's collapse. Potter's service on the high court (1868–1882) was the culmination of a distinguished career as attorney, historian, adjutant general, state legislator, U.S. congressman, and state commissioner of education.

Senator Sprague entered the employment of the trustee, and the plants of the Quidnick Company and the Sprague corporation were continued in harmonious operation until 1881. The hopes that the embarrassment of the Sprague corporations might be overcome during the three-year moratorium were not realized. The panic of 1873 left in its wake a business depression from which the country made a slow recovery. The effect upon the market for print cloths, the staple product of the Sprague textile factories, appeared in the uncontradicted statement made in later litigation that the trustee by 1881 had "incurred an unexplained loss of about $2,000,000" in the operation of the Quidnick Company and the A. & W. Sprague Manufacturing Company. The notes secured by the trust mortgage were defaulted, and the courts were busy with the trial of suits brought by creditors in a frantic effort to retrieve something from the disintegration of the trust estate.

Eventually open quarrels developed between the Spragues and Chafee, which resulted in a long series of sharply contested cases, in the trial and argument of which Rhode Island counsel were assisted by lawyers from other states, including Benjamin F. Butler of Massachusetts as counsel for Senator Sprague. Justice Elisha R. Potter of the Supreme Court, who dissented [in favor of Sprague] from every decision of his colleagues, a majority of the court, on the Sprague cases, died while the litigation was still in progress. Senator Sprague was divorced by Kate Chase Sprague and remarried.

With the announced purpose of removing from the Supreme Court justices whom he accused of participation in a plot to ruin him, and of obtaining from the people of Rhode Island a "vindication," he became the Democratic party candidate for Governor in 1883, and though unsuccessful in a campaign which the *Journal* declared had been without precedent because of extravagant expenditure of money by both parties, polled a remarkably large vote in spite of opposition by some Democrats who supported a third candidate.

Twenty years and a day from that hot afternoon of July 20, 1861, when as Governor he had rallied the Rhode Island Second Regiment at the battle of Bull Run in Virginia, William Sprague assumed command in Rhode Island and opened a battle to retrieve the Sprague factory property from sacrifice in forced sales to satisfy creditors. The contract under which the Quidnick Company had been delivering the fruit of its looms to the A. & W. Sprague Manufacturing Company for "finishing" was terminated on July 21, 1881, by the notice stipulated. Zechariah Chafee, trustee in possession of the Sprague factories that had been insolvent in 1873 and of other property conveyed to him for the benefit of creditors, was ousted as treasurer of the Quidnick Company. William Sprague, as president of the Quidnick Company, with Colonel Henry T. Sisson, hero of Little Washington, as agent and manager, ejected the superintendent of the Quidnick factory, took possession and continued operation. The Quidnick Company entered three actions at law and two suits in equity against the A. & W. Sprague Manufacturing Company, the bills in equity praying injunctions against sale of property unless and until ordered by the court.

Counter suits were entered by Chafee as trustee for the creditors of the A. & W. Sprague Manufacturing Company. The factories of the A. & W. Sprague Manufacturing Company were closed, as the business through which they had been operating was terminated by the action of the Quidnick Company. Thus the battle opened with heavy blows and with issues clearly defined; the stakes included possession of the largest textile manufacturing properties in Rhode Island, and the regeneration or ruin of the house of Sprague.

Besides charges against Chafee of inefficiency, if not of wanton and purposeful maladiministration hostile to Sprague interests, which were developed as the litigation proceeded, the refusal by Chafee to entertain proposals by William Sprague for a settlement with creditors and an open personal quarrel between Chafee and Sprague were pretexts for drastic action. Chafee in a bill in equity filed by him against the Quidnick Company made these allegations, all of which were significant: (1) "That said Sprague made sundry propositions to Chafee for a full settlement with the creditors, which were declined, whereupon William Sprague threatened that he would do all in his power, by litigation and otherwise, to embarrass the sales of the trust estate; (2) that one John Rooney of Brooklyn, alleged to be a person of small financial ability, offered to purchase all the trust estate upon terms stated in his offer, which is believed to be in the handwriting of William Sprague's counsel, and of which offer, 'Your orators, of course, took no notice whatever'; (3) 'that Thomas A. Doyle, the brother-in-law of William Sprague, made in writing to Nelson W. Aldrich,' one of the complainants, 'a proposition for the settlement of the indebtedness of the Spragues.'"

Famous Civil War general Benjamin Franklin Butler (1818–1893), called "The Beast" by Southerners, was a principal lawyer for William Sprague. Butler served one term as governor of Massachusetts (1882) and five terms as U.S. congressman from the Bay State.

Briefly, William Sprague, by 1881, had obtained funds or credit that made it possible for him to begin overtures for a settlement with creditors, but the trustee and other representatives of the creditors rejected offers made by Sprague and others on his behalf. In December, 1881, Benjamin F. Butler, as counsel for William Sprague, made a further offer to purchase the Sprague property, which was rejected. The situation late in 1881 might be summarized briefly as follows: (1) The Quidnick Company was operating under control and management of William Sprague; (2) the printing factories of the A. & W. Sprague Manufacturing Company had been closed; (3) a battle for possession of the Sprague property was being contested in the courts of Rhode Island.

At this time, and with reference to this situation, William Sprague had reason, if at no other time, for his assertion that a combination had been formed against him. As events progressed it became clear that there was no disposition to relent. The Sprague propeties were taken under the trust mortgage, and William Sprague was driven from one position to another as the mortgage was foreclosed. His enemies understood the vengeance of which he was capable, had he been permitted to return to power; they were determined that that should not occur.

Winthrop De Wolf, receiver of the Franklin Savings Bank, which was in liquidation because of the Sprague failure, sued the A. & W. Sprague Manufacturing Company in 1874, and recovered judgment in 1878 for $826,912.78, on which execution was issued and levied upon property of the Sprague corporation in Rhode Island. In April, 1879, De Wolf filed a bill in equity, seeking to set aside the trust mortgage of 1873, and other assignments of Sprague property to Chafee, thus to clear the property for sale for satisfaction of the judgment.

While the De Wolf judgment was unsatisfied, and the bill in equity was still pending, the Quidnick Company, in 1881, as part of William Sprague's campaign for recovery of the Sprague property, started three actions at law against the A. & W. Sprague Manufacturing Company, two in Rhode Island seeking recovery of $2,000,000 and $1,000,000, respectively, and the third in Maine for $500,000. Following the actions at law, the Quidnick Company filed two bills in equity, one seeking a lien on the property of the A. & W. Sprague Manufacturing Company for a claim of $2,000,000, and the second seeking a lien on shares of the Quidnick Company held by Chafee as collateral security for the trust mortgage of 1873.

The lawsuits and bills in equity were based upon an old claim of the Quidnick Company for $216,410.88 arising before the failure and assignment, and a new claim for $2,000,000 arising from a contract between the Quidnick Company and Chafee as trustee for the A. & W. Sprague Manufacturing Company. One of the bills in equity also accused Chafee of maladministration, specified as (1) using money belonging to the Quidnick Company to pay claims against the Sprague corporation; (2) buying with trust funds a judgment obtained by the Bank of Commerce; (3) applying funds belonging to the Quidnick Company to purchasing claims against the Sprague corporation, and (4) selling a large manufacturing plant, one of the Sprague factories, at much less than its fair value to a firm one of the members of which was "an active and influential member" of the creditors' committee; it requested an accounting, declaration of a lien in favor of the Quidnick Company, and an injunction against Chafee forbidding sales of trust property except under direction of the court. For practical purposes the Quidnick Company in these suits represented the Sprague family interest against the trustee and against the creditors, and the court procedure aimed to prevent further sale of the trust property by Chafee, whom the Spragues considered an enemy.

The proceedings in the first bill in equity were heard by Justices Potter,

Stiness and Tillinghast, until Justice Potter died, on April 10, 1882, and after Potter's death by Stiness and Tillinghast. The Court invariably divided, with Potter, always the minority, dissenting from the opinions of his colleagues. The first difference of opinion between the judges arose from their interpretation of the contract between the Quidnick Company and the A. & W. Sprague Manufacturing Company, already mentioned. Stiness and Tillinghast construed the agreement as a "stocking" contract, substantially a proposition by the Quidnick Company in these terms: "Make our cotton into prints in your mills, we paying all expenses. If on sale they bring more than a certain price, you shall have the excess." "By necessary implication, therefore," the court ruled, it said: "If they bring less than cost, it is our own loss, because our own goods have brought less than we have put out on them." On such a contract no liability for loss incurred in manufacture could arise unless from negligence or non-performance, neither of which had been alleged. The majority held that, while the Sprague corporation was not liable for any loss in the manufacture of print cloths, the Quidnick Company was entitled to an accounting on its allegations that Chafee had used funds of the Quidnick Company to pay claims against the trust estate.

Potter dissented, urging that the majority had read into the contract an interpretation which had not been urged by the counsel who had argued at the hearing, and which differed from the construction placed upon it by the parties themselves, as shown by the method of keeping accounts. Potter construed the contract as an agreement made by the Quidnick Company to assist the Sprague corporation by furnishing stock to operate the Sprague corporation's print works, the Sprague corporation being obligated to pay for stock out of the proceeds of sales, the Quidnick Company retaining title merely to protect its own interest while dealing with an insolvent corporation. Any other interpretation, he argued, would place the entire risk for the contract on the Quidnick Company, which, besides carrying the risk, could not possibly profit from the contract. Potter believed that the making of a contract with such terms was as inconceivable as the contract would be unenforceable for want of consideration.

Potter agreed with the majority "that no sale should be made except under the direction of the court," because "This would enable the court to see that all interests are protected; to prevent the trust property from being thrown upon the market in such amounts as to necessitate a sacrifice; to reserve from the sale or from the proceeds of sales enough to satisfy any liens that may be ascertained; to withhold from present sale any portion of the estate the title to which is so clouded as that it would not sell for a fair value, until the difficulties are removed; to prevent secret bidding; or to provide for a sale by a master of the court, all of which may be done upon proper proceedings to be advised by counsel and approved by the court."

The interpretation of the contract between the Quidnick Company and the A. & W. Sprague Manufacturing Company was vital. The ruling of the majority of the court tended to remove obstacles to a sale of the trust estate, which was opposed by the Sprague family; Potter's interpretation would have effected a postponement of sale until the cloud on the title attached to a lien in favor of the Quidnick Company had been removed. The majority of the court entered a decree on November 5: (1) declaring that the A.& W. Sprague Manufacturing Company was not indebted to the Quidnick Company under the contract; (2) ordering an accounting and repayment of money belonging to the Quidnick Company applied by Chafee to the payment of creditors under the trust mortgage; and (3) "it appearing that said property cannot be held to await such account, except at great and ruinous expense," directing Chafee to advertise and sell the property. The final order in the decree rested on the fact that the printing factories were standing idle, operations having ceased when the Quidnick Company terminated the contract for supplying gray cloth.

Potter, following his dissent from the majority's interpretation of the contract, dissented also from the decree ordering a sale, saying: "I do not think the court ought to make an order for the sale of the property so long as the title to it is in dispute. The decree for sale will bind no one who is not a party to the suit in which it is made, and it may therefore be argued that no harm can be done. In ordinary cases no mischief may be done. But here is an immense estate to be sold for the benefit of creditors, and if creditors appear and are represented in the suit, it by no means follows that the large creditors will look out for the interests of the smaller creditors as well as they do for their own. And it is a very common notion, too, that when a sale is made under order of court, the purchasers are sure of a good title. While the lawyers know that this is not so, and while we are apparently selling only lands, mills, stocks, etc., we may, in fact be selling only the privilege for having a lawsuit, and thus aid in misleading purchasers and promoting litigation.... The court ought to protect not only those who are bound by their decree, but also, as far as possible, those who may act honestly upon the faith of their decree."

Potter then urged the duty of the court to guard against decrees obtained by collusion, adding: "Even if the parties do not collude, they may have an interest of the same nature in the result. Now we know, not from hearing nor loose declaration, nor from statements by counsel in argument, which may be inaccurate, but from our own records, that the title to all, or nearly all, of the property now sought to be sold is in dispute." He then directed attention to the pending bill in equity filed by De Wolf to test the legality of the trust mortgage.

Chafee, on November 19, 1881, asked authority to lease the Baltic Mill property, in Connecticut, which was under litigation in Connecticut, and a decree was entered, accordingly, on December 3. Potter dissented on the grounds that Chafee had authority to act under the trust mortgage, and that the court could not give him any "power whatever over land in Connecticut." He argued also that there was no more reason for not selling the property in Connecticut because of encumbrances, than for not selling the property in Rhode Island, which was subject to the lien of the Quidnick Company, and the judgment and execution of De Wolf.

Two days later, the court decided that the Quidnick Company, having prosecuted its bills in equity, was not entitled to a remedy at law. It entered a decree on December 10, ordering discontinuance of the actions at law, and dissolving attachments. The Quidnick Company was enjoined against further prosecution of its action at law pending in Maine. Potter dissented for the reason that a motion for reargument of the bills in equity was pending.

Chafee advertised the trust estate for sale at public auction on December 8. On the morning of that day, Potter received a petition from depositors in the Franklin Savings Bank, asking permission to intervene, and granted an injunction against a sale within ten days. The injunction was dissolved by the court majority, which ruled that the depositors were not proper parties to the suit brought by the Quidnick Company, which sought only to reclaim "its own funds, which, it claims, have been unlawfully added to the property belonging to the creditors in the hands of the trustees." Potter dissented from the reasoning of the majority of the court, but joined with the others in dissolving the injunction, on the ground that the purpose of the injunction had been attained in so far as the depositors had been permitted to have their day in court on the question of intervening.

Previous to March 8, 1882, Chafee received several offers for the Sprague estates, and the court, after consideration thereof, ordered a sale at public auction at a price not less than $2,880,000, that being the figure named in a letter suggesting the public sale. Potter dissented; he had read the letter and interpreted it, not as an offer, nor as a promise to bid $2,880,000 if the property were offered for sale, but as merely a suggestion.

When the auction was opened no bidders appeared. Justice Potter's keen discernment had been justified by the course of events. He died, however, before the case was further heard. Sale at public auction having failed, the court rescinded the order for an auction and entered a decree which authorized Chafee to sell the Sprague estates at private sale at terms satisfactory to him. The court also adjudged Joshua Wilbour, Benjamin A. Jackson, Charles H. Sheldon, Jr., and William Binney, Jr., of the firm of Wilbour, Jackson & Co., which had made the suggestion of a sale at public auction, to be in contempt of court because of interference. The court, after a hearing on the question of contempt, failed to inflict a fine because Justices Stiness and Tillinghast did not agree as to the amount of the fine or the time at which it should be inflicted.

The embarrassing position into which the court had permitted itself to be drawn attracted attention beyond the borders of the state as well as in Rhode Island, and a New York newspaper printed an editorial holding the court up to ridicule because of dilatoriness if not complete inefficiency.

To the charge of dilatoriness, which was based on the term of almost ten years that had elapsed between the Sprague failure and the approach to a final settlement, Justice Stiness responded in a letter in which he reviewed the procedure before the court, and demonstrated that the Sprague case had not reached the court in the form of an action until 1881, nearly eight years after the making of the trust deed. The end was close at hand in 1882. The Sprague estate was sold by Chafee to the Union Company, a corporation chartered April 20, 1882, under an amendment to an earlier corporation charter. The incorporators of the Union Company included Wilbour, Jackson, Sheldon and Binney of the firm of Wilbour, Jackson & Co., which had been declared in contempt, besides Jesse Metcalf, William Binney and

Charles D. Owen. Alleged irregularity in the charter, suggesting unconstitutionality, was made the basis for procedures purposing to set aside the sale to the Union Company before the Sprague cases had been concluded.

Other decisions of the Supreme Court on cases incidental to the Sprague litigation tended to confirm the decision in the principal case. Thus the second complaint in equity by the Quidnick Company against Chafee as trustee for the A. & W. Sprague Manufacturing Company was dismissed for the reasons (1) that, as previously decided, the contract between the Quidnick Company and the Sprague Corporation had been a "stocking" contract, and (2) that the claim of the Quidnick Company against the A.& W. Sprague Manufacturing Company existing before the assignment had been settled and paid by the acceptance of trust notes under the trust mortgage. Potter dissented, renewing his objection to the court's interpretation of the contract. The court, Carpenter, Stiness and Tillinghast, JJ., sitting, held in 1884 that the conveyance of the Sprague property in 1873 to Chafee was a trust mortgage, and later in the same year that it was valid and not subject to attack as fraudulent in its effect on non-assenting creditors.

The court had previously, in 1883, sustained the conveyance to Chafee as binding him and the Spragues. In that particular case (a bill in equity to foreclose a pledge of stock as collateral to the trust deed), the Sprague family answered that the indenture had been made for the purpose of hindering, delaying and defrauding the creditors of the Sprague corporations, and asked to have the issue thus raised tried by a jury. To the complainant's objection, "Nemo allegans suam turpitudem audiendus sit" (No one may be allowed to plead his own fraud as a defense), the respondent answered "In pari delicto potior est conditio defendentis vel possidentis" (When both are equally guilty, the defendant or possessor prevails). The court held that a plaintiff or defendant, in law or in equity, who can make out his case without introducing into it a fraud in which his opponent and himself participated, may obtain relief in spite of any effort on the part of such opponent by plea or offer of proof to set up such fraud.

The court sustained the charter of the Union Company as constitutional, in spite of apparent inconsistency with Article XIV, section 17 [of the state constitution], which read: "Hereafter, when any bill shall be presented to either house of the General Assembly to create a corporation for any other than for religious, literary or charitable purposes, or for a military or fire company, it shall be continued until another election of members of the General Assembly shall have taken place and such public notice of the pendency thereof shall be given as may be required by law." Jesse Metcalf, William Binney, Charles D. Owen, Joshua Wilbour, Benjamin A. Jackson, Charles A. Sheldon, Jr., William Binney, Jr., their associates, successors and assigns, were incorporated June 3, 1881, under the "name of the Providence Car Trust Company, with full power and authority to make, manufacture, buy, sell, lease and deal in all kinds of railroad rolling stock and equipment, to buy, sell and deal in all kinds of railroad securities, and to accept and execute all trusts that may be committed to said corporation by any railroad corporation."

On April 20, 1882, the charter granted to the Providence Car Trust

Company was amended in such manner as to incorporate the same persons under the name of the Union Company, "for the purpose of manufacturing, bleaching, dyeing, printing and finishing cotton, woolen, worsted and other goods, with full power and authority to take, acquire, hold, manage, improve, lease, let, sell and convey real estate, to take, hold and dispose of stock in national banks and other corporations, and to transact any other business incidental thereto or connected therewith, and generally to do and execute all acts, matters and things which may be necessary or convenient to carry into effect the purposes of this act," etc.

The capital stock of the Providence Car Trust Company was $100,000, in shares of $100 each; of the Union Company, $1,000,000 in shares of $1000 each. It was argued that the charter of the Union Company was unconstitutional because (1) the petition for amendment had not been continued over the holding of a general election, and (2) the notice required by law had not been given. The court, Carpenter, Stiness and Tillinghast, JJ., overruled the objection that "the amendatory act amounted substantially to an act creating a new corporation," saying: "In order to sustain this position we ought to be satisfied beyond a doubt of the truth of two propositions: first, that an amendment to a charter which radically changes the purpose and power of the corporation is in effect the creation of a new corporation; and, second, that the amendment in this case was of such a radical character. We are not prepared to say that we could resolve these questions in favor of the defendant, even if there were no other consideration in the case. But there is an additional most weighty consideration. The act in question is one of very many acts of amendment equally radical and sweeping which have been passed by the General Assembly at different dates since the adoption of the Constitution. To hold that such acts are void would give rise to endless litigation. The uniform practical and legislative construction has been in favor of the validity of these acts."

The court also held that the notes issued by Chafee in accordance with the agreement for a three-year moratorium were negotiable, as certain in amount, although the right to pay by installments was reserved, but that notes issued as collateral security to a draft were not negotiable because the obligation was contingent. In this series of decisions the court had sustained the original conveyance to Chafee, the sale to the Union Company, and the Union Company itself.

With the major issues decided against the Sprague family, the process of completing the details of enforcing the trust mortgage of 1873 and the assignments supplementary thereto went steadily forward. The Supreme Court, Potter, Stiness and Tillinghast, JJ., in September, 1881, entered a decree enjoining the Quidnick Company, its officers, agents and servants, "from taking any corporate action prejudicial to creditors, and from contracting any debts or other obligations, or entering into any agreement that in any manner can be or become liens upon the corporate property or estate or subject it to liability, and from disposing of any part of the corporate estate or property, or otherwise changing its present condition," and appointed a special receiver, with direction to collect a certain claim due the company, and to apply the proceeds to insurance of the property and to payment of claims for labor and services.

The court subsequently sustained a demurrer to the bill in equity on which the injunction had been granted, on the ground that the bill was multifarious. Potter dissented from the reasoning of the majority, but concurred in the opinion that the bill was defective. Benjamin F. Butler, Roger A. Pryor and Andrew B. Patton appeared as solicitors and as counsel for the Quidnick Company. Butler and Patton assigned to Pryor, who was a member of the bar in New York, their claims for counsel fees against the Quidnick Company, and Pryor filed an action for counsel fees against the Quidnick Company in New York, and attached the claim which the receiver had been directed to collect, to recover the sum of $21,000. For this "interference" with the decree of the Supreme Court of Rhode Island, Butler, Patton and Pryor were called before the court for alleged contempt. Butler and Patton were excused, as having no control over the procedure in New York, and Pryor was enjoined from further procedure in New York and ordered to release the attachment. He did.

The bill in equity came up for further hearing, and in 1883 the court, Carpenter, Stiness and Tillinghast, JJ., declined to appoint a receiver for the Quidnick Company, on the ground that the injunction already in force protected the company and property amply, and that the evidence tended to show that the operation and administration under the direction of William Sprague was not detrimental. The court, Carpenter, J., thus summarized the situation: "The personal property of the company being in the hands of a custodian, and the company being enjoined from contracting any debt, and by consequence prevented from doing any business, the president of the company has been able to make an agreement with some persons of substance by which he continues the business, keeps the property in good order, and keeps the insurance rates at the lowest point, retains the operatives in employment at the mills, and pays the profits of the business, if any there be, to the use of the stockholders, without involving them in liability for any losses which may be made.... If we should retain the receiver in office, and advise him to the best of our ability as to the management by the mills, I could not venture to hope that the condition of the property would be more favorable."

The court later in the same year, 1883, facilitated the enforcement of an assignment of 4022 shares of the Quidnick Company as collateral security for the trust mortgage of 1873, by refusing to submit to a jury an issue raised by William Sprague's plea that the trust mortgage and pledge were fraudulent. With Chafee in control of the stock, William Sprague could have no further interest in operating the Quidnick Mill. The Quidnick Company, while controlled by Sprague, resisted an attempt to collect a bill for cotton purchased by Chafee, for the reasons alleged (1) that the cotton delivered was of poor quality; and (2) that the fact that Chafee bought cotton regularly at a price higher than the market rate was proof of fraud and collusion. The court found no evidence to sustain a claim that Chafee was imposed upon by the delivery of cotton of a lower grade than had been contracted for, and sustained the trial court's instruction to the jury with reference to the price paid, which the newspapers of the period show was higher day by day than the cotton market price in Providence. "There is nothing here that tends to show any imposition on Mr. Chafee. The fact, if true, simply tends to show incompetence on his part to buy cotton, which is no defence to the Quidnick Company. If he was a poor buyer that is their fault. Mr. King [the plaintiff-seller] had a right to sell them cotton for all he could get."

The Sprague factory property had been taken, and the Spragues had been ousted. The trustee and purchasers under him proceeded to obtain possession of the Sprague residences. One of these in Providence, the property in 1873 of Fanny Sprague, William Sprague and Amasa Sprague, was included in the trust mortgage of 1873 and was sold by Chafee to the Union Company. After the delivery of the trust mortgage, Rodman, a creditor, who had not accepted the composition, recovered judgment against William and Amasa Sprague, and levied execution on the residence. The latter was sold under the execution, and purchased by Inez Sprague, second wife of William Sprague.

In an action brought by the Union Company under the trust deed, the Supreme Court, Carpenter, Stiness and Tillinghast, JJ., sustained the trust mortgage as legal, and the Union Company's charter as constitutional, and confirmed a judgment against the Spragues. The court also allowed recovery for "damages for wrongful occupation" on the bond given by the Spragues when they appealed from the Common Pleas Court to the Supreme Court. But the tide stopped at Canonchet, the magnificent palace with eighty bedrooms at Narragansett Pier, where Senator William Sprague and Kate Chase Sprague had entertained the most brilliant society in America.

Kate Chase Sprague had departed, after divorcing William Sprague while he was fighting desperately to retrieve his fortune. To Canonchet he returned with his second wife, Inez Weed Sprague. A jury which heard an action of trespass and ejectment for possession of Canonchet against William Sprague on January 18 and 19, 1883, returned a verdict for the defendant, although the only question for the jury related to the fact of possession. The Supreme Court on July 18, 1885, ordered a new trial. William Sprague was not dispossessed; he sat on the porch at Canonchet with a shotgun across his knees when a sheriff called.

Time works curious changes. Justice John H. Stiness, who wrote most of the decisions in the Sprague cases and participated in others, was regarded by William Sprague as his worst enemy. Yet a son of Justice Stiness, Henry W. Stiness, married Inez Sprague, a granddaughter of William Sprague.

Amasa Sprague, brother of William and partner in the firm of A. & W. Sprague, married on November 12, 1873, a few weeks before the execution of the trust mortgage. When Amasa Sprague died on August 4, 1902, his widow, Harriet B. Sprague, instituted proceedings to establish a claim for dower against over 700 persons [who had acquired Sprague property from the trusteeship]. The suit was before the Supreme Court twice, and two decisions were rendered, in the course of which the court discussed the law of dower exhaustively. Edward C. Stiness, nephew of Justice Stiness, was a counsel for Mrs. Sprague in the dower cases. Justice Stiness died September 6, 1913; William Sprague died in Paris, September 11, 1915.

The Arctic Mill on the south branch of the Pawtuxet River was just one component of the vast Sprague holdings.

23

Legal historian Lawrence M. Friedman has written a superb chapter on the development of tort litigation in his impressive tour de force *A History of American Law* (2nd ed., 1985). Friedman shows that tort law grew "most explosively" in the second half of the nineteenth century. The Industrial Revolution—spreading, like the law of torts, from England to America— also "manufactured injury and sudden death, along with profits and the products of machines. The profits were a tempting and logical fund out of which the costs of the dead and injured *might* be paid… but lawsuits and damages might injure the health of precarious enterprise. The machines were the basis for economic growth, national wealth, and the greater good of society."

This dilemma of whether or not to compensate for injuries was first posed in railroad cases, for railroads were late-nineteenth-century America's greatest business. According to Friedman, railroad law and tort law developed together. Personal injury cases grew as fast as railroad trackage. To the railroads, which crisscrossed the state by 1870, urban-industrial Rhode Island added other potential tortfeasors—the textile industry, the base- and precious-metals industry, the rubber-goods business, the interurban horsecar system, and municipalities, especially Providence, with extensive public works projects.

Businesses developed several early defenses to negligence suits: (1) the fellow-servant rule, whereby a servant (employee) could not sue his master (employer) for injuries caused by the negligence of another employee; (2) the theory of contributory negligence, whereby the plaintiff had to prove not only that the defendant was negligent but also that he was faultless himself; (3) the doctrine of assumption of the risk, whereby a plaintiff could not recover if he willingly put himself in a position of danger; and (4) the theory of proximate cause, which required the act of the defendant to cause the injury with no other person, event, or situation intervening. All of these rules were initially embraced by Rhode Island courts during the formative period of tort law described in the following essay by Charles Carroll.

Despite the obvious political power of big business, legislatures in the various states sometimes heeded the voices of labor or the passenger-public. For example, in 1844 a pioneering Rhode Island law attempted to impose safety precautions to prevent the most common railroad tort—crossing accidents—by ordering "a bell of at least thirty-two pounds in weight" to be hung on every locomotive and sounded "at the distance of at least eighty rods" from a crossing until the engine passed the road. Railroads were also required by the law to post warning signs at every crossing, "of such height as shall be easily seen," with an "inscription...painted in capital letters, of at least the size of nine inches each, 'Railroad Crossing—Look out for the Engine while the Bell Rings,'" on each side of the signboard. This statute also imposed liability "for all damages sustained by any person" because of a noncomplying train.

By the end of the century more statutes creating liability were passed in Rhode Island and elsewhere, and courts were developing exceptions to those rigid doctrines of early tort law that placed a weighty burden on the injured party. William F. Micarelli, in his doctoral dissertation "The Rhode Island Supreme Court and Social Change, 1865–1900" (Catholic University of America, 1969), concludes that our court "was never so Darwinian as to remove business from the control of law, nor so reformist as to hamper the operations of industry."

Professor Friedman concludes his lucid summary of early tort law during the period covered by Dr. Carroll with an impassioned analysis of its rise and metamorphosis:

> The American landscape had subtly altered after 1850. Smokestacks were as dense as trees in the forest. In row on row of mean houses, in crowded cities, lived hundreds of poorly paid, landless workers. Each year, accident tore through these *barrios*, extracting its tax of dead and shattered bodies, ruined lives, destitute children. A finger of shame pointed at industry. Dissatisfaction was in the air. Labor denounced the system of tort law as cruel and inefficient. It *was* inefficient, if only because it no longer worked, because too many people had lost or were losing their faith in a harsh, simple system, as the lesser of two evils. Change was clearly on the way. Insurance and risk-spreading techniques were ready; cushions of capital reserves were ready; most important, perhaps an organized and restless working class pressed against the law with voices and votes.
>
> The rules of tort law, in twilight by 1900, were like some great but transient beast, born, spawning, and dying in the shortest of time. The most stringent rules lasted, in their glory, two generations at most. Had it been worthwhile? Was that span of time so precious? Would the economy have

suffered under other arrangements? It is impossible to know. There may have been some point to that short, bitter life, some virtue to the sacrifice of life and body; or then again it may all have been in vain.

Professor Charles Carroll, the author of this and the preceding essay, held a law degree from Harvard and a doctorate in education from Brown. These excerpts are taken from his *Rhode Island: Three Centuries of Democracy* (1932), a four-volume survey (two narrative and two biographical) that remains the definitive in-depth history of the state. Because of Carroll's legal training, it is also the general work that contains the most detailed and accurate information about Rhode Island's legal history. Carroll's specialty was education law. He served as state commissioner of education and wrote an authoritative study on *Public Education in Rhode Island* (1918) and a treatise entitled *School Law in Rhode Island* (1914).

The crew of a Mount Pleasant horsecar pose on Academy Avenue, Providence, about 1890. Horsecars such as this were familiar sights on the streets of Providence from their inception in 1864 to their demise in the mid-1890s. In addition to their benefits, the horsecars were responsible for many injuries to pedestrians, passengers, and company employees.

Development of the Law of Negligence in Rhode Island, 1872–1903

Charles Carroll

An essentially new type of litigation in Rhode Island appeared in 1872, when the Supreme Court rendered its first decision in a tort action based upon negligence. The suit sought damages for injuries to a carriage stored in a barn, and the negligence alleged was failure to provide a roof strong enough to resist the weight of snow (*Remington* v. *Sheldon*, 10 R.I. 218). Three years later the first action seeking damages for injuries incurred during employment reached the court, and the decision suggested the fellow servant rule, which became so important in later litigation alleging employment injuries (*Mann* v. *Oriental Print Works*, 11 R I. 152). Two negligence cases were before the court in 1878, in one of which the court outlined the general rule that an employee accepts the ordinary risks attending his occupation (*Kelley* v. *Silver Spring Company*, 12 R.I. 112). The other was the first negligence case against a public service corporation that reached the Supreme Court; the plaintiff sued the Providence Gas Company for injuries in his greenhouse arising from gas escaping from a leaking main (*Butcher* v. *Providence Gas Company* 12 R.I. 149).

It may not be assumed that negligence was not recognized as a cause of action for damages earlier than 1872, that settlements were not made without recourse at law, or that actions had not been tried in courts of inferior jurisdiction. The appearance of the cases noted in the Supreme Court indicated that damages had attained figures sufficient to warrant contests in the highest court, and also that the number of such cases was increasing and that their frequency necessitated an accurate statement of the legal principles to be applied.

Two of the early cases named manufacturing corporations and one a public service corporation as defendants; against such, a jury might be persuaded to return verdicts sufficient in amount to warrant appeals. Other early cases followed the general tendencies noted, the number of cases increasing rapidly with the expansion of public service corporations, and the development of larger manufactories. Included were actions for damages arising from (1) a street railway company's negligence in leaving a pile of snow after clearing tracks; (*Lee* v. *Union Railroad Company*, 12 R.I. 303); (2) a collision occasioned by careless driving on a public highway (*Baldwin* v. *Barney*, 12 R.I. 392); (3) the carelessness of a hospital intern (*Glavin* v. *Rhode Island Hospital*, 12 R.I. 411); (4) the death of a laborer employed in the construction of the Providence City Hall (*McCaughey* v. *Tripp*, 12 R.I. 449); (5) the escape of a horse to a public highway (*Fallon* v. *O'Brien*, 12 R.I. 518); (6) a defective cistern cover (*Bradbury* v. *Furlong*, 13 R.I. 5); (7) a defective stairway in a public building (*Wixon* v. *Newport*, 13 R.I. 454); (8) and carelessness in starting a street car while a passenger was alighting (*Rathbone* v. *Union Railroad Company*, 13 R.I. 709).

An amendment to the statutes permitting actions by relatives for damages in instances of negligence resulting in death favored the development of the new practice, which within a few years had grown to such an extent that it had become one of the most prolific and productive sources of income for lawyers. The latter might be classified in two categories, thus: Those who were counsel for plaintiffs seeking damages in actions based upon negligence and those who had become counsel for corporations defending themselves against claims for negligence.

Tort cases alleging negligence lengthened the dockets of courts, necessitated an increase in the number of jurymen drawn, aroused public interest because of the damages asked for and the large verdicts sometimes returned, and burdened the appellate division of the Supreme Court with appeals and requests for new trials involving close discriminations in decisions. In the desire to state an action somehow in such manner as to assure a trial by jury, a tendency to multiplicity in pleading developed, principally to avoid the demurrer interposed by a lawyer skilled in the technique of procedure to obtain a decision in chambers.

The profession and practice of law might be considered as having reached the golden age if the stories of almost fabulous retainers, and shares of large verdicts and of settlements negotiated out of court might be true. It was commonly stated and generally believed that law had become the most remunerative of the professions, as rumors were circulated that certain lawyers had received as fees in individual cases amounts that were larger than the annual earnings of some of the more prominent members of the bar in earlier days. Law had been a dignified and studious profession practiced in an environment of dusty, dingy offices and small courtrooms; now it had become the highway to wealth. The new type of lawyer chose an elaborate suite of offices in a modern building, with an imposing library, a corps of clerks, and sometimes a staff of younger lawyers serving an apprenticeship with the head of the "firm."

Courtrooms also were increased in size, and accommodations were provided for hosts of witnesses, large panels of jurymen, and the crowds of the curious who attended trials, which had become more dramatic than the theatre. Older easygoing methods of trial had been replaced by sharp practice to win advantage, and the presentation of evidence and examination of witnesses had undergone a revolution. Lawyers were being classified as specialists, and a new type of "trial lawyer" had appeared—a lawyer who tried jury cases for his colleagues at the bar. The "trial lawyer" or "jury trial lawyer" was practiced in the art of winning the jury, getting from his own witnesses the most of evidence favorable to his case, cross-examining the witnesses of the other party, and finally summing up the case for the jury. In the trial of cases involving large claims, several lawyers participated for the parties on each side.

Two backfires eventually tended to reduce the volume of this litigation—the practice of corpora-

The electric trolley made its debut in Newport in 1889 and in Providence in 1892. This more rapid and much more hazardous mode of transportation soon rendered the horsecar obsolete. In 1900 this trolley collision on the Providence-to-Buttonwoods line killed six passengers and seriously injured many others, including Lieutenant Governor Charles Kimball. Popular outrage focused on the unsafe operational practices encouraged by the corporate owners—the United Traction and Electric Company. In 1900 alone, the company reported 111 mishaps and 22 fatalities.

Riders, some perched precariously on the locomotive *Hercules*, are shown in this 1870s photo. The engine, a product of the Rhode Island Locomotive Works, ran on the Providence and Springfield Railroad, which began service in 1873 as the sixth major line to radiate from Providence. Despite the dreams of its promoters, the main tracks got only as far as the Burrillville village of Pascoag. The large number of railroad-related injuries contributed to the rise of the law of negligence.

tions in seeking promptly—if possible before a claimant had employed a lawyer—settlement and a release; and with reference to employment accidents, the workmen's compensation law. Meanwhile Rhode Island courts had developed three rules that tended to reduce damages: (1) the doctrine of contributory negligence (*Chaffee* v. *Old Colony Railroad Company*, 17 R.I. 600); (2) the fellow servant rule as applied to employees of the same corporation (*Gaffney* v. *N.Y., N. H. & H. R. R.*, 15 R.I. 456; *Brodeur* v. *Valley Falls Co.* 16 R.I. 448); and (3) the doctrine that an employee accepted all the ordinary risks of an occupation (*Kelley* v. *Silver Spring Co.*, 12 R.I. 112; *McGrath* v. *N.Y. & N.E. R. R.*, 14 R.I. 357). Other measures that tended to reduce "accident" cases were safety devices installed in factories and by public service corporations. The courts also introduced the practice of reviewing verdicts (*Dyson* v. *Rhode Island Company*, 25 R.I. 600) rendered by juries, and of granting new trials conditional upon remission of excessive verdicts.

The workmen's compensation act [passed in 1912] practically repealed the fellow servant rule, which excused employees from liability for injuries caused by the negligence of other employees on the ground that such negligence was among the ordinary risks of occupation assumed, and thus eliminated several early cases as precedents. It tended also to reduce litigation, both by establishing exact rules for damages and by setting up a simple procedure for action on claims without the intervention of a court. The courts had established other precedents that tended to limit suits, such as the rule that intervening negligence may break the causation and become paramount (*Mahogany* v. *Ward*, 16 R.I. 475), that negligence must be proved rather than assumed (*Gunn* v. *Union Railroad Company*, 22 R.I. 321, 579), and that there must be reasonable proof that a claimant for damages himself was careful in a dangerous situation (*Judge* v. *Narragansett Electric Company*, 31 R.I. 128; 23 R.I. 208).

One action for damages for negligence reached the Supreme Court seven times before final disposition (*Gunn* v. *Union Railroad Company*, 22 R.I. 325, 579; 23 R.I. 289; 24 R.I. 174; 26 R.I. 112; 27 R.I. 320, 432). A jury had returned a verdict for the plaintiff with damages assessed as $10,000. The defendant moved for a new trial for the reason alleged that the verdict was contrary to the evidence. The motion for a new trial was argued and granted. Plaintiff obtained an order for a reargument, and the court decided that a new trial may be granted, in the discretion of the court, even if there is evidence before the jury that will support the verdict. The order for a new trial was reaffirmed. Plaintiff then raised a constitutional question as to the right of a court to set aside a verdict in view of the constitutional safeguards of right and property. The constitutional question was decided adversely to the plaintiff on the ground that a court unquestionably has a right to grant a new trial if a verdict is in conflict with the evidence. At the second jury trial the plaintiff received a second verdict, and the case was carried to the Supreme Court on the refusal of the trial court to enter judgment on the verdict. The Supreme Court sustained the trial court. One defendant's petition for a new trial based upon the allegation that the verdict was against the evidence, the Supreme Court after argument entered judgment for the defendant. The plaintiff then raised a fresh constitutional question on the right of the court to reverse a verdict returned by a jury, and the court decided adversely, holding that in the instance of a verdict contrary to the evidence, the defendant was entitled to final judgment as a protection against continued litigation. The court denied a motion for reargument of the constitutional question.

In another action one of the parties raised a constitutional question as to the organization of the Supreme Court under the judiciary act of 1893, which divided the Supreme Court into an appellate division and a common pleas division, asserting that since 1893 the common pleas division had been an inferior court, and that the appellate division consisting of the chief justice and three justices assigned by him was a body so variable as to permit not less than 120 combinations. To this argument the court answered: "Some calculations in permutations and combinations have been made, to show of how many constituent elements the court may be composed under the present system. They are quite correct, and a like result can be shown as to the supreme court of the United States, or any other court whose quorum is less than their whole number. This, however, is a constitutional question, and such problems are not solvable by mathematics.... We have one supreme court with full jurisdiction upon the highest matters, and divisions for subordinate matters." The court denied a motion to dismiss a petition for a new trial, filed by the plaintiff who sought a second trial upon the ground of erroneous rulings and inadequacy of damages (*Floyd* v. *Quinn*, 24 R.I. 147). As a rule, however, the juries of the period were generous, if not extravagant, in awarding damages, and lawyers with cases against corporations could not be persuaded to settle out of court while juries were disposed to punish corporations.

Public service corporations experienced difficulty in retaining the services of good trial lawyers, in view of the possibilities of large fees to be won through successful actions against corporations. Eventually a shrewd corporation lawyer found a way out. In a case that was clear-cut the plaintiff claimed a jury trial, and was ready to proceed, when the defendant submitted to default and moved that the judge should assess the damages. The court denied the motion, and empanelled a jury to assess damages, which returned a verdict for the plaintiff in the sum of $2250. Defendant excepted, and filed a petition for a new trial on the grounds (1) that the court was in error in calling the jury, and (2) that the verdict was excessive and unjust. The appellate division denied the motion for a new trial and sent the case back to the common pleas division with directions to the court to assess the damages by approving or disapproving the award of the jury (*Dyson* v. *Rhode Island Company*, 25 R.I. 600). Substantially the court held that the "right of trial by jury... relates only to those civil cases or causes of action in which there has been an issue made by the pleadings of the parties—

where the facts alleged constituting the cause of action are denied and an issue of fact is formed which must be tried by a jury. Such a trial of an action has no application to an inquiry into damages, whether by the court or jury, after default, when the cause of action stands confessed." The decision meant that a corporation could default a case that involved no doubt as to liability, and have the damages assessed by the judge without a jury; and that the finding of a jury under the circumstances was not a verdict.

The decision of the court, written by Blodgett, J., recalled, in its massing of precedents and exhaustive examination of the point involved in its historical aspects with reference to even the earliest decisions in the Norman-English Year Books, the note summarizing the history of Rhode Island law occasionally appended by Justice Elisha R. Potter to an opinion. Aside from the consternation which the decision caused among the lawyers who were amassing riches through successful suits against wealthy corporations, the case as printed in the Rhode Island reports is most striking from a typographical point of view, as it incorporates, done in Gothic letters, ample quotations from the Year Books. The decision in the *Dyson* case, with that in the case of *Gunn* v. *Union Railroad Company*, tended to diminish the effectiveness of appeals to juries in civil cases, as (1) a defendant could avoid a jury trial by defaulting; and (2) the court assumed in the *Gunn* case the right to set aside verdicts held to be in conflict with evidence and to enter up judgment contrary to the finding of the jury.

Marsden Perry (1850–1935) was Rhode Island's most resourceful financier of his era and the man most responsible for the electrification and growth of a street railway system in the state. He created the Union Trust Company, a forerunner of Fleet Bank, acquired the fledgling Narragansett Electric Company, and chartered a transportation holding company—the United Traction and Electric Company. By the time Perry erected the Union Trust Building in 1902, he had rerouted the traction lines from Market Square (the hub of the horsecar system) to the corner of Dorrance and Westminster streets, bringing (as he boasted) "all of Rhode Island to Union Trust's doorstep." Cartoon from Cyrus Farnum's *Men of Providence in Cartoon*.

BIOGRAPHICAL PROFILES

James Burrill, Jr. (1772–1820), a brilliant leader of the early-nineteenth-century bar and a noted orator, was born in Providence and graduated from Brown University. After legal clerkships, first in the office of Theodore Foster and then under the tutelege of David Howell, he became state attorney general in 1797 at the age of twenty-five and served in that elective post until 1813, when he was chosen a member of the state's House of Representatives. Within a year he was elevated to the position of Speaker (1814–1816), after which he was made chief justice for a year.

Burrill was elected to the United States Senate as a Federalist in 1817, but he died in office on Christmas Day, 1820, after serving only half his term. During his short tenure he became chairman of the Senate's Judiciary Committee. His last major speech, in December 1820, was in opposition to the Missouri Compromise; because the measure banned Negroes and mulattos from settling in Missouri, said Burrill, it "was entirely repugnant to the Constitution of the United States" in that it distinguished between classes of citizens.

On the personal side, Burrill married Sally Arnold in 1797 and fathered four daughters. He was the great-grandfather of Rhode Island governor and U.S. senator Theodore Francis Green. The town of Burrillville, established in 1806, was named in his honor. Senator Burrill's older brother, George R. Burrill, who was also a distinguished lawyer and orator, is regarded as Rhode Island's first notable constitutional reformer.

In the estimation of his contemporaries, Tristam Burges (1770–1853) was a leader of the Rhode Island Bar during the first half of the nineteenth century. After briefly studying medicine, Burges enrolled at Brown, where he became valedictorian of the class of 1796. He was admitted to the bar in 1799 and soon became an accomplished lawyer and a leader of the Federalist party. He became a state representative in 1811 and chief justice of the Rhode Island Supreme Court for a one-year term in 1815. A powerful and acerbic speaker, Burges assumed the post of professor of oratory and belles lettres at Brown in 1815 and taught there until 1828. His career as lawyer and Brown professor was reenacted by his great-great-nephew Theodore Francis Green.

Burges served five terms in Congress from 1825 to 1835, engaging in several famous oratorical duels with the vitriolic John Randolph of Virginia. By the 1830s he had became a leader of the Rhode Island Whig party. In 1834 he was defeated for reelection, and in 1836 he was unsuccessful in his quest to wrest the governorship from Democrat John Brown Francis. Upon his return to private life he resumed the practice of law and commuted to court in Providence from his estate "Watchemoket Farm," then in Seekonk, Massachusetts, but since 1862 within the bounds of East Providence. Burges's death in 1853 ended what Abraham Payne called a brilliant yet "stormy career."

Despite its disapproval of the War of 1812, Rhode Island produced not only the foremost naval hero of that conflict, Oliver Hazard Perry, but also one of its most persuasive legal defenders, Henry Wheaton (1785–1848). This jurist, diplomat, and expounder of international law graduated from Brown in 1802 and practiced law in Providence until 1812, when his legal defense of the policies of Jefferson and Madison prompted Democratic Republicans in New York City to offer him the editorship of the *National Advocate*, their local party newspaper. Writing forcefully and with learning on the questions of international law growing out of the War of 1812, Wheaton was considered the mouthpiece of the Madison administration during his three-year wartime tenure with the paper. He was rewarded with the post of U. S. Supreme Court reporter in 1816 and performed that job with ability and with praise, from jurists and lawyers alike, until 1827, when he embarked upon a long and successful diplomatic career. In 1847 Harvard offered him a distinguished lectureship in civil and international law, but he died before he could assume this new position.

Notable as Wheaton's career was, his most enduring achievement was his work as an expounder and historian of international law. His classic study *Elements of International Law* (1836) went through numerous editions and translations. Its excellence has prompted historians to rank Wheaton with Marshall, Kent, and Story as major architects of the American legal system.

24

From its inception in the decade following the Dorr Rebellion as a mutated offspring of the Law and Order party, the Republican party dominated Rhode Island political life. It owed its ascendancy to many factors, not the least of which was the state's political system established by the constitution of 1843. That document, carefully drafted by the Law and Order coalition of upper-class Whigs and rural Democrats that vanquished Thomas Dorr, was designed to prevent the old-stock industrialist and the Yankee farmer from succumbing to the numerically superior urban proletariat, especially those of foreign birth and Catholic faith. When the Republican party formed during the 1850s in response to the slavery issue, it revived the Law and Order coalition of the preceding decade and adopted its nativistic posture, and it determined to use and preserve that party's constitutional checks upon the power of the urban working class.

Included in those checks were (1) a malapportioned Senate that gave a legislative veto to the small rural towns; (2) a cumbersome amendment process to frustrate reform; (3) the absence of procedures for the calling of a constitutional convention; (4) the absence (until 1889) of a secret ballot; (5) a General Assembly that dominated both the legislatively elected Supreme Court and the weak, vetoless (until 1909) governorship; and (6) a real estate voting requirement for the naturalized citizen. The last-mentioned check was eliminated by the Bourn Amendment (VII) in 1888, but it was replaced by a $134 property-taxpaying qualification for voting in city council elections. This requirement had the practical effect of preventing those at the lower socioeconomic levels, usually Catholic immigrants, from exercising control over the affairs of the cities in which they resided. This was true because the mayors, for whom all electors could vote, had very limited powers, while the councils, for whom only property owners could vote, were dominant, controlling both the purse and the patronage.

The famous political reformer James Quayle Dealey, of Brown University, contended in 1909 that "the political effect of this [voting] limitation is to place the control of municipal government in the hands of the

Republicans. The general vote which elects the mayor is usually Democratic in the five cities, but the property vote is strongly Republican. As the mayor has small powers in government, control over municipal affairs rests with the Republican organization. This limitation on municipal suffrage is a standing grievance on the part of Democratic, reform, and radical organizations and is pointed at as the only survival in the United States of the old-fashioned, colonial property qualifications." Nearly 60 percent of those who could vote for mayor were disfranchised in council elections.

As if constitutional checks were not sufficient, General Charles Brayton, legendary boss of the Republican party, for good measure engineered the enactment in 1901 of a statute designed to emasculate any Democrat who might back into the governor's chair by virtue of a split in Republican ranks. With a few limited exceptions, this "Brayton Act" placed the ultimate appointive power of state government in the hands of the Senate. In the aftermath of its passage a governor could effectively appoint only his private secretary and a handful of insignificant state officials.

By 1920 the Senate—the possessor of state appointive and budgetary power—was more malapportioned than ever. For example, West Greenwich, population 367, had the same voice as Providence, population 237,595! The twenty smallest towns, with an aggregate population of 41,660, outvoted Providence 20 to 1, although the capital city had over 39 percent of Rhode Island's total population. The Senate, said George F. O'Shaunessy, a Democratic congressman (1911–1919), was "a strong power exercised by the abandoned farms of Rhode Island."

The Progressive Era (ca. 1898–1917) was an age of national reform—political, economic, and social—but Rhode Island's reactionary constitutional system survived the period relatively intact. Boss Brayton and Nelson Aldrich proved more than a match for Lucius Garvin, James Higgins, Charles E. Gorman, Robert H. I. Goddard, Theodore Francis Green, Amasa Eaton, and other supporters of governmental reform. The Brayton-Aldrich combine even survived a national exposé by noted muckraker Lincoln Steffens, who in 1905 described Rhode Island as "A State for Sale."

Professor Chilton Williamson, author of the following essay, established his reputation as a leading authority on voting rights in America with the publication of *American Suffrage from Property to Democracy, 1760–1860* (Princeton, 1960). His analysis of Rhode Island suffrage from the Dorr War to the 1928 ratification of Amendment XX to the state constitution illustrates the importance of political nativism and ethnoreligious factors in Rhode Island political and constitutional history during the nine decades encompassed by his survey. While Williamson's narrative is otherwise both accurate and remarkably perceptive, his analysis of the purpose and effect of the Bourn Amendment to the state constitution (Article VII) misses the subtlety of the Republican maneuver to immediately enfranchise the recent immigrant rivals of the Irish Catholic Democrats for state elections. Most of the latter were native-born by 1888 and were therefore unaffected by the real estate requirement imposed upon naturalized citizens by the constitution of 1843. By 1888 Henry Bowen Anthony's constitutional check on Irish Catholic political participation had outlived its usefulness.

To the Hon. General Assembly of the State of Rhode-Island, at their May Session, A. D. 1846.

The undersigned, Citizens of the United States, resident in the State of Rhode-Island and Providence Plantations, respectfully set forth,

That under the Constitution and laws of the United States, the naturalized citizens of the United States, resident in Rhode-Island, have renounced all allegiance to any foreign power or government, and have been duly admitted to the rights and privileges of American citizens. And yet, your petitioners have to complain, that, by the existing Constitution of the State of Rhode-Island, the great majority of them are debarred from the most important political right, that of partaking, as voters, in the choice of their Representatives and other officers; inasmuch, as by a provision in said Constitution, no citizen of the State, born out of the U. States, can exercise the right of suffrage without being possessed of real property, which is impossible to many to obtain, and is a degrading brand placed upon all naturalized citizens, setting them apart as a peculiar, unworthy and disqualified class, to be shackled and held in suspicion, and continual objects of insult and derision.

The undersigned would further represent, that to render more marked the stigma which is thus affixed to naturalized citizens in Rhode-Island, the colored population of this State are allowed to exercise the right of suffrage, as freely as it is accorded to any white native citizen of the United States, thereby degrading naturalized citizens below the colored population.

The undersigned do not wish to be understood by this allusion to envy the colored population; on the contrary, they believe they have received nothing but what they are in justice entitled to: but, as the impression is abroad, that the colored race is inferior to the white and shaded population, the insult is more piercing.

The undersigned are not aware of anything in the character or conduct of naturalized citizens to warrant this illiberal, unjust and insulting distinction. They are useful members of the community; they contribute by useful labor and industry, to the prosperity of the community in which they live, as is evident to every unprejudiced mind; they do their full part in supporting institutions of government, learning and religion. They are ever ready, like the LAFAYETTES, STEUBENS, MONTGOMERIES, DE KALBS, KOSCIUSKOS, ST. CLAIRS, GATES and GALLATINS, on whom the success of American Liberty was so largely indebted in 1776 and 1812, and on all occasions of danger (as testified to by the most eminent Americans) to engage in the defence of the country and the home of their choice and adoption; and the undersigned challenge an investigation to show when and where naturalized citizens ever proved faithless to the confidence reposed in them, or shrunk from danger, or in what respect they are unworthy to exercise *all* the rights of American citizens.

The undersigned respectfully request your honorable body to take such steps towards an immediate alteration of that portion of the Constitution of this State, which requires a condition of naturalized citizens, not required of WHITE NATIVE CITIZENS OR COLOURED CITIZENS, conditions which are contrary to the true spirit and letter of the constitution and laws of the United States, and thus enable naturalized citizens to exercise freely and unshackled, the rights of the elective franchise, as given to them in good faith by the Constitution and laws of the United States, and by acting justly, wipe off the stain, that (should the law remain as it now is) would be a lasting stigma on our State, and a deliberate degeneracy from the liberal principles of its illustrious founder,—and,—your petitioners, as in duty bound, will ever pray.

This 1846 petition by Irish Catholic leader Henry J. Duff was the first of many formal attempts to remove the nativistic suffrage provision from the 1842 state constitution. It failed when the General Assembly rejected it in 1847.

Rhode Island Suffrage since the Dorr War, 1842–1928

Chilton Williamson

The adoption of a written constitution for Rhode Island in 1842 is a landmark in the evolution of Rhode Island democracy because it abandoned the old freehold qualification for the suffrage. Nevertheless it did not provide either a satisfactory or permanent solution to an issue in part responsible for the arresting phenomenon of the Dorr War. As a matter of fact, from about 1850 to 1928 suffrage issues were always in the background of Rhode Island politics. On at least two occasions they dominated the foreground.

The survival of the spirit of "Dorrism" into the twentieth century was due to aggravated tensions in Rhode Island, present it is true in other New England states but not in so acute a form. Hostility of country for city, of Protestant for Catholic, of the older stock for the newer, of conservative for liberal traditions have characterized Rhode Island politics to a greater degree probably than the politics of other New England states.

The clue to the relative power of these groups is to be found in the constitutional and statutory provisions with regard to suffrage and representation which favored the native-born, Protestant elements at the expense of Catholic, immigrant groups, and of the native-born who were poor.

The first struggle involving suffrage was the celebrated Dorr War. A striking analogy exists between this event and the passage of the first British Reform Bill in 1832. Probably neither would have occurred had not industrialization imposed such severe strains upon tile structure of government that only reform of suffrage and representation could offer relief. To achieve these aims, critics of the established order in Rhode Island after 1840 formed a non-partisan coalition composed of Democrats and even some Whigs who were angered by the indifference of their parties to democratic suffrage theory and practice. Merchants and manufacturers joined them because they resented the freehold qualification as well as overrepresentation of the farming communities. Many militia men and firemen who as foreign or even native- born working men, could not meet the property tests, became active in the movement because they thought their services to the community warranted a voice in government. Their ideas were based on the political theory of the "Loco-foco" wing of the Democratic party, to which a few members of even the "best families," including Thomas W. Dorr, were attracted. Democratic party professionals joined the movement hoping that reform would forever eliminate Whig creation of freeholds to defeat them at the polls and would increase their popularity at a time when they had been routed by the appeal of "Tippecanoe and Tyler too" in 1840.

It was sound strategy of the anti-Dorr elements to pit country against city, manufacturer against worker, Protestant against Catholic, native-born against foreign-born. By 1842, the solidarity of the Dorrite leaders had been undermined. When they attempted to displace the existing government by force, the "popular majority" in whose name they acted no longer

FRIENDS OF GOV. JACKSON,
READ THIS!

IRISH VOTERS!!!

We have just been informed that the Country towns are flooded with *Infamous Handbills,* misrepresenting the views of GOV. JACKSON as to the *Qualification of Foreign Voters!*-- It is well known that Gov. Jackson PROPOSED the *FREEHOLD QUALIFICATION* in the CONVENTION. The whole story that *Gov Jackson* is in favor of ABOLISHING that qualification is *utterly* and *totally without foundation!* It is manufactured by SAMUEL CURREY, a *Naturalized Foreigner* from NOVA SCOTIA, who has been HIRED to *MISREPRESENT* the views of GOV. JACKSON *and his friends.*

People of *Rhode-Island* believe not these INFAMOUS LIES manufactured by this *HIRED TOOL* of the Providence ARISTOCRACY!-- They are *INTENDED to DECEIVE you,* and thus prevent the election of GOV. JACKSON AND HIS PROX. They dared not *circulate* one of them in Providence, for they *knew it would be refuted forthwith!*

Friends of CHARLES JACKSON, are you willing to see *him* crushed by the FALSEHOODS and *MALIGNITY* of his bitterest enemies?---- *We know you are NOT!*

MANY WHIGS.

The opponents of Governor Charles Jackson, the chief executive who had liberated Thomas Dorr in 1845, tried to engineer the governor's defeat in 1846 by alleging that Jackson favored the repeal of the real estate restriction on naturalized voters. In this broadside Jackson's supporters assure native citizens that this claim is a "falsehood" and an "infamous lie." Jackson, the grandson of an Irish Protestant immigrant, lost the election to nativist Byron Diman, whose grandson John Diman became a Roman Catholic priest and founder of Portsmouth Priory.

existed. The *opera bouffe* events which followed brought success to Whig efforts to alienate Dorr's remaining followers from him.

Dorr lost the war; but not completely, for the victors found it expedient to write a constitution as Dorr had demanded. It was a foregone conclusion, however, that it would differ in many particulars from the Dorrite document of November, 1841. The anti-Dorr constitution was framed in 1842 and went into effect in 1843. It granted the right to vote to all adult, native-born citizens if they owned $134 worth of property, "real and personal," and, if not, upon payment of a $1.00 tax. The tax qualification for the very poor, native-born citizen was, in effect, a poll tax like that so prevalent until recently in the South.

The qualification for the naturalized citizen was different. It perpetuated, despite statements to the contrary, a freehold qualification. No adult male naturalized citizen was permitted to vote unless he owned a freehold worth at least $134. That sum was a holdover from colonial and Revolutionary days, expressed in terms of the American dollar instead of the English pound. By the 1880s, it was impossible to purchase a house in Providence without spending at least $2,000. If the freehold qualification had been $2,000, it is doubtful if any fewer foreign-born could have voted than under the $134 qualification.

Discrimination against the naturalized citizen could scarcely be reconciled with prevailing democratic theory, but it was extremely popular among nativist elements, Whig or Democrat. The Whigs, moreover, shared with Democrats a prejudice against the adult male who was not a property-owner or tax-payer in Rhode Island towns or in the City of Providence. Both the Dorrite and Whig constitutions denied such men a voice in the raising and expenditure of money in these units of local government. They justified this exclusion on the grounds that town and city poor would play fast and loose with other people's money and that they had no right to be represented in financial matters. The new constitution reflected this philosophy by prohibiting anyone from voting to raise money in town meetings and, in Providence, from voting to raise taxes and to elect members of the city council unless he was the owner of property, real or personal, assessed at $134.

The precise extent of enfranchisement under the new constitution will never be determined without laborious examination of the records of Rhode Island towns and of Providence, similar to R. E. Brown's investigation of voting in colonial Massachusetts. Democratic and Whig newspapers never agreed as to the proportion of the adult males who could vote under the old freehold qualification and under the new constitution. Democratic newspapers declared that prior to 1843 only about 30 per cent of the adult males could vote. Whig papers asserted that this figure was much too low because it represented percentages of actual, rather than of qualified voters. Both agreed, however, that the proportion of legal voters in the small, farming towns was very high. The situation in the newer industrial communities, containing a large, highly mobile and poor immigrant population, was different. In 1841, the *Providence Journal* estimated that only 1,886 persons were qualified to vote in Providence and that under "an extended suffrage" (presumably tax-paying) 3,862 would qualify. For the state as a whole it maintained that, of an adult male population of 26,000, in 1840, only 11,293 qualified and only 8,621 voted. Under an extended suffrage only 18,139 would qualify because of the very large number of aliens and temporary residents.

Industrialist Philip Allen (1785–1865) was an uncle and ally of Thomas Dorr. He served three terms as governor (1851–1853) and one term as U.S. senator from Rhode Island (1853–1859). Allen was a philanthropist and an advocate of equal voting rights for naturalized immigrants.

If these figures are correct, the new constitution increased the electorate by about 60 per cent. One would expect that the newly enfranchised would have flocked to the polls. On the contrary, the number of voters decreased after the constitution went into effect, despite prodding by the Democratic party and despite the increase of population in the eighteen forties. In 1843, 15,000 voted, in 1850, only 4,000: a number equal to about one-fifth of the adult male population. One Democratic newspaper maintained that no greater proportion of adult males voted in Rhode Island in 1850 than in Britain in the same year.

The Democratic party concluded from this evidence that further suffrage reform was indispensable to bring Rhode Island abreast of the democracy of other states, particularly New York. The real reason for the declining interest of voters, it claimed, lay in the fact that suffrage reform, coming at the "hands of enemies," had created a system "of elections without voters" in which citizens thought no more of voting than the "surfs" of Russia.

Democrats blamed this situation on the absence of a secret ballot, the payment of the registry tax, the exclusion of registry voters from electing members of the city council of Providence, and the freehold qualification for the naturalized citizen. The registry tax provision was singled out for particular condemnation. Democratic newspapers, in convincing detail, accused Whig employers of coercing their factory-hands by paying their registry taxes, escorting them to the polls, and on pain of dismissal requiring them to vote for Whig candidates. When, in 1850–1851, Democrats and Free Soilers in Massachusetts secured the passage of a secret-ballot law, Rhode Island Democrats fought the Whigs on suffrage and related issues, declaring that their state constitution was "one of the worst in the country" and "infinitely more calculated to disfranchise than to enfranchise."

Some Democrats favored comprehensive suffrage reform but others, aware of the prejudices of the native-born Protestants, sought simply to reform registry tax procedures and the abuses of the open ballot system. Whigs opposed any suffrage reform whatever, asserting that the situation in Rhode Island was unique. They argued that states such as Connecticut, Massachusetts and New York which had "unrestricted suffrage" had a majority of farmers and landowners to hold "the fluctuating masses" of cities in check. Rhode Island was in a different situation because it was fast becoming "one great workshop," composed of Catholics, foreigners and, it was intimated, of Democrats as well.

Despite Whig charges that they were reviving "Dorrism," Democrats won the election of 1851. Subsequently, they passed a bill requiring voters to cast their ballots in sealed envelopes and another permitting them to pay their registry tax a short time before actually voting rather than, as formerly, about a year in advance. Despite criticism from its liberal wing for not having gone far enough, the Democratic party appealed to the voters to support it because of those reforms which it had achieved. The voters, however, did not respond to the appeal, and the Democrats failed to win any further important elections before the Civil War.

But war, that prime mover of American suffrage reform, brought the issue to the fore again. When Lincoln called for volunteers after the firing on Fort Sumter, foreign-born young men were told that the reward for valor would be their admission to the suffrage upon the same terms as the native-born. When the military situation improved greatly, the Republican successors of the Whig party lost whatever enthusiasm they may have had for reform. With the help of Democrats who shared their fear of foreigners, Republicans rejected in 1864 a constitutional amendment designed to honor the post-Sumter commitment.

On the whole, the Republicans benefited much more than did the Democrats from maintaining a restricted electorate. The Republican machine based its success not only upon its policies regarding business enterprise and southern reconstruction, but also upon its control

The petitions of Charles E. Gorman (1844–1917), Rhode Island's first Irish Catholic lawyer, prompted a U.S. Senate investigation into voting abuses in Rhode Island that reached the conclusions recited below.

EXTRACTS FROM REPORTS 572 AND 427 MADE TO THE UNITED STATES SENATE IN APRIL AND MAY, 1880, BY A SELECT COMMITTEE OF WHICH SENATOR WILLIAM WALLACE OF PENNSYLVANIA WAS CHAIRMAN

Restricted suffrage, registry taxes upon poor men alone, statutory closing of the polls at sunset, instead of eight o'clock, as formerly, by which the operatives in the mill are prevented from voting, and the compulsory payment of the registry tax ten months prior to the general election in a Presidential year, cause great complaints upon the part of the poor men and foreign-born citizens in Rhode Island; and to these features of her laws many intelligent witnesses ascribe the small percentage of voters among her people and the large amount of corrupt practices in the elections of the State.

. . . .

Your committee believes that there are good grounds for the complaints made that the government of Rhode Island, under its present constitution, is nearer an oligarchy than a democracy. The disfranchisement of so large a percentage of her people, by systematic effort and rigidly-enforced statutes, the small vote cast for President at a hotly-contested election, the small number of votes cast for members of Congress in four successive elections, when contrasted with the number cast in other States in the same elections, the choice of members of Congress, governors, and Presidents by the votes of one out of every ten of the people, whilst other States cast one vote for every five of theirs, the maintenance of the rule of three-fifths for the amendment of her constitution, by which the will of the majority has been twice defeated, all compel us to recognize Rhode Island as different in her government, her institutions, and her policy from all of her sister commonwealths in the Union, and lead us to grasp at any provision of the Federal Constitution which, fairly construed, will grant us power to enforce, for her people, 'a republican form of government,' by which we mean a government by the whole people, for the whole people of the State.

Rhode Island is the only State in the Union in which native and foreign-born citizens stand upon different grounds as to State qualifications for the right of suffrage.

. . . .

Your committee reports that the rights of suffrage to *foreign-born* citizens of the United States is abridged by the constitution and laws of Rhode Island.

of registry voters. Respected, well-to-do Republican nominees for governor and other offices were expected to help finance, in return for nomination, the payment of the registry taxes of a key proportion of poor voters, as well as other party expenses.

Republicans benefited also from the property qualification for the foreign-born, whose influence was reduced to an absolute minimum. The situation was virtually the same with regard to the native-born voters. According to the *Providence Journal*, about 20 per cent of the 53,814 native-born potential voters did not register. Of the 31,913 foreign-born potential voters, 74 per cent were not naturalized; only 15 per cent of those naturalized could meet the freehold qualification. As a result of indifference and suffrage restrictions, only 53 per cent of adult males were voters. These facts justified the assertion that the same reasons for reform existed at this time as before the Dorr War because the same ratio was denied the suffrage as in 1840.

Henry Bowen Anthony (1815–1884), editor and then publisher of the *Providence Journal*, was elected governor in 1849 and 1850 and served as U.S. senator from 1859 until his death in 1884. Anthony was Rhode Island's most prominent nativist and a die-hard defender of the real estate requirement for naturalized voters. As a U.S. senator, Anthony led the fight to limit the Fifteenth Amendment to blacks ("race, color, or previous condition of servitude") and left such oppressed minorities as the Irish Catholics of Rhode Island and the Chinese of California unprotected by federal law.

To increase the size of the electorate, reformers founded the Equal Rights Association which in the late seventies and early eighties agitated the question of reform, reviving a stratagem as old as "Dorrism." This organization appealed to the Congress of the United States to intervene in the affairs of Rhode Island. Suffrage restrictions, it said, were the very antithesis of the Reconstruction policies of the Republican party. In particular, reformers tried to convince Congress that the suffrage restraints upon foreigners violated the "privileges and immunities" and the "equal protection of the laws" clauses of the Fourteenth Amendment as well as the intent of the Fifteenth. A Republican Rhode Island Senator, Henry B. Anthony, could think of nothing better in this embarrassing situation than to appeal to states' rights. "Since the days of nullification," one commentator remarked, "there has been no such powerful appeal for States' Rights as that of the Rhode Island Senator."

Within Rhode Island, the objectives of the Association were supported by the Greenback Labor party and the Knights of Labor. The Prohibition party which had secured a Prohibition Law in 1886 was urged, although unsuccessfully, to broaden the basis of its support by favoring suffrage reform. One speaker said wistfully and somewhat cynically that whichever party did so "would secure a great many votes." The leaders of the Woman's Suffrage movement avoided the issue by seeking the vote for women upon the same terms as the vote for men. With some exceptions, Republicans were distinctly cold to suffrage reform, so much so that as late as 1888 the *Providence Journal* warned them that continued intransigeance upon this issue was dangerous.

By a process of elimination, the Democratic party proved to be the only organization capable of securing reform. Nevertheless, many in that party were not anxious to change suffrage qualifications for reasons appreciated

Elizabeth Buffum Chace (1806–1899), shown here, and her colleague Paulina Wright Davis (1813–1876) led the fight for women's suffrage in Rhode Island during the second half of the nineteenth century. In 1868 they formed the Rhode Island Woman Suffrage Association. Shortly thereafter, Davis became the first historian of the national women's rights movement. Their goal was not achieved until January 1920, when the General Assembly ratified the Twentieth Amendment to the federal Constitution.

and respected by many Republicans. The outstanding reformers were often Democrats, but they were seldom in control. Indeed, some of them abused their fellow Democrats quite as much as they did Republicans.

In the last analysis, the Democratic machine could not forever condone a flagrant violation of democratic theory nor remain indifferent to the prime fact that many poor men were Democrats by conviction and wanted to vote. For many years the party postponed a decision, adopting the Republican practice of paying registry taxes, but it had more trouble getting funds to do so than did the Republicans. To such an extent did both parties pay registry taxes that it was estimated that 50 per cent of the voters had their taxes paid for them This practice elicited a southerner's comment that Yankees would soon have to be paid to celebrate the Fourth of July.

This pattern remained unchanged until 1886 when a bipartisan coalition removed the onerous discrimination against naturalized Civil War veterans, permitting them to qualify as voters on the same terms as the native-born. The agitation of the issue at this time led to such an increase of interest in suffrage reform as to encourage the Democratic party to adopt a reform platform in 1887. It called for the abolition of property and tax-paying qualifications, amid excitement of mass meetings highly reminiscent of the Dorr War.

The Republican party followed suit, but so tardily as to give color to the criticism that it acted merely from expediency. Whatever the reason, it was too late. The *Providence Journal* could truthfully state in 1887 that the power of the party was endangered for the first time since the Civil War. Republicans were also losing popularity because of their failure to enforce the Prohibition Law of 1886, because of their indifference to labor-capital relations and because they condoned the activities of Charles R. Brayton, the Republican "boss" who groomed the famous Nelson W. Aldrich for high office. "Boss" Brayton manipulated elections and nominations, kept the party in funds, and obtained for himself a lucrative post in the state government. Despite the presence at political rallies of Henry Cabot Lodge, especially imported for the occasion, the Republicans suffered at the hands of the voters as never before in the election of 1887.

Republicans saw the inevitability of reform and cooperated with the Democrats to pass suffrage legislation. The act dealing with voting qualifications, in the form of a constitutional amendment, was the work primarily of Augustus O. Bourn, Brown University graduate, rubber manufacturer, and twice Republican governor of the state. Although the Bourn Amendment abolished the property qualification for the naturalized citizen and the payment of the dollar tax for the native-born, it imposed a dollar tax upon all qualified voters, whether they voted or not, the proceeds to be spent upon the public schools. This tax was primarily a revenue measure rather than an effort to keep poor voters from the polls. An enforcement act of 1890, which provided for imprisonment for failure to pay this tax, sustains this interpretation of the major aim of the act. The more striking aspect of the amendment was its failure to allow the non-property owner to vote in financial town meetings and the application of this provision to all the cities which had achieved city status since 1842.

To an extent, therefore, the Bourn Amendment both enfranchised and disfranchised, thus confirming the charge that actually Republicans had won the election and that the Equal Rights Association had been captured by the more conservative Democrats. The amendment was attacked by representatives of the cities affected who termed it a dishonest bill and a snare and delusion. The real object, they said, was to forestall the calling of a constitutional convention which might create a strong executive with veto powers, and increase the representation of cities at the expense of the towns. One critic declared that the amendment would disfranchise 4,000 voters in Pawtucket and Newport, and 2,000 in Woonsocket. Friends of the amendment defended it on the grounds that no one believed "in letting down every safeguard to the prosperity of the state." Despite these criticisms, the Bourn Amendment was a decisive step towards political democracy. The voters ratified it in 1888, with a vote of 19,462 to 12,590. Only in this year did Rhode Island approximate the stage of democracy which most of the other states had reached before the Civil War; the restrictive features of the amendment did not occasion much discontent for many years.

This apathy came to an end with the first World War which, like the Civil War, brought in its wake a questioning of suffrage restrictions. A crusade to make the world safe for democracy could not fail to make Rhode Islanders more sensitive about their remaining suffrage restrictions. In addition, the Bourn Amendment did not prevent voting frauds, such as the assignment of wholly fictitious values to the personal property of those persons who would vote as they were told. Despite numerous violations of this sort, the amendment seems to have been generally enforced. Some persons were actually dropped from voting lists for city councils because the value of their automobiles had sunk below $134. Critics said also that in Providence only 20,670 persons voted for aldermen, whereas 54,696 voted for mayor and that, in the third ward, 50 percent of adult males were not qualified to vote. The Democratic candidate for mayor of Pawtucket said in the same year that in his city only 8,300 voted for general officers and mayor. The limited suffrage, he said, was the "key to the present situation in Pawtucket," i.e., Republican ascendancy. Moreover, so extensive was the practice of padding voting lists that it was alleged that the number of illegal voters in some city elections outnumbered the propertied voters, thus making a travesty of the Republican philosophy that those who owned the cities should control their finances.

Republican control of cities involved Republican engrossment of patronage. Democrats felt this situation with especial keenness. Republicans were in part correct in

Charles R. "Boss" Brayton (1840–1910), depicted in this *Journal* cartoon by Milton W. Halladay, manipulated both the legislature and elections in Rhode Island from the 1880s until his death in 1910. A longtime chairman of the Republican State Central Committee, Brayton often addressed the members of that group as "fellow machinists." He was able to control the General Assembly through old-stock rural legislators from the country towns, because each municipality, regardless of size, had one vote in the Senate. Brayton used the contributions of Providence businessmen to buy up the vote in these small towns, cynically remarking that "an honest voter is one who stays bought."

McCLURE'S MAGAZINE

VOL. XXIV FEBRUARY, 1905 No. 4

RHODE ISLAND: A STATE FOR SALE

WHAT SENATOR ALDRICH REPRESENTS—A BUSINESS MAN'S GOVERNMENT FOUNDED UPON THE CORRUPTION OF THE PEOPLE THEMSELVES

BY

LINCOLN STEFFENS

AUTHOR OF "THE SHAME OF THE CITIES"

ILLUSTRATED WITH PORTRAITS

THE political condition of Rhode Island is notorious, acknowledged, and it is shameful. But Rhode Islanders are ashamed of it. There is the shining truth about this state. Not many American communities are so aware of their political degradation, none has a healthier body of conservative discontent; and the common sense of this good-will, unorganized and impotent though it is, makes the Rhode Islander resent the interest of his neighbors. "Our evils are *our* troubles," he says; "they don't concern the rest of you. Why should we be singled out? We are no worse than others. We are better than some; we want to set things right, but can't. Conditions are peculiar."

This is all wrong. The evils of Rhode Island concern every man, woman, and child in our land. For example:

The United States Senate is coming more and more to be the actual head of the United States government. In the Senate there is a small ring (called the Steering Committee) which is coming more and more to be the head of the United States Senate. The head of this committee is Senator Nelson W. Aldrich, who has been described as "the boss of the United States," "the power behind the power behind the throne," "the general manager of the United States." The fitness of these titles is a question of national politics, and all I know to the point in that field is what everybody knows: that Senator Aldrich, a very rich man and father-in-law of young Mr. Rockefeller, is supposed to represent "Sugar," "Standard Oil," "New York," and, more broadly, "Wall Street"; our leading legislative authority on protective tariff, he speaks for privileged business; the chairman of the Senate finance committee, he stands for high finance. These facts and suppositions, taken together with the praises I have heard of him in Wall Street and the comfortable faith he seems to inspire in business men all over the country, suggest that we have in Senator Aldrich the commercial ideal of political character, and—if not the head—at least the political representative of the head of that System which is coming more and more to take the place of the passing paper government of the United States.

What sort of a man is Senator Aldrich? What school of politics did he attend, what

Brayton's electioneering tactics and those of his colleagues Nelson W. Aldrich and Marsden Perry prompted muckraker Lincoln Steffens to write a 1905 exposé, aptly entitled "Rhode Island: A State for Sale," for *McClure's Magazine*. Said Steffens: "The political condition of Rhode Island is notorious, acknowledged, and it is shameful."

suspecting that suffrage reform arose from Democratic determination to secure a fair share of jobs and political influence. One Republican dismissed the suffrage reform movement on the grounds that it had arisen for seven crass reasons: "five loaves and two fishes."

Suffrage restrictions were condemned also by leaders of various minority groups. Sons and grandsons of Irish, Italians, and French Canadians believed that their influence in either Republican or Democratic councils was not as great as their numbers and abilities warranted. Both parties had long since recognized the delicate nature of this problem. With varying degrees of success, they had endeavored to meet it by nominating even French Canadians to high office, now that they comprised about 20 per cent of the population. Nevertheless, descendants of immigrants who, by becoming tradesmen, lawyers or members of other professions, had gained middle-class status resented the Bourn Amendment because it fell particularly hard upon their fellows, if not upon themselves.

Because the two-party system did not represent a clear-cut division between the older and the newer stock, talk of reform caused trouble within as well as between the two major parties. On one occasion, when a Republican of the older stock attacked the growing influence of "minorities" in the government of Rhode Island, a fellow Republican of Italian extraction retorted, "If we who didn't come over in the *Mayflower* combined, there would be little or no representation by those who trace ancestry to the *Mayflower*."

If grievances of professional politicians and of descendants of immigrants had been the only impulses behind the renewed demand for reform, however, the movement would never have waxed so strongly after 1921. Poor residents of cities, regardless of origin, supported reformers. They were critical of the Bourn Amendment on the grounds that it had resulted in economy-minded city administrations, indifferent to the probems of twentieth-century urbanism: inadequate public improvements, recreational facilities, and police protection. Organized labor, particularly the United Textile Workers, denounced police brutality in strikes, and ridiculed the Republicans for condemning lynchings in the South, while ignoring humane legislation for a forty-hour week in Rhode Island.

Rhode Island traditions made the outcome of this situation almost predictable. Between 1922 and 1924 the spirit of Dorr was once more abroad in the state. The leaders of the newer movement included such Democratic "insurgents" as the well-born Peter Goelet Gerry, Harvard '01;

the able Irishman, William S. Flynn, Georgetown Law School graduate and Providence lawyer; and the colorful French-Canadian leader, Felix A. Toupin. As insurgent Democrats, they and their supporters secured control of the party convention of 1924. Once in command, they brushed aside the timid delegates from the smaller towns and launched a reform movement whose outcome is one of the great divides in Rhode Island's history.

Once again, Rhode Islanders appealed to their indigenous historical traditions. Roger Williams was quoted as having said that Rhode Island was a "Democracy" and Providence was again said to be governed by "an aristocracy created by the property qualification." Orators asserted, as had Dorr, that the people had an inherent right to change their government. If reformers were balked, they would urge the registry voters "to swarm from all over the State to the State House and in their thousands terrify the plutocrats by another bloodless revolution like that of Thomas W. Dorr." The situation was likened to that preceding Magna Carta, the Boston Tea Party, and the American Revolution.

Augustus O. Bourn (1834–1925)—a Bristol rubber-goods manufacturer, Brayton ally, and governor from 1883 to 1885—sponsored a pseudoreform in 1887 while a state senator. This Bourn Amendment to the state constitution (Article of Amendment VII), ratified in 1888, removed the real estate requirement for naturalized male citizens and allowed them to vote on the same basis as the native-born. In its practical effect, however, it immediately enfranchised the more recent ethnic arrivals to Rhode Island, such as the French Canadians, British, Germans, and Swedes—all of whom were inclined toward the Republican party.

Unfortunately, the Democrats failed to agree as to the extent of reform as well as how it was to be achieved. Some hoped only to reduce the number of "rotten boroughs" represented in the Senate, to increase the powers of the Governor, to abolish all property tests and to secure the passage of modern labor legislation. Insurgent Democrats, however, wanted to go further. They demanded a popular referendum on the subject of a constitutional convention for the purpose of overhauling thoroughly the machinery of government, as had Dorr in 1841.

The Republican organization chose to ignore this movement in a way reminiscent of Whig fatuity in scorning the earliest manifestations of Dorrism. The dramatic success of the Democrats in the elections of 1922 demonstrated forcefully the inexpediency of such a policy in the twentieth century. Henceforth, few Republicans cared to be so frank as to say, as one did, that reform would bring, among other undesirable things, "labor legislation galore."

Constructively minded Republicans responded to their defeat by adopting an attitude like that of the British Tory leader, Sir Robert Peel, who declared that the function of his party was to demolish untenable positions so that which remained could hold out longer. Republicans tried to prevent the consideration of Democratic legislation by sponsoring in January, 1924, a bill to abolish all property qualifications in towns and cities, incorporating, however, a measure to reduce town meeting control of finances by creating quasi-independent town budget commissions. Insurgent Democrats refused to support this measure as well as another Republican-sponsored bill to abolish all property qualifications except in towns.

Democrats had a different program in mind. A majority of them sponsored a bill in the lower house to abolish all property tests. Meanwhile, the insurgents in the Senate, working somewhat at cross-purposes with their colleagues in the lower house, sought not only suffrage reform but also a constitutional convention bill. Fearing that Democrats would control such a convention, Republicans opposed the bill as the greatest threat to Republican power since the Civil War.

Denied a convention by Republican opposition in the Senate, extremist Democrats launched a campaign to paralyze the legislative processes, like that of the Irish Home Rulers in the British House of Commons. So successful were they that, by May of 1924, the state was unable to pay salaries of some of its employees because Democrats refused to permit the passage of even the appropriation bill. Only funds borrowed from banks and trust companies prevented a total financial collapse.

On June 18, the situation became as tense as any since the Dorr War. On this day fighting broke out on the floor of the Senate between spectators and Senators, causing a hurried call for the police. The next day, some unidentified persons released bromine gas in the chamber, driving Senators from their seats. Republican Senators angrily retaliated by withdrawing to the uncontaminated atmosphere of Rutland, Massachusetts. They complained that the Democratic Lieutenant Governor, Felix A. Toupin, had kept them in continuous session, refusing to allow them to leave the chamber for "food, rest or any other purpose." The Senators vowed they would not return until promised that the Senate floor would be cleared of unauthorized persons and that their personal security would not again be jeopardized.

In the opinion of many, the insurgents had gone too far. For this reason the elections of November, 1924, were fought not so much upon the issue of reform but upon the highly emotional issue of "law and order." Although the *Providence Journal* favored reform, it was extremely critical of reformers' methods, particularly their conduct in the Senate during the previous June. "For a few lurid moments," it said, "the blockade of public business blazed up into the more violent semblance of plain revolution." The major issue of the campaign was neatly summarized by a Republican: "Toupin or American government." The Republicans won the election.

The sequel to Republican victory bears comparison with the aftermath of the anti-Dorr triumph of 1842. In both cases, the victors were compelled to concede a good deal to their opponents. The proposal for a convention was shelved as was that to abolish the property qualification in towns. Nevertheless, under pressure from Republican and Democratic newspapers, Republicans moved slowly to honor their electoral commitment to reform the suffrage and representation. Bowing to majority opinion, the legislature passed three bills in 1925 and 1926 in the form of amendments to the constitution. One provided for reapportionment of seats in the Senate, one provided for biennial registration, and one abolished the property qualification for voting in cities. Tax-payers in financial town meetings were authorized to submit to the qualified voters a plan to establish budget commissions. If this plan were accepted, the tax-paying qualification would be automatically abolished. In conformity with the constitution, these bills were passed a second time in the legislature in 1927. Ratification by a three-fifths' majority of the voters was now required to make them a part of that document.

A few Republicans resisted reform to the last. During the legislative session of 1927, a Republican introduced a bill to abolish the property qualification in cities, but to establish instead what critics called a southern-type poll tax. Under this measure no person, otherwise qualified, could vote unless he had paid a three dollar tax. The memory of the abuses of the registry tax under the Brayton regime was sufficient to make this a quite unreal proposal.

Despite public indifference at that time, the suffrage and other amendments were milestones in Rhode Island's history. According to Samuel Lubell, the suffrage amendment marked the coming of age of the more recent immigrant groups as well as of the Democratic party. In the larger perspective, the amendments are significant because Rhode Islanders had succeeded in their efforts to recover and to exceed the extent of political democracy of colonial times, despite the development of an industrial, urban society and the immigration of a people different in culture and religion. Thomas W. Dorr was the first great Rhode Island figure to see the problem clearly and to advocate a solution in harmony with the American democratic creed. The suffrage amendment of 1928 vindicated the position he had taken in 1842 and demonstrated that his great misfortune was to be born one hundred years too soon.

Dr. Lucius F. C. Garvin (1841–1922) ranks among Rhode Island's most tenacious reformers. This Tennessee native entered the state legislature in 1883, joining with attorneys Charles Gorman and Edwin McGuinness in the Equal Rights Movement of that era—an effort to remove the real estate voting requirements for naturalized citizens and to apportion the state legislature fairly. Garvin was elected to the governorship in 1902 and 1903 but was defeated in the gubernatorial elections of 1901, 1904, and 1905. He remained active in reform causes in his later years, and he died in 1922 while campaigning for reelection as state senator from Cumberland. Always the physician, Garvin made house calls to his patients until the day of his death at age eighty-one. Lincoln Steffens observed in 1905 that "this country doctor is the most singular figure in American politics."

BIOGRAPHICAL PROFILES

During the 1840s and 1850s there occurred a burst of literary activity in Providence that was unequaled since the Revolutionary era. Prominent among the local literati was the city's earliest historian, Judge William Read Staples (1798–1868). His *Annals of the Town of Providence* (1843), the first extended history of the city, is still a valuable source.

Staples was a member of Providence's first city council in 1832, an associate justice of the state Supreme Court from 1835 to 1854, and the court's chief justice from 1854 to 1856, when he resigned his high judicial post to accept the newly created position of state auditor (thus paving the way for the accession of Samuel Ames to the chief justiceship). History, however, was his great passion. He was an incorporator of the Rhode Island Historical Society (established in 1822) and its first secretary and librarian. In addition to the *Annals*, Staples's published works include a critical edition of Samuel Gorton's *Simplicity's Defense* (1835), a *Documentary History of the Destruction of the Gaspee* (1847), an annotated edition of the colony's famous 1647 code of laws (1847), and a history of Rhode Island's ratification of the federal Constitution entitled *Rhode Island in the Continental Congress* (1870), which appeared posthumously.

Two Providence attorneys and staunch advocates of political reform, Charles E. Gorman (1844–1917) and Edwin D. McGuinness (1856–1901), led the rise of the local Irish American community to a position of power and influence in opposition to the rural-based Republican machine of Henry Bowen Anthony and his successors. Gorman (shown top right) became the first Catholic admitted to the Rhode Island Bar (1865), the first to win election to the General Assembly (1870, from Wanskuck in North Providence, prior to that district's annexation by Providence), and the first to serve on the Providence City Council (1875). In the aftermath of the Democratic party's electoral victories in 1887, its first such win since 1853, Gorman was chosen Speaker of the House and then became U.S. attorney (1893) during the second administration of Grover Cleveland.

Gorman's most important legal foray was the publication of a learned treatise entitled *An Historical Statement of the Elective Franchise in Rhode Island* (1879), a work that he effectively presented to the Congress of the United States to demonstrate that the prevailing Rhode Island suffrage system was at variance with the newly enacted Fifteenth Amendment to the U.S. Constitution. His invocation of that amendment foreshadowed twentieth-century U.S. Supreme Court interpretations of the provision as it relates to state suffrage laws.

In the election of 1887 McGuinness, Gorman's protégé, was elected secretary of state, becoming Rhode Island's first Catholic general officer. In 1888 McGuinness (shown bottom right) turned to Providence politics, serving as alderman until 1893, when he made the first of his two unsuccessful bids for mayor. Victorious on his third try, in 1895 he became the city's first Irish Catholic chief executive, and he won reelection by a large majority the following year. Because of ill health he declined nomination for a third term. McGuinness's two mayoral terms were characterized by governmental reform, efficiency, and a relentless campaign against public utilities—such as the Union Street Railroad Company and the New York, New Haven and Hartford Railroad—that victimized or disregarded the consumer. He died in 1901, a month short of his forty-fifth birthday. In his obituary the *Providence Journal* called McGuinness's tenure "the first great triumph here for independence in politics," and one that was "particularly commendable."

Part Three

The Modern Era, 1898–1998: The Law as a Profession

25

At the dawn of the twentieth century our judicial branch was headed by a Supreme Court, consisting of a chief justice and six associate justices. The court sat as a body on constitutional questions, but it otherwise was divided, in accordance with the provisions of the Judiciary Act of 1893, into an appellate division of four justices and a common pleas division. In the case of *Floyd* v. *Quinn*, 24 R.I. 147, an ingenious member of the bar raised the question of whether Rhode Island, under the prevailing practice that permitted the chief justice to assign members to either the appellate or common pleas division, had one Supreme Court or 120 Supreme Courts—that being the number of different panels possible under the assignment system.

This conundrum challenged the court to make a searching analysis of its organization and jurisdiction. The newly formed Bar Association, especially attorneys Amasa Eaton and Charles E. Gorman, joined the quest for a more simple and efficient judicial system. The products of this reassessment were the Twelfth Amendment (1903) to the Rhode Island Constitution, which provided for a Supreme Court with final revisory and appellate jurisdiction, and the voluminous Court and Practice Act of 1905, consisting of 1,275 sections in 576 pages, which established a Supreme Court of five justices, a Superior Court with trial jurisdiction in law and equity, and a detailed code of court procedures.

The principal influence on the 1905 statute was the report of a seven-man study commission created in 1904 by the General Assembly to recommend judicial restructuring. This distinguished board consisted of Chief Justice John H. Stiness, its chairman, and Charles E. Gorman, Edward D. Bassett, Stephen O. Edwards, William A. Morgan, Nathan W. Littlefield, and Ellery H. Wilson. A useful account of court development from 1638 down to the modernization of 1905 is Francis I. McCanna, "Study of the History and Jurisdiction of Rhode Island Courts," *Journal of the American Irish Historical Society* 22 (1923), 170–195.

The creation of Rhode Island's modern judicial system is the subject of the following essay by Chief Justice Joseph R. Weisberger, who is only the second Rhode Islander (William H. Sweetland was the other) to serve as both presiding justice of the Superior Court and chief justice of the Supreme Court. With a reputation for erudition in both law and history, Judge Weisberger is a scholar in the tradition of such earlier chief justices as Stephen Hopkins, James Burrill, Jr., Job and Thomas Durfee, William R. Staples, Samuel Ames, and John H. Stiness.

The Founding of the Superior Court: A New Era in the Rhode Island Judicial System

Joseph R. Weisberger

The year was 1905. Victoria of England had been dead for four years, succeeded by her colorful son, Edward VII, who was affectionately called "the Uncle of Europe." In the United States, Theodore Roosevelt was President. He was walking across the world stage softly but carrying a big stick. He was soon to send the Great White Fleet on a voyage around the world in order to show the flag and demonstrate the ability to project American sea power. On the continent of Europe, intrigues had begun among the contending powers of France, Germany, Austria, Italy, the Balkans, and Russia that would ultimately cast the world into a maelstrom of war. The fierce ambition of Kaiser Wilhelm II had become apparent. The doting Franz Josef of Austria, sick with grief at the loss of his wife and son and the difficulties of holding his heterogeneous empire together, was slipping into feeble old age, relying more and more on his jingoistic ministers.

Nevertheless, in 1905 all seemed right with the world. The "proud towers" of European monarchy and aristocracy seemed to have an unshakable permanence. The Industrial Revolution and the Gilded Age had spread a surface prosperity throughout the western world. The pockets of poverty and oppression were neatly eclipsed by the glitter of wealth, pomp, and elegance.

In Rhode Island, on the front page of the *Providence Journal*, the Outlet Company advertised Hart, Schaffner & Marx suits, single- and double-breasted styles, beginning at $10.98 and running to a high of $16.98. High-quality candy was selling at fifty cents per pound for chocolates or French bonbons. The best-quality butter was advertised at thirty-two cents a pound. A two-family house consisting of nine rooms on each floor with bath and furnace could be purchased for $4,700. Shoes for men, women, and children were advertised at prices ranging from $3.50 up to a luxurious $5.00 per pair. Rhode Island was a beehive of industrial and commercial activity from South County to Woonsocket. Providence was among the great textile centers of the world. More than forty thousand persons were engaged in cotton- and woolen-textile manufacture in the state. In addition, Rhode Island was prominent in machine-tool, base-metal, and machinery manufacturing, and achieved further fame as the costume-jewelry capital of the nation.

The Rhode Island judicial system, however, was not efficient enough to meet the litigation needs of a population of approximately 450,000 people. Pursuant to the General Laws of 1896, the Supreme Court consisted of six justices in two divisions: the Appellate Division, which consisted of three members, including the chief justice, and a Common Pleas Division, in which any of the justices of the Supreme Court might be assigned by the chief justice to hold sessions in the various counties throughout the state.

Individual justices had jurisdiction to try civil actions at law relating to real estate (except actions for possession of tenements) and all other actions at law in which the amount of damages exceeded $300. The statute provided, nevertheless, that equity cases were triable not in the Common Pleas Division but in the Appellate Division before three justices. In addition, petitions for divorce were triable in the Appellate Division, as were all motions for new trial. This was, indeed, a cumbersome judicial system, since there were only six justices of the Supreme Court in both divisions.

Below the Supreme Court were twelve justices of the District Court, who sat in individual judicial districts from the First Judicial District in Newport to the Twelfth Judicial District in Woonsocket. These justices, and their clerks who could substitute for them, had jurisdiction to try criminal cases wherein the fine did not exceed $20 or the imprisonment did not exceed three months. District Court justices also had jurisdiction to try civil actions at law wherein the damages did not exceed $300, and they were authorized to try cases for possession of tenements or "estates let, or held at will or by sufferance."

Both civil and criminal cases tried in the District Court could be appealed with trial *de novo* to the Common Pleas Division of the Supreme Court. That court would also try in the first instance criminal cases in which the penalties exceeded the jurisdiction of the District Courts. Sessions of the Common Pleas Division were held at Bristol, East Greenwich, South Kingstown, Newport, and Westerly. Both the Appellate and the Common Pleas Divisions of the court were in vacation from the third Monday in July to the third Monday in September each year, with one justice on duty during that period.

Pursuant to Chapter 451 of the Public Laws of 1897, the membership of the Supreme Court was expanded to consist of a chief justice and six associate judges. Of this number, the chief justice and three of the associate justices constituted the Appellate Division. Any three of these justices constituted a quorum for the conduct of business. Equity cases and contested petitions for divorce were required to be heard before three justices. Petitions for new trial in jury-waived cases could be heard by a single justice of the Appellate Division, except if the gravity of the matter required that it be reserved for hearing before three justices. Two years later, pursuant to Chapter 649 of the Public Laws of 1899, a single justice of the Supreme Court assigned to the Appellate Division was authorized to try all petitions for divorce, whether contested or uncontested.

As a consequence, the manpower of the Supreme Court was divided into two groups, the Appellate Division and the Common Pleas Division. Equity cases, petitions for divorce, and actions for enforcement of mechanics' liens were authorized to be tried only in the Appellate Division, and many of these proceedings required three justices to try each case. The Common Pleas Division really consisted of only three justices who moved from one county to another at stated times throughout the year, except when the court was on vacation. It is, therefore, nor remarkable that a prominent member of the bar, Amasa A. Eaton, Esq., in a speech delivered before the Pawtucket Businessmen's Association on January 4, 1904, suggested that no more important subject would come before the General Assembly than the subject of the revision of the judicial system and the appointment of a commission to formulate specific recommendations. He pointed out that in all other states at the time, the highest court had become a court of appeals upon all questions of law, as well as in equity, but that in this state, only the Supreme Court could exercise jurisdiction in equity, and therefore there was no court to which an appeal could be taken.

By 1904 the constitutional provision that conferred equity powers solely upon the Supreme Court had been modified by Article XII of the Amendments to the Constitution, adopted November 3, 1903. This amendment enabled the legislature to confer equity powers upon such other courts as it might deem appropriate. In Mr. Eaton's words:

> The object of the amendment that has been proposed by the Bar Association of the State and that has been carried through mainly by their instrumentality and that of the members of the Committee on Judiciary of the General Assembly, is to provide lower courts with jurisdiction in all cases, both in law and in equity, and also to provide a court of last resort, a court of appeals, or Supreme Court, with final jurisdiction over all matters of law and equity.

The Court and Practice Act of 1905 was to bring about the realization of this goal. This act, remarkable for its scope and thoroughness, provided for a simple and easily understood judicial structure. The act recast the Supreme Court as a five-member appellate court, with jurisdiction over prerogative writs and with general supervisory and revisory authority over all other courts. It also established a new court, known as the Superior Court, which consisted of a Presiding Justice and five associate judges. These justices, like the justices of the Supreme Court, were to be elected by the General Assembly in Grand Committee, but they were to hold their offices during good behavior unless removed on impeachment or by concurrent resolution passed by three-fifths of the members elected to each of the houses of the General Assembly. The act provided that in case of removal, the Superior Court justice to be removed (unlike a justice of the Supreme Court) be served with a copy of the resolution of removal and be given an opportunity to be heard.

Any one justice of the Superior Court, then as now, constituted a quorum for all purposes. The Superior Court was given exclusive original jurisdiction of suits and proceedings in equity and all statutory proceedings following the course of equity, and of petitions for divorce, separate maintenance, alimony, and custody of children. The Superior Court was further given jurisdiction over actions at law involving real estate (except actions for the possession of tenements) and other actions at law in which the damages exceeded the sum of $500. It was given original jurisdiction of all criminal offenses save those within the jurisdiction of District Courts. It was also authorized to try and determine appeals from the District and Probate Courts of the state. Concurrent with the Supreme Court, it was given jurisdiction of writs of habeas corpus, mandamus, quo warranto and informations in the nature of quo warranto.

Chief Justice John Henry Stiness (1840–1913) chaired the seven-man blue-ribbon commission that recommended the Court and Practice Act of 1905. Stiness was admitted to the bar after service in the Civil War, and from 1865 to 1874 he conducted a private law practice. In 1874 he was elected to the General Assembly, and in 1875 his colleagues in the legislature appointed him an associate justice of the Supreme Court—a classic example of the absence of separation of powers in Rhode Island. Stiness's long service on the high court earned him elevation to the chief justiceship in 1900, and he served in that position until 1903. Stiness is best remembered for his authorship of "The Struggle for Judicial Supremacy," in Edward Field's cooperative history of Rhode Island (1902).

Liberal retirement provisions were enacted for justices of both the Superior and the Supreme Courts, applicable either after twenty-five years of service or, at age seventy, after ten years of service. Provision was made for sessions of the Superior Court in Newport (for Newport County), in East Greenwich (for Kent County), in Providence (for Providence and Bristol Counties) with sessions to be tried also at Woonsocket and Bristol, and in South Kingstown (for Washington County) with sessions to be tried also in Westerly. In short, the duties and sessions of the Superior Court as established by the Court and Practice Act of 1905 bore a very strong resemblance to the sessions that are presently provided by law.

The District Court [created in 1886] was unchanged as to personnel. Its members, too, were to be elected by the General Assembly in Grand Committee, and they were to hold office for a term of three years. The act also provided that justices of the District Court must be members of the bar. Oddly enough, no such requirement was set forth by statute for justices of the Supreme or Superior Courts, perhaps because the General Assembly felt that such a statute was unnecessary, since by custom it was firmly established that justices of the Supreme Court would be members of the bar, and it was assumed that a similar qualification would be insisted upon by the Grand Committee for members of the Superior Court as well. The act further required that the person elected clerk of the court of the Sixth [Providence] and Tenth [Pawtucket] Judicial Districts also be a member of the bar. District court judges were given jurisdiction in civil cases over actions at law wherein the damages did not exceed $500 and of actions for possession of tenements, and they were given criminal jurisdiction of crimes punishable by fine not exceeding $500 or by imprisonment not exceeding one year, or both. In addition, District Courts were authorized to conduct preliminary hearings in regard to probable guilt or innocence in respect to felony cases. All cases tried in the District Courts, whether civil or criminal, could be appealed with trial *de novo* in the Superior Court.

Thus it may be seen that the Rhode Island judicial structure as established in 1905 was very similar to the structure presently existing. However, it must be borne in mind that the six justices of the Superior Court then performed the duties now [i.e., 1986] being carried out by nineteen justices of the Superior Court, eleven justices of the Family Court, and seven members of the Workers' Compensation Commission. Moreover, additional duties have been conferred upon the District Court, which now consists of thirteen full-time justices. In 1905 the twelve justices of the District Court were part-time only.

No more eloquent indication of the litigation explosion could be cited than the increase in the numbers of judicial personnel during the last eighty years. Indicative also is the provision made in the Court and Practice Act for a vacation of the Superior Court from the second Monday in July to the

William H. Sweetland (1856–1931), first presiding justice of the Superior Court, moved to the Supreme Court bench in 1909. Eleven years later he was elected chief justice, and he served with distinction in that post until his retirement in 1929.

third Monday in September of each year, with one justice to be present on weekdays during that period from 10 A.M. to 1 P.M. Obviously it was not anticipated at its inception that the new court would be overburdened with backlogs. By contrast, it should be noted that the present-day courts are in session twelve months of the year, and yet, as shown by the most recent statistical reports of the court administrator, they are barely able to keep abreast of the ever-increasing flood of case filings. For example, the Family Court alone reported over 6,000 juvenile cases and approximately 600 contested domestic-relations cases. In Providence County, the Superior Court reported 5,105 civil cases pending trial and nearly 3,000 new felony cases filed. The justices of the new Superior Court in 1905 were not called upon to deal with such overwhelming amounts of litigation as now confront their successors, in spite of the substantial increase in the numbers of judicial personnel.

In its news coverage just prior to and succeeding the formation of the Superior Court, the *Providence Journal* did not greatly emphasize the structural changes that the new act would bring about, but rather seemed enormously preoccupied with the personalities of those who might be elected to the new positions. In its issue of May 4, 1905, the *Journal* reported the final adoption of the Judiciary Act (Court and Practice Act) and predicted that the judges would probably be elected the following day. This prediction proved erroneous. A headline in the paper's May 5 issue read:

> **FACTIONAL BATTLE AT STATE HOUSE.** Entire Legislature stirred up over bitter struggle for judicial honors.

Nevertheless, the new justices were finally elected by the Grand Committee on May 9, 1905. Their biographies, as reported by the *Journal*, are set forth below:

William H. Sweetland

William Howard Sweetland, who was elected Chief Justice of the Superior Court, was born in Pawtucket, December 19, 1856, and is the son of William and Nancy Greene (Howard) Sweetland. He attended the public schools in Providence and graduated from Brown University in the class of 1878. He was admitted to the Bar in this State in 1881. A Republican in politics, he has been a member of the school committee of this city, a Clerk of the House of Representatives, and prior to being made Judge of the Sixth District Court he was Clerk of the Court. Many civil cases come up in this jurisdiction, and Judge Sweetland's rulings have, with very few exceptions, been upheld by the Supreme Court in cases where an appeal has been taken. Judge Sweetland is actively interested in charitable and humane work, and is connected with several societies interested along those lines.

Darius Baker (1845–1926), one of the five original members of the Superior Court, served at every judicial level during his long career: he was Newport's judge of probate (1877–1898), District Court justice (1886–1905), Superior Court justice (1905–1913), and associate justice of the Supreme Court (1913–1919).

Willard B. Tanner

Willard Brooks Tanner is a well-known practicing attorney in this city and was born in Blackstone, Massachusetts, August 24, 1858. After receiving the usual preparatory school education he entered Brown University, graduating in the class of 1879 with the degree of A.M. He also attended the Boston Law School and was admitted to the Rhode Island Bar in 1881. He was Assistant Attorney General from 1891 to 1894 and Attorney General from 1897 to 1901. He is prominently identified with the Cranston Street Baptist Church and as a member of several clubs.

Darius Baker

Darius Baker of Newport was born in Yarmouth, Massachusetts, January 18, 1845, the son of Braddock and Caroline (Crowell) Baker. He attended the schools of his native town, Providence Conference Seminary, East Greenwich, now known as East Greenwich Academy, and Wesleyan University, Middletown, Connecticut, graduating from the latter in 1870. He was admitted to the Connecticut Bar in 1874 and later to the Rhode Island Bar, beginning practice in Newport in 1876. He was Judge of Probate from 1877 to 1898 and Justice of the District Court, First Judicial District, from 1886 to the present time. He is a veteran of the Civil War, having served as a Private in the 5th Regiment, Massachusetts Volunteer Militia. He is one of Newport's prominent attorneys.

Charles F. Stearns

Charles F. Stearns is the son of Henry A. and Kate Falconer Stearns and was born in Smithfield, R.I., July 27, 1866. He was educated in Mowry & Goff's School in this city and graduated from Amherst College in 1889 and from the Harvard Law School in 1893. He was admitted to the Rhode Island Bar in the latter year and has since practiced law in this city. He was Assistant Attorney General from 1897 to 1902 and Attorney General from this time until last year. He is a well-known club man and is identified with various societies.

Charles C. Mumford

Charles Carney Mumford is a member of the firm VanSlyck & Mumford, Attorneys. He was a graduate of Brown University in the Class of 1881 and was admitted to the bar in 1883. He was Assistant Clerk of the Court of Common Pleas in 1883–84 and Clerk of the Municipal Court 1884–85. From 1885–86 he was Assistant Attorney General of the State and was a member of the House of Representatives in 1893–94. In 1894 he was appointed United States Commissioner, holding that office for several years. He is a member of the University Club and the Metacomet Golf Club and has been President of the Churchmen's Club.

Charles F. Stearns (1866–1946) moved from the Superior Court to the Supreme Court in 1917. He assumed the post of chief justice upon the retirement of William Sweetland in 1929, only to see his office vacated on January 1, 1935, by the famous Bloodless Revolution.

George T. Brown

George Tilden Brown was born in West Greenwich, R.I., June 28, 1848, the son of Peter T. and Roxalana (Potter) Brown. He attended East Greenwich Academy, Newport High School and Brown University, graduating from the latter in 1873. In May 1875, he graduated from the Albany Law School with a degree of LL.B. and was admitted to the Rhode Island Bar in October of the same year. He was a member of the House of Representatives in 1877–78, 1887–88 and 1893 and 1894. From 1889–91 he was Senator from Providence and has been a candidate for Attorney General on the Democratic ticket on a number of occasions, although never elected.

In its issue of Tuesday, May 9, 1905, the *Journal* announced that the results of the Superior Court elections had won general approval and that the high character of the men chosen would add strength to the Republican party. A cartoon indicated that the chairman of the Republican State Central Committee had his way in securing the election of those favored by this party. Since a member of the court, George T. Brown, had been selected on the recommendation of the Democratic State Central Committee, it might be suggested that a token bipartisan gesture had been made.

In its editorial page for Wednesday, May 10, 1905, the *Journal* complimented the General Assembly by stating:

> As those who knew the average high standing of the members of the General Assembly in civic intelligence and political morality were confident from the first would be the result, they have, resisting all the temptations of unworthy influences, placed upon the bench of the new Superior Court a group of men that as a whole are a creditable representation of the legal profession of the State, are free from personal, political or pecuniary taint, are fully capable of the important duties awaiting them and have the deserved respect and approval of Rhode Island people. Besides thus meeting faithfully the immediate duty of the moment and assuring the continuance of the State judiciary on a high plane, they have at the same time once more vindicated the State as a whole and the Republican party organization in particular against the ignorant or prejudicial aspersions of those who have been wantonly vilifying the party leaders and the voters who tolerate them. This Republican Assembly, thus responsive to the worthiest impulses of its constituency and elected under a constitution out of which we have been asked to believe that no good can come, has certainly shown itself in this matter very far from untrustworthy and still farther from "degraded."

With that kind of sendoff from the *Providence Journal*, the new court could scarcely fail to be an outstanding success. Present-day members of the General Assembly would perhaps be astounded at the abundant praise that the *Journal* showered upon its predecessors. Unfortunately, the newspaper has rather steadily heaped opprobrium and scorn upon the present generation of legislators of both political parties.

In any event, the Superior Court of Rhode Island was a great success and continues to perform its duties with ability, vigor, and integrity down to the present time. As one who served as the eleventh Presiding Justice of the Superior Court for six years, and as a member of the court for twenty-two years, I can say without equivocation that I am most proud of my association with what I consider to be an outstanding judicial tribunal.

BIOGRAPHICAL PROFILES

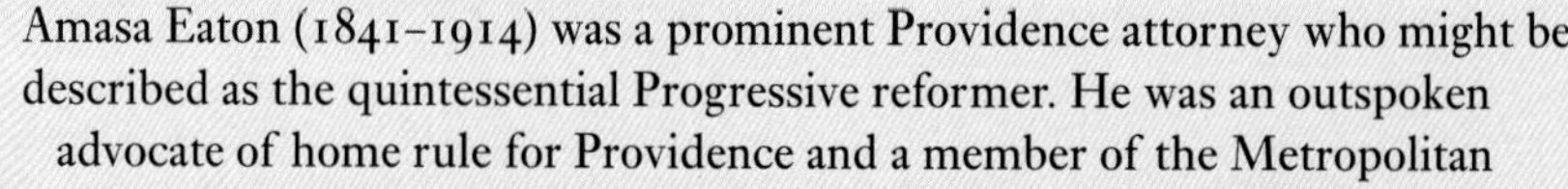

Amasa Eaton (1841–1914) was a prominent Providence attorney who might be described as the quintessential Progressive reformer. He was an outspoken advocate of home rule for Providence and a member of the Metropolitan Park Commission, the Blackstone Neighborhood Improvement Association, and various good-government organizations. He supported the local Equal Rights movement of the 1880s and advocated the implementation of the merit system and civil service reform. In one reformist essay he stated that "the routine business of government should be conducted on business principles" and "officeholders should be appointed on account of their fitness for the work to be done."

State constitutional change was Eaton's major concern. In 1899 he wrote a learned 128-page tract entitled *Constitution-Making in Rhode Island*, which traced the history of his subject and made numerous recommendations for reform, including women's suffrage, removal of all property qualifications for voting, a strengthening of the governor's powers, and municipal home rule. From 1903 to 1905 he played a leading role in advocating the establishment of Rhode Island's modern court system through his strenuous advocacy of the Court and Practice Act of 1905.

Attorney Eaton was such a persistent advocate of political, legal, constitutional, and social improvements that in the breadth of his reformist zeal he resembled Thomas Wilson Dorr. Undoubtedly it was this perceived similarity that led Eaton in 1908 to write an extensive (53-page) and highly favorable biographical sketch of Dorr for William Draper Lewis's multivolume *Great American Lawyers* series. That profile remains the best life of Dorr yet published.

By the turn of the century, several upwardly mobile Irish American attorneys had seized control of the organizational structure of the state's Democratic party and were persistently advocating economic and social reforms on behalf of the working class, as well as constitutional reforms that would lessen rural influence in state affairs and give lower-class ethnics (themselves included) political control over the cities in which they resided.

Attorney James H. Higgins (shown here), who had succeeded the colorful and dynamic fellow-lawyer John J. Fitzgerald as mayor of Pawtucket in 1903, won election in 1906 and again in 1907 as Rhode Island's first Irish Catholic governor. Though his efforts at reform were stymied by a Senate controlled by rural Republicans, in one celebrated triumph the feisty Higgins succeeded in ousting Boss Brayton from his unofficial State House office.

Galway-born attorney George O'Shaunessy (1868–1934) became another local Irish Catholic pathbreaker, securing election four times to the U.S. House of Representatives (1911–1919) as a Democrat. In 1913 the Irish began their unbroken sixty-two-year grip on the Providence mayoralty (1913–1975) with the victory of attorney Joseph H. Gainer, who much later (1946) would become a Bar Association president.

During the second decade of the twentieth century, Irish Democrats belatedly began their efforts to woo French and Italian voters away from their customary Republican allegiance by advancing such ethnic leaders as Alberic Archambault of West Warwick and Luigi De Pasquale and Louis W. Cappelli of Providence to high positions within the Democratic hierarchy. All three of these prominent attorneys later became judges.

26

The politically chaotic decades of the 1920s and 1930s in Rhode Island witnessed a major transition from Republican to Democratic control in state government. Economic unrest—stemming from such factors as the decline of the textile industry, the Crash of 1929, the ensuing Great Depression, and the local rise of organized labor—coupled with the development of cultural antagonisms between native and foreign stock to weaken the normal allegiance of local Franco-Americans and Italian Americans to the Republican party. Simultaneously, vigorous efforts by the Irish-led Democratic party to woo ethnics, key constitutional reforms such as the removal of the property-tax requirement for voting at council elections (Amendment XX in 1928), a shift in control of the national Democratic party from rural to urban leadership, the 1928 presidential candidacy of Irish Catholic Democrat Al Smith, and the social programs of Franklin D. Roosevelt's New Deal combined to pull the newer immigrant groups towards the Democratic fold by the mid-1930s.

A highlight of the turbulent twenties, and one of the most bizarre episodes in the history of any statehouse, was the stinkbombing of the Senate in June 1924. At that stormy session the Democratic minority, led by Senator Robert Quinn (later governor and judge) and Lieutenant Governor Felix Toupin, the presiding officer, staged a marathon filibuster to force weary Republicans to pass a constitutional convention bill that had already cleared the Democratic House. Toupin's strategy was to wear some of the elderly Republicans down and then call for a vote on the question when they snoozed or strayed.

In the forty-second hour of the filibuster, as the vigilant Democrats awaited the success of this scheme, Republican party managers authorized some thugs imported from Boston to detonate a bromine gas bomb under Toupin's rostrum. As the fiery Woonsocket politican keeled over uncon-cious, senators scrambled for the doors. Within hours most of the Republican majority was transported across the state line to Rutland, Massachusetts, where Toupin's summons could not reach them. There they stayed (Sundays excepted) until a new Republican administration assumed office in January 1925. Ironically, the defeat of the Democrats in the 1924 state elections was due in part to the fact that the *Providence Journal* wrongly accused them of the bombing. In that year the newspaper had much to gain from discrediting the Democrats, because Jesse H. Metcalf, brother of the *Journal*'s president, was the GOP candidate for U.S. Senate in the fall election.

Attorney William S. Flynn (1885–1966) served as representative from South Providence from 1912 to 1914 and from 1917 to 1922. In the latter period he emerged as Democratic minority leader, and in an upset caused by several Republicans miscues, he won the governorship in the election of 1922. During the final year of his two-year term, he supported the Senate filibuster designed to force the Republican party to grant the constitutional reforms for which he had long campaigned; and when the filibuster was broken by the detonation of a bromine gas bomb, and the Republican senators fled the state for a 6½-month self-imposed exile, his administration was discredited. Though it has since been discovered that Republican bosses commissioned the gassing, the *Providence Journal* blamed Flynn and the Democrats, perhaps because its candidate, Jesse Metcalf, was Flynn's opponent for U.S. senator in 1924. Flynn lost that election and held only minor appointive positions for the remainder of his political career, but his brother Edmund Flynn became chief justice in the aftermath of another legislative upheaval in 1935.

To stem the defection of Franco-Americans from the Republican party, Aram Pothier was summoned from retirement to battle Felix Toupin in the 1924 governor's race. With the Democrats unjustly blamed for the stink-bomb incident, Pothier and the GOP won a decisive victory. The turmoil that convulsed the state legislature in its 1924 session prompted the victorious Republicans, who gained decisive control of that body in the fall elections of 1924, to institute checks against the potential for such disruptions in the future. When the new legislative session opened in January 1925, the Republicans promptly sponsored a bill creating a Department of State Police. Rising violence in labor disputes and the need to enforce a statewide auto code were also motivating factors in the establishment of this uniformed statewide law-enforcement agency.

Shortly after passage of the state police statute on April 2, 1925, Governor Pothier appointed Everitte St. John Chaffee of Providence as the department's first superintendent. Chaffee, a military man who had compiled a distinguished World War I record as an officer of the 26th "Yankee" Division, was given comprehensive administrative authority over the new agency, a power that all subsequent state police colonels have wielded.

Nineteen twenty-four was only a temporary reversal in a seemingly inexorable political trend. By the General Assembly session of January 1935, Democratic leaders—especially Governor Theodore Francis Green, political boss Thomas P. McCoy of Pawtucket, state senator William Moss, and Lieutenant Governor Robert Emmet Quinn—were on the verge of achieving political ascendancy and ready to stage a governmental reorganization now known as the Bloodless Revolution. This bizarre coup, made possible by a controversial scheme that gave the Democrats narrow control of the state Senate in defiance of election-day returns, had a number of far-reaching effects: the repeal of the Brayton Act of 1901, which had placed the ultimate appointive power over the many boards and commissions that ran the state in the hands of the Republican-controlled Senate; the reorganization of the state government through the replacement of that commission system with the present departmental structure; the seizure of state patronage by the Democrats; and the dismissal of the entire five-member Republican Supreme Court. With vivid memories of the 1924 bombing, Quinn ringed the Senate chamber with state policemen and sheriffs to prevent the startled Republicans from escaping and preventing a quorum prior to the execution of the Democratic plan.

That bold strategy and its results are the subject of the following account by Professor Erwin L. Levine, the holder of a doctorate in political science from Brown University, who was teaching government at Skidmore College when he wrote a detailed two-volume biography of Theodore Francis Green. Levine's account of the Bloodless Revolution is taken from volume 1, *Theodore Francis Green: The Rhode Island Years, 1906–1936* (1963). The second volume deals with Green's long tenure in Washington as United States senator. Also helpful in understanding this colorful episode is Matthew J. Smith, "The Real McCoy in the Bloodless Revolution of 1935," *Rhode Island History* 32 (1973), 67–85.

Shortly after passage of the state police statute on April 2, 1925, Governor Pothier appointed Everitte St. John Chaffee of Providence as the department's first superintendent. Chaffee, a military man who had compiled a distinguished World War I record as an officer of the 26th "Yankee" Division, was given comprehensive administrative authority over the new agency, a power that all subsequent state police colonels have wielded. Chaffee personally selected the first troopers, most of whom had military experience, and established a training camp for them at his twenty-acre summer home in South Kingstown. Within hours of setting up the camp, the department suffered its first fatality when trooper John Weber of Newport was killed in a motorcycle accident on Post Road. Weber was to be a member of the first state police motorcycle patrol, shown here in this 1925 photo.

The Bloodless Revolution

Erwin L. Levine

> *Let us hope that the New Year may resurrect much delayed legislation of benefit to the State as a whole.*
>
> –Theodore Francis Green

Theodore Francis Green (1867–1966) was elected governor over incumbent Norman S. Case in 1932, a victory that came on his third try for the office after a long period of reformist activity in the politics of Providence and the state. A Yankee patrician who had taught Roman law at Brown, Green had served in the Spanish-American War and practiced law prior to winning a House seat from Providence in the Good Government campaign of 1906. After losing the governor's race in 1912 to popular Franco-American Aram Pothier, he became a charter member, and then chairman, of the prestigious Providence City Plan Commission.

Despite grumblings by various Democratic legislators over the increasing concentration of power in the executive branch, Governor Theodore Francis Green faced only one serious challenge in his party leadership in 1934. Pawtucket boss Thomas P. McCoy (who aspired to become State Chairman) attempted to form a coalition with Lieutenant Governor Robert E. Quinn (who aspired to become governor) and Congressman Francis B. Condon (who aspired to become United States senator) to wrest control from Green, former U.S. Senator Peter G. Gerry, and U.S. Attorney J. Howard McGrath; but apart from sound and fury the effort accomplished nothing. The McCoy coalition was defeated, 68 to 25, when it forced a vote on the chairmanship at a special meeting of the State Central Committee. The state convention went smoothly, all incumbent state officers and incumbent Congressmen John M. O'Connell and Condon being renominated, and Peter Gerry being chosen as the opponent to Republican Senator Felix Hebert.

For Green's opponent the Republicans chose Luke Callan, a popular Bristol contractor and war hero who in 1932 had been elected to the State Senate as an independent. Senator Hebert was renominated, and the rest of the slate reflected an effort to effect some balance of ethnic groups in the Republican ticket.

Callan conducted a vigorous, somewhat demagogic campaign. He referred to his own war record and pointed out that, while he was fighting in France, Green was "engaged in selling war stamps in Rhode Island." He sought favor with the workers by charging Green with cowardice in having called out the National Guard [in the 1934 textile strike], and sought favor in the rural districts by asserting that the Democrats planned to gerrymander the small towns out of their Senate seats. One sequence of exchanges on this matter probably planted the seed of a revolution that was about to come. Democratic State Senator William G. Troy, talking on the issue of representation in the Senate, casually remarked that "some skunkhunter from West Greenwich" had as much power in the State Senate "as a good citizen" from a larger community. In response, Callan and the Republicans promoted a series of "Skunkhunters' Rallies" at which they accused the Democrats of seeking to "steal our birthright through a Constitutional Convention." In a moment of enthusiasm at one such rally, Callan claimed that if the Democrats won control of both houses of the General Assembly, they planned to oust the State Supreme Court justices. This was a coincidental reference to what actually did happen, for the Democratic leaders had not yet conceived the idea. Quite possibly, it was Callan who gave it to them.

The Democrats geared their efforts to two things. On the general level, Green led a campaign identifying the Democrats' state program with the New Deal. Defending his own record in the relief program in Rhode Island, Green heaped lavish praise on President Roosevelt and the national administration, which he said had sought "to lift us out of our difficulties along the American road of intelligent self-help." The New Deal had pointed the way towards social security and insurance against unemployment, rendered bank deposits secure, repealed prohibition, ended manipulation of the stock market, and brought the re-employment of nearly four million people throughout the nation. Above all, the Governor asserted, the New Deal had "recreated hope and confidence in the hearts of men." Rhode Island Democrats had cooperated in these achievements, said Green, but a new political deal was also badly needed in the state, and Green told his radio audiences that the election of a Democratic legislature would do just that.

On the more specific level Green, Quinn, Senator Francis J. Kiernan, Edward J. Higgins, and a handful of other Assembly leaders decided to concentrate a great deal of effort in an attempt to win the State Senate seats in several key towns. Quinn was made chairman of this inner group in charge of operations, and even before the Democratic State Convention, efforts had been made to convince the Town Committees of Coventry, Johnston, North Smithfield, Portsmouth, South Kingstown, Tiverton, and Westerly to select competent Democrats as nominees for the Senate. Republicans had been elected from these towns in 1932, but the Democrats felt that they stood an excellent chance of winning them all in 1934. Green himself supplied most of the money for expenses in the town campaigns. Republican U.S. Senator Jesse H. Metcalf had not been as free as usual with his "registration" money, and this had caused some resentment on the part of Republican powers in the towns. Making a determined bid to wage strong fights in these communities, Democratic state headquarters supplied a great deal of printed matter and physical aid and several automobiles for the use of Town Committees and the candidates who had been selected by them.

In general, there was never any real doubt of the outcome of the state election in 1934. Gerry, riding for the most part on the magic of Roosevelt's name, more than made up for the beating Hebert had given him in 1928 by carrying every city but Cranston and Warwick as he swept to victory. Green was re-elected governor by a plurality 4,000 votes greater than his margin in 1932. The entire Democratic ticket, including O'Connell and Condon for Congress, was easily elected. The real interest in 1934 centered on the General Assembly. The Democrats won the normally Republican House seats in Cumberland, East Providence, Lincoln, Newport, Pawtucket, and Tiverton, carried twenty of the twenty-five Representative districts in Providence, and emerged with a comfortable margin of eight seats in the lower house. Democratic candidates for the Senate scored upset victories in four of the seven key towns—Johnston, North Smithfield, Tiverton, and Westerly. In addition, Bristol had also elected a Democratic senator, even though the town had voted for Callan in the gubernatorial contest.

In Coventry a very distressing thing had occurred on the night of the election. Lieutenant Governor Quinn had been informed by a Democratic watcher that about a hundred Democratic ballots had been literally destroyed so as to give the Republican candidate, Edwin H. Arnold, Jr., the Senate victory over Democrat J. W. Butler, by a plurality of only twenty-three votes. Coventry was at least temporarily Republican. In Portsmouth and South Kingstown the news was bad for the Democrats. On the night of the election, for a short while, the *Providence Journal*'s count had Democrats ahead in both towns. The returns in the morning, however, showed that in Portsmouth, Republican B. Earl Anthony had defeated Democrat Joseph P. Dunn 535 to 496, a plurality of thirty-nine. In South Kingstown, the same thing had happened, as Republican Wallace Campbell edged out Democrat Charles A. White, Sr., 1377 to 1321, a plurality of fifty-six. Democratic watchers told Quinn that the Republican town wardens had merely thrown out enough Democratic ballots, on the claim that they were defectively marked, to give the Republicans the victory.

With these three towns—Coventry, Portsmouth, and South Kingstown—in the Republican column, the State Senate apparently stood at twenty-three Republicans and nineteen Democrats. Quinn and the Democrats raised a clamor about Coventry, and two days after the election the Republican-dominated State Returning Board, with all of the Democratic state officers except Green looking on, recounted the ballots and declared Democrat Butler the victor 1490 to 1476. The vote in South Kingstown was also recounted later, but the board ruled that Republican Campbell had gained a net increase of five votes, and the count now stood Campbell 1369 and Democrat White 1308. Portsmouth was unchanged and since there were no reversals anywhere else, the State Senate stood at twenty-two Republicans and twenty Democrats.

Prospects for the passage of Democratic legislation now appeared dim. Democratic leaders held a series of meetings with Governor Green at his home in Providence, trying to find a way to reverse the decisions in Portsmouth and South Kingstown. Thirty-nine votes in the former town and sixty-one in the latter separated the Governor and the Democratic Party from control of the legislature. The combined houses, in Grand Committee, had a slight edge in favor of the Democrats, and in the event of a vacancy on the State Supreme Court, the Democrats would have the advantage. Nevertheless, without a majority in the Senate itself, the Democrats would be unable to pass any kind of reform legislation.

Attending the meetings with the Governor were Quinn; Attorney General John P. Hartigan; his first assistant William W. Moss; Senators Troy and Kiernan; House Speaker William E. Reddy; his deputy James Kiernan; chairman of the State Committee Thomas Kennelly; House leader Edmund W. Flynn; Higgins; and McGrath, who, despite his Federal position as United States Attorney, continued to mastermind many of the Democratic

Edmund W. Flynn (1890–1957), the younger brother of Governor William S. Flynn, was Tom McCoy's candidate for chief justice in January 1935. Prior to his elevation to the high court, Flynn had served for five years as a state representative from South Providence. He was a legal craftsman who played a major role in preparing the two most recent digests of Rhode Island's general laws in 1938 and 1956. After his death in office in April 1957, he was succeeded as chief justice by another McCoy ally, associate justice and former congressman Francis B. Condon of Pawtucket (1891–1965).

moves in 1934. The meetings were held in such secrecy that even the *Providence Journal* was taken completely by surprise at the events which transpired on New Year's Day, 1935.

Lieutenant Governor Quinn, convinced that the Republicans had won their elections in Portsmouth and South Kingstown by fraud, suggested that the State Senate itself had the constitutional right to recount the ballots cast in those towns. He based his opinion on Article IV, Section 6 of the State Constitution, which made each house "the judge of the elections and qualifications of its members." Although the Senate had never recounted ballots cast in any other election—there never had been any occasion to—there was no reason it could not invoke the power now. Quinn suggested that the ballots, which were deposited in the vault at the State House, be ordered out and given to a special Senate committee for scrutiny. The Lieutenant Governor was certain that if a senatorial recount were made, Democrats would be found elected to the Senate from Portsmouth and South Kingstown. After considerable discussion the Democratic leaders hit upon a plan to catch the Republicans by surprise. They decided to appoint a three-man Senate committee on the first day of the new session to examine and count the ballots of those towns. Wanting a trustworthy Republican on the committee, they settled on Archibald B. Kenyon of Richmond. The Democratic Senators were to be Francis J. Kiernan of North Providence and Edward F. Dwyer of Woonsocket. Confident they would win, but mindful of the need for discretion, they decided to withhold their plans from the rest of the Democrats in the legislature until the very last moment. The Governor expressed his approval of the plan.

One of the first things the inner group of Democrats agreed they would do after obtaining control of the Senate would be to pass a resolution declaring the State Supreme Court offices vacant. To do this, as with any bill, they needed approval of both houses. The Grand Committee would then replace the five Republican Supreme Court justices with three Democrats and two other Republicans. Some of the inner group wanted to have Democrats in all five judgeships, but Green insisted that if this were done the Democratic Party would be accused of doing just what it had been berating the Republicans for over the years. The two Republicans decided upon were Hugh B. Baker, a Yankee Protestant, and Antonio A. Capotosto, an Italo-American, two capable Superior Court justices. One of the Democrats was to be Congressman Francis B. Condon, upon whom almost all agreed. Green and Higgins particularly wanted Condon on the court in order to remove him as a threat for the United States Senate in 1936. For a Yankee Democrat the group selected William W. Moss, who had conducted much of Green's negotiations with the Federal government regarding RFC funds. Pawtucket's McCoy urged that the third Democrat be Edmund W. Flynn, the House Leader. Flynn urged it, too. Nevertheless, former Mayor of Providence Joseph Gainer was selected as the third Democratic judge.

The ethnic balance had been well kept: two Irish Democrats, one Yankee Democrat, one Yankee Republican, and an Italian Republican.

Moss was assigned the job of preparing a series of bills which would be rapidly introduced into the Senate and then the House. The bills were to declare vacant the Supreme Court judgeships and the office of High Sheriff of Providence County, abolish the office of Finance Commissioner, remove the Providence Safety Board from state control, and provide for the administrative reorganization of the state government. With Green's help, Moss carefully worked out the wording of the bills. Everything was in readiness for the coup, and on the Sunday before the opening of the 1935 legislative session, all the Democratic legislators, including the defeated senatorial candidates from Portsmouth and South Kingstown, gathered at the Governor's residence. They were told to attend a caucus at eleven on the morning of January 1 at the State House, at which time they would be told what was going to happen.

On Tuesday morning, January 1, all the Democratic legislators were brought into the scheme. Just one thing went awry. Edmund W. Flynn wanted to be the Chief Justice of the new Supreme Court. He had little use for Green personally and the feeling was mutual. Flynn was, however, a popular figure on both sides of the aisle in both houses, and he let it be known that unless he were made Chief Justice, there would be a great deal of trouble pushing the Governor's contemplated reforms through the House of Representatives, of which he was the majority leader. In the words of one member of the administration, "He held a gun to our heads." Flynn was supported by James H. Kiernan, who wanted Flynn's job as majority leader. Lieutenant Governor Quinn had been given the task of selling Gainer to the assembled Democrats in caucus, but working under the pressure of time, he was unable to convince them, and Flynn won out. No doubt, appeasement of McCoy, Flynn's Pawtucket ally, played a part in the decision also. In any event, the ethnic balance remained undisturbed and the Democratic caucus approved the scheme.

When the caucus had ended, Quinn called the Senate into its first session. The carefully planned scene was then enacted. Quinn ordered the Secretary of State, Louis Cappelli, to swear in all the senators-elect except Republicans B. Earl Anthony of Portsmouth and Wallace Campbell of South Kingstown. He had, he solemnly announced, been informed that a protest to their certification had been noted. Taken aback, Anthony and Campbell did not know what to do. Campbell's desk was replete with flowers from well-wishers and he was dumbfounded by Quinn's statement. With the Senate now evenly divided twenty to twenty and working without rules, Senator Troy stood and requested that the Lieutenant Governor appoint a special committee to procure the ballot boxes and ballots cast in certain towns at the last election. Troy's motion was seconded, as prearranged, by Senator Francis J. Kiernan, and before the Republicans knew what happened Quinn called for a voice vote and ruled it approved. The resolution was transmitted to the House, which concurred by a roll call vote of fifty-seven Democrats to forty-two Republicans, and then signed by

Governor Green, who was impatiently waiting for the bill. All this took place within a space of a few minutes. The Senate had been at ease awaiting the return of the resolution from the House, and the Republicans, realizing what was about to take place, began to leave the building in hopes of preventing a legal quorum from being presented in the Senate. Quinn, citing Chapter 24, Section 32 of the *General Laws*, which gives the presiding officers of both houses the right to compel attendance, issued warrants for the arrest of Republican Senators Daniel F. McLaughlin, Lester Simmons, and Archibald B. Kenyon, for whom the Democrats had plans. McLaughlin later left for dinner with two state troopers—the Superintendent of State Police had supplied about twenty-five troopers at the Governor's request—and Simmons was soon let off. Only Kenyon remained at the Capitol.

When the House had approved the first measure and Green had signed it, Quinn called the Senate back to order. He then appointed Senators Kiernan, Dwyer, and Kenyon to procure and count the ballots of Portsmouth and South Kingstown, to determine who had been elected senators from those towns. Waiting in Louis Cappelli's office all this time was Joe Atkins, the Republican Deputy Secretary of State, whom Cappelli had kept on. Atkins' duties had been to record the votes as counted by the State Returning Board and to take care of their security. He had the combination to the state vault, and to make sure that he remained until they were ready for him, the Democrats had stationed a State Trooper with him in Cappelli's office. Even lunch was brought to him while he waited, not knowing what was happening. After the special committee was named, Atkins was asked to open the vault. Upon the appearance of two burly state troopers, each of whom was carrying a large sledge hammer to smash it in, Atkins complied with the request. The ballots from the two disputed towns were then brought to a committee room. The discounted ballots, which had been separated from the counted ones, were mixed in with them and the entire amount recounted. The committee pored over the ballots, threw out some for improper markings, and came out with new totals. Kiernan, Dwyer, and Kenyon unanimously declared that Democrats Charles A. White, Jr. and Joseph P. Dunn had been elected from South Kingstown and Portsmouth. The special committee had actually rejected more ballots than the State Returning Board had. Prior to the special count, the votes had stood this way:

South Kingstown		**Portsmouth**	
Campbell (Republican)	1,369	Anthony (Republican)	535
White (Democrat)	1,308	Dunn (Democrat)	496
Total	2,677	Total	1,031

After the Senate count, the vote stood:

White (Democrat)	1,318	Dunn (Democrat)	520
Campbell (Republican)	1,292	Anthony (Republican)	510
Total	2,610	Total	1,030

Democrats now had twenty-two senators to the Republicans' twenty, and thus control of both houses of the General Assembly. Secretary of State Cappelli swore in the new senators and Senator Troy then moved in rapid-fire order for the consideration of the five major bills which Moss had drawn up.

The first bill vacated the office of Sheriff Andrews of Providence and the second vacated the five judgeships of the State Supreme Court. The Republican judges on the Court were granted large pensions on condition that they resign their offices by noon the following day. The first bill was passed by a voice vote and the second by a roll call vote, with Republican McLaughlin casting the lone dissenting ballot. Republican Senators Kenyon and Russell H. Handy were present but did not vote. The third bill wiped out the [legislatively appointed] Providence Safety Board and gave Governor Green the power to name a Public Safety Director for a thirty-day period. The fourth bill abolished the [legislatively appointed] office of Finance Commissioner and created the combined office of State Budget Director and State Comptroller, to be appointed by the Governor. These also passed by voice vote. The last bill was the most voluminous. In essence it merged the some eighty state commissions into ten departments, to become effective in sixty days. From the time the Senate reconvened to hear the report of the special committee to the adoption of the fifth measure at 7:32 P.M., only fourteen minutes had elapsed. The House quickly approved the Senate measures by roll call votes, along straight party lines, and Governor Green eagerly signed them into law.

By this time it was 10:30 P.M. and the Grand Committee (less almost all the Republican senators and representatives) met to fill the vacancies of Sheriff and judges of the Supreme Court. Philip E. Quinn of Providence was elected as Sheriff of Providence County and the agreed-upon slate of judges was duly elected. Theodore Francis Green was then sworn into office as governor for a second term. The time was 12:05 A.M., and the Governor read an abbreviated inaugural address containing recommendations for much that had already occurred.

While the Grand Committee was filling the new vacancies, Higgins, in the governor's car, delivered letters to the Providence Safety Board—Everitte St. John Chaffee, George T. Marsh, and Michael Corrigan. They were informed that they had been removed from office and were therefore no longer state officials. On the following day, the new Supreme Court justices, except for Condon, who was in Washington, were sworn into office and the "Bloodless Revolution" of 1935 was over.

Instead of being reorganized under a new state constitution, as Democrats had urged for so long, Rhode Island had been made over by the determination, the cleverness, the audacity, and the persistence of the Rhode Island Democratic Party. To justify the actions that had taken place on New Year's Day, Governor Green addressed a statewide radio audience. Praising the new regime, he said that the Democratic success made him feel "the spiritual presence of the Patron Saint of the Democratic Party in Rhode Island, Thomas Wilson Dorr." It was this spirit and Dorr's "indomitable advocacy of the rights of the people" that had led the Democrats on and would continue to do so.

While Democrats rejoiced, others cursed. Republicans attacked the coup as an unconstitutional, illegal, and dictatorial act. The *Providence Journal* condemned the haste with which the legislature had acted on the five bills, and charged that they were "not reforms but political maneuvers and reprisals." The Rhode Island Bar Association was aghast at the treatment of the Court, despite the fact that two Republicans had been appointed to the state's highest judicial body. Fred Perkins, secretary of the Association, was particularly vehement in his denunciation of Green and the Democrats. (Many years later Perkins himself would be elevated to the Supreme Court by a Democrat, Governor Dennis Roberts, who often looked upon the bench as a convenient place to deposit potential Republican opposition.)

Legally or not, the rotten-borough system had at last been beaten without benefit of a new constitution. The Democrats were now in control of both branches of the government and they believed they knew how to use their power. The state could be reorganized and, in the process, the spoils of victory could be distributed to the party faithful. The Rhode Island Democratic Party, however, had been built on a tenuous coalition of various ethnic groups. Whether the coalition could hold together was another matter. It did not take long to find out.

Flushed with their triumph on New Year's Day, the Democrats adopted new Senate rules which gave the power of committee assignments and choice of committee chairmen to the lieutenant governor. James H. Kiernan succeeded Flynn as majority leader, and by the end of January the infamous Brayton Law of 1901 had been repealed. The Governor's appointees became subject to confirmation by the Senate, not to substitution by it. Other major acts passed by the regular session of the 1935 General Assembly were a proposal for a constitutional amendment to extend voter registration through September 30, an appropriations bill for the fiscal year of July 1, 1934, to June 30, 1935, a $200,000 old-age pension bill, a resolution establishing a State Planning Board to chart the state's economic future, and a bill providing for a referendum to decide on the need for voting machines.

Progress ended there, for the distribution of patronage now began to occupy most of the Democrats' time. With the office of Finance Commissioner abolished, Green had appointed Thomas McCoy of Pawtucket to the newly created position of Budget Director and Comptroller. McCoy was more or less a political choice: he controlled about nine Democrats in the House—the balance of power—and placating him might help to ensure passage of the Governor's program. But McCoy was also an able administrator, and besides, since the budget director served at the governor's pleasure, Green could remove McCoy if he proved to be troublesome. James H. Kiernan was another, though not so serious, challenge to Green's influence in the House. House Democrats had their own battle over committee assignments, and Kiernan alienated many Democratic legislators by his dictatorial tactics and lack of finesse in handling them.

The appointment of Judges Baker and Capotosto to the Supreme Court had left vacant two Superior Court judgeships. Ethnic problems immediately arose, as Alberic A. Archambault, Felix Toupin, Patrick P. Curran, Mortimer A. Sullivan, and Luigi De Pasquale presented themselves as candidates. Green finally decided upon his old law partner Curran and former Democratic State Chairman Archambault, while, at the same time, he elevated Judge Jeremiah O'Connell to be the presiding justice of the Superior Court. These appointments made some people happy and upset others. The Senate approved the nominations and Republican Senator Handy conveniently voted on the Democratic side. (Green often reminded Handy of his debt to the Governor for placing him on the Horse Racing Commission, and when an occasional Republican vote was needed in a close contest, Handy could usually be prevailed upon to act accordingly.)

The sheriffs of the five Rhode Island counties offered another source of enlarged patronage. Democratic deputies filtered through Sheriff Philip E. Quinn of Providence County, and in late January the Grand Committee vacated the other four offices of sheriff and Democrats became sheriffs in Bristol, Kent, Newport, and Washington Counties. In addition, four Republican roving clerks of the Superior Court were turned out and replaced by Democrats. As Senator Troy so aptly put it, "The people of the State (had) issued a mandate to the Democratic Party to administer the affairs of the State."

Thomas P. McCoy (1883–1945), "the Prince of Pawtucket," is regarded as Rhode Island's closest facsimile to a genuine machine politician, but he was much more than just a powerful political boss. During the 1920s McCoy compiled a distinguished record as a Democratic representative in the General Assembly. There he supported legislation beneficial to working-class ethnics and advocated reorganizing and streamlining state government and strengthening the office of governor. A populist, McCoy also urged other important constitutional reforms to increase public participation in the political process. In 1930 he ran unsuccessfully for lieutenant governor as Theodore Francis Green's Democratic running mate, but in 1936 he won the Pawtucket mayoralty.

Motivated by a desire for the governorship, during the mid-1930s McCoy made frequent sorties from his power base in Pawtucket against the state leaders of his own party. Each time he was soundly repulsed. Although he was an architect of the Bloodless Revolution of 1935 and, briefly, state budget director, his Democratic rivals were not willing to trust him with the reins of state government, for they believed that if the Pawtucket chieftain were given the opportunity to control state patronage—a necessary factor in forging a statewide machine—their own positions would be in jeopardy. In 1945 Mayor McCoy died in office.

More than altruism and devotion to the cause underlay the speedy passage of the skeleton reorganization bill on New Year's Day. Consolidating the departments and commissions of the state also meant the creation of many new jobs for good Democrats. The problem was to determine who was to get what. Governor Green insisted that only capable people be appointed to any position, regardless of factional influences; even McCoy's appointment had fallen within this limitation. Nonetheless, necessity dictated that Green exercise great political prudence in screening the field of candidates for the new political plums. For example, thirteen Italo-Americans in the General Assembly requested Green to appoint Ernest Santagini as State Director of Public Works. Albert J. Lamarre, McCoy's man in Pawtucket, also wanted the post, and Franco-American groups urged him on Green. The Governor, however, wanted Charles F. McElroy, chairman of the Providence City Committee, in that position. This fight alone caused much bitterness in the ranks of the Democrats. Green began to realize the seriousness of his opposition when Representative Frank X. Shunney, the dog-loving Democratic representative from Woonsocket, urged that the Grand Committee fill all the posts—department heads as well as Superior and District Court judgeships—instead of allowing the Governor to do so with the consent of the Senate. This did not come about, but the possibility served as an additional caution to Green.

The fight over the selection of department heads went on into February. Senate Democratic caucuses finally accepted four of Green's appointees—Thomas Kennelly as Director of Taxation and Regulation, Dr. John E. Donley as Director of Welfare, James Rockett as Director of Education, and Edward McLaughlin as Director of Public Health—but Senate Democrats forced Burton K. Harris on Green as Director of Agriculture, and Republican aid was called upon to approve L. Metcalfe Walling as Director of Labor and Charles F. McElroy as Director of Public Works. Favors in kind were of course promised to the friendly Republicans. Throughout, McCoy fought Green's appointments behind the scenes, in an effort to place his own people in several key jobs. The department heads appointed divisional chiefs and other subordinates, and were thus a lucrative source of patronage.

Patronage squabbles continued. McCoy, wanting more to say on who should fill clerkships and other offices, continued to press Green, and for more than mere political reasons. He and Walter O'Hara, one of the original owners of the new race track, wanted Pawtucket to own its public utility facilities, which would give them control of the policies of the plant and thus an opportunity to corner the utilities market in the Blackstone and Woonsocket sections of the state. Green was aware of their plans and resisted them as best he could. McCoy's controls in the House extended not only to the nine representatives but also to the House Finance Committee, chaired by Harry Curvin, who was politically beholden to McCoy. James H. Kiernan also wanted more of a voice in patronage matters, and he was disgruntled with Green for personal reasons as well. Kiernan resented Green's desire to lead all the Democrats, and he also felt that Edward J. Higgins had usurped his own rightful position as Green's personal agent. Kiernan, after all, had started to work with Green before Higgins had come on the scene. In a word, Green was having a great deal of trouble with factions in his own party. Largely for that reason, major items of the Governor's program failed to pass the regular 1935 session of the General Assembly. One was the calling of a constitutional convention and the other was the appropriations bill for the fiscal year 1935–36.

In February Governor Green had requested from the State Supreme Court an advisory opinion on the legality of legislation calling for a constitutional convention. Back in 1883 a Republican Court had ruled in the negative, but now, soon before the Assembly ordinarily adjourned, the Court unanimously stated that the legislature could summon such a convention. The Court recommended, but did not require, a referendum on the necessity of the call. The issue of a new constitution, however, was lost in a factional struggle to determine the manner of selecting delegates to such a convention if one were held. One group of Democrats, led by Quinn, wanted a nonpartisan convention to draw up the new constitution. Another group, of which the Governor was a part, really wanted the convention dominated solely by Democrats. To ensure the latter, the proposal was made that party committees nominate delegates. Although this managed to get through the House, the Senate buried the measure completely. Some Democratic senators, including Dunn of Portsmouth, were genuinely afraid that a new constitution would not be in the best interests of their small towns. Quinn, as presiding officer, could also direct the Senate away from the proposal he personally disapproved. In any event, no constitutional convention was called.

No action was taken either on the annual appropriations bill. It was painfully apparent that Chairman Curvin of the House Finance Committee was holding up the bill in an attempt to force Green to come to terms with McCoy on the question of a municipal utilities system in Pawtucket. Green refused to give in, and a stalemate ensued. Two more of the Governor's pet projects, the prohibition of dual office holding and the requirement that sheriffs and clerks turn in fines and fees to the general treasury, never left the ground because Democrats, not Republicans, were now profiting from the existing system.

The regular 1935 legislative session, then, was indeed a spectacle. The first day had resulted in the Democratic take-over of the State Senate and the passage of measures which ousted Republicans from key positions. Most of the remainder of the session was spent in personal feuding over patronage, jealousies, and pet projects. The General Assembly suddenly adjourned on April 13, and Governor Green announced almost immediately that he would call a special session to reconsider measures that should have been acted upon earlier.

Two days later, at the Jefferson Day Dinner, Governor Green publicly excoriated McCoy and Kiernan for opposing him in the House. A thunderous ovation greeted the Governor at the conclusion of his address, and he was verbally supported by Lieutenant Governor Quinn. Realizing he had the support of the Democratic rank and file, Green decided to meet McCoy head on. The Governor openly blamed McCoy for holding up many bills in the House and attacked him for his selfishness. He then summarily ousted McCoy as Budget Director and promoted a talented young Italo-American Democrat, Christopher Del Sesto, to his place.

Green had often turned to radio to explain his position on various matters, and now he did so again to broadcast his impressions of the legislative session just concluded. He stressed the importance of the repeal of the Brayton Law and spoke of how efficient state government would become under the reorganization, but he also enumerated the legislature's failures and then proceeded to denounce the Democratic legislators who had held up bills because they wanted to use them for trading purposes. Green explained that he had removed McCoy from the position of Budget Director because he had "failed to act with the administration which was trying to procure the unconditional passage of the appropriation bill." Although McCoy had helped draft the bill, he had "sat silent while his intimate political friends and supporters wrecked the administration program." The open attack on McCoy had a salutary effect on Kiernan, and in early May he called Green the "most patient, ablest man who ever sat in the Governor's chair." McCoy was not so docile. He charged the Governor and Higgins with attempting to bribe a Democratic representative to abandon McCoy by offering a bit of direct patronage to him, a charge not without foundation.

To break the back of McCoy's control of the Pawtucket bloc in the House, Governor Green chose to deal with the Republicans. Green wanted five major things passed in the special session. These were 1) the reorganization bill amplifying the original measure passed on New Year's Day, 2) an appropriations bill, 3) the establishment of a Police Commission in Providence not subject to state control, 4) the addition of two judges to the Superior Court, and 5) the removal of all the district judges and a new slate to replace them. The Republican House leaders offered to support these measures if Green would abandon his plans for a constitutional convention, allow the Republicans a greater voice in selection of key personnel in the new administrative setup, and give one of the new Superior Court judgeships to a Republican. Green agreed, the bills were passed, and Green ceased to be concerned with McCoy and his henchmen.

Dealing with the opposition, a common thing among practical politicians, had been rewarding. For one thing, Green had not had to trade much, for a constitutional convention no longer seemed so important now that the Democratic Party was in control of the state. Second, and more important, by dealing with the Republicans and trading a *quid pro quo*, Green had thwarted McCoy's control of the House, which had often been more frustrating than being blocked by the Republicans. Later, under a different set of circumstances, he would be able to push McCoy even farther away. As for now, Green could be satisfied with having won a measure of control in the General Assembly. He had entered the regular legislative session in January without a majority in the Senate, and by the end of May, he had not only obtained relatively firm leadership of his party and thus of both houses, but had also learned a great deal about using the political weapons of an executive leader—patronage, the power of removal, and informal deals with the opposition party.

In the statewide elections of 1936, the Democrats called a moratorium on their intraparty feud long enough to secure control of every political plum except the malapportioned and traditionally Republican state Senate. The *Pawtucket Star*, owned by Walter O'Hara, the flamboyant managing director of Narragansett Race Track, ran this November cartoon depicting three principal architects of the Bloodless Revolution—U.S. senator-elect Green, governor-elect Quinn, and Pawtucket mayor-elect McCoy. The victorious trio is preparing to feast on the fruits of the upcoming December 1936 special session, called by Green and Quinn so that the outgoing General Assembly, with its lame-duck Democratic Senate, could enhance gubernatorial power in several areas, including the conferral upon the governor of the right to appoint sheriffs and clerks of the Supreme and Superior courts. This measure came on the heels of a 1935 Democratic raid upon District Court clerks and judges, which the new Supreme Court had upheld by a 3-to-2 margin in *Gorham* v. *Robinson*, 57 R.I. 1 (1936), a decision denying the applicability in Rhode Island of the doctrine of strict separation of powers.

Although McCoy also did well at this special session by securing the passage of an act increasing his control over Pawtucket's police and fire departments, he again failed to gain approval for his great obsession—municipal ownership of public utilities. Both Green and lawyer-lobbyist Cornelius C. Moore of Newport consistently blocked McCoy's populistic crusade against Blackstone Valley Gas and Electric and other utility companies.

Because of such opposition and his failure to secure greater statewide influence, McCoy moved closer politically to Walter O'Hara and would side with the *Star*'s publisher and track proprietor when O'Hara battled Governor Quinn in the notorious Race Track War waged by this determined duo during the autumn of 1937.

27

The genteel upbringing and business connections of Zechariah Chafee, Jr., described by his biographer Donald L. Smith, professor of communications at Pennsylvania State University, in the following excerpt from *Zechariah Chafee, Jr.: Defender of Liberty and Law* (Harvard, 1986), did not foreshadow Chafee's career as one of America's most influential civil libertarians. After earning an undergraduate degree at Brown, this scion of a prominent Rhode Island family graduated from Harvard Law School in 1913 and returned there to teach in 1916. For the next forty years his brilliant mind and wide-ranging legal interests earned him such accolades as that penned by Erwin Griswold, U.S. solicitor general (1967–1973) and dean of the Harvard Law School: "Zechariah Chafee, Jr.... was one of the most influential figures in American law and political thought in the first half of the twentieth century." Among Chafee's diverse achievements were a standard casebook on equity, a study of negotiable instruments, and the drafting of the Federal Interpleader Act of 1936, a statute creating federal court jurisdiction when persons of different states make conflicting claims to the same shares of stock or the same bank accounts.

Despite this impressive array of legal accomplishments, Chafee's greatest claim to fame was his authorship of *Freedom of Speech*, published in 1920 and greatly enlarged and revised in 1941 as *Free Speech in the United States*. It remains the classic analysis of this First Amendment right. Chafee contended that the test for free speech should consider not only the individual's interest in freedom but also the social desirability of injecting provocative thought into the marketplace. "Tolerance of adverse opinion is not a matter of generosity, but of political prudence," Chafee argued. Justice Oliver Wendell Holmes embraced this position in his famous dissent in *Abrams* v. *United States* (1919).

According to constitutional historian Paul L. Murphy, "Chafee, as one of the nation's leading civil libertarians in the 1920s, became involved with a number of vital issues. He served on commissions to probe owner autocracy and brutality in the mining regions of the East and he spoke out publicly against excessive use of the labor injunction to curtail legitimate union activities. In 1929 he headed a subcommittee of the Wickersham Commission which looked into police use of the 'third degree' and improper trial procedures. He played a prominent role in the American Bar Association's Commission on the Bill of Rights in the late 1930s, and in the 1940s served on the Commission on Freedom of the Press, afterward performing similar duties for the United Nations."

Despite his national prominence, Chafee was always a Rhode Island lawyer at heart. During the late 1930s he published a series of booklets on the state's major political and legal issues. His inaugural "Dorr Pamphlet," entitled *State House versus Pent House: Legal Aspects of the Rhode Island Race Track Row* (1937), analyzed the legal maneuvering leading to the declaration of martial law at Narragansett Park in October 1937 during the bizarre and bitter feud between Governor Robert Emmet Quinn and racetrack owner Walter O'Hara. This bold action by Quinn was roundly criticized by the libertarian Harvard professor.

Chafee's next two Dorr Pamphlets examined and lamented *The Constitutional Convention That Never Met*, a reference to the abandonment of the crusade for Rhode Island constitutional reform by the Democrats after they finally gained control of state government in the Bloodless Revolution and turned that government to their own ends by statute. In a fourth pamphlet Chafee reflected upon the Panic of 1873 in Rhode Island and the Sprague cases, while attempting to rehabilitate the reputation of his grandfather, the embattled Sprague trustee.

As might be expected, Chafee has a host of intellectual disciples and admirers. Their eulogies and reminiscences, interspersed with Chafee's own essays, were edited as *Freedom's Prophet* by Edward D. Re, chief judge of the United States Court of International Trade (Oceana Publications, 1981). Among the reminiscences are those by Rhode Island attorney Claude R. Branch, Supreme Court justice Thomas J. Paolino, and Senator John H. Chafee, nephew of the illustrious "prophet."

Zecharíah Chafee, Jr.: A Rhode Island Man

Donald L. Smith

On the wall of Zechariah Chafee's office at Harvard Law School hung a colored print of Thomas W. Dorr, who led the nineteenth-century political struggle known as the Dorr Rebellion. This movement, covering the period 1833-1849 but highlighted by armed revolt in 1842, sought to establish a People's Constitution and broaden the suffrage in Rhode Island. After the armed insurrection failed, Dorr was convicted of treason and spent twenty months in jail.

Obviously, Chafee admired Dorr. As well as keeping a portrait of him in his office, he gave the name of "Dorr Pamphlets" to a series of tracts about Rhode Island affairs he published privately during the 1930s and early 1940s. Each pamphlet bore this quotation from Dorr's speech to the jury at his trial: "I am no stranger in this State. I am a native citizen of Rhode Island, descended from Rhode Island ancestors, and inheriting Rhode Island principles and feelings. By birth, by blood, and by education, I am a Rhode Island man." But Chafee was also critical of Dorr, lamenting that "like many enterprising reformers, he lacked patience and judgment. If he had only been content to compromise on non-essential matters, the reforms he desired would have been peacefully granted. He would have been the first governor under the new Constitution instead of languishing in jail and ruining his health."

As a Rhode Island man, Chafee had been influenced by the Roger Williams tradition; he was, in fact, descended from Williams through his mother. He was also steeped in Providence's manufacturing tradition. Both sides of his family were industrialists, and he said both of his grandfathers "made a deep impression on me." He was born in Providence on 7 December 1885, the eldest of six children of Zechariah and Mary Dexter (Sharpe) Chafee. A ninth generation American, he was the fourth successive Zechariah descended from Thomas Chaffe, who arrived from England in 1635 and settled in Hingham, Massachusetts, near Providence. That the family had a modest beginning in this country Chafee humorously acknowledged in responding to a query about a Chafee coat of arms: "It is my opinion that if the family did sport a coat of arms, it would have acquired the same by false pretenses. The original ancestor... did not know how to write his name. Consequently, I suspect that he was not a member of the British nobility."

As for the name Zechariah Chafee, it was the source of both amusement and exasperation. Chafee's father, who ran the family iron foundry in Providence, once prepared a letter about misspellings of his name and sent it to commercial correspondents. "I appreciate that my first name (Zechariah) is today very uncommon," he wrote, "and that my family name (Chafee) is spelled in different ways by different branches of the family; and to write my full name (Zechariah Chafee), correctly, requires a moment of thought, and some care. If it were correctly spelled our amusement might be somewhat lessened, but here are some of the ways in which it comes to me." There followed a two-column listing of thirty-four misspellings of either or both names. A few of the choicer specimens: Jechuriah Chafer, Zebriah Chafee, Zenas Chafee, Ziehzien Chafee, Zarhariah Chaffee.

Zechariah Chafee, Jr.—the kind of name "borne by American millionaires in English musical comedies," H. L. Mencken wrote in a column praising *Freedom of Speech*—was more resigned to such misspellings. "This is one of the incidents of an unusual appellation," he told a magazine editor who apologized for getting his name wrong. The name provided still other light moments. In the spring of 1920 as the nation was recovering from the Red Scare, his friend Calvert Magruder, whose career included service on the Harvard Law School faculty and on the federal bench, wrote: "My stenographer first spelled your name Zach & when I corrected it to Zech she informed me that both are biblical—the former a King, the latter a Prophet. I'm sure, in these days, you prefer the Prophet to the King." As a way of saving time and energy, Chafee usually signed his correspondence "Z. Chafee, Jr."

Despite the problems the name caused him, he thought well enough of it to be mildly disappointed when the wife of his only surviving son, Zechariah Chafee III, chose another name for their son, but he tried to be philosophical about it: "I had some wishes that my own grandson might have borne [the] name, but my daughter-in-law wanted to call him after her own father and that settled the matter for me because I think the mother does the work and ought to be absolutely free to chose the name." Naturally, he was delighted when a grandnephew, the son of John H. Chafee, who has been Rhode Island governor and a U.S. senator, was christened Zechariah in 1951.

Zechariah, Jr., was in a sense a Chafee twice over. Both his parents, who were sixth cousins, could trace their bloodlines back to the original Thomas Chaffe. (Other spellings include Chaphe and Chaffee.) The line that descended on his father's side, Chafee liked to note, always lived within about a fifty-mile radius of Swansea—except for a period when his grandfather Zechariah worked in Pittsburgh. The grandfather, born the son of a stone mason in 1815, had begun working at the age of eleven; at seventeen, perhaps reflecting the Roger Williams spirit of the independent man, he went to Pittsburgh, where he spent two decades in the flour business, starting as a clerk. In 1845, prior to returning to Rhode Island permanently in 1852, he married a young woman from Providence named Mary Frances Buffington and started a family.

Back in Providence—a move made primarily because Mary disliked living in Pennsylvania—Zechariah acquired the High Street Foundry. After changing the name to Builders Iron Foundry, he built it into a solid business producing structural iron work prior to the development of steel-making processes; the firm also made castings for textile manufacturers and cannon for the Union Army during the Civil War. He became a member of several bank boards and of the Rhode Island Hospital Trust Company, and from time to time he was called upon to untangle the financial affairs of small businesses. Things went well for the Chafee family until the nation's financial structure was shaken during the panic of 1873.

This crisis, brought on by wild speculation in railroad construction and by business and agricultural overexpansions, toppled the powerful banking house of Jay Cooke in September. The Cooke collapse caused a drop in security prices, diminishing national income and resulting in considerable unemployment. Rhode Island's economy in particular was imperiled by the failure of the A. and W. Sprague textile empire whose assets totaled $19 million. How to prop up the tottering company was obviously a matter of statewide concern. The task would have been easier if there had been a federal law like the present-day one making it possible to reorganize financially troubled businesses. The eventual attempt at a solution, to simplify a complex story, consisted of naming Zechariah Chafee as the sole trustee of the Sprague estate. He insisted on this arrangement despite the fact that he knew nothing about the textile business and that his own company was a comparative dwarf, being capitalized at $150,000. For a time it appeared that he might be able to turn things around; but it was not to be, and ultimately the properties had to be sold piecemeal with creditors gradually paid off at about thirty cents on the dollar.

Although Chafee was never convicted of any wrongdoing, his role as Sprague trustee got him into various legal difficulties. For one thing, he bought up some of the claims against the company; this constituted speculation by a trustee in the trust property and caused him to be censured by the Rhode Island Supreme Court. And he was periodically taken to court by critics of his handling of the trust.

Partly because so much of his time was taken up by Sprague affairs, he asked his son to take charge at Builders Iron Foundry (BIF). This meant a change in the career plans of the man who became the father of Zechariah, Jr., for he had hoped to go west and become a banker. He ended up as president of the foundry upon his father's death in 1889. Besides altering his occupational plans, the Sprague affair made him somewhat distrustful of the legal profession because he blamed lawyers for at least some of his father's difficulties. And, according to some family members, this helps explain his later lack of enthusiasm for his namesake's decision to study law.

Although he would have preferred to be a banker, young Zechariah applied himself to improving the foundry. Under his leadership the firm added new lines, including components for the Venturi Meter, a fluid-measuring device used by municipal water works. Later, comparable devices were produced to measure steam, gas, and oil. During World War I, BIF made mortars, rifling machines, and shell casings for the government. At its peak the foundry had some 300 employees, many of them Italians. Wages were not exceptional—it was an open shop—but it was Chafee's policy to try to provide steady employment. The plant was considered a good place to work, and many employees encouraged members of their families also to seek jobs there. BIF was an important part of Providence's economy—but never as important as the much larger Brown and Sharpe Manufacturing Company owned by the family of Chafee's wife.

After his marriage to Mary Dexter Sharpe on 10 February 1885, Zechariah, Sr., was associated with Brown and Sharpe for a decade, including service as its secretary, while continuing to operate the foundry. Mary's father was Lucian Sharpe, son of Wilkes Sharpe, a Providence livery stable proprietor, and Sarah (Sally) Adams Chafee, another descendant of Thomas Chaffe. Lucian Sharpe and Joseph Brown started Brown and Sharpe as a partnership in 1853 after Lucian had served an apprenticeship with Joseph, a clock and watchmaker and general tinkerer. As befits one trained as a watchmaker, Lucian Sharpe was meticulously organized—a trait inherited by his daughter Mary.

The oldest of six children of Lucian and Louisa (Dexter) Sharpe, Mary Sharpe worked in her family's machine-tool business as a young woman; she maintained an interest in its affairs until her death in 1934, and at times was expected to resolve family differences within the company. As related by some members of the Chafee family, one such incident put her under great pressure. It involved a struggle between her brothers Lucian and Henry for control of the company. She had promised the older, Lucian, a brilliant eccentric generally considered unfit to run a large concern, that he would be granted the presidency originally denied him. Her inability to fulfill that pledge drained her emotionally and apparently contributed to her somewhat frail condition. An angry Lucian went to Paris and remained there in exile, while Henry had a long tenure as head of the firm.

A 1904 graduate of Brown University, Henry Sharpe became one of its illustrious alumni and served from 1932 to 1952 as its chancellor, or chairman of the Board of Trustees. A bachelor until his late forties, he was like an older brother to his nephew Zechariah, Jr., who was just a few years younger. They enjoyed one another's company and took trips together, journeying as far as Alaska in 1902 when Zech was sixteen. Later, they had sharp political disagreements, and Chafee's writings defending free speech for radicals were thought by Uncle Henry to be little short of treasonous. Yet they were always close friends and, apart from politics, greatly respected each other.

Zechariah Chafee, Jr., spent his early years on Hope Street on Providence's East Side in a house that was a wedding gift from Lucian Sharpe; not far away were Brown University and hilly streets lined with historical homes and churches. He was the first child in what amounted to two families of three children each, separated by a seven-year interval. Besides Zechariah, Jr., there were Henry, born in 1887, Elisabeth in 1889, John in 1896, Mary in 1897, and Francis in 1903. (After much teasing from his siblings about being "an accident," Francis asked his parents if this was true, to which they answered, "You're the only child who wasn't.") By the time of Mary's birth in 1897 the family had outgrown the Hope Street house; thus when Grandmother Chafee gave up her home in 1900, a year before she died, and moved to Boston to be closer to two daughters, Zechariah, Sr., moved his family to the house at 5 Cooke Street, also on the East Side, where he had been born. There he remained until his death in 1943.

The immediate neighborhood of 5 Cooke Street, whose spacious grounds had wisteria, a grape arbor, and a garden that provided fresh vegetables, was quiet but not elegant. A professor at Brown lived next door, another manufacturing family lived across the unpaved street, and two former Rhode Island governors had homes nearby. Beyond the immediate neighborhood lay the "high-rent district" to the north and a large Irish Catholic working-class parish to the south.

A three-story frame structure, the new home provided ample space for the children plus rooms for several servants. A cook and waitress were almost always in attendance, and at times there might be an upstairs maid as well as a nurse. For the three younger children, there was a governess. In a 1952 reminiscence Zechariah, Jr., noted that during his childhood the cook and waitress were both Irish Catholics and that a black nurse was among his earliest memories: "Her devotion and that later on of my [Chafee] grandmother's cook, who had been born a slave, make me feel I can never do enough to repay my debts to the [black] race."

At the age of ten, Zech enrolled in the University Grammar School, a small private boys' school that his father had attended. This followed an eventful summer at camp at Squam Lake, near Holderness, New Hampshire, where he formed what he always looked upon as his oldest friendship—with Harry Dana (Henry Wadsworth Longfellow Dana), then fifteen years old. It must have been an instance of friendship at first sight owing to similarities in character and temperament. Both had solid Yankee backgrounds—Dana's grandfathers were Richard Henry Dana, author of *Two Years Before the Mast,* and Henry Wadsworth Longfellow—and both were to become troubled by the fact that they enjoyed special privileges. And after both had become university professors, their outspokenness got them into trouble. In Dana's case it meant being fired from the Columbia University English Department in the fall of 1917 because of his pacifist activities. Chafee said he owed to Dana one of his key ideas, which he stated thus in *Free Speech in the United States*: "The real value of freedom of speech is not to the minority that wants to talk, but to the majority that does not want to listen."

Two years later, in September 1898, Zech entered Hope Street High School on the day it opened. With a student body representing a cross-section of the community, the school had excellent teachers drawn from defunct private schools as well as from the public system. His first teacher was Alice W. Hunt, who went on to head the Consumers' League of Rhode Island and to campaign for shorter hours for working women; the two corresponded for years about important social questions. The principal was Charles E. Dennis, whom he had for Latin and Greek. Of the instruction he received in the classical curriculum, he said, "What was learned there was 'for keeps' and I cannot conceive of a solider foundation for college." Schoolmates included two who became lifelong friends: George Hurley, who combined legal practice and Democratic politics in Providence after attending Oxford University, and Claude Branch, who practiced law in Providence and Boston with time out for service as special assistant to the U.S. attorney general in the Hoover administration.

Always bookish and somewhat frail, as well as lacking in physical dexterity, Zech was taken out of school in January 1900 for some outdoor seasoning. In the care of a "congenial couple," Mr. and Mrs. James Otis, Zech along with brother Henry journeyed first to southern California, where they stayed at Las Casitas Villa, about five miles from Pasadena. There he became somewhat smitten with one of the guests, a young violinist named June Reed, and met Mrs. C. P. Stetson, a feminist author of whom he wrote in his diary: "She's very jolly and one would not think she was a theorist." He rode horses, did some mountain climbing, and took drawing lessons in Pasadena, sometimes making the roundtrip on foot. But of course there was always time for books, as he later recalled in an essay, "Confessions of a Book Worm," printed in the Brown University literary magazine: "My head has been befuddled with books since I learned to read. My friends make vain attempts to cure me. One of them frequently tries to alarm me by saying that I know absolutely nothing except what I have gained from books. It is of no use; I am incurable. I swore off [once], and went out West for a horseback trip. On my return I found that among other books I had read a volume of De Quincy, an anthology of English poetry, half of a play of Molière's, three books of 'Paradise Lost,' and 'Childe Harold.'"

The California sojourn progressed from Pasadena to Montecito, near Santa Barbara, where he learned from a reader of tea leaves that he would be rich, famous, and well traveled—and "best of all" would marry the Providence girl who then appealed to him most. After Montecito, they visited Yosemite Valley and San Francisco before returning by train through Nebraska where "I really formed my Bryanite opinions." The summer of 1900 was spent in and around Providence, but then he and Henry were off again—to northern Maine, where during the autumn they helped a farmer and went to corn huskings with country boys and girls before resuming their studies.

During his career at Hope Street High he was best known for scholarship. He was on the football second team but his father would not let him play in games. As he wearied of being a model offspring, his deportment at times dipped below the norm. Once, after conspiring with most members of his Greek class to answer "unprepared" when called on, he was even kept after school. This event he gleefully chronicled as "The Greek Conspiracy," a narrative launched in a style like that of the Roman historian Sallust but later changed to "a very grandiloquent style like Gibbon's." And in the best Samuel Johnson tradition he sold typed copies of the narrative for fifteen cents each. A diary entry about this publishing venture, however, makes no mention of Johnson's dictum about writing for money.

Outside the classroom he displayed the outspokenness that made him a controversial figure during much of his career. On one occasion he took part in a lunchroom boycott—a fiasco anticipating lost causes to come; on another he campaigned for outdoor recess—a crusade resulting in his first personal encounter with censorship when, in the fall of his senior year, school officials forbade him to speak on the subject.

But there were triumphs, too. He won a medal for a reading called "The Hero of the Play 'Julius Caesar,'" in which he said of Brutus: "Though he errs often and acts wrongly and unwisely, he never does what he believes to be wrong; he is always true to his principles." With Chafee, sticking to one's principles was always regarded as "a very fruitful quality." And, despite *C* grades in declamation, he was valedictorian of the class of 1903. His commencement speech, opposing an alliance with England, concluded with a portent of the mature Chafee's view of America's role in the world: "Let us throw open our ports to all the world. Let us no longer think of enemies, but regard every nation as our friend. When we act 'with malice toward none, with charity for all' we shall be a people truly great, realizing the ideals of those who founded the Republic."

During his years at Hope Street High his diary became a confessional of the pangs and preoccupations of a typical teenager: having teeth straightened, flirting with girls, expressing doubts about the future, almost ceaselessly indulging in introspection. In the fall of 1901: "Mine is a life of ideals; shatter an ideal, and depression ensues; but soon a new ideal replaces that destroyed and all goes well." In the fall of 1902: "I confess it was rather a disappointment to me that I was not chosen [yearbook] editor-in-chief [his friend Hurley was]. Still, perhaps I lack the requisite executive ability."

And in the summer of 1903, as he prepared to enter Brown, he told his diary: "Father gave me a long talk this morning on my general conduct in college, the sum of it all being, to keep my mouth shut. Very much needed advice. I have decided, on his advice, to try for only two [prizes for entrance] examinations, Latin & Math. He says he does not care how many I try for as long as I don't get them, but I don't think I will waste my time preparing for exams I don't expect to get. His idea is that it is not well to start in with a big reputation, and that entrance prizes merely show excellence for preparation, not like other prizes for excellence in college work." But after changing his mind, he took three exams, in Greek as well as in Latin and math, and won a first prize for each. Consequently, the announcement of the awards by President Faunce at a convocation in the fall of 1903 was, in the words of Zech's friend Branch, "pretty monotonous."

At the time, Brown University had recently been made into a modern institution under the presidency of E. Benjamin Andrews, a fiery economist. He had quadrupled the faculty size, introduced many new courses, created a women's college (Pembroke), and put the graduate school on solid footing. He resigned in 1897 because the trustees had criticized his advocacy of free silver but soon withdrew the resignation. He left Brown, however, the next year, and after two years as superintendent of the Chicago schools became chancellor at the University of Nebraska. There, his dynamic leadership facilitated the efforts of Roscoe Pound, the head of the law school, to transform legal education, and he recruited E. A. Ross, a founder of American sociology, whose ideas about law helped shape the philosophy of law Pound later developed at Harvard. Pound's philosophy also was influenced by another pioneer sociologist—Lester F. Ward, who was on the Brown faculty when Chafee was studying there. Ward, who believed that man could use his mind and spirit to direct the laws of evolution to which all nature and all forms of life are subject, used the phrase "efficacy of effort" in referring to what an intelligent man could accomplish. Although Chafee took no course from Ward, later at Harvard he heard a great deal about efficacy of effort from his mentor Pound.

Also overlapping Chafee's undergraduate years at Brown was Alexander Meiklejohn, the dean of the university. Later, Meiklejohn became an innovative and controversial college president, who was fired by Amherst and subsequently headed an experimental college (dubbed "the Athens of the West") at the University of Wisconsin. Late in his long life he emerged as a First Amendment theorist whose book *Free Speech and Its Relation to Self-Government* Chafee criticized. Much more to the mature Chafee's liking was the First Amendment work of one of Brown's most distinguished alumni—Chief Justice Charles Evans Hughes, whose thinking about free speech was influenced by Chafee's writings.

Harvard Law School dean Roscoe Pound, an influential advocate of sociological jurisprudence and a critic of the long-dominant system of legal formalism, had a profound influence on Chafee's thought. During the Rhode Islander's second year at law school, 1911–12, Chafee sat in on several of Pound's lectures in legal theory and was "so thrilled" that he attended the class regularly. More than four decades later, as Chafee was preparing to retire, he still regarded the course as "one of the decisive influences on my life because it excited me about the possibilities of doing something to make the law better."

As a Brown undergraduate, Zech again concentrated on the classics, and came to revere one of his teachers—James Irving Manatt, who had been chancellor of the University of Nebraska when Roscoe Pound was a brilliant student of the classics as an undergraduate there. His interest in the classics was ignited early, as he related in an English composition written in 1904. During summers in the country when he was seven, he and his mother read from a book called *Stories of the Old World*. After they had finished reading about the Trojan War, he played with pointed sticks representing javelins: "Sometimes I was Patroclus, and would wage a long hand to hand combat with Sarpedon, a maple tree on the lawn. Sometimes I was Agamemnon or Ulysses. Most of all, I loved to be the swift-footed Achilles, son of Peleus. Shouting my war-cry, I would pursue an imaginary Hector around the walls of an imaginary Troy, until at last the javelin flew from my hands and quivered in the bark of some convenient tree."

In general, his freshman English compositions showed little of the delightful style that marked his mature writings, although he made some use of a construction ("on the one hand...on the other hand") that became characteristic of his prose. The theme "Small Boat Sailing" drew these professorial criticisms: "Except for slight incoherence in one paragraph, and for some colloquial phrases and misspelled words, this is clear and correct. But your style is rather plain and unliterary."

He cared about his writing—in fact, he longed to be a poet or novelist until he realized at Brown that he did not have much to write about—and strove to improve it. By the time of his graduation Brown publications had printed several informed and polished essays by him such as "Literary Conditions in the United States" and "Burton's 'Anatomy of Melancholy.'" Their originality, however, may be questionable; in donating various of his college papers, including English compositions, to the Brown University Archives in 1952, he told a librarian: "I blush now to think of the use that I made of some sort of encyclopedia of criticism, which was possessed by the old polygonal library. I fear there is more of this English in these papers than accords with my present views of the Law of Copyright."

As a freshman, he received two *H*'s (honors) in English, as well as in French, Greek, Latin, and mathematics. Only in gym did he earn a gentlemanly *C*. But, despite his campus reputation as a brain and a bookworn, he did not spend all his time reading. He enjoyed going to football games and sometimes took brother John, ten years his junior, with him; he was proud of being the author of the official class yell; he delighted in explaining that the class motto (from the Roman poet Tibullus), "*Non festa luce madere est rubor*," translated freely as, "It's no crime to get drunk when you beat Dartmouth."

He also pledged his father's fraternity, Alpha Delta Phi. Thanks to an agreement Zechariah, Sr., worked out with the fraternity's officers, Junior was spared the kind of hazing usually inflicted on pledges. But fraternity life was not always smooth; he found himself virtually alone in opposing his brothers' support of a new university rule permitting professionals to play on the varsity baseball team. The issue was hotly batted about in campus publications and at mass meetings after the Athletic Board voted in early February 1904, with only Meiklejohn and another professor dissenting, to repeal the amateur-athletics rule excluding from varsity competition athletes who played for pay in the summer. Zech's outspoken opposition to the rule change, Branch related, was "not appreciated" on the Brown campus: "Most of us cared more about a winning team than about amateur standing. He thought the professionals should be disqualified and eventually they were. It was an early example of his integrity." In a revealing diary entry Zech said of the incident: "I suppose I shall always be a minority man. It makes me rather lonely, though I am right... I have Father and my own convictions to give me courage."

Perhaps the extracurricular activity that gave him the most pleasure was his membership in The Sphinx, a recently formed intellectual society. He was chosen "to hear the Sphinx' riddles" in June 1905 when Arthur Upham Pope was president. A lifelong friend, Pope became executive secretary of the League of Oppressed People, went on photographic expeditions to Iran, and published *A Survey of Persian Art* and a biography of Maxim Litvinov, Soviet foreign commissar from 1930 to 1939, who advocated cooperation with the Western powers. "I had many delightful evenings as a member of this noble organization during my last two years at Brown," he recalled in 1955, "and consumed a great deal of Italian wine at an unlicensed restaurant in the Italian district. Fortunately the police did not raid the place while The Sphinx was meeting and eating."

At commencement in 1907 Zech closed out his undergraduate career by giving a speech entitled "The Future of American Poetry." He had not been nominated as a speaker, but President Faunce intervened and made sure the son of Zechariah, Sr., who had been a classmate at Brown, was part of the program. While his undergraduate record did not live up to the promise of the three entrance awards he won, he had accomplished a lot both in class and out. He made Phi Beta Kappa and received one scholarship prize, he contributed to campus publications and served as campus correspondent for the *New York Evening Post*, he was on the class debating team for two years and was president of the Civics Club and the Chess Club during his last year. Not winning a Rhodes Scholarship to Oxford was a major disappointment; that honor went to his friend Hurley. Of the academic assets he carried away from Brown, two proved to be of particular value: the facility to deal with general concepts acquired in a history of philosophy course; and "an everlasting source of delight" in the classics.

The summer after commencement he did go to Oxford—as part of a European trip. And then, fulfilling the role of obedient eldest son, he went to work at the foundry ("the family graveyard," he called it), where, he grudgingly recalled years later, he received some badly needed case hardening. Although there can be no doubt that his father would have wished for him to run the business eventually, Zechariah, Sr., believed that even a few years spent in the foundry might save his namesake from becoming hopelessly pompous. His deep concern about his son's future he expressed in a letter to a family friend, written in early 1909 during Zech's second year at BIF:

> As a child he was ever unconscious of any superiority in school over his fellows but the last two years in college he began to look upon himself as a scholar and to be a bit vain...As one of my friends says ...it is quite an injury to a man when he manifests any consciousness of intellectual superiority, and we felt that... if [Zech] kept in books the way he was doing, there was danger of that defect in his character ...I also felt that it is a great misfortune for any one [not to]...master or enjoy any form of work which comes in their way. Not to do this, it seems to me, is unmanly or un-American...
>
> ...With his temperament (he is pre-eminently trustworthy) and with some capacity and experience for practical affairs, I think very high positions are open to him...But, having had some practical experience, he must decide for himself. At present he is drifting towards law, which might not be a bad thing, although I think at present he is not strong enough for the study.

No single event—no blowup with his father, for example—precipitated Zech's decision to leave the family business and become a lawyer. If his father had not virtually commanded him to do so, he would not have worked for BIF in the first place. Once there, he tried to perform conscientiously the tasks assigned him, ranging from common laborer to company secretary. He also had a chance to write his first "book"—a catalog of the firm's products. But grinding out an occasional foundry price list could not end the frustration he felt as an intellectual who wanted to write but was convinced that he had nothing to write about. Conversations with his friend Branch, who was studying law at Harvard, contributed to his consideration of a legal career, and after three years at BIF he convinced his father that he should be allowed to follow Branch down the path of the law. "The study of law," he liked to say, "gave me something to write about." Although his father never quite forgave him for leaving the foundry, especially since he did so in favor of a profession whose integrity Zechariah, Sr., questioned, in an important sense Zechariah, Jr., never left. For he continued to be associated with BIF even after joining the Harvard law faculty, serving as a director and from 1944 to 1954 as chairman of the board.

After graduating in 1913 from Harvard Law School, where he finished second in his class (a fraction of a point behind Robert A. Taft), Chafee returned to Providence and practiced for three years with Tillinghast and Collins, a leading firm whose principal client was the Rhode Island Hospital Trust Company. The senior partners were William R. Tillinghast, a college friend of Chafee's father and a member of the BIF board until his death in the early 1930s, and James C. Collins, who, Chafee quipped, would turn down any job applicant who "lacked a Mayflower ticket." More than once after he became a professor, Chafee saw former students he had recommended get rejected by his old firm simply because they were not of old Yankee stock. Chafee had the right credentials, of course, and he was well liked by the senior partners. He looked upon Tillinghast as "always the ideal lawyer" and a man to whom he owed "a great debt," including the fact that Tillinghast had originally stimulated his interest in interpleader. And he maintained a close relationship with Collins until the latter's death in the early 1950s. Another good friend with the firm was Harold B. Tanner, who was made a partner at the same time as Chafee early in 1916. A few months later, Chafee left to start teaching, but the mails kept him in regular touch with his former associates, and for years some of his happiest times were weekends spent at Ninigret Lodge, situated on a pond in the woods of northern Rhode Island, with Collins, Tanner, Branch, and others, including Harvard faculty occasionally invited by Chafee. As well as good food and stimulating conversation, the group enjoyed long walks and, in winter, skating on the pond. Chafee, while others were drinking and playing cards, liked to just sit and read the *Atlantic Monthly*.

During his years with the firm, which he said paid its young men well and did not require them to work nights or Sundays except in major emergencies, Chafee never tried a case before a jury, handling instead mainly appellate cases. But his brief career as a working lawyer did not lack diversity. Cases he worked on alone or with others ranged from cruelty to animals to challenges to the will of a Newport multimillionaire, Theodore M. Davis; in the latter litigation, which engaged him off and on for almost a decade after he started teaching, he helped save Davis's famous Egyptian collection for the Metropolitan Museum in New York. Outside the firm, as a member of the Rhode Island Bar Association's Committee on Amendment of the Law, he was instrumental in drafting an intestacy statute but unsuccessful in trying to end imprisonment for debtors.

While in practice, he also was an unsuccessful Democratic candidate for the Providence City Council—a race he ran without consulting his father, who felt the outcome might have been different had he known of his son's intention and thus been able to line up support among his numerous community contacts. Certainly there was a need in Rhode Island for someone of Zechariah, Jr.'s, integrity. The worst kind of political corruption continued to infect the state long after the Dorr Rebellion, which did result in some constitutional reforms. Led by "the Blind Boss," Charles R. Brayton, the Republicans bought elections for decades, while Democratic desires for reform were thwarted by gross malapportionment. Conditions received national publicity in 1905, when Lincoln Steffens published an article in *McClure's Magazine* called "Rhode Island: A State for Sale."

During the 1930s Chafee, from his prestigious chair at Harvard Law School, published a series of articles in the *Providence Journal* and the *Evening Bulletin* in an effort to persuade Rhode Islanders of the need for a constitutional convention. His efforts ended up merely as one entry in his mental file of lost causes with which he was identified. Still, he always remained a loyal son of Rhode Island, a city-state like those of ancient Greece, for whose culture he felt such an affinity. His vision of what the state might become he expressed in a letter to Sinclair Lewis, written in 1942: "I have always felt that a city-state like Rhode Island offered unusual opportunities for an integrated community, something like Attica, but I am afraid that these opportunities have not yet been realized. One of the great advantages of Rhode Island is that the state is so small that everybody who counts can easily get to know everybody else who counts. It would also be possible for an enlightened citizen to get to understand the principal needs of the state and the claims of all the different groups. Jefferson had such an understanding of Virginia when he wrote his *Notes* at the end of the eighteenth century."

Professor Chafee is shown here testifying before the U.S. Senate Subcommittee on Constitutional Rights in 1955, just two years before his death in February 1957 at the age of seventy-one.

DORR PAMPHLET NO. 2

The Constitutional Convention That Never Met

First Part — 1935

BY

ZECHARIAH CHAFEE, JR.

Professor of Law in Harvard University
Member of the Rhode Island Bar

Articles and Documents on the Proposed Rhode Island Constitutional Convention

PUBLISHED AND SOLD BY
THE BOOKE SHOP, MARKET SQUARE, PROVIDENCE, RHODE ISLAND
Fifty Cents, Postpaid

Chafee, who always maintained a lively interest in Rhode Island politics, served as historian and critic of the state's political scene in the years immediately following the Bloodless Revolution. In his "Dorr Pamphlet No. 2," he described the failure of the divided Democratic party to make good on its long-standing promise to implement reform via a constitutional convention.

In "Dorr Pamphlet No. 1," Chafee had a field day chronicling the political battle called "the Race Track War," which brought Rhode Island's Democrats into national disrepute. In the fall of 1937 Narragansett Park became the focal point of the bitter Democratic party factionalism that had vexed state politics since the Bloodless Revolution of January 1935 brought that hungry party to power. Flamboyant Walter E. O'Hara had made huge donations to both major political organizations and employed numerous state legislators and party regulars in lucrative part-time posts at his track. He repeatedly lobbied for more racing dates and sought to limit the state's take of the betting handle. Lieutenant Governor Robert E. Quinn, intensely partisan but highly principled, resented what he viewed as O'Hara's baneful influence on state government, and when Quinn succeeded Green as governor in January 1937, the stage was set for a showdown between these two extremely combative Irishmen.

Former newsboy O'Hara had acquired two newspapers (the *Pawtucket Star* and Peter Gerry's *Providence Tribune*), which he merged in 1937 to create the *Star Tribune*. When Quinn intensified state surveillance of the track's operation (with the enthusiastic backing of the moralistic Sevellon Brown's *Providence Journal*), O'Hara declared war on Quinn in the pages of the *Star Tribune* and strengthened his relationship with Mayor Thomas McCoy and House leader Harry Curvin, two of Quinn's intraparty rivals.

The smoldering resentments ignited on September 2, 1937, when O'Hara's guards beat up and forcibly ejected *Journal* reporter John Aborn from the track. Quinn ordered his supporters on the State Racing Commission to investigate O'Hara's long train of abuses and rescind his right to operate Narragansett Park. When the commission promptly complied, McCoy used his influence with the new state Supreme Court (he had secured the appointments of Francis Condon of Central Falls and Chief Justice Edmund Flynn) to have the racing commission's ruling quashed. Quinn countered by directing the commission to cancel the track's fall racing dates, but once again the high court blocked the move. Meanwhile O'Hara let loose a barrage of libelous charges against the governor.

"Battling Bob" Quinn refused to be deterred. First he filed a criminal libel action against O'Hara, and then, on October 16, 1937, one day after the second Supreme Court ruling and two days before the park was scheduled to open, he issued a proclamation declaring that the track and its environs were in a state of insurrection justifying the establishment of martial law. Several hundred armed national guardsmen, such as those pictured here, joined with state police to cancel the fall meet. McCoy and Curvin, who doubled as Pawtucket's public safety director, dispatched the Pawtucket police, who wisely backed off.

Quinn won the battle, but the national embarrassment to Rhode Island caused by the Race Track War contributed to his defeat in 1938, when he ran ten thousand votes behind the remainder of the Democratic ticket. O'Hara suffered greater wounds: he was ousted as president and manager of the racing association by its stockholders; his newspaper went into receivership (after which the *Journal* acquired and destroyed much of the *Star Tribune*'s equipment); and he was indicted for illegal use of corporate funds (though the charges were later dropped). In February 1941 O'Hara died on Route 44 in a spectacular head-on auto crash, ending his turbulent career. Photo of National Guard troops from Zechariah Chafee, Jr., *State House versus Pent House: Legal Aspects of the Race Track Row* (1937).

28

The following selection, which is admittedly more political then legal, describes a development that arose from a highly publicized and highly controversial decision of the Rhode Island Supreme Court. This ruling, in the aftermath of the closely contested gubernatorial election of 1956, reversed the apparent victory of Republican attorney Christopher Del Sesto and gave the nod to incumbent Democratic governor Dennis J. Roberts.

The fact that Associate Justice Thomas Roberts, brother of the governor, was a member of the high court—though he abstained from voting—further offended the general public's sense of fair play and hurt the image of the court as an impartial tribunal. The technical soundness of the ruling was obscured by the popular belief that the will of the voters had been disregarded.

The court's decision in *Dennis J. Roberts* v. *Board of Elections et al.*, 85 R.I. 203, was not handed down until February 13, 1957, although it was made retroactive to inauguration day, January 1, 1957. It came in the form of a proceeding on petition for certiorari to review the action of the state Board of Elections in declaring Del Sesto the victor. The board's tally of absentee ballots had reversed the election-day machine returns, which had given Roberts a slight edge—190,259 to 190,052. A count of all the absentee votes by the Board of Elections, however, gave Del Sesto the governorship by a margin of 194,974 to 194,547. Roberts challenged this final total, asserting that many votes had been cast illegally. The court agreed.

Of the three categories of mail ballots—servicemen, civilian, and shut-in—the 3-to-1 court majority contended that the latter two types should be invalidated because of an inconsistency between statutory and constitutional provisions relating to the time when shut-ins and civilian absentees could vote. According to the court's analysis, Article of Amendment XXII (1944), dealing with servicemen, allowed the legislature to fix a time for balloting on a day other than election day, whereas Article XXIII (1948), dealing with civilians and shut-ins, did not. The failure of the latter amendment to allow the legislature discretion regarding the time for casting ballots necessitated recourse to Article XVI (1911), which had earlier been interpreted by the court to require voting only on election day. Therefore the portion of the existing 1953 statute governing shut-in and civilian absentee voting procedures that allowed voting prior to election day was unconstitutional. Its unconstitutionality, said the court, rendered void all ballots cast under its authority. To compound the confusion of the electorate, the court noted that Article XXI (1930) had modified Article XVI and enabled the General Assembly to allow absentee voting before election day, but XXI had been repealed by Article XXIII, and with it fell all of the voting laws based upon it, including the 1953 elections law.

This somewhat strained decision also strained public confidence in the judicial system. With all civilian absentee and shut-in voters disfranchised, Roberts was certified the winner, 192,315 to 191,604. Although Roberts lost the governorship in 1958 in a rematch with Del Sesto, he conducted a successful private law practice until his death in 1994 at the age of ninety-one. In addition, he served in a number of high-level civic posts, including chairmanships of the 1964–1969 state constitutional convention and the Board of Regents for Education. He was also a confidant of, and adviser to, President John F. Kennedy.

Smith's essay reveals that factors other than the Long Count decision contributed to the defeat of Roberts in the next gubernatorial election. The circumstances surrounding his 1956 victory diminished his stature and thus encouraged ethnic-based Democratic factionalism, not only among Italian American voters but among Franco-Americans as well. For such restive dissidents, the Long Count decision of the Supreme Court was more an opportunity than a grievance.

When Matthew J. Smith researched and wrote this essay, he was a recently elected state representative and a doctoral candidate in political science at Brown University, as well as the archivist of Providence College. Though not a lawyer, Smith was more than a mere academician. He would become Speaker of the House of Representatives in 1980 and state court administrator and clerk of the Rhode Island Supreme Court in 1988.

Though a man of integrity and firm religious convictions, Smith admired—and, to a degree, emulated—the Democratic leaders of the Bloodless Revolution, especially Robert E. Quinn, Thomas P. McCoy, J. Howard McGrath, and Dennis J. Roberts. In many ways he was their lineal descendant; and, to a lesser degree, so was Smith's colleague, Chief Justice Thomas F. Fay. But the political climate of the 1930s, which tolerated the Bloodless Revolution, and that of 1950s, which acquiesced in the Long Count, changed dramatically from the mid-1980s onward. Conduct that may have been routine in the era of patronage and partisanship was now regarded as unethical or worse.

Just as climatic change destroyed the dinosaurs, the hothouse growth of governmental reform undid Rhode Island's old-style political practitioners like Matthew Smith and Thomas Fay. They were among the last of a dying breed. In the early 1990s, for indiscretions that would have been business-as-usual in the 1950s, both Smith and Fay—men of basic honesty—were subjected to an intense media barrage that inspired legal sanctions against them, which, in turn, drove both from the high court offices they held. Both were victims of moralism run rampant.

Smith's essay on party realignment can be supplemented by Duane Lockard, *New England State Politics* (1959), which contains an insightful view of Rhode Island's political landscape during the period from the 1930s through the mid-1950s. Lockard's two chapters dealing with Rhode Island—"One Party Facade and Two Party Reality?" and "Politics on the Seamy Side"—speak volumes.

The Long Count and Its Legacy: Rhode Island Political Realignment, 1956-1964

Matthew J. Smith

Study of state political structures received scholarly impetus from V.O. Key's classic work, *Southern Politics*. Key used three models—multifactional, dominant faction and bifactional—to classify one-party states of Dixie. Following Key's lead, David Fenton used different paradigms to categorize midwestern states and Duane Lockard attempted to analyze the six-state New England region during the mid-1950s. The focal point of these studies was the post-1932 period and roughly the first decade following the close of World War II. In the case of Rhode Island, Lockard's commentary closed with the gubernatorial election of 1956, in many ways a turning point in the state's political history. Ensuing years saw a resurgent Republican party regain control of the executive branch and reestablish two-party competition for a number of general offices. The Democratic machine dominating Rhode Island politics since 1932 began to falter. Although Democrats regained the governorship in 1968, they have continually faced stiff competition for control of the executive.

The turnabout in Democratic party fortunes can be traced to a number of factors and events which reshaped political balance. Elements of this story are complex, but they shed new light on patterns of state political development and in several aspects reinforce the traditional cyclical interpretation of ways in which American parties gain and lose power.

Rhode Island's modern political development has been somewhat unique in comparison to that of her sister New England states and in general to that of the other forty-four members of the Union. These irregularities of evolution are due to basically conservative political leadership in the late nineteenth and twentieth centuries and to smallness, leading to what one prominent scholar has termed the "politics of intimacy," which fostered a parochial inbred power structure in both political parties.

Rhode Island did not experience any type of political, social or economic reform movement during the so-called progressive era. While the rest of the nation, including the South—except on racial matters—was penetrated by the spirit of change, this state was bound to a system of boss-controlled Republican government in which a rural-dominated and grossly malapportioned legislature held sway over a hapless executive branch which was at best ceremonial.

The Democratic election victory in 1932 and the famous "bloodless revolution of 1935" gave that party control of the state senate and ushered in a new era of Rhode Island politics. For the first time in the twentieth century the urban ethnic electorate—over eighty per cent of the state's population—had a voice in governmental affairs. Triumphant Democrats reorganized the archaic state government into a departmental system, expanded executive power to include personnel appointments and budget making, and eliminated Republican control of the judicial system. By the close of 1935 the entire fabric of state government had been rewoven by Democratic reforms which shape the state's development to the present day [i.e., 1976].

Over the next two decades Democratic leaders were quick to adopt New Deal and Fair Deal programs and were in the forefront promoting labor, social, and other progressive legislation for the state's workingmen. But they were in some cases reluctant, and in others unsuccessful, at reforming political machinery. In 1936 the party's call for a long promised constitutional convention was defeated at the polls. This setback guaranteed continuance of the malapportioned state senate until the Supreme Court's *Baker* v. *Carr* decision of 1962—in Rhode Island, *Reynolds* v. *Sims*—mandated the one man-one vote rule and ended apportionment inequities. After 1936 Democrats resorted to limited conventions for specific constitutional changes but never sought a total revision of the basic document until the Supreme Court's decision, which was the catalyst for an ill-fated convention which met in 1964. Solidly Democratic in delegate strength, this convention deliberated, bickered, and ultimately botched its mandate by taking four long years to produce a document which voters overwhelmingly rejected in 1968.

While constitutional change failed, other reforms also lagged. The General Assembly, with Democratic control in the House and rural Republican domination in the senate, resisted any attempt to reorganize its outmoded committee structure, and legislative conflicts of interest continued. A long discussed primary law was not adopted until 1947, a conservative statute labeling a voter for a twenty-six month period as a member of either major party. Rhode Island became the forty-seventh state to provide a primary system.

The retarded nature of Rhode Island's political evolution had a profound impact on both parties. GOP control in the pre-1935 period rested with a rural, white, Anglo-Saxon, Protestant hierarchy whose economic and social philosophy had definite pro-business and anti-immigrant overtones. With the exception of token acceptance of the French-Canadian community, Republicans failed to revamp their image until the mid-1950s. Democrats who emerged in leadership roles after 1935 rode the crest of anti-Republican attitudes created by the great depression and reinforced by the liberal New Deal. This generation of Democratic leaders engaged in what one author has called the "politics of revenge." While wrapping themselves in the mantle of national reform programs, they continued a high-powered patronage program featuring dual office-holding among state legislators and accommodation with business interests. In place of the rural Republican political apparatus Democrats instituted an urban-based brand of machine politics through which a small coalition of leaders maintained a tight grip until the gubernatorial election of 1956, when the party's electoral hegemony was jarred and then broken in the subsequent election.

In the post-1936 period the leadership in both parties remained fairly static. Democratic officeholders in the top echelons were young and ambitious. With the exception of Senator Theodore Francis Green they were

Irish. McGraths, Quinns, Fogartys and Robertses jockeyed for the governorship with the hope of advancing to national offices. J. Howard McGrath, elected governor in 1940, advanced rapidly, but in his haste to become senator in 1946 he left the door open to an Italo-American, lieutenant governor John O. Pastore, who claimed the governor's chair from McGrath's political ally, Dennis J. Roberts, mayor of Providence. Pastore duplicated this feat in 1949 and became senator when McGrath advanced to attorney general in the Truman administration. This move finally cleared the path for Roberts to run for governor in 1950.

But the decade of the 1940s had been costly for Democrats. The political ascendancy of Pastore and the phenomenal longevity of Green had created a bottleneck on the party's ladder of advancement. This impasse was reflected all along the state ticket where non-Irish members of the party's ethnic coalition eagerly awaited their turn to move up. Furthermore, the predicament extended to the new generation of Democratic leaders on the local level, who found themselves virtually without access to higher office.

The advancement bottleneck on the lower level was also due to the size of the state. Rhode Island is virtually a city-state, with Providence—at least until the late 1960s—the major ingredient in Democratic victories. Other urban areas were satellites of the central city and, acting in political unison with Providence, they constituted an impregnable bastion. Throughout the forties and into the fifties the party was ruled by this urban coalition to which Roberts fell heir in 1950. There was virtually no area in the state where a separate political base could be formed by an ambitious candidate. Unless a candidate was approved by party leaders, he could not enter its small governing circle or be picked to join its "ticket." In short, the Democratic political hierarchy resembled the Republican oligarchy of the pre-1935 era.

Republican leaders did not have to worry about a bottleneck occurring among their state office holders, for from 1932 to 1958 they elected only five, all in 1938. Their stagnation of another sort was the result of the GOP's failure to recognize political facts of life in Rhode Island. In a state whose population was over sixty per cent ethnic in origin and over eighty per cent urban in life style, Republican leadership was overwhelmingly Yankee and rural in its caste. Its Yankee establishment was the result of a sharp economic and social class dichotomy unique to Rhode Island's development. The rural nature of the party rested in its last bastion of strength—the state senate—where gerrymandered districts allowed small-town leaders to exert an inordinate amount of leverage over nominations to the state ticket. Again, the state's smallness worked in reverse for Republicans seeking access to party councils. The fledgling urban GOP was largely populated by ethnics who, in the case of the more prosperous Italian and French-Canadian elements, had pre-1935 Republican ties during the period the party had controlled the cities. Leadership in urban areas gravitated to ethnics such as Christopher Del Sesto or Felix Toupin, who had once been Democrats but were unable to find advancement in that party. Since few Republican inroads were made in the cities, their urban cohorts had small voice in GOP affairs.

Governor Dennis J. Roberts (1903–1994), who prevailed in the Long Count, entered politics shortly after his graduation from Boston University Law School in 1930. In 1934 he secured election to one of four Senate seats that Providence was allocated by the provisions of the recently ratified Nineteenth Amendment to the state constitution. As a protégé of Governor Green, Roberts advanced rapidly in the ranks of the Democratic party, becoming state chairman in 1938.

Along with Providence mayor James Dunne, a fellow attorney, Roberts was beaten in the Republican electoral sweep of 1938, a contest in which the national recession of 1937 and the scandalous Narragansett Race Track War of the same year hurt nearly every Democratic candidate on the state and local levels. This defeat proved to be a blessing in disguise, however, because the removal of the popular Democratic mayoral incumbent enabled Roberts to secure his party's endorsement against Republican-Good Government-Independent mayor John F. Collins in the campaign of 1940. In that banner year for the Rhode Island Democrats, Roberts defeated Collins by a 17,474-vote margin and began an efficient ten-year reign as Providence's chief executive, interrupted only by a leave of absence in 1943–44 to serve in the U.S. Naval Reserve, where he attained the rank of lieutenant commander in the Office of Strategic Services.

Roberts went from Providence to the governorship (1951–1959), only the second mayor in the city's history to accomplish that feat. In later life he returned to the practice of law and served in a number of high-level civic posts, including the chairmanships of the Board of Regents and the 1964 state constitutional convention. Roberts was also a confidant of, and adviser to, President John F. Kennedy.

Between 1932 and 1956, and possibly to the present, it could be argued that Rhode Island was basically a strong one-party state. Although Republicans gained the governorship in 1938, 1958, 1962, 1964 and 1966 elections, their victories did not reflect a strong grass-roots party movement, but rather opportunistic triumphs over a sometimes divided (1938), sometimes tarnished (1938, 1958, 1962), or sometimes disorganized (1966) Democratic party. Other Republican electoral victories were either in the rural-dominated state senate or with the popular President Dwight D. Eisenhower. Even control of the state senate seesawed back and forth until 1958 when Democrats gained control. Election statistics for the period reflect a pattern of this sort, but it is also clear that since 1956 the Republican party regained the ability to compete and win elections for the state's general offices. This turnabout in the electorate's voting habits, from solid Democratic margins to competitive two-party runoffs for major offices, can be traced to events within both parties during a crucial eight-year period, 1956–64.

The Roberts-Del Sesto race for governor in 1956 was a watershed for electoral changes of the next decade. Their bitter battle unleashed a tide of political undercurrents which rocked Democratic party structure and refocused Republican election strategy. Among more important trends were the following: a fracturing of Democratic unity as witnessed by emergence of the primary election as a vehicle for expression of discontent; resurgence of ethnic politics in both parties; lessening of the urban Democratic voting base; and loss of other traditional supportive groups.

Dennis J. Roberts seemed destined to become a United States senator. An Irish Catholic with natural leadership qualities, he had starred in football in high school and college, gone on to law school, and in 1934 had been elected to the state senate from Providence. By 1938 he was state party chairman allied to J. Howard McGrath, a leading Democrat. In 1940 Roberts wrested the nomination for mayor from powerful city treasurer Walter Fitzpatrick and, with the aid of Frank Rao, ousted Republican incumbent John Collins. During the next ten years as mayor he built the reputation of being an able and progressive administrator and an adept political leader. Although unable to move up to governorship in 1946, Roberts' future still looked bright. Theodore Francis Green was eighty-three in 1950 when Roberts was endorsed without opposition for governor and easily beat Eugene J. Lachapelle in the general election, and it seemed highly likely that Green would soon retire. Roberts moved quickly to consolidate his power. In 1951 Frank Rao became state party chairman and his reign was marked by tight party discipline and allegiance to Roberts.

But dreams of 1950 quickly became realities of 1956. Green had not stepped down from the United States Senate in 1954 when his term expired, and two years later his zest for Washington had not diminished. There was a logjam in the upper echelons of the party, and Roberts was forced to run for governor for the fourth time.

His rival in 1956 was a Democrat turned Republican, Christopher Del Sesto, who had earlier served as a Democratic appointee to highly responsible positions in state government. Del Sesto's disenchantment with Democrats came in 1944 when McGrath and others had vetoed his candidacy for lieutenant governor in favor of John O. Pastore. He subsequently joined the GOP and ran a losing campaign for mayor of Providence in 1952. But Del Sesto's road to the Republican nomination was not easy. After being denied the GOP nomination for governor by the rural "old guard" in 1954, Del Sesto won endorsement in 1956 and became the first Republican Italo-American candidate for governor of Rhode Island.

Christopher Del Sesto (1907–1973) was both a lawyer and a certified public accountant, with an expertise in taxation. During the Democratic coup of 1935 he became Tom McCoy's deputy in the state budget office and then succeeded McCoy after the latter's quick break with Governor Green. Feeling bypassed by the Democrats, Del Sesto later switched parties and became a formidable Republican candidate for governor. Despite his disappointing loss in 1956, Del Sesto persisted and turned the tables on Roberts in 1958. In turn, he lost to lawyer John A. Notte of North Providence in the Kennedy landslide of 1960. Del Sesto finished his productive career as an associate justice of the Superior Court.

Del Sesto's candidacy was a significant change in Republican strategy, which had made ethnic matches by pitting an Irishman against John Pastore in 1946 and by endorsing French-Canadian candidates in 1948 through 1952 elections, possibly in an effort to revive their pre-1932 alliance with that ethnic group. John G. Murphy in 1946 and Raoul Archambault, Jr., in 1952 had run reasonably well, but the GOP had not been able to pierce the New Deal Democratic ethnic coalition. Their endorsement of Del Sesto was in a way the last possible alternative Republicans could offer to break tripartite Democratic alliances.

Del Sesto's nomination was also a victory for the GOP's urban-liberal wing. The feud between more progressive city Republicans and the rural senatorial clique had been simmering since 1953, when the Republican state central committee had openly criticized their party counterparts in the senate for obstructionism and for dealing with Democrats. Senator George D. Greenhalgh of Glocester, leader of the group, and his state chairman, Herbert B. Carkin of Warwick, were able to prevent Del Sesto's candidacy in 1954. But two years later Del Sesto gained endorsement with the aid of William T. Broomhead of Barrington and strong Italo-American support from Providence.

The "long count" election of 1956 resulted in a tainted Roberts victory when the state supreme court invalidated absentee and shut-in ballots cast prior to election day on the grounds of a constitutional amendment specifying that all votes of this type be cast on the polling day. While the victory was costly to Roberts' image, a close examination of the election reveals that other significant factors were at work in 1956 having important long-term effects on the state's political life.

Ethnicity played a crucial role in the election for both Republicans and Democrats. Although ethnic politics was a way of life in Rhode Island—both parties had been systematically balancing tickets with French, Irish, Italian, and Yankee candidates since 1936—this was the first post-1935 contest in which sizable defections occurred statewide. No doubt, Del Sesto's totals were enhanced by the presidential year turnout and the Eisenhower triumph in Rhode Island, but the Roberts-Dean J. Lewis runoff in 1954 was the largest off-year vote in the state's history until that time and almost matched the turnout in 1958.

Comparison of Roberts' 1954 vote with that of 1956 in the Italian Federal Hill area of Providence, and examination of Roberts-Del Sesto returns from communities with sizable Italian populations, both reveal a dramatic swing to the Italo-American. During the campaign it was felt that

Del Sesto's ethnic origins would hurt him with Yankee Republicans said to be reluctant to endorse an Italian. But returns from three rock-ribbed rural Republican towns—Foster, Glocester, Exeter—show no vote cutting when results are compared to Yankee William T. Broomhead's totals. In short, it appears Del Sesto picked up important Italian Democratic votes and retained traditional GOP strength—there was no ethnic backlash.

Evidence represented in voting returns of this election are buttressed by campaign events. From late September until November, newspapers and airways were filled with stories and appeals about and to Italian voters. Roberts never injected nationality into his remarks, but the Democratic candidate for secretary of state John A. Notte Jr. did so unsparingly. He called Del Sesto a figurehead, implying that the Republican party had never been friendly to the Italian. "If the Republicans thought they could win, they would never have put up Del Sesto." Notte also announced that a Democratic poll showed Roberts winning by a three to one margin in the thirteenth ward, "heart of the biggest Italian-American district in Rhode Island." In the campaign's final week Notte addressed radio messages to his fellow Italians praising Roberts' work on the American committee on Italian migration to revise the quota system and noting his award from the Italian government of Grand Officer of the Order of Merit.

Other Democrats of Italian extraction continued the assault upon Del Sesto. When Assistant Attorney General Francis J. Fazzano learned that the GOP candidate was going to spend a day in Natick, a predominantly Italian area of West Warwick, he sneered, "He never knew where Natick was until he became a candidate." This was the pattern of attack by many others, and for Democrats their ethnic wooing ended with a massive rally on Federal Hill at which Senator John O. Pastore flailed away at Del Sesto and the Republican party.

Republicans were far from outdone. Del Sesto concentrated his campaign in predominantly Italian areas of the state. His only Providence headquarters were in Italian-populated wards. He challenged Roberts to campaign in Westerly or on Federal Hill, where Democrats had had bitter primary battles. Del Sesto's own visit to the "Hill" five days before the election was portrayed in a full page layout of pictures featuring the candidate conversing in Italian with a local woman shopper.

Ethnic strategies of both candidates in 1956 ignited an intense series of primaries and elections during the next eight years and beyond. In 1958 Roberts again faced Del Sesto with much the same type of campaign. Del Sesto's vote in the various districts and towns remained virtually the same, only this time the Republican won. Two years later Democrats nominated John A. Notte, Jr. to head a ticket that included Edward P. Gallogly in the second spot. The Notte-Del Sesto race clearly indicates a return by Italo-Americans to Democratic ranks, and Notte's pluralities in 1962 against Yankee John H. Chafee offer further evidence. The persistence of ethnicity as a factor in elections can be seen as late as 1970 when an Italian Republican challenged a Jewish Democrat.

Besides creating ethnic antagonisms, the Roberts win in 1956 intensified the logjam within the party. Before Democratic endorsements that year, Roberts had to dissuade West Warwick chieftain Michael DeCiantis from challenging him for the nomination and, in order to pacify Secretary of State Armand Coté's desires, the lieutenant governor's spot was given to the popular Frenchman against the advice of Italian leaders. This patchwork compromise did not work. Coté was quick to understand the precarious position of the governor due to his "victory" over Del Sesto, and within a year rumors of a primary challenge were in the air.

Armand Coté's political career in state politics was the result of J. Howard McGrath's desire to unite the Democratic party in the 1940 election. In order to pacify Thomas P. McCoy, political sachem of Pawtucket and a constant thorn in the side of the governing coalition of the party, McGrath offered McCoy the opportunity to name two spots on the state ticket. For one of these positions, secretary of state, McCoy chose Coté, an obscure first-term schoolcommitteeman from Pawtucket. From this fortuitous start Coté emerged as the top party vote getter by the 1950s. While it is difficult to determine Coté's motivations in 1958, it would be reasonably correct to assume that personal ambition coupled with the ethnic desire to have a Franco-American lead the party after two decades of Irish domination were factors in his determinations.

In order to challenge Roberts in 1958, Coté was forced to take the primary route because the Democratic state committee, the endorsing instrument, remained strongly in Roberts' control. A primary was at that time an untested method in Rhode Island politics; a primary law had been adopted in 1947 and, after a brief flurry of activity in both parties the following year, it had fallen into disuse on the state level as an instrument of change in party politics. There is little doubt that the rigid hierarchy of both parties which "anointed" candidates for the ticket contributed to this situation. Especially in the Democratic party, where victors of 1935 were very visible and active, party rank and file were quite docile about the decision-making process. It is ironic that by 1958 the rigidity remained and had created a situation with which party leaders were unable to cope.

The Roberts-Coté battle during summer 1958 was the first serious primary in the state's history. Coté and his capable campaign manager, Walter Kane of Smithfield, put challengers into the field for every state office except general treasurer, but the major race was for the top office and subsequent control of the Democratic party. The election could be classified as "crude" in the sense that the media was used to a small degree, reflecting the somewhat unsophisticated nature of Democratic campaigning and almost total reliance upon the concept of party "organization." With regard to issues, Coté relied upon criticisms of the governor that Del Sesto had leveled two years earlier and upon the theme that a change was needed. Unlike the 1956 election, little mention was made openly of nationality, but the Roberts camp made special efforts in Woonsocket to hold the French-Canadian vote. Roberts' ally in that city was Kevin Coleman, a highly respected reform mayor.

Tuesday, September 17, was a gloomy, rainy day as Democrats went to the polls. Surprisingly, Coté held a three hundred vote lead statewide before returns from Providence were counted. But that lead was shattered by an organization vote of two to one for the governor in his home city. The challenger ran very well in the Blackstone and Pawtuxet valleys, French-Canadian strongholds, carrying Pawtucket, Lincoln, Cumberland, Central Falls and West Warwick. His major disappointment was Woonsocket; although he carried the city by a 4,015 to 3,718 vote, the margin was far less than expected. Overall, Coté garnered almost 44 per cent of the vote and 50.4 per cent outside of Providence.

Roberts' fifth campaign for governor was a rematch of the 1956 affair. Del Sesto, after initial refusal, had again decided to be a candidate when his choice for state party chairman, William T. Broomhead, was selected to replace the Greenhalgh-Carkin combine. The day after the primary Del Sesto said that the results of the Democratic squabble forecast "a Republican landslide of unprecedented proportions." While his rhetorical prognosis was far from correct, the GOP candidate's narrow 6,230 vote plurality was dependent in part on the Democratic rupture of the previous September.

Journalists have attributed the GOP victory to a revenge-minded public, aroused by the "vote steal" of 1956, forcing retribution upon Roberts and his cronies. There is probably much to this idea, particularly among that group of voters highly interested in and aware of state affairs. But further analysis of election returns indicates that Roberts' strength dropped sufficiently in Coté strongholds so that in conjunction with the "long count" issue of 1956, the defection of Franco-Americans from the Democratic party cost the governor a fifth term. Contrasting Roberts-Del Sesto totals for 1956 and 1958 shows that the Del Sesto vote in Italian areas remained fairly static or declined slightly in terms of percentage. Comparing areas of Coté's strength against returns for the two candidates in each election indicates that Del Sesto's vote picked up significantly or remained approximately the same in a low turnout year, while Roberts' support and his margins dropped in every community. It appears that Democrats in those areas either abstained from voting or moved into the GOP column in sufficient numbers to maintain Del Sesto's totals. While results are not conclusive, the Roberts-Coté split may have been the key ingredient in Republican victory.

The Coté primary had several long term important implications. The hegemony of the Roberts-Rao organization was fractured and would be eliminated in 1960. With Roberts' defeat in the senatorial primary of that year, the state organization that had existed since 1935 was unable to regroup under strong leadership and declined rapidly. John A. Notte Jr. and John G. McWeeney, who emerged in 1960 as governor and state chairman respectively, were unable to cope with the new political environment.

Keystone of the political scene, at least for Democrats, was the primary election. Between 1958 and 1964 elections, the endorsed party candidate for governor faced serious challenges for the nomination. In each case the party's endorsement went to an individual from Providence opposed by candidates outside the party hierarchy. Although in every case except Clairborne Pell's in 1960 the state organization was victorious, each race further weakened it. This process stopped not for lack of ambitious men but for emergence of an extremely popular Republican governor in 1962.

The ascendancy of John H. Chafee made the Democratic nomination decidedly less popular. Even after his defeat in 1968, the Republican party had gained a new credibility, making Democratic endorsement no longer the major step to the governorship.

It is likely that primary campaigns among Democrats will continue for major offices. Upon the death of Congressman John E. Fogarty in 1967 a major free-for-all ensued for the endorsement, with Providence forces losing out to a newcomer from suburban Warwick, Robert O. Tiernan. Even defeat of the Providence "machine's" candidate for the congressional nomination did not forestall a primary race—former governor John A. Notte Jr., hoping to capitalize on the heavy concentration of Italo-Americans in the district, contested the nomination in a primary and lost in a very close election.

The state Democratic organization of the post-1935 era, while priding itself on political acumen, was myopic in understanding fundamental changes occurring in Rhode Island society. Within two decades, 1950–1970, Providence and its sister cities experienced significant emigration to suburban communities. There is little doubt that Providence's substantial decreases are reflected politically in Democratic gains in Warwick, Cranston, Johnston, and some South County communities. General Assembly delegations from suburban communities provide an accurate measure of this phenomenon. Beginning in 1956 and perhaps even earlier, Democratic strength in the malapportioned state senate began to increase. By 1958 the senate had gone Democratic (23–20), and this trend continued, receiving further impetus from court-mandated reapportionment in 1966 elections. Power in the state organization began to drift away from Providence's control as newcomers became aware of their influence. It is not surprising that the present [1976] governor and state chairman are from suburban areas.

The party hierarchy of the forties and fifties was also very complacent about extending organizational influence and control into suburban communities. Democratic victories in those areas were due not to an organization master plan but rather to diligence of local candidates who benefited from the population influx. Suburban Democratic parties that emerged were not bound by patronage or other loyalties to the state organization. Their rank and file, without constraints or viewpoints of traditional party leadership, developed an autonomous status which further weakened the state organization.

This political evolution produced new allegiances and power bases which emerged in the mid-sixties. Warwick provides the best example of this changing political environment. Traditionally Yankee in population and politics, this city was the recipient of substantial numbers of Irish-American Providence residents in the post-World War II period. Following the pattern of the Democratic surge of the thirties, a Yankee Democrat, Horace Hobbs, was elected mayor in 1960. Warwick's first Democratic senator in the modern era was an Irishman, Robert O. Tiernan, whose family had migrated from Providence in the fifties. The city's next mayor, Philip W. Noel, of French-Canadian and Italian extraction, became governor in 1972. Its General Assembly delegation presently consists of four

Irish-American Democrats, all formerly from Providence, in the senate and six representatives of either Italian or Irish extraction in the House.

Eclipse of the state Democratic party and its subsequent realignment occurred during a period in which the Republican party was undergoing an image overhaul and program modernization equally as significant to the state's political life. This metamorphosis was aided externally by emigration from Democratic cities and by a softening of organized labor's stance toward the GOP. These factors, in combination with internal changes in the party, led to a Republican resurgence in the sixties.

While it is difficult to measure, exodus to the suburbs by urban Democrats aided the GOP to the degree that party allegiance was not constrained by tight organizational control found in city organizations. It is highly likely that the ex-urbanites retained their party identification, but it was not reinforced or pressured due to relatively new and loosely structured suburban Democratic organizations. This circumstance made the newcomers susceptible to Republican overtures, provided that the candidate was attractive and moderate in his views.

Also aiding the GOP was the political "divorce" which terminated the long-lived marriage between organized labor and the Democratic party. Their squabbles began in the early fifties, were encouraged by the emergence of Republican Christopher Del Sesto in 1956, and smoldered during Roberts' fourth term from 1956 to 1958. With Del Sesto's victory in 1958, AFL-CIO leaders found that the GOP governor was not opposed to labor goals. His defeat two years later by John A. Notte Jr. seemed to revive the long-standing romance with Democrats, but within twenty-four months labor abandoned the Democratic party for an independent posture. A headline summed up union feelings— "R. I. Labor Charges Democratic Betrayal." Thomas F. Policastro, AFL-CIO president, charged the Notte administration with self-interest legislation to protect "race tracks and insurance companies." Further, labor leaders were highly annoyed at Notte's withdrawal of support for a state income tax and other legislation. The importance of the split between traditional allies is difficult to measure in terms of its effect upon voting behavior, because it is generally conceded that the impact of a union endorsement waned in the fifties. But in the vital area of finances the union disillusionment had an important impact on Democrats. By withholding funds from the state ticket in 1962 labor made its displeasure felt.

By 1962 the state GOP was a revamped party no longer carrying the image of a rural-dominated conservative organization. The election of 1956 began a reversal of the trend of Republican domination in the state senate, occurring ironically while the party was making a very creditable run for the governorship. Although the Republicans carried the senate that year by twenty-three to seventeen, Democrats took the seats in Tiverton and Lincoln and ran very well in Burrillville, Coventry, East Greenwich, Exeter, Jamestown, Portsmouth and Westerly. The combined Republican margin in those towns was approximately 1100 votes.

Two years later Democrats gained control of the upper branch by twenty-three to twenty with notable victories in Coventry, Burrillville and

Jamestown. This trend continued in the Kennedy election of 1960. The Democratic margin was twenty-eight to sixteen with notable victories in Warwick and Glocester, both Republican bastions in the modern era. The effect of this turnabout was clear. The rural Republican "old guard" had lost its power and subsequently its bargaining position in state GOP councils.

Augmenting this significant development was the activity of Christopher Del Sesto. In 1957 he removed Herbert Carkin as state party chairman against the wishes of George Greenhalgh, leader of the senatorial clique. Del Sesto's nominee, William T. Broomhead of Barrington, presented a youthful, more liberal image. A measure of the importance of this change was seen in the following year when Greenhalgh declined to run for the senate, thus depriving the rural wing of its most forceful leader. Broomhead's six-year tenure was marked by Del Sesto's 1958 win and the upset victory of John H. Chafee in 1962. Del Sesto's gubernatorial term provided the GOP with statewide patronage for the first time since 1939, to further strengthen the party.

By 1962 Republicans had rebuilt their organization to the degree that the party experienced its first real primary for a gubernatorial nomination. On the surface the bitter battle between John H. Chafee and Louis V. Jackvony Jr. appeared to be a traditional test between rural and urban wings of the party, but a close examination of the state convention and subsequent primary reveals that both candidates shared important support from rural Republican leaders. If anything, the primary appears to have been first and foremost an ethnic clash between Yankee and Italian elements in the GOP with urban-rural configuration a secondary consideration.

Competition for the Republican gubernatorial nomination began very early. In December 1961 two leading candidates, John H. Chafee of Warwick, house minority leader, and Louis V. Jackvony Jr. of Providence, director of the Department of Business Regulation in the Del Sesto administration, were both actively courting members of the GOP state central committee. Mentioned as possible contenders were former governor Del Sesto, Republican state chairman Broomhead, and Joseph H. O'Donnell Jr., a North Smithfield businessman whose father had been a party stalwart in that town.

As the June 6 endorsement date neared, the Jackvony-Chafee rivalry grew more intense amidst dinner meetings to woo delegates and formal openings of staffed campaign headquarters by both candidates. A poll of state committee members in mid-June showed none of the candidates having the fifty-seven votes necessary for victory but speculated that Chafee had forty-two, Jackvony forty-one, Broomhead ten, and O'Donnell three, with the remaining seventeen unwilling to make their choices known. Tension began to mount when Del Sesto withdrew his name three days before the meeting and publicly endorsed Chafee. One day later Broomhead dropped out, leaving his ten pledges free to support any of the other candidates.

The endorsement meeting at the new Colony Motor Inn in Cranston—a bitter five and one-half hour battle—took three ballots to decide upon a nominee for governor, with the emotionally spent 113-member body adjourning without choosing candidates for other state offices. On the first ballot Jackvony led with fifty-five to fifty-two for Chafee and five for O'Donnell. One vote was not cast on the first two ballots. On the second tally Chafee picked up two votes from each contender, giving him fifty-six to Jackvony's fifty-three and O'Donnell's three. In the climactic third ballot, after O'Donnell withdrew and released his supporters, Chafee went over the top with fifty-nine and Jackvony netted fifty-four. Amidst booing, cheering, and hissing, Chafee accepted the endorsement but Jackvony bitterly denounced the vote as unrepresentative and vowed a primary fight in remarks tinged with anti-Yankee animosity: "The Republican Party is in the unfortunate position of being the party that carries the mantle that it is not interested in the welfare of the ordinary citizen. He [Chafee] is the image of the conservative rich man who is not good for the people." This was to be Jackvony's theme throughout the primary campaign—portraying himself as the candidate of the "little man" vs. the candidate of the rich man.

Reconstructing the state central committee vote is difficult because it was a secret ballot, but from newspaper reports and subsequent events in the campaign it appears that the votes for the two candidates split along the following lines. Chafee carried Barrington, Burrillville, Charlestown, Coventry, East Greenwich, Exeter, Glocester, Hopkinton, Jamestown, Lincoln, Little Compton, Middletown, North Kingstown and South Kingstown. Added to these were two votes from Pawtucket and others from Providence and his home city of Warwick. Jackvony's support came from Providence, Cranston, Newport, East Providence, Westerly and Woonsocket with significant rural support in Narragansett, Tiverton, West Greenwich and Scituate.

While it is obvious that the bulk of Chafee's support came from the rural towns, it is highly doubtful that the split between him and Jackvony was strictly on the basis of the traditional rural conservative vs. urban liberal axis. Rather, it appears that among the so-called "senatorial clique" Jackvony had a definite edge in support. Such stalwarts as George M. Westlake and E. Rex Coman, both of Narragansett, Sam S. Tourtellot of Scituate, George D. Lewis of Tiverton, Romeo D. Asselin of Warren, George M. Leuth Jr. of Foster, and Louis E. Perreault of Richmond were all in the Jackvony camp. Former gubernatorial candidate of the Greenhalgh-Carkin combine, Dean J. Lewis, headed the challenger's campaign in Newport. Jackvony's campaign manager, William R. Halliwell Jr. of North Smithfield, was the son of the conservative Republican leader in northern Rhode Island.

Chafee's campaign aides and town leaders cannot be easily identified with old-line senatorial leadership. His campaign manager, Representative John Conley of East Providence, was a liberal urban Republican who had helped plan Chafee strategy as early as 1961. Probably most important was the support given to the endorsed candidate by Christopher Del Sesto and William Broomhead, GOP leaders who had broken the rural hegemony in the party six years earlier.

Results of the September 11 primary bear out the thesis that the battle was along ethnic lines rather than urban liberal versus rural conservative ideology. Chafee carried the urban centers of Providence, Pawtucket, Warwick, Westerly and Cranston while losing Central Falls by only four votes. Jackvony's strength came from Italo-American areas of Providence, Cranston, West Warwick and Warren. In almost every other area he ran poorly. Chafee's sweep was complete.

An examination of vote returns in Providence shows the extent of the ethnic split. Wards 1, 2 and 9 with large Yankee elements gave Chafee overwhelming pluralities while wards 4, 5 and 13 showed a strong preference for the Italian-American Jackvony. This trend can be seen in Cranston and other urban areas.

A factor in the turnout affecting Jackvony's Italo-American support was the fact that Democratic governor John A. Notte Jr. faced strong primary opposition from Kevin Coleman of Woonsocket. Due to prior legislation that mandated for the first time a same-day primary for both parties, Italian voters' ethnic allegiances were torn, and the vast majority opted for Democrat Notte whose victory was won with Providence's strong organization vote. This circumstance was somewhat offset by loss of Yankee Republican voters who had in 1960 voted in the Democratic primary for Claiborne Pell over Dennis Roberts, thus losing their right to vote in a Republican primary for twenty-six months. Estimates of this loss run from 4,000 to 40,000 with knowledgeable observers setting the figure at 12,000.

John Chafee went on to prove Jackvony's "can't win" label wrong, even in the face of the Italo-American's failure to support the GOP ticket. His victory ushered in a six-year Republican hold on the executive branch, beginning another political cycle.

State politics entered a new phase with the Chafee victory. Although Democrats were complacent about regaining the governorship in 1964—most viewed the 1962 election as an aberration—they again experienced a primary and an internal fight for control of the state chairmanship and for nominations to state offices, further weakening party structure. In the general election their candidate for governor was resoundingly beaten by the popular Chafee. In the eight years since 1956 the Democratic party had unintentionally lost unity of purpose, leading to resurgence of the GOP and enabling Republicans to seize the executive branch and regain credibility with voters.

Democratic leadership in 1956 was unable to clear the logjam for advancement to federal offices. Ethnic elements of the party's governing coalition therefore resorted to the primary election as a means of gaining power and advancement. This led to a series of ethnic primary conflicts which shook party discipline. After the emergence of Republican Christopher Del Sesto, a new, more intense round of ethnic politics developed which split the Democratic coalition.

Besides the primary election and intense ethnicity of the period, the Democratic party failed to develop a new strategy to meet the changing nature of Rhode Island society. Wedded to a "Maginot Line" mentality concerning the cities, leaders were negligent in cultivating a suburban organization under state party auspices. They relied instead upon the false notion that the GOP would never be a threat because the electorate was overwhelmingly Democratic.

This dream was not thoroughly dispelled until the debacle of 1964, and by that time it was too late to crush a Republican party that had used the politics of "personality" to leapfrog over Democratic organizational politics.

Thomas H. Roberts (1902–1976), a year older than his brother, the governor, received the same education—LaSalle Academy, Fordham University, and Boston University School of Law. He had moved from the Superior Court (to which he was appointed in 1951) to the Supreme Court in 1955, where he sat when the Long Count decision was rendered. Although he refrained from voting, the presence of the governor's brother on the high court caused many to question its impartiality. In 1966, upon the death of Francis Condon, Thomas Roberts became chief justice, and he held that post until his own death in 1976. His son, Dennis J. Roberts II, served three terms as state attorney general from 1979 to 1985.

As Christmas 1956 approached, the gubernatorial election was still unresolved. This *Journal* cartoon of December 23, 1956, shows the Rhode Island electorate watching the two contestants battle it out.

29

There is a tinge of irony to the fact that Rhode Island, the state that pioneered religious liberty and church-state separation in America, has in the past three decades become a leading source of major U.S. Supreme Court decisions relative to the Establishment Clause of the First Amendment. A fundamental reason for this seeming anomaly is that the state's predominantly Catholic population has fostered an interpretation of establishment at variance with the prevailing Supreme Court view. The high court has generally supported a wall of strict separation between church and state, prohibiting any direct governmental assistance to any religion. The Catholic view accepts government aid if it is evenhanded and does not support or advance any religious sect at the expense of another. Curiously, one of the most persuasive, succinct historical defenses of that position has been written by a Rhode Islander about a Rhode Islander.

Professor Mark DeWolfe Howe—late professor of law at Harvard, secretary to Justice Oliver Wendell Holmes, and author of *Cases on Church and State in the United States*—wrote a book entitled *The Garden and the Wilderness: Religion and Government in American Constitutional History* (1965), a title derived from a metaphor of Roger Williams. Here Howe demonstrates that the "wall of separation" phrase employed by the modern Supreme Court originated not with Jefferson but with Williams. However, "when the imagination of Roger Williams built the wall of separation, it was not because he was fearful that without such a barrier the arm of the church would extend its reach. It was, rather, the dread of worldly corruptions which might consume the churches if sturdy fences against the wilderness were not maintained." Howe contends that "there is a theological theory of disestablishment traceable to Roger Williams," and that "the Court, in its role as historian, has erred in disregarding the theological roots of the American principle of separation" in favor of Jefferson's secular view. Howe further states that the First Amendment's prohibitions at the time of their promulgation "were generally understood to be more the expression of Roger Williams's philosophy than that of Jefferson's." The conclusion

Howe eventually reaches is that the First Amendment was designed to prevent government interference with religion and not to prevent "government advancement" of religion generally. If Howe is correct, then the posture assumed by Rhode Island in the three major establishment cases that it has sent to the Supreme Court since 1971 does no violence to Williams's position on the relation of church and state.

During the tumultuous and ideologically divisive 1960s the liberal Warren Court rendered several decisions on the relationship between religion and education that ran counter to the "government advancement" view described by Howe. In Rhode Island most legislative efforts to aid the state's financially troubled Catholic schools were thwarted by this Court's new and expansive view of the First Amendment's Establishment Clause. In 1969 the state legislature passed an act to supplement the salaries of teachers in parochial elementary schools. After an ACLU challenge, the U.S. Supreme Court, in the landmark case of *DiCenso* v. *Robinson* (1971), struck down the measure because it provided "substantial support for a religious enterprise" and caused "an excessive governmental entanglement with religion." Shortly thereafter the federal District Court for Rhode Island invalidated a state school-bus law requiring towns to bus private-school pupils beyond town boundaries if necessary. This decision prompted the resourceful legislature to create regional bus districts to circumvent the court's ruling.

In 1973 the high court made its controversial decision on abortion in *Roe* v. *Wade*. Since that time the Rhode Island state legislature has displayed much more opposition to abortion than the general population, as evidenced by the decisive defeat of a pro-life amendment proposed by the 1986 state constitutional convention. Although abortion is basically a moral rather than a religious issue, in Rhode Island the battle has assumed sectarian overtones and church-state implications. Numerous laws to blunt the effect of *Roe* have passed the General Assembly, including one declaring that life begins at conception, another requiring spousal or parental permission for abortions, and another requiring the informed consent of the prospective patient, followed by a forty-eight-hour waiting period. Most of these laws have failed to pass constitutional muster in our federal District Court.

The next church-state issue to pierce the thin veil of local ecumenism involved the use of public funds for religious displays. Here Rhode Island produced another nationally significant case in *Lynch* v. *Donnelly*, 465 U.S. 668 (1984). In this confrontation the ACLU challenged the City of

Pawtucket's inclusion of a Nativity scene in its Christmas display. In a 5-to-4 decision Chief Justice Burger, speaking for the majority, dismissed the complaint in part because "it has never been thought either possible or desirable to enforce a regime of total separation" of church and state. The Court majority felt that in the predominantly secular context of Pawtucket's display, the primary purpose and effect of the Nativity scene were not to promote religion but only to acknowledge the spirit of the holiday season. The decision continues to generate interest and has prompted a book-length analysis entitled *The Christ Child Goes to Court*, (Temple University Press, 1990), by Wayne R. Swanson, professor and chairman of the Government Department at Connecticut College.

The final major establishment case, *Lee* v. *Weisman*, 505 U.S. 577 (1992), developed from a graduation ceremony at Nathan Bishop Middle School in Providence at which a student, Weisman, objected to the principal, Lee's invitation to clergymen to give the invocation and benediction. The Supreme Court ruled, in a 5-to-4 decision, that a school requirement that a student stand and remain silent during a "nonsectarian" prayer at the graduation exercise in a public school violated the Establishment Clause, even though attendance at the ceremony was completely voluntary. The student, said the Court, should not be required to give up her attendance at the graduation, "an important event in her life, in order to avoid unwanted exposure to religion."

The following essay by Patrick T. Conley and Fernando S. Cunha, a Providence attorney, is a case study, or anatomy, of the first Rhode Island establishment case, *DiCenso* v. *Robinson*, 403 U.S. 602 (1971). The Rhode Island controversy has been obscured because it was joined for decision with the Pennsylvania case of *Lemon* v. *Kurtzman*, which involved a law authorizing that state's superintendent of public instruction to reimburse nonpublic schools for teachers' salaries, textbooks, and instructional materials in secular subjects. Both cases, however, are significant as a statement of the Supreme Court's view of impermissible "entanglement." In fact, the three-prong test and other rulings associated with *Lemon* actually were part of the DiCenso decision!

For a survey of the church-state issue in Rhode Island, consult Conley, "Civil Rights and Civil Wrongs in Rhode Island: Church, State, and the Constitution, 1636–1986," *Rhode Island Bar Journal* 35 (June–July 1987), 14–19. In its original form this article was the keynote address to the 1997 annual meeting of the American Catholic Historical Association.

State Aid to Rhode Island's Private Schools: A Case Study of *DiCenso* v. *Robinson*

Patrick T. Conley and Fernando S. Cunha

Dr. William P. Robinson, Jr. (1913–1987), state commissioner of education, became the defendant in the salary supplement case. As a prominent Catholic layman, he was sympathetic to the motives of the law's supporters and assisted in drafting the statute. Robinson is shown here after receiving an honorary Doctor of Pedagogy degree from Providence College in 1964. The Rhode Island Higher Education Assistance Authority building on Jefferson Boulevard, Warwick, was dedicated in his honor in 1989.

In the January 1969 session of the Rhode Island General Assembly, House Majority Leader John Skeffington of Woonsocket, freshman Representative Robert J. McKenna of Newport, and several other prominent Catholic legislators sponsored "An Act Providing Salary Supplements to Non-Public School Teachers." The introduction of this measure precipitated a controversy in the land of Roger Williams over state aid to sectarian education that was ultimately resolved by the United States Supreme Court.

Necessary to a full understanding of the issues involved in the salary supplement case is a brief description of the sociopolitical structure of Rhode Island. According to the 1970 census, the state had a population of nearly 950,000. Of this number, approximately 600,000 were Roman Catholics according to estimates of the Diocese of Providence, a see coterminous with the state itself. Because Catholics comprise sixty-two percent of Rhode Island's inhabitants, a proportion far larger than that of any other state in the union, the Catholic Church can and does exert considerable influence, both direct and indirect, on Rhode Island's educational and political affairs.

The educational impact of the Church is more susceptible to measurement than is its political influence. In the area of elementary education, the domain with which this article is concerned, the Catholic role is substantial. In the peak academic year 1963–1964, parish-related grammar schools enrolled 38,455 pupils, or 28.3 percent of the elementary school population in Rhode Island. By 1969–1970, the year of the controversy discussed herein, enrollment in these schools was down to 29,340, or twenty percent of total school enrollment. Despite this decline, the Catholic effect on the educational system was still very significant.

A 1972 Rhode Island Department of Education report on public and nonpublic elementary education in the state revealed that a complete phase-out of Catholic elementary education would necessitate a $20,317,000 annual increase in the operating expenses of the public school system, a jump of 13.4 percent. Some urban centers would be even more adversely affected—the increased educational outlay in the heavily Catholic city of Pawtucket, for example, would be a whopping 26.6 percent.

Hence, for economic as well as the obvious religious and sociocultural reasons, many individuals in Rhode Island are committed to the continued existence of Catholic elementary schools. These institutions, however, are in a grave financial plight which has resulted in numerous school closings. The number of Catholic grammar schools reached a high of 112 in academic year 1966–1967. By the time of the salary supplement controversy of 1969–1970, the number was down to ninety-eight, and by the 1971–1972 school year the number had decreased to eighty-three. This alarming and precipitous decline has been caused by several factors: the enrollment and contribution drop in many city parishes due to the suburban exodus; rising educational costs due to inflation; the less competitive position of Catholic schools as a result of continually increasing government aid to public education; and the decline in vocations, the revolution in religious community life, and the proliferation of clerical "dropouts" which have combined to produce a critical shortage of religious teachers.

The clerical teacher shortage is the most significant cause of the economic ills of Catholic elementary education. It was to remedy this condition that the Salary Supplement Act was passed. Statistics on the teacher problem are alarming: In 1966–1967 there were 959 religious teachers, mostly nuns, in parish elementary schools throughout the state; in 1969–1970 the figure was 691; in 1971–1972 there was an incredible decline to 489. During this same 6-year period, the number of lay teachers rose from 205 to 328. The substitution of a lay for a clerical teacher means a threefold increase in salary costs for a parish school.

It was apparent to the sponsors of the Salary Supplement Act that the parish elementary schools were caught in a cruel dilemma. When the nuns left the schools, lay teachers had to be hired at salaries competitive with constantly rising public school stipends. To meet this cost, tuition had to be raised. The increase prompted some parents to avoid the additional levy by placing their children in free public schools. This move was facilitated by the fact that a Catholic school staffed by lay teachers does not appear to offer much of an alternative to public education. Thus, enrollments declined and schools were forced to close.

To stem this trend, public funding by the state government seemed necessary. Fortunately for the friends of parochial education, the General Assembly was even more Catholic in composition than its constituency. Both houses of the legislature were overwhelmingly Democratic, and the strength of the Democratic Party in Rhode Island derives from a fortuitous political coalition of ethnic Catholics forged during the late 1920s and the New Deal era—Irish, Italians, French, and Portuguese. The General Assembly, it seemed, would be very receptive to a program of state aid to private education. This body appeared especially amenable to a plan that would save the private institution experiencing the gravest fiscal difficulty—the Catholic elementary school. This was the religious, educational, and political setting in Rhode Island at the start of this legal drama. The curtain opened and the plot began to unfold when the January 1969 session of the General Assembly commenced.

At the outset of this legislative conclave, an important but unresolved question concerned the form which aid to private education would take. There were two proposals which received discussion. The first was a straight tuition grant to parents of private school children. This course of action was supported by the Rhode Island Chapter of Citizens for Educational Freedom (CEF). The local affiliate of CEF was, in fact, predominantly Catholic. The membership of this powerful educational group contained several prominent state legislators, including House Speaker Joseph Bevilacqua, Deputy House Leader Aldo Freda, and Robert J. McKenna, an irrepressible freshman representative from Newport. McKenna was an associate professor of politics at Salve Regina College, a specialist in church-state relations, and a prime mover in CEF.

The second legislative remedy for the fiscal ills of the nonpublic-schools was a proposal to pay a salary supplement to private school teachers of secular subjects. Advocates of this measure felt such a plan would ease the cost burden on private schools and make them better able to compete for qualified teachers. This proposal was designed to raise the salaries paid by private schools to public school levels. It should be noted that in 1971–1972 the average teacher's salary in the public schools was $9,322, while the average salary for lay teachers in Catholic schools was $6,000, or only 64.4 percent of the public school figure. The salary supplement proposal was favored by the Reverend Edward Mullen, superintendent of Catholic schools for the Diocese of Providence. Father Mullen was a lawyer, and he used his legal talents to prepare a draft of the salary supplement bill. Eventually, he prevailed upon CEF to support his recommendation.

Robert J. McKenna, a professor of politics at Salve Regina University and a specialist in church-state relations, was one of the plan's leading architects. A freshman representative in 1969, McKenna later became a state senator from Newport, then chairman of the Senate Finance Committee, and, still later, mayor of Newport. Presently he is chairman of the Rhode Island Higher Education Assistance Authority.

Shortly after the opening of the January 1969 session of the General Assembly, the original version of the Act was introduced by Representatives Skeffington and McKenna. Among those who assisted in its drafting were Professor McKenna, Father Mullen, and Dr. William P. Robinson, Commissioner of Education of the State of Rhode Island.

Interviews conducted by the authors yielded considerable information on the fate of the measure in the state legislature, but this story is much too detailed and inscrutable for treatment in an article of this scope. Some developments, however, are worthy of note. The original version of the measure would have allocated $1,500,000 in state aid, covered grades one through twelve, and provided a thirty percent supplement, an amount just sufficient to equalize public and private school salaries. Certain developments made some amendments necessary. First, Governor Frank Licht, who supported the bill, was beset with a revenue shortage and could spare only $400,000 to implement the measure. Second, Dr. Henry Brickell, a state educational consultant, issued a report on Rhode Island's nonpublic schools while the supplement bill was pending. In his report he analyzed four different types of nonpublic schools: (1) private non-Catholic institutions, (2) Catholic private schools, (3) Catholic diocesan high schools, and (4) Catholic parochial elementary schools. The first two cateogories were fiscally sound, the third in a slight economic bind, but the fourth group was experiencing a severe crisis, according to Dr. Brickell, and was in need of fiscal assistance.

On the basis of the Governor's budgetary limitations and Dr. Brickell's findings, the salary supplement bill was amended. Teachers at exclusive, well-to-do private schools, both Catholic and non-Catholic, were eliminated by the insertion of a clause providing that teachers were ineligible in a school where per capita expenditure per student for secular subjects was greater than the public school average. Next, high schools were eliminated, and, finally, the supplement was reduced to fifteen percent. These alterations lowered the necessary first year appropriation to $375,000.

Constitutionally, these amendments were significant. Under the original bill, according to advance estimates, $600,000 of the $1,500,000 allocation would have gone to teachers in non-Catholic private schools. Under the amended version, all $375,000 was to go to teachers in Catholic parish elementary schools. The amendments gave the bill a distinctly Catholic hue and rendered it more vulnerable to constitutional criticism under the "purpose and primary effect" doctrine of *Abington Township School District* v. *Schempp* (1963).

Another interesting aspect of the salary scheme concerned the role of the commissioner of education. Legally, he was the executive agent of the state Board of Education, but in the administration of the Act the commissioner was given an autonomous role while the influence of the board was negligible. Commissioner Robinson, a devout Catholic layman who assisted in the drafting of the bill, contended that this result was intended. Most of the seven-member state Board of Education were non-Catholics who had been appointed by a three-term non-Catholic Republican governor, John H. Chafee. Dr. Robinson, a vigorous supporter of salary supplements, was well aware that a majority of the board opposed the bill; hence, the board was circumvented.

In its final form, the Act empowered the commissioner to establish regulations for the disbursement of funds in February and June of 1970. Eligible for aid were those nonpublic school teachers who *exclusively* taught a subject required by the state, possessed a Rhode Island teaching certificate, and received a salary, including the supplement, which met the minimum salary paid to public school teachers. The effect of this last requirement was to prevent any cleric from receiving funds under the Act.

The measure's preamble declared that it was state policy "to provide a quality education for all Rhode Island youth." It then observed that approximately twenty-five percent of the state's elementary school population attended nonpublic institutions that were "finding it increasingly difficult to maintain their traditional quality." The preamble concluded that the state's policy of quality education for all "would be seriously impaired if the quality of education provided in said schools were to deteriorate." This rationale was accepted by the state's predominantly Catholic-Democratic General Assembly. The measure was reported to the floor by the House Health, Education, and Welfare Committee by a six to three vote which divided along party and religious lines; six Catholic Democrats versus three Protestant Republicans. The bill passed the whole house by a comfortable fifty-six to eighteen majority; fifty-two Democrats and four Republicans including minority leader Oliver Thompson, a Catholic and a cosponsor of the legislation, versus eighteen Republicans, most of whom were Protestant.

In the senate, the road was tougher. As the session drew to a close in early May, HEW Committee Chairman John McBurney informed the bill's manager, Representative McKenna, that he lacked the votes needed to report it to the floor. A vigorous eleventh-hour appeal by McKenna turned the tide and the measure was approved. The margin was eight to seven with Chairman McBurney casting the deciding vote. Once the bill came to public view before the entire senate, its fate was more secure. On the final day of the session it was carried by a twenty-six to thirteen margin in a vote which reflected political and religious divisions. On May 16, 1969, an apprehensive Governor Licht signed the Act privately and without fanfare; its effective date was July 1, 1969.

There were others concerned with the constitutionality of the Act. Paul McMahon, legal counsel to the Diocese of Providence, expressed his reservations to the diocesan chancellor Monsignor Daniel Reilly in a letter dated May 5, 1969. On the other side of the fence, the American Civil Liberties Union (ACLU) also entertained grave doubts concerning the Act's validity, and decided to challenge it. During the fall of 1969, the ACLU sought plaintiffs with standing to contest the law, and this course of action produced six volunteers—Joan DiCenso, Donald R. Hill, Ann Clayton, Alice Chase, Helen King, and Marie Friedel. Some had children in the public schools and all were taxpayers of the state. They provided the ACLU with the "case and controversy" prerequisite to a legal action in federal court. ACLU lawyers relied heavily on the decision of the Supreme Court in *Flast* v. *Cohen* (1968) to maintain a class action and establish standing to sue for the plaintiffs:

> The plaintiff-taxpayer's allegation in such cases [involving the establishment clause of the first amendment] would be that his tax money is being extracted and spent in violation of specific constitutional protections against such abuses of legislative power. Such an injury is appropriate for judicial redress and the taxpayer has established the necessary nexus between his status and the nature of the allegedly unconstitutional action to support his claim of standing to secure judicial review.

Once Joan DiCenso and the other plaintiffs had lent their status to the cause, the legal battle began. On December 16, 1969, Milton Stanzler, an able and experienced ACLU attorney, filed a twenty-four point complaint in the United States District Court for the District of Rhode Island. This taxpayers' complaint alleged in substance that Catholic schools were the primary baneficiaries of Rhode Island's Salary Supplement Act, that the goal of such schools is the propagation of the Catholic faith and that the statute, therefore, had as its purpose and primary effect the advancement of religion. The complaint also alleged that the statute constituted compulsory taxation in aid of religion in violation of the free exercise clause.

The defendants were Commissioner Robinson, General Treasurer Raymond H. Hawksley, and State Controller Charles W. Hill. They were named because of their roles in the disbursement procedure, and were sued in their public capacities. Section II of the complaint, entitled "factual allegations," contained fourteen assertions. While several dealt with the specific provisions of the Act, the most interesting charges were those which attempted to establish a connection between the measure and the Catholic Church. For example, the complaint made the following assertions: (a) "During the 1969 session of the General Assembly numerous spokesmen for

Milton Stanzler, a prominent Providence attorney well known for his legal expertise and his espousal of liberal causes, led the ACLU challenge to the salary supplement act. The measure's principal legal defenders were attorneys Richard P. McMahon and Charles F. Cottam and Attorney General Herbert F. DeSimone.

at least one religious body and organizations associated with at least one religious body strongly and publicly called for and supported legislation giving state financial assistance to church-operated schools"; (b) "The act will primarily benefit parochial elementary schools"; (c) "Under the language of the act substantially all payments ... will be made to teachers in religiously oriented schools"; (d) "The act on its face authorizes payments which support sectarian educational institutions"; and (e) the education in parochial schools is "conducted in an atmosphere conducive to the promotion of religious doctrine and one in which it is impossible to separate the sectarian from the secular." The complaint also alleged that as of October 10, 1969, all of the approximately 200 teachers who had applied to the commissioner of education for a salary supplement taught at religiously-oriented schools.

The third section of the complaint set forth the constitutional causes of action based upon the establishment and free exercise clauses of the First Amendment. The final section contained a fourfold prayer for relief, asking: (1) that a three-judge court be convened to declare the Act unconstitutional; (2) that the defendants be enjoined permanently from approving payment of any funds under the Act; (3) that a preliminary injunction be granted pending a trial of the issues; (4) "that the plaintiffs be granted such other and further relief as the Court may deem just and proper."

When Milton Stanzler filed the complaint with the clerk of the court he also filed his appearance as counsel for the plaintiffs. The summons was returned on December 17, 1969, indicating that it was duly served on the defendants and filed with the court. Service had been made on Americo Campanelli, a Rhode Island assistant attorney general, who accepted on behalf of Charles W. Hill, Raymond H. Hawksley, and William P. Robinson. On December 19, 1969, William J. Sheehan also entered an appearance as attorney for the plaintiffs.

Since the result which the plaintiffs sought was a permanent injunction against the disbursement of funds under a state statute on the grounds of unconstitutionality, the convening of a three-judge court was appropriate. The three-judge court legislation required that where an interlocutory or permanent injunction was sought to restrain the enforcement or operation of a state statute on the grounds of unconstitutionality, the application should be heard and determined by a federal district court of three judges. Therefore, on December 23, 1969, Chief Judge Bailey Aldrich of the First Circuit Court of Appeals designated Circuit Judge Frank M. Coffin and District Judge Hugh H. Bownes of the district of New Hampshire to sit with District Judge Raymond J. Pettine of the district of Rhode Island. Judge Pettine conducted all proceedings between December 16, 1969, the date on which the complaint was filed, and March 18, 1970, the date on which the three-judge court heard the case.

On December 29, an appearance was filed by Benjamin A. Smith, on behalf of the plaintiffs. W. Slater Allen, assistant attorney general, filed his appearance for the defendants on January 5, 1970, along with the answer to the complaint and a motion to dismiss. Judge Pettine denied this motion by written order on January 20, 1970. On January 21, 1970, a hearing was held on the plaintiffs' request for a temporary restraining order. Allan Shine and W. Slater Allen argued for their respective sides at this proceeding. Judge Pettine ruled that a temporary restraining order would not be issued at that time. On January 22, 1970, a separate motion for a temporary restraining order was filed. On February 9, 1970, this motion was heard with Mr. Shine and Mr. Allen again presenting arguments. Judge Pettine, by a written ruling on February 13, 1970, granted a temporary restraining order which was to run until the hearing date of March 18, 1970.

An important development occurred on February 11, when several additional parties filed motions to intervene as defendants. Appearances were made on behalf of the intervenors by Richard P. McMahon, William F. McMahon, Jeremiah C. Collins, Charles H. Wilson, and Edward Bennett Williams, who was principal counsel. The McMahons were Providence lawyers, while Williams, Collins, and Wilson were prominent Washington attorneys and partners in the same firm. These five lawyers represented a group consisting of private school teachers and parents who had children in Catholic elementary schools. The lead intervenor was John R. Earley. Judge Pettine filed an order giving this group leave to intervene under Rule 24 of the Federal Rules of Civil Procedure, which permits intervention in an action

> when the applicant claims an interest relating to the property or transaction which is the subject of the action and he is so situated that the disposition of the action may as a practical matter impair or impede his ability to protect that interest, unless the applicant's interest is adequately represented by existing parties.

These intervenors suggested that because of their status as parents and teachers they could raise constitutional issues related to public aid to private sectarian education that might not be properly asserted by the original defendants.

On March 18, 1970, the case went to trial before Judges Coffln, Bownes, and Pettine. On the trial day, an appearance for the plaintiffs was entered by Leo Pfeffer of New York, a nationally-known civil libertarian and authority on church-state relations. Pfeffer and Milton Stanzler were the principal trial counsel for the plaintiffs, W. Slater Allen represented the defendants, and Jeremiah C. Collins argued for the intervenors.

At the outset of the hearing, Slater Allen made a motion to dismiss which was disputed by Pfeffer. The court chose to reserve judgment on the motion. This tactic allowed the court to hear all the evidence in the case before deciding on the motion. A total of six witnesses were called and twenty-six exhibits were entered. The trial continued through March 19. On that day, summations were made by Jeremiah Collins for the intervenors and by W. Slater Allen for the defendants. Summation for the plaintiffs was conducted by Leo Pfeffer. The court then called for briefs to be submitted by April 6, 1970. On the final day of the trial, an appearance for the plaintiffs was made by Franklin C. Salisbury as *amicus curiae*. Salisbury was representing "Protestants and Other Americans United for the Separation of Church and State." The court granted Salisbury permission to submit his brief.

On March 20, 1970, the court allowed the temporary restraining order to lapse. This action was not contested by the plaintiffs, who waived their prayer for a preliminary injunction. According to Milton Stanzler, this action was a policy decision of the ACLU lawyers. They were mindful of the climate of opinion in Rhode Island, and they did not wish to penalize those teachers who had made contracts in good faith reliance upon the salary supplement law. Once the restraining order lapsed, Commissioner Robinson eagerly proceeded to grant the initial installment to those nonpublic school teachers who had qualified for payment.

The three-judge federal court delivered its anxiously awaited opinion on June 15, 1970, just prior to the time scheduled for the second installment of the salary supplement. The verdict was unanimous; all three jurists found that the Act was unconstitutional, with Judge Raymond Pettine concurring in the result but dissenting in part from the majority view.

At the outset, the question of standing was resolved in favor of the plaintiffs, with reliance placed upon *Flast* v. *Cohen* and *Doremus* v. *Board of Education* (1952). The court next concerned itself with findings of fact by examining "the statutory scheme," "the nature of the crisis leading to the statute," and "the parochical school system." The most significant findings from a constitutional perspective were these: (1) the commissioner of education required nonpublic schools to

> submit data concerning enrollments and total expenditures. If this data indicates a per pupil expenditure in excess of the statutory norm, an agent of the Commissioner must examine the books of the school in question in order to determine how much of its spending was attributable to secular education and how much to religious";

(2) Approximately 250 teachers had applied for aid, and "all of these applicants are employed by Roman Catholic schools";

> [T]he diocesan school system is an integral part of the religious mission of the Catholic Church. It is not that religious doctrine overtly intrudes into all instruction. Rather the combined conveniences of ready access to church and pastor, homogeneous student body, and ability to schedule throughout the day a blend of secular and religious activities makes the parochical school a powerful vehicle for transmitting the Catholic faith to the next generation.

On the basis of these findings, the court proceeded to formulate several conclusions of law. Surprisingly, the court rejected the purpose and primary effect standard of *Abington Township School District* v. *Schempp* despite its conclusion concerning the recipients of the supplement and notwithstanding the fact that the plaintiffs placed heavy reliance on this doctrine. The judges rejected the plaintiffs' attempt "to divine the 'true intent' of the legislature by inspecting the activities of the lobbyists," and asserted that the *Schempp* test contained deficiencies.

The court found the first and third findings of fact more persuasive.

Because of the nature of parochical schools, the court concluded that the Act provided "substantial support for a religious enterprise." In view of the supervisory role exercised by the commissioner, the court held that the "act results in excessive government entanglement with religion and thus violates the Establishment Clause of the First Amendment." The judges placed heavy emphasis on a test which the Supreme Court had devised only the month before in *Walz* v. *Tax Commission* (1970). The court in *DiCenso* determined that the *Walz* test of a statute's effect was "whether the degree of entanglement required by the statute is likely to promote the substantive evils against which the First Amendment guards." The Rhode Island law, the court stated, authorized a subsidy which must be annually renewed and one which "will inevitably excite bitter controversy." In addition, it created an "ongoing administrative relationship between government and the Catholic schools," and "may significantly limit the internal freedom" of those schools. Ironically, the *Walz* decision itself had sustained New York City's tax exemption on property used for religious purposes. In *DiCenso*, however, the *Walz* test was employed to invalidate "the kind of reciprocal embroilments of government and religion which the First Amendment was meant to avoid."

The court gave short shrift to the plaintiffs' free exercise claim, because there was "offered no testimony concerning... personal religious beliefs and practices, or lack thereof" and thus the plaintiffs had "failed to introduce the kind of particularized evidence necessary 'to show the coercive effect of the enactment as it operates against [them] in the practice of [their] religion.'" Finally, the court considered the equal protection claim of the teacher-intervenors and the free exercise claim of the parent-intervenors. The claim of the former asserted that a Salary Supplement Act restricted by judicial decree to aiding teachers in nonpublic but secular schools would deny equal protection because of discrimination against teachers of secular subjects on an impermissible ground, *i.e.*, religion. The court felt that such a distinction was "commanded by the Establishment Clause." Therefore, "even though religion in general may be a suspect classification, the mandate of the Establishment Clause provides an overriding justification in this case."

The parent-intervenors asserted that they

> [felt] in conscience bound to send their children to parochial schools which teach both secular subjects and religion. If, however, the quality of secular education [fell] too low in parochial schools, the parent-intervenors [contended that they might] well be forced to ignore the dictates of conscience by sending their children to public schools. To avoid this result, intervenors argue[d] that the free exercise benefits which flow from aid to parochial education should prevail over the establishment clause values protected by strict separation....

The court, however, rejected "the notion that the Free Exercise Clause demands affirmative state action to accommodate such personal evaluations when society at large has accepted the premise that religious and secular education can be successfully separated."

Judge Pettine authored a separate opinion concurring in part and dissenting in part. He agreed with the court's decision to apply the *Walz* test and noted the "excessive entanglements" inherent in the Act, but he denied the majority's contention that the Act's effect was "substantially to support a religious enterpise." He made the formidable contention that "[o]nly proof will establish that subsidization of an educational enterprise is subsidization of a 'religious enterprise,'" and observed that "there is unanimous unrebutted testimony from several teachers of secular subjects in Roman Catholic schools that religion does not enter into their teaching process."

On June 17, 1970, the judgment and order were formally entered: the defendants' motion to dismiss was denied, the Salary Supplement Act was held unconstitutional in that "it violates the First Amendment of the Constitution insofar as it authorized aid to teachers employed by denominational schools," and the defendants and their agents were permanently enjoined from making any payments or disbursements under the Act to teachers employed by denominational schools.

On the same day, W. Slater Allen and Richard P. McMahon filed an application for a stay, alleging that the injunction would create problems in the negotiation of teacher contracts in parochical schools for the 1970–1971 school year and that an appeal to the Supreme Court would be forthcoming. Judge Pettine denied the motion because he felt there would be "a loss to plaintiff taxpayers" of "a substantial sum of money when we realize the uncertainty of a date of final disposition" by the Supreme Court. An order expressing that rationale was promptly entered on June 17.

The defeated defendants lost no time in bringing their cause to the attention of the United States Supreme Court. Edward Bennett Williams filed an appeal for the intervenors on June 19, and Attorney General Herbert F. DeSimone performed a similar task for the defendants on June 25. DeSimone also appointed Charles F. Cottam, a special attorney general, to argue the case before the High Court. Cottam had a longstanding interest in church-state questions.

On June 26, the record on appeal together with a certified copy of the docket entries were mailed to the clerk of the Supreme Court. The appeals were taken pursuant to a statute which provides for a direct appeal to the Supreme Court from a three-judge district court. The appellants then appeared before Supreme Court Justice William Brennan, to request a stay. Justice Brennan denied the request, but was promptly overruled by the full Court. Thus, on July 1, a certified copy of the order granting a stay *pendente lite* was received from the high tribunal and filed in the Rhode Island district court.

Later in the month, jurisdictional statements were filed with the Supreme Court by the defendants and intervenor-defendants. In a curious move, the ACLU lawyers for DiCenso filed an answer to the jurisdictional statements which also urged the Court to decide the case. According to Milton Stanzler, this action was motivated by the desire of the ACLU to have the important issues raised by these cases finally adjudicated. This concern was shared by the intervenors, and accounted for the failure of the parties to erect procedural roadblocks which would have delayed court action at either the district or Supreme Court level. After examining the statements of the parties, the Supreme Court noted "probable jurisdiction" on November 9, 1970.

This action was the signal to the attorneys to prepare their final briefs for argument before the Supreme Court. The day of presentation came on March 3, 1971. Each side was allocated one-half hour on the Court's busy schedule. Edward Bennett Williams argued the cause for Earley, while Charles F. Cottam argued for Robinson. Leo Pfeffer and Milton Stanzler shared the rostrum in arguing the appellees' cause. Briefs were filed by all of the parties to the action. In addition, because of the significant constitutional questions raised by this case, six *amicus curiae* briefs were filed. Four urged affirmance (*viz.*, the American Jewish Committee, Protestants and Other Americans United for the Separation of Church and State, the Center for Law and Education at Harvard University, and the Connecticut State Conference of Branches of the NAACP), while two urged reversal (*viz.*, the National Catholic Education Association and the U.S. Department of Justice).

Warren Burger, chief justice of the U.S. Supreme Court (1969–1986), wrote the majority opinions in both *DiCenso* and *Lemon*, setting forth the threefold test that continues to be invoked in establishment-of-religion cases. Thirteen years later Burger upheld the City of Pawtucket's nativity display, writing for a 5-to-4 majority.

The Court studied the material presented to it, and nearly four months later it rendered its decision, consolidating the appeal in *DiCenso* with a similar Pennsylvania case, *Lemon* v. *Kurtzman*. A detailed summary of the Court's decision would be somewhat repetitious, for in essence the Court adopted the argument of the three-judge district court. The majority opinion, written by Chief Justice Burger, affirmed the lower court ruling by accepting its finding that the Act "fostered 'excessive entanglement' between government and religion" and "had the impermissible effect of giving 'significant aid to a religious enterprise.'" Justice Burger noted the "comprehensive, discriminating, and continuing state surveillance" required by the Act, and concluded that "[t]hese prophylactic contacts will involve excessive and enduring entanglement between state and church."

The free exercise issue raised by the intervenors was ignored in the opinion of the Court, as were the free exercise claims of the appellees. But Justice Douglas, joined by Justices Black and Marshall, touched upon these and other issues in an impassioned and far-reaching concurring opinion. In essence, Justice Douglas would have sustained every contention in the ACLU's original complaint. The concurring opinion concluded by affirming that "a history class, a literature class, or a science class in a parochial school is not a separate institute; it is part of the organic whole which the State subsidizes"—a whole that is permeated with religious values. In Justice Douglas' view, therefore, "the taxpayers' forced contribution to the parochial schools in the present cases violates the First Amendment."

Justice Brennan also filed a separate concurring opinion. Justice Brennan's historically oriented discourse concluded that "in using sectarian institutions to further goals in secular education, [the Salary Supplement Act does] violence to the principle that 'government may not employ religious means to serve secular interests, however legitimate they may be, at least without the clearest demonstration that nonreligious means will not suffice.'"

Justice White authored a lone dissent which urged a reversal of the district court decision. He observed, as had Judge Pettine, that "[t]he Court points to nothing in this record indicating that any participating teacher had inserted religion into his secular teaching." Justice White further argued:

> Where a state program seeks to ensure the proper education of its young, in private as well as public schools, free exercise considerations at least counsel against refusing support for students attending parochial schools simply because in that setting they are also being instructed in the tenets of the faith they are constitutionally free to practice.

Finally, the dissent contended that the Act did not violate the First Amendment since indirect benefit to religion from govemment aid to sectarian schools in the performance of separable secular functions does not convert such aid into an impermissible establishment of religion. This position, however, was unavailing. The Court immediately ordered the lower court judgment affirmed and sent notice of this decision to the clerk of the United States District Court for the District of Rhode Island.

Meanwhile, back in Rhode Island, payment of the June, 1971 salary supplement was causing some dispute. Commissioner Robinson was determined that the money should be disbursed. Therefore, on June 15, when the Supreme Court opinion was imminent, he ordered the supplement vouchers processed. He hoped to have the checks in the mail prior to the High Court's ruling so that in any event the teachers would be paid. Milton Stanzler revealed that the Rhode Island ACLU lawyers made a "policy decision" not to bring a suit to recover the three supplement payments which had been disbursed in February and June of 1970, and in February 1971. He felt that this was a "wise decision" in view of the climate of opinion in Rhode Island and also in view of the fact that the Pennsylvania plaintiffs in *Lemon* v. *Kurtzman* were rebuffed by the Supreme Court in an attempt to recover state funds which had been paid prior to the time when the act challenged by the litigants in that case was declared unconstitutional.

Charles Hill, the codefendant state controller, balked at Robinson's move and refused to disburse the funds. When the Supreme Court's decision was announced on June 28, the new attorney general, Richard Israel, decided that the Court's opinion was sufficient reason to cancel the June supplement. This action put to rest one phase of Rhode Island's aid to private education controversy, but the proponents of such aid have only left the field to return another day.

This peaceful Pawtucket Christmas display generated a storm of controversy culminating in the 1984 Supreme Court case of *Lynch* v. *Donnelly*, a split decision in which the high court showed some flexibility regarding the issue of establishment.

30

In an earlier essay, nineteenth-century lawyer Abraham Payne related personal, anecdotal insights regarding the legal practitioners of his era. Here I will do the same with reference to the three recent constitutional conventions in which I have been personally and prominently involved. Hopefully there will be no conflict between the objective historian and the subjective participant.

In December 1964 Rhode Island's first open, unlimited constitutional convention since 1842 convened. Its call had been approved and its delegates selected (81 Democrats and 19 Republicans) in the November 1964 general election. Early in 1965, as a young history professor at Providence College, fresh from the graduate school of the University of Notre Dame, I applied for a position on the convention's research staff, which was directed by Dr. Elmer E. Cornwell, Jr., professor of political science at Brown University, and his assistant, Dr. Jay S. Goodman (now both a professor of political science and a Providence attorney). This talented duo would eventually write a detailed analysis of the gathering, appropriately titled *The Politics of the Rhode Island Constitutional Convention* (1969), under the auspices of the National Municipal League.

Although tarnished by the Long Count of 1956, former governor Dennis J. Roberts secured election as convention chairman. As the convention began its work, however, a Democratic legislative faction under the lead of Family Court judge John F. Doris, a former Woonsocket state representative, took political control of the gathering.

The convention's blueprint for action was the well-crafted *Report of the Commission on Revision of the Rhode Island Constitu-*

William H. Edwards (1898–1976), constitutional scholar, civic leader, and senior partner in the law firm of Edwards and Angell, chaired a thirteen-member blue-ribbon commission which proposed a draft constitution in 1962 that has served as a basis for discussion of constitutional change ever since. Though Edwards criticized the partisan procedures for selecting delegates to the 1964 convention, he supported that body's final document and cochaired a statewide committee formed to secure its ratification.

tion, prepared in 1962 by a thirteen-member blue-ribbon legislative panel chaired by prominent Providence attorney and legal scholar William H. Edwards. Chairman Roberts diminished his influence with the Doris faction by championing a unicameral legislature, a radical innovation that the Edwards Commission had considered and rejected and that the General Assembly strongly opposed.

For more than three years the convention dragged on, hampered by factionalism and extremely cumbersome rules that made delay the order of the day. Since the Democrats controlled the convention by a lopsided majority, both the *Providence Journal* and incumbent Republican governor John H. Chafee repeatedly criticized the gathering and made political hay from its controversies and its conservatism. Ironically such prodding encouraged some significant reforms, and the document that was eventually submitted to the voters in April 1968 was a vast improvement on the existing state constitution.

Family Court judge John F. Doris (1917–1980) lost his bid to become chairman of the 1964 convention when Republican delegates supported former governor Dennis J. Roberts. However, Professor Elmer E. Cornwell and Jay S. Goodman, the historians of the convention, assessed the judge's role as follows: "John Doris emerged as the single most important figure in the whole body, not even excepting the Chairman. A former political magnate in the important Democratic stronghold of Woonsocket, and former member of the House of Representatives and deputy majority leader, he quickly came to be the recognized leader of the legislative group. He acquired this role in part out of sheer strength of personality and tactical ability, and in part by default. He is an extremely shrewd and forceful politician who automatically commands the right to lead men of less force and presence, without need of formal position to support his claims." Doris ended his career as an associate justice of the Supreme Court.

The proposed constitution, however, had a fatal image problem. The public began to judge it by its parentage—a squabbling, dilatory convention—rather than on its substance and its merit. Because I firmly believed then (as I do now) that every article in the 1968 constitution represented an improvement over the existing basic law, I wrote "A Statement in Defense of the Proposed Constitution" for publication in the January 1968 issue of the *Bar Journal*, and I resigned my research-staff position to organize a statewide ratification campaign. William Edwards came aboard as my cochairman and Roman Catholic bishop Russell J. McVinney, in a rare and unusual move, became our ratification group's honorary chairman; but neither faith nor reason would prevail. Behind the scenes, Judge Doris (who would later move to the Supreme Court) and Providence Democratic chairman Larry McGarry gave us various kinds of assistance. Even the *Providence Journal* eventually bestowed its grudging editorial endorsement upon the new document, but three years of negative news stories about the convention and its delegates had a much greater impact on public opinion.

Arrayed against ratification were a resentful and disappointed Chairman Roberts and the enormously popular Governor John Chafee, whom the ad firm of Fitzgerald-Toole had sold to the voters as "The Man You Can Trust." Bill Edwards and I "debated" Roberts and Chafee on prime-time TV, but the format insisted upon by the opponents of ratification did not produce a true debate—each side had a half hour in isolation to present its position.

The ratification referendum was held on April 16, 1968, the Tuesday after Easter. Although the convention's Public Information Committee was blocked by a Superior Court ruling from spending money to explain and promote the document, Governor Chafee gave a substantial sum to his public relations agency to run an incessant media blitz against the proposed constitution over the Easter weekend. To say that the anticonstitution ads were inaccurate and distorted would be a charitable understatement, but the negative campaign was a stunning success. The proposed basic law succumbed to the popular will by a 4-to-1 margin, 68,940 to 17,464.

Though constitutional change was stymied in 1968, such persistent issues as legislative pay, lotteries, four-year terms for state officials, suffrage, and grand jury reform prompted a call for a limited constitutional convention in 1973 to consider these specific items. By that date I had completed my doctoral dissertation on Rhode Island's constitutional development. Being politically ambitious and tired of the dull and subservient role of researcher, I secured the Democratic nomination for convention delegate from Cranston's Fifteenth Senatorial District. To prevent a partisan imbalance such as that which had afflicted the 1964 convention, the enabling statute called for each party to nominate one candidate in each of the fifty senatorial districts. Since nomination was almost tantamount to election, I achieved victory at the polls for the only time in my checkered political career, and, even then, I ran behind the Republican candidate with whom I was paired. With Alexander Hamilton, I can state emphatically that "this American political world was not made for me!"

Away from the scrutiny of the general public, I fared better. Despite the attempt at parity, some Democrats cheated the system and gave their party a 56-to-41 delegate margin, with 3 independents, in the 100-member convention. Because of my long-standing interest in Rhode Island constitutional issues, I had persuaded several of my political associates and fellow teachers, as well as a few former students, to run as delegates. Thus I had a strong nucleus of votes for convention chairman. Party leaders, however, wished to confer that distinction on William E. Powers of Central Falls, a former attorney general and retired Supreme Court justice. Though I had the votes to win, I withdrew in favor of Judge Powers for several reasons—some altruistic, some not. Powers was brilliant and eminent, and the chairmanship would be a nice capstone on his distinguished career, whereas I had time for such honors (or so I thought). In addition, by placating Larry McGarry and Charles Reilly, the Democratic state chairman, I hoped for their favor in my eventual quest for state office. Also, I extracted concessions for my withdrawal—the post of convention secretary, control of the limited patronage, and decisive influence in the selection of committee chairpersons.

Accordingly, my law associate Fernando S. Cunha became the convention's executive director, my former supervisor Elmer Cornwell became director of research, and Matthew J. Smith, my former student and boyhood chum, was appointed assistant director of a research staff that included such other former students as Paul Campbell, attorney Edward Newman, and Marjorie Tarmey, who had also been my research assistant when I chaired the Cranston Charter Review Commission in 1972.

In sharp contrast to its immediate predecessor, this convention ran smoothly, efficiently, and rapidly. It removed the last vestige of the ancient property qualification by eliminating the property-taxpaying requirement for participation in financial town meetings, and it enacted (with me as principal sponsor) a campaign finance disclosure amendment (now Article IV, Section 9, of the state constitution). In addition, the convention expanded the role of grand juries, gave eighteen-year-olds the vote, and removed the ban on state lotteries. Its proposals for a legislative pay increase and four-year terms for general officers were narrowly rejected by the voters.

However, the product of this convention that gave me the greatest personal satisfaction was the proposal that became Article of Amendment XLII (Article XIV of the present basic law). It streamlined the amendment process and set up a mechanism for the regular call of state constitutional conventions. I based the new amendment procedure upon a similar majoritarian provision in the People's Constitution of 1841, while the convention section stemmed from my belief that the failure of the constitution of 1843 to provide for the calling of constitutional conventions had been productive of political turmoil for nearly a century.

This reform, described editorially by the *Providence Journal* as "the most significant substantive alteration ever made in the state constitution," involved some sleight of hand by Judge Powers (who favored it) and myself. The 1973 convention was a conclave *limited* to the consideration of certain definite topics. Amendment procedures and constitutional convention calls

Professor Patrick Conley, secretary of the 1973 convention, presides over a session of that gathering. To his right is Helen Migliaccio of Cranston, the convention's vice chair. At the time of this photo, Conley had just completed his studies at Suffolk University Law School.

were not specified in our mandate, but we were charged with "revision of the election laws." Accordingly, I developed the far-fetched theory (with Justice Powers concurring) that amendments and conventions were within our purview because each procedure was submitted to the electors for approval. Hence I titled my proposed amendment "Election Requirements for Constitutional Revision" and sent it to the Elections Committee, which was headed by my academic colleagues Professor William T. Murphy, Jr., of Brown (chairman) and Professor Robert J. McKenna of Salve Regina (vice chairman). The amendment passed the convention on October 4, 1973, by a margin of 93 to 1. The lone dissenting vote was cast by Pawtucket Republican Ronald R. Gagnon (who would later attain a Superior Court judgeship and become my friendly nemesis on the Formal and Special Cause Calendar in a host of tax title cases). The Rhode Island Supreme Court later ruled in *Malinou* v. *Powers*, 114 R.I. 399, 333 A.2d 420 (1975), that the legislature's authority to limit the power of the 1973 convention to propose amendments that were outside the call legislation governing our agenda became moot, since there was no indication that any proposals were ruled out of order, and since the convention finally adopted a resolution (mine), and entertained others, that exceeded the restriction set forth in the enabling legislation.

As the convention prepared to adjourn without mishap on October 4, Judge Powers laughingly recalled the admonition of state Democratic chairman Charles Reilly at the outset of our deliberations one month before. "Keep an eye on this convention," Reilly had urged; "don't let the Republicans get out of hand." Ironically *an* eye was all we had between us. Powers, of course, was rendered sightless by a boyhood accident, and I am blind in my right eye. To take a cue from Hollywood, a movie of the proceedings of the 1973 convention might well be titled "My Left Eye."

Article of Amendment XLII was the proximate cause (to use a tort analogy) of the highly productive 1986 open convention, ably presided over by attorney Keven McKenna. I had difficulty establishing a permanent residence that year, so I did not run for delegate. I did, however, pen a detailed blueprint for constitutional change, which appeared as an article in the *Bar Journal* in May 1985.

Sensing my desire to be included and aware of my role in providing for the convention's call, President McKenna retained me as his paid general counsel. That post was short-lived, for many things had changed since my glory days in '73. For one, I had defected from the Democratic party in 1977 after Governor J. Joseph Garrahy turned a deaf ear to my requests for a state position, despite my chairmanship of his 1976 campaign advisory council. Mayor Buddy Cianci, sensing the rift, picked up my option in September 1977 and named me director of the Providence Crime Commission. I took the post in the belief that Cianci would challenge Garrahy for governor in 1978. When the polls said no, the mayor ran for reelection, pitting me, as Cianci's campaign adviser, against Frank Darigan (now Judge Darigan), a South Providence friend and a candidate of high integrity. Cianci's change of heart left me on the horns of a dilemma, but my plight evoked little sympathy from Matt Smith, Darigan's most powerful Providence ally. Things were never the same between us after that campaign.

Attorney Keven A. McKenna, a former Providence legislator, presided over the 1986 constitutional convention with effectiveness and efficiency.

After defeating both Darigan and attorney Fred Lippitt in 1982, Cianci was forced to resign as mayor when he pleaded nolo to a charge of assault in an incident with his former wife's lover. Citizen Cianci eventually took a job as a radio talk show host. In 1986, as the General Assembly debated the impeachment of Chief Justice Joseph Bevilaqua, Cianci conducted a media blitz against House Speaker Smith in an attempt to discredit the legislative leaders who were contemplating Bevilaqua's removal. When the attacks got quite detailed and personal, Smith assumed that I had supplied the ex-mayor with his "inside" intelligence. Actually Cianci, who always had his finger on the pulse of Providence, had acquired the information on his own. Nonetheless an understandably irate Speaker Smith called President McKenna with an ultimatum: either general counsel Conley goes or your convention funding goes. Thus ended, at least for now, my paid career as a constitutional reformer. Even my appointment as volunteer chairman of the Rhode Island Bicentennial of the Constitution observance was jeopardized by Cianci's charges. For months, until he was assured that I was innocent of smearing him, Smith held my appointment in abeyance, although the other eight members of the foundation had long been selected.

As Keven McKenna notes in his portion of the following essay, the 1986 convention did a fine job. Among its reforms was a provision banning convicted felons from public office (Article III, Section 2). Ironically, that provision was used in an attempt to block Cianci's return to the Providence mayor's chair after his 1990 election victory. Attorney Ronald W. Del Sesto (son of Christopher, the Long Count victim), William J. McGair, and I successfully persuaded the Supreme Court that the disqualification provision was prospective only and did not bar Cianci from taking office (see *State of Rhode Island ex rel. Floyd Edmund Webb III* v. *Vincent A. Cianci, Jr.*, 591 A.2d 1193).

In another notable reform, the 1986 constitution directed the General Assembly to establish an Ethics Commission (Article III, Section 8). This commission has since turned on its creator by invoking both conflict of interest and separation of powers arguments to deter legislators from serving on state administrative boards and commissions. The governor has requested an advisory opinion from the Supreme Court regarding the constitutionality of this long-standing General Assembly practice, and, as this book goes to press, I am an amicus preparing to argue a legal and historical justification upholding the constitutionality (at least in Rhode Island) of this legislative function. My brief (if one could give such a name to a 190-page treatise) is entitled "Neither Separate nor Equal."

This attempt by the Ethics Commission to bar members of the General Assembly from making appointments to, or serving on, state administrative boards and commissions poses a major constitutional question. In this century, only the 1935 Supreme Court advisory opinion relative to the power of the Assembly to call a constitutional convention rivals this issue in significance.

After tracing the appointive power of the Rhode Island legislature from its origins in the royal charter of 1663 through two constitutions to the present, I have made the following findings and conclusions: (1) the General Assembly has always possessed and exercised the power to create state boards and commissions of an administrative nature, to make appointments thereto, and to sit thereon; (2) Rhode Island, contrary to the assertions of the governor and the Ethics Commission, never adopted the federal model of separated powers, nor is that model binding upon the states; (3) Chief

Justice Samuel Ames, in the landmark decision of *Taylor* v. *Place* (1856), established the independence of the judiciary without enhancing the power of the governor; (4) the Rhode Island constitution of 1842 (which the 1986 convention left relatively intact) was a Whiggish document that exalted the legislative branch of government and reserved for the General Assembly nearly all of the power it had exercised under the chater of 1663; and (5) the Ethics Commission regulation that prompted the governor's request is an unconstitutional infringement upon the power of the legislature.

Principal counsel for the General Assembly in this classic struggle for political ascendancy is Lauren E. Jones, prominent appellate attorney and incumbent president of the Rhode Island Bar Association. Among my other colleagues in this defense of the General Assembly's power is Professor Elmer Cornwell, former parliamentarian of the House and aide to Speaker John Harwood. Another is political science professor Jay S. Goodman, who followed my route from doctorate to law school and is now a practicing attorney in Providence. In thirty-three years of constitution making, I have come to see the wisdom of the old French maxim: "The more things change, the more they remain the same!"

The Rhode Island Constitutional Conventions of 1964, 1973, and 1986: Getting Down to Basic Law

Patrick T. Conley and Keven A. McKenna

The 1973 Constitutional Convention was the eleventh such assemblage in Rhode Island history. The state had conducted six open or unlimited conventions [prior to 1973]. The first, in 1824, saw its mildly progressive product rejected by a two-to-one margin, and the second in 1834–35 never submitted its handiwork to the voters. The next three open conventions grew out of the constitutional controversy known as the Dorr Rebellion. The People's Convention of 1841 drafted a document which won the overwhelming approbation of the voters (13,944 to 52), but Thomas Wilson Dorr's attempt to carry this constitution into effect was thwarted by "law and order" conservatives who objected to the fact that the People's Convention had been called in an extra-legal manner without authorization from the General Assembly. The so-called Freemen's Convention of 1841–42 was the Law and Order Party's response to the demand for reform; it was legally called, but the conservative document which it framed was rejected by an 8,689 to 8,013 vote in March, 1842.

After Dorr was vanquished by the Law and Order coalition, a third convention was called in September, 1842. This conclave drafted our present state constitution, an instrument which went into effect in May, 1843. The next open convention was convened in December, 1964. That body's slow pace (the convention did not formally adjourn until February 17, 1969) and poor image were partly responsible for the rejection of its product in April, 1968 by a four-to-one margin.

The other five conventions have been limited assemblages which confined their deliberations to specific, predetermined constitutional questions. The first four conventions were held in 1944, 1951, 1955, and 1958 respectively. The final conclave was the 1973 convention.

These limited conventions have been called principally to effect constitutional change in a more rapid and less demanding manner than provided in the cumbersome amendment procedures of the state's basic law. From 1843 through 1973 a constitutional amendment which originated in the General Assembly required passage by two successive assemblies, a general election intervening, and then ratification by a three-fifths vote of the qualified electors. The limited convention became a device to circumvent this difficult, time-consuming process, because an amendment proposed by such a body only required a majority vote of the qualified electors voting thereon for ratification.

Of the six open conventions [held prior to 1986], only one resulted in constitutional change; and of the five limited conventions, the 1973 conclave produced the greatest change in the state's basic law. It would not be an exaggeration, therefore, to regard the 1973 convention as the second most productive gathering in Rhode Island history.

The General Assembly authorized the 1973 conclave by Chapter 98 of the Public Laws of 1973. Ironically, the proposed convention was nearly aborted by the voters. On the morning following the August 7 special election to elect delegates and authorize the gathering, the local press headlines read "Convention Call Loses by 26 Votes." Fortunately for the cause of constitutional reform, an official recount reversed the results—the convention won approval by a narrow ninety-two vote margin (21,302 to 21,210). Voter apathy and a ninety-degree day on August 7 resulted in an election which drew only eight percent of the state's eligible electors to the polls. Experts attributed opposition to the convention call to several factors: (a) the poor image of the recent 1964–69 convention, (b) a fear that the amendments proposed by the 1973 convention would be submitted to the voters as a package—an all-or-nothing proposition, and (c) public coolness toward a proposed legislative pay increase which the convention was authorized to discuss.

The fears of those who opposed the convention were largely dispelled by the efficient, workmanlike, bi-partisan nature of the body. It opened on September 4 and adjourned on October 4 in accordance with the instructions of the General Assembly; it rejected the package ballot in favor of an item-by-item referendum; and it took a broad view of its powers in the four areas opened to it by the General Assembly and the people (*viz.*, the grand jury, lotteries, election laws, and legislative compensation). This broad interpretation was especially evident in the delegates' response to the directive that they effect a "revision in the election laws." The convention regarded this instruction as enabling it to advance proposals dealing with such topics as financial disclosure of election contributions and election requirements for constitutional revision.

A total of ninety-one proposals for constitutional amendment were reviewed by the convention, and seven proposed amendments were submitted to the people for approval. Five of these proposals secured ratification by wide margins, including such important revisions as a codification and reform of the election article and a streamlined procedure for amending the state's basic law and for calling future open conventions at regular intervals. This latter amendment was perhaps the most significant substantive alteration ever made in the state constitution. Two proposals, one raising legislative pay to $2,000 per year and another giving four-year terms to the state's general officers, were rejected in close contests.

* * *

On November 4, 1986, Rhode Island entered a new era of constitutional history with the adoption by the voters of the redrafted and revised Constitution of 1986. After one hundred forty-three years, the Rhode Island Constitution had accumulated more than forty amendments, nullifying much of the original document and many of the early amendments. The result was a document difficult to read even for scholars and professionals in the law. Among the tasks taken up by the 1986 Constitutional Convention, then, was a redrafting of the Constitution, deleting sections nullified by amendment. The convention also directed its Committee on Style and

Drafting to rewrite each article in gender-neutral language, and to reorder the sections and articles in appropriate sequence.

The most important work of the convention, of course, was to adopt substantive proposals for submission to the voters. The convention, through its committees, sifted through more than two hundred ninety resolutions and ultimately adopted twenty-six for submission to the people. These were combined by common category into fourteen ballot questions. On election day the voters approved the redrafted document and seventeen substantive resolutions for change contained in eight of the fourteen ballot questions.

This constitution making combined the best direct and indirect democracy. The delegates of the people deliberated and argued, sometimes with great emotion, in deciding which of the scores of ideas presented were important enough to present to the electorate. The will of the people made the final choices for a new constitution.

Analyses of the popular will are always risky, but one may draw some tentative conclusions from the election results. The voters seem to have been skeptical about making structural changes in their government. Resolutions concerning the process of judicial selection, voter initiative, four-year terms, and local government were all defeated. On the other hand they were prepared to approve new ideas concerning the practice of government. Resolutions concerning campaign finance, ethics, citizen rights, and felon voting and office-holding were approved on election day.

When the convention reconvened for the last time after the election, the delegates accepted and signed a final version of the redrafted document which incorporated the approved resolutions into the Constitution. In this way the 1986 Constitutional Convention presented to the people of Rhode Island not simply a series of amendments, but a new and modern Constitution as well.

Democracy is a demanding system which requires strong commitment and constant attention from its citizens. There is nothing in the process of democratic government more important than the drafting of constitutions. There is little in the work of democracy that is more satisfying to its participants. The delegates to the 1986 Constitutional Convention worked for uncounted hours, without compensation, from January to December. That year carried them through agenda meetings and public hearings in every corner of the state, long and difficult committee deliberations, plenary sessions and public information forums. They served the demands of democratic citizenship with great distinction. In a world in which democracy is easier to attack than to sustain, the delegates of the convention and the voters of Rhode Island have honored this state's long and cherished democratic tradition.

RHODE ISLAND CONSTITUTIONAL CONVENTION

19  86

GET THE FACTS KNOW THE ISSUES

Shall the action of the Constitutional Convention in amending the Constitution in the following manner be ratified and approved?

1 ☐ YES ☐ NO
REWRITE OF THE PRESENT CONSTITUTION
Shall the Constitution of 1843 and the 44 amendments ratified since then be adopted as rewritten, in proper order, with annulled sections removed? Shall the Constitutional Convention publish the Constitution in proper form, including new amendments, if they are approved by the voters? (Resolution 86-00042 B)

2 ☐ YES ☐ NO
JUDICIAL SELECTION AND DISCIPLINE
Shall a non-partisan, independent commission be established to nominate judges for appointment by the general assembly in the case of supreme court vacancies and for appointment by the governor in the case of vacancies in other courts? Shall the commission have authority to discipline or remove all judges? Shall judges appointed hereafter be required to retire at 72 years of age? Shall the duty of the supreme court to give advisory opinions be abolished? (Resolution 86-00080 A)

3 ☐ YES ☐ NO
LEGISLATIVE PAY AND MILEAGE
Shall the daily pay of general assembly members be established at a sum equal to the average weekly wage of Rhode Island manufacturing workers, divided by a four-day legislative week (about $76), the speaker receiving twice that amount; and shall mileage compensation be equal to the rate paid U.S. government employees, such pay and mileage to be limited to 60 days per year? (Resolution 86-00094 B)

4 ☐ YES ☐ NO
FOUR-YEAR TERMS AND RECALL
Beginning in 1988, shall the governor, lieutenant governor, secretary of state, attorney general, general treasurer and members of the general assembly be elected to four-year terms and be subject to recall by voters? (Resolution 86-00028 A)

5 ☐ YES ☐ NO
VOTER INITIATIVE
Shall voters be empowered to petition certain laws and/or constitutional amendments onto the ballot for voter approval or rejection? Shall future constitutional convention candidates be elected on a non-partisan basis? (Resolutions 86-00001 B, 86-00136)

6 ☐ YES ☐ NO
ETHICS IN GOVERNMENT
Shall more specific impeachment standards be established? Shall an ethics commission be established with authority to adopt a code of ethics and to discipline or remove public officials and employees found in violation of that code? Shall the general assembly adopt limits on campaign contributions and shall the general assembly enact a voluntary system of public campaign financing, coupled with limitations on total campaign spending by participating candidates? (Resolutions 86-00047 A, 86-00060 A, 86-00145 A)

7 ☐ YES ☐ NO
BUDGET POWERS AND EXECUTIVE SUCCESSION
Shall the governor be constitutionally empowered to present an annual budget? Shall the speaker of the house become governor if both the governor and lieutenant governor die or are unable to serve? (Resolutions 86-00222, 86-00246)

8 ☐ YES ☐ NO
RIGHTS OF THE PEOPLE
Shall free speech, due process and equal protection clauses be added to the Constitution? Shall the state or those doing business with the state be prohibited from discriminating against persons solely on the basis of race, gender or handicap? Shall victims of crime have constitutionally endowed rights, including the right to compensation from perpetrators? Shall individual rights protected by the state constitution stand independent of the U.S. Constitution? (Resolutions 86-00033, 86-00032, 86-00140, 86-00002 B, 86-00171)

9 ☐ YES ☐ NO
SHORE USE AND ENVIRONMENTAL PROTECTION
Shall rights of fishery and privileges of the shore be described and shall the powers of the state and local government to protect those rights and the environment be enlarged? Shall the regulation of land and waters for these purposes not be deemed a public use of private property? (Resolutions 86-00003, 86-00004A)

10 ☐ YES ☐ NO
FELON OFFICE HOLDING AND VOTING
Shall felons' voting rights, removed upon conviction, be restored upon completion of sentence and probation or parole? Shall felons and certain misdemeanants be banned from holding office for three years after completion of sentence and probation or parole? (Resolutions 86-00149 A, 86-00025 B)

11 ☐ YES ☐ NO
LIBRARIES
Shall it be a duty of the general assembly to promote public libraries and library services? (Resolution 86-00098)

12 ☐ YES ☐ NO
BAIL
Shall the courts be authorized to deny bail to persons accused of the unlawful sale or distribution of controlled substances punishable by a sentence of ten years or more? (Resolution 86-00153 B)

13 ☐ YES ☐ NO
HOME RULE
Shall cities and towns with charters have more authority over local affairs, within the limits of the General Laws, including the power to tax and borrow with local voter approval (unless overridden by a three-fifths vote in the general assembly); to protect public health, safety, morals and the environment; to regulate local businesses and local planning and development? Shall new or increased tax exemptions pertaining to cities and towns be subject to local voter approval? Shall cities and towns be reimbursed for certain state-mandated programs? Shall charter adoption and amendment procedures be simplified? (Resolution 86-00196 B)

14 ☐ YES ☐ NO
PARAMOUNT RIGHT TO LIFE/ABORTION
To the extent permitted by the U.S. Constitution, shall all persons, including their unborn offspring, without regard to age, health, function, or condition of dependency, be endowed with an inalienable and paramount right to life; and to the extent permitted by the U.S. Constitution, shall abortion be prohibited, except that justified medical procedures to prevent the death of a pregnant woman shall be permitted? Shall the use of government monies to fund abortions be prohibited by the Constitution? (Resolution 86-00212 A)

VOTE
ON THE CONSTITUTIONAL QUESTIONS
TUESDAY, NOVEMBER 4th

As of 1986, the 143-year-old state constitution had been amended forty-four times, with suffrage requirements the most altered component. Although the amendment procedure was once very cumbersome, a change in the basic law can now be ratified by a majority of the whole membership of each house of the legislature, together with a majority of those electors voting thereon at a general election. This simpler process was accomplished in 1973 by Article of Amendment XLII, one of five changes successfully proposed by the limited constitutional convention of that year. In addition, Article XLII, sponsored by convention secretary Patrick T. Conley, professor of history and law at Providence College, provided a mechanism for allowing the voters to convene constitutional conventions on a regular basis at least once every twelve years. This amendment was described editorially by the *Providence Journal* as "the most significant substantive alteration every made in the state constitution."

The unlimited convention of 1986, which had the power to restructure Rhode Island's government, is Amendment XLII's direct legacy. That convention, chaired by Keven McKenna, made fourteen proposals (shown here) to the electorate in a November 1986 referendum. The most significant of these recommendations were a so-called "neutral rewrite" to delete annulled sections of the constitution and integrate the amendments into the main body of the document without substantive change; the establishment of a commission on judicial selection and discipline; a proposal to increase legislators' pay; the creation of an ethics commission; four-year terms for general officers and members of the General Assembly; voter initiative; a strengthening of the state bill of rights; greater home-rule powers for municipalities; and a very controversial provision prohibiting the use of government money to fund abortion and declaring the paramount right to life of all persons, including the unborn, to the extent permitted by the U.S. Constitution.

On November 4, 1986, Questions 1, 6, 7, 8, 9, 10, 11, and 12 were approved by the electorate, while the others failed to pass.

BIOGRAPHICAL PROFILES

One Rhode Island attorney who sought from the start to carve out his legal and political career on the national level was Thomas Gardiner ("Tommy the Cork") Corcoran (1900–1981), a leading draftsman and lobbyist for much of the legislation now labeled Franklin D. Roosevelt's New Deal. His college education began at Brown University, where he majored in the classics and served as class valedictorian in 1921. Corcoran remained at Brown to earn a master's degree in English in 1924 and then entered Harvard Law School, completing his legal education in 1926. At Harvard he came under the tutelage of Felix Frankfurter, the man who would bring him into the Roosevelt inner circle.

In 1926 Corcoran clerked with Supreme Court justice Oliver Wendell Holmes, with whom he formed a close association. After his year with Holmes, Corcoran joined a Wall Street law firm and became knowledgeable in the areas of securities and holding companies. By 1932 he returned to Washington to take a legal position with the Reconstruction Finance Corporation. Once back in the capital, he never left.

Recommended by Professor Felix Frankfurter, Corcoran joined the New Deal "Brain Trust" in 1933 and helped to draft such landmark laws as those creating the Securities and Exchange Commission, the Federal Housing Administration, the Tennessee Valley Authority, and the Fair Labor Standards Board. A Pawtucket-born son of an Irish immigrant, Corcoran often entertained Roosevelt with Irish ballads. On the serious side, Corcoran penned some of the president's important political speeches, especially during Roosevelt's second term, and coined FDR's famous phrase "rendezvous with destiny." For forty years after his retirement from government employ in 1940, Corcoran was one of Washington's most prominent and successful lawyer-lobbyists. For an in-depth study of his career, consult Monica Lynne Niznik, "Thomas G. Corcoran: The Public Service of Franklin Roosevelt's 'Tommy the Cork,'" a doctoral dissertation written at the University of Notre Dame in 1981.

Robert Emmet Quinn of West Warwick (1894–1975) was the nephew and protégé of Colonel Patrick Henry Quinn, a Democratic party potentate who engineered the creation of the town of West Warwick in 1913 as his political fiefdom. Patrick Henry, a lawyer-lobbyist, also served as president of the Rhode Island Bar Association in 1943.

The younger Quinn was a durable politician and a learned and talented attorney with degrees from Brown University and Harvard Law School. He rose from the state Senate (1923–1925 and 1929–1933), where he led the famous 1924 filibuster, to the lieutenant governorship (1937–1939), where he battled with Narragansett Park director Walter O'Hara in the ludicrous and nationally scandalous "Race Track War" of 1937. That episode, featuring Quinn, O'Hara, Pawtucket mayor Tom McCoy, and Chief Justice Edmund Flynn, became the subject of a *Life* magazine photo essay (November 8, 1937) aptly entitled "The War of the Wild Irish Roses"—a phrase coined by columnist Westbrook Pegler.

Although this much-publicized altercation, coupled with the economic recession of 1937, cost "Fighting Bob" reelection in 1938, Quinn remained in the forefront of Democratic politics. When his party returned to power in 1941 after Republican governor William Vanderbilt's brief interregnum, Quinn was appointed associate justice of the Rhode Island Superior Court, where he served for a decade (1941–1951). That tenure was interrupted by service in World War II. Quinn, a member of the U.S. diplomatic intelligence corps in World War I, received a leave of absence from his judgeship in 1942 to serve in the U.S. Navy as a lieutenant commander—a rank he held until January 1946, when he went on inactive duty as a captain. Both the army and the navy cited him for distinguished service.

Quinn's participation in both World Wars and in Rhode Island's bitter political conflicts of the 1920s and 1930s prompted President Harry Truman to appoint him as the first chief judge of the United States Court of Military Appeals in 1951. Quinn served with distinction on that tribunal until April 1975. A month after his retirement he died at the age of eighty-one.

31

The final essay in this centennial history has been written by the ultimate Bar Association insider—Edward P. Smith, executive director of the association from 1958 to 1989, a period of rapid growth and transformation. In a self-effacing manner Smith describes the organization's first century, especially the expansion of services and influence that occurred during his three-decade watch.

In 1886 *The Providence Plantations*, a commemorative history cclcbrating the 250th anniversary of the founding of Providence (which in the seventeenth century was nearly coterminous with present-day Providence County), listed 189 practicing attorneys in the county, most, of course, in the city itself. By 1898 that number had increased to well over 200. An intelligent estimate of the lawyer count in the remainder of the state—which, except for Newport, was basically rural—indicates that Rhode Island had no more than 300 lawyers when the state Bar Association was created in 1898.

Of course, not all lawyers immediately rushed to embrace a Providence-based operation in which membership was not compulsory. Indeed, as Smith shows, for the first six decades of its existence the association's membership was limited not only by geography but also by socioeconomic factors. During that early period socially prominent, well-to-do big-firm attorneys from the Providence area led the association and determined its policies and role.

The transition to the present broad-based, service-oriented organization with a membership exceeding 4,800—1,160 of that number women—began in the late 1950s, not coincidentally with Ed Smith's assumption of the position of full-time executive director. The bulk of Smith's essay—an affectionate, intimate reminiscence as much as a history—deals with the evolution of the Bar Association into its modern form. And who is more qualified to relate that story?

The Rhode Island Bar Association: Its First Century

Edward P. Smith

Origins and Early Progress, 1898–1957

In the archives of the Rhode Island Historical Society is the handwritten minute book of the Providence County Bar Association, which covers the period from 1795 to a final entry on October 3, 1844. In this entry it is stated that the meeting adjourned to October 5 "at the rising of the Honorable Court at noon to receive the report of the committee on the [forthcoming] centennial celebration." Thus there had been a Providence County Bar Association since 1745.

At the meeting on February 3, 1795, the "Gentlemen of the Bar" agreed at a gathering held in East Greenwich "to a set of principles of an Association." Among those principles was one that called for "a meeting of the Gentlemen of the Bar in this state for the purpose of promoting Harmony among the Members and supporting the Honor of the profession." No further records have been found beyond that one volume, yet its existence tells us that in addition to the Providence County Bar there was a Kent County Bar and possibly a Newport Bar Association, for the annual meeting of the 1795 group was to be held in Newport.

Bar associations throughout the nation were usually formed in local areas first, often as social clubs, discussion groups, and/or organizations for establishing law libraries—always a large part of a lawyer's overhead. The earliest date of a state bar association, as recorded in the 1995 directory of the National Association of Bar Executives, an affiliate organization of the American Bar Association, is that for the Kentucky Bar Association, founded in 1871. Obviously, local bar associations existed long before that. The NABE directory names the earliest as the Boston Bar, established in 1761.

The NABE directory lists fifty-three state bar associations. Three states (North Carolina, Virginia, and West Virginia) have two associations, one "unified" plus an "independent" association. There are thirty-two "unified" associations and twenty-one "independent" associations, including the three mentioned above.

The Rhode Island Bar Association, founded in 1898, is listed as the twenty-fourth oldest state bar association. There were only forty-five states at that time. Twelve other state bars were founded between 1871 and 1900. This surge of founding was caused by many post-Civil War factors and changes that forced lawyers, traditionally very independent and individualistic, to band together to protect themselves and their clients from the increasing number of self-appointed practitioners and the overwhelming explosion of complex legal and economic issues then facing society. Bar associations were a mechanism for improving the knowledge of lawyers, setting some training standards, and controlling the practice of law to safeguard the reputation of the profession and to protect clients who could be the victim of unethical practitioners. Bar associations—local, state, and national—have "done something" in areas that needed "something done." In 1898 Rhode Island was in the midst of a golden age of national influence. Manufacturers of textiles, rubber goods, jewelry, machine tools, steam and electric engines, and locomotives were all doing well. Huge fortunes had been made and were being made. Yet this opportunity was not spread universally.

In 1898 the Spanish-American War was fought after several years of debate about the Cuban situation. The actual fighting lasted only from April to August of 1898, but it resulted in the United States becoming a "world power," as some called it. Others called it colonialism, for along with Cuba came the Philippines and the Great White Fleet to protect it all.

As the lawyers throughout the nation were becoming aware of the great changes in our society, both financial and social, they began to form the needed professional societies to meet these needs. Rhode Island was not the first, but it did not ignore the problem.

In 1898 there were active, talented, conscientious groups of lawyers throughout the state in Newport, Pawtucket, Westerly, South Kingstown, Warwick, and Woonsocket, as well as in Providence. They saw what other states were doing and were ready to follow suit. The spark that ignited the action occurred when the prominent lawyer William A. Morgan proposed to Colonel Albert A. Baker, then first assistant city solicitor of Providence, the formation of a statewide association of lawyers in Rhode Island. Its purpose would be to maintain the honor and dignity of the profession, to promote the administration of justice, and to cultivate communication and the exchange of information among the members of the bar.

At that time there existed the Providence Bar Club, to which many prominent lawyers belonged. It was purely a social club, however, and was not what Messrs. Baker and Morgan had in mind. It was thought that the club might oppose a new organization out of loyalty to Judge Lorin M. Cook, its secretary and treasurer. Attorneys Morgan and Baker sought the aid of Francis Colwell, then city solicitor of Providence, a popular, well-respected, persuasive leader in the profession, to lead the organizational drive for the new association.

Francis Colwell (1833–1906) served as the first president of the Rhode Island Bar Association from its formation in 1898 until his death in 1906. A direct descendant of Roger Williams, Colwell clerked for Abraham Payne and then became Payne's law partner. Later he was affiliated in practice with Bristol's LeBaron B. Colt and Samuel P. Colt until the former became a federal judge and the latter was elected attorney general. Colwell served Providence as president of its common council, state representative, state senator, and, finally, city solicitor.

Committees were formed and letters were sent out to the members of the bar announcing the organization's purposes and urging action. The drive was successful, and soon a meeting was held at which a group of interested and dedicated lawyers announced the formation of the new organization. With low budgets and no staff, strong willing volunteers carried the load for the next sixty years. Many officers, particularly secretaries and treasurers, served for many consecutive terms. Most of the records we have of the work of the Association appear in the minutes, in the annual meeting reports, or in the news reports. Because Association work was so time-consuming, it was difficult for anyone but a lawyer from a large firm or one of independent means to serve. Small law offices just could not usually afford to neglect their practice to do the volunteer work of the Association. This early situation had its disadvantages, causing some to call the new group the "Providence Big Firm Association." It was an unfair criticism, but it was enough to establish the Association's elitist image.

It was not until 1958, during the presidency of Frank Cambio, that Edward P. Smith, first full-time administrator, was hired. Since that time there have been more presidents from smaller firms than from large ones. This trend has been true nationally as well. With the daily assistance of a staff, small-office members proved more willing and able to serve as bar leaders. Rhode Island was the first New England state to have a full-time paid administrator of its state bar association.

Services provided by the Association expanded rapidly with the hiring of a full-time director. The Rhode Island Bar Association Lawyer Referral Service, established in 1953, was the first such statewide service in the country. It was run by a part-time secretary before the full-time administrator was hired. Full-time staffing of the referral service followed quickly, as did expansion of the *Bar Journal* and implementation of a Blue Cross-Blue Shield program for members and staff (the group rate saved members double the amount of the Association's dues at the time).

Ada Lewis Sawyer (1892–1985) achieved the distinction of becoming Rhode Island's first female member of the bar when she became "a full-fledged attorney" in 1920 at the age of twenty-eight. Her triumph occurred in the same year in which Rhode Island women acquired the right to vote. After her graduation from Providence's English High School, Sawyer served successively as a stenographer, legal secretary, and clerk in the law office of Percy Gardiner. She performed her three-year clerkship in lieu of law school from 1917 to 1920 before successfully passing a bar exam that ranged over thirty subjects. During her long legal career Sawyer specialized in wills and trusts.

Membership grew rapidly on a voluntary basis in proportion to the new services provided. New committees were formed and met more and more often, better records and schedules were maintained, and "hot line" information was made available instantly both for the public and for members.

A more formal Continuing Legal Education program became possible with staff assistance in hiring space, printing materials based on Rhode Island law, and handling registrations. One immediate, visible accomplishment of the education program was that probate court practice became more uniform in the thirty-nine local probate courts of the state when William Graham, a well-known probate lawyer, drew up a written guide to the Rhode Island probate court practice system and gave lectures explaining it. There was no compulsion to adopt his system, but it proved so practical that most lawyers and probate courts implemented it voluntarily.

As the *Bar Journal*, the CLE courses, the Lawyer Referral Service, and the health and life insurance plans became known throughout the state, and not just in the Greater Providence area, bar leaders were anxious to get more participation from a wider geographic base. Agitation for a House of Delegates, based on lawyer population in the counties, became strong. Along with it came a group that felt it would better serve the profession if all lawyers could take part in the services and responsibilities of the profession via a "unified bar." This was not a new idea; it was first suggested in the early 1940s, but it had faded when its Rhode Island advocates ran out of energy. Much groundwork was required for its accomplishment, and although there are still challenges to it nationally and locally, with some modifications the basic "unified" concept has remained. The idea that the public and the profession both benefit when all lawyers take part is now accepted by most lawyers.

Because of the compulsory nature of the unified bar, the formation of bar foundations has increased. Bar foundations do not *require* contributions, so they become a vehicle for nonprofit, pro bono charitable works that a unified bar cannot do. The main examples are legal services for the poor and grants for law-related projects.

All of the services and good works of the Bar Association require some funding. Bar leaders are always looking for "non-dues income" that does not fall into the IRS's "unrelated business income" category for nonprofit organizations. Another source of such income is the Interest on Lawyers' Trust Accounts fund (IOLTA). This arrangement is a cooperative action between banks and the Bar Foundation by which interest on funds held in their clients' accounts are amassed and used for nonprofit educational or charitable purposes.

As we can see from this review, the work of the Bar Association has become widely diversified, quite technical, and certainly more voluminous. When the first full-time administrator was hired in 1958, the voluntary membership was five hundred. It is now, in 1998, over forty-eight hundred. What started with one full-time administrator and one part-time secretary has grown to a seventeen-person operational staff.

The Modern Era: Toward the New Millennium, 1958–1998

With the arrival of the one hundredth anniversary of the Rhode Island Bar Association and the approach of the twenty-first century, it is startling to look back at the last forty years and to review the changes that have occurred in the practice and administration of our legal system. It is very hard for the imagination to grasp what will be in store in the next century. Certainly there will be many more mechanical devices doing the research and recording of the law. However, the human element will always be present in what is often referred to as "the people's profession." Almost everything that affects a person's lifetime from birth to death and all the activities in between—such as property purchases and sales, marriages and/or marriage problems, injuries, estate planning, and settling of estates—will require a lawyer at some time or other.

We can feel proud of the conduct and growth of the profession over these past hundred years. In Rhode Island we have had many societal changes, and in almost all instances they have come with little, if any, bloodshed, unlike what we have seen in other parts of the world, other cultures, and other government systems. If the past foretells the future, we can expect that the eternal vigilance that is required to preserve freedom and liberty will be maintained by a legal profession that will accept the principle that all rights depend upon a corresponding responsibility of both those who govern and those who are governed.

As a democratic society changes, so also does its justice system and its bar associations. In the last forty years the societal changes in the United States and in Rhode Island have been massive in scope and kind. The Rhode Island Bar Association has responded and adjusted to these new circumstances in a variety of ways.

* * *

When the Bar Association began to hire the staff it needed for its administration and programs, it opened up opportunities for members of law offices of all sizes to take part in the planning and operating of its broad agenda. Two basic goals emerged and were pursued diligently. One was to get wider representation in the governance of the Association from members of all areas of the state, not just Providence and the immediate vicinity. Associated with this objective was the need to get all areas of the state to bear the burden of that governance.

A House of Delegates, elected from all sections of the state based on their proportion of the state's lawyers, was the logical first step. It was adopted in 1969 by the initiative of attorney Arthur J. Levy, a past president, in the form of a modified county system. This step helped to answer the complaint of some lawyers that the Association was a Providence organization. Now if outlying areas did not get representation, it was because of their own inaction.

The unification of the bar, or compulsory membership, was more difficult to achieve. While it had been talked about in Rhode Island as early as 1940, it did not get sufficient support, mainly because the Association was run entirely on a volunteer basis and was not capable of funding or managing the types of programs the lawyers needed. Once the staff was hired, unification became practical.

It was not until the promulgation of a Rhode Island Supreme Court order, effective October 1, 1973, that all lawyers were required to become members. It took several years of debate, polling of bar members, and petitions to the Supreme Court to achieve this result. Daniel J. Murray, a past president of the Association, wrote the petition and argued the Association's case.

With the unified bar, all lawyers benefit in some way from the Association's work, so all participate in the responsibility of funding and running it. Unification also provides a certainty of budget that allows the kind of long-range planning that was impossible when planning had to be based on a year-to-year guess at what the membership would be.

* * *

From 1898 until 1958 the address of the Rhode Island Bar Association was wherever the elected secretary's office was. In 1953 the Association hired space in the Phoenix Bank Building at 17 Exchange Street in Providence, and it was from there that the first statewide lawyer referral service in the nation was run by a part-time stenographer. It was a two-room suite consisting of a one-desk office of fifteen by twenty feet and a conference room of fifteen feet by thirty feet. The Executive Committee held its monthly meetings there, and it was available for any other committee that wished to schedule a meeting. The Westminster Street branch of Citizens Bank now occupies the first floor; the rest of the building is part of Fleet Bank's main office complex on Kennedy Plaza.

Edward P. Smith, the author of this essay, became the first full-time director of the Bar Association in 1958 during the presidency of Frank C. Cambio. His thirty-year tenure was productive and eventful.

When the new executive director was hired, these quarters were to become the home of the Bar Association and its new address. When Director Smith went to that office on the Friday before he was to start work in 1958, he told the part-time referral lady to expect him on the following Monday. "Oh, I'm glad you came in," she replied. "I'm quitting this afternoon, so I'll give you a quick run-through of the forms, files, and policies of the Referral Service." This change of paid staff was not a ceremonial event.

At the time Smith came aboard, Frank Cambio was president, William H. Edwards was president-elect, James H. Higgins, Jr., was secretary, and Arthur J. Levy was a past president. They were the main sources of training for the new director, informing him of what he was expected to do and how he should do it.

By 1975, after two modest expansions of the Phoenix Building quarters, the Association's office space was again too crowded. Since membership and activities had grown as a result of the 1973 establishment of the unified bar, the expansion of the Lawyer Referral Service, a more sophisticated Continuing Legal Education program, and the institution of other services, the decision was made to move to bigger and better quarters. Michael Monti was president then, and he led the search.

Brightly lit and well-arranged larger quarters were leased in the prestigious Industrial Bank Building, now known as the Fleet Bank Building. Soon new employees were hired—a director for the Referral Service and an assistant director, Helen Desmond McDonald—and new equipment was brought in. But the activities of the Bar Foundation, the Client Security Fund, and the Lawyers' Trust Fund soon dictated yet another move. In addition, the transition and expansion of Industrial Bank into Fleet Bank was under way, and the space occupied by the Association was desired by the bank. The need for ample space and the high leasing costs in the center of the city prompted the decision to buy rather than lease, and to move a short distance to the Remington Building at 91 Friendship Street, diagonally across from the Garrahy Court Complex.

Helen McDonald, Smith's assistant, succeeded him as executive director of the Bar Association in 1989. During her tenure the organization has experienced significant growth and expansion.

The Bar Foundation became the owner of the first floor and lower level as a condominium co-owner with an advertising agency, an investment firm, and two law firms. James Cardono was president of the Bar Association at the time of the new acquisition. A stellar cast of fund-raisers helped Cardono and Richard S. McMahon, Bar Foundation president, work out the complex details. Past president Edward F. Hindle was chairman and attorneys Bernard P. Campbell, William A. Curran (a past president), Peter J. McGinn, Robert F. Pickard, William J. Sheehan, and Allan M. Shine formed the "cabinet." It was the most ambitious effort up to that time in the Bar Association's finance and ownership history. The building was occupied in 1984 and was renamed the Law Center.

Interest on Lawyers' Trust accounts, administered by the nonprofit Bar Foundation, provided funds for many public-service projects and educational programs for the poor. These further increased public traffic and, again, the need for space and administrative staff. Helen McDonald assumed the executive director's post in 1989 amid a search for a new bar headquarters. Rents and/or purchases of property in the downtown Providence area of the size needed were prohibitively expensive, but the capital city was still the desired site for the Association's headquarters because it was also the major population hub of the state.

A relatively new building was found at 115 Cedar Street, about a half mile from the center of the city. The sale of the Friendship Street condo and the purchase of the new building took skill, time, and patience, but the experience of the previous purchase was a great help. Stephen A. Fanning, Jr., was now president of the Association, and Joseph Roszkowski, a past president of the Bar Association, was the Bar Foundation's president. In this centennial year the Cedar Street location remains the site of the Bar Association's headquarters. In the forty years between 1958 and 1998, the staff, the traffic, and the activities of the Association have increased from one person—the director, operating from eight hundred square feet of floor space—to the current staff of seventeen, occupying eight thousand square feet to house the added programs and equipment that serve the members and the public today.

* * *

The most important aim of the founders of the Rhode Island Bar Association was to form a group that would help lawyers help themselves in a professional way. Education, ethics, energy, honesty, and self-confidence are all requisites for being a good lawyer. The pitfalls are great too. No other profession faces the challenge of representing a client in an adversary system in an open public arena against an equally trained professional, with both closely regulated by the law and the traditional licensing system. Up to a hundred years ago most lawyer's organizations were local social clubs or local library cooperatives.

Small-office lawyers faced many challenges, especially in the economics of practicing law. Lawyers are very independent and strong-minded people, and it took a long time for them to realize that a good bar association could do remarkable things for its members if they really put their collective minds to it. Larger firms had resources of their own, but small offices did not. The tremendous expansion of technical and scientific endeavors forced lawyers, of both small and large firms, to cooperate with each other for their mutual benefit. The programs and expansion of bar services in the past hundred years has increased by geometric progression. The dedication of lawyer-members who have volunteered their time and skill to organizing and running the Bar Association is seldom given the credit it is due.

Bar associations turned a corner in membership services and public service in the 1940s. It was at that time that the American Bar Association changed its self-concept. Originally the ABA believed its mission was to be *The* Bar Association, with state, county, and city branches. By the 1950s the ABA had changed to actively and effectively promoting an association of other association members. State bar associations that had looked suspiciously at the ABA as a competitor now saw it as a resource of talent and technology on a national scale. Since there are more small-office lawyers than big-firm members, the ABA membership itself grew rapidly, with programs now reaching out to most lawyers, big-office and small.

The huge exchange of information and services that is available through cooperative planning would not have been dreamed of twenty or thirty years ago. A list of Rhode Island Bar Association committees, activities, and staff appears in the *Bar Journal*. These public services and membership services would not exist if not for the organized Bar Association.

* * *

Colin MacRae Makepeace (1890–1968), a graduate of Harvard College and Harvard Law School, had a private practice in Providence and served for a time as an assistant attorney general. In the 1950s Makepeace played a leading role in the organizational and structural growth of the Bar Association and served as its president in 1953.

One name that must be mentioned in this history is that of Colin MacR. Makepeace, who served as the Association's president in 1953. Those who were members of the bar then were awed by the amount of time he spent in Bar Association work and the dedication he brought to that task. Attorney Makepeace was a member of Tillinghast, Collins and Tanner, one of the large law firms of that time. It is said that he gave up a year's practice to be a full-time activist for improving the Bar Association. He kept in touch with what other bar associations were doing through their connection with the American Bar Association. He also was an advocate of further cooperation with the ABA, of hiring a full-time staff, and of establishing many more activities of service to members. It was during his administration that the Rhode Island Lawyer Referral Service was begun.

The Rhode Island Lawyer Referral Service was the first statewide plan in the country. Many other referral services existed in the United States, but none were operated statewide. Most others were county or city plans. Since many people did not know a lawyer, did not know how to get one, and were hesitant to approach lawyers because they were afraid the initial conference might cost them more than they were prepared to pay, they missed out on some of their rights and benefits under the law. A panel of lawyers was recruited, a first-conference fee was established, and referrals were made from this panel by rotation. It seems fundamental now, but only forty years ago it was a dramatic step.

Five years later, in 1958, when Frank C. Cambio was president and the full-time executive director was hired, the plan had grown considerably, both in the size of the panel and in the areas of the state that were represented. The program had become part of the Bar Association's regular staff operation.

Six years later, in 1964, the work of the referral service had expanded to such an extent and to such widely diverse areas of the law that the bar leadership decided that the service should have its own director, though it would remain within the Association. Sharon Kersh was chosen for the new post. The present Lawyer Referral Service director is Susan A. Fontaine.

* * *

In 1971 the national Bar Association's president-elect, Robert W. Miserve of Boston, stated that the most pressing need of the profession was to provide legal services to middle-income families at reasonable cost. Efforts throughout the country to provide such services centered around prepaid legal service plans similar to Blue Cross prepaid medical plans. Labor unions were beginning to investigate and promote plans for their members, and some insurance companies were doing the same thing. Most plans proposed at first were closed-panel plans, which meant that the sponsor picked, provided, and controlled the lawyers who would be participants in the plan. Bar associations, however, preferred open panels in which any practicing lawyer could be a participant. There were some who felt that closed-panel plans represented a conflict of interest, since the plans were controlled by the sponsor, and clients were denied free choice of attorney.

In June 1975 the leadership of the Bar Association took the initiative in organizing an open-panel prepaid legal-service program. The decision was made with the realization that if the Bar Association did not do it, no one else would. At an open general meeting, those present voted a thirty-dollar assessment per member to establish a fund of thirty thousand dollars. It was the first assessment in the sixty-five years of the Association's history. The change required legislation, so on May 21, 1976, the new procedure became law. Two attorneys on the prepaid legal-service committee, Frank E. Little, Jr., and Harold Demopulos (later elected Association president), traveled to Portland, Oregon, and Des Moines, Iowa, to visit operating plans. Midwest Insurance Company of Des Moines, the leader in this field, was willing to work with the Rhode Island Bar Association in installing a plan. Details for implementation included approval from the Insurance Division of the Department of Business Regulation, a charter for the prepaid legal-service committee, and the incorporation of the plan in this state. The plan is now over twenty years old, and it is successful. Without the efforts of the Bar Association, there would not be a nonprofit open-panel prepaid legal-service plan for all lawyers to join.

* * *

Over the last forty years many changes have occurred in the code of professional ethics for lawyers. In the 1960s the code of ethics was a Bar Association document, and the Rhode Island Supreme Court normally used it as its guideline in cases of lawyer discipline. However, the court was not required to use it, and since the Bar Association was not unified, it was not an official code. The Rhode Island Bar Association did not then, nor does it now, have any official standing in lawyer-discipline matters.

Because of the involvement of some lawyers in the Watergate scandal that occurred during Richard Nixon's presidency, concerns were raised about the issue of lawyer discipline. This concern resulted in the creation of a special American Bar Association committee, headed by retired U.S. Supreme Court justice William O. Douglas, to make a study of lawyer disciplinary systems in every state. The study group contacted each state, held regional meetings, and made recommendations for changes. Each state then determined what steps to take to ensure adherence by its lawyers to the highest ethical standards. Bar association staffs were increased, investigators were hired, and recommendations for action were quickly and forcefully presented to state supreme courts. The Rhode Island Supreme Court heard, studied, and then adopted the present code in 1988 for all Rhode Island lawyers.

* * *

In the late 1950s and early 1960s the Economics of the Profession committees of some state bar associations had advocated and promoted a "legal checkup" program for lawyers to send to their clients to review the status of the clients' wills, businesses, financial obligations, and other legal concerns. Complaints were received, however, that this was improper "lawyer advertising." Since the checkup was a device to help a client avoid problems, the ethical infraction was debatable, but some bar associations would not permit their members to promote legal checkups, nor were their public relations committees allowed to do so. In the early 1960s Rhode Island lawyers were allowed to advertise or put notices in the news media only when they changed their address, started a new firm, or were admitted to the bar.

Due to the increase in college attendance through the G.I. Bill and other methods of paying for college education, the number of law schools increased dramatically, as did the number of people being admitted to the practice of law. Many of the new lawyers felt that allowing just one notice of their admission left most of the general public unaware that they existed, and it constituted a violation of their "business freedom of speech." Over the years this problem was debated until eventually the United States Supreme Court approved lawyer advertising on "business freedom of speech" grounds.

Most bar associations across the county had opposed such advertising, fearing it could result in unprofessional boasting and diminish the stature of the profession. In some instances those fears were realized, but in most cases lawyers acted responsibly. At times the disciplinary system had to step in and moderate some of the advertising claims. The advent of television affected law advertising more than radio and print advertising did. It also had an effect on the issue of cameras in the courtroom, which now included TV cameras. More on this later.

* * *

During the last four decades of the twentieth century, several changes were made in our Rhode Island court system, and these have had considerable effect on the way justice and the legal profession function. The Rhode Island Constitution provided for a Supreme Court and such inferior courts as the legislature might from time to time determine. This system was modified in 1905 by the creation of the Superior Court, with jurisdiction over both criminal and civil cases. For many years that court handled domestic-relations problems as well. Since 1886 a District Court system, at first presided over by part-time judges, has handled entry-level cases. It was in the District Court that most citizens came in contact with the judicial system on a face-to-face basis. It handled traffic problems and criminal problems that could result in a year or less incarceration, and/or fines of less than $1,000, and it was limited to matters involving relatively small dollar amounts.

During the last forty years a Family Court was created to handle domestic relations cases, juvenile cases, and juvenile criminal cases. A short time later, during Governor Frank Licht's administration, the District Court system was changed to require full-time judges. This change was made because of the caseload, and also because of the feeling that part-time judges, who might be practicing lawyers in other courts, might have conflicts of interest that would disturb the public image of the justice system. The jurisdiction of the District Court as it pertains to monetary limits has been changed considerably from time to time. Other recently established courts include a system for traffic adjudication and a gun court and housing court in the city of Providence.

Ralph P. Semonoff (1918–1992) and his father, Judah, were the only father-and-son duo to lead the Bar Association. An association award for professionalism honors the younger Semonoff (shown here).

In the 1960s the Roman Catholic Diocese of Providence imposed on Catholic lawyers a prohibition against handling divorce cases between Catholic spouses. This prohibition no longer exists, and the number of divorce cases handled in the Family Court has grown significantly.

While speaking of courtrooms, one might mention a significant change in court procedures—the presence of cameras in the courtroom. This issue was debated nationally for many years until finally, by U.S. Supreme Court rule of January 17, 1983, cameras were admitted and regulations devised for how they would operate. Most of the nation's bar associations opposed cameras in the courtroom, which have turned trials in some spectacular cases into soap-opera-style entertainment shows. Now judges are more conservative in allowing cameras in the courtroom because of such cases as Rhode Island's von Bulow trial, the O. J. Simpson trial, and several others. The proponents of cameras assert that they can be educational. Most opponents contend that few, if any, people would watch entire trials, and few stations would show them; as a result, only heavily edited tapes would be shown, and these could distort the picture of the trial process while emphasizing the grandstanding tactics of some participants, including witnesses, jurors, lawyers, judges, and even court attendants.

In the early sixties the newest courthouse in the state of Rhode Island was the Providence County Courthouse, which had been completed in 1933. Some active courthouses were buildings that were built in the late eighteenth century. Modern facilities were very scarce indeed. It is only within the last twenty years that the Garrahy Judicial Complex in Providence, which houses District and Family courts, was built. Newer or remodeled court facilities are now open in Newport, Warwick, and Wakefield, but all are inundated by the modern flood of litigation.

* * *

President Johnson's "War on Poverty," in addition to other projects, set up legal-service programs for the poor who could not get such help through privately sponsored organizations. Most low-income people could not afford the legal services that might be needed in domestic or rental-housing problems. There were also changes in the law to allow increased access to the courts and to assist in the maintenance of more suits on product liability. The latter put more responsibility on industry to manufacture safer products and/or to disclose potential product weaknesses. Changes in the law that provided for punitive damages awarded to plaintiffs were considered to be an answer to the complacency of huge corporate manufacturers who could lose an occasional lawsuit and not be hurt too much. But the prospect of triple damages had a strong effect on such manufacturers.

Civil rights laws gave court access to people who felt they had been unfairly treated because of their sex, color of skin, weight problems, or so forth. The accumulation of such new causes of action has outstripped the programs to speed up the judicial process and to control the flow.

* * *

It is extremely important for professional people to keep informed of the rapid changes in our modern world. Each year local, state, and national legislatures change and create new laws by the thousands. Court decisions change or remove laws on constitutional grounds constantly. How do lawyers keep track of it all?

A lawyer's education definitely does not end with admission to the bar. That happy event puts the new lawyer under a greater obligation to maintain his or her competence. Until 1994 the programs for keeping up with changes in the law were run almost exclusively by the Bar Association, because Rhode Island had no local law school.

For purposes of education, the court issued copies of changes in procedures, the legislature published books of new laws or changes in the law for each session, and some commercial books, often written by local attorneys, were also published. For the small-office lawyer with cost and staff limitations, the task of keeping abreast was very hard. The Bar Association provided an affordable alternative and opportunity. Through the *Bar Journal*, which published articles on changes, recent decisions, and court calendars, and through the Committee on Continuing Legal Education, the Bar Association offered programs on Rhode Island law at in-state locations, with written outlines and texts virtually at cost. There was no one else to do it.

* * *

Our legal system must have a way of selecting our judges, but how it should be done and by whom has been debated for years. After the appointment to the bench comes the question of measuring a judge's performance, but who should do that? Popular election of judges nominated by political parties or by open primaries has been tried in some states and found wanting. Most states now favor life terms with tenure, unless improper behavior is charged. This security relieves the judge from running for reelection and feeling the need to make "popular" decisions to win votes and gain campaign funds.

On June 2, 1994, legislation created a Judicial Nominating Commission empowered to screen applicants for vacancies on all of Rhode Island's courts. The commission must recommend three to five names to the governor for every vacancy. The governor's selection from those recommended must be confirmed by the Senate, except in the case of Supreme Court justices, who must also be confirmed by the House.

Formerly the governor had the statutory power to select judges for the lower courts, subject to Senate confirmation, while the Rhode Island

Constitution formerly gave the House and Senate, sitting as the Grand Committee, the power to select Supreme Court justices. The new selection statute controlled lower-court selections immediately, but the new process did not go into effect for vacancies on the Supreme Court until November 1994, when the voters approved a constitutional amendment. This change, ratified by a margin of more than 2 to 1, also gave all judges tenure for "good behavior."

The nine members of the commission were sworn in on June 15, 1994. All were appointed by the governor, who has complete discretion to make four appointments, except that three of those appointees must be attorneys. The remaining five commissioners are selected by the governor from lists forwarded by legislative leaders, including leaders of the minority party. Members serve staggered four-year terms. The purpose of this new procedure was to eliminate, as much as possible, the role of politics in judicial selection.

With very few exceptions, our state has had good fortune in that our judges at all levels have been honest and competent. Yet in 1991 a number of separate events, resulting in part from an economic crisis, sparked a Brown University poll that showed that more than half (67 percent) of the Rhode Island public was dissatisfied with the state's legal system. This disapproval led then Supreme Court chief justice Thomas Fay to appoint a Rhode Island Supreme Court Ethics Reform Commission to study ways to improve the legal system and to make recommendations for implementing the changes.

In March 1992 the Ethics Reform Commission issued its findings in a sixteen-page report. It listed things the Supreme Court had already done to improve procedures and approved of them, but these were not enough. Therefore the ethics panel recommended that the Supreme Court should take the following steps: it should add public members to the Disciplinary Board and open the process to the public once probable cause has been found; to provide a broader range of sanctions, it should establish a court-wide judicial performance evaluation program to promote accountability and professionalism and include part-time judges in the code; and it should mandate an orientation program for newly appointed judges as well as a continuing education program for all attorneys. Most of the recommendations were adopted.

* * *

The practice of law has become widely diversified and technical as a reflection of our society. Now it is basically impossible for one person to be competent in all fields of law. In Rhode Island, by Supreme Court order, lawyers cannot hold themselves out as "specialists." However, by U.S. Supreme Court order, they can advertise. According to our Code of Professional Conduct, they are allowed to advertise areas of practice, but not rate themselves in comparison to other practitioners. The specifics are cloudy.

In a state the size of Rhode Island, there is no practical method to set up a specialization board for all the categories needed, and there are probably not enough clients in need of specialized service for most Rhode Island lawyers to limit their practice in any way and still make a living. Another complication results from the fact that a lawyer can be disciplined if he/she mishandles a case that he/she took without the necessary experience in that field. So a lot is left to the integrity and honesty of the lawyer and the alertness and vigilance of the Disciplinary Board.

* * *

In 1994 Roger Williams University established the first Rhode Island law school, now named the Ralph Papitto School of Law. With the cooperation of the Rhode Island Supreme Court and the hard work of the administrators and faculty of the new school, in 1997 it achieved its accreditation from the American Bar Association in the minimum time (three years) under the ABA rules. A new era in Rhode Island law and education has begun most auspiciously!

* * *

Perhaps the best way to end this history is to quote from the March 21, 1844, letter of William E. Richmond, Esq., to the Providence County Bar Association, which was then approaching its one hundredth anniversary. Richmond had served for thirty years as the secretary of that association, and he was now submitting his resignation. His closing paragraph reads: "In this benign result of liberal study, let us all rejoice, for it is obvious, and strikingly obvious, and all around us; in the junior members of our fraternity, it is full of promise for the future, a ready and trustful pledge for the preservation, in *our* community at least, of that *enlightened system of regulated liberty* [emphasis by the author], the richest inheritance which we have received, the most invaluable which we can possibly transmit."

Rhode Island Bar Association Presidents, 1898–1999

It is a great honor to be a Bar Association president, because one does not achieve this distinction easily. Longtime service to the profession and demonstrable legal ability must be presented by the candidate in order to be chosen over other candidates within a profession known to be highly motivated.

A Bar Association presidency is a costly office to hold in time, energy, patience, and the sacrifice of income as well. Some past presidents have kept time records of hours spent in Association work during their terms, and they have found that their presidential duties have cut their "billable hours" as much as one-third.

Serving as a spokesperson for the legal profession demands courage and diplomacy as well as clarity; it is a responsibility that cannot be delegated. To paraphrase Harry Truman, "The buck ends with the president."

A list of past presidents and their dates of tenure appears below. In 1941 a one-year term limit was established. It is impossible to include all of the projects and progress made in each term in this short history of the Bar Association, but the reader may correlate the developments chronicled in my essay with those leaders who presided over the Association during its first one hundred years.

RHODE ISLAND BAR ASSOCIATION PRESIDENTS, 1898–1999

*1898–1906	Francis Colwell
*1906–1908	William A. Morgan
*1908–1910	Dexter B. Potter
*1910–1912	Albert A. Baker
*1912–1914	Charles C. Mumford
*1914–1916	Richard B. Comstock
*1916–1918	William P. Sheffield
*1918–1923	Richard Comstock
*1923–1925	William B. Greenough
*1925–1927	George H. Huddy, Jr.
*1927–1929	John H. Murdock
*1929–1930	John H. Swan
*1930–1932	John H. Slattery
*1932–1934	James C. Collins
*1934–1936	Chauncy E. Wheeler
*1936–1938	Frederick W. O'Connell
*1938–1940	Herbert M. Sherwood
*1941	Henry C. Hart
*1942	Henry M. Boss
*1943	Patrick Henry Quinn
*1944	Fred B. Perkins**
*1945	Elmer S. Chace
*1946	Joseph H. Gainer
*1947	Harold B. Tanner
*1948	Fred A. Otis
*1949	James L. Taft
*1950	Andrew P. Quinn
*1951	Arthur J. Levy
*1952	James A. Higgins
*1953	Colin MacR. Makepeace
*1954	Henry J. Blais, Jr.
*1955	John P. Cooney, Jr.
*1956	William A. Graham
*1957	Judah C. Semonoff †
*1958	Frank C. Cambio
*1959	William H. Edwards
*1960	Willis L. Yatman
*1961	Sayles Gorham
*1962	James H. Higgins, Jr.
*1963	Francis J. O'Brien
1964	James C. Bulman**
1965	George C. Davis
1966	William R. Goldberg***
1967	Lee A. Worrell
*1968	James O. Watts
*1969	Joseph V. Cavanagh
1970	Daniel J. Murray

RHODE ISLAND BAR ASSOCIATION PRESIDENTS, 1898–1999 (*continued*)

*1971	Henry E. Crowe
*1972	Edward F. Hindle
1973	Julius C. Michaelson
*1974	Paul F. Murray
*1975	Michael A. Monti
1976	William A. Curran
1977	Harold B. Soloveitzik
1978	Seth K. Gifford
*1979	Ralph P. Semonoff†
*1980	James M. Shannahan**
*1981	Leo T. Connors
1982	Beverly Glenn Long****
*1983	Melvin A. Chernick
1984	James Cardono
1985	Harold W. Demopulos
1986	Joseph J. Roszkowski
1987	Lester H. Salter
1988	Scott K. Keefer
1989	William F. McMahon
1990	Susan Leach DeBlasio
1991	Stephen A. Fanning
1992	Alan S. Flink
1993	Bruce G. Pollock
1994	Mark S. Mandell
1995	Justin S. Holden
1996	R. Kelly Sheridan
1997	Richard W. MacAdams
1998	John A. Tarantino
1999	Lauren E. Jones

*Deceased
**Also served as judge of the Superior Court
***Also served as judge of the Family Court
****First woman president
†Father and son

Lawyer/Governors of Rhode Island

Since the founding of the Rhode Island Bar Association one hundred years ago, there have been twenty-eight state governors, sixteen of whom have been lawyers. Their names and years in office are:

James H. Higgins, Pawtucket (D)	1907–1909
William S. Flynn, Providence (D)	1923–1925
Norman S. Case, Providence (R)	1928–1933
Theodore Francis Green, Providence (D)	1933–1937
Robert Emmet Quinn, West Warwick (D)*	1937–1939
J. Howard McGrath, Providence (D)	1941–1945
John O. Pastore, Providence (D)	1945–1950
John S. McKiernan, Providence (D)*	1950–1951
Dennis J. Roberts, Providence (D)	1951–1959
Christopher Del Sesto, Providence (R)*	1959–1961
John A. Notte, Jr., North Providence (D)	1961–1963
John H. Chafee, Warwick (R)	1963–1969
Frank Licht, Providence (D)*	1969–1973
Philip W. Noel, Warwick (D)	1973–1977
Bruce G. Sundlun, Providence (D)	1991–1995
Lincoln C. Almond, Lincoln (R)	1995-

*Also served as judge of the Superior Court

The present headquarters of the Rhode Island Bar Association at 115 Cedar Street, Providence, was acquired in December 1990.

BIOGRAPHICAL PROFILES

Woonsocket-born lawyer J. Howard McGrath (1903–1966) was undoubtedly Rhode Island's most versatile politician of this or any era. A protégé of U.S. senator Peter Gerry, McGrath served successively as Democratic state chairman and U.S. district attorney in the 1930s and as Rhode Island's governor during the war years (1941–1945). In 1945 President Harry Truman appointed him U.S. solicitor general, and in 1946 J. Howard won election as U.S. senator. The following year Truman conferred upon the Rhode Islander the national chairmanship of the Democratic party. In 1949 McGrath gave up his Senate seat to become the U.S. attorney general. After resigning this post in 1952 amidst controversy, he returned to private business and the successful practice of law. In 1960 McGrath lost a comeback bid in a heated three-way Democratic senatorial primary to newcomer Claiborne Pell, the eventual winner.

McGrath's brilliant career as a lawyer-politician was deservedly recognized when the new Washington County Courthouse near Wakefield was formally dedicated on October 28, 1988, as the J. Howard McGrath Judicial Complex.

Justice William E. Powers (1907–1989) of Central Falls was one of Rhode Island's brightest major political figures of the century. He overcame the handicap of blindness, the result of a childhood accident, to rank second in his Boston University Law School graduating class. After five terms in the state House of Representatives (1939–1949) and thirteen years as probate judge in Cumberland (1936–1949), Powers served nine years as attorney general before his elevation in January 1958 to the state Supreme Court. Shortly after his accession, Judge Powers's achievements in the face of blindness were the subject of the nationally televised show "This Is Your Life."

Having stepped down after fifteen distinguished years on the high-court bench, in 1973 Powers reemerged to chair that year's highly successful state constitutional convention, and he later chaired the state's Solid Waste Management Corporation.

These and other posts of civic responsibility were his personal answer to the rhetorical question he raised in an address before the Bristol Rotary Club in 1939: "Why make basket-weavers, mattress-makers, or chair-caners out of everybody that's blind?" Powers's legal and civic contributions to Rhode Island were prominently acknowledged when the new state administration building at One Capitol Hill was dedicated in his honor.

Joseph G. LeCount (1888–1981) of Providence was Rhode Island's most prominent Afro-American attorney of the early twentieth century. In addition to his pioneering role in the legal profession, he was a leader in the local NAACP and a major force in the advancement of civil rights for blacks.

Born in Washington, D.C., LeCount grew up poor in the West End of Providence and was compelled to leave English High School prior to graduation to help support his family. After employment first as an elevator operator and then as a porter, LeCount saved enough money for a year's tuition at Howard University Law School in Washington. His failure to complete high school nearly prevented his enrollment, but Howard allowed him to take an entrance exam, and he passed it without difficulty.

After graduation LeCount returned to Providence and opened his practice. Along with his business activity, he embarked upon a lifelong campaign to improve the civil rights of black citizens. He was present at the creation of the Providence branch of the NAACP in 1914 and served as its president for many years. Although initially skeptical of the Providence Urban League, he eventually became involved with that organization when it proved its worth in advancing the condition of Afro-Americans.

LeCount was a stalwart supporter of the party of Lincoln, and his Republican loyalty led to appointments in the administrations of Republican fellow-attorneys Christopher Del Sesto and John H. Chafee. He was also a GOP leader in Providence's Third Ward—the Mount Hope section—and once held the state's highest Masonic office.

LeCount's lifetime of public service earned him many awards, including honorary doctorates from Providence College and Rhode Island College. When he retired from the practice of law in 1978 at the age of ninety, he was Rhode Island's oldest active attorney.

Florence Kerins Murray is, without question, the most prominent woman in the history of Rhode Island law. Born in Newport in 1916, she graduated from Syracuse University and Boston University Law School. Her early career included a teaching position on Prudence Island and a 4½-year tour of duty in the Women's Army Corps during World War II that earned her several decorations and the rank of lieutenant colonel.

After the war Murray returned to Newport and represented that city in the state Senate from 1949 until her appointment to the Superior Court on May 7, 1956, as its first female judge. After twenty-two years of distinguished service, she became presiding justice on April 4, 1978. She then became the first woman to serve on the state Supreme Court when the Grand Committee elevated her to the position of associate justice in October 1979, in which capacity she served for eighteen years.

During Murray's long judicial tenure she was involved with a host of boards and committees, holding positions as chairperson of the Rhode Island Committee on the Humanities and chairperson of the board of directors of the National Judicial College in Reno, Nevada. In recognition of her pioneering judicial role, she was awarded numerous honorary degrees and saw the Newport County Courthouse dedicated in her honor while she was still a sitting justice.

Though Judge Murray's professional and public life was replete with awards and accomplishments, she especially treasured her private life with her late husband and confidant, Paul F. Murray, U.S. attorney for Rhode Island, president of the Bar Association, and a highly respected legal and political practitioner.

Judge Murray has many worthy successors among lawyers of her gender. Today, Justice (and Dr.) Victoria S. Lederberg and Justice Maureen McKenna Goldberg hold seats on the five-member Supreme Court, while Judge O. Rogeriee Thompson sits on the bench as the first Rhode Island Afro-American woman to hold a Superior Court judgeship.

Rhode Island's most famous political figure of the postwar era was attorney John O. Pastore. Born in 1907 amid humble surroundings on Providence's Federal Hill, Pastore rose to become one of the nation's most influential and respected United States senators. The son of Italian immigrants, he is cited by the famous political scientist Samuel Lubell in his book *The Future of American Politics* as the individual who epitomized the rise of the Italian American to a position of political power and influence. As the first governor and the first U.S. senator of Italo-American stock, Pastore was enormously popular with Rhode Island's Italian community, but he also won the respect and support of a much larger constituency.

Pastore began the practice of law in Providence in 1932 and launched his career in politics shortly afterward, securing election as Democratic state representative from Providence in 1934. After one legislative term, he served a six-year stint as assistant attorney general and was also a member of the 1939 Providence Charter Revision Commission.

His big break came when partly chieftains J. Howard McGrath and Dennis Roberts selected him over fellow Italian American Christopher Del Sesto as Democratic nominee for lieutenant governor in 1944. Victorious in that election, he succeeded to the governorship on October 6, 1945, when McGrath resigned to become Harry Truman's solicitor general. After two convincing triumphs in gubernatorial elections, Pastore ran for the U.S. Senate in 1950 and defeated his Republican opponent by nearly seventy thousand votes. He assumed office (again as McGrath's successor) on December 19, 1950, and served with distinction for the next twenty-six years. Among his many important senatorial posts were the chairmanship of the Communications Subcommittee of the Senate Commerce Committee, where he was often referred to as "the conscience of the television industry," and the chairmanship of the Joint Committee on Atomic Energy.

Frank Licht was born in 1916 on the South Side of Providence to Jewish immigrant parents from eastern Europe. He graduated from Brown University in 1939 and received his law degree from Harvard in 1941. As a young man Licht espoused Zionism and assumed an increasingly active role in Jewish charitable agencies, especially the General Jewish Committee.

Alongside these accomplishments in Jewish community affairs, Licht developed a successful career first in law and then in state politics. As a supporter of Providence political potentate Dennis J. Roberts, he secured nomination and election to the state Senate from 1949 to 1956, when Roberts appointed him to the Superior Court.

In 1968 Licht left the bench to accept the Democratic gubernatorial nomination. As a tireless campaigner and an eloquent speaker, he upset popular incumbent John H. Chafee to become Rhode Island's first Jewish American governor. He won reelection in 1970 in a tight race with former attorney general Herbert F. DeSimone, but his support of a graduated income tax during his second term generated such controversy (particularly in view of his campaign pledge against such a measure) that he declined to run for a third term and returned to the practice of law, leaving Warwick attorney Philip W. Noel to battle DeSimone in another close election, in which Noel prevailed.

Just two months before his death on May 30, 1987, the state recognized Licht's many civic, legal, and political accomplishments by dedicating the Providence County Courthouse in his honor. For an informative account of Licht's rise to prominence, see Walter H. Conser, Jr., "Ethnicity and Politics in Rhode Island: The Career of Frank Licht," *Rhode Island History* 44 (1985), 96–107.

Sources and Permissions

PART ONE: FROM COLONY TO STATE, 1636–1790: THE FOUNDATIONS OF THE LAW

* 1. "The Colonial Foundations of Rhode Island's Legal System," by Patrick T. Conley, adapted from *Democracy in Decline* (1977), pp. 14–27, 36–45, and *The Statehouses of Rhode Island* (1988), pp. 8–13. Courtesy of the Rhode Island Historical Society (RIHS).

2. "Roger Williams and His Legacy," by Edwin S. Gaustad, from *Liberty of Conscience: Roger Williams in America* (1991), pp. 193–219. Courtesy of William B. Eerdmans Publishing Company.

* 3. "Murder of an Indian, 1638: Equal Treatment before the Law," by Glenn W. LaFantasie, from *Rhode Island History* 38 (August 1979), 67–76. Courtesy of RIHS.

4. "Jezebel before the Judges: Anne Hutchinson Tried for Sedition," by Richard B. Morris, from *Fair Trial* (1952), pp. 3–32. Courtesy of Alfred A. Knopf, Inc.

* 5. "Rhode Island's First Court of Admiralty," by Marguerite Appleton, from *New England Quarterly* 5 (January 1932), 148–158. Courtesy of the *New England Quarterly*.

* 6. "The Piracy Trial of Charles Harris and His Crew," by George Francis Dow and John Henry Edmonds, from *The Pirates of the New England Coast, 1630–1730* (1923), pp. 288–308.

* 7. "Women and the Legal Culture of Colonial Rhode Island," by Catherine Osborne DeCesare, adapted from a paper presented at a historical symposium, "Rhode Island Reconsidered," at Brown University, November 14, 1997.

* 8. "Stephen Hopkins: Chief Justice, Governor, and Signer," by Marguerite Appleton, from *A Portrait Album of Four Great Rhode Island Leaders* (1978), pp. 31–54. Courtesy of RIHS.

* 9. "The Uses of Law and the *Gaspee* Affair," by Neil L. York, from *Rhode Island History* 50 (February 1992), 3–18. Courtesy of RIHS.

*10. "First in War, Last in Peace: Rhode Island and the Constitution, 1786–1790," by Patrick T. Conley, from *Rhode Island Bar Journal* 35 (May 1987), 11–19; adapted from *Democracy in Decline* (1977), chapters 3, 4, and 5. Courtesy of the Rhode Island Bar Association (RIBA).

*11. "The Bill of Rights and Rhode Island," by Patrick T. Conley, from *The Bill of Rights and the States: The Colonial and Revolutionary Origins of American Liberties* (1992), pp. 123–161. Courtesy of Madison House Publishers.

PART TWO: FROM STATEHOOOD THROUGH THE NINETEENTH CENTURY, 1790–1898: THE LAW AS AN INSTRUMENT OF CHANGE

12. "William Peck—Rhode Island's First U.S. Marshal," by Donald W. Wyatt, from *Rhode Island Bar Journal* 34 (May 1986), 16–17. Courtesy of RIBA.

*13. "The First Judicial Review of State Legislation: An Analysis of the Rhode Island Case of *Champion and Dickason* v. *Casey* (1792)," by Patrick T. Conley, Jr., from *Rhode Island Bar Journal* 36 (October 1987), 5–9. Courtesy of RIBA.

*14. "The Broken Bond: Divorce in Providence County, 1749–1809," by Sheldon S. Cohen, from *Rhode Island History* 44 (August 1985), 67–79. Courtesy of RIHS.

15. "Attorney Thomas Dorr: Rhode Island's Foremost Political Reformer," by Patrick T. Conley.

*16. "The Dorr Rebellion and American Constitutional Theory: Popular Constituent Sovereignty, Political Questions, and *Luther* v. *Borden*," by Patrick T. Conley, from *Rhode Island Bar Journal* 41 (November 1992), 19–25, and *Rhode Island History* 50 (August 1992), 66–100; adapted from *Democracy in Decline* (1977), chapters 12 and 13. Courtesy of RIHS and RIBA.

17. "Death Knell for the Death Penalty: The Gordon Murder Trial and Rhode Island's Abolition of Capital Punishment," by Patrick T. Conley, from *Rhode Island Bar Journal* 34 (May 1986), 11–15. Courtesy of RIBA.

18. "Joseph K. Angell, Law Writer," by Sidney S. Rider, from *Rhode Island Historical Tracts* 11 (1880), pp. 3–25.

19. "Rhode Island Reports—1828–1885," by John R. Robinson, from *Rhode Island Bar Journal* 24 (May 1976), 5–7. Courtesy of RIBA.

*20. "Samuel Ames: The Great Chief Justice of Rhode Island," by C. Peter Magrath, from *Rhode Island History* 24 (July 1965), 65–76. Courtesy of RIHS.

21. "Reminiscences of the Rhode Island Bar [1840–1883]," by Abraham Payne, from *Reminiscences of the Rhode Island Bar* (1883), pp. 1–3, 7–14, 15–16, 27–29.

*22. "The Sprague Cases," by Charles Carroll, from *Rhode Island: Three Centuries of Democracy* (1932), 2:762–773.

*23. "Development of the Law of Negligence in Rhode Island, 1872–1903," by Charles Carroll, from *Rhode Island: Three Centuries of Democracy* (1932), 2:773–776.

*24. "Rhode Island Suffrage since the Dorr War, 1842–1928," by Chilton Williamson, from *New England Quarterly* 28 (March 1955), 34–50. Courtesy of the *New England Quarterly*.

25. "The Founding of the Superior Court: A New Era in the Rhode Island Judicial System," by Joseph R. Weisberger, from *Rhode Island Bar Journal* 34 (May 1986), 5–9. Courtesy of RIBA.

*26. "The Bloodless Revolution," by Erwin L. Levine, from *Theodore Francis Green: The Rhode Island Years, 1906–1936* (1963), pp. 173–187. Courtesy of Brown University Press.

*27. "Zechariah Chafee, Jr.: A Rhode Island Man," by Donald L. Smith, from *Zechariah Chafee, Jr.: Defender of Liberty and Law* (1986) pp. 58–76. Courtesy of Harvard University Press.

*28. "The Long Count and Its Legacy: Rhode Island Political Realignment, 1956–1964," by Matthew J. Smith, from *Rhode Island History* 35 (May 1976), 49–61. Courtesy of RIHS.

*29. "State Aid to Rhode Island's Private Schools: A Case Study of *DiCenso* v. *Robinson*," by Patrick T. Conley and Fernando S. Cunha, from *The Catholic Lawyer* 22 (Autumn 1976), 329–343. Courtesy of St. John's University Law School.

30. "The Rhode Island Constitutional Conventions of 1964, 1973, and 1986: Getting Down to Basic Law," by Patrick T. Conley and Keven A. McKenna, from *The Proceedings of the Rhode Island Constitutional Convention of 1973*, pp. 3–4, and *1986 Rhode Island Constitution: Annotated Edition*, pp. iii–iv.

31. "The Rhode Island Bar Association: Its First Century, 1898–1998," by Edward P. Smith.

*Documentation and/or bibliography in the original has been omitted.

Bibliographical Note

Apart from the numerous studies of Rhode Island constitutional development and the histories of judicial administration that are cited in the extensive bibliography of Patrick T. Conley's *Democracy in Decline: Rhode Island's Constitutional Development* (1977), to which the reader is directed, there has been very little written about Rhode Island's legal history per se. Early in the twentieth century Roscoe Pound, dean of Harvard Law School, challenged legal scholarship to seek deeper insights through a "sociological jurisprudence" which might put law into societal context with other institutions. Legal historians have been slow to respond to this challenge, and this reticence is very evident to anyone familiar with the literature of Rhode Island legal development. Perhaps the voluminous manuscript records at the recently organized Rhode Island Supreme Court Judicial Archives will tempt historians to correct this glaring deficiency in our state's legal literature. Time will tell.

For the reader seeking a broader knowledge of the history of local legal development, other scholarly works, in addition to the anthologized selections and the works cited in the introductory essays, may also be consulted.

Charles Carroll, *Rhode Island: Three Centuries of Democracy*, 4 vols. (1932), by a prominent lawyer-educator, is the best detailed general history of Rhode Island. Because of Carroll's legal training, his narrative includes a substantial amount of legal history in its broad sense. The final two volumes of this work are biographical and contain profiles of many prominent lawyers and judges of the early twentieth century.

Among the more specialized monographs of use to the student of legal history are Peter J. Coleman, *The Transformation of Rhode Island*, 1790–1860 (1969), which presents valuable information on business law; Joseph Brennan, *Social Conditions in Industrial Rhode Island, 1820–1860* (1940), which contains an informative chapter on law and society; and William F. Micarelli, "The Rhode Island Supreme Court and Social Change, 1865–1900" (doctoral dissertation, Catholic University of America, 1969), which deals with the economic and social impact of Supreme Court decisions in the Gilded Age.

Nearly eighty years ago Howard M. Chapin began the publication of Rhode Island's court documents in the *Records of the Court of Trials of the Colony of Providence Plantations* (1920–22), but only two slim volumes of trials were printed covering the period from 1647 to 1670. William R. Staples, ed., *Proceedings of the First General Assembly... and the Code of Laws Adopted by That Assembly in 1647...* (1847), contains historical and explanatory notes by Staples, a justice of the Supreme Court and a pioneering Rhode Island historian.

Other documentary material with explanatory narrative relating to the early Rhode Island justice system can be found in Dorothy S. Towle, ed., *Records of the Vice-Admiralty Court of Rhode Island, 1716–1752* (1936), with an historical introduction by Charles McLean Andrews, the premier historian of colonial America; Frederick B. Weiner, *Notes on the Rhode Island Admiralty, 1727–1790*, *Harvard Law Review* 46 (November 1932), 44–90; Harold D. Hazetine, "Appeals from Colonial Courts to the King in Council, with Especial Reference to Rhode Island," in the *Annual Report of the American Historical Association for the Year 1894*, pp. 299–350; and Zechariah Chafee, "Records of the Rhode Island Court of Equity, 1741–1743," *Proceedings of the Colonial Society of Massachusetts* 35 (1951), 91–118, which covers the brief span of this court's existence. The early laws of the colony and state are edited with occasional historical annotation by Secretary of State John Russell Bartlett, comp., *Records of the Colony of Rhode Island and Providence Plantations in New England*, 10 vols. (1856–65).

Older studies of the development of the state court system include Amasa M. Eaton, "The Development of the Judicial System in Rhode Island," *Yale Law Journal* 14 (1905), 148–170; John T. Farrell, "The Early History of Rhode Island's Court System," *Rhode Island History* 9 (1950), 65–71, 103–117, and 10 (1951), 14–25; Francis I. McCanna, "A Study of the History and Jurisdiction of Rhode Island Courts," *Journal of the American Irish Historical Society* 22 (1923), 170–195; and Robert A. Coogan, "The Foundations of the Rhode Island Judicial System," *Rhode Island Bar Journal* 1 (1964), 1–19.

Two recent studies of early Rhode Island law are useful: Mary Sarah Bilder, "The Origin of Appeal in America," *Hastings Law Journal* 48 (July 1997), 913–968, which focuses on the appeal as an equitable remedy using seventeenth-century Rhode Island and Massachusetts as case studies, and G. B. Warden, "The Rhode Island Civil Code of 1647," in *Saints and Revolutionaries: Essays on Early American History* (1984), ed. David D. Hall et al., pp. 142–149.

Crime and punishment in Rhode Island have attracted the attention of several legal historians. A very useful survey of early criminal law was written in the mid-nineteenth century by Chief Justice William R. Staples. His *History of the Criminal Law of Rhode Island* (1853) is learned and detailed. Also of interest is Constance D. Sherman, "Curious Crimes in Colonial Newport County," *Rhode Island History* 18 (1959), 116–118, and William D. Metz, "Thomas Mount," *Rhode Island Historical Society Collections* 20 (1927), 53–58, the account of a man executed in South Kingstown in 1791 for burglary. A criminal proceeding that sparked the interest of the late *Providence Journal* critic and historian Bradford F. Swan concerns the trial of a well-endowed seventeenth-century pervert with a penchant for cows: *The Case of Richard Chasmore, alias Long Dick* (1944). Swan also analyzed another early case: his "Frontier Justice in Newport, 1652," *Rhode Island History* 33 (1974), 3–7, covers the trial, conviction, and execution of Alexander Partridge, vigilante style, for an alleged murder committed in defense of his house.

Two famous nineteenth-century Rhode Island murder cases have been covered by legal historians: *Brotherly Love: Murder and the Politics of Prejudice in Nineteenth-Century Rhode Island* (1993), by Charles and Tess Hoffmann, analyzes the Gordon murder trial, while *Fall River Outrage: Life, Murder, and Justice in Early Industrial New England* (1986), by David Richard Kasserman, is an interesting account of the trial of the Reverend Ephraim Avery for the murder of Sarah Cornell (Fall River was a mill village in north Tiverton at the time of the homicide). A much briefer study of the Avery-Cornell affair is William Gerald McLoughlin, "Untangling the Tiverton Tragedy: The Social Meaning of the Terrible Haystack Murder of 1833," *Journal of American Culture* 7 (Winter 1984), 75–84. "'The Result May Be Glorious'—Anti-Gallows Movement in Rhode Island, 1838–1852," by Philip English Mackey, *Rhode Island History* 33 (1974), 19–31, details the movement to abolish the death penalty in Rhode Island. James F. Nutting, "The Poor, the Defective, and the Criminal," in Edward Field, ed., *State of Rhode Island and Providence Plantations at the End of the Century* (1902), vol. 3, pp. 389–490, is a detailed survey of the pre-1900 correctional system.

More recent criminal topics are the subject of Harold A. Phelps, "Frequency of Crime and Punishment [Providence and Bristol Counties, 1897–1927]," *Journal of the American Institute of Criminal Law and Criminology* 19 (August 1928), 165–180; William F. Powers, *In the Service of the State: A History of the Rhode Island State Police, 1925–1975* (1975); and Richard J. Maiman, "Constitutionalizing the Juvenile Court: The Impact of *In Re Gault* in Rhode Island" (doctoral dissertation, Brown University, 1972). Rhode Island's most famous modern criminal trial is analyzed by Alan M. Dershowitz, *Reversal of Fortune: Inside the Von Bulow Case* (1986), an irreverent account critical of the state judicial system, and William Wright, *The Von Bulow Affair* (1983).

Biographical and autobiographical literature on Rhode Island judges and lawyers is scarce. In addition to the materials printed or cited in the text of this volume on Stephen Hopkins, Thomas Wilson Dorr, James K. Angell, Samuel Ames, and Zechariah Chafee, scholarly works of this genre include Carl Bridenbaugh, *Silas Downer: Forgotten Patriot* (1974), a volume containing the life and writings of a Providence attorney who penned several essays challenging the right of Parliament to legislate for the colonies, and William M. Fowler, *William Ellery: A Rhode Island Politico and Lord of the Admiralty* (1973), a detailed study of the career of a Harvard-educated Newport lawyer who signed the Declaration of Independence and led the fight for ratification of the Constitution. Richard B. Carpenter, "James Mitchell Varnum, Esq.," *Rhode Island Bar Journal* 24 (March 1976), 2–3, 14–17, James M. Varnum, *A Sketch of the Life and Public Services of James Mitchell Varnum* (1906), and Donald A. D'Amato, *General James Mitchell Varnum (1748–1789): The Man and His Mansion* (1996), are biographical profiles of the lawyer who advocated judicial review in *Trevett* v. *Weeden* and became the first U.S. judge for the Northwest Territory.

Ralph G. Vaccaro, "The Politics of David Howell of Rhode Island in the Period of the Confederation" (master's thesis, Columbia University, 1947), traces the career of a Providence attorney who represented the state in the Confederation Congress; William E. Foster, "Sketch of the Life and Services of Theodore Foster," *Collections of the Rhode Island Historical Society* 7 (1885), 111–134, details the career of the Providence lawyer who became Rhode Island's first United States senator and the man for whom the town of Foster is named; Elizabeth F. Baker, *Henry Wheaton, 1785–1848* (1937), is a biography of the Providence lawyer who became the first official reporter for the United States Supreme Court and a leading authority on international law; and Henry L. Bowen, *Memoir of Tristam Burges* (1835), and Thomas J. Sullivan, "From Federalist to Whig: The Political Career of Tristam Burges" (master's thesis, University of Rhode Island, 1964), are accounts of a U.S. congressman, chief justice of the Supreme Court, and leader of the Rhode Island bar in the early national period. Thomas Durfee, ed., *The Complete Works of Hon. Job Durfee... with a Memoir of the Author* (1849), contains a life of Chief Justice Durfee, several of Durfee's charges to the grand jury, a sketch of Chief Justice Samuel Eddy, and some discourses on local legal history. John H. Stiness, *Memorial Address ...Walter Snow Burges* (1892), is the biography of a prominent Providence attorney and Supreme Court justice by a Supreme Court chief justice. Burges was a confidant of Thomas Wilson Dorr.

For modern members of the bar, consult Walter H. Conser, Jr., "Ethnicity and Politics in Rhode Island: The Career of Frank Licht," *Rhode Island History* 44 (1985), 97–107; Ruth E. Morgenthau, *Pride without Prejudice: The Life of John O. Pastore* (1989); and Arlene Violet, *Convictions: My Journey from the Convent to the Courtroom* (1987). The only detailed history of a Rhode Island law firm is Edward Winsor, *Edwards & Angell: A Firm History* (1978).

Among the most informative glimpses into the history of bench and bar are the anecdotal reminiscences of lawyers and judges. Nineteenth-century Rhode Island legal history has been enriched by several in-depth accounts. For the early decades, consult Wilkins Updike, *Memoirs of the Rhode Island Bar* (1842), by a prominent South Kingstown lawyer-politician. For the period from 1840 through the mid-1880s, Abraham Payne, *Reminiscences of the Rhode Island Bar* (1885), is a fascinating, detailed memoir that has furnished some material for the text of this volume. Chief Justice Thomas Durfee, *Gleanings from the Judicial History of Rhode Island*, (1883), updated as *The Judicial History of Rhode Island*, in

William T. Davis, ed., *The New England States* (1897), vol. 4, pp. 2362–2397, combines reminiscence with substantial historical narrative, as does the survey of Rhode Island law by Chief Justice Edward C. Stiness, "The Struggle for Judicial Supremacy," in Edward Field, ed., *State of Rhode Island and Providence Plantations at the End of the Century* (1902), vol. 3, pp. 91–169. Francis J. O'Brien, "Down Memory Lane," *Rhode Island Bar Journal* 20 (January 1972), 14–16, is a very brief reminiscence of lawyers active in the 1920s.

One-of-a-kind assessments of important Rhode Island legal topics of historical interest include Sidney S. Rider, "History of the Law Books of Rhode Island," *Book Notes* 33 (1916), 201–202, 204–207; Fred Volpe, "Rhode Island Advisory Opinions: Ghosts That Slay?," *Rhode Island Bar Journal* 25 (February 1977), 2–3, 8, 13, 15–17, 19–21, a history of Supreme Court advisory opinions from 1883 to 1974; and Catherine Ann Fisher, "Teacher Union Grievances and Arbitrations in a Rhode Island Public School System from 1966 to 1983: An Historical Analysis of Statutory, Case, and Contractual Law" (doctoral dissertation, Boston College, 1984).

The massive neofederal Providence County Courthouse, renamed the Licht Judicial Complex in 1987, was completed in 1933 after several years of construction. It houses the Supreme Court and the Superior Court for Providence and Bristol counties. The proposed park for its west approach shown in this 1931 architectural rendering has just become a reality. Sketch from the 1931 *Annual Report of the City Plan Commission*.

Appendix I

RHODE ISLAND SUPREME COURT (CHIEF JUSTICES) AND SUPERIOR COURT (PRESIDING JUSTICES)

The "Superior Court of Judicature, Court of Assize, and General Gaol Delivery" was established in June 1729. Until 1747 it consisted of the governor, deputy governor, and assistants.

In February 1746-47 an act was passed providing for the annual election of a chief judge and four associates.

In the Revision of 1798 the court's designation was changed to Supreme Judicial Court. The court was to be staffed by one chief justice and four associate justices.

Under Article X of the 1843 Rhode Island Constitution, one Supreme Court was established. The court, which has varied in size, now consists of one chief justice and four associate justices.

CHIEF JUSTICES OF THE SUPREME COURT

Gideon Cornell	1747 to 1749
Joshua Babcock	1749 to 1751
Stephen Hopkins	1751 to 1756
Francis Willett	1756 to 1756
John Gardner	1756 to 1761
Samuel Ward	1761 to 1762
Jeremiah Niles	1762 to 1763
Joshua Babcock	1763 to 1764
John Cole	1764 to 1765
Joseph Russell	1765 to 1767
James Helme	1767 to 1768
Joseph Russell	1768 to 1769
James Helme	1769 to 1770
Stephen Hopkins	1770 to 1776
Metcalf Bowler	1776 to 1777
William Greene	1777 to 1778
Shearjashub Bourn	1778 to 1781
Jabez Bowen	1781 to 1781
Paul Mumford	1781 to 1785
William Ellery	1785 to 1786
Paul Mumford	1786 to 1788
Othniel Gorton	1788 to 1791
Daniel Owen	1791 to 1795
Peleg Arnold	1795 to 1809
Thomas Arnold	1809 to 1810
Peleg Arnold	1810 to 1812
Daniel Lyman	1812 to 1816
James Burrill, Jr.	1816 to 1817
Tristam Burges	1817 to 1818

James Fenner	1819 to 1819
Isaac Wilbour	1819 to 1827
Samuel Eddy	1827 to 1835
Job Durfee	1835 to 1843

Under the Present Constitution Adopted in 1842

Job Durfee	1843 to 1848
Richard W. Greene	1848 to 1854
William R. Staples	1854 to 1856
Samuel Ames	1856 to 1866
Charles S. Bradley	1866 to 1868
George A. Brayton	1868 to 1875
Thomas Durfee	1875 to 1891
Charles Matteson	1891 to 1900
John H. Stiness	1900 to 1903
Pardon E. Tillinghast	1904 to 1905
William W. Douglas	1905 to 1908
Edward C. Dubois	1909 to 1913
Clarke H. Johnson	1913 to 1917
Christopher F. Parkhurst	1917 to 1920
William H. Sweetland	1920 to 1929
Charles F. Stearns	1929 to 1935
Edmund W. Flynn	1935 to 1957
Francis B. Condon	1958 to 1965
Thomas H. Roberts	1966 to 1976
Joseph A. Bevilacqua	1976 to 1986
Thomas F. Fay	1986 to 1993
Joseph R. Weisberger	1993 to

PRESIDING JUSTICES OF THE SUPERIOR COURT

William H. Sweetland	1905 to 1909
William B. Tanner	1909 to 1929
Edward W. Blodgett	1929 to 1932
Hugh B. Baker	1932 to 1935
Jeremiah E. O'Connell	1935 to 1948
Charles A. Walsh	1948 to 1951
G. Frederick Frost	1951 to 1959
Louis W. Cappelli	1959 to 1966
John E. Mullen	1966 to 1972
Stephen A. Fanning	1972 to 1972
Joseph R. Weisberger	1972 to 1978
Florence K. Murray	1978 to 1979
Anthony A. Giannini	1979 to 1991
Joseph F. Rogers, Jr.	1991 to

Appendix II

RHODE ISLAND ATTORNEYS GENERAL

In May 1650 the offices of "Atturney Generall for the Colonie" and "Solicitor" were created.

William Dyer, Newport, General Attorney	May 23, 1650 to 1651
Hugh Buitt, Solicitor	May 20, 1650 to 1651

In 1651 the Coddington patent separated the island towns from those on the mainland. No attorney general was elected for Providence-Warwick.

PORTSMOUTH AND NEWPORT

John Easton, Newport	May 17, 1653 to May 16, 1654

UNION REESTABLISHED

John Cranston, Newport	May 16, 1654 to May 20, 1656
John Easton, Newport	May 20, 1656 to May 19, 1657
John Greene, Jr., Warwick	May 19, 1657 to May 22, 1660
John Easton, Newport	May 22, 1660 to May 22, 1663
John Sanford, Portsmouth	May 22, 1663 to Nov. 25, 1663

Under the Royal Charter of Charles II, 1663

GENERAL ATTORNEYS

John Sanford, Portsmouth	1663 to 1664
John Easton, Newport	1664 to 1670
John Sanford, Portsmouth	1670 to 1671
Joseph Torrey, Newport	1671 to 1672
John Easton, Newport	1672 to 1674
Peter Easton, Newport	1674 to 1676
Weston Clarke, Newport	1676 to 1677
Edward Richmond, Newport	1677 to 1680
Weston Clarke, Newport	1680 to 1681
Edmund Calverly, Warwick	1681 to 1682
John Pococke, Newport	1682 to 1683
Weston Clarke, Newport	1683 to 1684
John Pococke, Newport	1684 to 1685
Weston Clarke, Newport	1685 to 1686
John Williams, Newport	1686 to —[1]
John Pococke, Newport	1690 to —[2]
John Smith, Warwick	1696 to 1698
John Pococke, Newport	1698 to 1700
John Rhodes, Warwick	1700 to 1701
John Pococke, Newport	1701 to 1702

Nathaniel Dyer, Newport	1702 to 1704
Joseph Sheffield, Newport	1704 to 1706
Simon Smith, Warwick	1706 to 1712
Richard Ward, Newport	1712 to 1713
John Hammett, Newport	1713 to 1714
Weston Clarke, Newport	1714 to 1721
Henry Bull, Newport	1721 to 1722
Daniel Updike, North Kingstown	1722 to 1732
James Honeyman, Jr., Newport	1732 to 1740

In December 1740 the act providing for the election of a general attorney was repealed, and a king's attorney was chosen for each county.

KING'S ATTORNEYS

James Honeyman, Jr., Newport County	1741 to 1743
John Walton, Providence County	1741 to 1742
Daniel Updike, King's County[3]	1741 to 1743
John Andrew, Providence County	1742 to 1743

In September 1742 the act was repealed and provision made for the election of one attorney general only.

ATTORNEYS GENERAL

Daniel Updike, North Kingstown	1743 to 1758
Augustus Johnston, Newport	1758 to 1766
Oliver Arnold, Providence	1766 to 1771
Henry Marchant, Newport	1771 to 1777
William Channing, Newport	1777 to 1787
Henry Goodwin, Newport	1787 to 1789
David Howell, Providence	1789 to 1790
Daniel Updike, North Kingstown	1790 to 1791
William Channing, Newport	1791 to 1793
Ray Greene, Providence	1794 to 1797
James Burrill, Jr., Providence	1797 to 1813
Samuel W. Bridgham, Providence	1813 to 1817
Henry Bowen, Providence	1817 to 1819
Dutee J. Pearce, Newport	1819 to 1825
Albert C. Greene, East Greenwich	1825 to 1843

Under the Present Constitution Adopted in 1842

ATTORNEYS GENERAL

Joseph M. Blake, Bristol	1843 to 1851
Walter S. Burges, Cranston	1851 to 1854
Christopher Robinson, Cumberland	1854 to 1855
Charles Hart, Providence	1855 to 1858
Jerome B. Kimball, Providence	1858 to 1860
Walter S. Burges, Cranston	1860 to 1863
Abraham Payne, Providence	1863 to 1864
Horatio Rogers, Jr., Providence	1864 to 1867
Willard Sayles, Providence	1867 to 1882
Samuel P. Colt, Bristol	1882 to 1886
Edwin Metcalf, Providence	1886 to 1887
Ziba O. Slocum, Providence	1887 to 1888
Horatio Rogers, Providence	1888 to 1889
Ziba O. Slocum, Providence	1889 to 1891
Robert W. Burbank, Providence	1891 to 1894
Edward C. Dubois, East Providence	1894 to 1897
Willard B. Tanner, Providence	1897 to 1901
Charles F. Stearns, Providence	1901 to 1905
William B. Greenough, Providence	1905 to 1912
Herbert A. Rice, Pawtucket	1912 to 1923[4]
Herbert L. Carpenter, N. Smithfield	1923 to 1925
Charles P. Sisson, Providence[5]	1925 to 1929
Oscar L. Heltzen, Providence[6]	1929 to 1930
Benjamin M. McLyman, Providence[7]	1930 to 1933
John P. Hartigan, Cranston	1933 to 1939
Louis V. Jackvony, Providence	1939 to 1941
John H. Nolan, Newport	1941 to 1949
William E. Powers, Cumberland	1949 to 1958
J. Joseph Nugent, North Providence[8]	1958 to 1967
Herbert F. DeSimone, North Providence	1967 to 1971
Richard J. Israel, Providence	1971 to 1975
Julius C. Michaelson, Providence	1975 to 1979
Dennis J. Roberts II, Providence	1979 to 1985
Arlene N. Violet, Providence[9]	1985 to 1989
James E. O'Neil, Narragansett	1989 to 1993
Jeffrey B. Pine, Providence	1993 to 1999

[1] Charter suspended by the Dominion for New England

[2] Gap in the records

[3] Name since changed to Washington County

[4] Longest term as attorney general under the constitution of 1843

[5] Resigned, June 10, 1929

[6] Appointed by the governor, June 10, 1929, after Charles P. Sisson resigned

[7] Elected by the General Assembly, January 16, 1930, and elected at the general election of November 4, 1930

[8] Elected by Grand Committee, January 21, 1958, after William E. Powers resigned, and elected at the general election of November 4, 1958

[9] First woman to be elected attorney general of an American state

Appendix III

JUDGES OF THE UNITED STATES DISTRICT COURT FOR THE DISTRICT OF RHODE ISLAND

Judge	*Date of Nomination*	*End of Service*
Henry Marchant (1741–1796)	July 2, 1790	August 30, 1796[1]
Benjamin Bourne (1755–1808)	December 21, 1796	February 20, 1801[2]
David L. Barnes (1760–1812)	January 6, 1802	November 3,1812[1]
David Howell (1747–1824)	November 12, 1812	July 30, 1824[1]
John Pitman (1785–1864)	December 16, 1824	November 17, 1864[1]
Jonathan R. Bullock (1815–1899)	February 9, 1865	September 15, 1869
John P. Knowles (1808–1887)	December 6, 1869	March 21, 1881
LeBaron B. Colt (1846–1924)	March 9, 1881	July 23, 1884[2]
George M. Carpenter (1844–1896)	December 18, 1884	July 31, 1896[1]
Arthur L. Brown (1854–1928)	December 8, 1896	June 10, 1927
Ira Lloyd Letts (1889–1947)	January 1, 1927	June 24, 1935
John C. Mahoney (1882–1952)	June 7, 1935	February 11, 1940[2]
John P. Hartigan (1887–1968)	February 12, 1940	January 12, 1951[2]
Edward L. Leahy (1886–1953)	January 12, 1951	July 22, 1953[1]
Edward W. Day (1901–1985)	October 1, 1953	March 19, 1976[3]
Raymond J. Pettine (1912–)	June 13, 1966	July 6, 1982[3]
Francis J. Boyle (1927–)	February 1, 1977	December 1, 1992[3]
Bruce M. Selya (1934–)	July 27, 1982	October 14, 1986[2]
Ronald R. Lagueux (1931–)	January 21, 1986	
Ernest C. Torres (1941–)	June 22, 1987	
Mary M. Lisi (1950–)	January 27, 1994	

[1]Died while serving
[2]Elevated to the First Circuit
[3]Assumed senior status
Second judgeship, 1966
Third judgeship, 1984

Appendix IV

UNITED STATES ATTORNEYS FOR THE DISTRICT OF RHODE ISLAND

U.S. Attorney	*Date of Commission*
William Channing	July 3, 1790
Ray Greene	January 27, 1794
David Leonard Burns	November 30, 1797
David Howell	May 30, 1801; January 26, 1802[1]
Asher Robbins	December 9, 1812
John Pitman	December 9 1820
Dutee J. Pearce	August 23, 1824; January 3, 1825[1]
Richard W. Greene	December 29, 1825, February 3, 1830; February 10, 1834; February 15, 1838; March 15, 1842[2]
Walter S. Burges	April 8, 1845; February 24, 1846[1]
James M. Clark	June 15, 1850
George H. Browne	April 19, 1853; March 14, 1854[1]
Wingate Hayes	April 16, 1861; July 22, 1861[1]
John A. Gardiner	March 20, 1871; February 26, 1875[2]
Nathan F. Dixon, Jr	March 1,1877; February 16, 1881; March 10, 1881[2]
David S. Baker	March 23, 1885
Rathbone Gardner	March 19, 1889
Charles E. Gorman	June 8, 1893; August 22, 1893;[1] August 23, 1897[2]
Charles A. Wilson	September 30, 1897; January 10, 1898;[1] January 21, 1902; December 19, 1905; January 11, 1910[2]
Walter R. Stiness	August 18, 1911
Harvey A. Baker	September 15, 1914; October 28, 1918[2]
Peter C. Cannon	June 9, 1920; March 7, 1921[1]
Norman S. Case	June 14, 1921
John S. Murdock	February 23, 1926
Henry M. Boss, Jr.	April 23, 1929; December 16, 1929[1]
J. Howard McGrath	March 20, 1934; March 21, 1938[2]
George F. Troy	September 5, 1940; March 10, 1941;[1] April 7, 1945; April 1, 1949; April 1, 1950[2]
Edward M. McEntee	July 3, 1952
Jacob S. Temkin	June 16, 1953
Joseph Mainelli	July 5, 1955; July 27, 1955;[1] July 18, 1959[2]
Raymond J. Pettine	April 14, 1961; May 22, 1965[2]
Frederick W. Faerber, Jr.	July 6, 1966
Edward Peter Gallogly	March 4, 1967
Lincoln C. Almond	June 20, 1969; December 4, 1973; November 12, 1981; August 4, 1986[2]

Everett C. Sammartino	June 1978[3]
Paul F. Murray	June 27, 1978
Edwin J. Gale	April 12, 1993
Sheldon Whitehouse	May 10, 1994
Margaret E. Curran	May 11, 1998; October 21, 1998[1]

[1]This date and the date immediately preceding represent court appointment and then confirmation of presidential appointment.

[2]Multiple dates represent subsequent reappointments.

[3]Sammartino was court-appointed only. His predecessor, Almond, resigned effective June 9, 1978, and his successor, Murray, was commissioned on June 27, 1978.

Anchoring the east end of Exchange Place (now Kennedy Plaza) in Providence, the classic-style Federal Building (center) has been the seat of the U.S. District Court since its completion in 1908. The federal bankruptcy court, presided over for a quarter century by Judge Arthur N. Votolato, is housed with other federal agencies in a modern office building at 380 Westminster Street. Photo ca. 1915, courtesy of the Rhode Island Historical Society.

Illustration Credits

Principal Sources:

RIHS Rhode Island Historical Society
RIBA Rhode Island Bar Association
PC Providence College Archives, Patrick T. Conley Collection
Cirker Hayward and Blanche Cirker, *Dictionary of American Portraits* (New York, 1967)
Mohr Ralph S. Mohr, *Rhode Island Governors for Three Hundred Years* (Providence, 1959)
Greene Welcome Arnold Greene, *The Providence Plantations for Two Hundred and Fifty Years* (Providence, 1886)

Chapter 1

Landing of Roger Williams: RIHS (RHi x3 2036)
Parliamentary patent of 1644: RIHS (RHi x3 6015)
Gorton's *Simplicities Defense*: RIHS (RHi x3 5301)
Dr. John Clarke: Portrait attributed to Guilliam de Ville, courtesy of the Redwood Library, Newport
Charter of 1663: RIHS (RHi x3 2289)
King Charles II: Greene, p. 41
Rhode Island counties: J. H. Cady, *Rhode Island Boundaries, 1636–1936* (1936), p. 15

Chapter 2

Roger Williams: Oil painting by Peter F. Rothermel, RIHS (RHi x3 3102)
Rev. John Cotton: Cirker, p. 134
Key into the Language of America: RIHS (RHi x3 19)
Rev. Cotton Mather: Cirker, p. 417
Rev. Isaac Backus: Cirker, p. 28
Thomas Jefferson: Cirker, p. 337
James Madison: Cirker, p. 409

Chapter 3

Massassoit: Sculpture by Cyrus O. Dallin, courtesy of the Pilgrim Society
Deed with markings: Providence City Archives
Edward Winslow of Plymouth: RIHS (RHi x3 2310)
Death of Miantinomi: Engraving by F. O. C. Darley from John W. DeForest, *History of the Indians of Connecticut* (1853)

Chapter 4

Anne Hutchinson: Photo of a sculpture by Cyrus Dallin from Helen Augur, *The Life of Anne Hutchinson* (1930)
Mary Dyer: Courtesy of the Social Law Library, Boston
William Coddington: Courtesy of the Redwood Library
Newport Quaker Meeting House: Lithograph by John Collins, RIHS (RHi x3 1133)

Chapter 5

Judge Nathaniel Byfield: Photo of a portrait by John Smibert, PC
Richard Coote: Courtesy of the Harvard College Library

Chapter 6

Newport harbor: Courtesy of the Newport Historical Society
Governor Dummer: Portrait by Robert Feke, courtesy of Governor Dummer Academy
Flag of pirate Thomas Tew: Courtesy of John Millar

Chapter 7

William Wanton: Mohr, p. 163
Edward Coke: Julius J. Marke, *Vignettes of Legal History* (1965), p. 207
Two Newport Colony Houses: Courtesy of the Newport Historical Society

Chapter 8

Stephen Hopkins: Courtesy of the Frick Art Reference Library
Samuel Ward: RIHS (RHi x3 628)
Title page, *Rights of Colonies*: RIHS (RHi x3 4291)
Title page, Silas Downer pamphlet: RIHS
Hopkins House: PC

Chapter 9

Gaspee burning: Steel engraving by J. Rogers after a painting by J. McNevin, Greene, p. 59
Joseph Wanton: Portrait by John Smibert, courtesy of the Redwood Library
Abraham Whipple: Portrait by Edward Savage, courtesy of the U. S. Naval Academy
Royal *Gaspee* proclamation: RIHS (RHi x3 727)
John Brown: Minature by Edward G. Malbone, courtesy of the New York Historical Society
Sabin's Tavern: Edward Field, ed., *State of Rhode Island: A History* (1902), I: 460

Chapter 10

Constitution referendum: RIHS broadside file
Renunciation of allegiance: Rhode Island State Archives
Country party ballot: PC
Paper money, 1786: PC
Convention call, 1790: RIHS broadside file
Benjamin Bourne: RIHS (RHi x3 1462)
John Howland: Portrait by James Sullivan Lincoln, RIHS (RHi x3 3101)
Courthouse, Kingston: RIHS (RHi x3 853)

Chapter 11

Catholic freemanship statutes, 1719 and 1783: Rhode Island State Archives
Touro Synagogue: Courtesy of Touro Synagogue
Code of 1647: PC
David Howell: RIHS (RHi x3 1944)

Indenture/Runaway slave: RIHS (RHi x3 4098 and 5780)
Slave ship *Polly:* Isidor Paiewonsky, *Eyewitness Accounts of Slavery in the Danish West Indies* (1989), p. 66
James DeWolf: Portrait, watercolor on ivory, artist unknown, RIHS (RHi x3 3070)
Manumission Act of 1784: Rhode Island State Archives
Bill of Rights and Proposed Amendments, 1790: RIHS broadside file

Part I Biographical Profiles

William Ellery: RIHS (RHi x3 786)
Theodore Foster: RIHS (RHi x3 756)
James Mitchell Varnum: RIHS (RHi x3 2018)
Henry Marchant: RIHS (RHi x3 1943)

Chapter 12

1790 census: PC
Ebenezer Knight Dexter: RIHS (RHi x3 4460)
William Peck gravestone: RIBA

Chapter 13

Silas Casey: Courtesy of the Society for the Preservation of New England Antiquities
John Jay: Cirker, p. 336
James Wilson: Cirker, p. 678
Casey Farm: Photo by Hartley Alley, PC

Chapter 14

Old State House, Providence: Photo by Lou Notarianni, PC
Courtship and marriage cartoon: Courtesy of the American Antiquarian Society
Providence Gazette advertisement: RIHS (RHi x3 5140)
Divorce graph: RIHS (RHi x3 8857)
Divorce statute: RIHS (RHi x3 8858)

Chapter 15

Sullivan Dorr House: RIHS (RHi x3 1564)
Sullivan Dorr: Portrait by Charles Loring Elliot, courtesy of the Providence Washington Insurance Company
James Kent: Cirker, p. 355
Thomas Wilson Dorr: Engraving by W. Warner from an 1845 daguerreotype, RIHS (RHi x3 2013)
Dorr's legal notebook: Copy in the possession of Patrick T. Conley

Chapter 16

Providence Ward 2 banner: RIHS
Suffrage badge: RIHS
Call for People's Convention: RIHS (RHi x3 6197)
People's Constitution: RIHS (RHi x3 6743)
Comparison of the two constitutions: RIHS broadside file

Anti-Irish broadside: RIHS (RHi x3 4355)
Samuel Ward King: Oil painting by John N. Arnold, RIHS
"The Paddy's Lament": Courtesy of the John Hay Library, Brown University
Law and Order caricature, Dorr's return to Providence: RIHS (RHi x3 1)
Henry Lord's sketch of Acote's Hill: RIHS (RHi x3 6586)
Benjamin F. Hallett: RIHS (RHi x3 586)
"The Four Traitors": RIHS (RHi x3 5683)
Legislative pardon of Dorr, 1854: RIHS (RHi x3 6688)

Chapter 17

State prison and cove: From a sketch in the Samuel W. Brown Scrapbook, RIHS
Amasa Sprague: Charles Hoffman and Tess Hoffman, *Brotherly Love* (1993), p. 7
General Thomas Carpenter: Portrait by James Sullivan Lincoln, RIHS
Judge Job Durfee: RIBA
Court report of Gordon trial: PC
Thomas R. Hazard and family: RIHS (RHi x3 5426)

Chapter 18

Class: Painting by James Calvert Smith, courtesy of the Litchfield Historical Society
Litchfield Law School exterior: Courtesy of the Litchfield Historical Society
Title page, *Law of Tide Waters*: PC
Sidney S. Rider: RIHS (RHi x3 8856)
Book Notes: PC

Chapter 19

Rhode Island Reports title page: PC
Justice Joseph Story: Cirker, p. 595
Thomas Durfee: Greene, p. 226

Chapter 20

Samuel Ames: RIHS (RHi x3 4213)
Samuel Bridgham: RIHS (RHi x3 4461)
"The Dorriad": PC
Old state arsenal, Providence: Arthur May Mowry, *The Dorr War* (1901), p. 185

Chapter 21

Law office of Samuel Y. Atwell: Courtesy of the Glocester Heritage Society
John Whipple: RIHS (RHi x3 6811)
Charles S. Bradley: Greene, p. 229
Walter Snow Burges: RIHS (RHi x3 8864)
Thomas Jenckes: Greene, p. 227
Abraham Payne: Courtesy of Brown University
Old Providence County Courthouse: RIHS (RHi x3 4539)

Chapter 22

William Sprague: RIHS (RHi x3)
Elisha R. Potter, Jr.: RIHS (RHi x3 5715)

Benjamin F. Butler: Cirker, p. 92
Arctic Mill: RIHS (RHi x3 6778)

Chapter 23
Horsecar: Courtesy of the R. L. Wonson Collection
Trolley crash: Courtesy of D. Scott Molloy
Locomotive *Hercules:* RIHS (RHi x3 2262)
Marsden J. Perry: Cyrus Farnum, *Men of Providence in Cartoon* (1906), RIHS (Rhi x3 4364)

Chapter 24
Duff petition: Rhode Island State Archives
Irish voters broadside: RIHS broadside file
Philip Allen: RIHS (RHi x3 4109)
U. S. Senate report, Wallace Commission: PC
Elizabeth Buffum Chace: RIHS (RHi x3 2388)
Brayton cartoon: Milton W. Halladay, *Cartoons by Halladay* (1914)
McClure's Magazine: PC
Augustus O. Bourn: Mohr, p. 273
Lucius Garvin: Mohr, p. 299

Part II Biographical Profiles
James Burrill, Jr.: RIHS (RHi x3 3026)
Henry Wheaton: Portrait by George P. A. Healy, RIHS (RHi x3 3099)
Tristam Burges: Greene, p. 83
William R. Staples: RIHS (RHi x3 4419)
Charles E. Gorman: Photograph from Thomas W. Bicknell, *The History of the State of Rhode Island...* (1920), biographical volume, Lister to Traver, opposite p. 201
Edwin D. McGuinness: RIHS (RHi x3 8904)

Chapter 25
John H. Stiness: RIHS (RHi x3 8742)
William H. Sweetland: RIBA
Darius Baker: RIBA
Charles F. Stearns: RIBA

Chapter 26
William S. Flynn: PC
State police: William F. Powers, *In the Service of the State: The Rhode Island State Police, 1925-1975* (1975), p. 38
Theodore Francis Green: Erwin Levine, *Theodore Francis Green: The Rhode Island Years* (1963), frontispiece
Thomas P. McCoy: Courtesy of the *Providence Journal*
Edmund Flynn: RIHS (RHi x3 8863)
Cartoon of McCoy, Quinn, and Green: *Pawtucket Star*, November, 1936, RIHS

Chapter 27

Roscoe Pound: Courtesy of Harvard University Law School
Chafee before the U.S. Senate: Donald L. Smith, *Zechariah Chafee, Jr.* (1986), p. 147
The Constitutional Convention That Never Met: PC
Martial law at Narragansett Park: Zechariah Chafee, Jr., *State House versus Pent House* (1937), p. 61.

Chapter 28

Dennis J. Roberts: Mohr, p. 335
Christopher Del Sesto: Mohr, p. 337
Thomas Roberts: PC
Long Count cartoon: Courtesy of the *Providence Journal*

Chapter 29

Dr. William P. Robinson: PC
Robert J. McKenna: Courtesy of Robert J. McKenna
Milton Stanzler: Courtesy of Milton Stanzler
Chief Justice Warren Burger: PC
Pawtucket Nativity display: Courtesy of the *Providence Journal*

Chapter 30

William H. Edwards: RIBA
Judge John F. Doris: RIBA
Dr. Patrick T. Conley: PC
Keven McKenna: Courtesy of Keven McKenna
Broadside of 1986 convention proposals: PC

Chapter 31

Francis Colwell: RIBA
Ada Sawyer: RIBA
Edward Smith: RIBA
Helen McDonald: RIBA
Colin Makepeace: RIBA
Ralph P. Semonoff: RIBA
Bar Association headquarters, Cedar Street: RIBA

Part III Biographical Profiles

Amasa Eaton: RIHS (RHi x3 8855)
James H. Higgins: PC
Thomas G. Corcoran: UPI photo, PC
Robert Emmet Quinn: PC
J. Howard McGrath: PC
William E. Powers: PC
John O. Pastore: PC
Florence K. Murray: PC
Joseph G. LeCount: RIBA
Frank Licht: PC

SPONSOR PROFILES

ROGER WILLIAMS UNIVERSITY RALPH R. PAPITTO SCHOOL OF LAW

Since its very conception, service to the Rhode Island bench and bar has constituted a key facet of the mission of the School of Law. The resources of the school provide significant assets to the professional community, enriching its intellectual, ethical, and moral vitality.

The *Roger Williams University Law Review* is published twice annually by a student editorial board. Commentary upon developments in the law of Rhode Island appears in articles written by practitioners, judges, and scholars, and in notes and comments authored by student-staff members. Each spring the *Law Review* surveys significant opinions of the Rhode Island Supreme Court from the previous term and previews cases currently before the court.

To address salient issues of concern to the state's legal community, the School of Law provides an appropriate venue for deliberation and debate by a community of critical scholars and engaged practitioners. A recent symposium addressing the separation of powers among the three branches of state government in Rhode Island provided a forum for scholarly discussion of a timely topic, with papers to be published in the fall 1998 issue of the *Law Review*.

Two specialized fields of endeavor at the School of Law are the Feinstein Institute for Legal Services and the Marine Affairs Institute. The former, dedicated to the provision of pro bono legal services in a myriad of forms, fosters inculcation of the spirit of service to the public. The Marine Affairs Institute takes advantage of our coastal setting to focus upon admiralty law, environmental regulation, and the international law of the sea. Drawing upon scholarly and pragmatic resources from the faculty and the admiralty bar, it sponsors an annual Maritime Law Symposium that draws attorneys and specialists from across the nation. Faculty members of the Marine Affairs Institute address leading-edge legislation and litigation in publications and seminars.

In state-of-the-art facilities, the School of Law's faculty complement of twenty-six full-time and thirty-one adjunct professors offers instruction in both a three-year day and four-year evening program, supported by a law library of more than 200,000 volumes. As a service to the bench and bar, classrooms are made available for continuing legal education programs, and access to the law library is a courtesy that the School of Law is pleased to provide.

At the three commencement ceremonies celebrated by the school since its inception, we were pleased to host and award honorary Doctor of Laws degrees to Associate Justice Anthony Kennedy of the United States Supreme Court, Chief Justice Juan Torruella of the First Circuit Court of Appeals, and Rhode Island Supreme Court Chief Justice Joseph R Weisberger, who declared that "the mission of a law school is not just to educate persons who wish to become members of the bar, but also to contribute to and enhance the legal culture."

In that reciprocally rewarding role, the Roger Williams University Ralph Papitto School of Law is pleased to play its proper part.

EDWARDS & ANGELL

Stephen O. Edwards

Walter F. Angell

In 1887 Mr. Walter F. Angell conceived the idea of getting a number of lawyers together, not in a partnership but merely to have adjoining offices for convenience and to pool their libraries so that excessive time would not have to be spent at the Bar Library looking up law. And so it was that Stephen Edwards, Walter Angell, Samuel Durfee, and Charles Bradley agreed to come together to form a nucleus which would attract other members.

As plans for uniting offices progressed, Messrs Edwards and Angell began to talk of uniting their businesses as well. Although this was not the original plan, both gentlemen were taking on more and more work, particularly of the office variety, with which trials interfered. They discussed the matter thoroughly and finally agreed to form a partnership on equal terms and upon the general plan that Edwards was to attend to all office business and Angell was to do the trial work.

The decision was finally reached and confirmed one night during the winter of 1893 at the corner of what is now Webster Avenue and Cranston Street in Cranston, where Edwards and Angell had arrived in the course of a long walk during which they discussed the matter for a final time.

Writing of the partnership he and Edwards had formed, Walter Angell wrote years later that "a real partnership between lawyers was, at that time, rather an unusual thing. They were jealous of each other and even feared to have their offices adjoining for fear one would get the other's clients, as we found when we endeavored to put into effect our first plan to gather a number of lawyers together in one place with a common library. Moreover, it was well known that we were both getting on, and the idea seemed to be that we ought to be rivals rather than associates. Of course, we did not hear all of this talk, but we heard some of it. The fact that we were to become partners was first communicated to us from the outside by John T. Blodgett, who said that someone had told him so and that he had replied that he felt certain that it was not true. Not a few of our individual clients expressed their doubts as to the wisdom of proceeding."

The gentlemen did have the wisdom to proceed, and on May 1, 1894, announcements were sent:

> *Mr. Stephen O. Edwards and Mr. Walter F. Angell announce that they have formed a copartnership for the general practice of the law, under the firm name of Edwards & Angell, and have taken offices in the Merchants Bank Building, No. 32 Westminster Street.*

Today, Edwards & Angell, LLP, has nearly 200 attorneys in seven offices. Since our founding in 1894, the firm has steadily evolved into a major regional law firm with offices in Providence and Newport, Rhode Island; New York City; Boston, Massachusetts; Hartford, Connecticut; Short Hills, New Jersey; and Palm Beach, Florida. E&A has structured its practice to anticipate, respond to, and adapt quickly to the economic, regulatory, social, and political challenges and opportunities that our clients face daily. As evidence of a strong interdisciplinary approach to client service, the firm's broad range of practice groups are organized by industry, business, or specialized legal services. These practice groups include Banking, Lending, Bankruptcy/Workout, Corporate, Health Care, Insurance and Reinsurance, Intellectual Property, International, Labor & Employment, Litigation, Media and Communications, Municipal Finance, Real Estate, Securities, Tax, Technology, Trusts & Estates, and Venture Capital and Emerging Companies. To insure timely and efficient service to our clients in these practice areas, Edwards & Angell incorporates a firmwide team approach while maximizing the use of state-of-the-art technology and highly professional paralegal and administrative staff.

Edwards & Angell, LLP, has earned the reputation of a distinguished community leader and spirited citizen. In addition to serving as directors and advisers to numerous community and civic organizations, Edwards & Angell attorneys have received awards for their steadfast commitment in providing pro bono services throughout the communities in which they live and work. The firm has grown steadily in the 104 years since it was established. Teamwork, commitment, technological advances, and dedication to both the community and our clients are the reason for the success of Edwards & Angell, LLP. Miss Viola Follis, Walter Angell's secretary from 1915 to 1948, once made the following statement: "May the succeeding generations of the firm continue to follow in the footsteps of its founders, and may there always be an Edwards & Angell to which people can take their problems with confidence and be sure of understanding and sound advice." This—the hope and dream of those who saw the beginning—remains the hope of this generation of the E&A family, continuing to link the firm's past with its future.

DECOF & GRIMM, P.C.

Leonard and Mark B. Decof

On May 1, 1975, Leonard Decof founded his firm under the name of Leonard Decof, Ltd. It was the first and only law firm in Rhode Island dedicated exclusively to litigation and trial of plaintiffs' cases. In the beginning, Leonard Decof was its sole member. A graduate of Yale University and Harvard Law School, he had decided to make trial advocacy his life's work. His credo was professionalism, excellence, and integrity. This philosophy has marked the work of the firm, which has evolved to the current Decof & Grimm. The firm has grown in twenty years to be nationally recognized, and the largest firm in Rhode Island devoted solely to the prosecution and trial of civil actions on behalf of plaintiffs. It presently numbers fifteen lawyers, with a support staff of twenty-two. Its lawyers are highly trained, experienced courtroom specialists who practice their profession in the spirit and with the philosophy of the firm and its founder.

Over the years Leonard Decof has become recognized nationally as one of the country's preeminent trial lawyers. He has won national recognition in the courtroom as well as at the lectern. He has tried in the trial courts and argued in the appellate courts many cases that established major precedent. Two examples are *Wilkinson* v. *Vesey*, the seminal medical malpractice case in Rhode Island, and *Williams* v. *United States*, a seminal case nationally, which established precedent for substantial damages for the wrongful death of a child. In the United States Supreme Court he has argued and won cases that set precedent in the areas of antitrust and constitutional law.

Leonard Decof has lectured at numerous law schools, including Harvard, Yale, Boston University, and Suffolk University. He has appeared regularly as instructor and lecturer before bar associations throughout the country, as well as the National Institute for Trial Advocacy, the Practicing Law Institute, the American Law Institute, the International Academy of Trial Lawyers, the International Society of Barristers, and the American Bar Association. He is a fellow and former president and dean of the International Academy of Trial Lawyers, a member of the American College of Trial Lawyers, the Inner Circle of Advocates, and the International Society of Barristers, and a diplomate of the American Board of Trial Advocates. He has twice received the Rhode Island Bar Association's award for excellence for outstanding service to the public.

Mark B. Decof, Leonard's son, has established his own place and reputation in the legal community. An experienced, thorough, and compassionate litigator, Mark Decof has tried to verdict many important cases, obtaining numerous verdicts in excess of a million dollars. He is recognized as one of the foremost plaintiffs' trial attorneys in Rhode Island, especially in the fields of medical malpractice and product liability. Mark Decof's skills as a trial lawyer have earned him election to the International Academy of Trial Lawyers and the American Board of Trial Advocates.

All of the firm's lawyers, particularly senior associates E. Paul Grimm, John S. Foley, and Vincent T. Cannon, are skilled litigators. The firm's mission is to offer to its clients the best representation possible. It is acutely aware of and responsive to its clients' needs. It pursues this mission conscientiously and diligently.

The firm has an abiding concern in cases affecting the public welfare and the public's rights. In 1992, at the request of the governor of Rhode Island, it undertook to represent the state to recover losses, in the hundreds of millions of dollars, suffered by the taxpayers as a result of the state's banking crisis, the greatest financial disaster in the state's history. In pursuit of those claims, the firm filed actions against hundreds of defendants. These actions were litigated in the state and federal trial and appellate courts and in the United States Supreme Court.

In addition to plaintiffs' tort cases, the firm handles select cases in the areas of civil rights, antitrust, and professional sports litigation.

RESMINI & CANTOR LAW OFFICES

Ronald J. Resmini

Ronald J. Resmini was sworn in before the bar in June 1969 while he was on leave from the United States Army Security Agency. Following three and a half years of active duty, where he attained the rank of captain, he began a clerkship for the Rhode Island Supreme Court under Justice William E. Powers.

As a private practitioner, Mr. Resmini became involved in the Indigent Defender Program. In addition, he was the assistant town solicitor for the town of Coventry, as well as a part-time instructor at Roger Williams Law School. A pre-law summer internship with the Neighborhood Legal Service Program provided him an added opportunity to be exposed to the needs of the individual.

With expertise developed from his clerkship with the Rhode Island Supreme Court, the law firm of Ronald J. Resmini became instrumental in clarifying numerous Rhode Island laws and statutes, as well as pursuing a successful appeal to the First Circuit of Appeals reviewing habeas corpus proceedings. Mr. Resmini argued numerous cases before the Rhode Island courts clarifying uninsured motorist law, including *Bush* v. *Nationwide Mut. Ins. Co.*, 448 A.2d 782 (R.I. 1982); *Manciacapra* v. *Sentry*, 517 A.2d 1041 (R.I. 1987); *Pin Pin H. Su* v. *Kemper Insurance Company*, 431 A.2d 416 (R.I. 1981); and *Digby* v. *Digby*, 120 R.I. 299, 388 A.2d 1 (1978), which abrogated the doctrine of interspousal immunity. The firm was further instrumental in the removal of the residence requirement for attorneys, primarily Rhode Islanders, seeking to practice in the state of Massachusetts.

After preparing over twenty legal handbooks, Mr. Resmini was requested by the Butterworth Publishing Company to author a two-volume treatise on tort law and personal injury practice. Mr. Resmini says that, at this point, he wisely began an association with attorney Daniel C. Pope, which resulted in the compilation of a two-volume work in the *Rhode Island Practice Series*, entitled *Tort Law and Personal Injury Practice* (Butterworth 1990, with annual supplements). Later, Mr. Resmini published a two-volume work entitled *Rhode Island Actions and Remedies*; a two-volume work on civil procedure after the major revision of the Superior Court rules of civil procedure, entitled *Rhode Island Civil Practice and Procedure* (Michie Law Publishers, 1996, with annual supplements); and a *Domestic Relations Handbook*. Also, Mr. Resmini has published many articles in the *Rhode Island Bar Journal* and law review articles in the *Suffolk University Law Review*, including "The Law of Uninsured Motorist Insurance," "The Law of Products Liability in Rhode Island," and "The Law of Domestic Relations in Rhode Island."

Senior partner Ronald J. Resmini has also served as a board examiner for the National Board of Trial

Advocacy. The firm has enjoyed the ranking for the past twenty years of A.V., the highest ranking available through Martindale and Hubbell.

The firm's constant efforts to expedite the handling of clients' cases resulted in the clarification of a venue case, *Placido* v. *Mello*, 492 A.2d 1226 (R.I. 1985), which allows Providence County cases to be litigated in Kent County, thereby reducing the time lag involved in waiting for disposition. Furthermore, the firm suggested a court-annexed arbitration plan to the Superior Court's then presiding justice Anthony Giannini some two years before the implementation of the current Court-Annexed Arbitration system. The IOLTA Program was chaired by Ronald J. Resmini after he initiated the request to establish such a plan following contact with the appropriate authorities at the Rhode Island Bar Association, informing the bar of the enormous amount of money in clients' escrow accounts, money that served to benefit only the banks holding those funds. The firm's involvement in assisting the bar and CLE has been long-standing and may well be responsible for securing CLE credits for attendance at seminars during the annual meetings of the Rhode Island Bar Association. This suggestion was submitted to Ms. Justice Florence Murray one year before its implementation. The firm's commitment to assist and improve the Rhode Island legal system is ongoing.

The current association of Resmini & Cantor, Ltd., resulted from the hiring of Mr. Paul S. Cantor some eight years ago, following Mr. Cantor's experience with a litigation defense firm in Boston, where he was managing trial attorney. Mr. Cantor is a graduate of Brandeis University and holds a J.D. and LL.M. (Tax) from Boston University. He is a member of the Massachusetts (1980) and Rhode Island (1984) bars and has been admitted to practice before the federal courts in both states.

Although involved in all legal matters, the firm concentrates its practice in personal-injury work and has continuously committed itself to civic, charitable, and professional organizations to improve the relationship of the law community to the general community which it serves. The firm has maintained an active practice in the Providence area, currently with offices at 155 South Main Street, Suite 400, Providence. It also has an office building in Seekonk, Massachusetts, at 41 Mink Street, to serve its Bristol County clients.

Left to right: Ronald J. Resmini, Ronald J. Creamer, M. Lee Capalbo, William A. Dickie, Arthur Ricci III, and Paul S. Cantor.

ADLER POLLACK & SHEEHAN INCORPORATED

The attorneys at Adler Pollack & Sheehan are known as aggressive advocates who tenaciously champion the interests of the firm's diverse clientele. Located in the heart of Providence's financial district at 2300 Hospital Trust Tower, the firm represents Fortune 500 companies, international corporations, emerging growth companies, family-owned businesses, public agencies, and private citizens in matters which are often national or regional in scope and focus.

The founders: Bernard R. Pollock (1926–1984), Walter Adler (1896–1991), and William J. Sheehan (retired).

Beginning as a three-lawyer practice in 1960, Adler Pollack & Sheehan's results-oriented performance and successful resolution of complex legal matters earned founding firm attorneys a reputation as tough negotiators in business deals and exceptional litigators in courtroom disputes. Over the years AP&S has grown both in size and practice to meet the increasingly sophisticated demands of the law and firm clients. In fact, in 1996 the firm added ten attorneys as part of its ongoing expansion of legal and technological resources.

The firm's rapid growth is a result of its outstanding record of achievement, the attorneys' genuine commitment to the ideals of the legal profession, and the firm's overall sensitivity to the diverse needs of business and industry. Today, as one of the largest law firms in the state, the firm remains on the cutting edge, known for its multidisciplinary approach, innovative legal solutions, and entrepreneurial spirit.

AP&S continues to be recognized both regionally and nationally. The firm's Litigation practice, one of the largest and most accomplished in southeastern New England, has been cited for numerous distinctions, including its selection by *The National Law Journal* for inclusion in the list of most significant victories by civil defendants. Both the Litigation and Environmental practices have been cited by the prestigious national trade journal *American Lawyer* for quality performance based on a survey of corporate counsel in the United States. The firm is one of a select group of law firms to serve as national trial counsel for the defense of complex national-brand product liability lawsuits for Fortune 100 companies.

Alder Pollack & Sheehan's dynamic Corporate practice is highlighted by its representation of clients in many substantial mergers, acquisitions, and divestitures throughout the United States, often totaling in excess of $500 million each year and involving unique tax, accounting, and earn-out structures. AP&S attorneys have been innovators in the field of labor relations and employment law by advancing precedent-setting case law, by addressing fast-breaking situations before problems arise, and by providing creative management solutions. Attorneys in the Real Estate practice counsel major corporate clients as well as financial institutions and individuals in some of the area's most significant and challenging real estate transactions, involving landmark Rhode Island properties as well as national and international real estate. Finally, AP&S Health Care attorneys advise clients in myriad engagements addressing critical issues in the complex health care marketplace.

At Adler Pollack & Sheehan, clients expect and receive quality, timely, and cost-effective representation aimed at furthering their individual and business interests.

THE RHODE ISLAND SUPREME COURT HISTORICAL SOCIETY

FORUMS FOR FREEDOM

RHODE ISLAND DEBATES THE BILL OF RIGHTS

A series of nine lively, public debates on the Constitutional rights of the people on the occasion of the 200th Anniversary of the First Ten Amendments.

FREE AND OPEN TO THE PUBLIC

OCT. 2	***FREEDOM OF SPEECH*** **WILLIAM P. MORRIS,** ACLU Free Speech Committee DEBATES **Robert G. Flanders, Jr., Esq.**
OCT. 8	***RIGHTS OF THE ACCUSED*** **Sanford H. Gorodetsky,** Former Commissioner of Public Safety DEBATES **John J. Hardiman,** Ass't Public Defender
OCT. 16	***FREEDOM OF RELIGION*** **Rev. Robert J. McManus,** R.I. Vicar for Education DEBATES **Rev. Dwight M. Lundren,** Senior Minister, First Baptist Church of America
OCT. 22	***FREEDOM OF THE PRESS*** **William P. Robinson, Esq.** DEBATES **Thomas E. Wright, Esq.**
OCT. 24	***EMINENT DOMAIN/LAND USE AND THE ENVIRONMENT*** **Dennis Esposito, Esq.** DEBATES **Mary E. Kay,** R.I. Department of Environmental Management Counsel
OCT. 30	***RIGHT TO PRIVACY: Pro-Choice vs. Pro-Life*** **Don E. Wineberg, Esq.** DEBATES **Kevin McKenna, Esq.,** Atty for Right to Life
NOV. 7	***RIGHT TO KEEP AND BEAR ARMS*** **Vincent Vespia, Jr.,** S. Kingstown Chief of Police DEBATES **Philip A. Sebella,** Director, Rhode Island Handgun Alliance
NOV. 14	***RIGHTS OF THE ACCUSED: Capital Punishment*** **Stephen J. Fortunato, Esq.** DEBATES **Rene Lafayette,** State Representative
NOV. 20	***STATES RIGHTS vs. POWER OF THE NATIONAL GOVERNMENT*** **Dr. John J. Carroll,** Univ. of Mass. at Dartmouth, Dept. of Political Science DEBATES **Stephen J. O'Rourke,** Chairman, Rhode Island Conservative Union

ALL DEBATES START AT 7:30 PM

SPONSORED BY

R.I. Supreme Court Historical Society
Hon. Florence K. Murray, *President*

R.I. Bicentennial Foundation
Dr. Patrick T. Conley, *Chairman*

The Rhode Island Supreme Court Historical Society was founded in 1988 through the initiatives of Justice Florence K. Murray. Although it dissolved in 1998 after Murray's retirement, the society sponsored numerous educational programs involving members of the bar, including the 1991 statewide forums in observance of the 200th anniversary of the Bill of Rights. During its brief existence the society funded or published such contributions to Rhode Island legal history as Patrick T. Conley and Albert T. Klyberg's *Rhode Island's Road to Liberty* (1990); Richard M. Deasy's edition of William R. Staples's *The Documentary History of the Destruction of the Gaspee* (1990), and Russell J. DeSimone and Daniel C. Schofield's *The Broadsides of the Dorr Rebellion* (1992).

PATRICK T. CONLEY

Conley delivers his second of four Law Day addresses to the state Supreme Court (1987).

Patrick T. Conley, a resident of Bristol with law offices in East Providence, is a sole practitioner. With a master's and doctorate in history with highest honors from the University of Notre Dame and a law degree from Suffolk University, Conley has pursued parallel careers as a professor of history and constitutional law (thirty years of teaching at Providence College), a businessman (rare-book dealer and real estate developer), an author (fourteen books, including this one, and dozens of articles), a practicing attorney, and a public service volunteer (including chairmanships of the Rhode Island Bicentennial Commission—ri76, the Rhode Island Bicentennial of the Constitution Foundation, the Cranston Historic District Commission, the Cranston Charter Review Commission, the Rhode Island Publications Society, the Providence Heritage Commission, the Bristol Statehouse Foundation, and the United States Constitution Council).

As a lawyer, Conley has divided his interest between the practical, bread-and-butter field of real estate law, with a particular specialty in tax-title litigation, and the scholarly domain of constitutional law and appellate work. He has written the definitive book on early Rhode Island constitutional development, *Democracy in Decline*, which was hailed by scholarly reviewers with such comments as "the depth of the research is astounding" and "the scholarship is meticulous."

The same acclaim greeted his two-volume study of the origins of the U.S. Constitution and the Bill of Rights—*The Constitution and the States* (1987) and *The Bill of Rights and the States* (1992), written with Dr. John Kaminski, director of the Center for the Study of the American Constitution at the University of Wisconsin. One reviewer described the award-winning set as "an invaluable teaching tool for the study of the colonial and early national constitutional history of the United States," while another termed Conley's analysis of the literature of the founding "a masterful treatment of the historiography of the framing and ratification of the Constitution"—a "sweeping, balanced, and lucid" treatise. Warren Burger, chief justice of the United States Supreme Court, wrote the introduction to *The Constitution and the States*.

Conley's most memorable practical forays into the field of constitutional law have been his services as research advisor to the 1964–1969 state constitutional convention, as secretary and delegate to the

1973 convention, and as general counsel to the president of the 1986 conclave. As a delegate in 1973, Conley was the principal sponsor of the clause in the article on elections that requires financial disclosure of political campaign donations, and he was sole sponsor of the section (now Article XIV) revising the amendment process and providing for the regular call of constitutional conventions. The *Providence Journal*, which Conley defeated in a libel case during the mid-1980s, editorially described this reform as "the most significant substantive alteration ever made in the state constitution."

In addition to his academic interest in constitutional law, Conley has established himself as the authority on the Rhode Island law of tax titles, arguing the arcane details of Title 44, Chapter 9, in more than a dozen cases before the Rhode Island Supreme Court. For years Conley and his investor-clients have purchased tax-title property throughout the state, but especially in Providence, where Conley's acquisitions and foreclosures caused him to be ranked by *Providence Business News* as the capital city's largest private landholder.

Conley assuming the chairmanship of the Rhode Bicentennial Commission (ri76) in 1975.

While pursuing what has been, at times, a controversial practice, Conley has been the subject of a full-length feature story in *Rhode Island Monthly* entitled "Dirt Rich," and he has been described in various *Journal* articles as the "tax sale king," the "mogul," and the "titan of titles." As one news story observed, "If there were national tax sales, Patrick Conley might be as well known as F. Lee Bailey. As it is, he seems to be the king of Rhode Island tax sales" (*Journal*, June 27, 1996).

Conley maintains a small vestige of the varied athletic pursuits of his youth in South Providence by competing in master's track and field. In recent years he has held the Eastern United States, New England, and Rhode Island titles in the javelin event. He has six children, the oldest of whom, Patrick Jr., is an assistant Providence city solicitor. Conley is married to the former Gail Cahalan of Central Falls, who assists him in his real estate ventures. His interests include travel, interior decorating, book and antique collecting, reading, fine dining, and all things historical.

In May 1995 Conley was inducted into the Rhode Island Heritage Hall of Fame — one of a handful of living Rhode Islanders who have been accorded that honor.

Conley and his wife, Gail, chat with U.S. Chief Justice Warren Burger prior to Conley's principal speech at Congress Hall, Philadelphia, on the 200th anniversary of the ratification of the Bill of Rights, December 15, 1991.

INDEX

COLOPHON

This book was laid out and typeset
in QuarkXPress on a Macintosh OS system.
The artwork was scanned
and processed with Adobe Photoshop.

Monotype Ehrhardt is the text face;
Bitstream Caslon Openface is used for display type
and Bitstream Zurich for captions.

The book was printed and bound
by Quebecor USA.